THE RIGHTS AND REMEDIES OF CREDITORS
RESPECTING THEIR DEBTOR'S
PROPERTY

THE RIGHTS AND REMEDIES OF CREDITORS RESPECTING THEIR DEBTOR'S PROPERTY

BY

GARRARD GLENN
OF THE NEW YORK BAR

SPECIAL LECTURER IN THE LAW SCHOOL OF COLUMBIA UNIVERSITY
JOINT AUTHOR OF EIKUS AND GLENN ON 'SECRET
LIENS AND REPUTED OWNERSHIP"

BOSTON
LITTLE, BROWN, AND COMPANY
1915

T
G4273c
1915

Copyright, 1915,
BY LITTLE, BROWN, AND COMPANY.

All rights reserved

Set up and electrotyped by J. S Cushing Co , Norwood, Mass , U S A
Presswork by S J Parkhill & Co , Boston, Mass , U S A

To
Professor Francis M. Burdick
and
Dean Harlan F. Stone
of the law school of columbia university
this book is gratefully
dedicated

PREFACE

The following chapters contain the substance of a special course of lectures delivered at the Law School of Columbia University, on the rights of creditors respecting their debtor's property. The aim of these lectures was to harmonize, as far as possible, the various statutes and doctrines which are scattered through the body of our law so as to demonstrate the system afforded by our jurisprudence for the realization of debts out of the debtor's property. I now offer these labors in completed form as an aid to the study of this system as a whole, and of the relation which each part of the system bears to the others.

I have not attempted an exhaustive discussion of any particular branch of the general subject. That would have obscured the single purpose for which the work was undertaken, and would do no special good, since many books have long since been written on all these different topics, ranging from treatises on executions to volumes on bankruptcy and receivers. But because, so far as I have gathered, none of these books attempts the task of synthesis to which the work that here follows is devoted, the present effort is put forth for what it may be worth to the student of our law and his brother of the bar as well.

Some of the ideas advanced in this book I have already suggested in the course of various articles which I have written for the *Columbia Law Review*, and my indebtedness to the writings of others is, I hope, sufficiently indicated by the marginal references in the course of the following pages.

GARRARD GLENN

NEW YORK,
September, 1914.

TABLE OF CONTENTS

CHAPTER I

		PAGES
The Creditor's Right of Realization, §§ 1–24		1–21
§ 1.	The Creditor has no Title to his Debtor's Property	1
§ 2.	Difference between Secured and General Creditors	2
§ 3.	The Creditor must have a "Claim upon the Debtor"	3
§ 4.	The Judgment as a "Claim upon the Debtor"	3
§ 5.	Double Effect of Judgment	3
§ 6.	The Right of Realization conferred by the Writ of Execution	4
§ 7.	The Judgment as the Original Source of the Right of Realization	5
§ 8	Limitations of the Common Law Execution	6
§ 9.	Failure of Statutes to cure These Defects	7
§ 10	Jurisdiction of Equity — the Judgment Creditor's Bill	8
§ 11.	Ancillary Character of this Jurisdiction	8
§ 12.	Prerequisites to Equitable Aid	9
§ 13.	Equality of Legal and Equitable Assets	11
§ 14	Representative Character of Bill	11
§ 15	Equality not Attainable by Common Law Procedure	12
§ 16.	The Equitable Jurisdiction did not confer Equality	13
§ 17.	Résumé of the Creditor's Procedure	14
§ 18	Apparent Exception. Absence of Judgment in a Strict Sense	15
§ 19.	Exceptions created by Statute	16
§ 20.	Enforcement of Foreign Judgment	17
§ 21.	Should there be an Exception where Debtor's Property is outside the State of his Residence?	18
§ 22.	Argument against allowing an Exception	19
§ 23.	Weight of Authority in Favor of Exception	20
§ 24.	No Other Real Exception	20

CHAPTER II

The Property Available for Creditors, §§ 25–60		22–48
§ 25	The Creditor may reach whatever the Debtor can Sell	22
§ 26.	Exception — Unlawful Assets	23
§ 27.	But All Lawful Property is Available to the Creditors	23

ix

TABLE OF CONTENTS

		PAGES
§ 28	Labor not an Available Asset	24
§ 29	The Property must have Existence in the Eye of the Law	24
§ 30	The Property must be taken with its Encumbrances	25
§ 31	Set-off as an Illustration	25
§ 32	Marshaling of Partnership Assets — Relation of Partnership and Individual Debts	26
§ 33	Rule of Marshaling in Case of Partnership's Insolvency	27
§ 34	Basis of Rule	28
§ 35	Income of Mortgaged Premises	30
§ 36	Extent of Creditor's Right — Property must be Alienable	31
§ 37	Corporate Franchises	31
§ 38	Claims against Government	32
§ 39	The Spendthrift Trust	32
§ 40	The "Self-created" Trust	33
§ 41	Trust created by Third Party	33
§ 42	Limitation over on Debtor's Insolvency	33
§ 43	Discretionary Powers in Trustee	34
§ 44	Statutory Rule of New York	35
§ 45	The Real "Spendthrift Trust"	36
§ 46	Is allowed in but Two States	36
§ 47	Powers	36
§ 48	Limitations of Market	37
§ 49	Stock Exchange Seat	37
§ 50	Contingent Remainder and Tenancy by the Entirety	38
§ 51	Right of Realization as limited by Statute	38
§ 52	Exemption Laws	39
§ 53	Life Insurance as a Subject of Exemption Laws	40
§ 54	The Provisions of the Bankrupt Act	42
§ 55	Former Conflict of Interpretation	42
§ 56	Present Rule as to Life Insurance in Bankruptcy	43
§ 57	The Question One of State Law	43
§ 58	Restoration of Status quo when Fradulent Transactions are set Aside	44
§ 59	Representatives of Creditors get no Higher Rights	46
§ 60	Agreements restricting the Creditor's Rights	47

CHAPTER III

THE FRAUDULENT TRANSFER. ORIGIN AND SCOPE OF THE
STATUTE OF FRAUDULENT CONVEYANCES, §§ 61–88   49–69

§ 61	Definition of Fraudulent Transfer	49
§ 62	Transfer as Distinct from Concealment	50

TABLE OF CONTENTS.   xi

		PAGES
§ 63	Inadequacy of Common Law	51
§ 64.	Equity's Jurisdiction never Tested	51
§ 65	Historical Reason	52
§ 66.	Historical Reason, Continued	52
§ 67	Historical Reason, Continued	53
§ 68	Adoption of Statute of Fraudulent Conveyances	54
§ 69.	The Statute the Corner Stone of this Branch of Law	54
§ 70.	Present and Subsequent Creditors	54
§ 71	Tort Claimant not a Present Creditor until Judgment is Recovered	55
§ 72.	Contract Creditors not necessarily Present Creditors	57
§ 73	Necessity of Judgment for Invocation of Statute	57
§ 74.	Procedure of Judgment Creditor — Levying upon the Transferred Property	58
§ 75.	Necessity of Regular Process	59
§ 76.	Another Method of Procedure	59
§ 77.	Procedure in Case of Real Estate	60
§ 78.	Inadequacy of Common Law Procedure	61
§ 79	Concurrent Jurisdiction of Equity in Case of Real Estate	62
§ 80	Concurrent Jurisdiction in Cases of Personal Property	64
§ 81	Subrogation of Surety	64
§ 82	The Statute gives merely a Right to Act	65
§ 83.	The Creditor must Act	65
§ 84	Assignability of Such Right	66
§ 85.	Effect of Statute on Third Parties	67
§ 86.	Validity of Fraudulent Transaction as between Immediate Parties	67
§ 87.	Opposing Views	67
§ 88	Validity of Transaction as against Third Parties who are not Creditors	68

CHAPTER IV

FRAUDULENT TRANSFER (*Continued*). PROPERTY AFFECTED BY
THE STATUTE, §§ 89–98 70–76

§ 89.	The Statute's Preamble	70
§ 90	The Statute's Omission of Equitable Assets	70
§ 91	Should an Equity Court nevertheless enforce the Statute in Cases of Equitable Assets?	71
§ 92	Lord Hardwicke's View	71
§ 93	Lord Thurlow's Contrary View	72
§ 94	Influence of Lord Thurlow's Rule	73
§ 95	Conflict of American Decisions	73

TABLE OF CONTENTS.

	PAGES
§ 96. Prevailing American Rule	74
§ 97. Statute not Applicable to Exempt Property	75
§ 98. Worthless Property	75

CHAPTER V

FRAUDULENT TRANSFER (*Continued*) METHODS OF ALIENATION,
§§ 99–109 77–86

§ 99.	The Effect of the Transfer is its Test	77
§ 100.	Illustrations	78
§ 101.	The Debtor's Inaction may have Fraudulent Effect	78
§ 102.	Another Expression of the Rule	79
§ 103.	Transfer need not be Direct	80
§ 104.	Illustrations from the Law of Partnership	80
§ 105	Fraudulent Use of the Corporate Entity	81
§ 106	Corporate Reorganization — Rights of Creditors against Purchaser at Foreclosure Sale	82
§ 107.	Early Decisions on this Question	84
§ 108	The Present View of the Supreme Court	85
§ 109	Corporate Reorganization — Rights of Creditors against New Corporation	86

CHAPTER VI

FRAUDULENT TRANSFER (*Continued*) VALIDITY OF GIFTS,
§§ 110–127 87–101

§ 110	The Proviso in Favor of the Innocent Purchaser	87
§ 111	No Proviso in Favor of Transferee unless he is a Purchaser	88
§ 112	Issues which Affect the Transferee	88
§ 113	Transferee cannot attack Validity of Creditor's Judgment	88
§ 114	Transferee's Privies are in Same Position	90
§ 115	Cases of Creditors' Estoppel furnish no Exception	90
§ 116	Hence a Donee's Case involves only an Inquiry as to the Debtor's Intent	92
§ 117	General Rule as to Debtor's Intent	92
§ 118	Is a Gift Fraudulent if Donor was indebted at the Time?	92
§ 119	The Early Rule — Lord Hardwicke's View	93
§ 120	Chancellor Kent's View — Reade *v* Livingston	94
§ 121.	Effect of the Hardwicke-Kent Doctrine	94
§ 122	The Contrary View — Prior Indebtedness should be only Presumptive Evidence of Fraud	95
§ 123	Prevalence of This View	97

TABLE OF CONTENTS xiii

		PAGES
§ 124.	Early American Origin of This Rule and its Final Triumph over the Hardwicke-Kent Doctrine in New York.	97
§ 125.	Both Rules present Questions of Law	99
§ 126.	Illustrations in Cases of Partnership and Corporate Reorganization.	100
§ 127.	Donee entitled to Subrogation	101

CHAPTER VII

FRAUDULENT TRANSFER (*Continued*) VALIDITY OF AN ALIENATION TO A PURCHASER, §§ 128-156 . . . 102-123

§ 128.	Situation of Purchaser Different from that of Donee.	102
§ 129	The "Saving Clause" of the Statute	104
§ 130.	Every *Bona Fide* Purchaser is Protected	104
§ 131	The Burden of Proof	105
§ 132	Relevancy of Evidence	106
§ 133.	The Debtor's Intent as determined by his Financial Condition	108
§ 134	The Debtor's Intent as determined by the effect of the Transaction	109
§ 135.	Where the Consideration is on Hand	109
§ 136.	Where the Debtor has disposed of the Consideration	109
§ 137.	Where the Debtor uses the Proceeds to prefer One Creditor over Another by Way of paying or securing his Claim The Early View	110
§ 138	Later Doctrine of Lord Justice James	111
§ 139.	The Supreme Court's Decisions	111
§ 140	Where the Debtor secretes, squanders or gives away the Consideration	112
§ 141	Nature of Consideration Necessary.	112
§ 142	Past Consideration.	113
§ 143.	Extent of Consideration.	114
§ 144	Good Faith	115
§ 145	Notice to Transferee.	115
§ 146.	Character of Badges of Fraud	116
§ 147.	Twofold Use of Badges of Fraud	117
§ 148	Vendor's Retention of Possession	117
§ 149.	The Sale in Bulk	118
§ 150	Sales in Bulk Statutes	118
§ 151	Agreements to withhold from Record	120
§ 152	Other Badges of Fraud	120
§ 153.	Case of Transferee who receives Notice before completing Payment of Consideration	121

TABLE OF CONTENTS

		PAGES
§ 154	The Common Law Rule	121
§ 155	The Equity Rule	121
§ 156	Extension of Doctrine	122

CHAPTER VIII

FRAUDULENT TRANSFER (*Continued*). RIGHTS OF SUBSEQUENT CREDITORS, §§ 157-172   124-136

§ 157.	Distinction in Principle between Present and Subsequent Creditors	124
§ 158	Early Rule in Cases of Gifts	125
§ 159.	Result of Rule	126
§ 160.	Present English Rule	126
§ 161	Discussion of the Two Rules thus far Stated	127
§ 162	Another Point of View Suggested	128
§ 163	The Prevailing American Rule	129
§ 164	The Doctrine as Stated in Iowa	129
§ 165	Criticism of This Statement	130
§ 166.	Other Statements of the Rule	130
§ 167.	Criticism of These Statements	131
§ 168.	Illustration of Express Intent	132
§ 169.	Illustration of Imputed Intent	132
§ 170	The Test Repeated	133
§ 171	Application of the Rule to Contract Claims	133
§ 172	Application of the Rule to Tort Claims	134

CHAPTER IX

REPUTED OWNERSHIP SOURCES OF THE DOCTRINE, §§ 173-205   137-156

§ 173	Definition of Subject	137
§ 174	Statute of Fraudulent Conveyances not Wholly Adequate	138
§ 175	Application of Statute of Fraudulent Conveyances	138
§ 176	Rule of Twyne's Case	138
§ 177	Separation of Ownership from Possession not Conclusive	139
§ 178	Secrecy not Conclusive	139
§ 179.	Separation Accompanied by Secrecy	140
§ 180	Other Cases Covered by Another Statute	141
§ 181	The Original "Reputed Ownership Clause" of the Bankrupt Statute	141
§ 182.	Present English Statute	141

TABLE OF CONTENTS

		PAGES
§ 183	The Statute as a Supplement to the Statute of Fraudulent Conveyances	142
§ 184	Limitations of the Reputed Ownership Statute — It only Applies in Cases of Bankruptcy	143
§ 185.	It does not Apply to Real Estate	143
§ 186.	Other Statutes Relating to Real Estate	144
§ 187.	Statute of Reputed Ownership does not Apply to Equitable Assets	144
§ 188	Lord Hardwicke's Interpretation of the Statute	145
§ 189	Statute's Application Limited to Trade Debts.	145
§ 190.	Criticisms of the Statute by English Courts	146
§ 191	Statute does not Apply to Stoppage in Transit.	147
§ 192	Statute does not Apply to General Assignment	147
§ 193	Statute does not Apply to Consignments or Conditional Sale	148
§ 194.	Reasons Assigned for these Exceptions	148
§ 195.	Reasonable Use of Commercial Custom	149
§ 196	Debtor's Status in the Business to which the Custom Appertains	149
§ 197.	Proof of Custom	149
§ 198	Absence of Similar Statutes in America	150
§ 199	View of the Illinois and Pennsylvania Courts	151
§ 200	Estoppel as American Substitute for Statute	151
§ 201	Estoppel the Spirit of the Statute	151
§ 202.	The American Doctrine of Estoppel	152
§ 203.	Exceptions to American Rule	154
§ 204	American Rule does not Apply to Choses in Action	155
§ 205.	Criticism of This Limitation	156

CHAPTER X

REPUTED OWNERSHIP IN THE LIGHT OF THE RECORDING ACTS, §§ 206–223 157–170

§ 206	General Nature of Recording Acts	157
§ 207	Statutes Relating to Real Estate	158
§ 208	General Nature of American Recording Acts as Affecting Land	158
§ 209	Distinction Between Creditors and Purchasers	159
§ 210	Statutes Protecting Purchasers but not Creditors	159
§ 211	Such Statutes do not Protect Judgment Creditors	159
§ 212	Purchaser on Execution Sale as Protected by Such Statutes	160
§ 213	Statutes Protecting Creditors as well as Purchasers	160
§ 214.	Recording Acts as Augmenting the Doctrine of Reputed Ownership	161

		PAGES
§ 215	Effect of Withholding Conveyance from Record	162
§ 216.	Withholding from Record raises only a Presumption	163
§ 217	Statutes Affecting Personal Property	164
§ 218	Tendency to Growth of Such Legislation	165
§ 219.	Classification of Statutes Affecting the Chattel Mortgage and the Conditional Sale.	166
§ 220.	Different Views as to Manner of Compliance.	167
§ 221	Necessity of Judgment for Action under Such Statutes	167
§ 222	Basis of Average Statute is Rule of Twyne's Case	168
§ 223.	Tendency to Extension of Legislation — Its Origin .	169

CHAPTER XI

REPUTED OWNERSHIP IN CONNECTION WITH PLEDGES, §§ 224–239 171–184

§ 224	Extent of Connection between Law of Pledge and Doctrine of Reputed Ownership	171
§ 225	"Pledges" of Choses in Action	172
§ 226	Doctrine of Casey v Cavaroc and Sexton v. Kessler	173
§ 227.	The Doctrine of "Equitable Pledge" is part of the Law of Specific Performance	174
§ 228.	The Strict Law of Pledges is Confined to Tangible Chattels	175
§ 229.	"Constructive Possession" as giving Room for Cases of Reputed Ownership	175
§ 230.	Symbolical Delivery and Notice of Possession	176
§ 231.	Illustrative Cases	177
§ 232	Custodian jointly Employed by Pledgor and Pledgee	178
§ 233.	Pledgor cannot be the Custodian	179
§ 234.	Confusion of Property	179
§ 235.	Possession by Third Party	180
§ 236	If Third Party's Possession is Manifest, Goods may Remain on Pledgor's Premises . .	181
§ 237.	Pledgor cannot be his own Warehouseman	182
§ 238	Fictitious Corporate Entity in Connection with Warehousing	182
§ 239	Validity of "Equitable Lien" on Chattels	183

CHAPTER XII

REPUTED OWNERSHIP IN CONNECTION WITH AGENCY, §§ 240–258 185–202

| § 240 | Class of Agency Arrangements Affected by Doctrine of Reputed Ownership | 185 |

TABLE OF CONTENTS. xvii

		PAGES
§ 241.	Definitions of Conditional Sale and Chattel Mortgage	186
§ 242.	Definition of Consignment	187
§ 243.	Essential Legality of Each Arrangement, Standing Alone	188
§ 244.	Method of Inquiry in Cases of Complication	188
§ 245	Illustrative case — Ryttenberg v Schefer	188
§ 246	Illustrative Case — Ommen v Talcott	190
§ 247.	Question — Whether Consignment or Sale?	191
§ 248	Disposition of the Goods	191
§ 249	Disposition of Proceeds of Sale	192
§ 250	Whether Sale is Absolute or Conditional	193
§ 251.	Rule in Cases of Conditional Sale and Chattel Mortgage	194
§ 252	Evolution of this Rule from the Particular to the General	195
§ 253.	Growth of Doctrine — Illustrative Cases	196
§ 254	Recordation of Agreement Immaterial	197
§ 255	Essentially False Character of such Arrangements	198
§ 256.	Opposing View of some Jurisdictions	199
§ 257	Trust Receipts	200
§ 258.	Confusion of the Decisions	201

CHAPTER XIII

REPUTED OWNERSHIP IN CONNECTION WITH MORTGAGES, §§ 259–278 203–219

§ 259	The "After-acquired Property Clause"	203
§ 260.	The Common Law Doctrine	204
§ 261	The Clause in the Light of Equity	205
§ 262.	Justice Story's View	207
§ 263	Concurring View of the House of Lords	207
§ 264.	The Clause has Limitations of Locality	208
§ 265.	American Courts not Unanimous	208
§ 266.	Intervening Act Required	209
§ 267	Early View in New York	210
§ 268.	The Corporate Mortgage — Mortgage of a Public Service Company	210
§ 269	The Corporate Mortgage — Mortgage of a Manufacturing Company	211
§ 270.	Judge Lowell's Opinion	211
§ 271.	Economics Basis for New York Doctrine	212
§ 272.	Early View of the Federal Courts	213
§ 273	Present View of the Federal Courts	214
§ 274	Exception in Favor of Railroad Mortgages	215

xviii TABLE OF CONTENTS.

	PAGES
§ 275. Reasons Given for Such Exceptions	216
§ 276 Rule Concerning Railroad Mortgages as Supplemented by Doctrine of Fosdick v Schall	217
§ 277 English View of the Present day	218
§ 278 English Rule is Based on the Recording Acts	218

CHAPTER XIV

EQUALITY OF DISTRIBUTION AS AN OBJECT OF ATTAINMENT
§§ 279–286 . . 220–225

§ 279 The Selfish System of Realization	220
§ 280 The System of Equal Distribution	220
§ 281. Equal Distribution an Object only in Case of Insolvency	221
§ 282. The Selfish Point of View	221
§ 283. The Principle of Equal Distribution	222
§ 284. Judicial Recognition of This Principle	222
§ 285 Common Ground of the Two Principles	223
§ 286 Relation of the Preferential Transfer to the Two Systems	224

CHAPTER XV

EQUALITY OF DISTRIBUTION AS ACHIEVED BY THE DEBTOR'S
VOLUNTARY ACT, §§ 287–292 . . 226–231

§ 287 Debtor cannot Secure Equal Distribution by Suit	226
§ 288 The General Assignment	226
§ 289 It must Prescribe Immediate Distribution	227
§ 290 Weakness of the General Assignment	229
§ 291 Validity of Preferences in General Assignment	230
§ 292. Status of Assignee	231

CHAPTER XVI

EQUALITY OF DISTRIBUTION (Continued). THE JURISDICTION OF
EQUITY, §§ 293–329 . . 232–260

§ 293 Inadequacy of Common Law Process	233
§ 294 Insolvency Alone Gives no Jurisdiction to Equity	233
§ 295 Basis of Equitable Jurisdiction — a Limited Fund Dedicated to the Payment of Debts	234
§ 296 First Exercise of Jurisdiction — Administration Bill	234
§ 297 The Grounds of Jurisdiction	234
§ 298. Conditions Imposed upon Plaintiff	236

TABLE OF CONTENTS. XIX

		PAGES
§ 299.	Jurisdiction Applied to Land as well as Personal Property	237
§ 300.	Equal Distribution Effected by Such Proceedings	237
§ 301.	Remains of This Jurisdiction in America	238
§ 302.	Survival of Jurisdiction in Federal Courts	239
§ 303.	Value of This Equitable Power under Modern Conditions	240
§ 304.	Administrative Jurisdiction of Corporate Assets	241
§ 305.	The "Trust Fund Doctrine" as a Description of Jurisdiction	242
§ 306.	Illustrations in the Case of Partnership	242
§ 307.	Illustrations in the Case of Statutory Liability	243
§ 308.	The Jurisdiction Arises in View of Insolvency	244
§ 309.	This Jurisdiction Limited in Exercise to America	244
§ 310.	Administration is not Dissolution	245
§ 311.	The Plaintiff cannot have Priority	246
§ 312.	"Collusion" not of Itself Improper	247
§ 313.	Jurisdiction Limited to Liquidation	247
§ 314.	Creditors' Committees Lawful	249
§ 315.	Jurisdiction not a Model of Perfection	249
§ 316.	Distribution of Property in Possession	250
§ 317.	Rights of Prior Lienor	250
§ 318.	Disposition of Pending Suits	251
§ 319.	Effect of Judgment Recovered after Receiver is Appointed	252
§ 320.	Disposition of Property not on Hand	252
§ 321.	Can Fraudulent Transactions be set Aside?	252
§ 322.	Receiver the Person to Sue in such a Case, if Any	253
§ 323.	The Question Considered from Standpoint of Principle	253
§ 324.	The Supreme Court's View	254
§ 325.	Precedents in Such Matters	255
§ 326.	Cases Distinguished	256
§ 327.	Extent of Court's Powers	257
§ 328.	Reasoning in Support of Contrary View	257
§ 329.	Answer to These Contentions	259

CHAPTER XVII

BANKRUPTCY AS A METHOD OF EFFECTING EQUALITY OF DISTRIBUTION, §§ 330–354 261–283

§ 330.	The System which is Needed	261
§ 331.	Bankruptcy Legislation Produces This System	262
§ 332.	Early English Legislation	263
§ 333.	Interpretation of These Statutes	264

		PAGES
§ 334	The Creditors' Representative	265
§ 335	Forcing the Creditors to Come In	266
§ 336	Double Object of the System	266
§ 337	Annulment of Outstanding Judicial Liens	267
§ 338	Annulment of Judicial Liens as Bearing on Status of Trustee	269
§ 339	Right of Trustee to Attack Fraudulent Conveyance	269
§ 340	Cognate Character of Statute of Fraudulent Conveyance and First Bankrupt Act	270
§ 341	Concurrent Jurisdiction of Law and Equity	272
§ 342	View in Some Jurisdictions	273
§ 343	Origin of Doctrine Concerning Preferences	273
§ 344	Trustee can Enforce All of the Creditors' Rights	275
§ 345	Position of Trustee under the Recording Acts	275
§ 346	Contrary Doctrine of Yeatman v Savings Institution	276
§ 347	Early Decisions under Present Statute	276
§ 348	The Amendment of 1910	277
§ 349	Trustee the Sole Representative	278
§ 350	Trustee's Status with Respect to Claims	278
§ 351	Trustee's Status with Respect to Stockholders' Liability	279
§ 352	Different Aspects of the Situation	279
§ 353	Procedure of Trustee	281
§ 354	Trustee's Status with Respect to New York Statutory Trust	282

CHAPTER XVIII

THE BANKRUPTCY TRUSTEE UNDER THE PRESENT NATIONAL ACT, §§ 355-385 284-306

§ 355	Present National Bankrupt Act	284
§ 356	Voluntary Bankruptcy	285
§ 357	Acts of Bankruptcy	285
§ 358	The Fraudulent Conveyance	287
§ 359	Concealment of Property	287
§ 360	The Preferential Transfer	287
§ 361	To Suffer or Permit, while Insolvent, a Creditor to Obtain a Preference through Legal Process, and not to Vacate it Five Days before Sale or Final Disposition of Property Taken under Process	288
§ 362	Debtor's Inaction with Respect to the Levy may Constitute Act of Bankruptcy	288

TABLE OF CONTENTS.

		PAGES
§ 363	Date of Lien	289
§ 364	Lien of "Equitable Levy"	289
§ 365	Other Acts of Bankruptcy	290
§ 366.	The Time Limit for the Occurrence of the Acts	290
§ 367	Relationship of Bankruptcy to Solvency	291
§ 368	Acts of Bankruptcy Unaccompanied by Insolvency	291
§ 369	Appointment of Receiver as Act of Bankruptcy	292
§ 370	What is Insolvency?	292
§ 371	Real Nature of Statutory Definitions	293
§ 372	Illustrative Cases	293
§ 373	Further Illustration — Appointment of Receiver	294
§ 374.	Territorial Limitations of Federal Courts	295
§ 375.	The Federal District as the Unit of Jurisdiction	295
§ 376.	Jurisdiction of the District Court	296
§ 377.	Character of Proceedings Prior to Adjudication	298
§ 378.	Appointment of Receiver in Bankruptcy	299
§ 379.	Ancillary Receivership	300
§ 380.	Title of the Trustee	302
§ 381.	Extraterritorial Powers of Trustee	303
§ 382.	Similar Powers of National Bank Receiver	303
§ 383.	Recognition of Title of Foreign Trustee to Personal Property — English Rule	304
§ 384.	Title of Foreign Trustee to Real Estate	305
§ 385.	Title of Foreign Trustee to Personal Property — American Rule	306

CHAPTER XIX

METHODS OF JUDICIAL LIQUIDATION OTHER THAN BANKRUPTCY
§§ 386–413 307–331

§ 386	Necessity of Statutory System	307
§ 387	Bankrupt Acts as Confined to Traders	308
§ 388	Insolvency Acts	309
§ 389.	Dual System thus Created, and its Omissions	310
§ 390	Conflict in American Ideas	311
§ 391.	Resulting Complexity of American System	312

A. *Personal Representative of a Deceased Debtor*

§ 392	Common Law Position of Executor	313
§ 393	Confusion in Early English Decisions	313
§ 394	Conflict in American Decisions	314
§ 395.	Doctrine under Modern Statutes	315

B *Committee of a Lunatic*

		PAGES
§ 396	Original Status of Committee	318
§ 397.	American Legislation	318
§ 398	Jurisdiction of Chancery Court under Modern Statutes	319
§ 399	Enforcement of Claims	320

C. *Assignee for Creditors*

§ 400	Assignee's Status under American Legislation	321
§ 401	Duty of Assignee under Such Statutes	322

D   *Statutory Receivers of Insolvent Corporations*

§ 402	Modern American Legislation	323
§ 403	Illustration — Practice under New York Statute	324
§ 404.	Status of Receiver	324

E   *Receivers of Banks*

§ 405	Resemblance of National Statute to English Statutes	325
§ 406	Federal Banks as Local Institutions	325
§ 407	Creative Legislation	326
§ 408	Statutes Afford Complete System for Winding-up	326
§ 409	Summary of Winding-up Provisions	327
§ 410	Statute Secures Equal Distribution	328
§ 411	Appointment of Receiver — State Control	328
§ 412.	Judicial Control of Receiver	330
§ 413.	Tendency to State Control in Laws Governing State Banks	330

CHAPTER XX

THE PREFERENTIAL TRANSFER AS INFRINGING THE RIGHT TO
EQUAL DISTRIBUTION, §§ 414–431 . . . 332–343

§ 414	General Considerations	332
§ 415	Preferences in Connection with the Trust Fund Doctrine	332
§ 416	State Laws Forbidding Preferences	333
§ 417	Preferences Forbidden by National Bank Acts	334
§ 418	Preferences under the National Bankrupt Act	335
§ 419	Superfluous Definitions in Statute	335
§ 420	Spirit of the Statute	336
§ 421.	National Bankrupt Act as Model	336
§ 422.	Passive Preferences	337
§ 423	Definition of "Transfer"	337

TABLE OF CONTENTS. xxiii

		PAGES
§ 424.	Illustrative Cases	338
§ 425	Illustrative Cases Continued	338
§ 426.	Exchange of Values No Preference	339
§ 427.	Test is the Diminution of the Debtor's Estate	340
§ 428.	Set-off as an Exception	340
§ 429.	Time Limit	341
§ 430.	Time Limit with Respect to the Recording Acts	341
§ 431.	Interpretation of Statute as to Time Limit for Recording Transfer	342

CHAPTER XXI

PREFERENCES (*Continued*) POSITION OF THE TRANSFEREE, §§ 432–450 344–358

§ 432.	"Intent to Prefer"	344
§ 433	Test is the Result of the Transfer	344
§ 434.	"Reasonable Cause to Believe"	345
§ 435	Ordinary Standard of Prudence	346
§ 436.	Transfer Pursuant to Previous Obligation	347
§ 437	Transfer must be in Payment of, or as Security for, a Previous Debt	347
§ 438.	Transfer is by Way of Performance or Recognition of Obligation	348
§ 439	Restoration of Embezzled Trust Funds	348
§ 440.	The Transfer must be of Debtor's Own Property	349
§ 441.	Explanation of Doctrine of Equitable Lien	350
§ 442	Illustrative Cases	352
§ 443	Agreement in the Alternative	353
§ 444.	Putting Mortgagee in Possession	353
§ 445.	Property must be Identified	353
§ 446.	Promise to Give Security	354
§ 447	Relation of Broker and Customer	355
§ 448.	Illustrative Cases	355
§ 449	Contract must have Mutuality	357
§ 450.	Good Faith Essential	358

CHAPTER XXII

RELATION OF NATIONAL AND STATE SYSTEMS OF JUDICIAL LIQUIDATION, §§ 451–471 359–375

§ 451	Supremacy of National Bankrupt Act	359
§ 452	Jurisdiction of Admiralty an Exception	360
§ 453	Question of Supremacy is One of Jurisdiction	360
§ 454.	Test for Determining Conflict of Jurisdictions	361

		PAGE
§ 455	Conflict Relates to Administration	362
§ 456	National Statute Suspends only the Decisions of the Particular Case	364
§ 457	Limitations of Bankruptcy Jurisdiction	365
§ 458	Other Courts' Powers are Territorially Limited	366
§ 459	Average Case Raises Question of Conflict of Laws	367
§ 460	Question in Connection with Jurisdiction where Debtor Resides	367
§ 461	Difficulty of Suing Absent Debtor	367
§ 462	Powers of Receiver outside Jurisdiction — Federal Rule	368
§ 463	Powers of Receiver outside Jurisdiction — Conflict among State Courts	369
§ 464	Powers of Statutory Receiver outside Jurisdiction	370
§ 465	Priority of Local Judgments	370
§ 466	Ancillary Receivers	372
§ 467	Nature of Ancillary Suit	373
§ 468	Duties of Ancillary Receiver	374
§ 469	Powers of Ancillary Court	374
§ 470	Jurisdiction of Federal Courts	374
§ 471	Dependent Jurisdiction of Federal Courts	375

CHAPTER XXIII

EXPENSES OF ADMINISTRATION, §§ 472–488 . . . 376–389

		PAGE
§ 472	Government does not Meet All the Expenses	376
§ 473	Expenses not Taxable as Costs	377
§ 474	Expenses are Chargeable against the Estate	377
§ 475	Services of Counsel	378
§ 476	Expenses of Administration as a Primary Charge	378
§ 477	Method of Estimating these Charges	379
§ 478	Allowances to Counsel other than Those employed by the Liquidator	380
§ 479	Requisites for Allowance to Counsel	381
§ 480	Continuance of Business by Liquidator	382
§ 481	Necessity of Receiver Borrowing Money to Continue Business	383
§ 482	Cannot Displace Vested Lien without Holder's Consent	383
§ 483	Liquidator's Pledge as against Rights of General Creditors Rule in Bankruptcy	384
§ 484	In the Absence of Statute	384
§ 485	Rule in the Case of Railroad Companies	385

		PAGES
§ 486.	This Rule should Apply to all Public Service Companies	386
§ 487.	Receiver's Certificates	387
§ 488.	Deficiency in Operation of Public Service Company	388

CHAPTER XXIV

DISTRIBUTION OF DEBTOR'S ESTATE — GENERAL CLAIMS, §§ 489–513 390–411

§ 489.	Creditors Primary Parties in Interest	390
§ 490.	Claims Capable of Assertion	391
§ 491.	Tort Claims	391
§ 492.	Judgments Founded on Torts	391
§ 493.	Interest on Claims	392
§ 494.	Mode of Establishing Claims	393
§ 495.	No Time Limits for Establishing Claims in Absence of Statute	394
§ 496.	Peculiarities of New York Rule	394
§ 497.	Protection of Distributing Officer	395
§ 498.	Liquidating Point for Claims	396
§ 499.	Corporate Dissolution — Conflict of Rules	396
§ 500.	Bankruptcy — Development of English Doctrine	398
§ 501.	Bankruptcy — American Doctrine	399
§ 502.	Restrictions of Early American Statutes	401
§ 503.	Restrictions on Contingent Claims should be Enforced only in Aid of Creditors	401
§ 504.	Contingent Claims in Cases of Corporate Dissolution	402
§ 505.	Ranking of Contingent Claims in Cases of Decedents' Estates and of Corporate Dissolution	403
§ 506.	Confusion in New York and Minnesota Cases	404
§ 507.	Whether Debtor's Liquidation is a Breach of His Contract	405
§ 508.	Right of Adoption, in General	406
§ 509.	What Obligations may be Adopted	407
§ 510.	Time Allowed Liquidator for Choice	408
§ 511.	Effect of Rejection	410
§ 512.	Effect of Adoption	410
§ 513.	Exception in Case of Public Service Companies	411

CHAPTER XXV

DISTRIBUTION (Continued). PRIOR CLAIMS, §§ 514–528 . 412–422

§ 514.	Nature of Prior Claims	412
§ 515.	Debts Due Government	413

TABLE OF CONTENTS

		PAGES
§ 516	Government Debts in National Bank Liquidation	413
§ 517.	Marshaling of Government Debts	414
§ 518.	Statutory Priorities in General	414
§ 519	Landlord's Lien on Tenant's Goods	415
§ 520.	Priority of Landlord's Lien	415
§ 521	Priority of Labor Claims	416
§ 522.	Priority of Supply Claims in General	417
§ 523	Equitable Doctrine in Case of Public Service Companies	418
§ 524.	The Decision in Fosdick v Schall	418
§ 525	Time within which Supplies must be Furnished	419
§ 526	Necessity for Liquidator to Obtain Further Credit	420
§ 527	Whether Doctrine Applies to Case Instituted by Creditor's Bill	421
§ 528	State Laws Embodying the Doctrine	421

CHAPTER XXVI

DISTRIBUTION (*Continued*) SECURED CLAIMS, §§ 529–545 . 423–436

§ 529	Secured Creditors have Interest in the Liquidation	423
§ 530	Position of Secured Creditor in Absence of Liquidation	424
§ 531.	Liquidation does not Deprive Mortgagee of Right to Realize on Security	424
§ 532	Rights of Mortgagee when Property is in Liquidator's Possession	425
§ 533.	Chancery Practice in Such Cases	426
§ 534.	Expenses of Preserving Property, and Liquidator's Charges	426
§ 535.	Relative Positions of Mortgagee and Liquidator	426
§ 536.	Bankruptcy Rule — English Legislation	427
§ 537.	American Bankruptcy Rule, and Practice Thereunder	428
§ 538	Security given by Surety — Federal Rule	429
§ 539	Defect of Bankruptcy Rule	431
§ 540	Limitations of Doctrine of Marshaling	431
§ 541	Early Chancery Doctrine	432
§ 542	Later Chancery Doctrine – Rule of Mason v Bogg	433
§ 543	Prevalence in America of Rule of Mason v Bogg	433
§ 544	Degree to which Rule of Mason v Bogg now Obtains	434
§ 545.	Problem of Notes Secured by Promissor's Bonds	435

CHAPTER XXVII

THE DEBTOR'S DISCHARGE, §§ 546–557 . . 437–445

§ 546. No Discharge at Common Law . . . 437
§ 547. Equity can Give no Discharge . . . 437
§ 548. Discharge under English System of Bankruptcy . 438
§ 549. Discharge in Present National Bankrupt Act . 439
§ 550. Discharge of Judgments — Tort Claims . . 439
§ 551. Test is whether Party could have Sued *Ex Contractu* 440
§ 552. Certain Judgments not Barred by Discharge . 442
§ 553. Creditor must have Notice of Bankruptcy . . 442
§ 554. Effect of Discharge 443
§ 555. Promise to Pay Discharged Debt . . . 443
§ 556. Extraterritorial Effect of Discharge . . 444
§ 557. Intervening Removal of Creditor . . . 445

INDEX 447

TABLE OF CASES

[The References are to Pages.]

A

Abbey v Deyo	24
Abbey Press, In re	50
Abraham v Plestoro	305
Abram Steers Lumber Co, In re	24
Acme Harvester Co. v. Beckman	248
Adler Goldman Comm Co. v. Williams	20
Aetna Bank v. Manhattan Life Ins. Co.	16
Ahearn v Prunell	59, 89
Aiello v. Crampton	338
Alabama Iron Works v. McKeever	16
Alderson v. Temple	274
Aldine Trust Co v Smith	46
Alexander v Relfe	325
v. Redmond	345, 346
Allen v Ferguson	444
v. Gray	64, 273
v Hollender	179
v. Luke	304
v. Massey	140
Alter v Clark	288
Alton Mfg Co, In re	299
American &c Co. v. Angelasto	416
American Bonding Co. v. Reynolds	413
American Brake Co. v Pere Marquette Ry.	245
American Can Co v. Erie Preserving Co	257
American Iron &c. Co. v. Seaboard A. L. Co	393, 427
American Nat. Bank v. Northwestern &c. Co.	30
American Pig Iron Co. v. German	177
American Sugar Ref Co v. Fancher	154
American Trust Co. v Metropolitan S. S. Co.	421
Ames, Ex parte	347
Ames v. Moir	404
Amory v. Francis	432, 434
Anders Push Button Co, In re	426
Anderson v Brown	315
v. Maltby	270
v Roberts	105
Angell v Draper	8
Annis v Butterfield	66
Anon	394
Anthony v Wood	8
Arrowsmith v Gleason	240
Atherton v Green	350
Atlantic Trust Co v. Chapman	386, 388, 389
Attorney General, Matter of	382
v Brewers Co.	381
v Guardian Mutual Life Ins Co	41
v. Old South Society	381
Audubon v Shufeldt	439
Austin v O'Reilley	415, 416
Auten v City Electric Co.	256
Aycock v. Martin	312
Ayres v McCandless	177, 178

B

Babbitt v. Dutcher	300, 303
v. Read	280
Babcock v Booth	314, 315, 316
v. Eckler	95, 97, 98
Backhouse v. Hunter	235
v Jett	315
Bailey v Hudson River R R Co.	187
v Timberlake	159, 160
Baker Company v. Bailey	343
Baker Notion Co, In re	429
Baker v. N Y Nat. Ex. Bank	187
Balch v. Wastell	8

TABLE OF CASES.

[The References are to Pages]

Baldwin v Hale	445	Binghampton Co, In re	424
v. Hosmer	372	Birbeck Bldg Soc, In re	245
v Short	109	Birkett v. Columbia Bank	443
Ball v German Bank	341	Blackburn v Gregson	144
Ballantine v. Ballantine	35	Black Pool Motor Car Co,	
Bank v Jagode	176	In re (1901)	348
v. Kennedy	304	Blackstaff Engineering Co.,	
v Sherman	302	In re	416
v Trebein	82	Blake v. Insurance Co	39
Bank of Bethel v Bank	241	v. McClung, 172 U S	
Bank of Scotland v Cuthbert	305	239	371
Banker's Surety Co v. Meyer		176 U S. 59	371
	239, 402	v. Williams	306
Banks, In re	299	Blakes, Ex parte	305
Barber v Barber	55	Blanchard v. Cook	209
Barcroft v Le Sieur	227	Blood v. Kane	239
Bardes v Hawarden Bank	297	Bluefields S S Co v. Steele	373,
Barker, Ex parte	398		375
Barnard v Onderdonk	424	Blue Mountain etc Co. v.	
Barnes v. Rettew	230	Portner	292, 294
Barnett, In re	416	Boese v King	364
Barron v. McKinnon	329	Bogen v Potter	291
Barrow, Ex parte	444	Bologh, In re	331, 417
Barth v Backus	371	Bond v. Willett	12
Barton v Sitlington	80, 205, 209	Boonville Bank v. Blakey	300, 301
v. Hasner	317	Boot v Wilson	404
Bass v Gilbert	392	Booth v Bunce	82
Bate v. Graham	317	v Clark	369
Bauer v Platt	243	v Kehoe	164
Bayard v Hoffman	74	Boston Iron Works v Boston	
Bazemore, In re	278	Locomotive Works	371
Beach v Hollister	38	Bosworth v. Association	278
Bean v. Smith	105	Bottom v National Ry.	
Beck v Burdett	11, 12	Building etc. Assn	375
Beekman v. Hudson River		Bourdillon v. Dalton	408, 411
Ry Co.	295	Bourne v Dodson	151
Beerman, In re	110	Bouslough v Bouslough	55
Beihl v. Martin	38	Boynton v. Ball	266
Beith v Porter	315, 317	Brackett v. Harvey	196
Belfast etc. Co, In re	292, 294	Bradley v. Benson	342
Benedict, In re	300	Bradley Co v White	288
Benedict v Deshel	345	Brandenburgh v Thorndike	227
Benfield v. Solomon	47	Brandon v. Robinson	34, 35
Bennett v Calhoun &c. Assn.	424	Brasher v Van Cortlandt	318,
Bergen v Carman	60		319, 320
Bergman v Lord	13, 35	Breck v Brewster	281
Bernard v Union Trust Co	388	Breeze v Brooks	163
Bernheimer v Converse	370	Brener, In re	150
Berthelon v. Betts	362	Brett v Carter	168, 199, 206, 208,
Berwind-White Coal Min.			211, 214, 219
Co. v. Metropolitan S S.		Bridgeport Ice Co. v. Meader	353
Co.	421	Briggs v. Austin	16
Bethel v Stanhope	314	v. Spalding	325
Big Four Company v Wright	343	Bright, Ex parte	149, 192
Biggs v French	351	Briswalter v Long	365
Bingham v. Jordan	275	Brook v. Bowman	154

TABLE OF CASES xxxi

[The References are to Pages]

Broderick's Will, *In re* 240
Brooks *v* Wilson 21
Brown, *In re*, 47 Hun 360 390
 79 N. Y. Misc 675 238
Brown, *Ex parte*, 4 Bro C. C.
 211 439
Brown *v* Allebach 374
 v. Chubb 75, 101
 v. Merchants Insurance
  Co 82
 v. McDonald, 1 Hill (S.
  C) 297 16
 1 Hill Eq 297 238, 256
 v. Schleier 114
 v. U S Button Co 440
 v Webb 220
Brundage *v* Chenoweth 129
Brunsden *v* Stratton 258
Bryant *v* Swofford Dry
 Goods Co 200
Buchanan *v* Smith 292
Buck, *Ex parte* 149
Buckingham *v* McLean 268
Bucknal *v* Roiston 63
Buehler *v* Gloniger 314
Buell *v* Buckingham 333
 v. Kanawha &c Co. 379
Buffalo Mirror Co , *In re* 406
Burdick *v.* Gill 120
 v Jackson 341, 352
Burkhalter, *In re* 388
Burlein Cornice etc Co , *In re* 384
Bulkingham *v.* Crouse 41, 42,
 43, 44
Burnham, *In re* 40
Burnham *v* Bowen 420
Burt *v* Rattle 48
Burton *v* Peters Salt Co 248, 249
Bush *v* Export Storage Co
 165, 177
 v. Moore 336
Bushnell *v.* Leland 329
Buswell *v* Supreme Sitting 372
Butcher *v.* Werskman 120
Butler *v* Baudovne 282
Butler Paper Co *v.* Goembel 293
Butters, *Ex parte* 269
Butterworth *v* Dignon &c
 Co 26
Button *v.* Rathbone 177

C

Cadogan *v* Kennett 52
Caesar *v* Bernard 294
Caldwell *v* Fifield 78

Cameron *v.* U S 50
Camp *v.* Niagara Bank 394
Campau *v.* Detroit Driving
 Club 248, 382
Campbell *v* Holyland 424
Candee *v.* Lord 89
Canton &c Co *In re* 278
Carbon Fuel Co *v* Chicago
 &c , Railway 420
Carey *v* Donohue 270, 345
Carnegie Trust Co , *In re*,
 206 N Y 390 413
 161 N Y App. Div
  280 394
Carr *v* Hamilton 406
Carson *v* Alleghany Glass Co 244
Cartwright *v* Wilmerding 180
Case *v* Bank 334
 v Beauregard 9, 28, 233, 242
 v Phelps 132
Casey *v.* Cavaroc 153, 171, 173
 v Societe 334
Cass *v* Realty &c Co 48
 v Sutherland 252
Cates *v* Allen 16
Catlin *v* Eagle Bank 333
Cattus, *In re* 201
Ceballos & Co , *In re* 271
Central Electric Co. *v.*
 Socorro Co 334
Central Improvement Co *v*
 Cambria Steel Co , 210
 Fed 696 21
 201 Fed 811 86
Central of Georgia Railway
 Co *v* Paul 84
Central Trust Co *v* Condon 427
 v East Tenn Railroad 420
 v Kneeland 215
 v. Marietta &c Ry. Co. 152
 v Morton Trust Co 26, 31
Century Throwing Co. *v.*
 Muller 153 201, 202
Chamberlain *v* Turner Co. 15
Chambers, Matter of 187
Chambers *v* Smith 34
 v Thompson 15, 222
Chapman *v* Brewer 298
 v Forsythe 442
Charavay *v* York Silk Mfg
 Co 201
Charles, *Ex parte* 56
Charles, *In re* 392
Charman *v* Charman 391
Chase *v.* Denny 205
 v Farmers &c Bank 298

TABLE OF CASES.

[The References are to Pages.]

Chatauqua County Bank v. Risley	250, 251	Cohen v Small	64
Chemical National Bank v. Armstrong	327, 433, 434	v U S	50
		Cono v Baron	186
		Coker v Shropshire	431
Chemung Canal Bank v. Payne	167, 169	Cole v Berry	194
		Coleman v Burr	99, 113
Chetwood, In re	330	Coler v Cunningham	443
Chicago &c Railway Co. v. Gould	390	Collender v Colonial Secretary	305
v Hall	40	Colonial Bank v Sutton	380
v Howard	84	v. Whinney, L R. 11 A. C 426	146, 151
Chicago Title etc Co v. Roeblings Co	293	11 App Cas 439	264
Christensen v. Eno	280	Colquitt v. Thomas	105
Christie v. Bridgman	443	Colston v. Austin &c Co.	288
Christophers t Garr	395	Columbia Real Estate Co., In re	340
Chubb v. Upton	270		
Chynoweth v Tenney	209	Comegys v Vasse	32
Citizens Trust Co v Tilt	358	Commercial Trust Co v Robert H Jenks Co	433
City Bank v Hamilton	163		
v Peacock	180	Commonwealth Bank v. Hall	39
Claflin v Claflin	34	Commonwealth Roof Co v North American Co.	409
v. Gordan	12		
v. McDermott	18	Compton v Golden Cycle Co	375
Claridge v Evans	270, 342	v Jesup	375
Clark etc Company, In re	383	Conklin v Shelley	194, 196
Clark v Clark	29	v. U S Shipbuilding Co.	246
v Isehn	175	Conkling v U S. Shipbuilding Co.	374
v Ray	366		
v Tippin	192	Conn. Mutual Life Ins. Co. v Spratley	18
Clark, In re	239		
Clarke v Centr. of Ga. Ry Co.	223, 249	Conover v Jeffrey	89
		Conrad v Fisher	180
v Rogers	336, 348, 440	v Hamner	378
Clayton v Exchange Bank	163	Constantein v Blache	222, 223
Clement v Cozart	97	Continental &c Bank v Chi &c Trust Co.	26
Clements v Moore	63, 117, 122, 347		
Cleveland v Chambliss	238, 255	Continental Securities Co. v Interborough R T Co.	241
Clough v Samuel	399		
Clowe v Seavy	38, 99	Cont Trust &c Co v Allis-Chalmers Co	223, 249
Clute v Emmerich	160		
Coats v Donnell	334	v Chicago &c Co	341
Cobb v Kempton	402	Cook County National Bank v. United States	327, 413
Coburn v Boston Paper Co	241		
Cockerell v Dickens	305	Cookson v Swire	168
Cockrill v Abeles	304	Cooper v Chitty	267
Codan, In re	25	v Payne	186
Coder v Arts	54, 111, 275	Copenian v. Gallant	142, 148, 151
v McPherson	347	Copland, Ex parte	28
Codrington v Johnston	30, 31	Cornell, In re	323
Codwise v Gelston	14	Cornell v Nichols Co.	279, 378
Coffin v Ray	161	Cotton Mfrs Co., In re	155, 358
Cohen, In re	155	Coulton, In re	396
Cohen v American Surety Company	364	Covert v Rogers	333
		Covington Bridge Co v. Shepherd	6
v. Parish	97		

TABLE OF CASES. xxxiii

[The References are to Pages]

Cowdrey v Galveston &c R R Co	378
Cowley v. McLaughlin	161
Coxe v Peruvian Limited	219
Crafts v. Belden	110, 111, 333
Crawcour v Salter	150
Crawford v Burke	441, 442
Crockett v. Phinney	121, 122
Cross v Carstens	230
Crossley v. Elworthy	135
Crosswell v. Allis	353
Crouse v. Frothingham	317
Crowe &c Company v Liquor &c Co.	187
Crower, Ex parte	28
Crumlin Viaduct Co, In re	146, 218
Cumberland Lumber Co v. Clinton Hill Lumber Co.	280
Curd v Miller	64

D

Dabney v The Bank	333
Dana v Bank	333
Daniel, In re	29
D'Aquila v Lambert	147
Darcy v Brooklyn Ferry Co	100
Dart v Wood	24
Darville v. Terry	114
Davenport v Alabama, etc Ry	384
Davis v Gray	257
v Owenby	160
v Schwartz	114, 120
v Snell	278
Dawson Bank v Harris	6, 16
Day v Cooley	128
v Goodbar	163
Dayton Hyd Co v Felsenthal	411
Dean v Plane	342
Deane v Caldwell	405
Dear, Ex parte	29
De Hierapolis v Lawrence	33
v Reilly	113
Delahunty, Matter of	320
DeLand v Bank	340
Demill v. Bedford	34, 35
Dempster, In re	301, 302
Demuth v. Kemp	9
Denny v Lincoln	277
Denton v Livingston	7
De Ruiter v. De Ruiter	56
Detroit, etc., Ry v Campbell	241

Deutschle & Co, In re	346
Dexter Horton Nat Bank v Hawkins	252
Dickinson v. Burrell	67
v Kempner	435
v Oliver	59, 169
Docker Foster Co, In re	291
Dodge v. McKechnie	224
Doe v. Ball	310
v Clark, 42 Ia 123	317
v Greenhill	8
Doney v. Clark	314, 317
Dooley v. Pease	195, 214
Douglas Company, In re	340
Downing Re	66
Dows v. National Bank	181, 201
Dox v. Backentose,	316
Drake v. Rice	74
Drexel v Pease	201
Drury v. Moors	176, 177
Dunbar v. Dunbar	400, 401
Duncan v. Treadwell Co	248
Dundas v. Dutens	72
Dunham v. Cinn etc Ry Co.	215
v. Cox	63
v. Waterman	228
Dunn v. Train	177, 179
Dunseath, In re	300
Duplan Silk Co. v Spencer	353
Duplex Press Co v. Clipper Pub Co.	257
Dupree, In re	290
Durrant v Mass Hospital	34
Dusenberry v Hoyt	443
Dushane v Beall	408
Dutton v. Morrison	271

E

Eameston v. Lyde	11, 12, 14
Earle v Conway	251
v. Fiske	158
v Robinson	186
East End Mantel Co, In re	277
East Tenn etc R R. v. Atlantic R. R	248
Ecklor v Wolcott	96
Eddy v McCall	207
Edge v Worthington	144
Edgell v Hart	196, 197
Edmonson v Meacham	74
Edwards v. Harben	117, 139, 148, 151, 315
Eisenberg. In re	365
Elliott v Teoppner	291

TABLE OF CASES.

[The References are to Pages.]

Ellis v. Vernon etc., Light & Water Co	386	First National Bank v. Hughes	228
Elmira Society v. Stanchfield	30	v. Pa Trust Co.	177, 178
Empire State Co v. Carroll County	393	Fitch, In re	368
Emslie, In re	289	Fitz, Ex parte	165
Engel v. O'Malley	39	Fleek v. Zielbauer	38
Engle v. Union Square Bank	340	Florence Sewing Mach Co v. Zeigler	122
Ernest v. Pere Marquette Railroad Co	370	Floyd, &c. Co., In re	422
Enrich's Brewery, In re	299	Flury v. Grimes	415
Equitable Life Ass. Co. v. Hughes	377	Fogg v. Blau	215
		Folger v. Putnam	288
Erickson v. Quinn	63	Ford v. Gilbert	290
Erie Lumber Co., In re	387, 416, 417	Forder v. Wade	235
		Fordyce v. Kansas City, etc Co.	25
Erlanger v. New Sombrero Phosphate Co	280	Forsythe v. Vehmeyer	442
		Forth v. Duke of Norfolk	8
Ernst v. Mechs & Metals Bank	107	Fort Wayne Electric Co v. Franklin etc., Co.	292
Estes, In re	61, 64, 65	Fosdick v. Schall	217, 255, 418
Estes v. Howland	314	Foster v. McAlester	220
Ethendge v. Sperry	195, 214	Fouche v. Brower	231
Evans v. Coventry	245	Fourth Street Bank v. Milburn Mills	182
v. Schoonmaker	372		
Everett v. Judson	43	Fowler, In re	372
Evertson v. Booth	424, 431	Fowler v. Jarvis-Conklin Co	223, 249
Exploration Mercantile Company v. Pacific &c. Company	360	Fox v. Gardner	90
		Frank v. Batten	195
		Franklin Bank v. Whitehead	182, 257
F		Fraser v. Levy	121
Fairview &c Co v. Ulrich	373	Freedman's Savings &c Co v. Earle	7, 8, 10, 13
Fanning v. Dunham	47		
Farmers' Bank v. Logan	201	Frelinghuysen v. Nugent	150, 152
Farmers' Loan & Trust Co v. Grape Creek Coal Co	210, 387	Freeman v. Pope	127
v. Oregon &c. Ry Company	386, 389	French v. Morse	401
		v. Winsor	12
Farrell v. Smith	250, 395	Friedman, In re	120
Faithing, In re	364	Friend v. Talcott	443
Faulk v. Steiner	299	Froment, Matter of	360
Faulkner v. Hyman	371	Frost v. Goddard	220
Faxon v. Ridge	167	v. Libby	317
Fechheimer Fishel & Co., In re	48	v. Warren	120
Federal Biscuit Co., In re	360	v. Yonkers Bank	160
Feigley v. Feigley	56	Fuller v. Ins Co.	302
Feldenheimer v. Tressel	15	v. Jameson	302
Fellows v. Lewis	75	Funerald v. Johnson	403
Fera v. Wickham	26	Funk, In re	365
Ferguson v. Ann Arbor R. R. v. Wilson	84, 208		
		G	
Fern v. Ward	41		
Fidelity &c Co. v. Roanoke Iron Co	418	Gableman v. Peoria etc Ry	375
		Gallagher v. Gingrich	379

TABLE OF CASES. XXXV

[The References are to Pages]

Gallison, In re	266
Galt, In re 120 Fed 443	195
120 Fed. 64	154
Galveston R. R. Co v. Cowdrey	204, 213, 216
Garcewich, In re	195, 198
Gardner v. Conn. Bank	228
v. Conn. Nat Bank	227
v. Kleinke	95
v. London etc Ry	245, 248
v McEwen	210
Garfield v Hatmaker	61, 75
Garland, Ex parte	365
Garrard v. Lauderdale	227
Garrison v Monoghan	24
Gassenheimer v. Kellogg	78
Gay v Hudson River Co.	425
v Bidwell	199
Geilfuss v Corrigan	177, 182
Gennort, In re	372
Germania &c. Co. v. Virginia &c Co.	382
Gerstman, In re	277
Gibson v East India Co	32
v. Love	118
v Stevens	181
v Warden	275
Gilbert v Vail	205
Gill v. Griffith	169
Gillespie v. J. C. Piles & Company	120
Gilligan, In re	195
Girard Trust Co. v. Mellor	174
Githens v Schiffler	111, 287
Glasgow v. Turner	24, 95
Glenny v. Langdon	278
Godden v. Crowhurst	35
Goding v. Rosenthal	403
Godschalk v. Sterling	120
Goodlander &c. Co. v. Atwood	340
Goodman v Wineland	96
Goodson v Ellison	227
Gordon v Southgate	334
Government etc Co v Manila	218
Gowing v Rich	74
Graff v Bonnett	35
Graham v Railroad	2
Grant v Humbert	320, 395
v Monmouth Bank	115, 345, 346
Grant Shoe Company v Laird	440
Grantham v Hawley	204
Gray, In re	30
Gray v Chase	44
v Rollo	26
Great Western Manufacturing Co, In re	358
Great Western Mining Co. v Harris	369
Great Western Telegraph Co v. Purdy	282
Green v Adams	55, 135
v McCrane	114
Greenberger, In re	416
Greenhall v C. T Co	302
Greenwald v Wales	115
Greenwood v Taylor	432
Greey v. Dockendorff	140, 155, 205, 297, 354, 425
Gregg v. Metropolitan Trust Co	419, 420
Gregory, In re	38
Griffin v Mutual Life	302
Griffith v Griffith	11
v Ricketts	227
Griswell v Pratt	362
Groome, Ex parte	267, 398
Grosvenor v Phillips	187
Grover v Wakeman	229, 230, 321
Guarantee &c Co. v Guaranty &c Co	413
Guaranty Co v Hanway	329
Guaranty Title &c. Co. v. Pearlman	301
Guardian Bldg Soc., In re	245
Guasti v Miller	443
Gunby v. Armstrong	374
Gutterson & Gould v. Lebanon Steel Co	248

H

Hadden v. Spader	72, 74
Haehnlen v Drayton	240
Haigh v. Grattan	380
Hale v. Frost	419
v. Met. &c. Co.	116
Hall v. Alabama Terminal Co.	54, 74
v Draper	343
v Stryker	89
Hall Company, In re	361
Hallenbeck v Donnell	30
Hallett's Estate, In re	51
Halstead, In re	100
Halsted v Forest Hill Co	250, 395
Hamilton Bank v Halsted	45
Hamilton, etc, Company, In re	46

TABLE OF CASES.

[The References are to Pages]

Hanover Bank v. Moyses	2, 285
Harding v. Mill River Corp.	406
Hardy v Fothergill	398, 399
Harkness v Russell	118, 139, 150, 151, 154
Harlan v Maglaughlin	129, 132
Harlem Savings Bank v. Larkin	2
Harmon v. Osgood	314
Harriman v Gray	45
v. Woburn Electric Light Co	209
Harrington v. Hart	37
Harris v Coe	166, 199
v. First National Bank	297
Harrison v Bowers	159
v. Dingman	394
v Sterry	306
Hart v. Clark	59
Harvey v Lord	304
v McDonnell	317
v Varney	68
Hassels v. Simpson	274
Hastings, Ex parte	318
Haston v Castner	256
Hattersley, Ex parte	150
Hawes v Leader	314
Hawkes, In re	220
Hawkins v Glenn	369
v. Learned	319, 365
Hayden v. Brown	303
v. Thompson	304
Hayes, In re	374
Hayes v Pierson	325
v Ward	431
Hayward v. Leeson	256
Head, In re	338
Heims Milk Co , In re	299
Helby v Matthews	192
Henderson v Mayer	416
Hendricks v Chilton	12
Hennequin v. Clews	442
Herkimer Bank v Brown	78
Hershberger, In re	425
Heryford v Davis	166
Hess v Hess	58, 59
Hevenor, Matter of	404
Hewit v Berlin Mach Works	166
Hibernia Insurance Co. v. Transportation Co.	82
Hibernia National Bank v. Lacombe	371
Hickerson, In re	163, 195
Hickey, In re	146, 264
Hickock v. Cowperthwaite	175
Higden v Williamson	265
Higginbotham v Holme	33
Hill v Harding	266
Hilliard v. Cagle	163
Hills v Sherwood	256
Hillyer v Le Roy	60, 250
Hilton v Ernst	358
Hines, In re	338
Hirsch, In re	120
H. K Porter Co v Boyd	183, 184, 257
Hobbs v. Hull	63, 272
Hodge, In re	120
Hodges v Hurd	167
Hoes v N. Y etc R R	372
Hoffman, In re	82
Hogan v. Walker	255
Holden v Stratton	43, 44
Holland v Cruft	314
v Holland	55
Hollins v. Briarfield Coal Co	21, 242, 247
Holmes v. Dowie	375
v Penney	34
Holroyd v Marshall	206, 207, 209, 218, 219
Holt v Everall	41
v. Henley	168
Holthausen, Ex parte	46, 352
Honegger v Wettstein	251
Hooks v. Aldridge	294, 360
Hooper v. Central Trust Company	387
Hopkins, In re	434
Horn v Pere Marquette Ry. Co	247, 252, 296
Houghton, Ex parte	405
Houghton v. Steiner	66
Howarth v Angle	282, 369
Howland v Carson	440
Hoyle v Plattsburg &c. R. R Co.	217
Hoyt v Godfrey	24, 75
Hubbard v Tod	322
Huddleston, In re	299
Hudgins v Kemp	109
Hudson River Power Co , In re	257
Huff v. Bidwell	382
Hughes, In re	360
Hughes v. Carey	199
Humes v. Scruggs	21
Humphrey v Tatum	167
Hun v. Carey	391
Hungerford v Earle	63, 151, 162
Hunt, In re	342
Hunt v. Doyal	271
v. Wyman	155

TABLE OF CASES. xxxvii

[The References are to Pages.]

Hunter v. Potts	305, 306
Hunters v Waite	99
Huntley v Kingman	114, 224, 230
Hurd v Elizabeth	369
v. New York & Commercial Steam Laundry	84, 86
Hurley v Atch &c Ry. Co.	407
Hyde v Woods	38

I

Idding v Bruen	278
Ideal Mfg Co. v Holland	127
Illingsworth v Holsworth	218
Importers Bank v Quakenbush	15
Imray v Magnay	4, 58
Ingram v Osborn	23, 76
Inman, In re	406
Inman v Mead	88, 89
Innes v. Lansing	243
International Trust Company v United Coal Company	387
Iron Clad Mfg Co., In re	436
Irvine v. N. Y. Edison Company	82

J

Jackson v DuBois	159
v Holbrook	60, 63, 250
Jacobs v Blair	370
v. Mexican Sugar Co.	245
Jacobson & Son Co , In re	241
Jacobson, In re	167
Jaeger v Kelley	114
Jaquith v Alden	336
Jennings v. Crystal Ice Company	86
Jerome v. McCarter	436
John Osborn's Sons Co , In re	393
Johnson, In re	114, 263
Johnson v Mills	402
v. Norris	391, 393
v. Trust Co.	220
v Waters	240
Jones v Boulten	113
v Clifton	37
v Green	58
v Marsh	258
v Springer	298
Jordan v Hall	362
v Laverty	100

Joseph v. Raff	333
Joslin v N J Springs Co	100
Joy v. Campbell	146, 148

K

Kain v. Larkin	98, 135
Kalkhoff v. Nelson	404, 405
Kaufman v Tredway	336
Kavanaugh v. McIntyre	442
Keene v Gaehle	250, 395
v Riley	15
Keep Shirt Co , In re	430
Keighthley v. Walls	74
Keller v Ashford	100
Kelley v. Buck	29
Kempner v Churchill	115
Kennedy v. Gibson	304
Kent v Lake Superior &c. Co.	384
Keppel v. Tiffin Bank	46, 429
Kerker v Levy	99
Ketcham v. McNamara	362
Kettle v Hammond	230, 274
Keystone Warehouse Co v Bissell	339
King v Ballett	7
v Dupme	71
v Malcott	402
v Pomeroy	304
Kingsley v First National Bank	334
Kingston Realty Co., In re	365
Kinmouth v White	14, 62
Kinnemon v. Miller	315
Kinney, In re	41
Kirkpatrick v. McElroy	394
Kiscadden v. Steinle	26
Kittier v Raynes	396
Klein, In re	359
Klein v Richardson	163
Klingamon, In re	183
Knapp v Milwaukee Trust Company	297
Kneeland v American Loan &c. Co.	386, 421
Knight, In re	360
Knowlton, In re	30
Koehlhefer v. Peterson	11
Kuhne v Law (S C)	13

L

La Montagne v. Bank of N Y	29, 30, 100
Lake, In re	348

TABLE OF CASES

[The References are to Pages]

Case	Page
Lake v Caushold	235
Land Title & Trust Co. v. Asphalt Co.	96, 245
Langford v Ellis	56
Langton v Hasten	206
Lanoy v. Duke of Athol	431
Lanphere v Lang	280
Lansing Works v Ryerson	287
Larkin, In re	99, 291
Lathrop Bank v. Holland	358
Lathrop Foundry v Highland	365
Latimer v. Batson	140
Lawrence v Nelson	240
Leaper v Falton	113
Lecouturier v Ickelheimer	239
Lee County v. Penberthy Company	377
Le Fevre v Matthews	370
Lehigh Valley R R v McFarland	377
Lehman v Van Winkle	163
Lehrenkauss v. Bonnell	114
Lemieux v. Young	119
Leonard v Bacon	259
v Simpson	313
Leverick v Meigs	187
Levi, In re	300
Lewensohn, In re	278
Lewis v Chase	311
Lewisohn v Stoddard	280
Lewkner v. Faulekner	57
Liberty Silk Co , In re	192
Lichtenberg v Herdtfelder	317, 322
Lindley v Ross	340
Lipman, In re	119, 301
Lloyd v. Fulton	97
Lobstein v Lehn	101
Locke, In re	340
Locke v Winning	274
Lockhart v Hardy	421
Loeb v. Flash	120
Loeser v Dallas	371
v. Savings Bank	342
Lofsky v Mauler	31
Longstreth v Pennock	416
Longworth v Longworth	56
Loos v. Wilkinson, 110 N Y 195, 18 N E. 99	121, 322
113 N Y 435, 21 N E 119	14
Lord v Bunn, 2 You & Coll Ch 98	35
Lothrop v. Drake, 91 U S 516	300
Lotte v American Silk Co , 159 Fed. 499	374
Loughbridge v Bolland, 52 Miss. 546	158
Louisville Co v Smith	377
Louisville Trust Company v Louisville Ry. Co	84, 85, 213
Louthan v. Hassell	114
Love v Railway Co.	375
Lovell v. Newman	298
Lovick v Crowder	58
Lowenberg v Levine	445
Lucas County v. Jameson	413
Ludden v Hazen	195
Ludington's Petition	231, 322
Ludington v Thompson	393, 394
Ludvigh v. American Woolen Company	191
Luedecke v. Des Moines Cabinet Company	84
Lufty In re	299
Luhrs v Hancock	61
Lush v Wilkinson	97, 126
Lydecker v Smith	16
Lyon v. Council Bluffs Bank	162

M

Case	Page
Mahon v. Ongley Electric Co.	371
McBride v Oriental Bank	369
McCaffrey v Woodin	210
McCarty v Light	337, 417
McCauley v McCauley	240
Mace v Cadell	148
McClum v. McClum	88
McClure v Campbell	371
McCullough v Porter	187
McDermott v Hannon	240
MacDonald v Daskam	353
McDonald, In re	347
McDonald v Chem. Nat Bk	341
v Williams	244
MacDougall, Ex parte	318
McGourkey v Toledo &c Co.	166, 215
McGraw v Mott	374
McGregor v The Bank	278
McIntosh v Ogilvie	305
v Ward	379
McKeithen v Walker	8
McKey v Lee	336
McLean v Johnson	317
McMahon v Allen	322
McMaster v Campbell	61, 66, 79, 278
McMullen Lumber Co. v Strother	239
McNaboe v Columbia Co.	348

TABLE OF CASES XXXIX

[The References are to Pages]

Case	Page
Macomber v Parker	140, 177
Malcolmson v Wappoo Mills	409
Malloney v Horan	45
Mandel, In re, 127 Fed 863	357
Mandeville v. Campbell	75
Manhattan Co. v Osgood	259
Manning v Patterson	271
Marbury v Brooks	231
Marine etc. Dry Dock Co., In re	214
Marsden v. Cornell	120
Marsh v Kaye	233, 244
Martin v. Baker	140
v Crosby	317
v Mathiot	154
v Pewtress	271, 274
Martindale v. Booth	116, 118, 139, 148
Marvin, In re	365
Mason v. Bogg	433
v Lord	10
Mathews v. Feaver	23, 113
Matthews, In re	435
Matthews v Hardt	358
Mattingly v Nye	89, 129
Maxim v Moss	443
May v Le Clair	296
v Wannamaker	371
Mayer v. Hellman	362, 363
Mayo Contracting Co., In re	346
Mayou, Ex parte	29, 81, 338
Meaux v Howell	60, 224
Mechanics Bank v Dakin	59
Mechanics & M. Bank v. Ernst	356
Melville v. Brown	58
Mendell, In re	110, 111
Mercantile Trust Co v. Baltimore etc. R R	248
v Kanawha Ry Co.	373
v. Pittsburg R R	251, 252
Mercedes Import Co, In re	360
Mercer, Ex parte	57, 97, 135
Merchants &c. Co. v Borland	41, 80
Merchants & Planters Nat Bank v Trustees	248
Merchants Bank v. Cook	345
Merrill v Nat Bank of Jacksonville	328, 428, 433, 434
Mershon v. Moors	201
Mertens, In re	425, 430
Merwin, In re	406
Metcalf v Barker	13, 289
Metropolitan Ry Receivership, In re	247, 249
Mettinger v Hendricks	282
Mexico Hardware Co., In re	278
Meyer v Attorney-General	403
v Pipkin	167
Michaels v Post	298
Miller v. Sherry	11, 14, 40
Millinser Co v Gallego Mills	181
Milliken v. Second National Bank	169
Mills v Northern Ry	2
Minnesota Harvester Works v Hally	187
Minot v. Thatcher	394
Mitchell v Beekman	82
v Mitchell	195
v Winslow	206, 214
Mitford v Mitford	46
Mobile Bank v McDonell	163
Monroe v. Smith	132
Montagne v Bank of New York	29
Montague v Hotel Gotham Co	346
Montgomery Webb Co v Dienelt	82
Moody v. Wright	209
Moore v Bonnell	371
v U. S Barrel Company	78
Moors v Drury	201
v. Kidder	201
v Reading	177
v. Wyman	201
Moran v Sturges	360
Morehouse v Giant Powder Co.	361
Morgan v Brindiett	268
v Wordell	25, 26
Morley, Ex parte	28, 29
Morrill v Noyes	216
Morris, In re	283
Morris v Carnegie Trust Co	417
v Geoghegan	76
v Morris	66
Moss, In re	44
Moss v. Gallamore	30
Moth v Frome	24
Mount v. Mitchell	239
Movius v Lee	325
Moyer v. Dewey	91, 278, 443, 444
Mueller v. Nugent	298
Mugge v. Ewing	64
Mulcahey v Strouse	427
Muncie Pulp Co, In re, 151 Fed 732	301
139 Fed 546	82
Munger &c. Co, In re	280, 282

TABLE OF CASES

[The References are to Pages]

Munson v Ellis	228	New York Security & Trust	
v Genesee Works	135	Co v Lombard	251, 397
Murphy, In re	365	New York Tunnel Co, In re	440
Murphy v Buggs	114	New York &c. Water Co,	
v. Murphy & Co	271	In re	365
Murray v. Judson	10	Niagara Radiator Co., In re	408
Musica v Prentice	301	Nichol v Eaton	34, 35, 36
Mutual Life Ins Co v. Belknap,	31	Nicholas v Lord	89
		Nichols v. Patten	68
Myer v. Car Co 3, 167, 168, 254, 255, 275, 423		Nicholson v. Schmucker	206, 353
Myers, In re	24	Nicols v Crittenden	123
Myers v Russell	36	Niederstein, Matter of	413
		Niles Tool Co v. Railway Co	420
N		Nisbett v Macon Bank	171
Nachman, In re	165	Nixon v Jenkins	273
Nash v Ely	167	Noble v. Holmes	58
National Bank v. Colby	326, 334	Norcutt v Dodd	258
v. Levy	78, 317	North Chi Rolling Mill Co. v Oregon &c Co.	26
v Rogers	180		
v Shackelford	120	Northern Counties Ins. Co, In re	407
National Bank of Newport v Natl. Herkimer County Bank	338	Northern Pacific Ry v. Boyd	86
		Noyes, In re	430
National City Bank v Hotchkiss	356	**O**	
National Hudson River Bank v Chaskin	164	Oakey v Bennett	305
		Oakland Lumber Co., In re	299
National Mercantile Agency, In re	300	O'Brien v East River Bridge Co.	294
National Shoe & Leather Bank v. Mechanics Nat. Bank	334	Ogden v Saunders	445
		Old Dominion Copper Co. v. Bigelow	280
National Trust Co. v Miller	237		
National Tube Works v Ballou	18	v Lewisohn	280
		Oliphant v St Louis &c Co	416
Neel v Clark	442	Ominen v Talcott 149, 190, 192	
Neff, In re	406	O'Neill v Int Trust Co	65
Nellis v. Clark	68	Orendorf v Budlong	63
Nelson v Camp	251	Osborne v Morse	314
New England Iron Co. v Gilbert Elevated Co.	408	Otis, Matter of	320
		Owen v. Body	228
New Haven Wire Co Cases	201	Oxenden v Lord Compton	318
New Oriental Bank, In re	402	Oxley, In re	414
New Orleans v. Fisher	89		
New Orleans, &c. R R Co v. Delamore	31	**P**	
New York County Bank v Massey	26, 341	Packman's Case	67
		Page v Edmunds	38
New York Economical Printing Co, In re	277	v. Rogers	46, 429
		v Way	35
New York &c., Ry Co v Beard	243	Pancoast v. Gowen	38
		Parker v Black	64, 273
New York etc., Co v. Saratoga Gas Co.	31, 210, 213	v Dykes	272
		v Sherman	119

TABLE OF CASES. xli

[The References are to Pages]

Parslow v. Weedon	258
Partridge v Gopp	93, 113
Paton v Northern Pacific Company	84
Patterson v Lind	373
Paxon v Fleming	360
Payne v Hook	239
Pease, In re	110, 117, 291, 347
Peeples v Tatum	64
Pelham v Aldrich	127, 129
Pennock v Coe	214, 215, 217
Pennoyer v Neff	18, 367
Pennsylvania Steel Co v. N. Y. City Railway Co., 198 Fed. 721	242, 245, 251, 386, 398, 411
v N Y City Railway Co., 208 Fed 168	421
Penny & Anderson, In re	198, 199
People v Am Loan & Trust Co.	393
v Board of Assessors of Albany	238
v. Commercial Alliance Life Insurance Co	397
v Globe Insurance Co	406
v. Granite Association	371
v Greer	440
v Luhrs	119
v Metropolitan Surety Co, 158 N Y. App Div 647	413
v. Metropolitan Surety Co, 205 N Y 135	403
v. Remington & Sons	433
v St Nicholas Bank	405
v Security Life Ins Co	41
v Sheriff	392
v Spaulding	392
Perkins, In re	195
Perlhefter, In re	29, 338, 340
Perrin, In re	341
Perry v Roberts	35
Peters v Irving	431
Petrie v Voorhis	402
Pettingill, In re,	345
Pfahler v McCrum	374
Pfohl v Simpson	243
Phelps v McDonald	305
Phenix Nat Bank v Waterbury	404
Philadelphia Warehouse Company v Winchester,	177, 178, 257, 260
Philmena, The	360
Phillips, In re	40

Phoenix Ins Co v. Abbott	19
Pickens, etc. Co , In re	292, 362
Pickstock v. Lyster	223, 224, 227, 230
Pierce, In re	365
Pierce v. Emory	216
v Hower	161, 163
Piquet v Swan	390
Pine v Trust Co	288, 336, 345
Pitts, In re	278
Pittsburgh Lead Co , In re	278
Pittsburgh v. S. S Trust Co	413
Pixley v Bennett	45
Planters Bank v Whittle	333
Platt v N Y etc Ry. Co	215
v N Y & Sea Beach Ry Co	216, 217
Pollard, Ex parte	352
Pollock v Jones	354
v Simon	113
Pond v Framingham R. R	2
Pope v Solomons	20
Portarlington, Lord, v Soulby	351
Porter Co , H. K v Boyd	183, 184, 257
Porter v Sabin	375
v Steel Company	204, 215, 420
Potter v Brown	444
v. Williams	257
Powder Company v Burkhardt	192
Powell, Ex parte	150
Pratt, In re	365
Pratt v Columbia Bank	346
v Curtis	272
v Wheeler	64, 273
Prentiss Supply Co. v Schirmer	166
Price v. Abbott	329
v Heybler	66
Prismall v. Lovegrove	147
Pruyn v. McCreary	370
Pryor v. Hill	231
Pullen v Hillman	445
Pulliam v Pulliam	239
Pyckstock v. Lyster	114

Q

Quenn v Weaver	334
Quincy Railroad Co v Humphrey	408

R

Rabbe v Astor Trust Co.	324
Raht v Attrill	387

TABLE OF CASES

[The References are to Pages]

Ramsden v Jackson	313	Rock v Leighton	313
v Ramsden	56	Rockford v Hackmen	35
Rand v Iowa &c Ry.	302	Rock Island Co v Freeman	338
Randolph v Scruggs	364	Rodgers, In re	177, 180
Raney, In re	166, 195	Rogers v. Page	120, 164
Rasmussen, In re	195	Rosenstock v. City of New York	32
Rathfon, In re	303		
Ray v Henderson	31	Rosett, In re	39
Reade v Livingston	93, 94, 125	Rosoff v Gilbert Transportation Co.	282
Receivers Philadelphia &c R R, In re	249	Ross, Ex parte	394
Redfield v Buck	127	Roth, In re	400, 405
Reese Brick Co, In re	340	Rouse, In re	69
Regina Music Box Co v Otto	334	Rouse v Merchants Bank	333
Reichwald v Hotel Co	333	Rowe v Page	362
Reiff, In re	279	Rowley v Bigelow	121
Reis, In re	399	Ruffin, Ex parte	2, 9, 115, 234
Relfe v. Rundle	370	Rung Furniture Co, In re	268
Remington Automobile Co, In re	282	Russel v Wynne	197
		Russell, Ex parte	132
Republic Life Ins. Co v. Swigert	256	Russell v Hammond	94, 125
		v Woodward	227
Restein, In re	384	Rust v Cooper	274
Reynolds, In re, Fed. Cas. 11723	361	Rutherford v. Alyea	238
		Ryall v. Rowles	143, 145, 148, 151, 152
153 Fed. 195	342		
Reynolds v Ellis	322	Ryberg v Snell	188
Rhawn v Pierce	371	Ryttenberg v Schefer	188, 192
Rheinstrom &c Co, In re	416		
Rice v Durham Water Co	375	**S**	
Richards, In re	337		
Richardson, Ex parte	365	Sabin v Camp	353, 354
Richardson v Shaw	350, 355	Sacker, In re	257
Richmond v Irons	304	Saeger v Aughe	123
Riddel v Munro	122	Sage v. Memphis, etc Ry.	246, 247
Riddle v First National Bank	394	Saggitary v Hyde	414
Rider v Kidder	258	St. Clair v Cove	18, 367
Ridgeway v Kendrick	95	St. John v Benedict	68
v. Underwood	127	St Louis etc Ry. Co. v Holbrook	384
Riggin v Magwire	401		
Riggs Rest Co, In re	288	St Louis Railroad v Cleveland Ry	420
Rinchey v Striker	59		
Ringol v. Biscoe	333	Salmon, In re	361, 364
Rippon v Norton	35	Salmon v. Bennett	97
Robbins v. Butcher	229	Sampter, In re	429
Roberts v Johnson	110	Sanders v Logue	135
v Lawrence	424	v. Watson	9, 20
Robins v Wooten	65	Sanderson v. Bradford	371
Robinson, In re	40	v Stockdale	16
Robinson v. Bank of Newberne	334	Sands v Codwise	44, 150
		v. Greeley	373
v Bates	45	Sanford v. Sanford	395
v Elliott	153, 195, 197, 212	Sarasohn v. Kamaiky	113
Rochester Distilling Co v Rasey	204	Sattler v Slonimsky	60
		Savage v Sherman	382

TABLE OF CASES

[The References are to Pages.]

Sawyer v Hoag	26	Smith v Bowker Torrey Co	2, 101
v Levy	69, 224	v. Collins	107
v Turpin	164, 340	v. Jones Lumber Co	250
Schenck, In re	271	v. Milles	267
Schenck v. Barnes	33	v Moore	107, 291
Schermerhorn v De Chambrun	68	v Reid	98
Schindler, In re	155	v Rumsey	64
Schless v. Thayer	38	Smith &c Piano Co , In re	199
Schloss v Schloss	248	Smith's Lessee v McCann,	
Schofield v Ute Coal &c Co	58	24 How. 398	7
Schreyer v. Scott	127, 131	Smithurst v Edmunds	207
Schumert & Warfield v Brewing Co	248, 291	Snohomish County v Puget Sound Bank	304
Scoggin v Schloath	109	Snow v Lang	65
Scott v Neely	9, 16	Southard v Benner 276, 277,	322
v Nesbitt	47	Southern Textile Co , In re	140
Scoville v Thayer	280, 282	Southworth v Morgan 280, 281,	282
Seager v. Aughe	123		
Seavey v Walker	177	Spader v Mural Decoration Co	397
Security &c. Co. v. First National Bank	223	Spalding, In re	14, 295
Security Warehousing Co v Hand	182	Spann, In re	99
Seeman v Levine	119	Speer v Speer	2
Senter v Williams	11, 14	Spelman v Freedman	317
Sessions v Romadka	410	Spencer v Duplan Silk Co	298
Severs v Dobson	57, 134	v. Taylor Creek Co	418
Sexton v. Kessler 155, 173, 174,	354	Spirett v Willows	93, 97
v Wheaton 129, 132, 161,	162	Sporza v German Bank	320
		Spragins, Ex parte	14
Sharp v Fitzhugh	271	Sprague v Cochran	206, 351
v Shea	160	v. Moore	382
Shaw, In re	177, 179, 180	Sprintz v Saxton	119
Shaw v Aveline	73	Spurrell v. Spurrell	223
v Standish	125	Spyer v Hyatt	25
Shears v Rogers	315	Stackhouse v Holden	155
Shelton v King	34	Stafford v. Bacon	444
Sheperdson's Appeal	366	Stanton v Ala. &c. Ry. Co	388
Shepherd v. Pepper	31	v. Hatfield	382
Shields v Anderson	316	v. Wooden	303
Sholes v Asphalt Co.	177, 179	Starin v Kelley	106
Shryock v. Boshore	362	Starks &c Co , In re	422
Shulthis v McDougal	297	Steam Vehicle Co . In re	338
Shults, In re	341	Steelman v Mattix	362
Silverman, Re	406	Stein, In re	365
Simonson v Sinsheimer, et al	364	Steinmeyer, In re	291
Singer v Jacobs	116, 347	Stephen v Olive	126
v National Bedstead Co	364	Stephens v. Gifford	177
Skilton v Codington 195, 196, 275, 276, 277		Sterndale v Hankinson	394
Skip, Ex parte	47	Stevens v Centr Bank	377
Skirm v Eastern Rubber Co	292	v Cody	7
Slater v Slater	24	Stevenson, In re	290
Sloan v Huntington	161	Stewart s Appeal	86
Slomka, In re	417	Stewart v Fagan	3
Small v. Oudley	118, 230	v. Moody	230

TABLE OF CASES

[The References are to Pages.]

Stiger, *In re*	358	Thompson *v* Cooper	381
Stirling *v.* Seattle &c Ry Co.	375	*v* Crane	75, 134
		v Fairbanks	205
Stockwell *v.* Silloway, 100 Mass 287	362	*v.* O'Sullivan	64
		v Parot	199
105 Mass 517	362	*v.* Reed	58
Stokes *v* Amerman	41, 42	*v* Thompson	293
Stokoe *v* Cowen	73	Thorp *v* Leibrecht	134, 135
Stone, *In re*	129	Tiffany, *In re*	283
Stratton *v.* Hale	34	Tiffany *v.* Boatmen's Savings Institution	103 108, 299, 347
Strauss *v.* Cunningham	104, 444		
Strawhan *v* Wheritt	298	*v.* Lucas	103, 104, 108, 299, 347
Strike's Case	44		
Stryker, Matter of	416	Tillinghast *v* Bradford	34, 35
Stubbins, *Ex parte*	111, 348	Tindle *v* Birkett	440
Studley *v* Boylston Bank	26, 341	Tinker *v* Colwell	442
Sturges *v.* Crowinshield	310, 359, 361	Tisdale Lumber Co *v.* Read Realty Co	289
Sturgis *v.* Wine Co	68	Tittle *v* Van Leer	227
Sturm *v* Boker	187, 192	Titusville Iron Company *v.* New York City	211
Sully, *In re*, 152 Fed 619	278, 390	Todd *v* Nelson	129, 130, 138
		v Weal	126
133 Fed. 997	380	Toland *v* Sprague	295
Sumner *v.* Hamlet	177, 179	Toledo etc Ry Co *v* Hamilton	215
Sunflower Oil Co. *v* Wilson	408, 409		
Sun Insurance Co *v.* Stebbins	30	Tolles *v* Wood	35
Swan Co *v* Frank	2	Toof *v* Martin	292
Swarts *v* Fourth Nat Bank	430	Toothaker Bros., *In re*	271
Swift, *In re*	406	Torrance *v.* Bank	354
Synnott *v.* Tombstone &c Co	47	Torrens *v* Hammond	365
		Towle *v* Am Bldg & Loan Soc	245
T		*v.* White	192, 193
Taft, *In re*	154	Towns *v.* Smith	107
Tailby *v.* Official Receiver	218	Townshend *v.* Windham	94
Talbott *v* Horton	65, 66, 69	Tracy *v* The Bank	252
Talcott *v* Levy	163	Traer *v.* Clews	67
Talley *v* Curtain	229	Tredegar Co *v* S A. L. Ry. Co	393
Tams *v* Bullitt	322		
Taney *v.* Pa. Nat Bank	182	Trefethen *v* Lyman	80
Tarbell *v* Griggs	17	Trego *v* Hunt	21
Taylor *v.* Insurance Co	373	Trenton Banking Co. *v.* Duncan	161
v Jones	71, 94, 125		
v Lauer	322	Trodger *v* Laughan	105
v Taylor	352	Trotter *v* Lisman, 199 N Y 497	17, 368
Telegraph Construction Co, *In re*	402	209 N Y. 174	369
Temple, *In re*	365	Troughton *v* Gitley	151
Terry *v.* Wiggins	37	Trueman *v.* Fenton	311
Thiveat, *In re*	118	Truitt, *In re*	288
Thom *v* Pittard	278	Trust Co *v* Miller	372
Thomas *v* Roddy	271	Trustees *v.* Anderson	78
v Sugarman	65, 359	*v* Greenough	378, 380, 381
v. Western Car Co	330	Tucker *v* Oxley	26
v. Woods	25	Tupper, *In re*	288

TABLE OF CASES   xlv

[The References are to Pages]

Turner v Richardson 304
   v Richardson 408, 411
Turville v Tipper 58
Twopenny v Peyton 34, 35
Twynne's Case 54, 117, 133, 140, 168
Tyler, In re 250

U

Underground Electric Rys
   v Owsley 240, 252
Underwood v Sutcliff 75
Union Bank of Brooklyn, In re 330, 366
Union Pacific R R Co , In re 212
Union Trust Co. v. Boker 18
   v. Bulkeley 356
   v. Illinois Midland Ry. 242, 245, 385, 386, 388, 420
   v. Wilson 176, 181
United Cigarette Mach. Co.
   v Winston Co 2
U S v Crawford 296
   v N. O Railroad Co 215
U S. Fidelity &c Company
   v Borough Bank 414
   v Bray 359
   v Carnegie Trust Co. 414
U S Trust Co v Wabash &c Ry Co 31, 409
U. S Wireless Company v. W E. Company 23
Upsher v Briscoe 91
Upton v Hubbard 371

V

Vail v. Hamilton 325
Vandegrift v. Cowles Engineering Co 408
Van Hausen v Radcliff 58
Van Iderstine v National Discount Co 111, 112, 275
Van Nest v Yoe 228
Van Tuyl v. Robin 331
   v Scharman 331
Van Wezel v. Van Wezel 392
Varnum v Hart 334
Veazie Bank v. Fenno 326
Verplank v Sterry 96, 98
Vickers v. Vickers 357
Virginia Iron etc Co v. Alcott 375

W

Wabash R R. Co v Adolbert College 250
Wadsworth v Schissebauer 63
Wager v Hall 117
Wagstaff, Ex parte 26
Wailes v Davies 79
Waite, In re, 1 Low. 207, Fed Cas 17044 29, 338
   99 N. Y 433 306
Walbrunn v Babbitt 116, 118
Walden, In re 118
Walker v. Burrows 46, 276
Walker, In re 13
Wall v Cox 64, 273
Wallace v Castle 187
   v. Dawyer 32
   v Treakle 11
Walsh v Raymond 250, 395
Walter Wood Co. v Van Storey 199
Ward, In re, 203 Fed 769 298
   161 Fed 755 365
Ward v. First National Bank 425
   v. Petrie 60
Warren v Moody 97, 127, 129
Washington Bank v. Eckels 329
Waterbury, In re 320
Waterman v. Bank 239
Waters v Taylor 248
Waters' Appeal 161
Watkins, Ex parte 147, 150
Watson, In re 120
Watson v Merrill 405, 406
Watts, In re 361
Wead v Central of Georgia Ry. Company 382
Wearing v Ellis 391
Weaver v. Haviland 9, 16
Webb v Armistead 228
   v Atkinson 314
   v. Jones 238
Weber v Weber 226
Weightman v Hatch 16
Weitzel, In re 365
Wells, In re 191, 199
Wells v. Hartford Manila Co. 403, 409
Wennell v Adney 443
Wentworth Lunch Co , In re 366
West v Filling 199
   v Skip 78
West Company v Lea 230
West Side Paper Company, In re 416

TABLE OF CASES.

[The References are to Pages.]

Case	Page
Western Tie Co v Brown	341
Westinghouse Company v. New Paltz Tract Company	166
Westmoreland v Powell	135
Wetmore v Markoe	439
v Tinslow	36
Wheat v Dingle	432
Wheaton v Daily Telegraph	252
Wheelock v Lee	47
Whelan v Enterprise Transportation Company	421
Whitcomb v Fowle	243
White, Ex parte	192, 193
White, In re	43
White v Benjamin	107
v. Ewing	375
v. Knox	393, 396
v. Megraw	394
Whitehead v Mallory	45
White's Bank v Farthing	12, 14
Whitfield v Brand	146, 156
Whitney v Dresser	393
Whittlesey v Becker & Co.	364
Whitwell v Warner	333
Wiggers, In re	391
Wiggins v Armstrong	3, 8
Wilcox v Jones	375
Wilder v New Orleans	251, 252
v Peabody	404
Wilkinson, Ex parte	147
Wilkinson v Paddock	14
Williams, In re	381
Williams v American Association,	11
v Clark	353
v Dyle	443
v Heard	32
v. Kirk	154
Willitts v Waite	373
Wilmer v. Railroad Co	248
Wilson Ex parte	30
Wilson v. City Bank	268
v. Nelson	268, 288
v Paul	237
v. State Savings Bank	366
v Trust Company	405
v Webb	222
Winchester v Charter, 102 Mass 272	97
v Charters, 12 Allen 606	131
Wing, Matter of	321
Wingfield, Ex parte	155
Winslow v Dousman	15
Wiseman, In re	411
Wiswall v. Sampson	250
Withernsea Brick Works, In re	434
Wittlesey v Becker & Co	364
Wolf, In re	348
Wolf v Stix	401
Wood, In re, 5 N B. R 421, Fed Cas 5271	353
Wood, In re, 210 U S 246	303
Wood v. Guarantee Trust Co.	418
v. Lowry	169
v Mann	105
v Wilbert &c Co.	296, 297
Wood & Selick v Vandeveer	241
Woodbury v. Sparrell Print Co	134
Woodruff v Jewett	250, 395
Woods v. Klein	271
Woodward v Marshall	229
v Saltwell	161
Woolridge v Boardman	107
Work v Coverdale	122
Worrall v. Harford	381
Worseley v Demattos	274
Worthington, In re	380
Wrede v Clark	38
Wright v Brown	120
v Campbell	188
v. Hart	119
v Nipple	134
v Nutt	431
v Sampter	116
v Simpson	432
v Wigton	231
Wrixon v Vize	394
Wurtz v Hart	432
Wyckoff v Scofield	31
Wyman v Fox	45

Y

Case	Page
Yeager v Wallace	256, 257
Yeatman v Savings Institution	276
Yeend v Weeks	134
York Mfg Co v Cassell	168, 298
Young v Billiter	273, 310
v Heermans	134
v. Hope	147
v. Upson	155, 156

Z

Case	Page
Zartman v Bank of Waterloo	211, 276
Zeiser v. Cohn	47, 82
Zimmerman, In re	40

THE RIGHTS AND REMEDIES OF CREDITORS RESPECTING THEIR DEBTOR'S PROPERTY

CHAPTER I

THE CREDITOR'S RIGHT OF REALIZATION

§ 1 The Creditor has no Title to his Debtor's Property
2 Difference between Secured and General Creditors.
3 The Creditor must have a "Claim upon the Debtor"
4 The Judgment as a "Claim upon the Debtor"
5 Double Effect of Judgment
6 The Right of Realization conferred by the Writ of Execution
7 The Judgment as the Original Source of the Right of Realization
8 Limitations of the Common Law Execution
9. Failure of Statutes to cure These Defects.
10 Jurisdiction of Equity — the Judgment Creditor's Bill
11 Ancillary Character of this Jurisdiction
12. Prerequisites to Equitable Aid.
§ 13 Equality of Legal and Equitable Assets
14. Representative Character of Bill
15 Equality not Attainable by Common Law Procedure
16 The Equitable Jurisdiction did not confer Equality
17 Résumé of the Creditor's Procedure.
18 Apparent Exception Absence of Judgment in a Strict Sense
19 Exceptions created by Statute
20. Enforcement of Foreign Judgment
21. Should there be an Exception where Debtor's Property is outside the State of his Residence?
22 Argument against allowing an Exception
23. Weight of Authority in Favor of Exception
24 No Other Real Exception

§ 1. **The Creditor has no Title to his Debtor's Property** From the standpoint of property rights in their broad sense, whether as viewed by courts of common law or of equity, there is no

1

relationship between the debtor and his creditor One is in the position of debtor when he owes a sum of money to another, —that is a broad enough definition for our present-purpose. But the existence of this debt does not confer upon the creditor any interest in the debtor's property The latter is free to pay the debt with any portion of his estate that he may select for the purpose, nor can he be constrained in his choice In the nature of things this must be so, because no man has any right in the property of another which is capable of enforcement unless either he has a legal title with respect thereto for which a common law possessory writ would lie, or transactions have occurred regarding the property in question which would authorize a court of equity to make directions with regard to the disposition of the property under one or the other of its many heads of jurisdiction, such as trusts, fraud, or the like. The mere existence of a debt would not justify either kind of court in moving. The debt itself confers upon the creditor no title in the debtor's property, nor does it raise any trust or equity therein. All other things being equal, a debtor holds his property free from any right of his creditors to specifically claim it or give directions with regard to its application, they have no title thereto, nor any equity therein [1]

§ 2 **Difference between Secured and General Creditors** If, by means of conveyance or agreement, the debtor has given the creditor the right to apply certain of the debtor's property to the payment of the debt, then a relationship has been created, but it is entirely apart from the right which the parties enjoy by reason of the mere existence of the debt. A creditor thus

[1] Hanover Bank v Moyses, 186 U S. 181, 22 S Ct 857, *Ex parte* Ruffin, 6 Vesey 119, 126, Swan Co v Frank, 148 U S 603, 13 S Ct 691, United Cigarette Mach Co v Winston Co, 194 Fed 947, Mills v Northern Ry, L R 5 Ch App 621, Pond v Framingham R R, 130 Mass 194, Graham v Railroad, 102 U S. 148, Smith v Bowker Torrey Co, 207 Fed 967. Hence they cannot appear in a partition suit affecting their debtor's land, Harlem Savings Bank v Larkin, 156 N. Y App Div 666, 142 N Y Supp 122, nor does the decree therein affect their rights, Speer v. Speer, 14 N. J Eq. 240

secured is none the less a creditor, as the Supreme Court has said, " every mortgagee is necessarily a creditor; a mortgage is in general but an incident to the debt it secures, and a mortgagee is nothing more than a creditor secured by a mortgage." [1] The difference, therefore, between a secured creditor and one who does not occupy that position, is that the former has a right of interference with the debtor's affairs so far as certain specified property is concerned, and the latter has not. We therefore shall part here from the secured creditor, for the moment, and confine ourselves to the case of one who holds no security

§ 3 **The Creditor must have a " Claim upon the Debtor."** To repeat, he has no interest in the property of his debtor. In the words of WOODS, J., having " simply a debt upon which he can sue at law," he has that right, and nothing more; he can sue and that is all [2] It matters not how wrongfully the debtor may have acted with respect to his estate — one of the purposes of this treatise is to discuss these possible wrongs — the creditor, in Chancellor Kent's language, " has no concern with these frauds, until he has a certain claim upon the debtor " [3]

§ 4. **The Judgment as a " Claim upon the Debtor "** What is the " claim upon the debtor " which the creditor must get in order to complain of the debtor's dealing with his estate? As the claim cannot be deduced from anything in the nature of the debt itself, it must be found elsewhere. And the only place where we can find it is reached by following the road pointed out by the cases already cited The debt being due, the creditor may sue upon it Unless the debt be meanwhile paid, that suit will result in a judgment

§ 5 **Double Effect of Judgment.** The judgment, thus obtained in a common law court, has a double effect Firstly, it determines, once and for all, that the debt is owing and unpaid. Secondly, it authorizes the creditor in whose behalf it has been

---

[1] Myer v Car Co , 102 U S 1
[2] Stewart v Fagan, 2 Woods 215, Fed Case 13,426.
[3] Wiggins v Armstrong, 2 Johns Ch 144

rendered — the "judgment creditor," as he may now be styled — to take enough of the debtor's property as may be necessary, sell the same at public outcry, and apply the proceeds to the satisfaction of his debt. That result is accomplished by means of the writ of execution This writ issues as of course upon the entry of the judgment. It directs the sheriff to "make" of the defendant's property sufficient money to pay the plaintiff's claim as stated in the judgment, and thenceforth the sheriff, in obeying these directions, "acts in the right of the creditor."[1] This, in the language of a classical writer, is "the last step, or putting the sentence of the law in force"[2]

§ 6 **The Right of Realization conferred by the Writ of Execution.** By means of this writ of execution, therefore, the creditor is judicially authorized to realize upon the debtor's property by means of seizure and sale. That is the direct effect of the modern form of writ in general use, — the writ of *fieri facias*, but three of the four original forms of execution of which this was one, had the same object, that, by one form of realization or another, the creditor should "make his money" out of the debtor's property. One of those forms of execution, the writ of *capias*, was not directed against the debtor's property, but against his body; yet it played its part, too, in the development of this branch of law which we are studying, as we shall see Nor does the fact, that originally the judgment creditor could take his debtor's body instead of his property, detract from the general proposition that the judgment gave the creditor an immediate interest in his debtor's property, because it was the creditor's option, not the debtor's, whether the judgment debt should be "made" out of the debtor's property or his liberty. The other three writs in general authorized the judgment creditor to make his money by either (*a*) seizure and sale of the debtor's personal property, or (*b*) possession of the debtor's real estate, or the enjoyment of its income, until the

---
[1] Parke, B, in Imlay v Magnay, 11 M & W 266
[2] 3 Blackst Com 411

debt should thereby be satisfied. To this day, in England, land is not subject to sale under execution, as distinct from use; in our States, on the contrary, commencing with a Colonial Act of the English Parliament, land is subject to sale, if the personal property seizable is insufficient to defray the judgment debt.[1]

§ 7. **The Judgment as the Original Source of the Right of Realization.** These distinctions, however, are of no importance to us, for they do not affect the principle that the judgment gives the creditor the claim upon the debtor's property which

---

[1] "After obtaining a judgment in his favor in an action at common law, the creditor was enabled by one of the provisions of the Statute of Westminster II (13 Edward I, c. 18) to choose whether to have execution upon the goods of the debtor by the writ which is still called the writ of *fieri facias* or to have a writ commanding the sheriff to 'deliver to him (all the chattels of the debtor saving only his oxen and beasts of his plow, and) the one half of his land, until the debt be levied upon a reasonable price or extent.' This power of the creditor to seize and sell half the debtor's land is now extended to the whole. The writ by which this is effected has ever since the Statute of Westminster II been called the writ of *elegit*." — Digby Hist. R. P. Ch. V.

"The remedy given to the judgment creditor by the English law was a sequestration of the profits of the land by writ of *levari facias*, or the possession of a moiety of the lands by the writ of *elegit*; and, in certain cases, of the whole of it by extent. In all these cases, the creditor holds the land in trust until the debt is discharged by the receipt of the rents and profits. This limited remedy against the real estate of the debtor was not deemed sufficient security to British creditors, in its application to the American colonies; and the statute of 5 Geo. II, c. 7, was passed in the year 1732 for their relief. It made lands, hereditaments, and real estate, within the English colonies, chargeable with debts, and subject to the like process of execution as personal estate. Lands were dealt with on execution, precisely as personal property.

"The practice of selling real estate under certain checks and modifications, created to prevent abuse and hardship, has been continued and become permanently established. The general regulation, and one prevalent in most of the States, is to require the creditor to resort, in the first instance, to the personal estate as the proper and primary fund, and to look only to the real estate after the personal estate shall have been exhausted and found insufficient.

"The right to sell real estate on execution reaches reversionary interests, and they are bound by the judgment. But in many of the States, the lands, after being taken by execution, are to be duly appraised by commissioners, or a sheriff's inquest, and set off, and posses-

he formerly lacked; it gives him, by one form or another, the right to realize his claim out of the debtor's property. Without the judgment, there is no such right No execution can be issued without a judgment, and no lawful levy can be made without an execution Therefore, first of all, the creditor must have a judgment. "A creditor, merely as such, and without a judgment," says the North Carolina Court, "cannot pursue and get satisfaction out of the debtor's property This is undoubtedly correct, for without a judgment for the debt .
the creditor has no claim upon his debtor's property." [1] The judgment, in short, gives him the necessary right of interference with the debtor's property, as a preliminary to realization of the debt by disposition or use of it

§ 8 **Limitations of the Common Law Execution** The common law courts, however, were forced to recognize a distinct limitation upon the exercise of this right. The writ of execution could not touch anything but that which the common law court could recognize as property. If the debtor had title to land, the writ of *levari facias* could be levied, giving the creditor the right to collect the rents and profits. If the debtor

---

sion delivered to the creditor in the execution, by metes and bounds; and they operate as a conveyance of the debtor's title, and a payment on the judgment to the amount of the valuation The return of the officer when recorded passes the title The debtor is likewise allowed a reasonable time to redeem This is the case in Maine, New Hampshire, Vermont and Massachusetts, and the debtor is allowed a year to redeem, except in Vermont, where it is only six months

"In those States in which the sheriff sells the land, instead of extending it to the creditor, he executes a deed to the purchaser, and it is held that the sheriff's sale is within the statute of frauds, and requires a deed, or note in writing, of the sale, signed by the sheriff In the New England States, with the exception of Rhode Island, the sheriff's official return of the proceedings under the execution constitutes the title of the creditor, as does the sheriff's return of the inquisition upon the *elegit* in England, and no deed is executed, for the title rests upon matter of record In New York every judgment and final decree are a lien on the real estate of the debtor from the docketing of the same, and affect equally his after-acquired lands" — 4 Kent Com. 428, see also Covington Bridge Co *v* Shepherd, 21 How. 112.

[1] Dawson Bank *v* Harris, 84 N C. 206.

owned tangible chattels, the writ of *fieri facias* could be levied, and the seized goods could be sold. But if the debtor had something which in a practical sense was property on which he himself could realize at any time, but which was not capable of being the subject matter of a common law possessory action, no writ of execution would avail Such was the case where the debtor owned an interest in a trust estate. " At common law judgments could not be levied upon estates merely equitable, because courts of law did not recognize any such titles and could not deal with them " [1] Nor could the debtor's interest in any choses in action be taken in execution, because, even if such an interest was represented by instrument under seal, there was no way of realizing on it by passing title to a purchaser, in view of the impossibility of assigning a chose in action.[2]

§ 9 **Failure of Statutes to cure These Defects.** Nor were these difficulties ever effectually cured by statute in most jurisdictions The English statute to which we have already referred, which made land in the Colonies subject to execution, was considered as not intended to interfere with the established distinction between law and equity, and hence as not subjecting an equitable interest to be taken under the writ of *fieri facias*[3] A direct attempt also signally failed. The tenth section of the Statute of Frauds[4] made a " fee simple " trust interest subject to execution in favor of the creditors of the *cestui que* trust, in like manner as though he had owned the legal title. But this statute has been of little practical use. In the first place it only applied to a " fee simple " interest, and hence left as they were all trust estates measured by the life of the *cestui que* trust, and as if this was not enough, the courts, starting with King v Ballett,[5] cut down the statute's direct application to

---

[1] Freedman's Savings &c. Co. *v* Earle, 110 U. S. 710, 4 S Ct. 226
[2] Com. Dig. title Execution, c 4, Denton *v.* Livingston, 9 Johns 96, Stevens *v.* Cody, 14 How 528
[3] Smith's Lessee *v.* McCann, 24 How 398.
[4] 29 Car II, c 3.   [5] 2 Vern 248

"cases where the *cestui que* trust is entitled to the full and exclusive benefit and enjoyment of an estate, the legal title of which is vested in another"[1] — in other words, a dry trust of infrequent occurrence. So it may be affirmed that in practically every instance of an equitable interest, whether in real or personal property, the common law court cannot aid the judgment creditor.[2] And while of late years statutes have rendered tangible evidences of debt liable to execution, yet the tendency in some States is to construe these statutes strictly, with the result that while the sheriff can levy upon such property if he can find it, he can bring no action to reach it when it has been fraudulently encumbered or transferred.[3]

§ 10. **Jurisdiction of Equity — the Judgment Creditor's Bill.** It was natural that the Court of Chancery should extend its aid to the creditor who otherwise would have suffered in such cases. This impulse the Court recognized almost as soon as the public began to seek its aid, as finally happened in course of time. The ancillary jurisdiction which thus started was invoked by what is known as a judgment creditor's bill. The creditor, who for one or the other of the reasons above given had failed to obtain seizure of his debtor's property under execution, filed in the Court of Chancery a bill asking that court to compel the debtor to turn over to a receiver his interest in the property in question, so that the court could sell it and pay the proceeds thereof to the complaining creditor in satisfaction of his debt.

§ 11. **Ancillary Character of this Jurisdiction.** Now when the Court of Chancery acts upon such a bill it acts purely in aid of the judgment, and consequently it is necessary that a judgment be shown.[4] This requirement is inexorable. The Court

---

[1] Freeman on Executions, Sec. 187; Doe v. Greenhill, 4 B & Ald 684; Forth v. Duke of Norfolk, 4 Madd 503.

[2] See McKeithen v. Walker, 66 N C 95.

[3] Anthony v. Wood, 96 N Y. 180.

[4] Angell v. Draper, 1 Vern 399; Balch v. Wastall, 1 P Wms 445; Wiggins v. Armstrong, 2 Johns Ch 144; Freedman's Savings &c Co v. Earle, 110 U S. 710, 4 S Ct. 226. Even under a statutory system of trusts, such as exists in New York to-day, none but a judgment

of Chancery recognized the creditor as having no interest in the debtor's property other than such as can be given him by means of a mandate of a law court. Hence without a judgment a debtor has no standing to complain. This has been pointed out in numerous cases. Thus, in Case *v.* Beauregard [1] it was held that there is nothing in the nature of a partnership to give the creditors an equity in the firm property so as to enable them to follow it into the hands of third persons by means of a bill in chancery, the court saying:

"It is indispensable, however, to such relief, when the creditors are, as in the present case, simple-contract creditors, that the partnership property should be within the control of the court, and in the course of administration, brought there by the bankruptcy of the firm, or by an assignment, or by the creation of a trust in some mode. This is because neither the partners nor the joint creditors have any specific lien, nor is there any trust that can be enforced until the property has passed in *custodiam legis*. Otherwise the property can be followed only after a judgment at law has been obtained and an execution has proved fruitless."

The Supreme Court has thus repeated the doctrine: [2]

"In all cases where a court of equity interferes to aid the enforcement of a remedy at law, there must be an acknowledged debt, or one established by a judgment rendered, accompanied by a right to the appropriation of the property of the debtor for its payment, or, to speak with greater accuracy, there must be, in addition to such acknowledged or established debt, an interest in the property or a lien thereon created by contract or by some legal proceeding."

§ 12. **Prerequisites to Equitable Aid.** Hence the decision in Weaver *v.* Haviland [3] that the statute of limitations on such an

creditor is recognized as able to bring an equitable action to reach his debtor's interest in a trust estate, Demuth *v* Kemp, 159 N Y. App Div 422, 144 N Y.'S 690

[1] 99 U S 119. To the same effect is *Ex parte* Ruffin, 6 Vesey 119
[2] Scott *v* Neely, 140 U S 106, 11 S. Ct. 712; to same effect, Sanders *v* Watson, 14 Ala. 198
[3] 142 N. Y. 534, 37 N E. 641.

action does not commence running until the creditor gets judgment "Until his claim had ripened into a judgment," said the Court, "the plaintiff stood as a general creditor merely"[1]

Having thus established his right to realize out of the debtor's property, how much further must the creditor go in order to induce the equity court to give him the run of the debtor's "equitable assets"? The Supreme Court has answered that question as follows:[2]

"But in other cases, when the object of the bill is to obtain satisfaction of the judgment, by a sale of the equitable estate, it must be alleged that execution has been issued This is not supposed to be necessary wholly on the ground of showing that the judgment creditor has exhausted his remedy at law, for, if so, it would be necessary to show a return of the execution unsatisfied, which, however, is not essential. But the execution must be sued out, for if the estate sought to be subjected is a legal estate and subject to be taken in execution, the ground of the jurisdiction in equity is merely to aid the legal right by removing obstacles in the way of its enforcement at law, and if the estate is equitable merely, and therefore not subject to be levied on by an execution at law, the judgment creditor is bound nevertheless to put himself in the same position as if the estate were legal, because the action of the court converts the estate, so as to make it subject to an execution, as if it were legal. The ground of the jurisdiction therefore is, not that of a lien or charge arising by virtue of the judgment itself, but of an equity to enforce satisfaction of the judgment by means of an equitable execution. And this it effects by a sale of the debtor's interest subject to prior encumbrances, or according to circumstances, of the whole estate, for distribution of the proceeds of sale among all the encumbrancers according to the order in which they may be entitled to participate"

---

[1] While a creditor is privileged to set aside usurious liens upon his debtor's property, it is only after he has secured a judgment that he is in such "privity" with the debtor as to come within the terms of the usury laws, Murray v. Judson, 9 N Y. 73, Mason v Lord, 40 N Y 476

[2] Freedman's Savings &c Co. v Earle, 110 U S 710, 4 S Ct 226.

§ 13. **Equality of Legal and Equitable Assets.** Nowhere has the equity point of view been better stated than in the passage quoted [1] {The chancery court, in short, should not require the creditor first of all to exhaust his search among the debtor's legal assets, that would not be consistent with its idea that the interests which it protects must pay for their protection The holder of an equity of redemption in mortgaged premises, who can to-morrow realize upon it by sale, should not object to his creditor realizing upon it to-day, nor has he any equity to require the creditor to realize first upon some other of his property. All the debtor's available property, legal or equitable, should go to meet his debts, in the view of the court of equity, and a creditor who has judgment should be compelled to no election.[2] By parity of reasoning, if it relates to specific real property, then, on properly describing it, the bill when filed operates as a *lis pendens* which will bind an interlocutory purchaser,[3] but on the other hand, it is not essential from any other aspect that the bill should be so specific.

§ 14. **Representative Character of Bill.** The creditor may, if he pleases, file his bill in his own behalf alone, or in behalf of such creditors similarly situated as may desire to make themselves parties to the bill These, under the well-settled practice, can intervene at any time prior to the interlocutory decree of distribution But it would appear to be settled that only judgment creditors can come in, because no one who is without a judgment is eligible to intervention [4] And it is equally well

---

[1] There is, however, much confusion on this point In New York, for example, the courts require that the execution be returned unsatisfied, Beck *v* Burdett, 1 Paige 305 No real harm is done by this requirement, of course, but the rule mentioned in the text seems more consonant with reason

[2] Miller *v* Sherry, 2 Wall 237, Griffith *v* Griffith, 9 Paige 315

[3] Williams *v* Am. Ass'n, 197 Fed 500; Koehlhefer *v* Peterson, 82 N. Y. Misc 180, 143 N Y S 353

[4] Eameston *v* Lyde, 1 Paige 637, Senter *v* Williams, 61 Ark 189, Wallace *v* Treakle (Va), 27 Gratt 479 "The first question in this case is as to the rights of the other judgment creditors of the defendants, and whether they are necessary parties. It might be sufficient in

settled that the creditor need not make his bill representative even to this extent. He can, at his option, bring the action exclusively in his own behalf, in which event no other creditors can intervene.[1] It follows that, although it is optional with the plaintiff to permit other creditors to intervene, yet it is by no means necessary, and indeed the other creditors are not in any sense of the word necessary parties to the bill.[2]

§ 15 **Equality not Attainable by Common Law Procedure.** Now, however far we may have gone, it is apparent that equality of distribution was not the aim of the procedure under review. Obviously, this must be so with common law process. The common law was essentially incapable of effecting equality of distribution, because a court can only consider the parties to the record. In behalf of judgment creditor A who has first levied on the debtor's only property, the court must give full effect to his judgment and execution as against creditor B who levied later. A must be paid in full before the others can have anything, and if there is not enough to go around, that cannot be helped. And so it is obvious that, if left to the common law for the realization of his claim against the insolvent debtor, the creditor must be first on the ground with his execution.[3] That is the sole point that a common law court had power to determine, — who was first in order of time.[4] If the

this case to say they do not stand in the same right with the complainants, as it does not appear by the answer that executions in those causes have been actually returned unsatisfied, which was necessary to give them any right to come into this court for relief. Beck v Burdett, 1 Paige, 305 " — Chancellor Walworth in Eameston v Lyde, 1 Paige 637, 638.

[1] Eameston v Lyde, *supra*, Claflin v. Gordon, 39 Hun 54
[2] White's Bank v Farthing, 101 N. Y. 344, 4 N E 734
[3] At common law the date of levy upon the sheriff's taking possession related back to the teste of the writ. The injustice of this procedure, however, which by *ex post facto* process would annihilate the title which a purchaser, innocent of the writ's issuance, had acquired from the judgment debtor, led to the Stat. 29 Car. II, c 3, sec 16, by which priority was determined according to the actual date of levy, as between conflicting executions. This is the modern rule. See Bond v Willett, 31 N Y. 102
[4] French v. Winsor, 36 Vt. 412; Hendricks v Chilton, 8 Ala 641.

case embraced features which called for such equitable doctrines as marshaling, election, or the like, the common law court was powerless to give relief.[1]

§ 16 **The Equitable Jurisdiction did not confer Equality.** In extending its aid to the judgment creditors the Court of Chancery took no broader view It paid the same respect to the priorities. It was always the practice of the chancery court to give priority of payment to the creditor who first filed his bill, as against other creditors who filed later bills or intervened in the cause instituted by the first bill. The reason for that rule was that the equity court was acting in the whole matter purely in aid of the legal right to payment evidenced by the judgment, and accordingly, when its own process had seized assets applicable to the purpose for which the plaintiff came into court, that purpose must be fulfilled, and the intervenors must take what was left. Hence the plaintiff upon filing his bill obtains at once what is known as an "equitable levy," that is, the same right to priority in payment out of all assets by means of the receivership as though he had been able to get these assets by means of execution. This right of equitable levy is as firmly established as any point in this practice [2] In a comparatively late case, PITNEY, V. C., has made a distinction between the case of real "equitable assets," that is, assets that were, by their nature, not subject to execution, and "legal assets," that is, property subject to execution but which had been fraudulently encumbered so that equitable process would be convenient for the injured creditor In the first of these cases, the Vice Chancellor says, the doctrine of "equitable levy" should have full place, but not in the second, because

[1] Kuhne v Law (S C), 14 Rich L R 18
[2] Metcalf v. Barker, 187 U S 165, 23 S Ct 67 , Bergman v Lord, 194 N Y 70, 86 N E 828, Freedman's Sav & Tr Co v Earle, 110 U S 710, 4 S Ct. 226 The same rule applies in the modern substitute for the judgment creditor's bill, in the shape of supplementary proceedings — the creditor who first institutes such proceedings has the prior right of realization, Re Walker, 157 N. Y App Div 609, 142 N Y S 972.

there, the property being subject to levy at law, the liens of the creditors' judgments or executions should be recognized to the same extent as in a court of law.[1] In strict logic, it is hard to criticize this view, though it seems never to have been adopted by the Supreme Court.[2] But laying these distinctions aside, it is clear that in no sense is the procedure by creditor's bill a winding up of the debtor's affairs, it has no characteristic of a fair liquidation. True, it portions out the debtor's assets among those creditors who are parties to the action, but it does not do so on a basis of equality. On the contrary, the distribution is wholly upon a basis of priorities — first comes he who has made the "equitable levy," then come those others who have obtained liens by their judgments and executions, and again in the order of their seniority.[3] So the same "race of diligence" is as necessary with the creditor's remedy in equity, as it is essential to his being made whole by common law process.[4]

§ 17. **Résumé of the Creditor's Procedure.** Thus there is provided, by the one procedure or the other, a method by which the creditor may realize on his debtor's assets, whether they consist of "legal" or "equitable" assets. First of all, he must get a "claim" upon the debtor's property, and he does that by means of a judgment. Upon that judgment is issued a writ of execution relating to the debtor's property, and then, *pari passu*, by physical seizure under the writ, or by aid of the Court of Chancery, invoked by means of a "judgment creditor's

[1] Kinmouth v. White, 61 N. J. Eq. 358, 48 Atl. 952
[2] See Miller v. Sherry, 2 Wall. 237.
[3] Codwise v. Gelston, 10 Johns. 507, 522; *Ex parte* Spragins, 44 S. C. 65, 21 S. E. 543; Senter v. Williams, 61 Ark. 189, 32 S. W. 490; Wilkinson v. Paddock, 57 Hun 191, 11 N. Y. S. 442; White's Bank v. Farthing, 101 N. Y. 344, 4 N. E. 734.
[4] "If the creditor whose execution is first returned unsatisfied pursues the race of legal diligence, by the commencement of a suit here, he will obtain the reward of his vigilance; but if he abandons the pursuit, or lingers on the way, before he has obtained a specific lien, he has no right to complain if another creditor obtains a preference by superior vigilance." Chancellor Walworth in Eameston v Lyde, 1 Paige 637, 640. For a late example of such encomiums see *In re* Spalding, 139 Fed. 244, 248.

bill" filed after the issuance of the execution, the debtor's property, whether cognizable at law or in equity, may be gathered in to meet the amount declared in the judgment to be justly due. There is the whole scope of the creditor's remedy, so far as it relates to the extent of the debtor's property; by such means the creditor originally reached the debtor's property, and by those means he reaches it to-day, however one or the other of these methods may be enlarged or atrophied by statute.[1] Nor has any system of bankruptcy or winding up added to the score; the creditors of an insolvent debtor, by means of any such procedure, can reach nothing that a single creditor could not have touched under execution or judgment creditor's bill.[2] So we may well feel free to start our general inquiry with the cognizance of the ideal system of remedial procedure thus afforded. Before leaving this point, however, we must examine the exceptions, real and apparent, which have arisen in certain of our States.

§ 18. **Apparent Exception. Absence of Judgment in a Strict Sense.** Let us first dismiss the apparent exception which we

---

[1] The modern tendency has been to provide a statutory substitute for the judgment creditor's bill by means of "supplementary proceedings" in the common law court at the foot of the judgment. Thus the "Judgment Act," 1–2 Vict c 110, made cash and choses in action subject to seizure and sale by means of a "charging order"; and in our country supplementary proceedings at the foot of the judgment afford a more or less complete substitute for the judgment creditor's bill. Importers Bank v Quackenbush, 143 N Y. 567, 38 N. E 728. However, this procedure is not considered as more than cumulative, the courts still having jurisdiction of judgment creditor's bills, Feldenheimer v Tressel, 6 Dak 265, 43 N. W 94, Chamberlain v Turner Co, 66 Neb. 48, 92 N. W 172. Some statutes expressly reserve this ancient jurisdiction, Winslow v Dousman, 18 Wisc. 479

[2] The only qualification to the above is this. In England creditors could realize upon the debtor's land by sale, as distinct from use, only by means of bankruptcy proceedings. Hence in Chambers v Thompson, 4 Bro. C C 434, to a bill filed to discover whether the defendant had committed an act of bankruptcy, it was pleaded that the discovery would subject the defendant to a forfeiture of his land. This plea was overruled, as we shall see. If a trader died before an adjudication of bankruptcy, his land could not be sold, until by Stat 47 Geo. III, c. 74, this defect was cured. See Keene v Riley, 3 Mer. 436

often encounter, where the creditor may reach equitable assets although he has not obtained what is technically a judgment This, however, should give us no trouble, but rather should illustrate the principle involved It is not necessarily a judgment as such that is required, but a judicial determination which gives the creditor the right to obtain satisfaction without more from the property of the defendant. From this it follows that a technical judgment is not necessary so long as these requisites exist Thus where a party had purchased on foreclosure sale but refused to complete title, whereupon the court made a damage order against him, it has been held that such an order authorizes a judgment creditors' bill, because, as the court said, "it is not questioned that an execution may issue."[1] And in Ætna Bank v. Manhattan Life Ins. Co[2] it was held that where a chancery decree had been made adjudging the plaintiffs to be entitled to the payment of money from the defendants, such a decree serves the same purpose, because out of it the chancery court, by its own procedure, will see to it that the plaintiff makes his money[3]

§ 19. **Exceptions created by Statute.** In some jurisdictions statutes have made considerable inroads. In certain States the two actions may be joined, and the plaintiff, in one judgment, recovers both a determination of the amount due him and a charging order upon the debtor's equitable assets.[4] In New York, on the contrary, the Code has never been allowed to overturn the idea that this equitable proceeding is purely ancillary to a judgment, and the right to realize upon the equitable assets does not arise until a judgment has been obtained.[5]

[1] Lydecker v Smith, 44 Hun 454 [2] 24 Fed. 769
[3] Woightman v Hatch, 17 Ill. 281, Brown v McDonald, 1 Hill (S C) 297
[4] Dawson Bank v Harris, 84 N. C. 206, Ala Iron Works v McKeever, 112 Ala 134, 20 So 84, Sanderson v. Stockdale, 11 Md 563 These statutes, however do not bind the Federal Courts, which vigorously apply the rule stated in the text, Scott v Neely, 140 U S. 106, 11 S Ct 712; Cates v. Allen, 149 U S 451, 13 S Ct. 883, 977.
[5] Briggs v Austin, 129 N. Y. 208, 29 N. E. 4, Weaver v Haviland, *supra*

§ 20 **Enforcement of Foreign Judgment** More difficulty has been occasioned on the point of jurisdiction. This situation presents itself in two aspects. First is where the creditor has obtained the judgment in a foreign jurisdiction. If the proceeding in equity is merely ancillary to the judgment, it would follow that the chancery court can only aid a judgment which it can recognize as such. If the judgment has been rendered by a court of a foreign jurisdiction, how can the chancery court aid it? That question presented itself to Chancellor Walworth, sitting in the New York Court of Chancery, in a case where the plaintiff had obtained a judgment in the United States Circuit Court for the Southern District of New York, and then filed, in the State Chancery Court, a judgment creditor's bill. This bill the Chancellor dismissed, saying that "there was not a sufficient foundation laid for the exercise of the jurisdiction" of his court[1]. The Chancellor was careful to note, however, that the plaintiff could easily obtain, in the New York courts, a fresh judgment and thus put himself in the proper position, and to reserve for future decision the question whether his court, upon the basis of comity, might not "interfere to aid the parties in the collection of a judgment of a court of the United States, or of a sister state, upon any sufficient grounds of equity appearing upon the face of the bill to show that the exercise of such a jurisdiction was necessary to prevent a failure of justice." And very recently the Court of Appeals of New York has decided that a creditor who had obtained a judgment in the courts of another State was in no position to reach by means of an action in equity equitable assets located within the State of New York[2]. The court again reserves the question whether this rule might be relaxed if it had been impossible for the creditor to obtain a fresh judgment in the New York courts. The Supreme Court of the United States has reached the same result. "the bill," it says, "must set forth a judgment

[1] Tarbell v. Griggs, 3 Paige 207
[2] Trotter v. Lisman, 199 N. Y. 497, 92 N. E. 1052.

in the jurisdiction where the suit is brought."[1] The soundness of these decisions seems unquestionable. The plaintiff could have obtained a fresh judgment within the jurisdiction where sat the chancery court whose aid he was invoking; and that being so, why should the court be asked to aid a foreign judgment? No hardship would result from holding the plaintiff to the logic of the situation, because the debtor, apparently, was within the jurisdiction and thus available for a fresh action at law, and there was no reason why the plaintiff should not be remitted to that course.

§ 21 **Should there be an Exception where Debtor's Property is outside the State of his Residence?** We now reach the other aspect of this question, upon which, as we have seen, the New York courts were careful to reserve their opinion, — where real hardship would result from insistence upon the prerequisite of a judgment. The cases presenting this question are where the debtor resides in one State, and his property is located in another. The creditor can obtain a judgment in the State where the debtor resides, but as we have seen he cannot, on strict principle, ask the chancery court of the State where the property is located to give ancillary aid to the judgment. He cannot obtain a valid judgment in the latter State, because he cannot obtain personal service of process upon the debtor, and a general judgment otherwise obtained would be a nullity.[2] Of course the process of foreign attachment, which is of force to-day in every state by virtue of statute, solves the difficulty to a considerable extent. If the statute is broad enough to permit equitable assets to be taken as well as legal assets under the writ of attachment, the suit upon the debt may be begun by seizure of the property under the writ of attachment, and

---

[1] National Tube Works v Ballou, 146 U. S 517, 13 S Ct 165, Claflin v McDermott, 12 Fed 375; Union Trust Co v. Boker, 89 Fed 6

[2] Pennoyer v Neff, 95 U S 714; St Clair v Cox, 106 U S 350, 1 S Ct 354, Conn Mutual Life Ins. Co. v Spratley, 172 U. S 602. 19 S Ct 308

the summons may be served by publication alone, with the result that a judgment may be obtained which will be valid with respect to the attached property.[1] But some attachment statutes are not so broad in their effect, and there was a time before which they did not exist in some States at all, so the difficulty is by no means in all aspects theoretical. In such a case may the creditor invoke the aid of the equity court in the State where the equitable assets are located, without showing a judgment against the debtor? In some jurisdictions statutes may guide us to a conclusion, but let us ignore them in our consideration.

§ 22. **Argument against allowing an Exception.** To answer this question affirmatively, one must override many difficulties. First of all is the principle we have already discussed, that this sort of relief is purely ancillary. Putting that aside, we face the basic principle that equity acts *in personam*. If the debtor is not within the jurisdiction to obey the court's command as to the disposition of his property, how can the court help the creditor? All it could ever do was to direct the debtor to turn over the property to the proper officer for sale or other disposition in favor of the creditor, and enforce its command by imprisonment of the debtor for contempt until obedience result. If the debtor is not present for imprisonment or obedience, what can be done? Should the court take jurisdiction for a vain thing? These considerations led the Alabama court to hold itself to be powerless in such a case, the court saying:

"I have not been able to find any case where the mere absence of the debtor from the country, has been held to give a court of equity jurisdiction, independent of statute provisions, and according to the general rule on the subject, if the matter was cognizable in equity, but the defendant was not within the jurisdiction of the court, no suit could be entertained, or relief

---

[1] Cases cited *supra*. In Massachusetts, by statute, the process of attachment may be aided by a bill in equity "in the nature of an equitable trustee process, as distinguished from a creditor's bill," Phoenix Ins Co v Abbott, 127 Mass 558.

afforded See Mitford's Pl. 30, note a. To remedy this defect, various statutes have been passed, in the several states of the Union, and also in England, and it is by virtue of these statutes, that courts of equity proceed against absent defendants, who are necessary parties to the bill, even where the subject matter is of a pure equitable nature And if a court of equity must look to statute aid, to enable it to proceed against an absent defendant, when the subject matter is properly within the jurisdiction of a court of equity, it would follow, that the mere absence of a defendant from the jurisdiction, could not enable a court of equity to take jurisdiction of a matter of pure legal cognizance, as the collection of a simple contract debt "[1]

§ 23. **Weight of Authority in Favor of Exception.** The weight of authority, however, is the other way. If by any other method it is possible to apply the property to the satisfaction of the creditor's claim, as where it is in the possession of a third person who is within the jurisdiction, the chancery court should act, according to this view [2] Against logic though it may be, necessity really supports this exception In a nation consisting of many sovereignties, such as ours, the debtor cannot be expected to abide in physical proximity to his property, in many cases artificial State lines separate them, and our courts, none of whom, State or federal, can reach with their process beyond the borders of the particular State where they sit, cannot afford in a case of this-kind to leave principle undistorted to the exclusion of justice

§ 24. **No Other Real Exception.** There is no other real exception to the general rule we have discussed [3] Confusion is sometimes created by the language used in cases dealing with the status of creditors when the debtor's property is already in the hands of the equity court for distribution, having

---

[1] Sanders v Watson, 14 Ala 198
[2] Adler Goldman Comm Co v Williams, 211 Fed 530, and cases there cited, Pope v Solomons, 36 Ga. 541
[3] The opinion in Adler Goldman Comm Co v Williams, supra, bristles with instances of alleged exceptions, but the authorities cited, upon examination, will reduce themselves to one or the other of the heads of discussion enumerated in the text.

§§ 23-24]   THE CREDITOR'S RIGHT OF REALIZATION.   21

been brought there under a certain distributive jurisdiction possessed by equity, which will hereafter be examined It is sufficient here to note that whenever that situation occurs, then a judgment is not required of the creditor in order to enable him to participate in the distribution of the property, because, as the property is already in court for distribution among the creditors, their claim upon it is thereby postulated [1]

[1] The foreclosure of a mortgage upon all or part of the debtor's property would not seem to constitute such a distributive proceeding, Hollins v Briarfield Coal Co , 150 U S 371, 14 S Ct 127. The creditors have no standing in such a suit, nor is the decree therein binding upon them so far as it affects the validity of the mortgage or the regularity of the proceedings, Brooks v Wilson, 125 N Y 256, 26 N E 258, Humes v Scruggs, 94 U S 22 If, however, creditors have been allowed to become parties, and the issues involved have become such that the final decision will necessarily involve the determination of the validity of the creditor's claims, then obviously their validity must be determined, although the claims are not represented by judgments Central Improvement Co v Cambria Steel Co , 210 Fed. 696. Of course this constitutes no departure from the general rule

CHAPTER II

THE PROPERTY AVAILABLE FOR CREDITORS

§ 25 The Creditor may reach whatever the Debtor can Sell
26 Exception — Unlawful Assets
27. But All Lawful Property is Available to the Creditors
28 Labor not an Available Asset
29 The Property must have Existence in the Eye of the Law
30. The Property must be taken with its Encumbrances.
31 Set-off as an Illustration
32 Marshaling of Partnership Assets — Relation of Partnership and Individual Debts
33 Rule of Marshaling in Case of Partnership's Insolvency
34. Basis of Rule.
35 Income of Mortgaged Premises
36 Extent of Creditor's Right — Property must be Alienable
37 Corporate Franchises.
38 Claims against Government
39. The Spendthrift Trust
40 The 'Self-created' Trust
41 Trust created by Third Party.

§ 42. Limitation over on Debtor's Insolvency.
43 Discretionary Powers in Trustee.
44 Statutory Rule of New York
45 The Real "Spendthrift Trust"
46 Is allowed in but Two States
47 Powers
48 Limitations of Market.
49 Stock Exchange Seat
50 Contingent Remainder and Tenancy by the Entirety.
51 Right of Realization as limited by Statute
52 Exemption Laws
53. Life Insurance as a Subject of Exemption Laws.
54 The Provisions of the Bankrupt Act
55 Former Conflict of Interpretation
56 Present Rule as to Life Insurance in Bankruptcy
57 The Question One of State Law.
58 Restoration of Status quo when Fraudulent Transactions are set Aside
59 Representatives of Creditors get no Higher Rights
60 Agreements restricting the Creditor's Rights

§ 25 **The Creditor may reach whatever the Debtor can Sell.**
From what has already been said, the general proposition is

apparent that the creditor is entitled to realize on whatever property the debtor may himself be able to realize on. In other words, whatever the debtor can lawfully alienate, that in turn the creditor can reach. From whatever angle it may be viewed, this proposition remains the same, and every opposite case simply reflects its likeness.[1]

§ 26 Exception — Unlawful Assets. The substantial exception that should immediately be made is where the property is of an unlawful character, so that it would be wrong to let the creditors have it even for what it is worth. Thus in United States Wireless Company v. W. E. Company,[2] it was held that the creditors of one who had infringed a patent were not entitled, by means of bankruptcy proceedings, to realize on the apparatus which the debtor had constructed in pursuit of his infringement. The reason for that decision is clear. No equity court would have permitted the debtor to dispose of apparatus whose very existence constituted an infringement of another's lawful monopoly, and therefore, as the debtor would have been restrained from realizing on this apparatus by means of sale, the creditors were likewise prohibited. They acquired, in other words, no higher right than the debtor himself had. The fact that a man owes debts does not add to the sum of his property rights, and confers no additional right on his creditors. They must work out their rights through his; and hence if he has nothing, they have nothing.

§ 27. But All Lawful Property is Available to the Creditors. On the other hand, whatever he has is theirs. Therefore it is not for the debtor to say that his property is of no value; that is a point for the creditors to determine,[3] unless, indeed, the court might be disposed to object to its time being occupied

---

[1] There seems to have been one exception. Copyhold estates were apparently not subject to the claims of creditors, unless the custom of the particular manor prescribed otherwise, Mathews v Feaver, 1 Cox C C 278

[2] 198 Fed 385

[3] Ingram v Osborn, 70 Wisc 184, 35 N W 304.

with valueless controversy, and so asserts its ancient right of abstention which is expressed in the maxim *de minimis non curat lex*.[1]

§ 28 **Labor not an Available Asset** The courts have never brought themselves to consider that a debtor's labor is an asset for the benefit of his creditors. There are obvious reasons of convenience for this rule. The creditors cannot compel the debtor to labor for them, nor have the courts any method of providing for such a case. Hence, if the debtor's efforts have enhanced some one else's property, that gives the creditors no lien on the improved property or rights therein.[2]

§ 29. **The Property must have Existence in the Eye of the Law** In like manner, if a thing has not yet come into existence so as to be recognized as property under the ordinary rules of law, there is nothing for the creditors to take. The prospects of an heir constitute no property for himself or his creditors.[3] Likewise, an author's unpublished manuscript has no existence as property. The author must secure a copyright in order to have an asset himself, until he does that he has nothing and hence his creditors have nothing, as was held in Dart *v.* Wood.[4] As against this case, however, may be set off the decision in *In re Myers*,[5] where it was held that the goodwill of a physician's practice did not pass to his trustee upon his being adjudged a bankrupt. In view of the trend of the law toward considering the goodwill of any business or profession as a transferable asset,[6] this decision would seem wrong in its result. But that

---

[1] See Garrison *v.* Monoghan, 33 Pa. St. 232; Hoyt *v.* Godfrey, 88 N Y 669

[2] To give away one's labor constitutes neither a fraudulent conveyance, Abbey *v* Deyo, 44 N Y. 343, Glasgow *v* Turner, 91 Tenn. 163, 18 S W 261, nor a preferential transfer, *Re* Abram Steers Lumber Co, 112 Fed 406 Hence the creditors can get no rights in the property of a third party, however much the debtor's labors may have enhanced its value, Abbey *v* Deyo, *supra;* Glasgow *v* Turner, *supra*

[3] Moth *v.* Frome, Amb 394.

[4] 40 Mich 399   [5] 208 Fed. 407

[6] Slater *v* Slater, 175 N Y 143, 67 N E 224, Trego *v* Hunt, 1896 App Cas 7

makes little difference in the end, because the court announces nothing contrary to the principle above mentioned. The court simply thought that the goodwill of a physician's practice was not really a transferable asset, and therefore held that his creditors could not realize upon it.

§ 30. **The Property must be taken with its Encumbrances.** Likewise, although the debtor may have a property right, it may be so burdened with servitudes in favor of others as to amount to nothing from a practical standpoint. The creditors must take the property with the servitudes; they cannot have their choice. If the debtor owns land subject to an easement, it is obvious that the creditors must take it as it is, thus burdened.[1] Thus the right of dower, which the debtor's wife has at common law, passes with his land into the hands of the creditors, and they must allow for it. In a few jurisdictions, statutes have subordinated the wife's dower right to the claims of her husband's creditors,[2] but unless the legislature has thus intervened, the wife's right cannot be barred.[3]

§ 31. **Set-off as an Illustration.** Another illustration is the case of set-off. The debtor may have a chose in action, and to it his creditors are entitled, but if the person indebted on this obligation himself has a claim against the common debtor, then, as he could set it off against the common debtor's suit if brought, so he can do the same if his fellow creditors attempt to enforce it.[4] In order to make sure of the matter, all bankrupt acts,

---

[1] Thus, if land has been occupied by a public service company under condemnation proceedings, but the value has not been paid, the creditors of the company can realize upon this real estate only after payment of the amount adjudged as representing the value thereof, Fordyce v. Kansas City, etc. Co., 145 Fed. 566.

[2] E g. in Pennsylvania, Re Codari, 207 Fed. 784. In England, by Stat 3-4 Wm. IV, c. 101, land which a debtor charges by will with the payment of his debts passes free of his wife's dower. See Spyer v. Hyatt, 20 Beav. 621.

[3] Thomas v. Woods, 173 Fed. 585.

[4] "The provision for the set-off of mutual credits is old." Morgan v. Wordell, 178 Mass. 350, 59 N. E. 1037, referring to the original statute 4-5 Anne c. 17, allowing set-off as a plea in actions at law.

from the middle of the eighteenth century [1] to the present day have provided for set-off of mutual debts and credits.[2] But as the Supreme Court has said, these provisions really add nothing; they express merely what was the law in their absence [3] Set-off, then, is a right subject to which the debtor's choses in action must be taken; of this, as a general proposition, there can be no question [4] This is not the place to discuss the different aspects of the law of set-off, whatever that is, the creditors, in collecting their debtor's notes and accounts, are subject to it, and it is only pertinent here to observe that there is one quite notable difference between the rules applied in two important jurisdictions. In New York, to defeat the creditors, the set-off must be of debts both matured,[5] whereas in the Federal Courts it is not necessary that both debts have matured, if one party is insolvent.[6]

§ 32 **Marshaling of Partnership Assets — Relation of Partnership and Individual Debts.** As further illustration of the principle that the creditor is entitled only to what his debtor has, and must therefore work out his rights through the debtor and subject to his burdens, we may cite the so-called marshaling of partnership assets in the case of insolvency. The rule is well settled that a partnership is in no sense an entity, but,

[1] Stat 5, Geo II, c 30, Sec. 28; *Ex parte* Wagstaff, 13 Vesey 65
[2] Natl Bankruptcy Act of 1898, Sec 68, see Morgan *v* Wordell, 178 Mass 350, 59 N E 1037; Gray *v* Rollo, 18 Wall. 629, Tucker *v* Oxley, 5 Cranch 34, for a review of similar provisions in our earlier Acts.
[3] Sawyer *v* Hoag, 17 Wall 610
[4] N Y County Bank *v.* Massey, 192 U S 138, 24 S. Ct 199, Studley *v* Boylston Bank, 229 U S. 523, 33 S Ct 806; Continental &c. Bank *v* Chi &c Trust Co , 229 U. S 435, 33 S Ct. 829; Butterworth *v* Dignon, &c Co . 208 Fed 381 The only apparent exception is in the case of a stockholder who has not paid in full for his stock He cannot, upon the company becoming insolvent, offset against this unpaid balance a debt due him from the company, Sawyer *v* Hoag, 17 Wall 610; Kiscadden *v* Steinle, 203 Fed 375 This is due to the "trust fund doctrine" of which we shall hear more later
[5] Fera *v* Wickham, 135 N Y 223, 31 N E 1028; Centr. Trust Co. *v* Morton Trust Co , 200 N Y 577, 93 N. E 975.
[6] North Chi Rolling Mill Co *v* Oregon &c Co , 152 U S 596, 14 S. Ct. 710.

on the contrary, that all partnership obligations are simply joint obligations of the partners. In the ordinary case the partnership owns certain firm assets, which are therefore the joint property of the contracting parties; and each individual partner owns also property in which the others have no concern Of course in the case of any joint obligations, the creditor who brings suit is entitled to satisfy his judgment out of the joint assets, and also out of the individual assets of such partners as he may have succeeded in serving with process, so that in the average case the firm property and the individual property of the partners must both respond to the joint debts in the shape of partnership obligations. In addition, however, it usually happens that each partner owes individual debts, and *per contra*, if the individual creditor recovers a judgment against the partners that judgment may be satisfied out of the partners' interest in the partnership assets, as well as the individual property of the partner.

§ 33. **Rule of Marshaling in Case of Partnership's Insolvency.** Now, when a partnership is insolvent, that is, the firm assets are insufficient to meet the firm debts, then, whatever may be the ratio of the partners' individual assets to their individual debts and the firm debts, the rule became well settled at an early date in the equity courts that partnership property should be first applied to the payment of partnership debts, and that each partner's individual property should be first applied to the payment of his individual debts. This leaves the individual assets of the partners as a secondary resource to firm creditors after they have exhausted the firm assets and the individual creditors have been paid, and also leaves the partners' interests in the firm as a secondary resource for the individual creditors after they have exhausted their respective debtors' personal estate As stated by JAMES, L J., "the mode in which that sort of thing is done is this· that if there be two estates, a joint estate and a separate estate, the court takes care that the joint assets are applied in payment of the debts of the joint creditors before any part of them goes to the separate creditors."[1] This rule, as laid down by Lord COWPER, L C.,[2] though overruled by Lord THURLOW,[3] has become the prevailing rule in our country[4] and is now established by the Bankrupt Acts of both England and America as the rule of administration of all bankrupt partnerships[5]

§ 34 **Basis of Rule.** This right, however, is worked out not on any distinct equity principle of marshaling, but simply on the principle that the creditors should be restricted to the rights of the partners themselves The partners have agreed, by forming a partnership, that the firm assets shall first meet firm debts, and that their individual assets must first be applied to taking care of their individual debts. A partnership is a business in which certain assets of each partner are launched, and to these in course of time are added the assets gained by the firm's activity It is but natural that each partner expects the firm property to meet the firm debts Of course if these are insufficient then he must make good the deficiency with his individual means, but, before he should be called upon to apply from his private purse the amount necessary to meet the firm obligations, the partner's natural desire would be that the firm assets, as primarily dedicated to that end, be called upon. Hence the well-settled doctrine above mentioned This primarily is not the right of the creditors They have no lien on either the partnership or the individual assets.[6] It is the right

[1] *Ex parte* Morley, L R 8 Ch App 1026
[2] *Ex parte* Crower, 2 Vern 706. [3] *Ex parte* Copland, 1 Cox C. C 420
[4] Burdick on "Partnership," 2d ed, p 282 *et seq*
[5] Nat'l Bankr Act of 1898, Sec 5 English Bankrupt Act of 1883, Secs 43, 59. Outside of the cases coming within the administration of the Bankrupt Act, this rule applies only in equity for the simple reason that at law a firm creditor has the right to proceed at once against the firm assets and also the individual assets, and per contra the individual creditor has the right to proceed at once against the individual assets and his debtor's interest in the partnership, Burdick on "Partnership," 2d ed, p 277 *et seq* It is only when by some means a court of equity acquires jurisdiction to administer the partnership estate that the other rule can be applied
[6] Case v Beauregard, 99 U S 119.

of the partners themselves, and the rights of the creditors can be worked out on this line only through the primary rights of the partners. As illustrating this, we may mention the doctrine, equally well settled, that no agreement between the partners, or between the firm and any transferee, can shut off the firm assets from this prime duty of taking care of the firm debts Every intendment is taken against such a construction, and so; in the absence of express words, every transfer of firm assets by the partnership to a successor firm is deemed to be subject to the payment of the firm debts [1] The same rule applies to the transfer of one partner's interest to another. In *Ex parte* Dear [2] it was held that, where partnership articles provide that a certain firm asset shall belong to one of the partners on dissolution, it still is subject to its burden of paying partnership liabilities because the articles did not expressly provide to the contrary. MELLISH, L J , said that the question was whether the partner by the articles, made long in advance of the firm liquidation, could be considered as selling to the other partner this important right As stated in an Illinois case, " the presumption that arises, in the absence of anything to show the contrary, is that in the valuation upon which the sale is based, the debt of the selling partner is taken into account and charged to him, and the value of his interest is thereby reduced to that extent so that it is actually paid in that way." [3] This being a reciprocal right, the transfer of it by the firm or an individual partner, as the case may be, may well constitute a fraudulent transfer [4] or a preferential transfer, as the case may be [5] On the other hand, if there are no firm assets, then the

---

[1] Kelley *v* Buck, 143 N Y App Div. 546, 128 N Y S. 918, La Montagne *v* Bank of New York, 183 N Y. 173, 76 N E 33; *Ex parte* Morley, L R 8 Ch App 1026, *Ex parte* Dear, 1 Ch. Div 514; *In re* Daniel, 75 L T 143

[2] 1 Ch Div 514

[3] Clark *v* Clark, 45 Ill App. 469; Kelley *v* Buck, 143 N Y App. Div 546, 128 N Y S 918

[4] *Ex parte* Mayou, 4 De G J & S 664

[5] *In re* Waite, 1 Low 207, Fed Cas 17,044; See also *In re* Perl-

firm creditors should share the individual assets equally with the individual creditors, by parity of reasoning, for surely the partners never intended to subordinate their partnership affairs to a degree which would be attained if the partnership creditors, in such a case, were postponed [1]

§ 35 **Income of Mortgaged Premises** Again, we find this principle illustrated in the conflicts that so frequently have arisen between one holding a mortgage on premises, on the one hand, and the mortgagor's creditors on the other, concerning the rents of the premises after default. At common law, a mortgage of land passed title, and the mortgagor held merely as tenant at will of the mortgagee But even under the common law system the mortgagee was not entitled to collect the rents until after he had entered the premises upon default, and then had no right to require from the mortgagor an accounting for rents already collected.[2] In most of our states the mortgagee's only remedy, on default, is to institute a foreclosure suit, as the mortgage is regarded as conferring merely a lien instead of passing the legal title If the mortgagor is insolvent, or the mortgaged property is obviously inadequate to secure the debt in default, the mortgagee is entitled to have the rents collected for his account by means of a receiver, during the pendency of the foreclosure suit.[3] In such a case the mortgagee is entitled to all rents that may accrue after his entry, and also those due at the time of his entry but not collected by the

hefter, 177 Fed 299. And so when one firm transfers its assets to another the first firm being insolvent, the court presumes that it was intended the transferee should pay the debts of the other; and consequently none of the new partners, as between himself and his fellows, misappropriates the firm assets when he uses them to pay debts of the old firm La Montagne v Bank of N Y., 183 N Y 173, 76 N. E 33

[1] Re Gray, 208 Fed 959 The above principles can be carried out through the most complicated situations As an illustration see Re Knowlton, 202 Fed 480

[2] Ex parte Wilson, 2 V & B 252, overruling Moss v Gallamore, 1 Doug 266, Codrington v Johnston, 1 Beav 520

[3] Sun Insurance Co v Stebbins, 8 Paige 565; Elmira Society v Stanchfield, 160 Fed. 811, Am Nat Bank v Northwestern &c Co, 89 Fed 610, Hallenbeck v Donnell, 94 N Y 312.

mortgagor.[1] But until the mortgagee actually makes such an entry by means of his receiver, he has no claim on the rents which can prevail against the rights of the other creditors.[2]

§ 36 **Extent of Creditor's Right — Property must be Alienable** It is now time to narrow somewhat our proposition, since we have sufficiently described its general outline The point we must now emphasize is this: The creditors are entitled only to the debtor's alienable property The right of the creditor, as we have already seen, is not possessory The right is to realize on the debtor's property, not to own it Hence the creditor cannot realize on anything which the debtor cannot realize on; the creditor cannot for his own benefit, cause to be alienated by judicial sale, anything which the debtor cannot sell.

§ 37. **Corporate Franchises.** Two illustrations will suffice One appears in the shape of corporate franchises. The franchise to be a corporation is not alienable The corporation therefore cannot mortgage or sell it But the additional franchises granted to a public service company, necessary to the functions of its being, may be alienated or mortgaged as an incident to the physical properties used in the corporate operations. We need not go into the fine lines of distinction that present themselves in this connection, it is enough to state, as a self-evident proposition, that the creditors of any corporation so circumstanced are entitled to realize upon all franchises which the corporation had power to alienate or hypothecate [3]

[1] Shepherd v Pepper, 133 U. S 626, 10 S Ct 438, Lofsky v. Maujer, 3 Sandf Ch 71, Wyckoff v Scofield, 98 N. Y 475, Ray v Henderson, 110 Ill. App 542, Codington v. Johnston 1 Beav 520; Mutual Life Insurance Co v Belknap, 19 Abb. N C 345 a decision at Special Term to the contrary effect, does not seem well founded

[2] "The earnings of a corporation from its business prior to the time possession is actually taken of its property by a mortgage trustee or receiver belong to its general creditors in preference to mortgage bondholders "— N Y Security &c. Co. v Saratoga Gas Co, 159 N Y. 137, 53 N E 758, Central Trust Co. v Morton Trust Company, 200 N. Y. 577, 93 N E 975, U. S Trust Co. v. Wabash &c Ry. Co., 150 U S 287, 14 S Ct 86, and cases there cited.

[3] New Orleans &c. R R Co v Delamore, 114 U S 501, 5 S Ct. 1009

§ 38. **Claims Against Government.** On the other hand, it is a general principle that a government employee cannot assign his claim for salary, public policy forbidding the proposition. It follows that creditors will not be permitted to reach any such claim even under the broadest statute authorizing realization by means of garnishment or supplementary proceedings.[1] But a claim against the government, based upon an outright award, which cannot be dismissed on the rather fine-spun theory that, like a government salary, it is a "gratuity" or "donation,"[2] occupies a different status. If, in compensation for losses suffered by certain of its citizens, the government has set apart a fund to be apportioned among them, the claim of each citizen, when ascertained, is assignable, is therefore a property right, and hence is available to his creditors.[3]

§ 39. **The Spendthrift Trust.** The law of trusts furnishes other good examples in the doctrine concerning the so-called "spendthrift trust." This subject has been discussed so thoroughly in a notable book,[4] that the only value of the present commentaries is to afford, if possible, a new setting for the thoughts there expressed. It all comes to the same end, because, as that learned author points out, the general rule to-day is what the common law rule always was, that whatever belongs to a debtor belongs to his creditors. The idea of the spendthrift trust involves only the question whether one's property in a trust estate can be hedged about in such manner as to secure it from the claims of his creditors. Of course, as to existing creditors the proposition is simple; it would be whether the matter constituted what is commonly known as a fraudulent

[1] Wallace *v.* Dawyer, 54 Ind. 501; Rosenstock *v.* City of New York, 101 N. Y. App. Div. 9, 91 N. Y. S. 737.
[2] Tindal, C. J., in Gibson *v.* East India Co., 5 Bing. N. C. 262.
[3] So the Supreme Court has held in two cases where our government had received from a foreign government a sum of money in settlement for injuries done to citizens of this country, Comegys *v.* Vasse, 1 Pet. 193 (Spanish claims), Williams *v.* Heard, 140 U. S. 529, 11 S. Ct. 885 (Alabama claims).
[4] Gray, "Restraints upon Alienation," second edition.

conveyance On the other hand, the question whether limitations as to future creditors can be created has nothing to do with the doctrine of fraudulent conveyance, and belongs to the domain of the rule above cited.

§ 40. **The "Self-created" Trust** We will start with a trust created by the debtor for himself If a man creates a trust for the benefit of himself, his creditors need do no more than place themselves in his shoes, and the trust will fall. The debtor created the trust out of his own assets, with himself as *cestui que* trust, so of course his creditors are entitled to the income and, indeed, if they please, to call for a conveyance of the principal, because the debtor could have done so. Now, if the debtor has gone further and piled on top of the trust for himself a remainder over to a third person in the event of his own insolvency, then the situation is more difficult. In the few cases found, this scheme has not been allowed, and the remainder over has been declared void.[1] Professor Gray puts these decisions on the basis of public policy;[2] Lord Eldon[3] puts his decision on the ground that the remainder was "a fraud on the bankrupt laws"; and between these theories the opinions of the judges fluctuate It is indeed difficult to go deeper than that into their justification.

§ 41 **Trust Created by Third Party.** But when we come to the case of a trust created by a third party for the debtor's benefit then we are on firmer ground, and can draw our lines with logic. If the trust was solely for the debtor's benefit then of course the creditors are entitled to its enjoyment But the creditors cannot reach the trust in any case where limitations have been created which, broadly speaking, are of two kinds

§ 42 **Limitation over on Debtor's Insolvency.** First is where the trust is so limited by way of remainder over, the condition

---

[1] Higginbotham *v.* Holme, 19 Ves. 87; Schenck *v.* Barnes, 156 N. Y 316, 50 N E 967, affirming 25 N Y App. Div. 153, 49 N Y S 222, De Hierapolis *v* Lawrence, 115 Fed 76
[2] Gray, *op cit*, Sec 91   [3] Higginbotham *v* Holme. *supra*

of which is the very condition of the debtor's insolvency, that *ipso facto* with his insolvency the trust interest passes from him. As where a trust is created for the benefit of A, but if he should become bankrupt or insolvent, then the income shall be paid to B, and the principal likewise to B or C, — in fact, any limitation over by whose operation, upon A's becoming insolvent, his interest ceases Now in any such case the creditors of A cannot keep this limitation from taking effect, for the very good reason that A himself could not They can get no better rights than A had He could enjoy or alienate only this limited right, and so his creditors can realize only upon it as it is So long as A is solvent, the question is academic, because he can pay his creditors, and they never have to realize on this limited right, when he becomes insolvent the limitation takes effect, and there is nothing for them to realize on That is the proposition established by good authority [1] and as Professor Gray points out [2] it is all that was actually decided in the famous case of Nichols *v.* Eaton [3] of which more will be said later.

§ 43 **Discretionary Powers in Trustee** Second is the case where the trust is so limited that the debtor never is entitled to principal or income, but the trustee is allowed discretion to apply so much of the income as he may please to the debtor's support In any such case the debtor has no rights through which the creditors can work out theirs; as the debtor cannot force the trustee to exercise his discretion in his behalf, neither can the creditors force him [4] In like manner such discretion may be imposed with respect to the payment of the principal

---

[1] Demill *v* Bedford, 3 Ves. 149; Brandon *v.* Robinson, 18 Ves. 429; Tillinghast *v.* Bradford, 5 R I 205; Shelton *v.* King, 229 U. S. 90, 33 S. Ct 686

[2] "Restr Alien.," 2d ed., Secs. 251-5

[3] 91 U S 716.

[4] Stratton *v* Hale, 2 Bro. C. C. 490; Durrant *v* Mass. Hospital, 2 Low 575, Fed Cas. No 4188; Twopenny *v.* Peyton, 10 Sim 487, Chambers *v* Smith, 3 App. Cases 795; Claflin *v.* Claflin, 149 Mass 19, 20 N. E 454, Holmes *v* Penney, 3 Kay & J. 90; Shelton *v.* King, 229 U. S. 90, 33 S. Ct. 686.

of the trust fund, and, at least until it is paid, the creditors have nothing [1]

§ 44 **Statutory Rule of New York.** In New York, the attempt to reorganize the law of trusts by means of statute has resulted in a peculiar doctrine. An express statute in the case of real estate,[2] and an analogous rule which the courts apply to personal property,[3] render creditors unable to reach any part of the income from a trust estate except " the surplus beyond the sum necessary for the education and support of the beneficiary." [4] Yet there is room for the other doctrine as well A discretionary power may be given trustees in behalf of a

---

[1] Ballantine v Ballantine, 152 Fed 775; aff'd 160 Fed 927. A statement of the entire rule may thus be gathered from Nichols v Eaton, 91 U S 716, 721-2 "A will which expresses a purpose to vest in a devisee either personal property, or the income of personal or real property, and secure to him its enjoyment free from liability for his debts, is void on grounds of public policy, as being in fraud of the rights of creditors, or as expressed by Lord Eldon in Brandon v Robinson (18 Ves. 433), 'If property is given to a man for his life, the donor cannot take away the incidents of a life-estate.' Taking for our guide the cases decided in the English courts, the doctrine of the case of Brandon v Robinson seems to be pretty well established. It is equally well settled that a devise of the income of property, to cease on the insolvency or bankruptcy of the devisee, is good, and that the limitation is valid, Demmill v Bedford, 3 Ves. 149, Brandon v. Robinson, 18 id 429, Rockford v Hackmen, 9 Hare, Lewin on Trusts, 80 c VII, Sec 2, Tillinghast v. Bradford, 5 R. I 205. . The cases on this point are well considered in Lewin on Trusts, above cited, and the doctrine may be stated that a direction that the trust to the first taker shall cease on his bankruptcy and shall then go to his wife or children is valid, and the entire interest passes to them, but that if the devise be to *him* and his wife or children, or if he is any way to receive a vested interest, that interest, whatever it may be, may be separated from those of his wife or children, and be paid over to his assignee, Page v Way, 3 Beav 20, Perry v Roberts, 1 Myl & K 4; Rippon v Norton, 2 Beav 63, Lord r Bunn, 2 You. & Coll Ch 98 Where, however, the devise over is for the support of the bankrupt and his family, in such manner as the trustees may think proper, the weight of authority in England seems to be against the proposition that anything is left to which the assignee can assert a valid claim, Twopenny v Peyton, 10 Sim 487; Godden v Crowhurst, id. 642."

[2] New York Real Pr Law, Sec 98

[3] Graff v Bonnett, 31 N Y 9

[4] Bergman v Lord, 194 N Y. 70, 86 N E 828, Graff v. Bonnet, 31 N. Y. 9; Tolles v Wood, 99 N. Y 616

given beneficiary, and in such a case his creditors can reach nothing.[1]

§ 45. **The Real " Spendthrift Trust "** All of this is quite far from the idea of a "spendthrift trust" as thus expounded by Mr Justice Miller in Nichols v Eaton.[2]

"But while we have thus attempted to show that Mrs. Eaton's will is valid in all its parts upon the extremest doctrine of the English Chancery Court, we do not wish to have it understood that we accept the limitations which that court has placed upon the power of testamentary disposition of property by its owner."

The Court then goes on to express its view that a trust is valid which, although enforcible by the *cestui que* trust, is expressly rendered exempt from the claims of his creditors

§ 46 **Is allowed in but Two States.** But this bold dictum has never taken hold It did not express the law, and has made much confusion, but no law. The result of all of the cases since that decision is stated by Professor Gray that in only two States can spendthrift trusts be created, viz Pennsylvania and Massachusetts. And even in Massachusetts a spendthrift trust cannot be created by one for his own benefit[3]

§ 47 **Powers.** Another angle of the proposition is afforded by that peculiar feature of real estate law where a man has a power over property which, while he can exercise it, he cannot

---

[1] Myers v Russell, 60 N Y Misc 617, 112 N Y S 520; Wetmore v Truslow, 51 N Y 338 The opinion in the first case cited thus states the proposition "The amount to be paid to Albert B Hilton depends upon the judgment and discretion of the executors He is entitled to receive only such a sum as they consider necessary, proper or expedient for the support and maintenance of himself and his family If in the judgment of the executors they deem it unnecessary, improper or inexpedient that the whole income of the estate should be paid to Albert B Hilton, the balance retained by them remains a part of the trust estate, to which the children of Albert B Hilton are entitled . The plaintiff, as creditor, has no greater right to this balance than that of the *cestui que* trust, Wetmore v. Truslow, 51 N. Y 338, and the latter has no right to it at all " — Myers v. Russell, 60 N Y Misc 617, 112 N Y S 520.

[2] *Supra*

[3] *Op. cit.*, Sec 177.

alienate It must follow, if the principle we are dealing with is sound, that his creditors cannot have the power exercised for their benefit; and such indeed has been established by the few decisions that can be found upon this point.[1] If, under the principles of real property law, the debtor could not alienate the power, then his creditors cannot have it in satisfaction of their claims. In Jones v Clifton,[2] the debtor had created a trust for the benefit of his children reserving a power of reduction. It was held that such a power could not be exercised by the creditors of the settler, nor would the court compel him to exercise the power for their benefit. As the court said, the power "is not an interest in the property which can be transferred to another, or sold on execution, or devised by law . . . Nor is the power a chose in action. It did not, therefore, constitute assets."

§ 48 **Limitations of Market** Again to repeat, the test is whether the debtor himself can sell the thing in question It does not matter that his market is limited by positive restrictions; if he has any market at all, the creditors in turn can avail themselves of that market.

§ 49. **Stock Exchange Seat** This is illustrated in the case of a debtor who owns a seat upon a mercantile exchange, such as the Stock Exchange of New York and the like The rules of such institutions generally provide that the purchaser of a seat cannot avail himself of the rights thereby conferred unless his personality is approved by some governing committee of the institution. Although this of necessity limits the salability of the seat, nevertheless, it is a salable asset, and consequently, as is now well settled, it is available to the creditors of the debtor Then, in realizing upon the seat, the creditors have to find a purchaser who will pass muster with the governing committee In other words, the creditors are bound by the rules of the Exchange in their efforts to realize upon property

[1] Harrington v Hart, 1 Cox Ch 131 Jones v Clifton, 101 U S 225 For the rule under the New York statutory system of trusts, see N Y. Real Prop Law, Sec. 149; Terry v. Wiggins, 47 N Y 512.
[2] 101 U. S. 225.

whose existence and enjoyment are governed by such regulations.[1]

§ 50. **Contingent Remainder and Tenancy by the Entirety.** If further illustration were needed, we have it in several instances of real estate tenure. Take the contingent remainder. The common law viewed it not as an estate, but a mere possibility, and hence it was inalienable and the remainderman's creditors could not apply it to their debts. But in a jurisdiction where, by statute, contingent remainders are alienable, it must follow that the remainderman's creditors can realize upon his interest.[2] Again, consider the peculiar rules surrounding tenancy by the entirety. Since the interest of each spouse depends entirely upon the tontine chance of surviving the other, it follows that the creditors of neither can take the property or seek partition.[3] But on the other hand, the creditors of the survivor, wheresoever their claims accrued, can realize on the property.[4]

§ 51. **Right of Realization as limited by Statute.** There is one thing more to reckon with. The creditor's right to realize upon the debtor's property is often limited by state laws governing the conduct of the debtor's business. In nearly every state at the present date, in certain classes of business a party is required, as a prerequisite to engaging in such a business, to

---

[1] The rule stated in the text was established by the Federal Courts in a consistent line of decisions, Hyde v Woods, 94 U S 523, Page v Edmunds, 187 U. S. 596, 23 S Ct 200; Re Gregory, 174 Fed 629. The New York Courts are in accord. Wrede v Clark, 132 N Y. App Div 293, 117 N Y S 5. The case of Pancoast v. Gowen, 93 Pa St. 66, is not to the contrary. As the Supreme Court points out in Page v Edmunds, supra, all that was held in the Pennsylvania case was that a "seat" was not property in the narrow sense of 'liability to be levied upon and sold under a fi fa.'" But, as we have seen, the creditor has remedies in addition to the writ of execution commonly known as a "fifa."

[2] Clowe v Seavy, 208 N Y. 496, 102 N E. 521

[3] Beihl v Martin, 236 Pa St 519, 84 Atl. 953; Schliess v Thayer, 170 Mich 395, 136 N W 365

[4] Beach v Hollister, 3 Hun 519, Fleek v. Zielbauer, 117 Pa. St. 213, 12 Atl. 420.

deposit with a state official in money or quick security, a certain sum which shall be applied in the case of his becoming insolvent to the payment of his debts.[1] Instances of such provisions are to be seen in the case of state laws regulating the business of insurance and banking, where it is almost uniformly required that any corporation, before engaging in such a business, shall make such a deposit with the State Comptroller or other similar officer, thus in effect providing an insurance fund against such debts as may be created in the course of the business thus instituted. Within recent years the State of New York has made a similar requirement in the case of an individual engaged in the business of banking within the State.[2] In a recent case, it was held that the object of this State was to protect only creditors residing in New York, and therefore when the debtor became insolvent only such a limited class of creditors were entitled to resort to this fund for satisfaction of their claims.[3] The reason for that decision was that the law, as construed by the court, "indicates only a purpose to protect persons living or doing business in this State, over whom alone it could rightfully exercise jurisdiction." Obviously this decision does not affect the general principle above discussed. It involves simply the case of a State requiring the debtor to set apart certain of his assets for the benefit of a certain class of creditors. In the absence of such a statute there would have been no doubt that all of the creditors could have resorted to this particular fund for payment wherever it could have been found.

§ 52. **Exemption Laws.** The mention of statutes leads us to an important topic. In the United States there is a widespread system of statutory exemptions, by means of which, to a degree

---

[1] See for an excellent instance of such a statutory marshaling under the Georgia Code, Commonwealth Bank v Hall, 203 Fed 366.

[2] General Business Law, Sec. 25, as amended, by Laws of 1910, c 348, and Laws of 1911, c 393. See Engel v O'Malley, 219 U S 128, 31 S Ct. 190, for a full discussion of the policy and objects of this statute.

[3] In re Rosett, 203 Fed 67; Blake v. Insurance Co., 209 Fed 309.

varying according to the policy of the particular State, a certain portion of the debtor's property is exempt from the claims of his creditors These statutory exemptions, whatever they may be styled, whether homestead rights or the like, must always be reckoned with because, in one form or another, they are to be found in the body of the statute law belonging to every American State.[1] The present National Bankrupt Act recognizes such exemptions and allows the debtor the benefit of those provided by the law of the State where he resides.[2]

§ 53 **Life Insurance as a Subject of Exemption Laws** As an illustration of this policy, which in some states allows a debtor to carve out a portion of his real estate as a homestead right exempt from the claims of his creditors, and in others allows him merely the tools of his trade or profession,[3] may be mentioned the case of life insurance policies A policy of life insurance in effect represents accumulated payments by the insured which, if he dies within a limited period, result in a payment to

---

[1] See note in 14 Columbia Law Review, p. 64 In Miller v Sherry, 2 Wall, at p 245, learned counsel thus stated in the course of his argument "As respects the homestead reservation The law which thus protects a man and his wife and children from a cruel and remorseless creditor, and gives to them at least a humble home,— one peaceful shelter from the misfortunes of the world, — is a law which does infinite honor to the refinement of America Such a law was quite above the civilization of our British ancestors; they have never yet reached it, though they have before them in ancient Rome record of the honor that was given to the 'domus in qua pater decessit, in qua minores creverunt' It is a law worthy of honest support from every court in the land It will receive it from this, the highest of them all This statute prohibits a forced sale of the homestead upon any process or order from any court of law or equity " Compare this with Professor Gray's criticism, that these laws "have been carried to an extent which it would not be easy to justify on any sound principles of ethics or political economy " — "Restr Alien," 2d ed, Sec 263 n

[2] National Bankrupt Act, Sec 6 The claiming of such an exemption, however, is governed by the practice prescribed by the Act Re Burnham, 202 Fed 762 Instances of such exemptions are to be found, among others, in the following cases. Re Robinson, 206 Fed 176, Re Zimmerman, 202 Fed 812 Chicago &c R R Co v Hall, 229 U S. 511, 33 S Ct. 885; Re Phillips, 209 Fed 490

[3] See for instance, New York Code of Civil Procedure, Secs 1390–1

his estate or the beneficiary under the policy, but if he lives beyond a certain period, result in his being entitled to receive from the insurer certain cash, in addition to having his insurance continued, or, in some instances, in substitution of the latter right. When this stage has been reached the policy is said to have a cash surrender value. As has been said, this cash surrender value is composed of " the excess in the premiums paid over the annual cost of insurance, with accumulations of interest." [1] As the Supreme Court has noted, nearly every insurance policy of the present day " will be found to have either a stipulated surrender value or an established value, the amount of which the companies are willing to pay " [2] When a policy reaches this stage, it bears out the remark of Vice Chancellor PITNEY that " there is no mystery or charm about life insurance It is not the means of creating wealth, nor yet a contract of mere indemnity, as is that of fire and marine insurance. It is in its most usual form, simply a mode of putting by money for savings." [3] Apart from the question of fraudulent transfer, in connection with laying by such treasures for the benefit of another by means of a policy of life insurance, there is no doubt that unless restrained by statute this cash surrender value is an asset available to the creditors.[4]

---

[1] *In re* Kinney, 15 Fed 535
[2] Burlingham *v.* Crouse, 228 U S 459, 33 S Ct 564.
[3] Merchants &c Co *v* Borland, 53 N J Eq 282, 31 Atl 272.
[4] Merchants &c Bank *v* Borland, *supra*, Holt *v* Everall, 2 Ch. Div 266, Fern *v* Ward, 80 Ala 555, 2 So 118; Stokes *v* Amerman, 121 N Y 337. 24 N E 819 The point has been precisely put by the New York Court as follows. "Contracts for the future payment of money depending upon conditions to be performed are not for any reason growing out of their uncertain character exempt from the claims of creditors. Unmatured life insurance policies have been treated by the courts as possessing a present value in the distribution of the assets of insolvent insurance companies (People *v* Security Life Ins Co, 78 N Y 114, 34 Am Rep. 522, Att'y-General *v* Guardian Mutual Life Ins. Co, 82 N Y 336) and we perceive no reason why the interest of a judgment creditor in such a contract, arising under the statute permitting a wife to insure her husband's life, may not be declared and protected by the courts The wife cannot be compelled to assign the policy, nor can her interest therein, represented by premiums to the

§ 54 **The Provisions of the Bankrupt Act** The present Bankrupt Act has covered the matter as follows.

"Sec. 70a. The trustee of the estate of a bankrupt, upon his appointment and qualification, . . . shall in turn be vested by operation of law with the title of the bankrupt, as of the date he was adjudged a bankrupt, except in so far as to property which is exempt, . . . provided that when any bankrupt shall have any insurance policy which has a cash surrender value payable to himself, his estate, or personal representatives, he may within thirty days after the cash surrender value has been ascertained and stated to the trustee by the company issuing the same, pay or secure to the trustee the sum so ascertained and stated and continue to hold, own and carry such policy free from the claims of the creditors participating in the distribution of his estate under the bankruptcy proceedings, and otherwise the policy shall pass to the trustee as assets."

§ 55 **Former Conflict of Interpretation.** Until very recently the federal courts were in a conflict upon the proper construction of this provision, which has been described by the Supreme Court as follows.

"The one favors the view that only policies having a cash surrender value are intended to pass to the trustee for the benefit of creditors. The other, conceding that the proviso deals with this class of policies, maintains that policies of life insurance which have no surrender value, pass to the trustee under the language of Section 70a immediately preceding the proviso which reads: 'Property which, prior to the filing of the petition, he could by any means have transferred, or which might have been levied upon and sold under judicial process against him.'"[1]

extent of $500, be affected by any proceedings on the part of such creditor. But the interest of a creditor which attaches to a contract of life insurance, in virtue of the statute, and by reason of the fact of payment by the judgment debtor of premiums in excess of $500, may be declared by a court of equity and impressed upon the contract in an action where the company issuing the policy and all persons interested therein are parties, though the money secured thereby is not due" — Stokes v. Amerman, 121 N. Y. 337, 24 N. E. 819

[1] Burlingham v. Crouse, 228 U. S. 459, 33 S. Ct. 564

§§ 54-57   THE PROPERTY AVAILABLE FOR CREDITORS   43

§ 56. **Present Rule as to Life Insurance in Bankruptcy.** The court, in the case just cited and another case decided at the same term,[1] has settled this controversy. It has laid it down that any policy passes to the creditors under this Section unless it has a cash surrender value, and then only for the purpose of realizing its value by the cancellation of the policy. In reaching this conclusion, the Supreme Court considered that Congress must have had in mind, at the time this resolution was adopted, the fact that exemption statutes existed protecting this peculiar sort of investment for the benefit of the debtor or his family.[2] As the Bankrupt Act, in Section 6, gives to every bankrupt the full benefit of all exemptions allowed him by the laws of the state of his domicile, the provisions of Section 70a of the Act above quoted apply only in the absence of a specific exemption under the state law. So in effect it may be said that the creditors under the Bankrupt Act are entitled to have the cash surrender value of the policy, only when (a) it has a cash surrender value, and (b) the law of the state where the debtor resides does not specifically exempt this value from the claims of the creditors.[3]

§ 57 **The Question One of State Law.** The reader, therefore, must look to the statutes of the particular state where the controversy arises to determine whether an exemption is created for the bankrupt in his life insurance. An illustrative statute is that of New York, at present composing Section 52 of the Domestic Relations Law, which in effect provides that in the case of a debtor with a wife and children or with merely a wife, the wife may take out insurance on her husband's life payable to her or her children, and the husband may, up to the amount

---

[1] Everett v Judson, 228 U. S 474, 33 S Ct. 568
[2] See Burlingham v Crouse, 228 U S 459, 33 S Ct 564, where the court said "It is the twofold purpose of the Bankruptcy Act to convert the estate of the bankrupt into cash and distribute it among creditors and then to give the bankrupt a fresh start with such exemptions and rights as the Statute left untouched."
[3] Holden v Stratton, 198 U. S 202, 25 S. Ct. 656, Re White, 174 Fed. 333

of $500 per annum, pay the premiums on such insurance out of his own estate; and that such a policy is in no way available to the claims of the husband's creditors [1]

§ 58. **Restoration of Status quo when Fraudulent Transactions are set Aside** The foregoing discussion has already led us into the domain of matters whose general aspects are reserved for later chapters But this could not well be avoided, and it is hoped that the reader will pardon the further encroachments that follow, as necessary to round out the present inquiry. The principle that a creditor is entitled only to what his debtor has, is well illustrated by cases where the debtor has put property beyond the reach of the creditors' process by means of fraudulent transfer or preference. When the creditors succeed in retaking the property, they are entitled to acquire no more than what they would have had if the wrongful transaction had not occurred. Of course they are entitled to acquire just as much as that, and hence the debtor must account to them for the intervening rents, profits and income of the property in question [2] On the other hand the debtor should be entitled to offset on this accounting any genuine improvements which he may have made on the property during this interval; certainly that should be the position of equity, and if the creditor proceeds in equity the court should put him upon these terms. That is the doctrine of the well-reasoned case of Loos v Wilkinson,[3] and the only case which has been found to the contrary [4] seems wholly indefensible. In like manner, if the transferee has paid off a mortgage existing upon the property, he is entitled to deduct the amount thus expended from the value of the property as returned to the creditor The creditors should not "undertake

---

[1] Other instances of state law exemptions are mentioned in Burlingham v Crouse, 228 U S 459, 33 S Ct 564; Holden v Stratton, 198 U S 202, 25 S. Ct 656; In re Moss, 206 Fed. 350
[2] Sands v Codwise, 4 Johns 537; Gray v Chase, 184 Mass 444, 68 N. E. 676
[3] 113 N Y. 435, 21 N E 117.
[4] Strike's Case, 1 Bland Ch (Md) 57.

to compel the fraudulent grantee or transferee to respond to them for an interest in property which he did not seek to get, and which his grantor or vendor did not have to convey or transfer to him In such a case the plaintiffs are without any equity on which to base a right of recovery."[1] In like manner, where a transfer of land is set aside the debtor's wife is entitled to a restoration of her dower rights therein, even though she had joined in the deed conveying the property to the fraudulent grantee[2] Of course this reasoning would not apply to a case where the conveyance was made before the marriage, because then, the property having passed from the husband before the marriage, he was never seized of it during coverture, and when the creditors recapture it the wife has nothing to claim.[3] This same idea, of restoration of the *status quo*, appears when the creditors sue by means of a representative such as a trustee in bankruptcy Where a debtor has preferentially transferred property to a creditor, and the trustee has recovered this property for the benefit of the estate, the Federal courts have allowed the preferred creditor to come in as a general creditor on

---

[1] Hamilton Bank *v* Halsted, 134 N Y. 520, 526, 31 N E. 900.

[2] "The principle which governs is this The release of an inchoate right of dower which a married woman makes by joining in a conveyance with her husband, operates against her only by estoppel An estoppel must be reciprocal, and binds only in favor of those who are privy thereto A release of dower can be availed of then only by one who claims under the very title which was created by the conveyance with which the release is joined. A release to a stranger to that title does not extinguish the right of dower, Harriman *v* Gray, 49 Me 537 It shows no privity of estate or connection of any kind between the doweress and the tenant, Pixley *v* Bennett, 11 Mass 298. But when a creditor of the husband pursues him to judgment and attacks as fraudulent and sets aside as valid the deed from him, joining in which the wife has released her right of dower, he does not connect himself with the title which that deed has created and with which the release of dower is connected. He sets up the title of the husband as it existed before the fraudulent conveyance, and stands in hostility to the title which it has given Not being a party to the release or in privity with it he may not set it up in bar of dower. (See Wyman *v* Fox, 59 Me. 100; Robinson *v*. Bates, 3 Metc 40)"—Malloney *v*. Horan, 49 N. Y. 112, 119

[3] Whitehead *v*. Mallory, 4 Cush 138

the distribution of the estate, notwithstanding the language of 57g of the Bankrupt Act by which such action is allowed only when the creditors surrender the preference In spite of the preference being taken from the transferee by force of a judgment, the courts still allow the proof of claim.[1] Mere lapse of time in effecting the surrender creates no estoppel.[2]

§ 59. **Representatives of Creditors get no Higher Rights** So we are brought back to the general proposition with which we started; by means of the procedure which we examined in Chapter I, the creditors are entitled to realize on whatever property of the debtor the latter may have been able to realize on. None of the additional remedies afforded to creditors by way of liquidation proceedings, which we shall later examine, ever gave the creditors less than that, and none ever gave them more The representative of the general body of creditors, whose existence is a primary feature of every such liquidation proceeding, whether he be styled assignee in bankruptcy, trustee in bankruptcy, receiver, or liquidator, and whatever may be the source of his appointment, never did more than take the debtor's property in the same plight and condition in which the debtor left it, the creditors' representative gets no higher or better interest in the debtor's affairs than the debtor had He is not a purchaser for a valuable consideration, at most he occupies no higher status than that of a judgment creditor.[3]

[1] Keppel v Tiffin Bank, 197 U S. 356, 25 S Ct. 443, Page v Rogers, 211 U S 575, 29 S Ct. 159.

[2] *In re* Hamilton etc Co, 209 Fed 596. Recently Section 57g of the Act has been amended so as to allow a similar proof on the part of one who, so far from merely receiving a preference, has actively participated in the fraudulent transfer of the debtor's property to him

[3] Walker v Burrows, 1 Atk 267, Mitford v Mitford, 9 Ves 87, *Ex parte* Holthausen, L R. 9 Ch. App 722; Aldine Trust Co v Smith, 181 Fed 449 We shall recur to this subject in a later connection, but for a general discussion of this self-evident proposition, reference may be made to an article in 6 Columbia Law Review, at p 562 The only difference of opinion that has been formed in this connection, arose under the usury laws The well-settled chancery rule, of course, is that as a condition of being relieved against a usurious obligation a court of equity will require the plaintiff to pay the principal with in-

§ 60 **Agreements restricting the Creditor's Rights** We may now safely leave the proposition with a passing word as to its application to particular creditors who may have circumscribed their general rights by express agreement with the debtor. If the debtor's agreement binds certain of his property to the payment of all or a great part of his debts, the validity and effect of such an agreement will be considered under the head of liquidation,[1] and requires no discussion here. If the debtor binds certain of his property to the payment of a particular debt, then whether the creditor thus favored is merely a secured creditor (of whose rights, so far as they affect the other creditors, we shall hereafter speak) or occupies a more narrow status, depends upon whether this creditor has agreed to look only to the particular property for the payment of his debt. If that is the case, then his status is not so much that of a creditor as it is that of a *cestui que* trust. He needs no judgment to give him a claim upon this property, because he already has the claim by express agreement, but on the other hand he cannot sue on his debt, because that would result in a judgment giving him a claim on the rest of the debtor's property as well, which would violate his agreement. He is therefore restricted to the particular property under all circumstances.[2] There is nothing to confuse in this. Nor is there any difficulty in the case where a particular creditor agrees to subordinate his claim to those of

---

terest at the lawful rate, Scott *v* Nesbitt, 2 Cox Ch 183, 2 Bro C C 641, Fanning *v* Dunham, 5 Johnson Ch. 122. At an early date it was held that assignees in bankruptcy were not subject to this rule, *Ex parte* Skip, 2 Ves 489, Benfield *v*. Solomon, 9 Ves 84. On the other hand, the New York Court of Appeals has held that a trustee in bankruptcy is still subject to the rule, although in New York a statute has abolished this requirement as to the original borrower, Wheelock *v* Lee, 64 N Y. 242

[1] In this connection should be read Zeiser *v* Cohn, 207 N. Y 407, 101 N E 184, where a debtor conveyed land to A in consideration of A's promise to pay certain of the vendor's debts. It was held that the vendor's specified creditors were entitled, by subrogation, to enforce against A the vendor's equitable lien upon the land for the amount of the debts thus assumed by A

[2] Synnott *v* Tombstone &c Co , 208 Fed 251.

all the other creditors He can make such an agreement, but it has its effect The contractor is no longer a creditor; call him what you will, shareholder or partner according to the nature of the agreement, his privity is thenceforth with the debtor.[1]

[1] Burt v Rattle, 31 Ohio St 116, Cass v Realty &c Co, 148 N. Y. App Div. 96, 132 N Y S 1074, aff'd 206 N. Y 649, 99 N. E. 1105; Re Pechheimer Fishel & Co, 212 Fed 357

CHAPTER III

THE FRAUDULENT TRANSFER ORIGIN AND SCOPE OF THE STATUTE OF FRAUDULENT CONVEYANCES

§ 61 Definition of Fraudulent Transfer
62 Transfer as Distinct from Concealment.
63 Inadequacy of Common Law
64 Equity's Jurisdiction never Tested
65 Historical Reason
66 Historical Reason Continued
67. Historical Reason Continued
68 Adoption of Statute of Fraudulent Conveyances
69. The Statute the Corner Stone of this Branch of Law
70. Present and Subsequent Creditors
71 Tort Claimant not a Present Creditor until Judgment is Recovered
72. Contract Creditors not necessarily Present Creditors
73. Necessity of Judgment for Invocation of Statute
74. Procedure of Judgment Creditor — Levying upon the Transferred Property.

§ 75. Necessity of Regular Process
76 Another Method of Procedure
77. Procedure in Case of Real Estate
78 Inadequacy of Common Law Procedure
79 Concurrent Jurisdiction of Equity in Case of Real Estate
80 Concurrent Jurisdiction in Cases of Personal Property
81 Subrogation of Surety
82 The Statute gives merely a Right to Act
83 The Creditor must Act.
84 Assignability of Such Right.
85 Effect of Statute on Third Parties
86 Validity of Fraudulent Transaction as between Immediate Parties
87. Opposing Views.
88 Validity of Transaction as against Third Parties who are not Creditors.

§ 61. **Definition of Fraudulent Transfer.** We have considered the methods by which the creditor is allowed to realize his claim upon the debtor's property, and the different kinds of property interests, enjoyed by the debtor, upon which the creditor may realize Having thus appraised the creditor's right of realization, it is now in order to view the wrongs upon that right which the debtor is capable of inflicting. First of these wrongs, in the nature of a logical progression of study, should come the numerous varieties of evasion which are commonly described under the heading of fraudulent transfer or fraudulent conveyance. Such a situation is presented in any case where the debtor has so dealt with the title to the property as to put it beyond the reach of the creditor's remedy unless, on some principle other than those governing the devolution of title, the courts can allow the creditor to realize upon the property despite the transfer.

§ 62. **Transfer as Distinct from Concealment** "Title" is used advisedly in the above connection, as connoting an idea apart from the mere concealment of the property. If the debtor merely hides his property from his creditor, that sort of case presents no difficulty, so far as our present inquiry is concerned The creditor must find the property, of course, but when he finds it he may realize on it. Bankruptcy statutes may penalize such conduct on the debtor's part,[1] as incident to a judgment creditor's bill, the creditor may have the right of discovery concerning the debtor's estate, a right which is preserved in the modern "order of examination" which may be obtained in the course of supplementary proceedings; and the right of examining the bankrupt as to the extent of his estate has always been a feature of bankruptcy proceedings[2] But the concealment of property is not of interest to us, because it effects no real violation of the creditor's right, such as it has already appeared to us to be. What we are concerned with now is the case where, by the debtor changing in some way

[1] See Section 29b of the Bankrupt Act of 1898, punishing acts of concealment Such a statute, however, may be construed as embracing a fraudulent transfer as well as mere acts of concealment. Cohen v. U S, 157 Fed 651
[2] See Section 21a of the Bankrupt Act of 1898, Cameron v U. S, 231 U S 710, 34 S Ct 244; Re Abbey Press, 134 Fed 51

the title to his property, the creditor is forced to assert something more than the right to realize on the debtor's property, and to ask the privilege of realizing on something that was formerly the debtor's property, but is no longer his at present

§ 63. **Inadequacy of Common Law.** On what common law principle can the creditor make such a request? Take the ideal case, where A, the debtor, gives his goods to B in order to prevent C, A's creditor, from realizing his judgment upon them It is obvious that the common law court cannot give relief All it could ever do, as we have seen, was to give C a writ of execution, allowing C to make his money out of A's property. But if A has transferred the legal title to this property to B, then the sheriff, however he may be C's servant in levying the writ of execution, cannot levy upon the goods, because they are not A's goods, the legal title is in B, and the writ directs a levy upon A's goods. True, B derived title from A, but that makes no difference, since all the sheriff can ask is, where is the title now?

§ 64. **Equity's Jurisdiction never Tested.** Could equity give relief in the case put? That question must remain unanswered; like many other questions suggested by the study of our law, the accidents of history have rendered it academic. We know that equity has at least once given relief in a case, long before the time of the great statute we are approaching, and apparently without reference to the statutes which preceded it[1] Looking back from present-day vantage ground, however, although we may presume to say that all these wrongs could have been righted if left to what JESSEL, M R., has styled " the gradual growth of equity,"[2] the fact is that in the begin-

---

[1] Case in Cal. of Chancery, 1 XCIX (1477) Selden Society, Select Cases in Chancery, p XLI Plaintiff was appointed to a rectory. His predecessor had allowed the church choir and parsonage house to become dilapidated, but to prevent any claim against his representatives, he made no will, but gave all his goods to defendant by deed of gift Decree for plaintiff in the sum of 26 marks

[2] *Re* Hallett's Estate, 13 Ch D 696.

ning the matter was not left to the Court of Chancery. On the contrary, the merchants of England went to Parliament for relief, and legislation, not equity, was the first agent of progress.

§ 65. **Historical Reason.** If we are to seek a reason for this choice of legislation over equity, it can be found, it is submitted, in the history of the Court of Chancery. The evil doings of debtors were recognized facts of daily existence long before the merchant public of England acquired the habit of going to the Court of Chancery with their grievances. Even prior to the publication of English reports, and in the dawn of English institutions, the practice was common for a debtor to convert his property into money and then with the money enjoy life to the exclusion of his creditors.[1] The great Statute of Fraudulent Conveyances [2] was by no means the first attempt of the English Parliament to legislate against the evils so graphically portrayed in its recitals.

§ 66. **Historical Reason Continued.** No less than three Statutes of Fraudulent Conveyances were passed prior to the reign of Queen Elizabeth,[3] and as far back as the time of Edward III, Parliament forbade practices which have not yet wholly

---

[1] The recitals in the Statute of 50 Edw. III, c. 6, would almost precisely apply to some present-day practices: "Divers people (it states), do give their tenements and chattels to their friends, by collusion thereof to have the profits at their will, and after do flee to the franchise of Westminster, of St. Martin's Le Grand of London, or other such privileged places, and there do live a great time with an high countenance of another man's goods and profits of the said tenements and chattels, till the said creditors shall be bound to take a small parcel of their debt, and release the remnant." Of course, in those days it was necessary for the debtor to flee to sanctuary in order to escape imprisonment for debt. Nowadays a fraudulent debtor does not need the protection of Westminster, because imprisonment for debt has been abolished. So far as his personal liberty is concerned, he can, to quote the words of the old Statute, "live a great time with an high countenance of another man's goods," wherever he pleases, instead of being bound by the jail liberties.

[2] 13 Eliz. c. 5.

[3] See Bigelow, "Fraudulent Conveyances," 11, *et seq.* These statutes alone can justify Lord Mansfield's view, Cadogan *v.* Kennett, 2 Cowp. 432, that, prior to the Statute of Elizabeth, the common law courts had power to aid in a case of fraudulent conveyances.

ceased. On the other hand, in the days of Crecy the Court of Chancery was hardly a mercantile court, nor had its stature grown much in this respect when, several centuries later, the great Act of Elizabeth was adopted, and the development of this branch of the law began. Even then the Court of Chancery was not in the highest public esteem. Though bishops no longer of necessity presided over it, yet the court had become subject during the time of Henry VIII to the charge of being too free with the process of injunction, or rather of abandoning control of that writ to the sister Court of Star Chamber.[1]

§ 67. **Historical Reason Continued.** In addition, the Chancery was still too much a part of the Royal Court, and the stain of scandal was upon that court at the time of Elizabeth's accession. Not only had the Lord Protector Somerset amassed, to the common knowledge, a mighty fortune while in office, not only had certain of his friends, after his fall, been made to disgorge vast sums of public money embezzled;[2] it was not enough for the Receiver-General of Yorkshire to "buy my own land with my own money" as King Edward VI dryly records, but the taint had reached the sanctuary of the Court of Chancery. The King himself records in his journal that Beaumont, Master of the Rolls, confessed "how he, being judge in the Chancery, between the Duke of Suffolk and the Lady Powis, took his title, and went about to get it into his hands, paying a sum of money, and letting her have a farm of a neigh-

---

[1] In the reforms demanded by the Catholics of the North in 1536 was the following "That the common laws may have place, as was used in the beginning of your Grace's reign; and that all injunctions be clearly decreed, and not to be granted unless the matter be heard and determined in Chancery." Froude, "History of England," ch 13. See also Roper, "Life of More," 42-3, for an account of a controversy Sir Thomas More, while Chancellor, had with the common law judges over this vexed question of injunctions.

[2] "Sir Thomas Smith and Sir Michael Stanhope were made to refund £3000 each of public money which they had embezzled. Sir John Thynne as much as £6000." Froude, "Reign of Edward the Sixth," ch. 4.

bor of his, and caused an indenture to be made falsely with the old Duke's counterfeit hand to it by which he gave these lands to the Lady Powis."[1] If there was little tendency on the part of the merchant body to look to the Court of Chancery for aid when it was in the hands of such men as Archbishop Warham and Sir Thomas More, it is hardly likely that they would have considered the court as improved by the presence of men of this other type.

§ 68. **Adoption of Statute of Fraudulent Conveyances** At any rate the merchants of England obtained their relief from another source, they went to Parliament. And so the year 1570 was marked by the Statute of Fraudulent Conveyances,[2] which declared void as against his "creditors and others," all the debtor's transfers of property when made with intent to hinder, delay or defraud them.

§ 69. **The Statute the Corner Stone of This Branch of Law.** This statute has passed with the common law into all our States, it is a part of every bankrupt act, and however re-enacted in modern dress it may be to suit the taste of our legislators, it is always present with us.[3] Though it had its predecessors, as we have seen, yet for all practical purposes it may be considered as the first of its kind, for, while the others were ignored, the statute of Elizabeth came under the attention of Lord Coke, who, it may be said, put it into the common law with his marvelous gloss in the famous case of Twyne.[4] You cannot read far in the law of fraudulent conveyances before you come to Twyne's Case; it is Coke who introduces you to the statute.

§ 70. **Present and Subsequent Creditors** The statute makes "void, frustrate and of none effect" as against creditors "and

---

[1] "King Edward's Journal," printed in Burnet's Collectanea, cited in Froude, *op cit.*
[2] 13 Eliz c 5
[3] Coder *v* Arts, 213 U S. 223, 29 S Ct. 436, Hall *v* Alabama Terminal Co, 143 Ala 464, 39 So 285, 2 L. R A (N. S.) 130
[4] (1601) 3 Co. Rep 80b.

others " any transfer of property by the debtor, when made with intent to hinder, delay or defraud them. The first question is, who are " creditors," and for whom is the word " others " intended? We may leave out of account, in the latter connection, purchasers of the property, a later statute of the same reign [1] protected them in terms, so the word " others " was left by legislative intent, to apply to persons who were in the same situation as creditors, in the minds of the framers of the statute If we fix our attention on the obvious point of division in the consideration of this subject, the time when the fraudulent transfer is effected, we come at once to an understanding of the legislative intent "Creditors" applies to those who were creditors at that moment; "others" are those who were not then creditors, but subsequently became so The distinction in this connection, therefore, is between present and subsequent creditors, and with this choice of nomenclature we may feel free to proceed.

§ 71 **Tort Claimant not a Present Creditor until Judgment is Recovered.** What is a present creditor? Obviously, one to whom the debtor is presently indebted.[2] Take two extreme

---

[1] Stat 27 Eliz c 4

[2] At this point we should inquire whether an alimony decree would constitute a wife a judgment creditor In bankruptcy such a decree has been held not to be a provable or dischargeable claim, and no English authority can be found for the proposition that she is a creditor, because in England an alimony decree was essentially a personal direction from the ecclesiastical court, and before any punishment even for contempt could be inflicted it was necessary for the wife to invoke the ancillary aid of the court of chancery   (See Barber v Barber, 21 How. 582) It is upon this historic line that the federal courts in bankruptcy have refused to consider an alimony decree as a provable or dischargeable debt, as we shall hereafter see This is somewhat inconsistent when we note that the state courts have tended almost uniformly toward holding an alimony decree as creating a creditor within the meaning of the statute, and thus enabling the wife, after obtaining a decree of divorce to attack a fraudulent conveyance made by her husband   (Holland v. Holland, 121 Mich 109, 79 N W. 1102, Bouslough v Bouslough, 68 Pa St 495, Green v Adams, 59 Vt 602, 10 Atl 742) The Michigan court said "It was also noticed that this statute is not limited to creditors, but extends to other persons, and is not limited to debts but extends to suits, damages, forfeitures

cases. If the debtor has committed a tort upon the person of another, or his property, for which an action in trespass would lie, it is apparent that until judgment is recovered in the action, the injured party is not a creditor. Until that time he has a mere personal cause of action, which does not pass to his estate if he dies, and which he cannot assign or pledge. When the plaintiff recovers a judgment, it will partake exactly of the characteristics of other judgments, and then of course he is a creditor, but there is never a moment of time prior to the entry of the judgment when he can be considered as a creditor. This is illustrated by proceedings in bankruptcy, the benefits of which are only open to persons who are creditors at a fixed date. A difference of opinion formerly existed in the English courts with regard to the provability of a tort claim upon which a verdict had been recovered at the time of the bankruptcy, but upon which judgment had not been entered. In Langford v. Ellis[1] it was held that the cause of action existed before the verdict, and that when the verdict is obtained the damages become a debt, and the judgment when entered operates back to the date of the verdict. This view, however, was overruled in *Ex parte* Charles[2] which referred the entire question to the date of judgment, as distinct from all else. So far is

and demands. . . . While not in the strict letter a creditor, she comes within the terms other persons; and while not strictly speaking delayed in the collection of a debt, she is hindered, delayed and defrauded out of her demands." The courts indeed have gone further and will allow the wife, pending a suit for divorce, to obtain an injunction forbidding the transfer of property. (De Ruiter v. De Ruiter, 28 Ind. App. 9, 62 N. E. 100; Feigley v. Feigley, 7 Md. 537.) In fact the only limit which any courts have placed upon this, is that they will not allow an independent suit for the purpose prior to or unconnected with a suit for divorce. (See Ramsden v. Ramsden, 91 N. Y. 281; Longworth v. Longworth, 144 N. Y. App. Div. 187, 128 N. Y. S. 1064.) It would seem that it was never necessary to rest these decisions upon the statute of fraudulent conveyances. Ample authority could be found under the general jurisdiction of the court which attaches of necessity to the primary jurisdiction of divorce causes.

[1] 3 T. R. 539; 4 T. R. 570.
[2] 16 Ves. 256; 14 East. 198.

this point free from doubt, that in an early case [1] the chancery court considered that tort debts, even when reduced to judgment, should be postponed, on setting aside a fraudulent conveyance, to contract debts. But while this view of course no longer obtains, there is no doubt even at the present day that a tort claim does not constitute a debt. In the words of LINDLEY, L J., until the injured party recovers judgment, the tort feasor is " not in fact indebted at all." [2]

§ 72. **Contract Creditors not necessarily Present Creditors**
By parity of reasoning, persons having a contractual connection with the debtor may yet, at a given moment of time, be in the position of subsequent creditors If the terms of such a contract are contingent, so that, unless certain things outside of the parties' control occur, no debt at all will arise, then we have, at any time before such conditions eventuate, the case of a subsequent creditor A single instance will suffice for purposes of illustration, — where the debtor has guaranteed the obligation of another Unless the principal defaults, the surety is not liable, and the principal may never default Consequently at no time before the principal's default is the obligee in the position of more than a subsequent creditor of the guarantor. As is said by BEARDSLEY, C J, "At the time in question they were not creditors of the donor It is readily admitted that they were such in a sense that entitled them to the remedies provided in the act for the prevention of frauds to purchasers," [3] that is, they were subsequent creditors

§ 73. **Necessity of Judgment for Invocation of Statute**
Both classes of creditors, present and subsequent, are protected by the statute, within limitations which we shall hereafter study. In the immediate connection, however, we should note that no party, of either class, can invoke the statute unless he has a judgment. The statute added nothing

---

[1] Lewkner *v* Faulckner, 1 Prec Ch 105, 1 Eq. Cas Abr 148, pl 5.
[2] *Exp* Mercer, 17 Q. B D 290
[3] Severs *v*. Dobson, 53 N. J Eq 633, 34 Atl 7.

to the scale of the creditor's rights except by preventing frauds upon his right of realization, but its application predicates a creditor who by his judgment has secured the right of realization. The creditor cannot say that the debtor should or should not have transferred certain property until he has the mandate of the court authorizing him to make his money out of the debtor's property. As has been said by DENIO, J., "When a conveyance is said to be void against creditors the reference is to such parties when clothed with their judgments and executions, or such other titles as the law has provided for the collection of debts."[1] And as said by BRONSON, J.,[2] a fraudulent sale "cannot be impeached by a creditor at large It must be a creditor having a judgment and execution or some other process which authorized a seizure of goods."[3]

§ 74 **Procedure of Judgment Creditor — Levying upon the Transferred Property.** When the creditor thus has his judgment conferred upon him, he then is in the position to invoke the statute of Elizabeth He does it by literally following its terms and treating the conveyance of the property as void The conveyance thus being void, the creditor can act as though it had never been made and cause the sheriff to levy upon the property if it can be reached.[4] If the debtor has conveyed the

[1] Van Hausen v Radcliff, 17 N. Y 580
[2] Noble v Holmes, 5 Hill 194.
[3] Jones v Green, 1 Wall 330, Schofield v Ute Coal &c Co, 92 Fed 271, Thompson v Reed, 202 Fed 870.
[4] Turville v Tipper, Latch's Rep 222; Imray v Magnay, 11 M & W 267, Lovick v Crowder, 8 B & C 132, Hess v Hess, 117 N. Y. 306, 22 N E 956. Thus, if A levies under his judgment, but fraudulently leaves the property in the debtor's possession, B on obtaining judgment, can take it in execution, Lovick v Crowder, *supra* When the process of foreign attachment came into general use with us, a difficulty arose in this connection upon which complete agreement has not yet been reached Can the plaintiff cause the sheriff, under such a writ, to seize property which the defendant has fraudulently transferred? In New Jersey this question is answered in the negative, the plaintiff cannot, in advance of his judgment, seize property which is not at that time the defendant's, under the authority of the statute of Fraudulent Conveyances, because *non constat* he may ever obtain a judgment, Melville v Brown, 16 N. J. L 63 The New York rule

goods after the writ has been issued to the sheriff, but before the latter has actually levied, the creditor can cause the sheriff to sue for infraction of the modern lien which he has from the issuance of the execution.[1] Or if the debtor has created a fraudulent lien upon the property, the sheriff, after levying, may contest the lien by such methods as would be proper, considering his right of possession. As has recently been said: "A sheriff who levies upon chattels by virtue of an execution acquires a special property therein and may sue any one who takes them from his possession, as for goods rescued, either to recover the possession thereof or damages for their conversion."[2]

§ 75. **Necessity of Regular Process.** Of course, for such a levy the process must be perfect, as otherwise, there being no judgment to authorize the levy, the plaintiff and the sheriff are trespassers. The plaintiff cannot justify under the Statute of Elizabeth because he has not reached the point where he can invoke it. This is illustrated by Ahearn v. Prunell[3] where a judgment creditor levied on goods which had been fraudulently transferred, and a proper statutory return of the levy was not filed. It was held that the creditor and the sheriff were liable to the transferee in trespass, the court saying that "the plaintiff's bill of sale can only be successfully assailed by a legal attachment."

§ 76. **Another Method of Procedure.** Such is the way of the statute in its aid to the creditor so far as his common law procedure is concerned. And it is his only way in the courts of common law with this exception, that, according to good

---

appeared to be to the contrary, Hess v. Hess, 117 N. Y. 306, 22 N. E. 956; Mech Bk v. Dakin, 51 N. Y. 519, Rinchey v. Stryker, 28 N. Y. 45, but the recent case of Hart v. Clark, 194 N. Y. 403, 87 N. E. 808, limits these cases to justifying the defense of a sheriff who has succeeded in levying, against the claimant, while forbidding an affirmative action by that official to reach property withheld by the claimant.
[1] Hess v. Hess, 117 N. Y. 306, 22 N. E. 956.
[2] Dickinson v. Oliver, 195 N. Y. 238, 88 N. E. 44.
[3] 62 Conn. 21, 25 Atl. 393.

authority,[1] an action on the case will lie at the suit of the injured judgment creditor, against the debtor's transferee, for damages measured by the value of the property thus removed from the possibility of his realization.

§ 77. **Procedure in Case of Real Estate.** This method of procedure was more common with the debtor's personal property than with his real estate. In England the common law procedure was seldom if ever resorted to in the case of the debtor's land, because, as we have seen, the English writ of execution against land never authorized its sale, but only its use or the collection of its profits. If then the land was in the possession of another, claiming under a title derived from the debtor, or the debtor had transferred its profits by way of rent-charge or the like, the difficulties in the way of a levy were too great, and the creditor went into equity for relief as a matter of course. In our States the susceptibility of land to sale under execution gave the creditor, as a theoretical matter, the same rights of levy and sale, in despite of a fraudulent conveyance or encumbrance, as he possesses in the case of personal property.[2] The right of the creditor thus to act, however, must be carefully distinguished from his right to the statutory lien which is now universal in this country. In every State, statutes make a judgment a lien upon the debtor's land from the moment of the proper entry of the judgment. But if the debtor has fraudulently conveyed his land before the entry of judgment, the creditor, despite the Statute of Elizabeth, can derive no aid from his claim of lien. The land is not the land of the debtor because he has conveyed it. It is true that such a conveyance is void as against any creditor, but the two statutes are distinct and do not supplement each other. If the creditor relies upon the statutory lien which arises from the judgment, he must

[1] Meaux v. Howell, 4 East 1; Sattler v. Slonimsky, 199 Fed. 592. See, however, Ward v. Petrie, 157 N. Y. 301, 51 N. E. 1002, where some doubt is cast upon the proposition.
[2] Bergen v. Carman, 79 N. Y. 148; Hillyer v. Le Roy, 179 N. Y. 369, 72 N. E. 237; Jackson v. Holbrook, 36 Minn. 494, 32 N. W. 852.

show that the title to the land is in the debtor. This does not deprive him of the benefit of the Statute of Elizabeth, but he must act under that statute solely and derive no help from the other In the language of a leading case

"The operation of the lien of a judgment being limited by statute to the property then belonging to the judgment debtor, is not a mode prescribed by which a creditor may attack a conveyance fraudulent as to himself, or assert any right as such against the grantor therein. This lien is constructive in its character, and is not the result of a levy or any other act directed against this specific property It is the creature of the statute and cannot have effect beyond it." [1]

§ 78. **Inadequacy of Common Law Procedure** But these common law remedies were inadequate for all purposes. While the creditor was never remitted to his action on the case for damages, still even the realizing procedure which we have described found the same limits as those we have considered under the first chapter The statute could not enable the creditor to realize on any property upon which the sheriff could not have levied had it never been fraudulently sold or encumbered. Thus all "equitable assets," and all choses in action were still outside of the common law procedure To repeat, the statute did not add to that procedure; it simply enabled it to be used in defiance of titles created by the debtor. And in addition, the statute, by this very failure to add to the common law measure of relief, left one vast domain unprotected by the common law process, in the case of a fraudulent transfer, which was open to its reach in the absence of such conduct on the debtor's part. We refer to all cases involving real estate In the case of a fraudulent transfer of real estate, the creditor finds practical difficulties in the way of the common law procedure which do not exist with respect to personal

[1] *In re* Estes, 3 Fed 134; McMaster *v* Campbell, 41 Mich 513, 2 N W 836, Luhrs *v.* Hancock, 181 U S 567, 21 S Ct 726, Garfield *v* Hatmaker, 15 N. Y. 475.

property Such difficulties have been well described in a New Jersey case as follows:¹ "It was found in practice that in such cases sales by the sheriff under a judgment and execution, before any declaration had been made by a competent court as to the character of the previous conveyance by the judgment debtor, produced only a nominal sum, and then, if the purchaser procured his title to be validated by a judgment in ejectment, he still held his judgment unsatisfied against the judgment debtor, although he may have obtained value enough in the land to have paid it. And if, in such case, after purchasing at sheriff's sale, without resorting to ejectment, he came into this court, as he might do, to have the title derived under the sheriff's deed declared valid, this court granted relief only upon condition that he should give credit on his judgment for the fair value of the land."

§ 79. **Concurrent Jurisdiction of Equity in Case of Real Estate.** All these difficulties resulted in the Court of Equity creating the same ancillary jurisdiction, invoked by judgment creditor's bill, in cases of fraudulent conveyance, that it exercised in the creditor's aid in other cases affecting the debtor's estate.² But there was this addition, that whereas if the debtor

---

¹ Kinmouth v White, 61 N J Eq 358, 48 Atl 952.
² The same rule as to "equitable levy" applies in this practice as in the other, there being, as we have seen, a difference of opinion as to whether it should apply to equitable assets as distinct from legal assets (see Ch I, § 16) The same conflict of view occurs with regard to the necessity for issuing execution. In New York, as we saw (Ch I. § 16), both the issuance of the execution, and its return unsatisfied, are required in all cases, whereas the Federal view is that while the issuance of the execution is necessary, its return is not a prerequisite. In the present connection still a third distinction is thus suggested. "It is not necessary for him to take out execution upon his judgment. The judgment constitutes a lien upon the land, and there is no necessity of compelling the creditor, as a mere matter of form, to incur the further expense at law of issuing an execution. It is, perhaps, most advisable for him to do so. It may avoid a contest with the subsequent execution creditor, for although the judgment is a lien upon the land, an execution upon a subsequent judgment acquires, upon its delivery to the officer by virtue of the statute, a prior lien upon the property. But if it is the personal property

had not fraudulently transferred his property, the creditor could come into equity only to reach nonleviable assets, or true "equitable assets," under the jurisdiction as extended to cases of fraudulent conveyance the debtor had the option of invoking the aid of equity as an alternative to the common law remedy in the case of legal assets. With regard to real estate, that is undoubtedly so, in the vast majority of courts the concurrent jurisdiction of equity is fully recognized. It was doubted in an early English case[1] but a century later we find the concurrent jurisdiction of equity declared to be an undoubted fact,[2] and that is clearly the prevailing American view. The option thus given the creditor between the legal and equitable remedy has been put in this way:

"A judgment creditor seeking relief against prior fraudulent conveyances of land has the choice of three remedies. He may sell the debtor's land upon execution issued on his judgment, and leave the purchaser to contest the validity of the defendant's title in an action of ejectment; or, secondly, he may bring an action in equity to remove the fraudulent obstruction to the enforcement of his lien by execution, and await the result of the action before selling the property; or, thirdly, he may, on the return of an execution unsatisfied, bring an action in the nature of a creditor's bill, to have the conveyance adjudged fraudulent and void as to his judgment, and the lands sold by a receiver or other officer of the court, and the proceeds applied to the satisfaction of the judgment, as in the case of equitable interests the debtor's assets are reached and applied."[3]

of the debtor which the creditor wishes to reach and appropriate to the payment of his judgment, he must take out an execution upon his judgment before he can exhibit his bill; for it is by the execution, and not by his judgment that he acquires a lien upon the personal property.'—Dunham v Cox, 10 N J Eq 437, 466-7; Wadsworth v Schissebauer, 32 Minn 84, 19 N W 390

[1] Hungerford v Earle, 2 Vern 261

[2] Hobbs v Hull, 1 Cox, 446, the first case to be found is Bucknal v Roiston, Prec Ch 287

[3] Jackson v Holbrook, 36 Minn 494, 32 N W 852; Erickson v Quinn, 50 N Y 697, 15 Abb Pr N S 166; Dunham v Cox, 10 N J. Eq 437; Orendorf v Budlong, 12 Fed 24; Clements v Moore, 6 Wall 299

In Massachusetts apparently jurisdiction is denied to equity[1] But as pointed out in *In re* Estes[2] the Massachusetts courts did not possess equity jurisdiction until a late date, and a proceeding by attachment was adequate, or considered to be so, by the Massachusetts courts.

§ 80 **Concurrent Jurisdiction in Cases of Personal Property** When it comes to personal property which is not of such a nature as to constitute equitable assets, it would seem that equity should have no concurrent jurisdiction, since the creditor's common remedies are adequate And so it has been determined in New York of late years, when trustees in bankruptcy, as representatives of creditors, began to flood the courts with actions in equity to recover chattels which could just as well have been gathered in by means of replevin suits[3] In the Federal courts, on the contrary, a broader rule was laid down, which gives concurrent jurisdiction to equity in all cases of fraudulent transfers, irrespective of the nature of the subject matter,[4] and to this rule they have adhered, though with some regret.[5]

§ 81 **Subrogation of Surety.** In this connection, one point more remains. If a surety has paid a judgment recovered against his principal, there is a difference of opinion whether he should be subrogated to the rights of the judgment creditor and thus be able to maintain an equitable action to set aside fraudulent transfers made by the judgment debtor. In Smith *v.* Rumsey[6] and Curd *v.* Miller,[7] it has been held that he should be so subrogated But the contrary has been held in Peeples *v* Tatum[8] and Mugge *v.* Ewing[9] The test, it seems to

---

[1] Pratt *v.* Wheeler, 6 Gray 520, Thompson *v.* O'Sullivan, 6 Allen 303   [2] *Supra*
[3] Allen *v* Gray, 201 N. Y 504, 94 N E 652 The same rule was applied to actions by trustees to recover preferential transfers of chattels, Cohen *v* Small, 120 N. Y App Div 211, 105 N. Y. S. 287; aff'd 180 N Y 568
[4] Wall *v* Cox, 101 Fed 403   [7] 7 Gratt. (Va)185
[5] Parker *v* Black, 151 Fed. 18.   [8] 1 Ired Eq (N. C) 414.
[6] 33 Mich 133.   [9] 54 Ill 236

us, should be whether the principle of subrogation could operate to the extent of leaving the judgment alive so as to entitle the surety to levy on his principal's estate.

§ 82 **The Statute gives merely a Right to Act.** From the foregoing, it is apparent that however the statute may describe the transfer as void, in reality it does no more than confer a course of action upon the creditor It would follow that the creditor may if he pleases affirm the transaction in a given case. If the creditor should affirm the transaction, then that ends the matter, he has elected his course, and he cannot afterwards bring a suit to set it aside [1] "Such a conveyance," says the court in *In re* Estes,[2] "is not as has sometimes been supposed, utterly void but is only so in a qualified sense Practically it is only voidable, and that at the instance of creditors proceeding in the mode prescribed by law " While naturally it requires a good deal to show such an affirmance or waiver,[3] still, if it occurs, the courts will hold the parties to the consequences Thus, a trustee waives a mortgage given by way of a preference when he sells the equity, expressly admitting the mortgage as an existing encumbrance;[4] and a creditor who takes a second mortgage of property to secure his own debt, stipulating that it shall be subject to a first mortgage, held by a third party, cannot afterwards assail the validity of the first, as constituting a transfer in fraud of his rights as a creditor.[5]

§ 83 **The Creditor must Act** Furthermore the creditor who desires relief must act. All he has is a right of procedure, and he must therefore proceed, and that, too, along the lines already indicated A mere disaffirmance, without more, has no effect, and no collateral attack upon the transaction, by the creditor

---

[1] Robins *v* Wooten, 128 Ala 373, 30 So 681, Snow *v.* Lang, 2 Allen 18; Thomas *v* Sugarman, 218 U S 129, 30 S Ct 650.
[2] *Supra.*
[3] Thomas *v* Sugarman, *supra*
[4] O'Neill *v.* Int. Trust Co , 183 Mass 32, 66 N E 424. As will be seen, in this respect the case of a preferential transfer is similar to that of a fraudulent conveyance
[5] Talbott *v.* Horton, 31 Minn 518, 18 N W 647.

or his privies, will avail His only course is to proceed with the process of realization by the means allowed him, as above described, and he can obtain no decision affecting the property by any other course.[1]

§ 84. **Assignability of such Right** Viewed in this light, the cases holding that such a cause of action is not assignable[2] seem unimpeachable in their reasoning. In Annis v. Butterfield[3] it was held that a trustee in bankruptcy could not sell a naked right to set aside the conveyance of property fraudulently made. The Bankrupt Act, as amended in 1910, provides[4] that a trustee in bankruptcy "as to all property not in the custody of the bankruptcy court, shall be deemed vested with all the rights, remedies or powers of a judgment creditor holding an execution duly returned unsatisfied" All this means, however, is that the trustee is in exactly the position of a creditor who is in a position to file a bill to reach equitable assets or to set aside a fraudulent conveyance, so that this amendment cannot be said to have changed the rule of the case last cited Nevertheless the Circuit Court of Appeals for the Second Circuit has recently decided that such a cause of action can be transferred[5] This decision seems wrong in principle. As is pointed out in McMaster v Campbell,[6] until the creditor gets the decision of a court setting aside the transaction, he has nothing but a right of procedure It is a well-settled rule of equity that a naked right to have the court set aside a transfer of property cannot be assigned. A cause of action in equity cannot be assigned unless with it goes property which is the subject matter of the cause of action. Thus, if A is induced by B's fraud to part with his (A's) property to B, A can sell his right to the property together with the right to re-

---

[1] Price v Heubler, 63 Conn 374, 28 Atl 524, Houghton v. Steiner, 92 N Y App Div 171, 87 N Y S 10, Talbott v Horton, *supra*.
[2] Annis v Butterfield, 99 Me. 181, 58 Atl 898, McMaster v Campbell, 41 Mich. 313, 2 N W 36, Morris v Morris, 5 Mich 180
[3] *Supra*.
[4] Sec 47a.
[5] *Re* Downing, 201 Fed 93
[6] *Supra*

cover it in equity But he could not merely sell the right to bring an action [1] In the present case, as we have seen, the creditors never were vested with the debtor's property. They have nothing but a right of procedure to bring that property into the scope of their process of realization, but they never were originally vested with the property. Therefore the Downing case seems to have been decided wrongly

§ 85. **Effect of Statute on Third Parties** So far we have considered this subject as bearing on the direct rights of the creditors against the debtor and persons to whom in one way or another he transfers his property. We should now consider the effect of the transaction where the rights of the creditor are not before the court for decision

§ 86 **Validity of Fraudulent Transaction as between Immediate Parties.** How stands such a fraudulent transaction as between the parties to it, the debtor and the transferee who is not a purchaser in good faith? The creditor can upset the transaction, but if the creditor does not act, what may either party do as against the other? Of course neither may deny that the transfer has been made; as was held in Packman's Case,[2] a gift made in fraud of the donor's creditors is good against the donor and his privies. The real inquiry is concerned with such undertakings of the parties as remain unfulfilled. Can either party sue the other upon any such covenant, or have equity's aid for the enforcement of any trust connected with the transaction? In some states statutes forbid the enforcement of any " secret trust " in connection with the transfer of real estate,[3] but, statutes out of the question, what should the court do in such a case?

§ 87. **Opposing Views.** In view of all we have considered, it would seem that as between the parties the transaction would be perfectly valid, if the creditor has not attacked it, why

---

[1] Dickinson v. Burrell, L R. 1 Eq 337, Traer v Clews, 115 U S 528, 6 S Ct 155
[2] 6 Co Rep 80.   [3] *Infra*, § 96.

should not the parties abide by their agreement? Consequently, if any covenant of the transaction remains to be enforced, the courts should enforce it at the suit of the proper party against the other, and listen to no plea that the transaction was in fraud of the creditors, since the latter are not before the court, and if they have not already done so, may yet affirm the transaction. That is the view taken in Massachusetts and Maine,[1] and it is hard to answer the argument of the Massachusetts court that " the transaction was not *in turpis causa* and therefore void, but was valid until avoided." [2] Nevertheless the weight of authority is to the contrary, at least in all cases of active participation on the part of the transferee The courts of this persuasion exercise their peculiar personal right to refuse to hear a controversy which involves the affirmance of a transaction involving moral turpitude, and withhold their help from either party to the transaction as against the other In such cases, as between the grantor and the grantee, the title remains where it has been placed, and neither can afterwards assert any right against the other based upon the original transaction or any term of the bargain made in connection therewith [3] In New York, the courts have particularly insisted upon this proposition. Both the courts of equity [4] and the courts of law [5] have refused to hear such cases.

§ 88. **Validity of Transaction as against Third Parties who are not Creditors** But as against third persons who were not parties to the original transaction nor yet assert themselves as creditors, a transfer given in fraud of the purchaser's creditors or by way of preference is valid because the third party, whether he be a junior incumbrancer or subsequent transferee of the

---

[1] Harvey v Varney, 98 Mass 118, Nichols v. Patten, 18 Me. 229
[2] Harvey v Varney, *supra*
[3] Schermerhorn v De Chambrun, 64 Fed 195, Sturgis v. Wine Co, 206 Fed 849
[4] St John v. Benedict, 6 Johns 111
[5] Nellis v. Clark, 9 Wend. 24.

property, is in no position to raise the question. He cannot assert the rule of *par delictum* to which we have adverted because he was not a party to the fault. He cannot attack the transaction by virtue of any other principle, because it is valid against all other assaults save the direct proceeding that a creditor, acting in his own right as such, may institute.[1]

[1] Talbott *v.* Horton, *supra,* Sawyer *v* Levy, 162 Mass 190, 38 N. E. 365; *Re* Rouse, 208 Fed. 181

CHAPTER IV

FRAUDULENT TRANSFER (CONTINUED). PROPERTY AFFECTED BY THE STATUTE

§ 89 The Statute's Preamble
90 The Statute's Omission of Equitable Assets
91 Should an Equity Court nevertheless enforce the Statute in Cases of Equitable Assets?
92 Lord Hardwicke's View
93 Lord Thurlow's Contrary View.
§ 94 Influence of Lord Thurlow's Rule
95 Conflict of American Decisions
96 Prevailing American Rule
97 Statute not Applicable to Exempt Property
98. Worthless Property

§ 89 **The Statute's Preamble.** The next question we have to consider under the Statute of Elizabeth is its extent with regard to the debtor's property. The preamble of the statute refers to " as well lands and tenements as goods and chattels "; and in the operative section it refers to the " lands, tenements, hereditaments, goods and chattels, or any of them, or any lien, rent, commission or other profit or charge out of the same lands, tenements, hereditaments, goods and chattels " This is a pretty broad description of property as it was known to the average common law practitioner in 1570, but it is not as broad as it should have been from a modern point of view, because it wholly omits equitable assets

§ 90. **The Statute's Omission of Equitable Assets.** Formerly we discussed the property which a creditor could reach where his debtor owned it, and that discussion proceeded upon the assumption that the debtor had not transferred any of his property or gone through any of the legal forms affecting the passage of title to it On the contrary, when we come to the property covered by the Statute of Fraudulent Conveyances, we are apt to find ourselves hampered by the statute itself if we are to go by its terms in order to reach a fraudulent conveyance So long as the debtor possesses his property the courts are on broader ground in giving the creditors the right of realization upon it, but when the debtor has passed the title to his property to some one else, then the courts, in order to aid the creditors in realization, must follow the terms of the statute, for outside of the statute they have no power at all. And if we go by the terms of the statute alone, we shall find ourselves confined by the language above used, which applies only to chattels, real and personal, and the various interests in real estate which the common law recognizes as alienable. In short, there is an important omission in the descriptive parts of the statute. It does not include choses in action or equitable interests of the various sorts which nowadays are commonly recognized.

§ 91. **Should an Equity Court nevertheless enforce the Statute in Cases of Equitable Assets?** We have seen that by the means of common law process or judgment creditor's bill, the creditor could realize on all such interests so long as the debtor had them When the debtor has fraudulently conveyed them, is this right to be denied because the statute only described one class of property? Is the equity court to say that because the statute did not forbid the fraudulent alienation of equitable assets, therefore the Court of Chancery cannot prevent such acts?

§ 92. **Lord Hardwicke's View** Lord Hardwicke was the first to answer this troublesome question. In two notable decisions, Taylor *v* Jones[1] and King *v.* Dupine,[2] he held that an interest in a trust estate was within the "equity" of the statute The reasons for these decisions were unfortunately not fully reported, but Lord Hardwicke's reasoning seems to have been this. This Court of Chancery by the exercise of its equitable jurisdiction on the subject of trusts, and by

[1] 2 Atk 600   [2] 2 Atk 603 n

that jurisdiction whereby it protected when necessary the interest of the assignee of any chose in action, had in effect created a species of property, of which the common law courts knew nothing, but which by his time had become an important part of the economic fabric. Although the statute did not cover this sort of property, yet as the statute had a basis of sound morality and equity, the Chancery Court, in dealing with its own peculiar kind of property, should enforce the same principle. It was easy for the court to carry this idea into effect All it had to do was to refuse to allow a man to avail himself of such rights by the aid of equity when he had acquired them in a manner condemned by the statute. This thought is well expressed by Woodworth, J.. " The doctrine," he says, " is calculated to lessen the temptation to fraud, when it is seen that a court of equity is armed with legitimate power, not only to detect fraud in its most secret recesses, but to wrest from the dishonest debtor his property not liable to execution in whosesoever hands it may be placed." [1]

§ 93 **Lord Thurlow's Contrary View.** But a more narrow judge succeeded Lord Hardwicke, with unfortunate results. In Dundas *v.* Dutens [2] Lord Thurlow overruled Lord Hardwicke's decisions and held that equitable assets were not within the meaning of the statute, because the statute did not describe them; and, there being no statute, the court was powerless The reason for his decision is this: " These things," he says, " such as we call debts, etc., being choses in action are not leviable. They could not be taken upon *levari facias* " In other words, Lord Thurlow made the test whether the property was subject to execution; if so, then the statute covered it; if not, the court of equity could give no relief. Historically Lord Thurlow was right, because the framers of the statute, as we have seen, contemplated no relief to anybody but a creditor who by means of common law process had

[1] Hadden *v* Spader, 20 Johnson 554.
[2] 1 Ves. Jr 196.

reached or could have reached the property by means of execution. The broader view taken by Lord Hardwicke, however, commends itself to one who appreciates the methods of reasoning by which the jurisdiction of equity has spread in so many modern instances.

§ 94. **Influence of Lord Thurlow's Rule** But, however that may be, the view of Lord Thurlow has prevailed in England and theoretically remains as law there at the present day. If the property in question is reachable by common law process, then the Statute of Fraudulent Conveyance opens to cover it, otherwise not. Thus, after the Judgment Act of 1 and 2 Victoria c. 110, which made money, bonds and choses in action subject to execution by means of a charging order, like the American method of supplementary proceedings or garnishment, the Court of Chancery held that, since the statute now covered them, it would lend its aid to the judgment creditor to reach such property when fraudulently conveyed.[1]

§ 95. **Conflict of American Decisions** In America the courts of the various states divided between the rule laid down by Lord Hardwicke, and that expounded by Lord Thurlow. As the latter decision appeared after the separation from England, Lord Hardwicke's rule was technically part of our inheritance of the common law, but nevertheless the courts seemed to have felt free to decide according to their convictions as to the soundness of the respective rules. A few courts followed the idea of Lord Thurlow and made the test whether the Legislature, up to that time, had made choses in action subject to execution. Such was the view expressed in Shaw v. Aveline,[2] and to such a pass was the idea carried in Indiana that, when a statute allowed choses in action to be reached by supplementary proceedings, it was held that the courts of equity were not thereby vested with any additional power,

---

[1] Stokoe v Cowen, 29 Beav. 637; See Bigelow, "Fraudulent Conveyances," pp 70-1.
[2] 5 Ind 380.

and hence could not by means of a creditor's bill set aside the transfer.[1] This is more narrow than Lord Thurlow's view, because he allowed that the Chancery Court would take jurisdiction if any form of execution could have reached the property. That is the doctrine in still other States. As the Massachusetts Supreme Court has stated, the only question which a Court of Chancery should consider is whether the transfer "is voidable by any form of judicial process"; if so, the Court of Chancery may lend its own aid to a creditor and not require him to stick to the statutory process.[2]

§ 96. **Prevailing American Rule.** The prevailing American view, however, which was first expressed in a dictum of Chancellor Kent[3] and later definitely held in New York[4] is in favor of the view of Lord Hardwicke.[5] The idea maintained by these courts is illustrated by the case where the debtor lays out his money in the purchase of land, but causes the purchaser to take title in the name of a third party. According to well-settled principles of equity, this transaction creates a resulting trust in favor of the debtor. In those States where Lord Hardwicke's view is followed, the creditors of the beneficiary of such a trust can apply his interest to the satisfaction of their claims, because the equity court will not enforce such a trust except upon that condition.[6] In New York, as part of the statutory system of trusts to which we have referred, it is enacted that such a conveyance shall be presumed to be fraudulent as against the creditors of the trust's creator, and that

---

[1] "A defendant might be worth millions, and yet if his wealth consisted of choses in action, he could successfully defy his creditors . . . the remedy afforded here, for the state of the law thus declared, is found in proceedings supplementary to execution," Keighthley v. Walls, 27 Ind 384, 386
[2] Drake v Rice, 130 Mass 410
[3] Bayard v Hoffman, 4 Johns Ch 450.
[4] Hadden v Spader, 20 Johnson 554
[5] See Hall v. Alabama Terminal Company, 143 Ala 464 39 So 285 2 L. R A (N S) 136
[6] Edmonson v Meacham, 50 Miss. 34, Gowing v. Rich, 1 Ired (N. C) 553

the legal title shall be held in trust for them [1] This statute, it has been held, has abrogated the equitable doctrines to which we have adverted, and in any such case creates an express trust for the creditors in question.[2] But there is this qualification, that the trust is only for the benefit of creditors having a claim upon the debtors' property, and hence none but a judgment creditor can enforce the trust.[3] And the terms of the statute are strictly applied in this, that only the creditors themselves can enforce the terms of this express trust, no representative of creditors has standing in their behalf [4]

§ 97 **Statute not Applicable to Exempt Property.** And lastly, a common sense qualification must be observed The rules which we have considered can be invoked only where real injury has resulted The statute does not refer to property which is not available for the creditors; the court should not be asked to do a vain thing. Thus if the property in question is exempt from process under the local homestead or exemption laws, the courts cannot be asked to concern themselves with its disposition So long as the debtor had the property the creditors could not reach it, and the most that the statute can do is to enable the debtor to overlook the intervening alienation. The transfer of exempt property, therefore, can work no wrong upon the creditors of the transferor.[5]

§ 98 **Worthless Property** A similar idea has actuated some courts where the property in question was plainly worthless In Hoyt v Godfrey,[6] it was held that if the debtor releases, without consideration, a debt owing him by a person who is worthless, such a transaction does not constitute a fraudulent conveyance. From a practical aspect, this decision

[1] R P Law Sec 94
[2] Garfield v Hatmaker, 15 N Y 475.
[3] Brown v Chubb, 135 N. Y. 175, 31 N E 1030, Mandeville v Campbell 45 N Y App Div 512, 61 N Y S 443
[4] E g A receiver appointed in supplementary proceedings has no standing Underwood v Sutcliff, 77 N Y 58
[5] Thompson v Crane, 73 Fed. 327, Fellows v Lewis, 65 Ala 343
[6] 88 N. Y. 669

was just, because the question came up in connection with the New York statute which allows an order for arrest to be issued in a case where the defendant has made a transfer of his property with intent to hinder, delay or defraud his creditors The court was doubtless moved by the consideration that it would be a hardship to imprison a man because he had released a worthless debt, and in effect had not injured his creditors On the broad proposition, however, that the court will not give its aid in the case of worthless property, the decision, though supported in Pennsylvania,[1] has met with marked disfavor in Wisconsin,[2] with whose court, in strict principle, the best of the argument must be admitted to lie.

[1] Morris v Geoghegan, 33 Pa St 234
[2] Ingram v. Osborn, 70 Wisc 184, 35 N W 304.

CHAPTER V

FRAUDULENT TRANSFER (*CONTINUED*) METHODS OF ALIENATION

§ 99 The Effect of the Transfer is its Test
100 Illustrations
101 The Debtor's Inaction may have Fraudulent Effect
102 Another Expression of the Rule
103 Transfer need not be Direct
104 Illustrations from the Law of Partnership
105 Fraudulent Use of the Corporate Entity.

§106 Corporate Reorganization — Rights of Creditors against Purchaser at Foreclosure Sale
107. Early Decisions on this Question.
108 The Present View of the Supreme Court
109 Corporate Reorganization Rights of Creditors against new Corporation.

§ 99 The Effect of the Transfer is its Test The next thing to consider is the method of alienation at which the statute strikes The language of the statute is very wide. It refers to "all and every feoffment, gift, grant, alienation, bargain and conveyance and all and every bond, suit, judgment and execution " This is broad enough to cover every conceivable transaction whereby the title to property or the extent of one's interest therein is affected. We must also take this in connection with equally emphatic language which the statute uses in another place. By its terms the statute strikes at any method of alienation which hinders, delays or defrauds creditors It follows that any dealing in the debtor's property which has the effect of hindering, delaying and defrauding his creditors constitutes a case within the condemnation of the statute That which would hinder, delay or defraud a creditor is an act that would prevent his realizing on the debtor's property

Any alienation or dealing in the property which would have that effect is condemned by the statute.

§ 100 **Illustrations** Taking the instance of an active mode of alienation, we have the case of a deed of land, or a bill of sale of chattels accompanied by delivery. From that the transition to other methods of alienation is gradual, but sure. For instance, a mortgage is a method of alienation which is within the meaning of the statute [1] The equity courts, in those jurisdictions which have adopted Lord Hardwicke's view, and considered that the spirit of the statute should be applied to the jurisdiction of equity over equitable interests and choses in action, have adopted the same view Thus it is clear that the cancellation of a chose in action belonging to the debtor may constitute a fraudulent transfer Two typical cases in this connection may be cited In Moore v United States Barrel Company [2] it was held that if a corporation releases a stockholder from his liability to pay for his stock in full, that release is fraudulent as against the creditors of the corporation. In Trustees v. Anderson [3] it was held that if A purchases land subject to a mortgage, assuming the payment of the mortgage, a subsequent release of this liability is fraudulent.

§ 101 **The Debtor's Inaction may have Fraudulent Effect** Not only may an act on the part of the debtor constitute an alienation within the meaning of the statute, but mere passivity on his part may often in principle accomplish the same result. Under the very terms of the statute, an alienation may be effected by means of permitting the levy of an execution, and so it has been held [4] Thus, if a debtor arranges for an attachment to be levied upon his property by a friendly creditor, he may properly be accused of having violated the statute [5]

---

[1] Natl Bank v Levy, 127 N. Y. 549, 28 N. E 592
[2] 238 Ill 544, 87 N E 536
[3] 30 N J Eq 366
[4] West v Skip, 1 Vesey 239; Caldwell v Fifield, 24 N J. L. 150, Herkimer Bank v Brown, 6 Hill 232
[5] Gassenheimer v Kellogg, 121 Ala. 109, 26 So. 29.

We may go even further than that If a mortgage has in fact been paid, but the mortgagor, in order to enable the mortgagee to withdraw the property from the claims of his creditors, does not cancel the mortgage of record, but allows it to remain open as a lien, that is a case within the terms of the statute.[1] In the same connection, we may refer to the case of Wailes v. Davies,[2] where it was held that allowing a favored person to "jump" a mining claim, may well constitute a fraudulent transfer.[3]

§ 102. **Another Expression of the Rule.** How can the result of these decisions be shortly expressed? Simply by joining to the language of the statute above stated, the principle which we have already studied, concerning the creditor's right of realizing on his debtor's property. As we have seen, the creditor has the right to realize on any property which the debtor himself could have realized on by means of sale. If, then, the debtor creates, by any method of transfer or contract known to the law, an outstanding interest in his property so that when the operation is completed the debtor has less of a property right than he had before, then the debtor has made a fraudulent transfer. One should look to the result of the operation, and ask oneself the simple question whether, as a result, the debtor's estate has been diminished If such is not the case, then, no matter how complicated, devious or suspicious the transaction was, it did not constitute a fraudulent transfer. Thus a power of sale in a valid mortgage does not even potentially diminish the debtor's estate if it provides that the surplus moneys realized from any sale made under the power shall be paid to the debtor. All the debtor is entitled to is this surplus money, and so long

---

[1] McMaster v Campbell, 41 Mich 513, 2 N. W 836
[2] Wailes v Davies, 158 Fed. 667.
[3] The court said "Here there was no formal conveyance of the lands by corporate action Wailes knowingly acquired a title to the property which had been owned by a corporation, through the negligence of the corporation itself, the connivance of a portion of its stockholders, and with the active assistance of others The purpose was clearly fraudulent." — Wailes v. Davies, 158 Fed 667, 677-8

as the terms of the power of sale insure his getting it, his creditors have nothing to complain of.¹ But any provision which could be otherwise construed would be governed by the principle we are discussing

§ 103 **Transfer need not be Direct.** As we have seen, in order to have a case of fraudulent transfer it is not necessary for the debtor to do anything. It is sufficient if he lets the other party do something, provided that the result of the operation is that his available property interests are lessened. Nor is it necessary for the debtor to make a transfer direct to the transferee. Any mode of transfer by the debtor, which has the effect we have already mentioned, comes within the terms of the statute If the debtor, instead of giving his property to another, lays it out to that other person's use, it all comes to the same result. An illustration is the case where the debtor, instead of giving A money, spends the money in erecting buildings on A's lands which, by virtue of the well-known principles of the law of real estate, *ipso facto* become the property of A That is a fraudulent transfer just as much as if the debtor had given the money to A directly² In the same way, if the debtor purchases the benefits of a contract for another, he has made a fraudulent conveyance just as much as if he had given the money to his friend and the latter in turn had purchased the contract. Such a case is where the debtor takes out insurance upon his own life in favor of a friend and pays the premiums thereon That constitutes a fraudulent conveyance. There is nothing mysterious about such a transaction; the debtor's money simply did not go where it belonged, to his creditors. It went to the use of somebody else, and that is what the Statute condemns³

§ 104 **Illustrations from the Law of Partnership** An excellent illustration may be gathered from the law of partnership

---

[1] Barton *v* Sithngton, 128 Mo. 164, 30 S W 514
[2] Trefethen *v* Lyman, 90 Me. 376, 38 Atl 335
[3] Merchants Insurance Company *v.* Borland, 53 N J Eq 282, 31 Atl 272

As we have already seen, it is a principle of courts of equity to handle partnership assets in the event of insolvency so as to secure the claims of partnership creditors to partnership assets to the exclusion of individual creditors. Now any transaction between the partners, which in the last analysis causes the disappearance of property which otherwise would have been on hand for the purpose of this marshaling process, is a fraudulent operation. Take the case where partners A and B are insolvent both as a firm and individually. A transfers his share in the firm to B, so that this share will be B's personal asset. B's individual creditors may thus be entitled, by virtue of this assigned claim, to satisfy their debts out of the partnership assets ahead of A's individual creditors, and also ahead of the partnership creditors. That is a plain fraud, and the court will not allow it to stand.[1]

§ 105. **Fraudulent Use of the Corporate Entity.** An interesting lot of cases in this connection are concerned with the frequent attempt to use the corporate entity for the purpose of covering a transaction which otherwise would obviously be within the principles we have above discussed. If, for instance, a man is insolvent and conveys all his property to a corporation organized by himself for that purpose and controlled by him, is it necessary to resort to any elaborate principles of reasoning to allow his creditors to reach this property? Of course the existence of the corporation must be respected wherever it appears, but it is not necessary, in order to reach a just result, to go into the question of regarding or disregarding the corporate entity. The fact is that by an operation set in motion by the defendant an interest has been created in his property which did not exist before, and its result is to lessen the amount of the debtor's property available for the realization of his creditors' claims. It is not necessary to go any further than that, to reach the conclusion that such a transaction constitutes a fraudulent operation within the meaning of the statute.

[1] *Ex parte* Mayou, 4 De G. J. & S. 664

Therefore the pioneer case of Bank v. Trebein [1] which so decided, and which has been frequently followed,[2] laid down no astounding principle. The debtor there had consummated a fraudulent operation, and the fact that he created and used a corporation for the purpose made no more difference than if he had induced an individual to act for the purpose of a holder of title. The same principle applies where the debtor, instead of being an individual, is a corporation. If it transfers its assets without consideration to another corporation organized for that purpose, it does not matter whether the stock of the new corporation is owned by the stockholders of the first company. The same decision must be made in any event. The available property of the first corporation has been lessened as a result of the operation, and that is all that it is necessary to say.[3]

§ 106 **Corporate Reorganization — Rights of Creditors against Purchaser at Foreclosure Sale**. Another angle of this proposition is to be seen in the case of corporate reorganization. With the average public service or large industrial corporation, there are usually three sets of parties in interest, the stockholders, the holders of bonds which are secured by a mortgage upon practically all of the company's property, and the general creditors without security. Of course the strict logic of the situation is this: the owner of the corporate property is the

---

[1] 59 Ohio State 316, 52 N. E. 834.

[2] *In re* Hoffman, 102 Fed. 989; Booth *v* Bunce, 33 N. Y. 139; Montgomery Webb Co *v* Dienelt, 133 Pa. St. 585, 19 Atl. 428; Hibernia Insurance Co *v* Transportation Co., 13 Fed. 516.

[3] Booth *v* Bunce, 33 N. Y. 139; Brown *v* Merchants Insurance Company, 16 Fed. 140; Mitchell *v* Beekman, 64 Cal. 117, 28 Pac. 110; *In re* Muncie Pulp Company, 139 Fed. 546. Care should be taken, however, to distinguish the case of a merger of corporations pursuant to a statute providing for such a thing. In such cases as that, where the statute itself protects the claims of the creditors by providing that the assets of the new company shall be subject to the claims of the creditors of the old company, there is nothing fraudulent in the two corporations availing themselves of the statute, Irvine *v* N. Y. Edison Company, 207 N. Y. 425, 101 N. E. 358; Zeiser *v* Cohn, 207 N. Y. 407, 101 N. E. 184.

corporation itself, and the stockholders own nothing of the corporate property as such The first lien upon the corporate property is held by the bondholders by virtue of the mortgage which secures their bonds, and the general creditors are entitled on the winding-up only to what remains of the property after the bonds have been satisfied in full Now the modern reorganization of a corporation's affairs often involves the endeavor to effect a union between the interests of the stockholders and the bondholders by means of foreclosure of the mortgage securing the bonds and a purchase of the property at the foreclosure sale in the joint interest of both classes. This practice, however, can find no justification in view of the principles we have discussed. If the property is insufficient to meet the claims of the bondholders, the latter have the remedy of foreclosure, which means, after application to a court of equity, a judicial sale of the property and the application of the proceeds to the payment of the bonds, with only the surplus going to the general creditors. If the property, however, is bought in on the sale by the bondholders and stockholders, and in turn they form a new corporation which will own the property, they enjoying the result through their common ownership of the new corporation's stock, a fraudulent operation has been effected on the general creditors of the old company. The former stockholders of that company are the last persons in the world to talk about the law applying to the corporate existence, because they themselves have ignored that law by taking part in a purchase of the property upon foreclosure sale If the forms of law had been gone through with, that property would have been sold to the general public for a real consideration which the bondholders would have pocketed, and that would have ended the matter But actual practice does not follow that course The parties in interest will not permit the property to go to the public on such a sale, for the simple reason that the sale would bring too little, so they take it over themselves. As the Supreme Court has said :

"We must therefore recognize the fact, for it is a fact of common knowledge, that, whatever the legal rights of the parties may be, ordinarily foreclosures of railroad mortgages mean, not the destruction of all interest of the mortgagor and a transfer to the mortgagee alone of the full title, but that such proceedings are carried on in the interests of all parties who have any rights in the mortgaged property, whether as mortgagee, creditor or mortgagor."[1]

§ 107 **Early Decisions on this Question.** The first case on this subject is Chicago &c Railway Company v Howard[2] There a railway was sold at foreclosure and was purchased by a combination of bondholders and stockholders under an arrangement whereby 84 per cent. of the purchase price was to go to the bondholders, and 16 per cent. to the stockholders in the shape of stock of a new corporation which was to be formed to take over the property when purchased at the block It was held that such a transaction was fraudulent as against the general creditors not secured by the mortgage. "The rule," said the Court, "is well settled that stockholders are not entitled to any share of the capital stock, nor to any dividend of the properties, until the debts of the corporation are paid" But however strongly the Supreme Court stated its position in this case, the lower courts did not seem to have fully grasped its significance. While it was followed by the Circuit Court of Appeals for the Fifth Circuit[3] and by several of the State courts,[4] a positive decision to the contrary was made in Paton v Northern Pacific Company.[5] There it was held that the transaction really made no difference as to the creditors of the old company, because the stock was given at the expense of the

[1] Louisville Trust Co v Louisville Railway, 174 U S 674, 19 S. Ct 827.
[2] 7 Wall 392
[3] Central of Georgia Railway Company v Paul, 93 Fed 878.
[4] Luedecke v. Des Moines Cabinet Company, 140 Iowa 223, 118 N W. 456, 32 L. R. A. (N. S) 616, Hurd v New York & Commercial Steam Laundry, 167 N Y. 89, 60 N. E 327, Ferguson v Ann Arbor R. R , 17 N Y App Div. 336, 45 N. Y S 172
[5] 85 Fed 838

bondholders, so that there was no basis on which it could be said that the creditors had been defrauded of anything to which they were entitled.

§ 108. **The Present View of the Supreme Court** This difference of view did not remain long, however, because the following year, in Louisville Trust Company *v* Louisville Railway [1] the Supreme Court affirmed its previous decision. What happens in such a case, in the court's opinion, is that the bondholders promise to give the interest in the new corporation to the stockholders of the old, in order to secure a waiver of any objections which the latter might have to the way in which the foreclosure proceedings may be conducted, and that therefore, in effect, this operation is consummated at the expense of the general creditors In addition to its language already quoted, the court said :

"Assuming that foreclosure proceedings may be carried on to some extent at least in the interests and for the benefit of both mortgagee and mortgagor (that is, bondholder and stockholder), we observe that no such proceedings can be rightfully carried to consummation which recognize and preserve any interest in the stockholders without also recognizing and preserving the interests, not merely of the mortgagee, but of every creditor of the corporation In other words, if the bondholder wishes to foreclose and exclude inferior lienholders or general unsecured creditors and stockholders, he may do so; but a foreclosure which attempts to preserve any interest or right of the mortgagor in the property after the sale must necessarily secure and preserve the prior rights of general creditors thereof This is based upon the familiar rule that the stockholder's interest in the property is subordinate to the rights of creditors, first of secured and then of unsecured creditors And any arrangement of the parties by which the subordinate rights and interests of the stockholders are attempted to be secured at the expense of the prior rights of either class of creditors comes within judicial denunciation " [2]

[1] 174 U S 674, 19 S Ct 827
[2] Louisville Trust Co *v* Louisville Railway, 174 U. S 674. 19 S. Ct 827. The same doctrine was recently followed by the C. C. A , 8th

§ 109 **Corporate Reorganization. Rights of Creditors against New Corporation.** The same result has been reached in a case where a corporation transferred all its assets to another corporation, in consideration of the stock of the new corporation being issued direct to the stockholders of the old. What difference did that make? The ultimate result was the same. The creditors of the old corporation were limited in the available property on which they might realize, and so the transaction was fraudulent as to them [1]

Circuit, in Central Improvement Company v Cambria Steel Company, 201 Fed 811, by the Supreme Court of Tennessee in Jennings v Crystal Ice Co , 159 S W Rep. 1088, and very recently again by the Supreme Court in Northern Pacific Ry v Boyd, 228 U S 482, 33 S Ct 554. In that case the plaintiff, a creditor of the old company, sued the new company on a debt of the old, and it was held that he could recover. Of course after the reorganization, the stockholders may be let in if it has not previously been so arranged, Stewart's Appeal, 72 Pa. St 291

[1] Hurd v New York &c Steam Laundry, 167 N. Y. 89, 60 N E 327.

CHAPTER VI

FRAUDULENT TRANSFER (*CONTINUED*) VALIDITY OF GIFTS

§ 110 The Proviso in Favor of the Innocent Purchaser
111 No Proviso in Favor of Transferee unless he is a Purchaser
112 Issues which affect the Transferee.
113 Transferee cannot attack Validity of Creditor's Judgment
114 Transferee's Privies are in Same Position
115 Cases of Creditors' Estoppel furnish no Exception
116 Hence a Donee's Case involves only an Inquiry as to the Debtor's Intent
117. General Rule as to Debtor's Intent
118 Is a Gift Fraudulent if Donor was indebted at the Time?
§ 119 The Early Rule — Lord Hardwicke's View
120. Chancellor Kent's View — Reade v. Livingston
121 Effect of the Hardwicke-Kent Doctrine
122. The Contrary View — Prior Indebtedness should be only Presumptive Evidence of Fraud.
123 Prevalence of This View
124 Early American Origin of This Rule and its Final Triumph over the Hardwicke-Kent Doctrine in New York
125 Both Rules present Questions of Law
126 Illustrations in Cases of Partnership and Corporate Reorganization
127 Donee entitled to Subrogation

§ 110. **The Proviso in Favor of the Innocent Purchaser.** The statute provides that an operation such as we have examined shall be void as against creditors, present or subsequent, when made with intent to hinder, delay or defraud them, unless — and this is by way of a proviso — the party receiving the property from the debtor received it in good faith and for a consideration. The statute thus requires the inquiry in each case, as to the debtor's intent first, and then as to the presence of certain facts which may affect the position of the transferee. If the transfer is made without consideration, then it is not necessary to consider the transferee's position. The proviso protects him only when in good faith he has purchased.

§ 111. No Proviso in Favor of Transferee unless he is a Purchaser. When, however great his good faith, the transferee has not purchased the property, but has received it as a gift, the statute requires us to consider only whether the debtor made the gift with intent to hinder, delay or defraud his creditors. So in any case of a gift, the sole question is the debtor's intent. If he has the intent described by the statute, then, as against his creditors, the gift is void, and no further inquiry is necessary, because there is no saving clause in favor of the donee

§ 112 Issues which affect the Transferee. The transferee, in other words, has no concern with the transactions between the debtor and the creditor except as they bear upon four issues: (1) the debtor's intent in making the transfer, (2) the nature of the transfer, in respect to the presence or absence of a consideration, (3) the good faith of the transferee, in the event that the transfer was supported by a consideration, and (4) the lawful ability of the creditor to realize upon the property in question. The first three of these questions will be discussed in this and the next two succeeding chapters The fourth has been discussed in Chapter III. With the consideration of one or more of these points, as the particular case may require, the court's duty to the transferee ends. He is not concerned in any other of the transactions that may have occurred between the debtor and his creditors, nor with any defenses that may avail to either in respect thereto.

§ 113. Transferee cannot attack Validity of Creditor's Judgment Hence the prevailing view is that the transferee cannot, in defense to any proceeding by the creditor, attack the validity of the latter's judgment, in so far as it determines the amount due the plaintiff and his status as a creditor In Massachusetts [1] and Texas [2] it has been held that he may, because, to quote from

---

[1] Inman v. Mead, 97 Mass 310
[2] McClum v. McClum, 3 Tex 192.

Hoar, J ,[1] " he was not a party or privy to the plaintiff's judgment He has therefore a right to avoid it by plea and proof if his rights would be injuriously affected by it " But the majority of courts hold that the transferee has no such right, he can attack the judgment and other proceedings only as to their validity as such. If he can show that the judgment or execution was a nullity by reason of fraud, or a failure to comply with the essential rules of practice governing such matters that course is open to him,[2] but that is as far as he may go. He cannot show that the plaintiff was not in fact a creditor, and properly entitled to the judgment so declaring.[3] There is no difference, in this respect, between the different forms of remedial procedure which the creditor might follow, the same rule applies to both. " The specific objection that the purchaser has no day in court to controvert the creditor's debt would apply with the same force where the seizure was under an execution issued on a judgment. In that case the judgment would be conclusive as to the judgment creditor's debt, though there, as in this case, the fraudulent grantee would have no opportunity to try the question of its existence." Thus spoke Judge Denio in Hall v. Stryker,[4] referring to the pioneer case of Candee v Lord[5] There the reasoning which leads to the conclusion above stated is thus set forth

" In creating debts, or establishing the relation of debtor and creditor, the debtor is accountable to no one unless he acts *mala fide*. A judgment, therefore, obtained against the latter without collusion is conclusive evidence of the relation of debtor and creditor against others · first, because it is conclusive between the parties to the record, who in the given case have the exclusive right to establish it; and second, because the claims

[1] Inman v Mead, *supra*.
[2] Ahearn v Purnell, 62 Conn 21, 25 Atl 393
[3] Nicholas v. Lord, 193 N. Y. 388, 85 N. E 1083; Mattingly v Nye, 8 Wall 370; New Orleans v. Fisher, 180 U S 185, 21 S Ct. 347, Conover v Jeffrey, 26 N J. Eq. 36.
[4] 27 N. Y. 596
[5] 2 N. Y. 269.

of other creditors upon the debtor's property are through him, and subject to all previous liens, preferences or conveyances made by him in good faith. Any deed, judgment or assurance of the debtor, so far at least as they conclude him, must estop his creditors and all others. Consequently, neither a creditor or stranger can interfere in the *bona fide* litigation of the debtor or retry his cause for him, or question the effect of the judgment as a legal claim upon his estate A creditor's right, in a word, to impeach the act of his debtor, does not arise until the latter has violated the tacit condition annexed to the debt — that he has done and will do nothing to defraud his creditors.

"Where, however, fraud is established, the creditor does not claim through the debtor, but adversely to him, and by a title paramount, which overreaches and annuls the fraudulent conveyance or judgment by which the latter himself would be estopped. It follows from the principles suggested, that a judgment obtained without fraud or collusion, and which concludes the debtor, whether rendered upon default, confession, or after contestation, is, upon all questions affecting the title to his property, conclusive evidence against his creditors to establish, first, the relation of creditor and debtor between the parties to the record, and second, the amount of the indebtedness."

§ 114. **Transferee's Privies are in same Position** The same principle applies of course to all persons claiming through the transferee, or holding the property in question under his orders, by virtue of any agency, trust or contract. Such a case is Fox v Gardner.[1] There the property transferred consisted of a chose in action, and it was held that the debtor thereon after notice of the nature of the transaction, could not properly pay the debt to the transferee, but should have held it for the benefit of the creditors, at his peril

§ 115 **Cases of Creditors' Estoppel furnish no Exception.** Of course in a given case the creditors may have estopped themselves from the benefit of this doctrine above discussed. But such a case constitutes no exception to the rule; rather is the doctrine affirmed thereby, because the assertion of an

[1] 21 Wall 475.

estoppel predicates a right, but urges extraneous matter, in the shape of the party's conduct, to prevent its enforcement in the particular case This is illustrated by the two cases of Moyer v. Dewey [1] and Upsher v. Briscoe [2] In Moyer v. Dewey, the debtor had made certain fraudulent transfers. Later he received a discharge in bankruptcy. Thereafter he confessed judgments founded on the debts which had existed prior to his discharge, thus waiving the benefits of his discharge; and the judgment creditors brought suit to set aside the original transfer. It was held this discharge in bankruptcy could not avail the transferee, as it was personal to the debtor. In Upsher v Briscoe, on the contrary, the debtor, having passed through bankruptcy and been discharged, transferred certain property to the defendant. Thereafter the plaintiffs procured judgments against the debtor, who did not plead his discharge It was held that the discharge was nevertheless a defense available to the transferee, because " she is entitled to the full benefit of the position in which she stood at the time the alleged fraudulent transfer was made and to all defenses resulting therefrom " The difference between the two cases is simply this . in the first case, at the time of the transfer the debtor owed the debt upon which the creditor later sought to realize. That fixed the creditor's right to realize his claim on all property which the debtor then had. A supervenient event which operated, without the creditor's consent, to discharge the debtor's personal liability could not alter the creditor's right of realization upon property which had been on hand prior to the discharge ; the latter was a defense, personal to the debtor, which would protect property he might acquire after the bankruptcy but was bereft of any *ex post facto* effect. In the second case, however, the debtor had been discharged of his indebtedness prior to the transfer The creditors had let him get the discharge and remain with the property as his own. Hence he was free after that to deal with it as his own, and the creditors who had thus stood by were

[1] 103 U S. 301   [2] 138 U. S 365, 11 S Ct 313

properly prohibited from later interference with it. The question there was one of estoppel, and the estoppel prohibited the creditors from asserting their usual rights.

§ 116. **Hence a Donee's Case involves only an Inquiry as to the Debtor's Intent.** Therefore, in the present connection we need no longer deal with the position of the transferee, so far as he is in the position of a donee as distinct from one who has furnished a consideration for the transfer. Let us therefore address ourselves to the question, under what circumstances may a debtor who gives away his property be considered as having done so with intent to hinder, delay or defraud his creditors?

§ 117. **General Rule as to Debtor's Intent.** At the outset of this study, we will find one thing to be certain. In the ascertainment of the debtor's intent the courts have never departed from their ordinary standard of reason. They have never doubted that the rule applies in these, as in all other cases, that a man is to be taken as having intended the natural consequences of his acts. There was never a difference of opinion on this point; on the other hand there was a considerable difference of opinion upon the application of the principle.

§ 118. **Is a Gift Fraudulent if Donor was indebted at the Time?** The undoubted object of the statute is to prevent the debtor from putting wrongful obstacles in the way of his creditor's right of realization. The creditor, as we have seen, has, after securing his judgment, a general right of realization upon his debtor's estate. There never was a principle, whether of law or equity, which restricted the creditor, in the exercise of this right, to one portion of the debtor's estate rather than another. We must not overlook the rule which we have already noted in passing and shall have occasion to examine again,[1] that the personal property of the debtor is the primary fund to which the creditor should resort. But that is not an exception, from the present point of view, because both classes of property are responsible for their owner's debts, and even if it were an ex-

[1] *Supra*, § 6, n. 3; *Infra*, § 300.

ception, it is not of much importance, because there are many cases where a debtor may own only one class of property So taking it as granted, for the purpose of this discussion, that the creditor with judgment may reach here and there as he will for different portions of his debtor's property in order to realize his debt, we are brought to this question — does the gift by the debtor of any part of his property in itself indicate an intent on his part to hinder, delay or defraud his creditors? In view of the result we have just reached above, one method of reasoning would give us an answer in the affirmative If to the creditor belongs the choice of his debtor's assets for realization, then any act by the debtor which restricts the exercise of this privilege would seem to violate the statute. It would not matter how many different sorts of assets remained for the creditor's choosing after the transfer of one piece of property had been made, because it was the creditor's right to say whether he would make good his claim out of that particular piece of property. Consequently, if the donor owed any debts at the time of the gift, he must have intended to hinder, delay and defraud the persons to whom these debts were owing, because *pro tanto* the effect of his gift was to restrict their range among his assets And a logical result would be, to use Lord Westbury's words, that "if the debt of the creditor by whom the voluntary settlement is impeached, existed at the date of the settlement, and it is shown that the remedy of the creditor is defeated or delayed by the existence of the settlement, it is immaterial whether the debtor was or was not solvent after making the settlement "[1]

§ 119. **The Early Rule — Lord Hardwicke's View.** In general, that was the position the courts at first took upon this question. Chancellor Kent[2] credits Lord Hardwicke with having originated the doctrine, but even prior to his incumbency the same result had been reached by Lord Henley[3] who said that "an aliena-

---

[1] Spirett *v* Willows, 3 De G J & S 293
[2] Reade *v* Livingston, 3 Johns Ch 481
[3] Partridge *v* Gopp, 1 Eden 153, Ambler 596

tion cannot be made *bona fide* and voluntarily where a man is largely indebted at the time. For every man ought to be just before he is generous. . . . It seems more reasonable that a gift should be fettered in this manner, than that creditors should be left to the mercy of ill-disposed debtors." Later, Lord Hardwicke put the powerful impetus of his approval behind this view, emphatically stating it on several occasions.[1] He took it, to use his words, "that a man, actually indebted, and conveying voluntarily, always meant to defraud creditors."[2]

§ 120. **Chancellor Kent's View — Reade** *v* **Livingston.** In our country a chancellor of equal intellectual attainments adopted the same view. In Reade *v* Livingston,[3] Chancellor Kent followed the opinion of Lord Hardwicke, stating his ideas of the matter as follows:

"The conclusion to be drawn from the cases is, that if the party be indebted at the time of the voluntary settlement, it is presumed to be fraudulent in respect to such debts, and no circumstance will permit those debts to be affected by the settlement, or repel the legal presumption of fraud. The presumption of law in this case does not depend upon the amount of the debts, or the extent of the property in settlement, or the circumstances of the party. There is no such line of distinction set up, or traced in any of the cases. The attempt would be embarrassing, if not dangerous to the rights of the creditor, and prove an inlet to fraud. The law has, therefore, wisely disabled the debtor from making any voluntary settlement of his estate, to stand in the way of his existing debts. This is the clear and uniform doctrine of the cases, and it is sufficient for the decision of the present cause."[4]

§ 121. **Effect of the Hardwicke-Kent Doctrine.** "This decision," in the words of the New York Court of Appeals, "assumed as a principle of law, that a voluntary conveyance was

---

[1] Russel *v* Hammond, 1 Atk 13; Taylor *v.* Jones, 2 Atk 600; Townshend *v.* Windham, 2 Vesey Sr 10.
[2] Townshend *v.* Windham, *supra*.
[3] *Supra*
[4] Reade *v* Livingston, *supra*

void as to any and all then existing creditors, without regard to the question of intention, because it might ultimately operate to defeat the collection or payment of their debts."[1] That is not quite a fair statement, in so far as it speaks of a disregard of the debtor's intention It is true that Chancellor Kent's doctrine prevents inquiry into the actual intention of the debtor in the particular case, but that is because the court, in the ascertainment of the debtor's intention, applied certain standards which constrained a judicial answer in all such cases. To repeat, a court, acting under the rule of Reade v. Livingston, proceeds logically enough once its premises are granted It holds the debtor to the reasonable consequences of his acts, and, as a gift of any property by a man owing any debts has an inevitable tendency to restrict the creditor's choice among the debtor's property for the realization of his claim, then the debtor must have intended to restrict the creditor's choice, therefore, concludes the court, the debtor must have intended to infringe the creditor's right to choose Such is the doctrine of Reade v Livingston, which has found place in many of our States.[2]

§ 122. **The Contrary View — Prior Indebtedness should be only Presumptive Evidence of Fraud** This is, however, by no means the universal doctrine, and a different answer to the question above propounded finds support not only in the weight of modern authority, but in sound reason as well The theory of Reade v Livingston has this weakness, that it mistakes an incident of the creditor's primary right for the right itself The creditor's primary right is to realize his claim in full, and for that purpose he is permitted to range at will among the debtor's assets, since the debtor has no right which he can urge to stop the creditor at any point. But when the debtor, prior to the creditor's invasion, has alienated a portion of his property he has done no wrong, because the creditor's right is to realize

---

[1] Babcock v. Eckler, 24 N Y 623
[2] Gardner v Kleinke, 46 N J Eq 90, 18 Atl 457, Glasgow v Turner, 91 Tenn 163, 18 S W 261, Ridgeway v Kendrick, 208 Fed 849

only upon such property as is on hand at the time of his incursion upon the debtor's estate. The statute should be given a reasonable construction, it permits the creditor to ignore the debtor's transfer when it hinders, delays or defrauds him. But if the debtor leaves enough property on hand to meet the creditor's claim, how is he hindered, delayed or defrauded? In other words the right of realization is protected fully, and that being so, the incidental right of roving should not be allowed as a factor of consideration. This is illustrated by Goodman v. Wineland [1] where, at the time a creditor sued to set aside a fraudulent conveyance, the debtor had recovered his solvency. The court held that while it would not dismiss the bill, yet it would make a decree "limiting a day for the payment of the claim or otherwise so as to preserve to the grantee the property conveyed by him, while at the same time securing the creditor." And the same idea governs the courts in charge of liquidation proceedings in refusing permission to the creditor's general representative, such as a trustee in bankruptcy, to attack any fraudulent transfer unless the assets already on hand are insufficient to discharge the creditor's claims.[2] The test, according to this view, may be shortly stated in the words of Spencer, J.,[3] "whether the grantor was indebted to such a degree that the settlement will deprive the creditors of an ample fund for the payment of their debts." If there are several creditors, the remaining property must be sufficient to pay them all in full, if there is one creditor, it must be sufficient to pay him in full. The debtor's intent should be judged by whether he was insolvent when he made the transfer, and thus necessarily diminished a fund already insufficient for the creditors' claims, or the result of the transfer was to leave him insolvent. The debtor's insolvency as connected with the transfer is thus the

[1] 61 Md. 449
[2] Land Title &c Co v Asphalt Co, 121 Fed. 587; aff'd 127 Fed. 1, Ecklor v Wolcott, 115 Wisc 19, 90 N W 1081
[3] See Verplank v Sterry, 12 Johns 556

real question; hence if he becomes insolvent afterward, through supervening causes which he could not control, he has made no fraudulent transfer.[1] Of course, the existence of indebtedness at the time he made the transfer should not be ignored, whether or not it existed to the extent of actual or potential insolvency It should have its weight as a *prima facie* case of fraudulent intent, but the transferee should be allowed to rebut this case by showing that the remaining assets of the debtor were sufficient to meet the debt. In short, according to this view " prior indebtedness is only presumptive and not conclusive evidence of fraud, and this presumption may be explained and rebutted "[2]

§ 123 **Prevalence of This View** This is the rule which the majority of the courts follow at the present day. In England, Lord Hardwicke's doctrine, which Chancellor Kent made his own, as we have seen, was never fully accepted,[3] and Spirett v. Willows,[4] the last case in line with Chancellor Kent's view, seems to be no longer in favor, insolvency as existing at the time of the transfer, or as resulting from it, is now the test there.[5] In some States of our country this is made the rule by statute.[6] In other States it has come to be the law through decision.[7]

§ 124 **Early American Origin of This Rule, and its Final Triumph over the Hardwicke-Kent Doctrine in New York.** This doctrine was announced by the highest court of Connecticut prior to the decision of Reade v. Livingston.[8] But

---

[1] Lloyd v. Fulton, 91 U S. 479.
[2] *Ibid*
[3] See Lush v Wilkinson, 5 Vesey 384, and Babcock v. Eckler, *supra*
[4] 3 De G J & S 293.
[5] Exp Mercer 17 Q. B D. 290
[6] As Georgia, Lloyd v. Fulton, 91 U S 479, Cohen v. Parish, 105 Ga 339, 31 S E 205, and North Carolina, Clement v Cozart, 112 N C 412, 17 S E 486.
[7] Winchester v Charter, 102 Mass 272; Warren v Moody, 122 U S 132, 7 S. Ct 1063, Bigelow, "Fraudulent Conveyances," p 210
[8] Salmon v Bennett, 1 Day N S. 525

Chancellor Kent dismissed this Connecticut case from consideration with these words:

"The court do not refer to authorities in support of their opinion, and, perhaps, they may have intended not to follow, strictly, the decisions at Westminster Hall under the Statute of 13 Eliz I can only say that, according to my imperfect view of those decisions (and by which I consider myself governed), this case was not decided in conformity to them, but I make this observation with great deference to that court."

Despite this rather contemptuous criticism, however, the idea expressed by the Connecticut judges has prevailed, even in the State of the great Chancellor's residence In New York considerable dissent from Chancellor Kent's idea soon appeared,[1] and when the Revised Statutes were adopted, they contained a provision that in every case the question of fraudulent intent shall be one of fact[2] This effectually annihilated the "presumption of law" which the Chancellor declared arose in the case of a gift by one who owed any debts at all;[3] but it has not deprived the courts of their right to judge the debtor's acts by the standards to which we have adverted. Although the statute created certain confusion which has only lately been dispelled,[4] the rule in New York may now be regarded as settled in accordance with the prevailing view, that a gift is not fraudulent unless it renders the debtor insolvent or was made while he was insolvent, and that prior indebtedness at the time of the transfer raises a presumption of fraud,

---

[1] See Verplank v Sterry, *supra*, and Babcock v. Eckler, *supra*
[2] See this provision as it now appears in R. P L Sec 265, and Pers Prop Law Sec 237.
[3] Babcock v Eckler, *supra*
[4] In Kain v Larkin, 131 N Y 300, 30 N E 105, the first division of the Court of Appeals held that no inference of law arose from the fact of existing indebtedness, and that consequently there was no duty on the debtor to go ahead with the evidence when such facts had been shown In the same term the other division of the same court held exactly to the contrary in Smith v Reid, 134 N. Y 568, 31 N E 1082, saying that the rule is well settled that a voluntary conveyance by one indebted at the time is presumptively fraudulent

which, however, can be rebutted by showing that enough assets were left to meet all the creditors' claims [1] The statute, in short, has had no further effect, as a clever writer has said, than to put the trial court to the necessity of stating its decision as to the debtor's intent in the shape of a finding of fact rather than a conclusion of law [2] But the New York Court of Appeals does not even go that far Although it is forbidden to pass upon questions of fact, yet it reversed the decision of a referee, who found, as a fact, that the debtor had no fraudulent intent, because the other facts which he also found, concerning the debtor's solvency at the time of the transfer, demonstrated his fraudulent intent " as a matter of law " [3]

§ 125. **Both Rules present Questions of Law** To repeat, both of the theories we have examined are alike in this — they reduce the question of the debtor's intent to one of law. The one theory rests upon the existence of indebtedness at the time of the transfer, the other involves an inquiry as to the transferor's solvency at that time; but whether governed by the one theory or the other, no court will permit the actual intention of the debtor to prevail, if it was contrary to the legal effect of his acts What a debtor says his intention was at a given time is of no avail as against his acts; [4] and more, what he proves his intention was avails nothing as against what the facts show his intention to have been, according to legal theory. " It is of no consequence," says the New York court, " that the transferee had no intent to hinder, delay or defraud the creditors of the transferor. A person cannot successfully put his property beyond the reach of his creditors by a transfer which secures it to himself and his children, even though the transferee may have the best of motives and be ignorant of his fraudulent intent." [5]

---

[1] Kerker v. Levy, 206 N Y 109, 99 N E 181; Clowe v. Seavy, 208 N. Y. 496, 102 N E 521
[2] Fowler's " Real Property Law," p 728
[3] Coleman v Bun, 93 N Y 17
[4] Re Spann, 183 Fed 819, Re Larkin. 168 Fed. 100
[5] Clowe v. Seavy, supra, Hunters v. Waite, 3 Gratt (Va) 26

§ 126 **Illustrations in Cases of Partnership and Corporate Reorganization** Illustrations of the common ground upon which both theories meet, is found in those cases where, as the result of a business transaction, all of the assets of one business concern are transferred to another. As between the parties to such a transaction the presumption would arise that the transferee, as part of the bargain, agreed to pay the transferor's debts Such a case was La Montagne v Bank of New York.[1] There one partnership transferred all its assets to a new partnership, and afterwards the managing partner of the new concern paid some of the old firm's debts with the new firm's property. It was held that this did not constitute a fraud as against his partners, because of the natural presumption that the new firm intended to pay the debts of the old firm, and the presumption should obtain since otherwise the transaction would be fraudulent. And as against the creditors of the old concern such a case is easy of solution. Neither a corporation, a partnership nor an individual can give all his property away to another, even though the latter agrees to pay the debts of the transferor. The creditors of the transferor, not being a party to such a contract, are not bound by it [2] Of course if a creditor accepts the situation and manifests his acceptance by any positive act a complete novation is effected, and he then has a new debtor in place of the old one.[3] On the other hand, he may, doubtless, treat the matter as a fraudulent operation and follow the transferred assets accordingly [4] It is, of course, needless to say that he must be reasonably prompt in signifying his choice, for a real choice is offered him, and any delay on his part may estop him from treating the matter as a fraud upon him, especially where the vendee has since become insolvent [5] But if the transfer

---

[1] 183 N Y 173, 76 N. E 33.
[2] Darcy v Bklyn Ferry Co, 196 N Y 99, 89 N E 461, 26 L. R A. (N S) 267, Jordan v Laverty, 53 N J L 15, 20 Atl 832, Keller v. Ashford, 133 U S 610, 10 S Ct 494
[3] Joslin v N J Spring Co, 36 N. J Law 144
[4] Darcy v. Bklyn Ferry Co, supra   [5] Re Halstead, 204 Fed. 117.

is of only part of the old concern's assets, and those remaining suffice to meet its debts, then its creditors, according to the modern theory above discussed, have no claim upon the transferee, for it is not a fraudulent conveyance, nor is there any reasonable presumption that the latter agreed to pay the transferor's debts [1]

§ 127. **Donee entitled to Subrogation** From the very fact that the donee is held to the measure of a rule of law rather than a question of fact, a certain rule in his favor has resulted. In Illinois [2] and New York [3] the rule has been established that in the case of any conveyance which involves merely constructive fraud of this kind, the grantee may hold the property as security for any debt honestly due him, so far as a court of equity is concerned. In short, if the creditors invoke the aid of equity to set aside a gift which was made while the donor was insolvent, but without any actual fraudulent intent on the part of donor or donee, the court, as a condition to giving relief, will require the creditors to let the donee make good out of the property any debts that may be due him by the donor.

[1] Smith v Bowker Torrey Co , 207 Fed 967
[2] Lobstein v Lehn, 120 Ill. 549 12 N E. 68
[3] Brown v Chubb, 135 N Y 174, 31 N E 1030

CHAPTER VII

FRAUDULENT TRANSFER (*CONTINUED*) VALIDITY OF AN ALIENATION TO A PURCHASER

§ 128. Situation of Purchaser Different from that of Donee
129. The "Saving Clause" of the Statute
130. Every *Bona Fide* Purchaser is Protected
131. The Burden of Proof.
132. Relevancy of Evidence.
133. The Debtor's Intent as determined by his Financial Condition.
134. The Debtor's Intent as determined by the Effect of the Transaction
135. Where the Consideration is on Hand.
136. Where the Debtor has disposed of the Consideration
137. Where the Debtor uses the Proceeds to prefer One Creditor over Another by Way of paying or securing his Claim. The Early View
138. Later Doctrine of Lord Justice James

§ 139. The Supreme Court's Decisions
140. Where the Debtor secretes, squanders or gives away the Consideration
141. Nature of Consideration Necessary.
142. Past Consideration
143. Extent of Consideration.
144. Good Faith
145. Notice to Transferee
146. Character of Badges of Fraud
147. Twofold Use of Badges of Fraud
148. Vendor's Retention of Possession
149. The Sale in Bulk
150. Sales in Bulk Statutes.
151. Agreements to withhold from Record
152. Other Badges of Fraud.
153. Case of Transferee who Receives Notice before completing Payment of Consideration
154. The Common Law Rule
155. The Equity Rule
156. Extension of Doctrine

§ 128 **Situation of Purchaser Different from that of Donee.** In the last chapter we considered the case of a gift, as affected by the Statute of Fraudulent Conveyances. We must now consider quite a different case, where the transferee has given a consideration for the transfer. Unless the statute is mandatory to the contrary, the presence of this additional element must at once alter our entire point of view, because when we have a sale of the debtor's property instead of a gift, we are entering a domain of conflicting rights. Against the right of the creditors to realize from their debtor's property comes the right of the debtor to deal with this property in the course of business, and also the right of the community to deal with the debtor in the course of business. Nothing is truer as a general proposition than what the Supreme Court has said in the litigation arising over the bankruptcy of the Boatman's Savings Institution. There it was unequivocally announced that the mere fact that a man is insolvent, or indeed that bankruptcy proceedings or other proceedings for the winding up of his affairs are pending against him, do not constitute a reason why he should be compelled to suspend all his business operations. It is not wholesome that his business should be paralyzed by the mere fact of his insolvency. He should be allowed to continue with his affairs, if he continues with them in the proper course of business and receives value for what he transfers; because, after all, the creditors would not be injured if value comes in, in return for value going out [1] As the Supreme Court said in one of these cases

"Clearly all sales are not forbidden. It would be absurd to suppose that Congress intended to set the seal of condemnation on every transaction of the bankrupt which occurred within six months of bankruptcy, without regard to its character A policy leading to such a result would be an excellent contrivance for paralyzing business, and cannot be imputed to Congress without an express declaration to that effect The interdiction applies to sales for a fraudulent object, not to those with an honest purpose. The law does not recognize that every sale of property by an embarrassed person is necessarily in fraud of the Bankrupt Act If it were so, no one would know with whom he could safely deal, and besides, a person in this condition would have no encouragement to make proper efforts to

---

[1] Tiffany v Lucas, 15 Wall 410, Tiffany v. Boatman's Savings Institution, 18 Wall. 375

extricate himself from difficulty. It is for the interest of the community that every one should continue his business, and avoid, if possible, going into bankruptcy, and yet how could this result be obtained if the privilege were denied a person who was unable to command ready money to meet his debts as they fell due, of making a fair disposition of his property in order to accomplish this object." [1]

§ 129 **The " Saving Clause " of the Statute** After annulling all transfers when made with intent to hinder, delay or defraud the creditors of the transferor, the statute adds a saving clause, by way of proviso, that nothing contained in the Act shall extend to property which is " upon good consideration and *bona fide* " transferred to one " not having at the time of such conveyance . . any manner of notice or knowledge of such covin, fraud or collusion as aforesaid." This " saving clause " appears in every reenactment of the statute in one form or another, but however the provision may actually appear in the modern dress of the statute in any jurisdiction, its essential nature as a saving clause or proviso is not destroyed The same method of treating the particular case is followed, and the same rule as to the burden of proof is observed. The case is not within the statute if, in the end, it reveals (*a*) a consideration supporting the transfer and (*b*) good faith on the transferee's part.

§ 130. **Every Bona Fide Purchaser is Protected** And in this connection an important point must be noted. The statute, it will be observed, does not limit its protection to the first person who received the property from the debtor, on the contrary it protects, by a fair reading, any person who in good faith paid a fair consideration, whether he purchased it directly from the debtor or from some one who in turn had purchased from the debtor. On the face of the statute, therefore, we may conclude that even if the first purchaser acted in bad faith, yet the ultimate purchaser is immune if he acted in good faith.

[1] Tiffany *v* Lucas, 15 Wall. 410.

In other words the statute aims to protect the title of a *bona fide* purchaser, no matter at what time or place he became such That was the view taken in England at an early date "The valuable consideration, wherever it occurs, entirely obliterates the fraud so that it can never again in any shape affect the transaction"[1] In Anderson *v* Roberts[2] Chancellor Kent reached a different conclusion, but his decree was reversed by the Court of Error[3] and the rule there laid down has prevailed in this country[4] As said by Spencer, C. J, in Anderson *v* Roberts,[5] "the principle is that although a deed be fraudulent in its creation, yet by subsequent matter it may acquire validity in favor of a purchaser for valuable consideration, and where two persons have equal equities, the maxim applies."

§ 131 **The Burden of Proof** To repeat, the statute avoids a conveyance made by the debtor with intent to hinder, delay and defraud his creditors, and then by way of a proviso protects a *bona fide* purchaser for a good consideration How stands the rule with regard to the burden of proof in such a case? On the face of the statute one might say that after the debtor's bad intent is proven, the case is won unless the transferee comes in under this saving clause and secures absolution by showing that he purchased for a consideration and in good faith But that conclusion, so broadly stated, is not correct, because it conflicts with the general principle that whoever states an affirmative must demonstrate it Whoever attacks a transfer must maintain the burden of showing that it was a fraudulent transaction instead of an ordinary transaction, and it does not matter whether by reason of the circumstances of the particular case the transferee is in the position on the record of plaintiff or

---

[1] Trodger *v* Laughan, 1 Siderfin 133, Robertson, "Fraudulent Conveyances," 497.
[2] 3 Johns. Ch 371.
[3] 18 Johns. 515.
[4] Colquitt *v.* Thomas, 1 Ga 258; Bean *v* Smith, 2 Mason 252, Fed. Case No 1174, Wood *v.* Mann, 1 Sumner 506, Fed. Case No 17951
[5] 18 Johns. 515.

106 THE RIGHTS AND REMEDIES OF CREDITORS. [CHAP VII.

defendant An excellent illustrative case is Starin v. Kelly[1] There goods had been sold to the plaintiff by A One of A's creditors issued an execution upon his judgment against A, and the sheriff levied upon the goods in question under a judgment which had been obtained against A. The plaintiff brought replevin against the sheriff for the goods, setting up his title by purchase from A The sheriff defended on the ground that the sale was a fraudulent transfer, and therefore by virtue of the statute no title passed to the plaintiff. The Court of Appeals, in reversing the judgment below by reason of the improper method in which the cause had been tried, stated the rule as follows

"To maintain the issue on the part of the defendant it was sufficient for him in the first instance to show Besson's fraudulent intent in making the sale. Then it was for the plaintiff to show that he purchased the property for a valuable consideration His title would then be unimpeachable unless the defendant should make it appear that he had previous notice of Besson's fraudulent intent or that he participated in the fraud. Under the statute, a creditor assailing a transfer of property as fraudulent may succeed by simply showing a fraudulent intent on the part of the vendor, or such intent on the part of the vendee. If, however, the vendee shows that he paid a valuable consideration for the property transferred to him, then proof of the fraudulent intent of the vendor only is not sufficient; then there must be proof also of a fraudulent intent on the part of the vendee or that he had notice of the vendor's fraudulent intent."[2]

§ 132 **Relevancy of Evidence** In short, the burden of proof is on the creditor throughout, but he is aided, in the progress of his case, by the ordinary presumptions that would naturally obtain But in the end his case, as made out on the pleadings and all the proofs, his own and the transferee's, must show (a) the debtor's fraudulent intent, (b) that the transferee, though having given a good consideration, was not acting in

[1] 88 N Y 418.   [2] Starin v Kelley, 88 N. Y. 418.

good faith and without notice. This is illustrated by the decisions on points of evidence that often arise on the trial of such cases Evidence going to show the fraudulent intent of the debtor is admissible, although not connected, at the time, with any knowledge or complicity on the transferee's part. Thus, to show the debtor's intention to defraud, evidence of his financial condition at the time of the transfer is material for reasons which we shall presently see To show his condition, and his knowledge of it, the debtor's books of account are admissible, that they bind him cannot be doubted [1] And in like manner any other admission made by him as to his financial condition is admissible, such as a tax report, entirely irrespective of its truth [2] The transferee cannot object to the admission of such documents in evidence. If he was acting in good faith, he cannot be held, no matter what these documents show; if he was acting in bad faith, then they are cumulative evidence against him also, his bad faith meanwhile being established by evidence aliunde [3]

[1] Smith v. Moore, 199 Fed 689, White v. Benjamin, 150 N Y. 258, 44 N. E. 956.
[2] Ernst v Mechs & Metals Bank, 201 Fed 664; Towns v Smith, 115 Ind 480, 16 N E 811; Woolridge v Boardman, 115 Cal. 74, 46 Pac 868 As stated in Ernst v Mechs & Metals Bank, *supra*
"The exception to the admissibility of the books is not good. They were not put in evidence to prove a sale and delivery of any securities represented by any item contained in them, or the loan of any money, but to show whether the bankrupts were solvent or insolvent at a given time If they were not admissible for that purpose no one could be proved insolvent without proving separately every item of liability and every asset by common law proof The law requires nothing of the sort, but allows any one's books in evidence, even if not a privy, to show whether he is insolvent or solvent upon proof that they are in fact his books duly kept in his business for the purpose of showing his financial condition "
[3] Cases cited *supra* The rule is thus stated, for cases tried by jury, in Smith v Collins, 94 Ala 394, 10 So. 334:
' Whenever the financial condition of the debtor is material, whatever throws light on this question is admissible To make such testimony available as against the purchaser, there must be additional proof, such as knowledge or notice of the condition of the vendor debtor, or of facts suggesting further inquiry, and which, if honestly followed up, would lead to a knowledge of his condition The court

§ 133. **The Debtor's Intent as determined by his Financial Condition** This renders it necessary to consider, first of all, the debtor's fraudulent intent. We considered that in connection with gifts, in the last chapter; but the case of a gift is not the same as that of a transfer for value, in this regard. In the case of a gift, as we saw, the debtor's intent was really a question of law, connected, according to one theory, with his indebtedness at the time of the transfer, or, according to another theory, with his insolvency as attendant upon, or caused by, the transfer. But when we have the case where the transfer represents value received, the mere insolvency of the debtor, or his being indebted at the time when it was made, is not sufficient. Because he is indebted, or even insolvent, must a man quit a business which consists essentially of the transfer of property? No, has answered the Supreme Court.[1] Insolvency of course is an element of consideration, upon that the decisions above cited on the question of evidence are predicated, but it is not, as in the case of a gift, the necessary limit of our inquiry. If the insolvent debtor sells a piece of property for a fair consideration, he has not hindered, delayed or defrauded his creditors, because the consideration received by the debtor is there for them to realize upon, all that has happened is a mere transmutation of the debtor's estate from one form of property into another, and the creditors may realize just as much on their claims as if the transmutation had not occurred. And even if, after thus changing his estate from one form of property into another, the debtor loses part of the new property he has received, this loss cannot be charged to the original transfer unless, by a logical chain of events, the one was the natural result of the other. The debtor's intent, therefore, must be determined

should not exclude testimony which is competent against one party because not competent against another party to the suit. The testimony should be received, and its bearing limited and explained to the jury."

[1] Tiffany v Lucas, *supra*, Tiffany v Boatman's Savings Institution, *supra*.

by some standard in addition to that furnished His condition is worthy of consideration, but another and equally important inquiry must be made.

§ 134 **The Debtor's Intent as determined by the Effect of the Transaction** That inquiry is, what effect did the transaction have upon the amount of the debtor's estate? Did the transaction, including not only the transfer, but what so followed it as to appear a logical portion of the debtor's entire plan, result in a material diminution of the value of the debtor's estate? That, it seems to us, is the real inquiry. The cases where this inquiry is pertinent are of infinite variety in circumstance and opinion, but the principles above discussed avail to reduce them into certain classes.

§ 135 **Where the Consideration is on Hand.** First is where the debtor has done nothing out of the ordinary with the consideration which he has received, and consequently it is either on hand, or has been lost through circumstances entirely disconnected with the transfer in question In any such case the courts cannot hold that the debtor intended to injure his creditors, unless the consideration was so grossly inadequate as to justify such a belief [1] Other things being equal, great must be this disparity between object and price before the courts can impute this intention to the debtor. Such a disparity appeared in Scoggin v. Schloath [2] where one hundred dollars was paid for land worth two thousand. And the courts are prone to take a very strict view where a part of the stipulated consideration is paid in a fictitious thing, because there the debtor himself has received less than he knew the property was worth.[3]

§ 136 **Where the Debtor has disposed of the Consideration.** Second is the case where the debtor has disposed of the consideration under such circumstances as to justify the conclusion that the transfer, by which he received the consideration, was

---

[1] Hudgins v. Kemp, 20 How. 45, Baldwin v Short, 125 N Y 553, 26 N. E. 928
[2] 15 Ore. 380, 15 Pac. 635.   [3] Baldwin v Short, *supra*.

merely part of a larger scheme by which the creditor's right of realization may be impeded In these cases the gist of the creditor's grievance is, not the size of the consideration received, but the disposition which the debtor made of the consideration when he got it, the receipt and the disposition being connected in a logical chain of events. These cases, in turn, divide themselves into two classes, (a) where the debtor uses the proceeds of the transfer to prefer a certain creditor by way of paying or securing his claim, (b) where the debtor secretes the consideration from his creditors or gives away the consideration. We shall take these cases in order.

§ 137. **Where the Debtor uses the Proceeds to prefer One Creditor over Another by Way of paying or securing his Claim. The Early View.** As we shall see, the common law courts viewed a preferential transfer as lawful, and the Chancery Court, while deprecating the practice, felt unable to give any affirmative relief in such a case As we shall also see, however, preferential transfers were viewed as impliedly forbidden by the terms of any statute which provided for the distribution of an insolvent debtor's effects among his creditors, with the result that a representative of the creditors, appointed in proceedings under such a statute, could by means of plenary suit, recover the property thus transferred [1] As a result, until a very recent date, it was the rule that if a transferee had reason to believe that the debtor intended with the proceeds of the sale to prefer certain of his creditors over others, then upon the debtor's being adjudged a bankrupt the bankruptcy trustee could set the transaction aside in behalf of the creditors; because, in aiding the debtor to give a preference, the transferee was participating in a wrong upon his creditors [2] In most of these cases, the creditor who was preferred had reasonable cause to believe that it was intended to prefer him, but in Crafts v Bel-

[1] *Infra,* § 343-4
[2] Crafts v Belden, 99 Mass 535, Ex. Mendell, 1 Low 302, Fed. Case No 9418, Re Pease, 129 Fed 446, Re Beerman, 112 Fed. 663, Roberts v Johnson, 151 Fed 567.

den¹ the preferred creditor was wholly in the dark Nevertheless the Supreme Court of Massachusetts held that "the sale would be void although the benefit of the preference might inure, not to the transferee, but to another and *bona fide* and wholly innocent creditor who by reason of his innocence could retain his payment " ²

§ 138. **Later Doctrine of Lord Justice James.** This doctrine, however, met with the emphatic disapproval of Lord Justice James,³ and the weight of his opinion started a movement in America which has led to a termination of its sway In Githens *v* Schiffler⁴ the view of Lord Justice James was followed, and thus doubt arose on the general proposition Meantime the Supreme Court was proceeding towards the same end

§ 139. **The Supreme Court's Decisions.** In Coder *v.* Arts,⁵ the Supreme Court drew a new distinction between a preference and a fraudulent conveyance, holding that a preference was essentially honest, and was valid unless forbidden by the express terms of a Bankrupt Act, and that the present Bankrupt Act, in forbidding preferences, did not affect the character of a preference as an essentially honest thing This logically led to the decision that if the only purpose of the debtor, in effecting a transfer of his property, is with the proceeds to prefer certain creditors, then that purpose does not predicate a fraudulent intent That was the decision in Van Iderstine *v* Nat Discount Co⁶ It is flatly at variance with Crafts *v* Belden and *In re* Mendell,⁷ and indeed with all the other cases cited in that connection The court indeed distinguishes the later cases on a line which is of value as indicating the court's point of view, although, were it worth while, it would be possible to demonstrate that the distinction is not justified by the facts of the cases in question Those "cases under the present statute," said the court, " relate to transactions in which the transferee

---
¹ *Supra*
² Crafts *v* Belden, *supra*
³ Exp Stubbins, 17 Ch D 58.
⁴ 112 Fed 505
⁵ 213 U S 223, 29 S Ct 436.
⁶ 227 U S 575, 33 S Ct 343.
⁷ *Supra*

was practically the representative of the preferred creditor, and where consequently, the conveyance was so much subject to attack as though it had been made directly to him "[1] That, therefore, is the line drawn for our future direction

§ 140 **Where the Debtor secretes, squanders or gives away the Consideration** The cases are so numerous and so infinite in their variety, that to give specimens of the frauds practiced would serve no good end. Reduced to last analysis, however, the situation in any such case is this. The creditor does not find on hand the consideration which the debtor received. Then a number of questions suggest themselves. What became of it? Has it in turn been transmuted into other property? If so, where is that property? Is this last of the value of the first? If not, why the disparity, and what caused the loss of the missing increment of value? If the result of these inquiries is to demonstrate that the debtor has in the honest course of fair dealing lost the consideration, then there is no relation of cause and effect between this loss and the original transfer. But if any other case appears, and the consideration, or its equivalent, is not on hand, then the question for determination is whether the disappearance of the consideration was part of the debtor's plan when he effected the transfer, if that is so, then the debtor's intent, as condemned by the statute, is apparent This question the courts determine by the presence or absence of circumstances going to show the debtor's purpose, but discussion of these badges of fraud will be reserved until we get into that consideration of the transferee's position which it is now our duty to begin

§ 141 **Nature of Consideration Necessary.** In order for the transferee to have any position at all, he must be a purchaser for a consideration. If he has given no consideration which the law recognizes as such, that is, a consideration, in the shape of a promise or an act, which would support a count in assumpsit, then he has given no consideration in the meaning of the statute.

[1] Van Iderstine v. Nat. Disc Co., *supra*

Despite the latter's use of the adjective "good" as prefixed to "consideration," that is settled. The consideration required must certainly amount to what, from the standpoint of the law of contracts, is known as a consideration, that is, it must be such a thing as would support a promise founded thereon. It follows, therefore, that natural love and affection is not a consideration.[1] An interesting illustration is afforded by Colman v Burr.[2] There the defendant, being insolvent, conveyed property to his wife in consideration of her agreement to perform domestic duties in connection with caring for the defendant's aged mother, who lived with them. It was held that the common law doctrine still remained in New York to the extent that a husband and wife could not contract for the rendition by her of domestic services, inasmuch as the marriage obligation bound her to render these services without compensation; and that, as there was no consideration for the transfer, it should be set aside, on the principles governing gifts which we have heretofore considered.[3] On the other hand, marriage forms a consideration within the meaning of the statute, as it does in the law of contracts.[4]

§ 142 **Past Consideration.** The statute, however, presents this exception to the modern principles of contract law, that a "past" consideration, if it would have originally supported an action of assumpsit, will support a transfer. If the debtor pays or secures a creditor, therefore, this preferential transfer does not constitute a fraudulent conveyance. That is not what the statute aimed at; it was not a bankruptcy law, and did not aim

---

[1] Matthews v Feaver, 1 Cox C. C 177; Partridge v Gopp, 1 Eden 153, Amb 596
[2] 93 N Y 17
[3] *Supra*, Ch VI
[4] Jones v Boulter, 1 Cox C C. 288, De Hierapolis v. Reilly, 44 N Y App Div. 22, 60 N. Y S 417, aff. 168 N Y. 585, 60 N E 1110; Sarasohn v Kamaiky, 193 N Y. 203, 86 N E 20 The terms of the agreement of course must be clear and the marriage must follow as an act clearly stipulated in the agreement, Pollock v Simon, 205 Fed 1005.

to secure equality of distribution.¹ Hence it was always clear that a past due debt was a sufficient consideration for the transfer " It is not necessary," said the New York Court of Appeals, " to show a new consideration, as the transaction amounts to nothing more than the voluntary preference of one creditor over another " ² Even if the transferee knows all the circumstances, and the effect of the transaction, it was never considered that this showed a want of good faith on his part. It was his natural instinct to desire to be paid or secured, there is nothing censurable in that, and he was not to be placed in the same class as a transferee under the circumstances we have discussed under the last heading. If, as has been stated, it is done " without fraudulent design and simply to prefer the favored creditor," the case is not within the Statute of Fraudulent Conveyances.³ As a result therefore, we may say that at common law a preference was valid and did not constitute a case within the Statute of Fraudulent Conveyances⁴ Nor could a court of equity on general principles take any other position, because there, as in favor of one creditor over another, the court felt itself compelled to recognize the same right of preference.⁵

§ 143 **Extent of Consideration.** Having such a legal consideration, its extent, other things being equal, is immaterial. Unless it was so grossly inadequate as to amount to a badge of fraud, as we shall use that term hereafter, the ratio of consideration to property is of as little importance in this connection as it is in the ascertainment of the debtor's intent;⁶ in short, the same principle applies throughout with regard to

---

¹ Fry, J., in *In re* Johnson, 20 Ch D 389.
² Murphy *v* Briggs, 89 N Y 446, Lehrenkrauss *v* Bonnell, 199 N Y 210, 92 N. E 637
³ Green *v.* McCrane, 55 N J Eq. 436, 37 Atl 318
⁴ Huntley *v* Kingman, 152 U. S 527, 14 S Ct 688, Davis *v* Schwartz 155 U S 631, 15 S Ct 237, Darville *v.* Terry, 6 H & N 807, Pyckstock *v* Lyster, 3 M & S 371
⁵ Louthian *v* Hassell, 4 Bro. C C 167.
⁶ Brown *v* Schleier, 194 U S 18, 24 S Ct 558, Jaeger *v.* Kelley, 52 N. Y 274.

consideration. With regard to the debtor, the size of the consideration is important only as showing the presence or absence of a fraudulent intent; with regard to the transferee, it is important only as showing his good faith. So we are led to this, as the final portion of our study, the question of good faith.

§ 144. **Good Faith.** The statute protects the purchaser when the conveyance is made in good faith to one having neither knowledge nor notice of the fraud. This language requires little in the way of judicial interpretation; such a task would produce nothing beyond synonyms. LORD ELDON has defined "good faith" as simply meaning fair dealing,[1] and that is good enough for our purposes.

§ 145. **Notice to Transferee.** What is sufficient to put the transferee on notice? All that can be said on that point is that he is held to the reasonable and natural standard of an ordinary man. Mere suspicion is perhaps not enough,[2] but anything constituting more than a ground of suspicion is certainly sufficient. Of course the transferee's motive is immaterial. He may, as the New York Court of Appeals has said, have in fact been actuated only by a desire " to secure a good bargain for himself," but, nevertheless, his conduct may be culpable.[3] It is not, therefore, a question of nomenclature, of defining good faith or anything else, but of holding a man to the natural and reasonable consequences of his acts. If the transaction is in the usual course of business, then there must be something extraneous to put the transferee on notice. But if it were itself unusual, and out of the ordinary course of business, or if anything in it would reasonably excite suspicion, then a duty is put on the transferee to " take the proper steps to find out the pecuniary conditions of the seller." And for that, " all reasonable means pursued in good faith must be used for this purpose."[4] Once

---

[1] Exp. Ruffin, 6 Vesey 119
[2] Grant v. Monmouth Bank, 97 U. S. 80
[3] Greenwald v. Wales, 174 N. Y. 140, 66 N. E. 665.
[4] Kempner v. Churchill, 8 Wall. 632

put on his guard, if the transferee " chooses to remain ignorant of what the necessities of the case require him to know, he takes the risk of the impeachment of the transaction." [1] That is the only practical rule which can be applied. To allow the transferee's degree of intelligence or experience as a test would, as has been aptly said, " put a premium upon ignorance and encourage its assumption " [2]

§ 146. **Character of Badges of Fraud.** In weighing the probabilities of the transferee's good faith, courts have resort to the so-called badges of fraud. Their character must not be misunderstood. Of themselves, they conclusively prove nothing, but they have probative value of varying force. No one of them is conclusive in law,[3] but their value is of greater or less degree according to the particular case.[4] We must remember that the transferor is always in the position of knowledge for better or worse. He is held to ordinary standards of reason in (*a*) the knowledge of his condition, and (*b*) the consequences that would flow from the contemplated act. The transferee, on the other hand, does not always positively know the circumstances, but that is not necessary. An actual agreement to defraud need not be shown.[5] Of course an actual conspiracy carries the case, but a conspiracy is not a necessary element. All needed on the part of the transferee is lack of good faith, and in order to ascertain that we need merely to inquire whether he should have been warned by the facts which he did know. Consequently, as the Supreme Court has said, " the rule of evidence is well settled that circumstances altogether inconclusive if separately considered may, by their number and joint operation, especially when corroborated by moral coincidences, be sufficient to constitute conclusive

[1] Walbrunn *v* Babbitt, 16 Wall. 577, 582; Wright *v*. Sampter, 152 Fed 196
[2] Wright *v*. Sampter, 152 Fed 196
[3] Martindale *v*. Booth, 3 B. & Ad. 498
[4] Hale *v* Met &c Co , 28 L J. N. S 777.
[5] Singer *v* Jacobs, 11 Fed. 559

proof." [1] In the words of the same court, the transferee, once warned, cannot "continue recklessly with guilty knowledge" [2]

§ 147. **Twofold Use of Badges of Fraud** These badges of fraud, therefore, have a twofold purpose (a) in proving the transferor's intent, and (b) in showing the bad faith of the transferee. For instance, where the transferor's books show on their face his insolvency — this is a two-edged sword. It proves the transferor's bad faith, because he is familiar with his own books, and if the transferee had access to them his bad faith would be shown by his refusal to examine them. If he had examined them he would have found out that the transferor was insolvent, and would thus have been put upon further inquiry, and, when having an opportunity to examine them, he refrains from so doing, the result is the same [3]

§ 148. **Vendor's Retention of Possession** These badges of fraud are numerous, but it is only necessary to notice a few For instance, the earliest is, in the case of a sale of chattels, the retention of possession by the vendor. The inference of fraud from such a circumstance is reasonable because the essence of a sale always has been delivery, and if there is no delivery, then there is something peculiar about the transaction That is what Twyne's Case [4] comes to, and in some States, as New York,[5] this doctrine now appears as part of the statute law, but this circumstance may be met by other facts showing that the retention was really innocent. It raises no absolute presumption of law, but simply one of fact. At one time in our history, a confusion of this idea with the doctrine of reputed ownership, to which we will come, led as noted a jurist as Mr. Justice Buller to state that retention of possession in such a case raises a conclusive presumption of law [6] This dictum was

[1] Wager v. Hall, 16 Wall. 584, 601-602.
[2] Clements v Moore, 6 Wall 786.
[3] In re Pease, 129 Fed 446, 452
[4] 3 Co Rep 80b
[5] Personal Property Law, Section 34
[6] Edwards v. Harbin, 2 Term. Rep. 587.

most unfortunate because it led to a confusion of opinion and of law which has existed to this day in some places. In several States this dictum has been followed as expressing the common law,[1] while in several other States, the same rule is established by statute as well as by decisions[2] But this doctrine of Buller, J , unsound in principle as it was, did not long survive elsewhere. In England it was decisively overruled in Martindale v. Booth[3] and that case expresses the prevailing rule of this country[4]

§ 149 **The Sale in Bulk.** Another badge of fraud of long standing is the "sale in bulk." That term describes the case where a tradesman or merchant, instead of selling his commercial assets in the usual course of business, sells them all at once and at a loss. Now that is a transaction so out of the usual course of business as reasonably to excite inquiry. A man's purpose in doing a thing like that is apt to be wrong, and the transferee is held to notice of that fact That doctrine was laid down as long ago as Small v Oudley[5] and has universally existed ever since[6]

§ 150 **Sales in Bulk Statutes** Of late years this doctrine has been in the course of passage into the body of our statute law. It appears in the 35th Section of the National Bankrupt Act of 1867, but was omitted from the successor Act of 1898. That however makes little difference, as the bankruptcy courts can enforce the corresponding statutes of the States[7] and nearly every State to-day has such a statute. Some years ago the American Bar Association recommended a uniform sales in bulk statute for adoption by the various States, and it was adopted

---

[1] See Harkness v Russell, 118 U S 663, 7 S Ct 51, Gibson v Love, 4 Fla. 217
[2] See Bigelow, "Fraudulent Conveyances," p 385
[3] 3 B & Ad 498
[4] Harkness v. Russell, supra
[5] 2 P Wms 427
[6] Walbrunn v Babbitt, 16 Wall 577, In re Walden, 199 Fed 315; In re Thiveat, 199 Fed 319
[7] See cases cited infra, p 119

by many of them.[1] This form of statute made a sale in bulk void unless the transferor's creditors were notified of the proposed transfer, prior to its making, and public record was made of the transaction within a limited time. Although very little doubt had been entertained as to the constitutionality of such a statute, in view of the fact that the courts had always considered such a transaction as certainly not within the inalienable rights of man, still the New York Court of Appeals took occasion to declare this form of statute, as adopted by the New York Legislature, to be unconstitutional.[2] The Legislature of New York then reënacted the statute with the modification that a transaction, consummated without complying with the terms of the statute, should be only presumptively fraudulent as against the creditors of the vendor; and this statute has been upheld.[3] But meanwhile the uniform statute as recommended by the Bar Association was upheld by the Supreme Court in a carefully considered opinion,[4] and, if we may judge by a recent dictum of the Court of Appeals, we may conclude that the original statute, if reënacted now in New York, would receive that court's approval.[5] The result is that to-day among our States will be found two classes of statutes regarding sales in bulk. One, following the model condemned in Wright v. Hart,[6] but upheld in Lemieux v. Young,[7] makes the transaction void as against the creditors of the vendor unless the statutory requisites are complied with. The other, framed to comply with the doctrine of Wright v. Hart,[8] makes it only presumptively fraudulent.[9]

---

[1] See American Bar Association Reports, vol 34, p 1099.
[2] Wright v Hart, 182 N Y 330, 75 N E 404
[3] Sprintz v Saxton, 126 N. Y App. Div 421, 110 N Y S. 585; Seeman v Levine, 140 N. Y. App Div 272, 125 N. Y S 184, N. Y. Pers Prop Law, Sec 44   [6] *Supra*
[4] Lemieux v. Young, 216 U S 174   [7] *Supra*.
[5] People v Luhrs, 195 N. Y. 377, 89 N E. 171   [8] *Supra*.
[9] The New Jersey Act was applied by the Federal courts in *In re Lipmann* 201 Fed. 169, and the New York statute in Parker v Sherman, 201 Fed. 155.

§ 151 **Agreements to withhold from Record** Another badge of fraud is to be found in the case of an agreement to withhold a transfer from record. In most of our States to-day, a mortgage or deed of real estate needs no record to be effectual as against the grantor's or mortgagor's creditors. So far as such recording acts go, the mere negligence of a mortgagee or grantee to record an instrument raises no presumption of fraud,[1] but this omission may indicate fraud, when taken in connection with other suspicious features of the particular case.[2] Even where the statute requires the recording of a chattel mortgage in order for it to be valid as against the mortgagor's creditors, the mere omission to comply with the statute in stating the true amount of the debt thereby secured, has but slight weight as an indication of fraud, when standing alone.[3] But on the other hand, a positive agreement to withhold a transfer from record is a very different matter. That is a more cogent badge of fraud, because the only obvious reason for such an agreement would be some design upon the rights of the grantor's creditors.[4] It is undoubtedly "a circumstance constituting more or less cogent evidence of the want of good faith."[5]

§ 152 **Other Badges of Fraud.** Other badges of fraud there are — many of them in fact — and each of them bears on its face its reason for existence. For instance, reselling at a loss undoubtedly indicates fraud,[6] purchasing goods by means of a system of check kiting indicates dishonesty of purpose,[7] so do dishonest books[8] and the debtor's destruction of his books[9]

---

[1] Butcher v Werskman, 204 Fed 330
[2] Marsden v Cornell, 62 N Y 215
[3] Frost v. Warren, 42 N Y. 204, *In re* Watson, 201 Fed 962
[4] Rogers v. Page, 140 Fed 586, aff 211 U S 575, 29 S Ct 159; Davis v Schwartz, 155 U S 631, 15 S Ct 237, *In re* Watson, 201 Fed. 962, National Bank v Shackelford, 208 Fed. 677
[5] Rogers v Page, *supra*
[6] Wright v Brown, 67 N Y 1, Loeb v Flash, 65 Ala 526
[7] Gillespie v. J C Piles & Company, 178 Fed. 886
[8] *In re* Friedman, 164 Fed 131
[9] Godschalk v Sterling, 129 Fed 580, Burdick v Gill, 7 Fed 668; *In re* Hirsch, 194 Fed 562, *Re* Hodgo, 205 Fed. 824

And so far have the courts gone that even contemporaneous frauds are admissible in evidence to show a fraudulent purpose in this connection, provided that the grantee knew of their existence [1]

§ 153. **Case of Transferee who Receives Notice before completing Payment of Consideration.** So far we have discussed the transferee's position as it existed at the time the transaction was completed But there are, of course, numerous cases where the transferee receives notice of the debtor's fraudulent purposes before he has paid all or part of the consideration. What are his rights in that sort of case?

§ 154. **The Common Law Rule.** So far as the meaning of the statute was concerned, the common law and equity courts agreed that the statute, by "purchaser," meant one who had paid in full the consideration in the shape of cash or property. A mere promise to pay or deliver, although binding, was not a good consideration within the meaning of the statute, however different might have been the legislative intent if expressed in the present day of a credit system. As a result, if the purchaser had not paid all of the agreed consideration he was not protected by the face of the statute But on this point the common law courts diverged from the courts of equity The common law courts would not regard one as a purchaser unless he had paid all the agreed consideration, and they had no way of protecting him even for the portion he had paid, since there was no common law principle which could stop the creditor from pursuing his common law remedy [2]

§ 155. **The Equity Rule** On the other hand, the equity courts could give relief to the transferee by refusing their aid to the judgment creditor except upon condition If the transferee had paid nothing at the time he was put on notice, the court would not tolerate his consummating the transaction,

---

[1] Rowley v Bigelow, 12 Pick 3; Fraser v Levy, 6 H & N. 15; Loos v. Wilkinson, 110 N Y 195, 18 N. E 99
[2] Crockett v Phinney, 33 Minn 157, 22 N W. 292.

but for what he had paid on account before he was put upon notice, the Chancery Courts will allow him to retain the property as security, and allow the creditors to take the property only upon the condition that they refund to the transferee these innocent advances.[1] It has been doubted whether this doctrine can apply to personal property,[2] but Riddell v Munro[3] holds that it does, and no good reason can be seen for any discrimination in this regard. Equity protects the transferee by virtue of its jurisdiction to specifically enforce the obligations of parties relating to the transfer or disposition of specific property. In short, it raises a trust with respect to the property in behalf of a person who has advanced money on the faith of an agreement that upon its full performance he may have the title to the property. In the present case the agreement becomes impossible of completion at the moment when the transferee receives notice of the transferor's fraudulent intent, but the equity court finds it possible to protect the transferee to the extent of the money which he has already advanced under the agreement, giving him an equitable lien upon the property to that extent. Consequently, in this class of cases the mere fact that the property is personalty instead of real estate should make no difference, because the transferee's remedy at law would be inadequate in either case, and the property is just as specifically identified in the one case as the other.

§ 156. **Extension of Doctrine** This doctrine has been carried a logical step further. Although the purchaser has paid nothing when he discovers the fraud, yet if he is in such a position that he is compelled to pay anyhow, a court of equity will protect him, allowing him to retain the property as security for the amount for which he is thus obligated This situation occurs where the transferee has given purchase money notes for the

---

[1] Clements v. Moore, 6 Wall 299, Florence Sewing Mach. Co. v. Zeigler, 58 Ala 221, Work v Coverdale, 47 Kans 307 27 Pac 984.
[2] Crockett v Phinney, supra, Florence &c. Co v Zeigler, supra
[3] 49 Minn 532, 52 N W 141.

property, and the transferor has negotiated some of them in due course As the transferee has no defense to the notes which have been negotiated, equity will protect him to the extent of allowing him to hold the property as security *pro tanto*[1] But he does not need this protection if all his purchase money notes have thus been negotiated Then he is a purchaser within the meaning of the statute, according to the view of the Indiana Supreme Court, because the value stipulated has been given, the grantor having realized on that value by his negotiation of the notes.[2]

[1] Nicols *v* Crittenden, 55 Ga 497.
[2] Seager *v.* Aughe, 97 Ind 285.

CHAPTER VIII

FRAUDULENT TRANSFER (*CONTINUED*). RIGHTS OF SUBSEQUENT CREDITORS

§ 157 Distinction in Principle between Present and Subsequent Creditors
158 Early Rule in Cases of Gifts
159 Result of Rule
160 Present English Rule
161 Discussion of the Two Rules thus far Stated
162. Another Point of View Suggested
163 The Prevailing American Rule
164. The Doctrine as Stated in Iowa
§ 165 Criticism of This Statement.
166 Other Statements of the Rule
167 Criticism of These Statements
168. Illustration of Express Intent
169 Illustration of Imputed Intent.
170 The Test Repeated.
171 Application of the Rule to Contract Claims
172. Application of the Rule to Tort Claims

§ 157 **Distinction in Principle between Present and Subsequent Creditors.** We must now consider the situation where persons, who become creditors after the transfer is made, assert that it was a fraud upon their right of realization. In the nature of things, a proposition of law to support a claim of this sort cannot be stated very broadly. The right of the creditor is to realize upon his debtor's property, but there never was a right to realize on everything that at one time or another had been the debtor's property. While the statute protects, under the name of creditors, those to whom the debtor owed money although they had not yet obtained judgments upon their claims, and consequently forbade the debtor to transfer his property so as to impair their prospect of realization when they should obtain judgments, that was as far as it went. By its use of the word "others," it included subsequent creditors in its prohibition of transfers by the debtor, but of necessity the interpretation of the statute in this regard should proceed upon narrower lines It must be remembered that the statute forbids a transfer by a debtor only when it is made with intent to hinder, delay or defraud his creditors, whether present or subsequent In the end, as we have seen in our discussion of the rights of present creditors, the question is of the debtor's intent When his intent in regard to his subsequent creditors is concerned, we should draw the line tighter, or else, by means of intolerable restrictions founded upon artificial presumptions, the freedom of action which one should have with respect to his own affairs would be most unjustly abridged. Of this as a general proposition there was never a doubt. It was recognized in Shaw *v.* Standish [1] that a conveyance might well be void against present creditors, and good against those who extended credit afterward, and to the same effect was the opinion of Lord Hardwicke [2] To use the words of Chancellor Kent,[3] "it seems to have been long since settled, that if the party be not indebted at the time, and has no fraudulent views, a subsequent creditor cannot impeach a prior settlement, on the mere ground of its being voluntary."

§ 158. **Early Rule in Cases of Gifts.** Notwithstanding, we find at the outset an artificial rule relating to the validity of gifts as against subsequent creditors, just as we found it in regard to present creditors, and emanating from the same high authorities. In Taylor *v.* Jones [4] Lord Hardwicke advanced the proposition that if the donor was indebted at all at the time of the transfer, then his subsequent creditors could set it aside, because, as the present creditors had this right, it should be extended to the subsequent creditors on that basis of equality upon which rests the equitable doctrine of marshaling In Reade *v* Livingston [5] which we have discussed in Chapter VI, Chancellor Kent supported this view by way of dictum, assert-

---

[1] 1 Vern 326
[2] Russell *v* Hammond, 1 Atk. 15.
[3] Reade *v.* Livingston, 3 Johns Ch 481.
[4] 2 Atk. 600
[5] *Supra*

ing " that indebtedness at the time will defeat a post-nuptial voluntary settlement, and that if it be set aside in favor of a creditor at the time, all the subsequent creditors are let in on the principle of equal apportionment, or marshaling of assets."

§ 159 **Result of Rule.** Thus a rule, peculiar to the courts of equity, was started, and a line of cleavage was established, whereby in equity a creditor of a certain class was given privileges which he did not have at law Up to now, as we have seen, the Chancery Court only gave ancillary relief to the creditor in cases arising under the statute, by virtue of this theory of marshaling, it undertook to give the subsequent creditor a right of realization of which a common law court, which knows no doctrine of marshaling, could not conceive. Nor was this doctrine restricted to equitable assets; it applied to all assets, and created, therefore, in favor of the subsequent creditor, a distinct equity in the debtor's general estate, under color of the Statute of Fraudulent Conveyances.[1]

§ 160 **Present English Rule.** In common with the doctrine of Lord Hardwicke and Chancellor Kent respecting the validity of gifts against present creditors, this rule did not long maintain undisputed sway In England strong opinion to the contrary was expressed in Stephen v Olive,[2] and in Lush v. Wilkinson[3] by Lord Alvanley, M. R. "To show any existing debts, however trifling and inevitable," he said, "would not surely support a presumption of fraud in fact, no voluntary settlement in any possible case could stand, upon that construction." The result finally reached by the English courts is that if the conveyance was fraudulent as against the existing creditors, under the principle discussed in the last two chapters, and

[1] The curious feature of this doctrine in its application was that, although it professed to rest on a rule of equity whose design is to secure equality of distribution, yet a single creditor was allowed to avail himself of it, and obtain the usual priority by superior diligence in filing his bill See Todd v Weal, 49 Ala. 266; Bigelow, "Fraudulent Conveyances," p 108 n
[2] 2 Bro C C. 90
[3] 5 Vesey 384

they still remain unpaid, a subsequent creditor can file the bill himself, or come into such distributive proceedings as the present creditors may have instituted.[1] This view practically amounts to this The court does not trouble to draw the line between the creditors when once it has a fraudulent conveyance which would be voidable if no further debts had been contracted, provided the original debts, or some of them, remain in existence. In many of our States that is the view as well,[2] and some of the lower federal courts have adopted the same view.[3]

§ 161 **Discussion of the Two Rules thus far Stated.** This doctrine of the modern English courts has much to support it, provided, of course, that in determining whether the transfer was fraudulent as to the present creditors, resort be had, not to the artificial test prescribed by Chancellor Kent and Lord Hardwicke, as discussed in Chapter VI, but to the sounder tests which represent the modern views. Thus, if a man gives away his property while insolvent, or the effect of the transfer is to leave him insolvent, then there is no good reason for discriminating between his present and his subsequent creditors. If a "present" creditor can complain of the transaction and set it aside, why should others be excluded because they became creditors later? On the other hand, if at the time of the transfer the debtor was solvent though indebted, or if he later becomes solvent, and in either case pays off those debts which he owed at the time of his transfer, on what principle of reason can later creditors attack the transfer? What if he was indebted at the time, since he was able to pay his debts and did pay them? To

---

[1] Freeman v Pope, L R 5 Ch App 538, Ideal Mfg Co v Holland, 1907 2 Ch. 157, Bigelow, 'Fraudulent Conveyances," p. 95
[2] Redfield v Buck 35 Conn 328, Pelham v Aldrich, 8 Gray 515. See Bigelow, "Fraudulent Conveyances," p 99
[3] Ridgeway v Underwood, 4 Wash C C 129 Fed Case No 11815 It must be remembered, however, that despite such early decisions as Warren v Moody, 122 U S 132, 7 S Ct 1063, the Supreme Court has prescribed that all federal courts, including itself, shall follow, in cases of fraudulent transfer, the law of the State where the property is located, Schreyer v Scott, 134 U S 405, 10 S Ct 579

128   THE RIGHTS AND REMEDIES OF CREDITORS   [CHAP. VIII.

allow recovery would be to allow a creditor to search all his debtor's past transactions without hindrance as to limitations of time or of cause and effect. That is the logical result of the Hardwicke-Kent doctrine, but can it be tolerated in view of the exigencies of the modern economic state? Is it not obvious, therefore, that some other mode of reasoning should be adopted?

§ 162   **Another Point of View Suggested**   Unless the creditor is to have a lien upon the debtor's entire past, the courts should refuse to give a subsequent creditor relief unless the prior transfer is connected with the present debt by some process of causation. To put it in another way, it seems clear that the subsequent creditors should not be heard unless they can show that the debtor intended to defraud them, just as the statute says. And in reaching the debtor's intent the imminence of the debts in question must appear in connection with the transfer   Such is the case where a man is already insolvent when he makes a gift, or it leaves him insolvent, and then, without paying his present creditors, he passes along until some one puts his affairs into the course of liquidation   No distinction should be drawn between the two classes of creditors, because the intent to defraud the one is just as clear as the intent to defraud the other. This is illustrated by the following language of the Massachusetts court.[1]

"This is not a case of voluntary conveyance which would be good against subsequent creditors if not tainted with any fraud. The jury have found that the conveyance to the tenant was made with a fraudulent purpose. The instruction requested is based upon the assumption that the only ground upon which subsequent creditors can impeach a conveyance by their debtor, is that it is made with specific intent to contract future debts to them and avoid the payment of the same This is not the law. It is well settled that if a debtor makes a conveyance with the purpose of defrauding either existing or future creditors, it may be impeached by either class of creditor, or by an assignee in insolvency or bankruptcy who represents

[1] Day v Cooley, 118 Mass 524

both. As it was proved in this case that the grantor had an actual fraudulent design which was participated in by the grantee, it is immaterial whether the demandants are to be regarded as subsequent or existing creditors as to the conveyance."

§ 163. **The Prevailing American Rule** In short, the test should be whether the debtor, at the time of the transfer, had in mind the future obligations that were to accrue, and made the transfer with a view to lessening his available estate against the time of their realization. Such is the view that has been adopted in a number of our jurisdictions, whose courts reduce all such cases to the test we have just stated. The cases, according to this, arrange themselves under two heads: (1) The debtor has remained in such control of the property as to induce the belief that it was still his own, or (2) the transfer was made under such circumstances as to show an intention to contract the debt in question while removing the property from its reach. Among the States whose courts maintain such views are New York, Massachusetts and Pennsylvania [1] While of late years the federal courts have abstained from expressing any views of their own on such questions, preferring to follow the law of the particular State of the property's location, yet earlier decisions of the Supreme Court have most emphatically been to the same effect [2] But although the courts of these States seem agreed upon this rule in actual application, yet they have not been equally happy in its expression.

§ 164 **The Doctrine as Stated in Iowa.** The Supreme Court of Iowa has laid it down as follows: [3]

"(1) A conveyance which is merely voluntary, and when the grantor had no fraudulent view or intent, cannot be im-

---

[1] Todd v. Nelson, 109 N Y. 316, 16 N E 360, Harlan v. Maglaughlin, 90 Pa. St. 293, Pelham v. Aldrich, supra; Brundage v Chenoworth, 101 Iowa 256, 70 N W 211; Re Stone, 206 Fed 356
[2] Sexton v Wheaton, 8 Wheat. 229; Warren v Moody, 122 U. S 132, 7 S Ct 1063; Mattingly v Nye, 8 Wall 370
[3] Brundage v Chenoworth, supra

peached by a subsequent creditor. (2) A conveyance actually and intentionally fraudulent as to existing creditors, as a general rule, cannot be impeached by subsequent creditors. (3) If a conveyance is actually fraudulent as to existing creditors, and merely colorable, and the property is held in secret trust for the grantor, who is permitted to use it as his own, it will be set aside at the instance of subsequent creditors The second rule above laid down is subject to some exceptions, among which may be mentioned cases in which the conveyance is made by the grantor with the express intent and view of defrauding those who may thereafter become his creditors, cases wherein the grantor makes the conveyance with the express intent of becoming thereafter indebted; cases of voluntary conveyances, when the grantor pays existing creditors by contracting other indebtedness in a like amount, and wherein the subsequent creditors are subrogated to the rights of the creditor whose debts their means have been used to pay; cases in which one makes a conveyance to avoid the risks, or losses, likely to result from new business ventures, or speculations "

§ 165. **Criticism of This Statement.** This is not a good statement, because the second heading admits of too many exceptions Thus, in addition to those which the court enumerates may be cited the case already put, where an insolvent debtor gives away his property, and then contracts subsequent debts, paying nobody. No court has cut off the subsequent creditors in such a case; the general rule, as we have seen, is to let them in, since the debtor must have intended to defraud all his creditors, those on hand and those to come.

§ 166. **Other Statements of the Rule.** The New York Court of Appeals makes this classification .[1]

"The theory upon which deeds conveying the property of an individual to some third party have been set aside as fraudulent in regard to subsequent creditors of the grantor has been that he has made a secret conveyance of his property while remaining in the possession and seeming ownership thereof, and has obtained credit thereby, while embarking in

[1] Todd *v* Nelson, *supra*

some hazardous business requiring such credit, or the debts which he has incurred were incurred soon after the conveyance, thus making the fraudulent intent a natural and almost necessary inference, and in this way he has been enabled to obtain the property of others who were relying upon an appearance which was wholly delusive "

And the Supreme Court of the United States has followed in the same strain : [1]

"From these authorities it is evident that the rule obtaining in New York, as well as recognized by this court, is, that even a voluntary conveyance from husband to wife is good as against subsequent creditors, unless it was made with the intent to defraud such subsequent creditors; or that there was secrecy in the transaction by which knowledge of it was withheld from such creditors, who dealt with the grantor upon the faith of his owning the property transferred ; or that the transfer was made with a view of entering into some new and hazardous business, the risk of which the grantor intended should be cast upon the parties having dealings with him in the new business "

§ 167. **Criticism of These Statements** These statements are too narrow, as there are cases besides those which they mention ; we need only enumerate the instance already used for purpose of illustration. It would therefore seem better to adopt the broad rule which appeared as a conclusion from the foregoing discussion, that a transfer, whether by way of gift or for value to one who is not a *bona fide* purchaser, is fraudulent as to subsequent creditors if the debtor had the prospect of these future debts in mind when he made the transfer In the words of the Massachusetts court, there must be " an intent on the part of the grantor to contract debts, and a design to avoid payment of such debts, by the conveyance of his property." [2] This fraudulent intent is to be gathered either from (1) direct evidence as to the debtor's state of mind, or (2) the circumstances of the transfer in connection with the circumstances under

---

[1] Schreyer v Scott, *supra*
[2] Winchester v Charters, 12 Allen 606.

which the future debts arose, tested by the principles of causation.

§ 168 **Illustration of Express Intent** An instance of express fraudulent intent is furnished by Harlan v. Maglaughlin [1] There the Pennsylvania Supreme Court, in setting aside a transfer on the application of a subsequent creditor, stated the presence, among the "elements necessary for a test case" of "an expressed apprehension of a claim for damages" In the case as made up on the record, it appeared that the debtor told a friend "that he was in a good bit of trouble, and that he was going to put what he had, his property, over into Belle's hands," Belle being the name of his wife, the grantee.

§ 169 **Illustration of Imputed Intent.** An instance of the second class is where a man, about to enter a hazardous business which is to be done largely upon credit, settles his available property upon his wife In such a case, to use the words of Jessel, M. R., "The grantor virtually says, if I succeed in business, I make a fortune for myself If I fail, I leave my creditors unpaid" That, continues the Master of the Rolls, "is the very thing that the Statute of Elizabeth was meant to prevent." [2] In such a case as that, it matters not about the present creditors, whether a small amount was left to pay their claims or not, the intent was evident to contract debts and remove the means of meeting them, so it is a case within the statute.[3] The circumstances of the two transactions must bear a relation of causation, they must depend upon each other in that respect; and that is all. If they do not thus connect, no fraudulent intent can be imputed to the debtor In such consideration, time, among other things, is a factor. Thus in Sexton v. Wheaton [4] in holding that there was no fraud in such a case, the court notes that it did not appear "that any of the debts which pressed upon Wheaton at the time of his failure were

[1] *Supra*
[2] *Ex parte* Russell, 19 Ch D 588; Monroe v. Smith, 79 Pa St. 459.
[3] Case v Phelps, 39 N Y 164. [4] *Supra*.

contracted before he entered into commerce in 1809, which was more than two years after the execution of the deed." But time alone may not be controlling, it did not control the decision in that case, for it also appeared that when the transfer was made, the debtor " had no view to trade." Hence, continues the court, " although his failure was not very remote from the date of the deed, yet the debts and the deed can in no manner be connected with each other; they are as distinct as if they had been a century apart "

§ 170. **The Test Repeated.** The above, indeed, is such a clear case under the statute that both the New York Court of Appeals and the Federal Supreme Court have considered it as one of the two chief cases The other is the case where the debtor remains in apparent ownership of the property, so as to induce the inference that the subsequent creditors were misled into extending credit by this circumstance Of these cases we shall speak in another connection,[1] so no more need be said of them here But there are still other groups of cases which illustrate the rule above suggested, and demonstrate that the judicial classifications we have quoted are too narrow In all such cases, it is believed, the first question to be asked is, is there direct evidence showing the debtor's intent, as in Harlan v. Maglaughlin, which we have already instanced? If that question is answered in the negative, then the inquiry should be as to the circumstances of the transfer, and the circumstances under which the debt in question was contracted If they join themselves in a chain of causation, then the transfer is within the statute.

§ 171. **Application of the Rule to Contract Claims** In the application of such a rule, should there be a distinction between debts founded in contract, and those which spring from judgments based upon torts? In the first class the point of inquiry ought to be whether the contract existed when the transfer was made, or whether its creation was within the debtor's contemplation. If so, then he ought to be considered as having contem-

[1] *Infra*, Chapter IX.

plated, in addition to the contract, the possibility of a breach of it by himself from which indebtedness would result. Thus if, at the time of the transfer, the debtor was surety on an undertaking, should he not be considered as making the transfer in anticipation of the principal's subsequent default and inability to make good, which event would make the surety liable? The general current of decisions is in the affirmative; " A contingent claim," says the Alabama Supreme Court, " is as fully protected as a claim that is certain and absolute " [1] In the same way, a tenant who transfers his property prior to a breach of a covenant contained in the lease defrauds his landlord within the meaning of the statute [2] In Severs v. Dobson [3] a contrary result was reached in the case of a guaranty made by the debtor; but that case has been distinguished by a lower court of the same State, as concerned with the artificial rule of Reade v Livingston, and as deciding only the question whether the transfer was to be conclusively presumed fraudulent, because, at its date, the donor was presently indebted to other parties.[4]

§ 172. **Application of the Rule to Tort Claims** The case of a tort liability is quite different. If, at the time of the transfer, the debtor has invaded the rights of another, and thus has given occasion for an action for damages, or if, indeed, he is being sued upon a cause of action which, though nominally contractual, may be classed with tort actions in respect to the rule of damages governing it, such as the breach of promise to marry, then can his transfer be considered as having been made with a view to defraud the plaintiff in realizing upon such a judgment as might be obtained? If the artificial Kent-Hardwicke idea is followed, the answer would depend upon whether the defendant owed any debts at the date of the transfer. If the sounder rule

---

[1] Yeend v Weeks, 104 Ala. 331, 16 So 165; Thomson v Crane, 73 Fed 327; Young v Heermans, 66 N Y 374; Wright v Nipple, 92 Ind 310
[2] Woodbury v Sparrell Print Co , 187 Mass 426, 73 N E 547.
[3] 53 N J Eq. 633, 34 Atl. 7
[4] Thorp v Leibrecht, 56 N J Eq 499, 39 Atl 361.

above discussed is to apply, then the answer would depend upon whether the debtor's circumstances at the time of the transfer were such that he could have anticipated the recovery of a judgment sufficient in size to be materially injured by the transfer. If he was insolvent, or the transfer rendered him insolvent, then this subsequent judgment creditor should be considered as defrauded together with the present creditors But if the transfer left him able to pay his existing debts, can it be said that he intended to defraud this subsequent judgment creditor? Both the English Court of Appeal [1] and the New York Court of Appeals [2] have decided that such a transfer was not fraudulent But Kain v. Larkin was decided on a question of law as to whether there was a rebuttable presumption as to fraud from the fact of existing indebtedness, and the English decision may be rested on Lord Esher's view of this circumstance — that the action was for breach of promise, and the size of the verdict was largely determined by an accident which the transferor could not have foreseen In Sanders v Logue [3] the same result was reached, but the case is distinguishable in this, that the deceit, upon which the judgment was based, was connected with the purchase of property, and *non constat* the plaintiff might have elected to repudiate the transaction instead of suing for damages. In general, the rule seems to be that one who recovers a judgment for unliquidated damages, whether based upon tort or contract, is a subsequent creditor, if the transaction upon which the judgment rested related back to the date of the transfer.[4] Although in some States a contrary view is entertained,[5] the sound doctrine seems to be that which Malins, V. C., thus enunciates [6]

[1] Exp. Mercer, 17 Q B D 290
[2] Kain v. Larkin, 131 N Y. 300, 30 N E 105
[3] 88 Tenn 355, 12 S W 722.
[4] Thorp v Leibrecht, *supra;* Westmoreland v Powell, 59 Ga. 256, Munson v. Genesee Works, 37 N. Y App Div. 203, 56 N. Y. S 139, Crossley v. Elworthy, L R 12 Eq. 158
[5] Green v Adams, 59 Vt 602, 10 Atl. 742
[6] Crossley v Elworthy, *supra.*

"I must, as I am bound by the verdict of the jury to do, attribute to Mr Elworthy the knowledge that he had made erroneous statements to Mr. Crossley in 1865 and those erroneous statements made him liable for a debt which he did not calculate upon when he executed the settlement, for he did not know till 1867 that the action would be brought. But the result of the action was to prove him to have become indebted in 1865, when he made the false representations by which the liability was created. I do not say that the debt would have been sufficient of itself to invalidate the settlement, but it was a circumstance which, considering the way he was involved in transactions with this company, ought to have led him to pause."

CHAPTER IX

REPUTED OWNERSHIP SOURCES OF THE DOCTRINE

§ 173. Definition of Subject
174. Statute of Fraudulent Conveyances not Wholly Adequate.
175. Application of Statute of Fraudulent Conveyances
176. Rule of Twyne's Case
177. Separation of Ownership from Possession not Conclusive.
178. Secrecy not Conclusive
179. Separation Accompanied by Secrecy
180. Other Cases Covered by Another Statute.
181. The Original "Reputed Ownership Clause" of the Bankrupt Statute
182. Present English Statute
183. The Statute as a Supplement to the Statute of Fraudulent Conveyances
184. Limitations of the Reputed Ownership Statute It only Applies in Cases of Bankruptcy.
185. It does not Apply to Real Estate
186. Other Statutes Relating to Real Estate
187. Statute of Reputed Ownership does not Apply to Equitable Assets
188. Lord Hardwicke's Interpretation of the Statute
§ 189. Statute's Application Limited to Trade Debts
190. Criticisms of the Statute by English Courts
191. Statute does not Apply to Stoppage in Transit
192. Statute does not Apply to General Assignment
193. Statute does not Apply to Consignments or Conditional Sale
194. Reasons Assigned for these Exceptions
195. Reasonable use of Commercial Custom
196. Debtor's Status in the Business to which the Custom Appertains.
197. Proof of Custom
198. Absence of Similar Statutes in America.
199. View of the Illinois and Pennsylvania Courts
200. Estoppel as American Substitute for Statute
201. Estoppel the Spirit of the Statute
202. The American Doctrine of Estoppel.
203. Exceptions to American Rule.
204. American Rule does not Apply to Choses in Action.
205. Criticism of This Limitation.

§ 173. **Definition of Subject.** The situation with which we will now deal is where a man, not the owner of property, is held out as the owner under such circumstances as would be reasonably calculated to induce the extension of credit to him upon the faith of his apparent ownership. In such a case, when he becomes insolvent, the question is whether the true owner can assert his title to the property in question as against the persons who have become creditors of the apparent owner.

§ 174. **Statute of Fraudulent Conveyances not Wholly Adequate** The Statute of Fraudulent Conveyances is not adequate for all the cases presenting this question. The statute is insufficient because it applies only to transfers by the debtor of property previously owned by him, and cannot cover the case of property never owned by the debtor, but of which he was placed in possession with indicia of ownership

§ 175 **Application of Statute of Fraudulent Conveyances.** So far as it goes, however, the Statute of Fraudulent Conveyances is adequate It can vindicate the rights of subsequent creditors where, to use the words of the New York court, "the debts were incurred soon after the conveyance, thus making the fraudulent intent a natural and almost necessary inference, and in this way he (the debtor) has been enabled to obtain the property of others who were relying upon an appearance which was wholly delusive."[1]

§ 176. **Rule of Twyne's Case.** In any such case the doctrine of Twyne's Case,[2] that the separation of the possession from the ownership is a badge of fraud, would apply. "The donor," said Coke of that case, " continued in possession (of the goods) and used them as his own, and by reason thereof he traded and trafficked with others, and deceived and defrauded them " Therefore, continued Coke, in his advice to the reader, " immediately after the gift, take the possession of them " Thus arose the well-settled doctrine under the statute of Fraudulent Conveyances, in all cases where that statute could apply, that where the debtor had transferred the title of property to another, the

---

[1] Todd v. Nelson, 109 N Y. 316, 16 N E. 360.
[2] 3 Co Rep 80b.

separation of ownership from possession was a badge of fraud. If later, the subsequent creditors could not satisfy their debts out of the other property, then the transfer of the property in question would be set aside in their favor. The rule, however, was subject to two important qualifications.

§ 177. **Separation of Ownership from Possession not Conclusive** The first was that the separation of ownership from possession was not conclusive in favor of the creditors, it was a mere badge of fraud, which could in a proper case, be overcome At one time the contrary was thought to be the case In Edwards v. Harben,[1] Buller, J, pronounced in favor of the view that the separation of possession from ownership was conclusively fraudulent in every case where chattels were concerned, and consequently a conditional sale agreement (of which we will have more to say later) was void as matter of law, as against the creditors of the vendee This decision is out of place here, because the case did not come within the Statute of Fraudulent Conveyances at all, by virtue of the distinction we have already noted, since the vendee never transferred the property, but rather received it as a bailment,[2] but it is well to mention it in the present connection, as its doctrine is broad enough to apply to proper cases of fraudulent conveyance But it was overruled in Martindale v Booth[3] where the conditional sale was upheld, the court announcing that the separation of possession from ownership was not an universal badge of fraud, and that in certain cases the separation raised not even a presumption of fraud.

§ 178 **Secrecy not Conclusive** The second qualification involves another badge of fraud mentioned in Twyne's Case — secrecy. The gift, Coke notes, " was made in secret, *et dona clandestina sunt semper suspiciosa* " Therefore, he counsels the reader, let the transfer " be made in a public manner, and

---

[1] 2 T R 587
[2] *See* Harkness v Russell, 118 U. S. 663, 7 S. Ct. 51.
[3] 3 B & Ad 498

before the neighbors, and not in private, for secrecy is a mark of fraud "[1] But here again we must not take this too unreservedly. Of itself secrecy is not a characteristic that will annul every transaction While undoubtedly "the fewer secret liens and trusts there are the better,"[2] there can be no doubt as well that the mere secrecy of a transaction is not the controlling factor in determining the rights of creditors, whether under the Statute of Fraudulent Conveyances or otherwise[3]

§ 179. **Separation Accompanied by Secrecy** But separation of ownership from possession, accompanied by secrecy, does furnish, in certain respects, a strong case for the relief of subsequent creditors under the Statute of Fraudulent Conveyances. In Martin v Baker[4] it was laid down that, as against a creditor levying on goods in the debtor's possession but claimed by another, the transaction by which the claimant acquired title was no fraud under the statute if it was not consummated secretly, but was notorious in the community The same opinion was voiced by Bayley, J, who considered the question as whether "the circumstances under which he has the possession are known in the neighborhood."[5] "Possession is much to be regarded," said Abbott, C. J, in the same case, "but that is with a view to ascertain the good or bad faith of the transaction" That is also the view of our courts;[6] in some States, in fact, this doctrine has been expressed in the State's reenactment of the Statute of Fraudulent Conveyances Speaking of such a statute, as of force in Missouri, the Supreme Court described its object as "to prevent parties from being misled by apparent ownership of property, where real ownership does not exist, but where a secret transfer has been made to another."[7]

[1] Twyne's Case, *supra*
[2] Lacombe, J, in *Re* Southern Textile Co., 174 Fed. 523.
[3] Greey v. Dockendorff, 231 U. S. 513; 34 S. Ct. 166.
[4] 1 M & S 251
[5] Latimer v. Batson, 4 B & C 652
[6] Macomber v. Parker, 14 Pick 497.
[7] Allen v Massey, 17 Wall. 351

§ 180 **Other Cases Covered by Another Statute** It is now time, however, to look beyond the limited range of the Statute of Fraudulent Conveyances for some standard of authority which can be applied to those many cases of reputed ownership to which the statute just mentioned could not apply. Going back to the early days, our search is rewarded by another statute, of almost contemporaneous date. Outside of the Statute of Fraudulent Conveyances, the doctrine of reputed ownership began in England with a statute, and it ends to-day in England with a statute.

§ 181 **The Original " Reputed Ownership Clause " of the Bankrupt Statute** In 1623 an Act of Parliament was adopted " for the further description of a bankrupt and relief of creditors against such as shall become bankrupts, and for inflicting corporal punishment upon the bankrupts in some special case." [1] The 11th section of the statute thus provides:

"If at any time hereafter any person or persons shall become bankrupt, and at such time as they shall so become bankrupt shall by the consent and permission of the true owner and proprietary have in their possession, order and disposition, any goods or chattels, whereof they shall be reputed owners, and take upon them the sale, alteration or disposition as owners, that in every such case the said commissioners or the greater part of them shall have power to sell and dispose the same, to and for the benefit of the creditors which shall seek relief by the said commission, as fully as any other part of the estate of the bankrupt."

In other words, Parliament provided that in such a case as above mentioned, if the party became a bankrupt the property thus held by him should be applied as part of his general estate to the payment of his creditor. This was the famous Reputed Ownership Clause which has ever since formed part of the law of England as a part of its bankrupt system.

§ 182. **Present English Statute.** It has been reenacted in

[1] 21 Jac I c 19.

142   THE RIGHTS AND REMEDIES OF CREDITORS.   [CHAP IX

every successive English bankrupt law; and thus appears today in Section 44 of the Bankrupt Act of 1883 [1]

"The property of the bankrupt divisible amongst his creditors and in this act referred to as the property of the bankrupt . . shall comprise the following particulars. . . . All goods being at the commencement of the bankruptcy in the possession, order or disposition of the bankrupt in his trade or business, by the consent and permission of the true owner under such circumstances that he is the reputed owner thereof, provided that things in action other than debts due or growing due to the bankrupt in the course of his trade or business, shall not be deemed goods within the meaning of this section"

§ 183. **The Statute as a Supplement to the Statute of Fraudulent Conveyances.** This statute supplements the Statute of Fraudulent Conveyances The latter, in the proper case, condemns the separation of possession from ownership where the property has been transferred by the debtor. The Reputed Ownership Statute applies not only to such a case as that, but also to cases where the debtor has never made a transfer, but has merely received the delivery of property. In the first reported case which arose under this statute [2] counsel argued that it should be given the same narrow scope as the Statute of Fraudulent Conveyances. The counsel making this point referred to the preamble of the Act, which referred to bankrupts transferring their goods, and submitted that this restrained the words of the "Reputed Ownership Clause" to cases where the debtor had made a sale to another but had not delivered possession, as distinct from the case where the third party had put the debtor in possession of the goods, retaining, however, the title thereto But Lord Cowper, L C, held to the contrary and although Lord Hardwicke and Chief Baron Parker afterwards thought that, on abstract principle, Lord Cowper was wrong in not allowing the preamble of a statute to control its

[1] 46-7 Vict. c. 52
[2] Copeman v Gallant, 2 Eq. Cases Abr 113 pl 2; 1 P Wms 314.

enacting clauses,[1] yet they did not overrule him, and his view remained as law concerning the scope of the Reputed Ownership Clause

§ 184. **Limitations of the Reputed Ownership Statute — It only Applies in Cases of Bankruptcy** On reading this clause, we will observe several limitations which require discussion, and to these let us now address ourselves.

First, the Statute only applied in cases of bankruptcy, that is, where a debtor's property had, by virtue of a statute, been taken into the custody of the court for general distribution among his creditors No single creditor, therefore, can demand its application in aid of either an execution or a judgment creditor's bill When we consider the original intent of bankrupt statutes, however, we can understand this restriction. No historical accident, such as attended the enactment of the Statute of Fraudulent Conveyances, led to the doctrine of reputed ownership starting with a statute The bankrupt acts, in those days, applied only to traders, persons engaged in commerce. It was in connection with commerce that the majority of cases of reputed ownership arose Furthermore, no case of reputed ownership can really arise unless the debtor is insolvent, or at least his creditors cannot readily find enough of his property to satisfy their claims, outside of the property which the third party claims as his own. The bankrupt statutes were originally designed for cases where, by reason of the debtor's supposed evil machinations, his creditors cannot find enough assets to meet their claims. These considerations led to the doctrine of reputed ownership finding its origin in a bankrupt act

§ 185. **It does not Apply to Real Estate.** Secondly, the statute does not apply to real estate This was an exception of point, because from early times the bankrupt acts affected the debtor's lands as well as his goods. The reason for the discrimination, however, was the same as before; the statute applied to traders, traders did not deal much in lands, and a case of re-

[1] Ryall v Rowles, 1 Vesey Sr 348

puted ownership was not so apt to occur in the case of real estate as in situations concerned with tangible chattels. Consequently Kenyon, M R., was right despite the regrets which he professed, in holding that an equitable mortgage of land constituted by the deposit of title deeds was not within the statute.[1]

§ 186 **Other Statutes Relating to Real Estate.** At a much earlier date than the Statute of Fraudulent Conveyances, for that matter, an attempt had been made to reach, by legislation, certain situations of reputed ownership with respect to lands. The Statute of Uses, passed in the time of Henry the Eighth, professed, among other things, to redress the grievances of creditors, who were often misled into believing that the *cestui que use* had the legal title to land of which he was possessed, only to learn that the legal title rested in a trustee, so that no writ of *levari facias* or *elegit* could avail.[2] How this statute eventuated is a story that belongs to the domain of real property law; but we may notice in passing that, when the State of New York adopted a statutory system of trusts, allowing but four kinds of trusts in real estate, her statutes included a provision[3] that no express trust not set forth in writing should be valid as against subsequent creditors of the *cestui que* trust, the object of this provision being to "discourage secret liens."[4]

§ 187 **Statute of Reputed Ownership does not Apply to Equitable Assets.** Thirdly, this statute, like the Statute of Fraudulent Conveyances, did not cover either class of equitable assets, whether choses in action or equities in property. This omission made no difference with regard to the average equitable interest in property, because it would be rare that any situation of reputed ownership could arise in that connection But

---

[1] Edge v Worthington, 1 Cox Ch. 211. Likewise Blackburn v. Gregson, 1 Cox Ch 92, where Lord Thurlow applied the statute to land, seems wrong
[2] See article on the Statute of Uses in 27 Harvard Law Review, p. 115.
[3] Now Sec 104 of the Real Prop. Law
[4] Fowler, "Real Prop Law," 2d ed., p. 420.

choses in action furnished more of a difficulty. It may be said that no one can be in the apparent ownership of a chose in action, because there is no possibility of an effective ostentation of ownership by means of possession. Presently we shall examine the uniform judicial opinion which exists in the United States to that effect, but as we are now dealing with the English statute alone, let us see how the English courts treated this omission

§ 188. **Lord Hardwicke's Interpretation of the Statute** The question first arose in a case before Lord Hardwicke, who summoned several common law judges to aid him in its decision.[1] There the subject matter consisted of tangible property used in partnership operations, and also book debts and accounts receivable which had accrued to the partnership in the course of its operations. Lord Hardwicke applied to these choses in action the same doctrine which we saw him use in connection with the Statute of Fraudulent Conveyances[2] As property rights in choses in action really owe their existence to the doctrine of equity, the court of equity ought to follow, in enforcing rights to choses in action, the spirit of any statute which has been enacted concerning legal titles. The Reputed Ownership Clause was intended to cover property owned and used by a trader The equity court should apply its terms to choses in action when owned by a trader, and used by him in his business. That was the result the Lord Chancellor reached, and thus, in his opinion, he carried out the object of the statute, which was "to prevent traders from gaining a delusive credit by a false appearance of substance to mislead those who deal with them"[3]

§ 189 **Statute's Application Limited to Trade Debts** Lord Hardwicke's decision extended no further than to book debts and bills receivable which had been acquired in the course of business, and later decisions emphasized this limitation The

---

[1] Ryall v Rowles, *supra*
[2] *Supra*, Ch IV
[3] Ryall v Rowles, *supra*.

146 THE RIGHTS AND REMEDIES OF CREDITORS. [CHAP IX.

statute does not apply to any other class of choses in action, such as shares of stock or the like.[1] Such property, says Lord Redesdale, whose opinion Baron Parke has characterized as the best exposition of the doctrine,[2] is not to be considered as in the debtor's control by virtue of any "unconscientious permission" of the true owner.[3] The present statute covers the matter in the section already quoted, the reputed ownership clause expressly applies to debts due or to grow due to the bankrupt in the course of his trade or business, and hence excludes all others.

§ 190. **Criticisms of the Statute by English Courts.** Thus limited and thus construed, the Reputed Ownership Clause has passed through English judicial history to the present day. But its benefits have never been extended beyond the subject of bankruptcy, and it has always been regarded with more or less disfavor This state of mind towards the statute has prevented its inclusion in other statutes providing for the general distribution of a debtor's effects; there was no such clause in the Insolvent Debtors' Acts, and there is no such clause in the Companies Acts,[4] although in England, as well as here, the average "trader" of to-day may be an incorporated company instead of an individual or a partnership While undoubtedly it is "a rough approach to that justice which is meted out by the law of estoppel,"[5] it is, as Christian, L J, described it, "probably the only instance of our law in which not only purposely but avowedly the property of one man is laid hold of to answer the debt of another."[6] The common law courts of England, however, are largely to blame for the general dislike which the statute encounters. At their hands it received a construction

[1] Joy v Campbell, 1 Sch & Lef 328, Colonial Bank v. Whinney, L R 11 A C 426
[2] Whitfield v Brand, 16 M & W 282
[3] Joy v Campbell, *supra*
[4] See opinion of Lord Fitzgerald in Colonial Bank v. Whinney, *supra;* Re Crumlin Viaduct Co, 11 Ch D 755.
[5] Ewart on Estoppel, p 301
[6] *In re* Hickey, 10 Irish Rep. Eq 129

which rendered it almost unbearable It was held that it was immaterial whether the creditors extended credit before or after the ostentation of ownership was effected, and that the true owner could with impunity remove the goods at any time prior to the bankruptcy, although credit may have been actually extended on the behalf of the bankrupt's apparent ownership.[1] In the middle of the nineteenth century Pollock, C B., described the doctrine of reputed ownership as having been completely out of fashion for at least forty years[2] This is, however, an extreme statement A more accurate commentary is afforded by the language of Lord Selbourne, " that the courts have of late years looked more narrowly and closely to the real weight and value of the facts which tend on the one hand to confirm and on the other hand to exclude the representation of ownership "[3]

§ 191 **Statute does not Apply to Stoppage in Transit.** In general, indeed, the operation of the statute was restricted to cases within the limits of good sense The courts soon came to put certain limits upon its operation, which would permit honest transactions of commerce to go uninjured In one of the earliest cases where the right of stoppage in transit was recognized, it was held that although goods had been delivered to the carrier and the latter for the purpose of sale was the agent of the vendee, yet if the vendee became bankrupt the goods could be stopped in transit. That was the unreported case of *Ex parte* Wilkinson[4] before Lord Hardwicke. There Lord Hardwicke said, " as there was no possession in the bankrupt, no appearance of credit on the goods, nor any payments made, the agent had a right to stop them "

§ 192 **Statute does not Apply to General Assignment** The first case which has been found under the statute was decided

---

[1] Young *v* Hope, 2 Ex. 105, Ewart, " Estoppel," 300–1
[2] Prismall *v* Lovegrove, 6 L T N S 329
[3] *Ex parte* Watkins, L R 8 Ch App 520-32
[4] *Ex parte Wilkinson*, in Ch Mar 21, 1755, cited by counsel in D'Aquila *v* Lambert, 2 Eden 75

at an even earlier date by Lord Cowper in 1716.[1] It appeared that A made a general assignment for the payment of his debts, but the assignee later became a bankrupt. The Lord Chancellor held the case not to be within the statute, because the assignment " was with an honest intent."

§ 193. **Statute does not Apply to Consignments or Conditional Sale.** Then Lord Mansfield came to the Chief Justiceship of the King's Bench, and straightway the common law courts proceeded to lay down certain wholesome exceptions to the statute. In Mace v. Cadell,[2] it was held that goods in a factor's hands do not fall within this description. This was followed by two cases which illustrate the distinction presently to be stated. In Edwards v. Harben[3] there is a notable dictum by Buller, J., that a conditional sale was void as matter of law if the vendee was let into possession of the bargained property. But in Martindale v. Booth[4] this was overruled, and it was held that, if such a possession had been made one of the terms of the original contract, no case of ostensible ownership was presented.

§ 194. **Reasons Assigned for these Exceptions.** On what principle can these exceptions be recognized? Lord Mansfield, in holding that goods in a factor's possession are not available to creditors under the statute,[5] states as the reason that the goods were not " put into the hands of the factor for a fraudulent purpose." Lord Cowper, in Copeman v. Gallant,[6] in holding that a general assignment was not within the statute, says that it is because the debtor executed the instrument " with an honest intent." As said by Mr. Justice Burnett[7] the separation of possession from ownership is not a badge of fraud " unless as calculated to deceive creditors." Lord Redesdale[8] makes the test whether possession had " unconscientiously " been left with the insolvent.

[1] Copeman v. Gallant, 2 Eq. Ca. Ab. 113.
[2] 1 Cowp. 233.
[3] 2 T. R. 587.
[4] 3 B. & Ad. 498.
[5] Mace v. Cadell, *supra*.
[6] *Supra*.
[7] Ryall v. Rowles, *supra*.
[8] Joy v. Campbell, *supra*.

§ 195. **Reasonable Use of Commercial Custom.** It does not suffice to deduce from this that good faith is the test. That is a convenient working proposition, but it will not wholly suffice Practically we will have to say that while good faith in one sense is the test, yet in deciding whether the transaction is in good faith, we must determine whether it involved a reasonable use of a commercial custom. For example, the relation of principal and factor is well known, and, other things being equal, a party should not be made to suffer under the terms of the statute because he followed a well-recognized commercial usage in intrusting his goods to the factor for sale.

§ 196. **Debtor's Status in the Business to which the Custom Appertains** But the mere fact that a commercial custom has been followed is not in itself sufficient. It must be attended by all the usual circumstances of the honest transaction If it were not known in general that a person was a factor, if his status as such is not established in the community, then, of course, if he takes goods on consignment as a factor, the true owner must in some wise give notice to the public that, with respect to these particular goods, the bailee is not acting on his own account and with his own property [1] This point has been graphically put by Jessell, M. R., as follows:

"If a man says to his creditors, 'I carry on business as a merchant and factor,' can the creditor say, 'I give you credit on the faith that any goods in your warehouse belong to you, not as a factor, but as a merchant'? The creditor knows that, by reason of the business carried on, the goods may not belong to the debtor, and it cannot be said that credit was given on the faith that the goods were his own." [2]

§ 197. **Proof of Custom** This principle has been carried to a great extent in England within late years, in favor of elimi-

---

[1] *Ex parte* Bright, 10 Ch. D 566, *Ex parte* Buck, 3 Ch. D 795; Ommen v. Talcott, 188 Fed. 401.
[2] *Ex parte* Bright, 10 Ch Div. 566

nating from the statute transactions permitted by customs of trade. To quote Lord Selborne, " A custom known to the whole trade, and to all persons dealing with the trade, surely is as well advertised, perhaps better advertised, than it would be by a notice posted over the door." [1] In connection with this, the English courts have reached the point of taking judicial notice of a custom in a particular trade after it has been proven several times in previous cases. Thus, while we find frequent instances where the existence of a custom has been proven as a particular fact, such as the custom of selling pianos on the installment plan [2] and a custom of wine merchants in Liverpool, [3] it is not always necessary to prove the existence of the custom. There is a point where the courts begin to take judicial notice of its existence, the test being whether the custom has " existed so long and been so extensively acted upon, that the ordinary creditors of the debtor in his trade may be reasonably presumed to have known it " [4] The courts can reach that result of their own motion, or they may be compelled to do so by the fact that in many cases the existence of the custom has been uniformly demonstrated by evidence.[5]

§ 198. **Absence of Similar Statutes in America** The Statute of James which contained the Reputed Ownership Clause did not pass to the American States by inheritance, because it was part of a bankrupt act, and the States did not inherit the bankruptcy system of England. In the first national bankrupt act of 1800, this clause appeared,[6] but it is not a part of any of the later bankrupt acts, nor was it ever a part of the statute law of any of our States.[7]

[1] *Ex parte* Watkins, L R. 8 Ch App 520.
[2] *Ex parte* Hattersley, 8 Ch Div 601.
[3] *Ex parte* Watkins, L R 8 Ch App 520
[4] Mellish, L J , in *Ex parte* Powell, 1 Ch Div. 501, 508
[5] Crawcour v Salter, 18 Ch Div 30, *Ex parte* Powell, 1 Ch Div 501. *In re* Brener, 166 Fed. 930
[6] See Sands v Codwise, 4 Johns. Ch 536
[7] Freelinghuysen v Nugent, 36 Fed 229, Harkness v. Russell, 118 U. S 663, 7 S Ct 51

§ 199. **View of the Illinois and Pennsylvania Courts.** A curious mistake, however, has been made by the courts of Illinois and Pennsylvania with regard to this situation. Overlooking the fact that the Reputed Ownership Statute is not part of our inheritance, and overlooking as well the fact that the particular decision in question had been overruled in England, it has been thought that Edwards v. Harben [1] expresses a principle of the common law in its decision that a conditional sale is void as a matter of law as against the vendee's creditors.[2]

§ 200. **Estoppel as American Substitute for Statute.** Outside of this instance it may confidently be said that reputed ownership in this country must be left to something other than a statute of reputed ownership. Nevertheless an effective substitute for this statute has been found in that principle of equity known as estoppel.

§ 201. **Estoppel the Spirit of the Statute.** As we have seen, the statute in itself is a "rough approach" to the principle of estoppel. As said by Parker, C. J., the statute's object was simply "to prevent that false credit which was destructive to trade."[3] The first decision under it was Copeman v Gallant [4] which we have already examined. Prior to this decision, however, the Court of Chancery had said by way of dictum, that "a deed, not at first fraudulent, may afterward become so by being concealed or not pursued, by which means creditors are drawn in to lend their money."[5] Later Lord Camden expressed the same idea,[6] placing the creditors in such a case "within

---

[1] Edwards v. Harben, *supra*.
[2] This mistake was pointed out by Mr Justice Bradley in Harkness v Russell, 118 U S. 663, 7 S Ct 51
[3] Ryall v. Rowles, 1 Vesey Sr. 348
[4] *Supra* Both Lord Hardwicke, Bourne v. Dodson, 1 Atk 154, and Lord Fitzgerald, Colonial Bank v. Whinney, 11 App Cas 412, seem to be in error in considering that the statute had almost become obsolete prior to Lord Hardwicke's time
[5] Hungerford v Earle, 2 Vern. 261
[6] Troughton v Gitley, Amb. 630

the principle that if a man having a lien stands by and lets another make a new security, he shall be postponed." And finally, Lord Hardwicke directly applied the estoppel principle in Ryall v Rowles[1] That case, though not within the terms of the statute, was, as he considered, within its spirit. He held that book accounts of a partnership could come within the statute although it applied only to goods and chattels, because the choses in action as to their title and assignment were peculiarly creatures of equity, and the court recognized that the statute should apply the same principle to this peculiar class of property. He states that "the general view and intent of the provision now under consideration was to prevent traders from gaining a delusive credit by a false appearance of substance to mislead those who would deal with them" Then he said that "as to the choses in action comprised in these securities, where it is admitted none could pass but in equity, equity ought to follow the law in this case, if in any."

§ 202 **The American Doctrine of Estoppel.** It remained for a great equity judge in America to finally put the seal of approval on this idea In Freelinghuysen v Nugent[2] Mr. Justice Bradley, after referring to the fact that this statute did not exist in America, stated that its principle is just and "wherever the case occurs equity will favor the application of the principle" This principle is "that possession with the appearance of ownership renders property liable for the debts of the possessor to those who have given him credit on the faith of it" Long before these words were spoken, however, and perhaps half unconscious of why they were doing it,[3] the Ameri-

---

[1] *Supra.*   [2] *Supra.*
[3] A few judges besides Mr Justice Bradley have recognized the part that estoppel plays in the formation of the American doctrine Thus in Central Trust Co v Marietta &c. Ry Co , 48 Fed. 872, Pardee, J , in holding that an unrecorded car trust agreement was valid as against a prior mortagor, said

"As to third persons and subsequent creditors who have dealt with the railway company as the apparent owner of the property in its possession, there would be no difficulty in treating the property as belong-

can courts had entered upon a course which has led to the establishment in this country of a general principle, founded upon the idea that the possession of tangible property usually leads to the extension of credit. So far as the Statute of Fraudulent Conveyances can cover such decisions, they may be referred to it for their justification; so far as the cases lie without the province of that statute, and many of them necessarily must for the reasons already stated, they can be justified only by the principle of estoppel, even if the courts, in deciding them, failed to touch bottom in their reasoning. But none may gainsay that there is a principle of force in this country's courts which rights the true case of reputed ownership in favor of creditors, and that too, without the artificial restraints which, as we have seen, limit the application of the English statute. With us the wrong is repaired at the instance of a single judgment creditor or of any representative of creditors, instead of the remedy being available only to a trustee in bankruptcy, and no unjust ideas have found place in the body of the law which has thus been created. All that is needed is a case where a debtor, now insolvent, is in possession of property belonging to another, who has allowed the debtor to remain in possession under such circumstances as make him the apparent owner of the property. The creditor, in such a case, may use that property in the satisfaction of his debt, without proving that he extended credit in reliance upon the ostensible ownership thus appearing. As the Supreme Court has said, "men get credit for what they apparently own and possess";[1] and as Mr Justice Bradley has said in another case, "if the debtor remains in possession, the law presumes that those who deal with him do so on the faith of his being the unqualified owner of the goods"[2] To require proof by the complaining creditor

ing to the railway company on the doctrine of estoppel, but there can be no estoppel between the appellee and the Central Trust Co. claiming the property as acquired by the railway company."

[1] Robinson v Elliott, 22 Wall 513
[2] Casey v. Cavoroc, 96 U. S. 467.

would be impracticable "A rule of law so restricted," says the Supreme Court of Pennsylvania, "would be of very little value. It rarely occurs that a man can prove what it was that induced him to give credit."[1] Hence, the presumption, as that court has said, "is that every man is trusted according to the property in his possession." Creditors, says the South Carolina court, "are legally presumed to give credit on the faith of the property in their debtor's possession."[2] We must assume, says the Missouri court, "that in business affairs property is a basis of credit."[3]

§ 203 **Exceptions to American Rule.** The same exceptions to this general rule that we found in the English decisions exist with us. Thus the possession of a factor is not considered as coming within the equity principle.[4] In American Sugar Refining Co v Fancher[5] it was held that an unpaid vendor who discovers his vendee's insolvency may exercise his right of rescission and retake the goods, though the vendee's affairs have meanwhile passed into the hands of a general assignee. The court referred to the fact that there was no evidence that the creditors had advanced anything on the faith of the vendee's possession of the goods, "assuming that that element would have had any bearing on the case." It is submitted that it would have no bearing, because the right of the vendor to rescind on the discovery of the insolvency was just as well founded in law as in the doctrine of reputed ownership itself. In short, our doctrine of reputed ownership is subject to those exceptions that the exigencies of trade customs may demand. Thus the conditional sale agreement, as such, is lawful except in Illinois and Pennsylvania, where a misunderstanding exists that has already been mentioned.[6] And so the sale or return agreement,

[1] Martin v Mathiot 14 Serg & R 214
[2] Brock v Bowman, 1 Rich Eq Cas 185
[3] Williams v Kirk 68 Mo App 457
[4] Re Taft, 133 Fed 411, Re Galt, 120 Fed 64.
[5] 145 N. Y 552, 40 N E 206.
[6] Harkness v Russell, supra.

which really amounts to a sale of goods with an option to the vendee to return them within a limited time [1] has been upheld,[2] and so with the installment plan of supplying fixtures for a factory.[3] In short, as the Circuit Court of Appeals, Third Circuit, has said, " the exigencies of trade and commerce have caused many exceptions to be made to the rigid rule . . . by which the divorce of title from possession is declared either evidence of fraud or to be fraudulent *per se* "[4] Later we shall go more fully into these exceptions to the general rule, as well as attempt a more complete study of the rule itself; for the present let us stop with the realization that there is such a rule, and that its exceptions are of the general nature already described.

§ 204. **American Rule does not Apply to Choses in Action.** One important point, however, should be made at this juncture. The American doctrine of reputed ownership does not apply to any class of choses in action [5] As the Supreme Court has recently said, " the rule of the English statutes as to reputed ownership may extend to debts growing due to the bankrupt in the course of his business, but we have no such statute."[6] Not only have we no such statute, but our courts believe that the principle we have mentioned cannot, as to choses in action, take the place of the statute The reason for this has been stated by Judge Ward [7] as follows:

"The public does not know what stocks, bonds or notes a merchant has and therefore does not give him credit because of them. . . . The visible possession of chattels apparently

[1] Hunt *v* Wyman, 100 Mass 198
[2] *Re* Schindler, 158 Fed 458, Exp Wingfield, 10 Ch D. 591.
[3] *Re* Cohen, 163 Fed 44
[4] Century Throwing Co *v* Muller, 197 Fed 252.
[5] Stackhouse *v* Holden, 66 N Y App Div 423, 73 N Y S 203, Sexton *v*. Kessler, 172 Fed. 535, aff'd, 225 U S 90, 32 S Ct 657; Young *v* Upson, 115 Fed 192; *Re* Cotton Mfrs. Co , 209 Fed 629, Greev *v* Dockendorff, *supra*
[6] Greey *v* Dockendorff, *supra*.
[7] Sexton *v* Kessler, 172 Fed 535

owned by the possessor creates a wholly different situation. In respect to such property the law prohibits secret liens against creditors "

As is stated by another judge,[1] "the dealings had with mercantile houses are always with knowledge that available bills and accounts receivable may be so used as to procure credit on capital "

§ 205. **Criticism of This Limitation.** In principle this would seem to be too sweeping a generalization, and the line drawn by the English statute, which includes trade debts, would seem to be nearer the true line of distinction. The entire doctrine of reputed ownership rests upon a generalization which with the refinement of processes of commerce becomes more and more archaic; perhaps Baron Parke is near the truth when he says that people get credit nowadays for other reasons than the mere physical possession of goods;[2] but it would certainly not seem a more violent generalization to say that people get credit on account of the visible possession of goods than it is to affirm that they never get credit from acting as the owners of accounts receivable in the way of collection, suit, and the like.

[1] Ray, J , in Young *v.* Upson, *supra*.
[2] See his colloquy with counsel in Whitfield *v* Brand, 16 M. & W. 282.

CHAPTER X

REPUTED OWNERSHIP IN THE LIGHT OF THE RECORDING ACTS

§ 206. General Nature of Recording Acts
207. Statutes Relating to Real Estate.
208. General Nature of American Recording Acts as affecting Land
209. Distinction Between Creditors and Purchasers
210. Statutes Protecting Purchasers but not Creditors
211. Such Statutes do not Protect Judgment Creditors
212. Purchaser on Execution Sale as Protected by Such Statutes
213. Statutes Protecting Creditors as well as Purchasers
214. Recording Acts as Augmenting the Doctrine of Reputed Ownership

§ 215. Effect of Withholding Conveyance from Record
216. Withholding from Record raises only a Presumption.
217. Statutes Affecting Personal Property
218. Tendency to Growth of Such Legislation
219. Classification of Statutes Affecting the Chattel Mortgage and the Conditional Sale
220. Different Views as to Manner of Compliance
221. Necessity of Judgment for Action under Such Statutes
222. Basis of Average Statute is Rule of Twyne's Case
223. Tendency to Extension of Legislation — Its Origin

§ 206 **General Nature of Recording Acts** In the early part of the nineteenth century recording acts became a feature of American jurisprudence, and about the middle of that century, in a lesser degree, they appeared in the English system. Their general characteristic is the requirement that transfers affecting the title to property, or creating interests therein, shall be recorded in some public office provided by law for that purpose. Their study involves a consideration of the kinds of property affected by these statutes, and the classes of persons, having a present or subsequent interest therein, for whose benefit such statutes are enacted and whom their provisions

157

protect. We shall pursue this study only in so far as it may be necessary to learn how far such laws may affect the doctrine of reputed ownership.

§ 207 **Statutes Relating to Real Estate.** Taking up first the kinds of property affected by these statutes, we may follow the usual distinction between real and personal property. Let us first take real estate. In all of our States are statutes requiring that every instrument conveying an interest in real estate shall be recorded. In England, with the exception of property located within a relatively small area, there is no statute requiring or authorizing the transfer of any interest in real estate [1].

§ 208. **General Nature of American Recording Acts as affecting Land.** In America, the statute law of every State requires public registry of such a conveyance. It is not the object of such statutes to add any requisites to the validity of the conveyance between the parties to the transaction; with their interests the statutes are not concerned. What these statutes seek to accomplish is the protection of subsequent traffickers in the land — in short, to protect those who might subsequently choose to acquire interest in the land. Any such statute therefore, affords, as is intended, a modern substitute for securing the notoriety formerly created by livery of seizin.[2] "A deed duly signed, sealed, and delivered," says the Massachusetts court, "is sufficient, as between the original parties to it, to transfer the whole title of the grantor to the grantee, though the instrument of conveyance may not have been acknowledged or recorded. The title passes by the deed, and not by the registration. . . . But when the effect of the deed upon the rights of third persons . . . is to be considered, the law requires something more, namely, either actual notice, or the further formality of registration, which is constructive notice."[3]

[1] See Williams, "Real Property," 242
[2] Loughbridge v Bolland, 52 Miss. 546.
[3] Earle v. Fiske, 103 Mass 492

§ 209. **Distinction Between Creditors and Purchasers.** When we consider the sanction of these laws, or the consequences of noncompliance, we are led to inquire as to the extent of protection they afford. The persons protected by the statutes relating to real estate differ in the various States, broadly speaking, they are of two classes, first, subsequent purchasers in good faith of the property, and second, the creditors of the person who has conveyed but whose conveyance has not been recorded In all the States the first class is protected, in others, creditors are protected to a greater or less degree

§ 210 **Statutes Protecting Purchasers but not Creditors** An example of the first class is New York, whose statute [1] excludes creditors by every fair intendment, since, with regard to transfers of real estate, its only penalty for failure of compliance is this:

"Every such conveyance not so recorded is void as against any subsequent purchaser in good faith and for a valuable consideration, from the same vendor, his heirs or devisees, of the same real property, or any portion thereof, whose conveyance is first duly recorded."

§ 211 **Such Statutes do not Protect Judgment Creditors.** Consequently the courts of States having such statutes as that give an unrecorded deed or mortgage the fullest effect as against creditors. A creditor, even with judgment, cannot be considered as a purchaser, within the words of the statute or otherwise [2] From our previous study we can appreciate that this is so, but it may not be amiss to repeat a cardinal truth in the following language of the Alabama court

"All he has acquired or can acquire is a mere general inchoate lien upon the lands or estate of his debtor subject to execution; and a court of equity will not suffer the lien to be so employed that property which in equity and good conscience

---

[1] Real Prop. Law Sec 291
[2] Jackson v Dubois, 4 Johns. 216; Bailey v Timberlake, 74 Ala 221, Harrison v. Bowers, 200 Mo. 219, 98 S W. 770.

belongs to another than the debtor shall be taken and applied to the satisfaction of the judgment." [1]

§ 212. **Purchaser on Execution Sale as Protected by Such Statutes.** There is, however, a difference of opinion whether a purchaser on an execution sale is protected by the language of the statute. In Missouri it has been held that although a judgment creditor is not a purchaser, yet if he levies upon the land and causes it to be sold under execution, one who purchases the property at that sale is a purchaser in all the sense of the statute, and entitled to its protection. The creditor, of course, says the court, gets no interest in the property by virtue of his judgment and hence is no purchaser. But if he levies upon the property and sells it, then that purchaser " is the first person who acquires an interest in the property, and is the person who is to be affected by notice either actual or constructive." [2] The New York courts take the opposite stand. They consider that one who purchases on an execution sale gets no rights superior to the holder of the unrecorded mortgage, because of the usual rule that a purchaser on a judicial sale takes only the interest of the judgment debtor, for whose benefit the recording act was not passed.[3]

§ 213. **Statutes Protecting Creditors as well as Purchasers.** In other States creditors are expressly protected by the statute. Such a State is New Jersey, and its courts have held that the only question is whether the judgment creditor himself has notice of the unrecorded lien. If he had no such notice then it matters not that the purchaser on the execution sale has notice. "It is obvious that unless the protection of the statute is to be extended to the purchaser at the execution sale, the judgment creditor cannot have the full benefit of the statute." [4] In Massachusetts, by means of what Mr. Justice Holmes has

[1] Bailey v. Timberlake, *supra*
[2] Davis v. Owenby, 14 Mo. 170.
[3] Frost v. Yonkers Bank, 70 N. Y. 553; Clute v. Emmerich, 99 N. Y. 342, 2 N. E. 6
[4] Sharp v. Shea, 32 N. J. Eq. 65

described as a strained fiction,[1] a creditor, from the time of his judgment, is considered as a purchaser in good faith, and hence he, or the purchaser on his execution sale, takes priority as against the holder of an unrecorded mortgage[2] The only limitation on this Massachusetts rule is where the interest of the judgment debtor itself was unrecorded In such a case the levying creditor takes only the actual interest of the judgment debtor subject to all other unrecorded prior liens. "We think," said the court, "that he must take what accident throws into his net as he finds it, and that he cannot claim the benefit of a fiction to get more than his debtor really owned."[3]

§ 214 **Recording Acts as Augmenting the Doctrine of Reputed Ownership** So far as recording acts of this class expressly protect creditors, as in Massachusetts and New Jersey, they fall into the same category as the recording acts relating to personal property, and require no further discussion at this point. But such statutes as those of New York, Alabama and Missouri, although not intended for the protection of creditors, have worked to that end, nevertheless, and have augmented the domain of the reputed ownership doctrine As we have seen, in England that doctrine does not apply to real estate With us, thanks to the recording acts, it does to a certain extent While the custom of registering land transfers, indeed, will often operate to prevent the presumption of ownership in one in whom the record title does not lie,[4] yet, on the other hand, it suggests in many cases a mode of affording presumptive ownership by the simple expedient of withholding the latest deed from record.[5] In the absence of recording acts, people always investigated the facts relating to the ownership of land.

---

[1] Cowley v. McLaughlin, 141 Mass 181, 4 N E. 821.
[2] Woodward v Sartwell, 129 Mass 210; Coffin v Ray, 1 Met. 212
[3] Cowley v McLaughlin, *supra*
[4] Sexton v Wheaton, 8 Wheat 229
[5] Trenton B'king Co v Duncan, 86 N Y 221, Sloan v Huntington, 8 N. Y. App Div 93, 40 N Y S 393, Pierce v Hower, 142 Ind 626, 42 N. E 223, Water's Appeal, 35 Pa St 523

Of course if on an investigation the conveyance was concealed from the investigator, a presumption would arise in favor of the creditors, as was pointed out in Hungerford v. Earle [1] where the court says that "a deed not at first fraudulent may afterwards become so by being concealed or not pursued, by which means creditors are drawn in to lend their money." But outside of such a special case, no presumption could really arise. The framers of the statute of reputed ownership had this in mind when they restricted its scope to chattels, and to-day the reputed ownership portions of the English Bankrupt Act are likewise restricted.

§ 215 **Effect of Withholding Conveyance from Record.** But such recording acts as do not in terms protect the creditors, have nevertheless led to their protection by the fact that they afford a natural and obvious way of giving the publicity to every transaction in real estate. If a party does not take advantage of this means of publicity, it is a natural presumption that no transfer has been made. Consequently the withholding of an instrument from record may lead to a presumption of ownership, in the presence of a recording act, which would not have arisen in its absence. Although the recording acts may not require the registry of the deed in order to be effectual as against the transferor's creditors, yet a proper case of reputed ownership may arise none the less, resting, as has been said,[2] on "a familiar principle not dependent upon the statute." If such a transfer is withheld from record by agreement and not by mere inadvertence, the doctrine is universal that such a transaction is void as against the creditors of the transfer or mortgagor who remains in possession. As was long ago pointed out, the very existence of recording acts may afford opportunities for the ostentation of ownership by the simple expedient of withholding deeds from record.[3] In later times

---

[1] 2 Vern. 261.
[2] Lyon v. Council Bluffs Bank, 29 Fed. 566.
[3] Sexton v. Wheaton, *supra*.

such cases have arisen and to them the doctrine of estoppel has been applied. Such is Talcott *v.* Levy [1] There a man conveyed property to his wife, but did not record the deed. The husband continued in possession and apparent ownership, and contracted debts in his business. It was held that his creditors were entitled to treat the property as belonging to their debtor, the court referring to the obvious "design to obtain credit by means of tainted possession and apparent ownership." Such secret transfers, the court continues, "have a direct tendency to induce persons to credit the apparent owner on the faith of his apparent ownership and where they are made without any new consideration they should not, in justice to creditors, be upheld to their prejudice." Numerous other decisions are to the same effect.[2]

§ 216 **Withholding from Record raises only a Presumption.** The courts, however, have never brought themselves to declare that a mere withholding of record raises an absolute presumption of fraud. Hilliard *v.* Cagle,[3] which laid down a rule of law against an unrecorded conveyance in favor of creditors, has always been considered as having gone too far [4]. The mere withholding from record of itself raises no presumption, but additional circumstances in connection with it may have that effect. If the lack of record was due to no understanding at all and the circumstances of the parties were such that some excuse for the lack of recording could be seen, then there is no

---

[1] 29 Abb N C 3, 20 N Y Supp 440, aff'd 3 N. Y Misc. 315, aff'd 143 N Y. 636, 37 N E. 826

[2] Clayton *v* Exchange Bank, 121 Fed 630, Lehman *v* Van Winkle, 92 Ala 443, 8 So 870, Pierce v Howei, 142 Ind 626, 42 N. E. 223; City Bank *v* Hamilton, 31 N. J Eq. 159, *In re* Hickerson, 162 Fed. 345, Hilliard *v* Cagle, 46 Miss 309 In two cases, Breeze *v.* Brooks, 71 Cal 169, 9 Pac 670, 11 Pac 885, Mobile Bank *v.* McDonell, 87 Ala. 736, 6 So 703, a contrary view appears. But the Alabama case has been criticized and practically overruled Lehman *v.* Van Winkle, 92 Ala 443, 8 So 870, Clayton *v* Exchange Bank, 121 Fed 630

[3] 46 Miss 309

[4] Day *v* Goodbar, 69 Miss. 687, 12 So 30; Klein *v.* Richardson, 64 Miss 41, 8 So 204

case of reputed ownership Thus in Sawyer v Turpin [1] a mortgage had been given but not recorded, the mortgagor meanwhile remaining in possession. Later, and just prior to the bankruptcy, a new mortgage was given and was recorded It was held that the mortgagee should prevail over the mortgagor's creditors because the "evidence did not justify the assertion that there was, in fact, an agreement that the bill of sale should not be recorded or that possession should not be taken under it" There must be more than a mere omission to record. We must have something to show an intention to create, as against the creditor, a secret arrangement which should not be allowed to prevail to his injury The omission to record the instrument of itself simply constitutes " more or less cogent evidence of the want of good faith " [2]

§ 217 **Statutes Affecting Personal Property.** Let us turn now to the recording acts affecting transfers of personal property. In all of our States are statutes requiring the registration of (a) chattel mortgages, where, as is generally the case, possession of the mortgaged property is not delivered to the mortgagee, and (b) contracts of conditional sale, where, as is always the case, that being part of the bargain, possession of the stipulated chattels is delivered to the vendee In England, the Bill of Sale Act of 1854,[3] and its successor Act of 1878, covers such agreements, with respect to chattels, where ownership is separated from possession, in any such case the instrument evidencing the agreement must be registered, or it shall be void against the creditors or bankruptcy trustee or liquidator of the party in possession Such statutes do not apply to mortgages, sales or pledges of choses in action; they are construed as relating only to " goods and chattels which can be moved from one place to another, and the possession thereof thus changed " [4] Nor do they relate to pledges of chattels, of whose

[1] 91 U. S 114 [2] Rogers v Page, 140 Fed 586 [3] 17-18 Vict. c 36.
[4] Booth v Kehoe, 71 N Y. 341, National Hudson River Bank v Chaskin, 28 N Y App. Div. 311, 51 N Y. S. 64.

essence, as we shall hereafter see, is delivery of possession. A contract of pledge, unaccompanied by change of possession, therefore, can find no auxiliary in a recording act. " The registration of such a claim would not sustain it, and the failure to do so would not defeat it." [1] Nor are contracts creating merely the relation of principal and factor within such statutes, because, as we shall see, no consignment agreement partakes of the nature of a conditional sale or of a chattel mortgage.

§ 218. **Tendency to Growth of Such Legislation.** Of late years, however, there has been a tendency on the part of State legislatures to extend the recording acts to such excepted cases, and that, too, for the benefit of creditors of the person who is in possession but bereft of the title. Thus the New York Legislature in 1911 passed an act requiring the recording of commission house loans to which we will presently come,[2] and at the very moment of writing there is a bill pending in the New York Legislature to require assignments of book accounts to be recorded. And South Carolina now has a recording act which applies to all "bailments" of chattels as well as chattel mortgages and conditional sales.[3] This statute, however, marks the limit of legislation on this subject, and there is still doubt as to the legislative intent.[4] We may therefore leave the extreme verge to which we have been thus carried, and return to the average statutes affecting chattel mortgages and conditional sales.

[1] Bush v. Export Lumber Co., 136 Fed. 918; *Ex parte* Fitz, 2 Low. 519; Fed. Case 4837.
[2] Laws of 1911 c. 326, amending Pers. Prop. Law Sec. 45.
[3] Laws of 1910, No. 401, now Sec. 3740 of Code of 1912.
[4] In *In re* Nachman, 212 Fed. 460, Judge Smith held that where the petitioner delivered to the bankrupt certain samples of cloth in order that the bankrupt might obtain orders for the petitioner to make suits of clothes from the samples, this was not a bailment within the language of the Act, the court considering that a reasonable construction must be given to the statute, saying among other things that "were there any charge here of fraud or intended fraudulent evasion of the statute, the result might be otherwise." There is also an intimation that consignments would not be within the meaning of the statute.

§ 219. **Classification of Statutes Affecting the Chattel Mortgage and the Conditional Sale.** These may be divided into two classes, according to whether they protect creditors of the party in possession. In some States, as New York, an unregistered chattel mortgage is void as against creditors of the mortgagor in possession, as well as *bona fide* purchasers,[1] whereas the only unregistered conditional sale agreement that is void against the creditors of the vendee in possession is one covering railway equipment,[2] all others being void, by the terms of the statute, against *bona fide* purchasers alone, and consequently valid as against creditors.[3] In other States, as Connecticut, an unregistered contract of conditional sale is void against the creditors as well as the purchasers.[4] In some States, in addition to recording a contract, marking the property is also required.[5] In most of the States at the present day special provision is made for the recording of agreements under which railroad corporations are accustomed to purchase their equipment and rolling stock. These agreements, while properly, it would seem in principle, contracts of conditional sale, very often take a more elaborate form by which the property is delivered to a trustee in trust to hold it until the purchase money notes have been paid, the railway company, however, to have the use of it meanwhile. In such cases the contracts have been considered as chattel mortgages, and therefore record thereof is essential to their validity against the railway company.[6] In most of the States, however, special statutes exist requiring these agreements to be recorded, and also the property to be plainly marked with the name of the vendor.[7]

---

[1] Lien Law, Sec 230
[2] Pers Prop Law, Sec 61
[3] Pers Prop Law, Sec 62; Prentiss Supply Co. v Schirmer, 136 N. Y 305, 32 N E 849, Westinghouse Co v New Paltz Tract Co, 32 N Y Misc 132, 65 N Y S 644, Hewit v Berlin Mach Works, 194 U S. 296, 24 S Ct 690.
[4] See Harris v. Coe, 71 Conn. 157, 41 Atl. 552
[5] See Re Raney, 202 Fed 1000
[6] Heryford v Davis, 102 U. S 235, see also McGourkey v. Toledo &c Ry Co, 146 U S 536, 13 S Ct 170
[7] See N Y. Pers Prop Law, Sec 61, above cited.

§ 220 **Different Views as to Manner of Compliance.** Still further diversities may be noted with respect to the manner of compliance with these statutes. While there is no difficulty on the requisites of such laws as to change of possession, the ordinary tests being applied,[1] yet the laws of the States differ as to the manner of registration. Thus, in Missouri, a mortgage transferring both real and personal property is sufficiently registered as to its chattel mortgage features, by recordation as a real estate mortgage,[2] while in New York such an instrument, to be valid against the mortgagor's creditors, must be registered as a chattel mortgage, as well as recorded in the manner provided for conveyances of real estate [3]

§ 221. **Necessity of Judgment for Action under Such Statutes** There is, however, no difference of opinion on the proposition that no creditor can take advantage of the omission to comply with such a statute unless he has obtained a judgment In some States this qualification appears in the statutes, only judgment creditors in terms being protected, but whether so stipulated or not. there is no doubt that creditors are in no position to avail themselves of the benefits of such a statute until, by obtaining judgment, they have enabled themselves to realize upon their debtor's property.[4] Therefore if, before the creditor reaches this position, possession is restored to the party having legal title, as where the mortgagor delivers possession to the mortgagee, the statute has been complied with, and the creditor cannot invoke it.[5] This view is further illus-

---

[1] Thus the mortgagee may be considered as having received possession if delivery is made either to him, or his agent If the property is already in the possession of a third party, his attornment in the shape of recognition of the mortgagee as entitled to call for immediate possession, constitutes a delivery to the mortgagee Nash v. Ely, 19 Wend 523, Hodges v Huid, 47 Ill. 363

[2] Faxon v Ridge, 87 Mo App 299.

[3] Chemung Canal Bank v. Payne, 164 N. Y. 252 58 N. E. 101

[4] See Re Jacobson, 200 Fed 812, Myer v Car Co, 102 U S. 1; Meyer v. Pipkin, 136 Fed 396

[5] Humphrey v Tatman, 198 U S 91, 25 S Ct 567 See on this point as well as others connected with the subject of this chapter

trated by the difficulty which the courts had with the status of the trustee in bankruptcy under the present National Bankrupt Act. Until 1910 the Supreme Court considered that the trustee did not occupy the status of a judgment creditor within the meaning of these statutes, and hence could not in behalf of creditors take into his control property of which the possession had been separated from the ownership in the course of noncompliance with such a State law.[1] But the amendments of 1910, of which we shall hereafter speak more at length,[2] having expressly given the trustee the status of a judgment creditor for all purposes, the Supreme Court has recently held that he is entitled to all the privileges which the recording acts of the various States extend to judgment creditors[3] In short, as the same court long ago observed,[4] these statutes are just like the Statute of Fraudulent Conveyances in that none but a judgment creditor is entitled to their advantages.

§ 222. **Basis of Average Statute is Rule of Twyne's Case** Mention of the Statute of Fraudulent Conveyances remits us to a consideration of the general features of these acts. So far as they protect creditors, and relate to tangible chattels (which, until very recently, they exclusively did, as we have seen), they are traceable to the rule of Twyne's Case[5] that a sale unaccompanied by delivery of possession is presumptively fraudulent as against the vendor's creditors All that these statutes do is to make the rule absolute instead of presumptive.[6] These statutes, therefore, do not repeal the Statute of Fraudulent Conveyances or restrict the doctrine of reputed ownership; on the contrary they "add another

an article by Professor Williston, of Harvard Law School, in 19 Harvard Law Review, p 557 et seq.
[1] York Mfg Co. v Cassell, 201 U S. 344, 26 S Ct 481.
[2] Infra § 348
[3] Holt v Henley 232 U S 637, 34 Sup Ct Rep 459.
[4] Myer v. Car Co , supra
[5] 3 Co Rep 80b, discussed in Chapters VIII and IX
[6] See opinion of Lord Blackburn in Cookson v. Swire, L. R. 9 A. C 653, Lowell, J , in Brett v. Carter, 2 Low 458, Fed. Case No. 1844.

to the grounds on which a mortgage of personal chattels shall be void "[1] As the New York Court of Appeals has said

"It will be observed that under the statute relating to the filing of chattel mortgages, such an instrument may be void without being tainted by any inherent vice It is declared to be void simply because it is not filed On the other hand, a chattel mortgage, though filed in strict compliance with the statute, may be actually fraudulent and therefore void."[2]

So far as these statutes apply, they avoid the necessity of referring to any doctrine outside of the rule written on their face If such a statute provides that an unrecorded transfer shall be void as against the creditors of the debtor, there is no need of going further. The statute applies to the case within its terms, and the policy of the courts is to give it the fullest enforcement in a case where it applies.[3]

In thus making absolute the presumption which Twyne's Case sanctioned, some of these statutes have gone very far While the law of reputed ownership started off with the presumption of fraud prescribed by that case, yet, as we have seen, the day arrived when no such presumption was allowed to have place in the case of a conditional sale;[4] although doubtless it would apply in the case of a chattel mortgage, where title passes but possession remains — exactly what Twyne's Case condemns. Therefore those State laws which require registration of a conditional sale agreement have in effect restored an exploded notion, that a conditional sale should be considered as fraudulent, while such States as confine the penalties of their registration laws to the case of an unregistered chattel mortgage are more in accord with judicial opinion on this subject

§ 223 **Tendency to Extension of Legislation — Its Origin.** On the other hand, when we find States, like New York and South

---

[1] Wood v Lowry 17 Wend 492; Gill r Griffith, 2 Md Ch. 271; Milliken v. Second Natl. Bank, 206 Fed 14
[2] Chemung Canal Bank v Payne, 164 N Y 252, 58 N. E. 101.
[3] Dickinson v Oliver, 195 N Y 238, 88 N E 44.
[4] See Ch. IX.

Carolina, requiring the registration of certain classes of consignment agreements, which were never touched by the rule of Twyne's Case or the doctrine of reputed ownership, then we are brought close to the subject matter of the ensuing chapter. As we saw, the use of the ordinary forms of commercial transactions was not condemned by the doctrine of reputed ownership. But the abuse of these forms, according to one or the other of the prevalent tendencies of the day, has necessitated the laying down of certain rules of law upon whose consideration we shall now enter. These recording acts of our later day, when taken in connection with modern rules as they will appear upon the reading of the ensuing statutes, may be considered as a new effort by legislation to keep pace with the growth of the law, and perhaps again to outstrip it.

CHAPTER XI

REPUTED OWNERSHIP IN CONNECTION WITH PLEDGES

§ 224. Extent of Connection between Law of Pledge and Doctrine of Reputed Ownership.
225. "Pledges" of Choses in Action
226. Doctrine of Casey v Cavaroe and Sexton v Kessler
227. The Doctrine of "Equitable Pledge" is Part of the Law of Specific Performance
228. The Strict Law of Pledges is Confined to Tangible Chattels
229. "Constructive possession" as giving Room for Cases of Reputed Ownership
230. Symbolical Delivery and Notice of Possession
§ 231. Illustrative Cases
232. Custodian jointly Employed by Pledgor and Pledgee
233. Pledgor cannot be the Custodian
234. Confusion of Property
235. Possession by Third Party
236. If Third Party's Possession is Manifest, Goods may remain on Pledgor's Premises
237. Pledgor cannot be his own Warehouseman
238. Fictitious Corporate Entity in Connection with Warehousing
239. Validity of "Equitable Lien" on Chattels.

§ 224. **Extent of Connection between Law of Pledge and Doctrine of Reputed Ownership** The idea of a pledge originally involved two things, (1) the subject matter was tangible personal property, and (2) the delivery of its possession to the pledgee and the latter's continued possession of it were essential.[1] That is still true to-day, so that there is no room for the doctrine of reputed ownership on the basis of these categorical conceptions. So far as the inquiry is whether, in the given case, a pledge was created at all, the pledgor's creditors are proceeding on the lines laid down in Chapter II, and are working out

[1] Nisbett v Macon Bank, 12 Fed. 686; Casey v Cavaroc, 96 U S 467

171

their rights through the debtor's. But modern refinements in the shape of "equitable pledges" of intangible personal property, and, in the case of chattels, arrangements which do not clearly show a transfer of possession, make it necessary to inquire as to the extent to which the doctrine of reputed ownership connects with the law of pledge.

§ 225 "**Pledges**" of **Choses in Action.** And firstly, as to intangible personal property, choses in action, to be short. Referring to the first principle frequently mentioned in the preceding chapters, a chose in action cannot, technically speaking, be the subject of a pledge, because no common law court can recognize and enforce its assignment. The assignability of a right of this kind depends upon the aid which, if necessary, the equity courts will give to the assignee. Consequently, any doctrine concerning the pledging of a chose in action in reality does not depend upon common law conceptions, but is a branch of the equitable jurisdiction under which the court forces parties to specifically perform their engagements. All the pledgee has in such a case, in the last resort, is the right to ask the equity court for relief and protection — to compel the pledgor and his privies to leave him in that enjoyment of the rights in question for which the pledge agreement stipulated. It follows that the equity court, in responding to such applications, is free to follow its own ideas, without being bound by common law strictness, and in thus doing, such a court is apt to use the same standards which it has set up in other branches of its jurisdiction over contracts. The first, and almost the last, of such tests which should be applied to a case where one party, the pledgee, has, at the outset, performed his side of the agreement by making the loan, is that of certainty. The property should be clearly identified, and the control should be recognized as being in the pledgee. With these requisites, a delivery of the documents representing the rights in question is not essential. And when such an agreement is thus so specific that the courts will specifically protect the pledgee's rights, there is no further inquiry possible in behalf of the pledgor's creditors. They have no rights superior to his, at least in America, because, as we have seen, our courts allow no rule of reputed ownership to apply to dealings concerning choses in action

§ 226 **Doctrine of Casey v Cavaroc and Sexton v. Kessler** All of this is illustrated by two decisions of the Supreme Court. In Casey v. Cavaroc [1] a debtor wishing a drawing account upon a foreign banker arranged to set aside securities to secure his drawings These securities were not delivered to the foreign banker, but instead the American drawer put them aside in his safe marked with the foreign banker's name In Sexton v Kessler [2] the same situation arose except that at the outset of the transaction a memorandum of the securities then set aside was delivered to the American agent of the foreign banker. In each case it was agreed that the borrower from time to time might withdraw securities from the packet, substituting other securities of equal value In Casey v Cavaroc, however, as part of the agreement as viewed in the light of the parties' conduct, the borrower did not keep the banker advised of substitutions as they were made, and often did not replace withdrawn collateral with its equivalent in value. In Sexton v. Kessler, on the other hand, whenever a withdrawal was made, a substitute security was placed in the packet, and the banker was advised of the details In Casey v Cavaroc the Supreme Court held that the foreign banker had no specific lien on the collateral which could prevail against the pledgor's creditors In Sexton v Kessler an exactly opposite decision was made, the banker's lien being held to be in all respects valid The distinction on this ground between the two cases may be stated as this in the one case the agreement was specific, and in the other it was not. In Casey v Cavaroc, the foreign banker at no time knew what securities were on hand, because he was not kept advised of the substitution of securities from time to time. In Sexton v. Kessler, the foreign banker was at all times advised

[1] *Supra.* [2] 225 U S 90, 32 S. Ct 657.

of substitutions At all moments he knew just what his security consisted of, and at all moments the American customer knew just what was kept apart for the banker. There was thus certainty, not only at the outset of the agreement, but throughout its continuance. There was also good faith in the arrangement It was made at the outset as a condition upon which the foreign banker would lend money at all. This proposition is well put in the opinion of NOYES, J., in the lower court:

"In considering the case from any point of view one thing is apparent from the outset, and that is the good faith of the parties. Another thing is also apparent — the New York house intended that the securities in question should afford protection to the Manchester house for their acceptances, and the latter supposed that they were obtaining protection. Both parties acted upon the assumption that that which they did accomplished something The New York house furnished security in the form desired by the Manchester house, and the latter accepted the former's drawings upon that security The transaction, if invalid, is only so because in contravention of some stated or positive legal principle, and it cannot be declared invalid without inflicting great hardship upon the Manchester house." [1]

§ 227 **The Doctrine of " Equitable Pledge " is Part of the Law of Specific Performance** It must be said that the point of view above suggested, by virtue of which all questions of the pledge of choses in action are considered according to the standards of equity in its jurisdiction over contracts, is suggested more by the Supreme Court's later pronunciamento than its first. In Casey v Cavaroc, the entire opinion traveled along the lines of common law conceptions, the pledge was invalid because of the want of some sort of delivery, the pledgee did not have or maintain possession. On the same line of reasoning have followed many cases of which we may mention only one, — Girard Trust Co v Mellor [2] There a firm, desiring

---

[1] Sexton v Kessler. 172 Fed 535.   [2] 156 Pa St. 579, 27 Atl. 626.

to secure the underwriters of a certain venture, inclosed in an envelope certain notes which, with a list of the persons intended to be protected, they placed in a tin box. This box they deposited with a safe deposit company, the package being properly indorsed. It was held that this deposit was invalid as against the bankers' creditors, the entire reasoning being based on the common law doctrine of pledge. But in Sexton v. Kessler, Mr. Justice Holmes put the proposition in its actual form when he reduced the validity of any " equitable pledge," in all cases and when all is said or done, to a " question of more or less." That is what every case of specific performance does — the court's power to decree for the claimant is always there to exercise, but its discretion must depend, to a final degree, on the so-called " equities " of the case at bar. Specific performance is a question of " more or less "; so, properly viewed, is the doctrine of equitable pledge, because it belongs to the domain of specific performance.[1]

§ 228. **The Strict Law of Pledges is Confined to Tangible Chattels.** When we come to tangible personal property, however, we enter the domain of the real law of pledge. There is no doctrine of more or less here, and the common law idea of the pledge must prevail, since equity has no exclusive jurisdiction.

§ 229. **" Constructive Possession " as giving Room for Cases of Reputed Ownership.** If the older ideas had been adhered to, no case of pledge could raise a question of reputed owner-

[1] With this in mind, the cases which allow one, who lends upon the security of bills and accounts receivable, to permit the borrower to handle and collect the collateral in his own name, and ostensibly in his own right, — cases of such class being Clark v Iselin, 21 Wall 360; Hickock v Cowperthwaite, 210 N Y 137, — make no inroad, upon the real law of pledge, as the common law courts apply it to tangible chattels. There is no reason why the borrower should not do the collecting, as agent for the lender. There is certainty about the agreement and the subject matter ; nor does possession of such vouchers as may represent the accounts cut any figure, because, as we saw in the last chapter, the doctrine of reputed ownership does not apply to choses in action.

ship, since in any such case we would find that the pledgee got possession of the goods at the outset, and thereafter continuously remained in possession, thus giving no chance for misleading the pledgor's creditors. But of modern times difficulty has been caused by practices which, while never departing from the technicalities of the common law regarding possession, nevertheless effectually conceal the fact of actual possession from the outside world. In such cases the doctrine of reputed ownership applies. In other cases the refinements push themselves over the line, and the courts must hold that there was no pledge at all. Such cases are Drury v. Moors[1] and Bank v. Jagode[2] of which HOLMES, J., spoke when he mentioned "cases in which the so-called power of the exclusive bailee gradually tapers away until we reach those in which the courts have held, as matter of law, that there was no adequate bailment."[3] Such cases as these last, of course, raise no question of reputed ownership — that sort of distinction we have already made in this chapter — but in the discussion of cases which do raise this question, it is sometimes necessary to deal with the other class as well. Let us deal with the cases so far as we may.

§ 230. **Symbolical Delivery and Notice of Possession.** In one large class of cases it is impracticable physically to transfer the property because of its bulk. A symbolical delivery may be made which is good between the parties, but the pledgee must thereafter maintain possession of the property either personally or through his own agents. At this point enters the doctrine of reputed ownership. So far as the pledgor's creditors are concerned, symbolical delivery and a show of custody may bind pledgor and pledgee, but, as the transaction concerns property which the creditors can see, there must also be visible indications of the pledgee's possession. There

[1] 171 Mass. 252, 50 N. E. 618.
[2] 186 Pa. St. 556, 40 Atl. 1018.
[3] Union Trust Co. v. Wilson, 198 U. S. 530, 25 S. Ct. 766.

must be a change of possession, and then the pledgee must maintain possession, under such circumstances that the public may know the facts. In the absence of a recording act applying to pledges, the only way public notice can be given is by affixing inscriptions upon the property itself, showing the existence of the pledge. That is the rule established by the weight of modern authority.[1] In Massachusetts and Maine, indeed, the earlier view was much more lax, the tendency being to the view that, once a transfer had been made, it was proper to leave the pledgor in possession, provided he acted in the right of the pledgee, and as the latter's agent.[2] But the later view in Massachusetts is to the contrary,[3] inclining to the doctrine above mentioned, which forbids, under any circumstances, the pledgor, or the latter's servants as such, having control of the property. Under this view, merely marking the property as the pledgee's is putting the cart before the horse. If the pledgee does not maintain possession, he has no pledge, despite public notice to the contrary. It is only when he has a pledge that he must give notice of it, either by the nature of his possession, or signs on the property.[4] Let us now examine a few illustrative cases.

§ 231 **Illustrative Cases** In American Pig Iron Company v German [5] a quantity of pig iron was pledged and left on ground belonging to the pledgor, a furnace company. It was located apart from the other iron and painted with the pledgee's

---

[1] American Pig Iron Company v German, 126 Ala 194, 28 So. 603, Ayers v McCandless, 147 Pa St 49, 23 Atl 344, Philadelphia Warehouse Company v Winchester, 156 Fed 600, First National Bank v Pennsylvania Trust Company, 124 Fed 968, Dunn v Train, 125 Fed 221, *In re* Shaw, 146 Fed 273, Bush v Export Storage Company, 136 Fed 918; Sholes v. Asphalt Company, 183 Pa. St 528, 38 Atl 1029; *In re* Rogers, 125 Fed 169

[2] Sumner v Hamlet, 12 Pick. 76, Macomber v Parker, 14 Pick 497; Dunn v. Train, 125 Fed 221

[3] Drury v Moors, 171 Mass 252, 50 N E 618, Moors v Reading, 167 Mass 322, 45 N E 760

[4] Geilfuss v Corrigan, 95 Wisc. 651, 70 N. W. 306, 37 L R A 166, Button v Rathbone, 126 N Y 187, 27 N E 266; Stephens v Gifford, 137 Pa. 219, 20 Atl 542. Seavey v Walker, 108 Ind 78, 9 N E 347.

[5] 126 Ala. 194, 28 So 603

initials. This segregation was held sufficient Likewise in Ayres v. McCandless [1] lumber piled in the mill yard of the vendors and so marked was held to be properly segregated for the purposes of the vendee So in Phila Warehouse Co v Winchester,[2] the warehouse company loaned money to the bankrupt company, taking from it as collateral leases of portions of its premises on which goods intended as security were situated. The warehouse company appointed a custodian of the leased premises and of the property The custodian maintained possession, and continuously maintained on the property, in a number of conspicuous positions, signs and placards which indicated that the warehouse company was the only one specifically interested in the pledged property. The bankrupt also had some of its own property on these premises But as the court says, this operated if anything to the detriment merely of the bankrupt, because the public would most probably assume that all the property within the inclosure was pledged, including the unhypothecated stock of the bankrupt, instead of believing that none of the property was under lien. In First National Bank v. Penn Trust Co ,[3] the facts were the same as in Phila Warehouse Co v Winchester, but during part of the time the signs were not on the property. This, however, was not the fault or done with the consent of the lienor, and so his rights were not thereby affected The court said

"It is not suggested that the bank had any knowledge of the removal of the signs or that it did not replace them so soon as their removal was brought to its notice The effect of a remarking of the billets was not to create a new lien or to acquire a preference for an antecedent debt between the parties."

§ 232 **Custodian jointly Employed by Pledgor and Pledgee.** The courts have gone a step further than this, and have held that even if the custodian of this segregated property is a joint

[1] 147 Pa. St 49, 23 Atl. 344.
[2] 156 Fed. 600.
[3] 124 Fed. 968

employee of the lienor and the bankrupt, the hypothecation is nevertheless valid.[1] As the Circuit Court of Appeals, First Circuit, has said, this sufficiently shows "that the goods are actually set apart in the keeping of the special bailee with authority to notify third persons that they are held in pledge and to remove the goods if found necessary for the safety of its principal." [2]

§ 233 **Pledgor cannot be the Custodian** But the debtor himself cannot be the custodian because obviously there is nothing in such a case to rebut the natural presumption of his free ownership.[3] In Sholes v. Asphalt Company [4] the Asphalt Company attempted to pledge certain asphalt blocks which were stored in the pledgor's yard. Nothing was done to carry the pledge into effect. The goods were not separated, marked, or in any way distinguished from the other assets of the company It was held that the pledge was invalid as against a receiver appointed on a creditors' bill "Even in such cases," says FELL, J , viz of constructive delivery, "the want of constructive or symbolical delivery or of some act whereby the goods pledged may be distinguished and set apart from the other goods in the possession of the pledgor has not been excused "

§ 234 **Confusion of Property.** Even in such jurisdictions as still consider it lawful for the pledgee to leave the pledgor in possession, segregation is insisted upon. The separation must be real and not merely formal. Tagging the goods with the owner's name is sufficient, if properly done.[5] The most obvious case to the contrary recently arose in Maine, where, the bankrupt being made the custodian of the pledged goods, they were tagged with initial letters which, by the understanding between the parties, indicated that the marked goods belonged to the claimant. But as against the creditors of the bankrupt, who

[1] Dunn v Train, 125 Fed 221 , Sumner v Hamlet, 12 Pick. 76.
[2] Dunn v Train, 125 Fed 221
[3] In re Shaw 146 Fed 273.
[4] 183 Pa St. 528, 38 Atl 1029
[5] Allen v Hollender, 128 Fed 159.

180   THE RIGHTS AND REMEDIES OF CREDITORS.   [CHAP. XI.

possessed no cipher for these signals, it was held that the goods belonged to the bankrupt.[1] And the same result was reached in another court, where "upon each pile of bags of seed for which the warehouse receipts or warrants were issued there was placed a small tag, which might be discovered upon careful search."[2]

§ 235 **Possession by Third Party.** The same proposition arises in the case where goods are in the custody of an independent third party. The bailee's own creditors, of course, might be misled, and as to their rights we must apply the considerations found in Chapter IX. But the bailor's creditors cannot be misled, because their debtor is not in possession, and the independent character of the bailee in possession will put them upon their inquiry. Such is the case of goods stored with a warehouseman. Any inquiry as to the present ownership of the goods leads to an inquiry as to the present ownership of the warehouse receipt. As between the original depositor and his vendee or pledgee, the attornment of the custodian is not necessary to a transfer of possession;[3] and as against the depositor's creditors there is no ostentation of ownership, since the possession by the independent third party puts them on their inquiry as to the present whereabouts of the muniments of title which represent the goods in his custody. It matters not what sort of a bailee it may be, just so that the bailee be free from the general control of the bailor. This proposition is brought out in National Bank *v* Rogers.[4] In that case S & Company borrowed money from the plaintiff, giving a note which recited that they had deposited with the plaintiff as collateral certain goods. S. & Company at the same time gave the plaintiff a paper whereby they acknowledged

[1] *In re* Shaw, 146 Fed 273
[2] *In re* Rodgers, 125 Fed. 169
[3] Conrad *v* Fisher, 37 Mo. App 352, 8 L. R A 147, City Bk. *v* Peacock, 103 Ga 171, 29 S. E 752; Cartwright *v.* Wilmerding, 24 N. Y 521
[4] 166 N Y. 380, 59 N E 922.

receipt of the merchandise from the plaintiff and agreed to hold
the goods in trust for him, and to give him the proceeds in case
of sale The goods at that time were in the custom house.
S. & Company took possession of the goods. While these
chattels still remained among S & Company's general mass of
merchandise they were taken possession of by an assignee for
the benefit of creditors It was held that the plaintiff was
entitled to the property, the court saying that "effect could
be given to the intention of the parties by holding Sholes &
Company strictly to the letter of their contract" This was
quite right, because it was not the plaintiff's fault that S. &
Company had not segregated the goods At the time he made
his contract with them the goods were segregated by being in
the custom house, and in the absence of proof that the plaintiff
had agreed to allow S & Company to mingle the goods with
their own, he was entitled to them, even against S & Company's
creditor In like manner, where one's goods are in the custody
of a third party, as warehouseman or common carrier, the receipt of the latter for the same may be dealt in as a commercial
instrument without fear of any doctrine of reputed ownership [1]

§ 236. **If Third Party's Possession is Manifest, Goods may
Remain on Pledgor's Premises.** We can carry this proposition
yet further without impairing its symmetry If the bailee
is openly independent, the physical location of the goods need
not be separate from the bailor's own premises That is illustrated by the practice under the Federal statutes imposing an
excise tax on certain classes of goods These statutes permit
the producer to keep the goods on his own premises until he
sells them, at which time the tax may be paid upon his furnishing a bond to the government, conditioned upon his not removing the goods until the tax is paid and a proper release of

---

[1] Dows v. Bank, 91 U S 618 And this is true even if the deposi-
tary be not a duly licensed warehouseman. Gibson v Stevens, 8
How 383, Millhiser Co v Gallego Mills, 101 Va 579, 44 S E 760,
Union Trust Co v Wilson 198 U S 530, 25 S. Ct 766

the goods has been obtained In such a case, the Supreme Court has lately held, a valid pledge of the goods may be made by the delivery of a memorandum describing them, since the situation is the same as though the government had possession of the goods on premises of its own. "The building is his," said the court, "but the government is in complete control." [1] But there is the limit; the bailee must have "complete control," not the bailor.

§ 237. **Pledgor cannot be his own Warehouseman** This leads to certain observations on the practice of warehousing From what has already been said, it is apparent that one cannot be his own warehouseman, and issue his own warehouse receipts covering his own property. That is a contradiction of ideas, and the only effect of such a "receipt" is that it personally binds its signer to hold that much of his property subject to the claim of another But that is not a pledge, if anything it is a chattel mortgage, which should be recorded. That was the decision in Fourth St. Bank v. Milburn Mills,[2] where a bankrupt milling company issued grain certificates each calling for a certain quantity of wheat or flour stored in its grain tanks or mill, to be delivered to the holder on demand. A number of these securities it hypothecated for a loan It was held by the Circuit Court of Appeals, Third Circuit, that these unrecorded certificates conferred no right as against the trustee in bankruptcy of the milling company [3]

§ 238 **Fictitious Corporate Entity in Connection with Warehousing** A more elaborate attempt, however, is revealed in Security Warehousing Company v Hand [4] The contest there was over the possession of certain property, between the trustee of the Racine Knitting Company and the appellant, the Ware-

[1] Taney v Penn Nat Bk, 232 U S 174; 34 Sup Ct Rep. 288
[2] 172 Fed 177.
[3] Franklin Bank v Whitehead, 149 Ind 560, 49 N E 592, 39 L R A 725, Geilfuss v Corrigan, 95 Wisc 651, 70 N W 306, 37 L. R A 166
[4] 206 U. S. 415, 27 S Ct 720

housing Company, which was a New York corporation engaged
in the so-called business of "field warehousing" in Wisconsin
It occupied no warehouse of its own, but leased certain premises
from the knitting company at Racine This place was occupied
by the knitting company with its goods to be sold, and the
goods were placed on the premises really occupied by the knitting company, although in form leased by it to the warehousing
company. So-called warehouse receipts were given to the
knitting company by the warehousing company, acknowledging
the receipt of the property at such place. These receipts were
in turn pledged by the knitting company to various banks
It was held that the trustee of the knitting company was entitled to the property on hand Mr. Justice Peckham, who
delivered the opinion, said .

"It is a trifling with words to call the various transactions
between the knitting company and the warehousing company
a transfer of possession from the former to the latter. There
was really no delivery and no change of possession, continuous
or otherwise The alleged change was a mere pretense and
sham. . . The security company gave no evidences to the
passer-by, no business was sought from the public, the only
property within the enclosures was the knitting company's.
The knitting company did not want storage room, but col-
laterals, which the security company agreed to furnish for a
commission upon the amount thereof, plus all expenses The
security company's only agents on the scene were the agents
of the knitting company, who cared for and shipped out its
goods. That this was the only business contemplated is disclosed by the agreement that the knitting company should be
restored to full possession of the premises at any time it returned the outstanding receipts. This, in our judgment, was
not warehousing within the law of Wisconsin "

§ 239. **Validity of "Equitable Lien" on Chattels** Such
cases, in short, are precisely like *Re* Klingamon [1] and H. K
Porter Co *v.* Boyd [2] In *Re* Klingamon, goods were sold on

[1] 101 Fed 691.   [2] 171 Fed 305.

credit and delivered to the vendee, who agreed to hold them as "pledged and hypothecated" for the purchase price. In H. K. Porter Co. v. Boyd, after certain locomotives had been delivered to the vendee under what amounted either to an absolute sale, or a conditional sale which, under the law of Pennsylvania, was invalid and therefore amounted to an outright sale, the parties agreed that the vendee should hold the locomotives as "equitably securing" the balance of the unpaid purchase price. In neither case was there a pledge, whatever else it was, but rather an attempt, by agreement, to give the vendor a lien upon property sold to the vendee. At most it created a chattel mortgage for the purchase money, and the lack of record vitiated it as against the creditors of the party in possession.

CHAPTER XII

REPUTED OWNERSHIP IN CONNECTION WITH AGENCY

§ 240. Class of Agency Arrangements Affected by Doctrine of Reputed Ownership
241. Definitions of Conditional Sale and Chattel Mortgage
242. Definition of Consignment
243. Essential Legality of Each Arrangement, Standing Alone.
244. Method of Inquiry in Cases of Complication
245. Illustrative Case — Ryttenberg v. Schefer
246. Illustrative Case — Ommen v. Talcott
247. Question — Whether Consignment or Sale?
248. Disposition of the Goods

§ 249. Disposition of Proceeds of Sale
250. Whether Sale is Absolute or Conditional
251. Rule in Cases of Conditional Sale and Chattel Mortgage
252. Evolution of this Rule from the Particular to the General
253. Growth of Doctrine — Illustrative Cases
254. Recordation of Agreement Immaterial
255. Essentially False Character of such Arrangements
256. Opposing View of Some Jurisdictions.
257. Trust Receipts
258. Confusion of the Decisions

§ 240. **Class of Agency Arrangements Affected by Doctrine of Reputed Ownership** As we have seen in the Tenth Chapter the doctrine of reputed ownership left unscathed certain arrangements which the courts considered as based upon sound mercantile usage. These arrangements may be classified as cases of (1) consignment, (2) conditional sale, (3) chattel mortgage with the mortgagee in possession The recording acts of modern times have made certain inroads, whose extent we have studied in Chapter X We are now, however, to consider the way in which the doctrine of reputed ownership may apply to these transactions irrespective of the recording acts, assuming in each case compliance with any recording act that may have application. Despite the general statement with which this chapter opens, there is a certain application of the doctrine of reputed ownership in this connection. The doctrine, it is true, applies to no transaction of any of the three classes above named when it stands alone. But of modern times the tendency is toward arrangements which combine more or less the relation of consignment with one or the other of the other two relations. It is to such combinations, rather than to the separate classes, that the doctrine of reputed ownership has distinct and vigorous application

§ 241 **Definitions of Conditional Sale and Chattel Mortgage** Let us first analyze each of these separate classes of transactions ·

A conditional sale occurs where A agrees to sell certain goods to B for a price to be paid at a future date, and, pending the payment of the price, allows B to have possession of the goods In the case of a chattel mortgage, B, owing A a debt, mortgages to him certain chattels. A chattel mortgage passes the legal title, and the mortgagee is therefore entitled to possession. In the average case, however, it is arranged that the mortgagor shall remain in possession of the goods until default So the arrangement includes a bailment, by virtue of which the mortgagor remains in possession of the goods although the title, separate therefrom, is in the mortgagee. But the mortgagee none the less has the title and is, in case of default, entitled to a writ of seizure of the goods.[1] Each case, therefore, of chattel mortgage or of conditional sale presents a case of possession separate from the title In each case, also, the title secures a debt. In the case of a chattel mortgage the debt secured is the loan, and in the case of a conditional sale it is the purchase price of the goods. There is of course this difference, that a conditional sale after all is a contract of sale and is distinct from a mere security arrangement securing a debt; and therefore if the vendor on default retakes the goods the contract is rescinded, and he has no claim for a deficiency.[2]

[1] Coiro v Baron, 158 N. Y App Div 591, 143 N. Y. S. 853
[2] Earle v Robinson, 91 Hun 363, 36 N. Y S 178, aff'd 157 N Y 683, 51 N E 1090, Cooper v. Payne, 111 N. Y. App Div 785, 97 N. Y S 863, aff'd 190 N. Y. 512, 83 N. E. 1124, Minnesota Harvester

§ 242. **Definition of Consignment** The usual case of a consignment is where A delivers his goods to B to sell for him as his agent In such a transaction, of course, the intention is not to pass the title of the goods to the consignee, on the contrary the mere possession passes, the title being reserved in the consignor [1] The proceeds of sale belong to the principal and are his property, so that the vendee is under the absolute duty to turn the same over to the principal, and his default amounts to a fraudulent conversion.[2] Nor is this relation complicated in point of law by any of the incidents which often are attached. A factor may well guarantee to his principal the accounts of the parties to whom he sells the goods; in fact, this is as usual as it is natural in a case where the principal is not familiar with the factor's territory and the trade conditions therein, or the soundness of the factor's customers But this collateral incident simply leads one to consider the agent as "a factor who has sold for cash."[3] A factor who makes advances on account has a lien on the goods or the proceeds of their sale for his advances and other charges[4] Hence he can maintain replevin or trover for the goods, and can enforce his lien on them by sale, retaining from the proceeds the amount of his advances and paying his principal the surplus.[5] But all of this makes him none the less a factor

Works v Hally, 27 Minn 495, 8 N W. 597 In New York, however, at present day there is little more than this distinction because the statutes (Personal Property Law, Sec 65) provide that the vendor, upon retaking the goods, must, at the vendee's request, sell them at public auction and apply the proceeds of sale to the payment of the debt, paying over the surplus to the vendee, thus conferring on the vendee what practically amounts to an equity of redemption, Crowe &c. Co. v Liquor &c. Co., 154 N Y. App Div 373, 139 N Y S 587.

[1] Sturm v Boker, 150 U S 312, 14 S Ct 99, McCullough v Porter, 4 Watts & S (Pa) 535
[2] Wallace v Castle, 14 Hun 106; Leverick v Meigs, 1 Cow. 644.
[3] Leverick v Meigs, 1 Cow 644
[4] Baker v N Y. National Exchange Bank, 100 N Y 31, 2 N E 452, Matter of Chambers, 17 N. Y App Div 340, 45 N Y S 264
[5] Grosvenor v Phillips, 2 Hill 147, Bailey v. Hudson River R R. Co., 49 N. Y. 70.

§ 243. **Essential Legality of Each Arrangement, Standing Alone.** Such cases as these occasion no difficulty, the trouble lies with those ahead of us, where more than any one of these different relations appear. The question to be determined in each such case is whether the transaction is of either of the regular classes, viz whether it is a consignment arrangement as last above described, or a security arrangement in the shape of a chattel mortgage or conditional sale The point of transition from the one category to the other is where we must halt. At that point we meet the doctrine of reputed ownership.

§ 244 **Method of Inquiry in Cases of Complication.** Our method of inquiry in any such transaction should be to start with the question — what does it pretend to be? That should be followed by the inquiry, is the transaction what it pretends to be, and nothing more, or does it also include the elements of one of the two other relationships? The use of this method may be illustrated by the case of a pretended consignment agreement. If this agreement is what it pretends to be, then there should be a transfer of possession of the goods in question from consignor to consignee The essence of a consignment agreement is a bailment, and there is no bailment until the delivery of possession.[1] If there has been no change of possession, then there has been no consignment. This method of inquiry is illustrated by two recent cases.

§ 245 **Illustrative Case — Ryttenberg v Schefer** In Ryttenberg v Schefer[2] the firm of Radon & Co. was engaged in the woolen goods business, both as factors for other people and as dealers on their own account They made an agreement with Schefer to transact all business through him. For that purpose

[1] Wright v Campbell 4 Burr 2046 Even after goods have been shipped by the principal to the factor the factorage agreement does not begin to operate until the factor has received them from the carrier, and until that time, he not being in possession of the goods, the right of stoppage in transit exists, irrespective of any factor's lien, Ryberg v Snell, 2 Wash. C. C , 294, 403; Fed. Cases, Nos. 12189, 12190

[2] 131 Fed. 313.

they assigned the lease of their premises to Schefer, and agreed that all goods then or thereafter owned by them, and all then or thereafter consigned to them by others, should be considered as consigned by their respective owners to Schefer as factor for sale upon commission. Schefer agreed to advance to Radon & Co two thirds of the net market value of the goods consigned, an account of sales to be furnished monthly, and Schefer to discount such sales for the respective consignor, charging therefor a certain commission. Upon the supervening bankruptcy of Radon & Co. the controversy arose as to four things. (*a*) goods on hand consigned by other people, (*b*) outstanding accounts for the sale of such goods, (*c*) goods owned by Radon & Co., (*d*) outstanding accounts representing goods owned by Radon & Co and sold. HOLT, J., reached the following conclusions. (*a*) As to the goods on hand belonging to outside consignors, Schefer was entitled to their possession, because by the agreement Schefer had acted as factor instead of Radon & Co. There was no reputed ownership claim possible on the part of Radon's creditors as to these goods, because, had Radon never made any agreement with Schefer, Radon's creditors could not claim them. "The entire title and right of possession therefore," said the court, "was either in the consignors or in Schefer." (*b*) As to the outstanding accounts for the sale of such goods, the same conclusion was reached. (*c*) As to goods bought by Radon & Co., a different conclusion was reached, the court saying that no change of possession ever occurred, and that therefore Schefer could not be considered as the factor for Radon. An assignment of the lease made no difference because "it was part of an agreement by which it was understood that Radon & Co were to continue their occupation of the premises and were in fact to pay the rent." The signs on the door made no difference, because "I do not think,' said the court, "that these signs indicated with any clearness who was the tenant or actual occupant of the premises." In short there was no change of possession so that one could affirm that Schefer was Radon's factor "A man cannot consign a thing to another by simply saying that he consigns it any more than he can deliver it by mere words. The goods . . remained in the possession and custody of Radon & Co and not of Schefer." (d) As to the accounts receivable representing goods belonging to Radon & Co and sold by them, the same conclusion was reached, because, as already stated, the goods were never in the possession of Schefer and so he could not claim a factor's lien on the accounts for advances.

§ 246 **Illustrative Case — Ommen** *v* **Talcott.** In Ommen *v* Talcott[1] a similar controversy arose. The John A. Baker Notion Co, engaged in the notion business, agreed to constitute Talcott its sole factor, and to consign to him its entire stock of goods at all times for sale upon commission, Talcott to make advances on the goods. The Baker Company agreed to assign to Talcott a lease of its premises, and the sign of Talcott was to be placed on the premises. The Baker Company later passing into bankruptcy, the controversy arose as to goods on hand and accounts receivable for goods sold. As to goods on hand, the court held that Talcott was not entitled to their possession, because there never had been a delivery of the goods to Talcott so that the latter could be considered as a factor in possession. The signs on the door of both parties had no effect, because it was not an inappropriate designation of premises where the Baker Company conducted its business and where Talcott also had quarters for the transaction of some business of his own. "It is absolutely essential," said the court, "to the validity of a factor's lien for advances, that the property consigned shall be delivered by the consignor to consignee." As to the accounts receivable for goods sold, however, the court reached a somewhat different conclusion. The contract provided that all accounts where advances had been made on the goods by Talcott should pass to Talcott and be billed on his bill head. The court held that this was a complete assignment

[1] 188 Fed 401.

of each such account, and that, therefore, as to every account so assigned before the defendant had reasonable cause to believe in the insolvency of the Baker Company, this was not a preferential transfer

§ 247. **Question — Whether Consignment or Sale?** Once having ascertained that there has been a transfer of possession, the next question is whether the transaction partakes of the nature of a consignment or of a sale, and, in the latter case, whether it is an outright sale or conditional sale The question we are now to consider has been well stated,[1] as this. "Were the goods put in the hands of the one party by the other, to be sold for him and on his account, creating the relation of principal and factor; or were they turned over to such party, to be treated and disposed of as his own, being responsible to the other simply for the price? In the one case we have a trust or bailment, the goods throughout being those of the consignor or principal, as well as the moneys received for them. In the other, there is a sale " In determining this question, we must have regard to two features of the agreement in each case, viz. the disposition of (1) the goods and (2) the proceeds of sale of the goods. Sufficient authority for this assertion is to be found, among others, in the case of Ludvigh *v.* American Woolen Co,[2] where these furnished the only heads of discussion, the court at length finding the contract involved to be " a consignment agreement with the net proceeds of sales to be accounted for to the consignor, and with the right to return the unsold goods." Let us then, without more, address ourselves to these two subjects.

§ 248 **Disposition of the Goods.** With regard to the goods, there are several requisites to be complied with in order that we may consider the transaction as a consignment The first relates to the identity of the goods If, as the Supreme Court has said, the consignee is under obligation to return the goods, " in the same or some altered form," there is a consignment;

[1] *In re* Wolls, 140 Fed 752.   [2] 231 U S 522; 34 S Ct 161.

but "when there is no obligation to return the specific article, and the receiver is at liberty to return another thing of value, he becomes a debtor to make the return, and the title to the property is changed, the transaction is a sale."[1] Thus, if a patentee is to manufacture patent articles for the account of a concern which supplies him with the raw material for that purpose, and the nature of the transaction gives the consignee room for discretion as to using the identical materials or exchanging them for others, the transaction is a sale and not a consignment.[2] If, then, the factor has not the right to return to the principal the goods which he is unable to sell, then we have no consignment agreement but a sale, because the essence of a consignment is that the goods are the principal's. If the agent can never return the goods to the principal, then, on the other hand, the principal is never entitled to call for the goods, and all of this contradicts the idea of agency and bailment.[3] Another test has sometimes been suggested,[4] whether the factor keeps the goods of his principal separated from his own. But this test is not really essential except where otherwise the public might be misled, as in the case where a factor is not generally known to be such in the business, or where the delivery of possession at the outset has been but symbolic at best.[5]

§ 249 **Disposition of Proceeds of Sale.** Turning now to the proceeds of sale, the test is simply whether the proceeds belong to the principal or to the factor. If the factor is bound to pay to the principal a fixed price for the goods whether he sells them or not and can keep the proceeds of sale so long as he complies with this condition, then it is obvious that the relation of principal and factor does not exist. This is illustrated by *Ex parte*

[1] Sturm v Boker, 150 U S 312, 14 S Ct 99
[2] Powder Co. v Burkhardt, 97 U S 110, *Ex parte* White, L. R 6 Ch App 397, aff'd under name of Towle v. White, 29 L T. N. S 78; *In re* Liberty Silk Co., 152 Fed 844
[3] Helby v Matthews, 1895 App Cases, 471
[4] Clark v Tippin, 9 Beav 284, 292
[5] See Ommen v Talcott 188 Fed 401, *Ex parte* Bright, 10 Ch. Div. 566, Ryttenberg v. Schefer, 131 Fed 313

White.[1] The firm of Towle & Co. had the custom of sending cotton yarn to the bankrupt, upon the terms that the bankrupt could make it up into goods and sell the same to whatever customers and on whatever credit he chose. A list of prices accompanied the goods so sent, and at the end of each month the bankrupt rendered an account of the yarn sold and the following month paid Towle & Co. for the quantity sold according to the price list. The issue arose on the attempt by Towle & Co to trace moneys in the hands of the bankrupt as specific trust money held for them by their agents. The Court of Appeals held against them and the House of Lords affirmed the judgment. The reasoning of the court is thus expressed by MELLISH, L J.

"If the consignee is at liberty according to the contract between him and his consignor to sell at any price he likes and receive payment at any time he likes, but is to be bound, if he sells the goods, to pay the consignor for them at a fixed price, and a fixed time, in my opinion, whatever the parties may think, their relation is not that of principal and agent. The contract of sale which the alleged agent makes with his purchasers is not a contract made on account of his principal, for he is to pay a price which may be different, and at a time which may be different from that fixed by the contract."

§ 250 **Whether Sale is Absolute or Conditional.** This reasoning brings us to the consideration of the other arrangement — the security agreement. If in the case of pretended consignment the proper elements of consignment do not appear as above stated, the transaction must amount to a sale. If the parties intend between themselves that title to the goods shall not pass to the consignee, the transaction is not a consignment transaction, but it may none the less be a conditional sale. So the next step in our procedure is to ascertain whether a conditional sale with powers of resale conferred upon the consignee can be valid as against the latter's creditors. And that

[1] L. R. 6 Ch App. 397, aff'd under name of Towle v. White, 29 L. T N. S 78

in turn naturally brings us to a consideration of the requisites of a security arrangement, whether chattel mortgage or conditional sale of the kind above discussed, with respect to the creditors of the debtor in possession.

§ 251 **Rule in Cases of Conditional Sale and Chattel Mortgage.** The principal reason why the common law viewed with complacency a security arrangement of chattels with the debtor in possession was that such an arrangement did not contemplate or permit the debtor's reselling the goods. As the New Jersey court has said,[1] " where the vendee is in possession under a conditional contract of sale, he has no property to convey to the purchaser ", nor was it ever intended that he should have, because neither instrument ordinarily confers any power of sale. In fact, having regard to the essential nature of the arrangement as securing a debt, such power of sale as is necessary should be given to the secured creditor, in order that he may realize on his debt by sale of the property if necessary. But no such power of sale should be given to the debtor in order to fulfill any of his own purposes. If the lender allows the borrower any power of sale, it can properly be for only one purpose, namely, to liquidate the debt which the goods secure. No other purpose should be tolerated. It would follow that the power must be coupled with the restriction that the proceeds of sale shall be immediately and unreservedly turned over to the lender in reduction or extinction of the debt To that extent it is proper for the debtor to be given a power of resale because, to paraphrase the language of the New York Court of Appeals, " it simply creates the debtor agent to do what the statutes and public policy require the lender himself to do, or to excuse himself for not doing, viz to make immediate and direct application of property of this description when it is mortgaged to the payment of the debt." [2] But if the instrument allows the borrower to do anything else with the proceeds of sale than apply

[1] Cole v Berry, 42 N J L 308.
[2] Conklin v. Shelley, 28 N. Y. 360.

it in extinction of the debt, it is void as against the borrower's creditors.[1]

§ 252. **Evolution of this Rule from the Particular to the General.** This rule is supported by the great body of authority.[2] Its history in New York is very illuminating. At first the tendency was to regard the matter as one of fact in the particular case, and thus the courts were prone to leave to the jury as a question of fact the issue of bad faith in the particular transaction. Thus in Frank v. Batten[3] the court held that the question of good faith was one for the jury to decide, the transaction there being a conditional sale of lumber. In Ludden v. Hazen,[4] which was a case of a sale of whisky to be retailed by the vendee to his customers, the court held as a matter of law that the transaction was invalid. But the growth of this doctrine has been from the particular to the general, culminating in the laying down of certain positive rules of law on the subject. The net result at the present day is simply this, that if the debtor is allowed, by the terms of the original agreement, to resell the goods and is not required forthwith to turn over the proceeds of the sale to the owner in reduction of his debt, the other creditors of the debtor may treat the goods as the latter's own, notwithstanding the terms of the agreement between the debtor and his mortgage creditor.

[1] Robinson v. Elliott, 22 Wall 513, In re Garcewich, 115 Fed 87, Skilton v. Coddington, 185 N. Y. 80, 77 N. E. 790.

[2] The federal courts in such matters profess to follow the State law (Dooley v. Pease, 180 U. S. 126, 21 S. Ct. 329, Ethridge v. Sperry, 139 U. S. 266, 11 S. Ct. 565), but they have ascertained the State law to be in accordance with the foregoing in a great number of jurisdictions. In Maine (In re Perkins, 155 Fed 237), in North Carolina (Mitchell v. Mitchell, 147 Fed 280); in Oregon (In re Rasmussen, 136 Fed 704), in Iowa (In re Hickeson, 162 Fed 345), and in Illinois (In re Galt, 120 Fed. 443) the District Courts have given it their approval. It has also been approved by the Circuit Court of Appeals of the Seventh Circuit (In re Gilligan, 152 Fed. 605). In some States, as Texas, this doctrine is announced by statute (In re Raney, 202 Fed 996)

[3] 49 Hun 91, 1 N. Y. S 705.

[4] 31 Barb 650

§ 253 **Growth of Doctrine — Illustrative Cases.** In Edgell v Hart [1] a chattel mortgage upon a stock of goods in a retail store permitted the mortgagor to sell the goods in the course of trade, the mortgage to embrace all other goods which might afterwards be put in the store. The court held that this transaction was fraudulent as matter of law, saying:

"The law adjudges that they intended what the writing expresses, and it would be incompetent for either party to show, if they were possessed of the most persuasive evidence, that they designed the instrument to have a different operation from the one the law assigns to it . . . The existence of such a provision out of the mortgage or in it would invalidate it as matter of law, and where the facts are undisputed this court should so declare. The manifest tendency of such arrangements to defraud creditors by giving to the mortgagor a false credit, and their incongruity with the just and legal idea of a mortgage are in my mind sufficient to condemn them."

In Conkling v Shelley,[2] on the other hand there was a chattel mortgage with an oral agreement that the mortgagors should continue in possession and sell the goods, paying over all the proceeds to the mortgagee This was held valid as against the mortgagors' creditors, the court saying that the agreement "was simply creating them (the mortgagors) agents to do what the statutes and public policy required the mortgagees themselves to do, or to excuse themselves for not doing, viz. to make immediate and direct application of property of this description when it is mortgaged to the payment of the debt." The two cases of Brackett v. Harvey [3] and Skilton v Codington [4] filled up the gaps in this proposition. In Brackett v. Harvey, the mortgagor was authorized to accept business paper for the sale, which the mortgagee agreed to take in payment *pro tanto* of the debt, and use a portion of the proceeds in the purchase of other property which should become subject to the lien of the

[1] 9 N Y. 213
[2] 28 N Y. 360
[3] 91 N Y 214
[4] 185 N Y 80, 77 N E 790.

mortgage This was held valid as against the mortgagor's creditors In Skilton *v* Codington the mortgagor was permitted to reserve from the proceeds of sale enough money to meet the expenses of his business, and this was held invalid as against the mortgagor's creditors

While some remarks of Judge FINCH in Brackett *v.* Harvey appeared to base the creditor's rights entirely on the Statute of Fraudulent Conveyances, the language of the court in Edgell *v* Hart[1] would seem to put it more on the ground of the effect such transactions would have in inducing credit And we have even more redoubtable authority to the same effect In a pioneer decision by the United States Supreme Court, where, no State law applying, it was free, as it said, to follow its own rule, a mortgage of this kind was held void. The defense was that the mortgage had been recorded and therefore the record would afford public notice, but the court said

"Manifestly it was intended to enable the mortgagors to continue their business and appear to the world as the absolute owners of the goods and enjoy all the advantages resulting therefrom It is idle to say that a resort to the record would have shown the existence of the mortgage, for men get credit by what they apparently own and possess, and this ownership and possession had existed without interruption for ten years. There was nothing to put creditors on their guard. On the contrary, continued possession and apparent ownership were well calculated to create confidence and disarm suspicion."[2]

§ 254. **Recordation of Agreement Immaterial** The question of recording or nonrecording of the instrument has nothing to do with the court's point of view As we have seen in Chapter X, a conditional sale agreement does not have to be recorded in New York to be valid as against creditors, and yet, on the other hand, in a leading case in the federal

[1] *Supra*
[2] Robinson *v* Elliott, 22 Wall. 513, 525, followed by Russel *v* Wynne, 37 N. Y. 591.

courts sitting in New York, such an agreement has been held void as against creditors. There a conditional sale agreement permitted the vendee to sell and dispose of a line of wearing apparel at such prices as he might desire, paying to the vendor at stated intervals fixed prices which were provided by the vendor at each delivery of goods. It was filed as a conditional sale agreement, but filed or unfiled, its effect was the same, the court held that it was fraudulent " as matter of law "[1]

§ 255 **Essentially False Character of such Arrangements** The difficulty with such a transaction is that it has none of the genuine attributes of any one of the classes of bailment, to which we have already referred. If a conditional sale agreement or a chattel mortgage permits the mortgagor to sell the property and put the money in his pocket, but provides that if he should buy more property the same should be subject to the lien of the mortgage, that is in itself a negation of the terms of the security; so that, as the court said in the Garcewich case,[2] the security provisions are nothing more than the expression of a confidence. Nor does such a transaction constitute the relationship of principal and factor, because the mortgagor or vendee, as it may be, by paying a fixed sum of money can keep the goods and resell them at a profit for himself. As pointed out in a recent case, this departs from the idea of principal and factor, " for a factor cannot make a profit by his agency, nor a valid purchase for himself and receive a commission for his services."[3] The same view is taken by the English courts in the case of *Ex parte* White which we have already discussed. There under a consignment arrangement, by which the consignee should make up the consigned stuff into goods and sell it at whatever price he might please, paying only fixed prices to the consignor, it was held that moneys received from such sales were not trust moneys in the hands of the consignee as against

---

[1] *In re* Garcewich, 115 Fed. 87.
[2] *Supra*
[3] *In re* Penney and Anderson, 176 Fed 141.

the latter's creditors, because the transaction was not one of principal and factor, whatever else it might be

§ 256 **Opposing View of Some Jurisdictions** Such is the doctrine which is supported by the weight of authority,[1] the federal Supreme Court itself, as we have seen, being in accord with it, and therefore with the more assurance, may it be submitted as the rule the most in accord with reason At the same time, however, the concession must be made that this is not the law of all the jurisdictions. In several circuits the federal courts have construed the law of the States where the property in question lay as supporting such arrangements [2] and we have several more States so declaring by their highest courts [3] In Connecticut, the vendee under a conditional sale contract may be allowed to sell at any price, paying only a fixed price to the vendor, because, as the courts reason, all he is under obligation to do is to pay the purchase price of the goods, and it does not matter what he does with it if the vendee chooses to give him that freedom. In Harris v. Coe [4] the question, as the Connecticut court viewed it, was "whether . . . there was either an absolute sale of the goods to Mamory, or such a conditional sale as under the provisions of Chapter 212 of the Public Acts of 1895 was invalid as against the defendant" The court held that the agreement was not a sale because " it was the *bona fide* intention of the parties that the title to the goods should not at any time pass to Mamory, but that he should receive and sell them for plaintiff," and for the same reason it was not a conditional sale because there was never any intention that Mamory could get title into himself. It made no difference

---

[1] *In re* Wells, 140 Fed 732; Penney v Anderson 176 Fed 141; Thompson v Paret, 94 Pa St. 275, West v Fulling, 36 Ind App. 617, 76 N. E. 325

[2] Walter Wood Co v Van Storey, 171 Fed 375 (North Carolina); *Re* Smith &c Piano Co, 149 Fed 111 (Eighth Circuit), Brett v. Carter, 2 Low 458; Fed Cases 1844

[3] Harris v Coe, 71 Conn 157, 41 Atl. 552, Gay v Bidwell, 7 Mich. 519, Hughes v Cary, 20 Iowa 399

[4] *Supra*

that M had the right to sell the goods at any figure he pleased "though bound to account to the consignor at a fixed price." "Whatever may have been the decisions of courts elsewhere," said this tribunal, "it has been distinctly held in this State that such power in the consignee does not of itself render a contract intended to be one of consignment, a contract of sale, that such right in the consignee is not inconsistent with the retention of ownership by the consignor." A recent decision of the United States Supreme Court, but professedly based upon the law of Arkansas where the transaction arose, is to the same effect. There a stock of dry goods was delivered by a wholesale to a retail house under an agreement reserving title, but providing that the goods could be resold in the ordinary course of business It was, however, expressly provided that the title not only to the goods but to all the proceeds of sale should be vested in the vendor "until the full purchase price and agreed value of the same shall be paid." The Supreme Court held that this transaction was a valid conditional sale.[1]

§ 257 **Trust Receipts** With all this in mind, let us turn to the cases upholding the so-called form of trust receipt. The trust receipt system for the importation of merchandise is this if one desires to import merchandise from abroad or from a distant place and has not the money with which to pay for it, he applies to a local banker for an advance on the collateral constituted by the goods purchased This banker, through his correspondent, buys the goods at their place of sale and brings them home. Upon their arrival they are delivered to the importer under a so-called trust receipt, which gives the importer the right to sell the goods to such persons as he may select, and at such prices as he may determine, but paying to the banker the amount which had been advanced on the credit of the goods, it being stipulated that the banker, until the time that the goods are sold, retains the title thereto.

The test of the validity of such an agreement should be as to

[1] Bryant *v* Swofford Dry Goods Co., 214 U S 279, 29 S Ct. 614

the disposal of the proceeds of sale. If those proceeds belong to the banker, then there is no doubt but that the transaction is valid. If, on the other hand, the proceeds of sale belong to the importer, then, under the majority view, the transaction is invalid, whether recorded as a chattel mortgage or conditional sale, or not As it is expressly provided that the proceeds of sale belong to the banker, up to the amount of his advances, the decisions upholding such transactions as against the creditors of the importer are well founded.[1]

§ 258 **Confusion of the Decisions** The early cases, logically enough, recognize the transaction as one of conditional sale because, as is said, "at the outset as one of the first steps in the process, the legal title is lodged in the plaintiff not to leave it until the payment of the draft"[2] As stated in a later case, "where a commercial correspondent however set in motion by a principal for whom he acts, advances his own money or credit for the purchase of property and takes the bill of lading in his own name, looking to such property as the reliable and safe means of reimbursement up to the moment when the original principal should pay the purchase price, he becomes the owner of the property instead of its pledgee, and his relation to the original mover in the transaction is that of an owner under a contract to sell and deliver when the purchase price is paid"[3] This idea was carried out in other cases where the transaction was held to amount to a conditional sale.[4] Other cases, however, have considered the transaction as constituting, not a conditional sale, but something in the nature of a mortgage.[5]

---

[1] *In re* Cattus, 183 Fed 735, Century Throwing Company *v.* Miller, 197 Fed 252
[2] Farmers' Bank *v* Logan, 74 N Y 568
[3] Moors *v* Kidder, 106 N Y 32, 12 N E 818; Dows *v* National Bank, 91 U S 618, Moors *v* Wyman, 146 Mass 60, 15 N E 104
[4] New Haven Wire Co cases, 57 Conn 352, 18 Atl 266, 5 L R A. 300, Mershon *v* Moors, 76 Wisc 502, 45 N. W 95, Moors *v.* Drury, 186 Mass. 424, 71 N. E. 810
[5] Charavay *v* York Silk Mfg. Co , 170 Fed 819; Drexel *v.* Pease, 133 N. Y. 129, 30 N. E. 732.

In the latest case on the subject, the court, while considering that "an authority to sell and account for the proceeds to the owner does not destroy the title reserved to him," considered that the question really did not arise. There the silk held under a trust receipt was delivered to a throwster for throwing into yarn. The throwster endeavored under a statute [1] to hold this silk for a prior indebtedness owing it by the importer. It was held that this could not be done, because the trust receipt arrangement does not affect the doctrine of reputed ownership, and therefore the throwster could not claim to have been misled into any belief that the silk belonged to the importer.[2]

[1] 3 Compiled Statutes of N J, 1910, p 3140, Sec. 60, a similar statute exists in New York, Lien Law, Sec 185
[2] Century Throwing Co v Muller, 197 Fed 252.

CHAPTER XIII

REPUTED OWNERSHIP IN CONNECTION WITH MORTGAGES

§ 259. The "After-acquired Property Clause"
260. The Common Law Doctrine
261. The Clause in the Light of Equity
262. Justice Story's View
263. Concurring View of the House of Lords
264. The Clause has Limitations of Locality
265. American Courts not Unanimous
266. Intervening Act Required
267. Early View in New York
268. The Corporate Mortgage — Mortgage of a Public Service Company
269. The Corporate Mortgage — Mortgage of a Manufacturing Company.

§ 270. Judge Lowell's Opinion
271. Economic Basis for New York Doctrine
272. Early View of the Federal Courts
273. Present View of the Federal Courts
274. Exception in Favor of Railroad Mortgages
275. Reasons Given for Such Exceptions
276. Rule Concerning Railroad Mortgages as Supplemented by Doctrine of Fosdick v. Schall
277. English View of the Present Day
278. English Rule is Based on the Recording Acts

§ 259. The "After-acquired Property Clause." We now come to the last feature of a security arrangement which affects the interest of creditors, and that is the "after-acquired property clause" of a mortgage. This is of universal presence in every mortgage by which the needs of a mercantile concern are financed. Such a mortgage usually conveys all the real and personal property of the mortgagor which he may then have on hand. The "after-acquired property clause" supplements this omnibus transfer by mortgaging a large part, if not all, of the borrower's future. It usually provides that all acquisitions to the mortgaged property, at any time placed on the mortgaged premises during the term of the mortgage, in addition to or substitution for anything existing at the date of the mortgage, and all other property, real or personal, which the mortgagor thereafter might acquire, shall be subject to the lien of the mortgage

§ 260 **The Common Law Doctrine.** A court of law would have no difficulty with this clause Of course such personal property as might be added to real estate in the sense that it may become part of the real estate within the meaning of the law of fixtures, would pass under the lien of the mortgage, but that is because a fixture, once becoming part of land, cannot be removed, and hence passes with the land wherever the latter goes under a pre-existing title.[1] But as to all after-acquired property that does not in law become part and portion of pre-existing property, the mortgage alone cannot have effect. It would amount to nothing but a contract to mortgage such property as the borrower thereafter might acquire. When the borrower acquires the property, he should perform his contract and mortgage the property. If he fails thus to perform he has broken his contract, but he has not mortgaged the property. It did not pass by his agreement, because at that date he did not own it, and one cannot transfer what he has not [2] On the other hand, the agreement to mortgage the property in advance has an important effect if it is followed up by consummation So far as any passage of title is concerned, the subsequent property is absolutely free unless after its acquisition the mortgagor, by means of a supplemental instrument, conveys the property, or the mortgagee takes possession with the mortgagor's consent But such a subsequent transfer would be supported by a sufficient, though precedent, consideration as to avoid its being considered as a voluntary conveyance within the meaning of the Statute of Fraudulent Conveyances The mortgagee under such circumstances is clearly a purchaser

---

[1] See Galveston R R Co v Cowdrey, 11 Wall 459, Porter v Steel Co., 122 U S 267, 7 S Ct 1206 On the subject matter of this chapter see 19 Harv Law Review p 557, et seq

[2] Grantham v. Hawley, Hobart 132; Rochester Distilling Co. v. Rasey, 142 N. Y 570, 37 N. E 632.

within the meaning of the statute, and, having furnished in good faith his consideration, is entitled to the transfer.[1] There may be some room for doubt whether he would be entitled to keep the property as against a trustee in bankruptcy if he received the transfer after he had acquired notice of the transferor's insolvency, since it might be avoided as a preferential transfer in a jurisdiction which does not attribute the qualities of a trust to the after-acquired property clause, of which we are about to speak. Nevertheless the courts sitting in such States have uniformly refused to adopt such a view, and have considered this intervenient act as not capable of constituting a preferential transfer under any circumstances.[2] But it may well be questioned whether these decisions are still possessed of their former strength, since of late the Supreme Court has come fully to the point of saying that a transfer for a past consideration is preferential, unless either the necessary elements of a preference do not exist or the agreement is such that a court of equity would force the specific performance of its terms.[3]

§ 261 **The Clause in the Light of Equity.** That brings us to the consideration of this clause in the light of equity jurisprudence. While undoubtedly one cannot grant what he has not, it is also clear that one may make such an agreement with regard to the disposition of property, present or future, as would justify an equity court in enforcing specific fulfillment of the obligations thus assumed. In such a case there exists, with respect to the property from the moment of its acquisition,

---

[1] Barton v. Sithington, 128 Mo. 164, 30 S. W. 514.
[2] Thompson v. Fairbanks, 196 U. S. 516, 25 S. Ct. 306, Chase v. Denny, 130 Mass. 566, Gilbert v. Vail, 60 Vt. 261, 14 Atl. 542
[3] See *infra*, Ch XX Cf. these remarks of Mr. Justice Holmes in Greey v. Dockendorff, 231 U. S. 513, 34 S. Ct. 166, "There may have been a moment when the goods could have been attached, or when, if insolvency had been made known, as in Nat'l City Bank v. Hotchkiss, it would have been too late to make the promised lien good. But in this case, the lien was acquired before any knowledge of insolvency, and before any attachment intervened."

an equitable lien. This is illustrated by Langton v. Hasten.¹ There a ship, while on a whaling voyage, was mortgaged " with all oil and head matter and other cargo which might be caught or brought home on the said ship on and from her then present voyage " Upon arrival of the ship at her home port with a cargo thus acquired, a judgment creditor levied upon the cargo, whereupon the mortgagee filed a bill to have the cargo declared subject to his lien It was held " that for some purposes at least, by contract an interest in a thing not in existence at the time of the contract may, in equity, become the property of the purchaser for value," and that in the particular case the lien was enforceable as against the creditor. Undoubtedly creditors are in no sense of the word purchasers for value, so as to cut off any genuine equity in the debtor's property ² It is very hard, therefore, to prevent the reasoning used in the case of the ship's voyage from applying to any case of after-acquired property, with the result that the mortgagee, by virtue of his contract alone, should have a lien upon any property which may be acquired, at least in so far as certainty may be predicated of the agreement So far, then, as it may identify the after-acquired property with reference to a particular place, there is much room for the argument in favor of equitable intervention. Such a case is where the mortgage covers a manufacturing plant *in esse*, and also all goods that thereafter may be acquired by the mortgagor and located upon the premises occupied by the plant, in the nature of manufactured stock, raw material, fixtures, or supplies For any such case there is very high authority for the view that the mortgage confers upon the mortgagee a specific equity in all the after-acquired property, as and when it comes within the description afforded by the mortgage.³

---

[1] 1 Hare 549
[2] Sprague v Cochran, 144 N Y. 104, 38 N. E. 1000, Nicholson v Schmucker, 81 Md 459, 32 Atl 182; Mitchell v. Winslow, 2 Story 630, Fed Cas. 9673
[3] Holroyd v Marshall, 10 H. L. C 191, Mitchell v Winslow, 2 Story 630, Fed Cas 9673, Brett v. Carter, 2 Low. 458; Fed Cas

§ 262. **Justice Story's View.** The pioneer of this doctrine was Mr Justice Story. In Mitchell v. Winslow,[1] the mortgage covered machinery or tools on hand or which might at any time within four years be acquired by the mortgagor. It was held that the mortgagor's assignee in bankruptcy did not take title to any machinery acquired within four years. Mr Justice Story said " that wherever the parties by their contract intended to create a positive lien or charge either upon real or upon personal property, whether then owned by the assignor or contractor, or not, or, if personal property, whether it is then *in esse* or not, it attaches in equity as a lien or charge upon the particular property as soon as the assignor or contractor acquires a title thereto against the latter, and all persons asserting a claim thereto under him, either voluntarily or with notice or in bankruptcy."

§ 263. **Concurring View of the House of Lords.** Later, in Holroyd v. Marshall,[2] the House of Lords reached the same result in an issue between the mortgagee and a judgment creditor of the mortgagor who had levied upon some of the after-acquired property. The reasoning of the court is thus summarized by Lord Westbury ·

"A contract for a valuable consideration by which it is agreed to make a present transfer of property passes at once the beneficial interest, provided the contract is one of which a court of equity will decree a specific performance. In the language of Lord Hardwicke the vendor becomes a trustee for the vendee, subject, of course, to the contract being one to be specifically performed. And this is true not only of contracts relating to real estate, but also of contracts relating to personal property, provided that the latter are such as a court of equity would direct to be specifically performed. A contract for the sale of goods, as for example, 500 chests of tea, is not a contract which would be specifically performed, because it does not relate to

---

1844, Eddy v. McCall, 71 Mich 497, 39 N W 734, Smithurst v. Edmunds, 14 N J Eq 408

[1] *Supra*   [2] *Supra*

any chests of tea under contract; but a contract to sell 500 chests of the particular kind of tea which is now in my warehouse in Gloucester, is a contract relating to specific property, and which would be specifically performed.'

§ 264. The Clause has Limitations of Locality It follows, of course, that a contract by which the mortgagor agrees to give a mortgage upon property to be placed upon a particular spot is a contract which comes within Lord Westbury's definition, and of which the mortgagee could ask specific performance. This would answer for the average case where the general mortgage covers an industrial plant or railroad lines within whose confines the after-acquired property is apt to be brought. Nor can it go further, in sound reason An agreement to mortgage all property that the mortgagor might thereafter acquire and place on a particular spot identifies the property, at least to some extent But an agreement to mortgage everything on earth that the mortgagor thereafter might acquire is really not a security agreement at all, rather does it attempt to give the lender a lien upon the borrower's earning power itself, it savors more of vassalage than of hypothecation That is the distinction taken by the Michigan courts in Ferguson v. Wilson,[1] where the "equity" of the clause was refused with respect to property acquired outside of the business in which the mortgagor was engaged and in which the other mortgaged property was used That, indeed, draws the line of distinction too loosely, to our way of thinking, but it is better to do that than to entertain the views of Judge Lowell, who, for his part, was in favor of pushing the doctrine of Mitchell v Winslow à l'outrance [2]

§ 265 American Courts not Unanimous But such ideas as Judge Lowell's have met with a serious check in the State courts of this country Many of our courts indeed have refused ear to any feature of the "equity" of the after-acquired

---

[1] 122 Mich. 97, 80 N W 1006.
[2] See Brett v. Carter, supra

property clause, and whether sitting in equity or at law, will attribute to it value only if it has been performed

§ 266 **Intervening Act Required** This contrary view seems to find accurate expression in the argument which occurred in Holroyd v Marshall,[1] where it was suggested that some "intervenient act to perfect the title in trust" was necessary In many of our States this is the rule Such a State is Massachusetts The pioneer case on this line is Moody v. Wright,[2] where the court says·

"The difficulty that presses in the present case is the want of any binding original contract which *per se* could have force and effect to change the after-acquired property, without some further act by the parties after the property should have come into existence Such act we deem to have been necessary to perfect the title of the petitioner whether his rights to property in such after-acquired articles are sought to be enforced in equity or at law"[3]

This intervening act need not, however, be the voluntary act of the mortgagor. It is sufficient if possession is taken by the mortgagee even against the will of the mortgagor, as by replevin suit[4] As is said by the Massachusetts court

"Formerly it was thought that such a covenant would take effect only if the mortgagor as well as the mortgagee acted under it Under the more liberal doctrine of later cases, which does not require the delivery of the property by the mortgagor, it is well settled that as against attaching creditors or assignee in insolvency, the title does not pass nor the mortgage take effect upon the after-acquired property, either at law or in equity, unless possession is taken under it"[5]

---

[1] *Supra*. [2] 13 Met. 17.
[3] Blanchard v Cook, 144 Mass 207, 11 N E. 83, Harriman v Woburn Electric Light Co, 163 Mass 85. 39 N E 1004; Barton v Sitlington, 128 Mo 164, 30 S W 514, Chynoweth v Tenney, 10 Wis. 397
[4] Barton v Sitlington, *supra*.
[5] Harriman v Woburn Electric Light Co, 163 Mass 85, 39 N. E. 1004

§ 267. **Early View in New York** In New York this doctrine has had a very interesting history. In McCaffrey v. Woodin[1] the views expressed in Holroyd v. Marshall were distinctly approved But that case is not of value in our study, because the question there arose as between the lessor and the lessee of a farm with respect to crops subsequently raised thereon. There never has been any question that the parties to such an agreement are bound and their subsequent privies are likewise bound, so that a clear distinction exists between their right on the one hand and that of the creditors on the other.[2] On the other hand, when the New York courts were faced with the direct question whether such a clause would be enforced as against the creditors of the mortgagor, then they speedily resolved a positive rule on the subject. At an early date the Court of Appeals, in dealing with an agency case of the kind we have previously discussed, doubted the validity of the after-acquired property clause as such,[3] but the question did not squarely present itself until it came up in connection with the modern form of corporate mortgage.

§ 268 **The Corporate Mortgage — Mortgage of a Public Service Company.** This sort of instrument presents itself in two aspects In the case of a public service company mortgage, where no stock of goods is dealt in, the after-acquired property clause generally stands alone. In New York Security etc. Co. v. Saratoga Gas Co ,[4] the question was whether earnings of the mortgagor derived between the date of the execution of the mortgage and the date of foreclosure, on hand in the shape of cash and book accounts, should be paid to the trustee under the mortgagee or to the receiver appointed in sequestration proceedings instituted by creditors of the mortgagor. It was held that to the latter belonged this fund. The court stated

[1] 65 N Y. 459
[2] Farmers' Loan & Trust Co. v. Grape Creek Coal Co., 63 Fed. 891.
[3] Gardner v. McEwen, 19 N. Y. 123.
[4] 159 N Y. 137, 53 N E. 758.

that to reach the opposite result " would deprive the unsecured creditor of the fund upon the faith he may have given credit to the mortgagor during the time when the latter was permitted to deal with and use it as his own."

§ 269 **The Corporate Mortgage—Mortgage of a Manufacturing Company.** In the case of a corporate mortgage executed by a manufacturing concern, however, the after-acquired property clause is accompanied by articles of the nature of those we examined in Chapter XII, permitting the mortgagor to sell off goods as it manufactures or acquires them, fresh acquisitions in turn becoming subject to the lien. The New York court has dealt with such a mortgage in two late cases In Zartman v Bank of Waterloo [1] the rule of the Saratoga Gas case was extended to the case of tangible personal property of the mortgagor as well as the earnings derived by it from the conduct of the plant covered by the mortgage, the court observing that " the general unsecured creditors had little, if anything, to rely upon except the shifting stock which, directly or indirectly, they themselves had furnished " In Titusville Iron Company v New York City [2] it was laid down that, although the after-acquired property clause would be enforced as against the mortgagor and purchasers from him with notice, it would not be enforced as against the mortgagor's creditors, the court saying " It seems settled law, at least in this State, that they will not be enforced as against creditors "

§ 270 **Judge Lowell's Opinion** Directly opposed stands the case of Brett v. Carter,[3] where Judge Lowell undertook to uphold the conjunction of the after-acquired property clause and the mortgage clauses such as we discussed in Chapter XII. The burden of his grievance against the contrary view is that it constitutes a reversion to " the harsher doctrine of fraud in law," whereas " a conveyance for a present valuable con-

[1] 189 N Y 267, 82 N E 127
[2] 207 N Y 203, 100 N E 806
[3] 2 Low 458, Fed Cas 1844

sideration is never a fraud in law on the face of the deed, and if fraud is alleged to exist it must be proved as a fact."

§ 271 **Economic Basis for New York Doctrine** It is submitted, however, that Judge Lowell's denunciation is scarcely sound. So far as the mortgage clauses discussed in Chapter XII are concerned, the Supreme Court answered him in Robinson v. Elliott,[1] which we cited in the chapter above mentioned. That decision does not rest upon the law of a particular State, as Judge Lowell suggests, on the contrary it expresses the Supreme Court's own views,[2] and to them we again refer, as we did in the last chapter So far as the after-acquired property clause is concerned, several considerations occur in support of the New York doctrine That doctrine resulted from the court's recognition of the way corporations nowadays are financed Instead of the investor putting his money into the stock of the corporation, he puts it into the corporation's mortgage bonds, so that in effect the corporation starts in business with a first lien, in favor of its investors, upon all its property. Then, by the after-acquired property clause it is sought to fasten this same lien upon subsequent property. Long ago Judge Lowell himself called attention to the fact, which he considered regrettable but well known, that all railroads in America were financed entirely on the basis of borrowed money[3] The same may be said of most large industrial companies The New York courts were not blind to this economic fact, and rightly or wrongly they felt it was incumbent upon them, if the ordinary rules of law would in any way allow, to restrict this lien of the investor as much as possible, so as to give the creditors of the company, by whose credit alone it is able to continue in business, a fair chance at some of the assets Of course the courts could not upset a lien with which the corporation starts business in favor of the investor, that is, the lien upon property

[1] 22 Wall 513
[2] See discussion of the decision in Ch XII
[3] *Re* Union Pacific R. R Co, 10 N B R. 178, Fed. Case No 14376.

already on the premises, although, as we have already seen, the courts will not allow even that lien to subsist upon property of which the mortgagor is given the right to dispose in the course of business unless he is required to turn over all the proceeds to the mortgagee. But while as to real estate and fixtures already on hand the courts cannot upset the lien, yet in the event of a foreclosure they will not allow the stockholders to take any profit in the purchasing company. That, as we have already seen, is the rule of Louisville Trust Co v Louisville Ry. Co [1] and the cases following it "We must therefore recognize the fact," said the Supreme Court, "for it is a fact of common knowledge, that whatever the legal rights of the parties may be ordinarily, foreclosures of real estate mortgages mean not the destruction of interest of the mortgagor and the transfer to the mortgagee alone of the full title, but that such proceedings are carried on in the interests of all parties who have any right in the mortgaged property, whether as mortgagee, creditor or mortgagor." When it comes to property afterwards put upon the premises, the New York court, following the same idea, has cut off the investor from the lien attempted by means of the after-acquired clause This clause depends upon the active aid of a court of equity. The court refuses that aid because, as it has said, "the foreclosure of a corporate mortgage does not necessarily mean a sale of the property in the ordinary sense It simply means a reorganization conducted by or in behalf of the bondholders. . . We think that justice and equity are best promoted by limiting the right of lien of the bondholders to such earnings only as shall accrue after the mortgagee, trustee, or the receiver shall have actually taken possession. The earnings prior to that time should in equity be awarded to the general creditor." [2]

§ 272. **Early View of the Federal Courts.** The attitude of the federal courts on this question is a matter of considerable

[1] 174 U S 674, 19 S Ct 827
[2] New York etc Co v Saratoga Gas Co., 159 N Y 137, 53 N E 758.

interest In the beginning, as we have seen, Mr. Justice Story decided in favor of the after-acquired property clause as constituting a valid lien against the creditors of the mortgagor.[1] In Pennock v. Coe [2] the Supreme Court distinctly adopted the same view in an issue which arose between the holders of first mortgage bonds upon a railroad and the holders of second mortgage bonds who, however, instead of relying upon the mortgage security, had sued upon their bonds to judgment and levied upon the after-acquired property as judgment creditors This in turn was followed by LOWELL. J., in Brett v. Carter,[3] so we may say that if the federal courts had been free to adopt a general rule of their own on such questions, independently of the State decisions, they had already established the rule in line with Holroyd v Marshall

§ 273. **Present View of the Federal Courts.** But a change has come of later years in the attitude of the federal courts towards creditors' rights. Commencing with the case of Etheridge v. Sperry [4] and continuing to the present day [5] the Supreme Court has laid down the rule that the validity of any grant, mortgage or lien upon real or personal property, both as between the parties and as against their respective creditors, is to be determined by the laws of the State where the property is situated at the time of the controversy The result is that at the present date the validity of the after-acquired property clause is a matter of State law rather than of federal rule. It was thus ruled by the Circuit Court of Appeals, Second Circuit, in In re Marine etc. Dry Dock Co.[6] where the court said "The mortgage contains the after-acquired property clause. This has been held valid and effective by the federal courts, but the case at bar must be disposed of in accordance with the decisions in the State courts."

[1] Mitchell v Winslow, *supra*
[2] 23 How 117.
[3] *Supra*
[4] 139 U S 266, 11 S Ct 565.
[5] Dooley v Pease, 180 U S 126, 21 S Ct 329
[6] 144 Fed 649

§ 274 **Exception in Favor of Railroad Mortgages** The Supreme Court, however, has given many times expressions showing its views in favor of the after-acquired property clause. In the cases where this has occurred, railway mortgages have always been involved, and this has led one jurist to make the suggestion that the case of a railroad mortgage constitutes an exception to the general rule forbidding the validity of such clauses as against creditors.[1] With the exception, however, of Pennock v Coe [2] the Supreme Court has never directly passed on the validity of such a mortgage as against the creditors of the mortgagor. All of the other Supreme Court cases in which the validity of these clauses has been insisted upon have involved quite different issues [3] Undoubtedly, the Supreme Court has entertained the view that there is something in the nature of a railroad security which

---

[1] Platt v N Y etc Ry. Co , 17 N. Y Misc. 22, 39 N Y. S 871.
[2] *Supra*
[3] Thus in Galveston Railroad Co v Cowdrey, 11 Wall 459, and Porter v The Steel Co., 122 U S 267, 7 S Ct 1206, the question arose between the mortgagee and one who had sold to the railroad property necessary for the construction of its right of way, such as rails and ties It was held that those articles when laid down constituted part of the railroad, and that the intention to reserve title to them, however well expressed, could not be effective in view, not only of the ordinary law of fixtures, but of the after-acquired property clause in question In Central Trust Co v. Kneeland, 138 U S 414, 11 S Ct 357, the issue was between the holders of a second mortgage and the holders of a first mortgage Similar issues were decided in Dunham v Cinn etc Ry Co , 1 Wall. 254 (contractor's lien), and Toledo etc Ry Co v Hamilton, 134 U S. 296, 10 S Ct 546 (mechanic's lien) In McGoinkey v Toledo etc. Co , 146 U S 536, 13 S Ct 170, it was held that a vendor of cars and other like "loose property suitable of separate ownership and separate liens," U S v N O Railroad Co , 12 Wall 362 may reserve a title by means of conditional sale which would be effective as against the mortgagee, but that the intention to do so must be clearly manifested. Finally in Fogg v Blair, 133 U S 534, 10 S Ct. 363, it was held that a debt of the mortgagor which the purchaser on foreclosure sale assumes has precedence over a mortgage given by the purchaser in order to secure bonds which shall constitute part of the purchase price That leaves us then with Pennock v Coe as the sole authority for any statement to the effect that the Supreme Court will sanction the after-acquired property clause as against creditors

might differentiate it from other property. Thus in Galveston Ry. Co. v Cowdrey[1] the court said that "to hold otherwise would render it necessary for a railroad company to borrow money in small parcels as sections of the road were completed and trust deeds could severally be given thereon."

§ 275 **Reasons Given for Such Exceptions** The general view of the State courts accords with this theory. Upon the reasoning that the charter or statute authorizes the company to mortgage not only its properties but its franchises as well, railroad mortgages on after-acquired property have been upheld.[2] In Pierce v Emory[3] the court said that the mortgage "would convey to the mortgagees all the right and power which the corporation had to acquire and hold property, if the power to acquire and hold property is one of the rights and franchises of the corporation, . . . and the subsequently acquired property would pass under the mortgage as incident to the right of acquiring and holding it." In other States the matter is regulated to this end by statute.[4] In New York the courts have reached the same result, by an ingenious reading of the statute requiring that railroad mortgages need not also be filed as chattel mortgages.[5] "By this act," said the court, "the status of such property, so far as it relates to liens by way of mortgage, is made practically subject to the same rules and is placed upon the same footing as real property." Therefore, as there may be an equitable lien on after-acquired real property, it was evidently the intention of the Legislature to make a railroad company's equipment, although personal property in the view of the New

---

[1] *Supra.*
[2] Pierce v Emory, 32 N. Y 484, Platt v N Y & Sea Beach Ry. Co , 9 N Y. App Div 87, 41 N. Y S. 42, aff'd 153 N Y 670, 48 N E. 1106 , Morrill v Noyes, 56 Me 458
[3] *Supra.*
[4] See Jones, "Corporate Bonds," § 42
[5] N. Y Lien Law, Sec 231

York courts,[1] "subject to the same rules so far as practical as apply to liens upon real property."[2]

§ 276. **Rule Concerning Railroad Mortgages as Supplemented by Doctrine of Fosdick v Schall** In point of fact, however, this exception in favor of railway mortgages can do little harm to creditors. The average unsecured creditor of a public service company has a debt for labor or supplies. If he has not waited too long for his money, he will find himself protected, in the event of the company passing into the hands of a foreclosure receiver, by the statutory priority which the laws of most States accord him.[3] The origin of these statutes, as we shall see, was the doctrine created by the Supreme Court in Fosdick v. Schall,[4] that an equity court should not extend its foreclosure process to the holder of a mortgage except upon the condition that priority of payment, out of the mortgaged property, be accorded to all those who, for an antecedent period whose limit was later fixed at six months, had supplied it with labor and material necessary to its operation. Thus the same court which in Pennock v. Coe[5] had enforced the after-acquired property clause against the unsecured creditors of a railway company, now, in high despite of the mortgagee's rights, extended to the bulk of the creditors this remarkable sort of priority. Why this was done sufficiently appears in the following extract from the opinion of the court.

"The business of all railroad companies is done to a greater or less extent on credit This credit is longer or shorter as the necessities of the case require. . . . The mortgagee has his strict rights which he may enforce in the ordinary way If he asks no favors, he need grant none But if he calls upon a court of chancery to put forth its extraordinary powers and grant him purely equitable relief, he may with propriety be required to submit to the operation of a rule which always applies in such cases, and do equity in order to get equity."

[1] Hoyle v Plattsburg &c R R Co , 54 N Y 314
[2] Platt v N Y. & Sea Beach Ry Co , *supra*
[3] See *infra*, § 528   [4] 99 U. S. 235.   [5] *Supra*

218   THE RIGHTS AND REMEDIES OF CREDITORS.   [CHAP XIII.

§ 277. **English View of the Present Day.** It may be noticed that on all the points discussed in this chapter and the one preceeding, where the rule of reputed ownership was involved, few English cases were cited That is for the very good reason that there are none of aid, since, with regard to all security arrangements, the English courts take a line that carries them very far from the prevailing American doctrines.

§ 278. **English Rule is Based on the Recording Acts** In England the courts profess to be guided entirely by the statutes There is, as we have seen, a reputed ownership clause in the Bankrupt Act There is no such clause in the Companies Acts; and the omission of such a clause from such a comprehensive statute settles the question as far as the English courts are concerned. They do not recognize as a substitute any rule based on estoppel.[1] As a result the after-acquired clause of an English corporate mortgage is enforceable, because the Companies Acts contain no reputed ownership clause.[2] In like manner the after-acquired clause is enforceable in any other kind of mortgage, because chattel mortgages nowadays have to be recorded under the Bill of Sales Act, and that record, as the court considers, is sufficient for all things.[3] The only limit which has been placed by the English courts is that the charge cannot be enforced as to income which had accrued before the grantee had made entry either personally or by means of a receiver; but that is really no limitation on the mortgagee's rights as such, for reasons we have already considered.[4] Under recent amendments to the Companies Acts, corporate mortgages must now be registered, and if not are void as against the company's creditors. Under these amendments a floating charge if not registered is void under the statute,[5] but if regis-

---

[1] *Re* Crumlin Viaduct Co , 11 Ch Div 755.
[2] Tailby *v* Official Receiver, 13 A C 523.
[3] Holroyd *v* Marshall, 10 H L C 191
[4] Government etc Co *v.* Manila, 1897 A. C. 81. The same rule of course prevails with us See Ch II.
[5] Illingsworth *v.* Holsworth, 1904 A C. 355.

tered the floating charge is fully enforced.[1] Such is the idea of Judge Lowell likewise, to pin everything to the recording Acts, and leave the case alone, beyond the simple inquiry whether the mortgage was recorded.[2] Such is the view adopted by the House of Lords in Holroyd v. Marshall,[3] "the present case," said Lord Chelmsford, "meets any possible difficulty upon the subject of notice, because it appears that the instrument was recorded as a bill of sale." There are, as we have seen, many American courts who agree with that idea. There are many others, as we have also learned, who strongly disagree with it. The result has been the addition to our jurisprudence, so far as any rule which is not universally accepted can be an addition, of a certain doctrine which at least is not out of tune with present-day conditions.

[1] Coxe v. Peruvian Limited, 1908 1 Ch. 604.
[2] Brett v. Carter, *supra*.
[3] *Supra*.

CHAPTER XIV

EQUALITY OF DISTRIBUTION AS AN OBJECT OF ATTAINMENT

§ 279. The Selfish System of Realization
280 The System of Equal Distribution.
281 Equal Distribution an Object only in Case of Insolvency.
282 The Selfish Point of View
§ 283. The Principle of Equal Distribution
284 Judicial Recognition of This Principle
285 Common Ground of the Two Principles
286 Relation of the Preferential Transfer to the Two Systems

§ 279. **The Selfish System of Realization.** To the present point we have considered the right of realization which every creditor possesses and may exercise for his own ends alone, and the wrongs which the debtor is capable of inflicting upon that right. We have seen that both equity and law concurred in giving the creditor, who availed himself of the respective remedies which they afforded, a priority of satisfaction over all creditors who should later institute proceedings in their own behalf. Upon this foundation has been constructed an enormous body of doctrine whose outlines we have studied in the preceding chapters. In no part of this is any duty recognized as owing by one creditor to another, no principle of sodality has place in this system. No creditor owes any duty of trust or confidence to the other, on the contrary, each may sue his debtor or compound with him on any basis he may please [1]

§ 280 **The System of Equal Distribution.** We are now to consider another body of law, of at least equal importance and

[1] Brown v. Webb, 20 Ohio 389, Frost v. Goddard, 25 Me 414, Johnson v Trust Co, 104 Fed. 174, Foster v McAlester, 114 Fed. 145, Re Hawkes, 204 Fed 309

extent, of concurrent growth with that which we have considered, and founded upon quite an opposite principle Both systems exist to-day, but the latter has always superseded the first in cases where it has application, and has within itself forces that make for progress portending still further encroachments The object of the system is equality of distribution in a case where the debtor's assets are insufficient to pay the creditors in full, and our study shall be of the means of attaining this object which the available statutes and principles provide

§ 281 **Equal Distribution an Object only in Case of Insolvency** If the judgment debtor is solvent in the broad sense when the creditor issues execution, that is, has enough assets to meet his debts in full when property which he has fraudulently dealt with has been brought back, it is obvious that the remedies we have considered are sufficient. And hence it would hardly seem to have been necessary for the courts so frequently to reiterate the well-established doctrine that a solvent debtor owes no duty of trust or otherwise to his creditors with respect to his property.[1] But if the debtor is insolvent, that is, if all of this property is not sufficient to meet all of his indebtedness, clearly a different situation is presented. What would one say is the right of the creditor?

§ 282. **The Selfish Point of View** The answer depends upon whose interest we are considering If we have in mind only the interest of a particular creditor who has obtained a judgment, we should say that if this particular creditor could levy ahead of any one else on something that the debtor owned, it is immaterial whether the other creditors found something on which they could levy. And if the debtor had property which was such in a practical sense, but not so recognized at common law, in short, rights enforceable only by aid of a court of equity, then this creditor would feel that the Court of Chancery should give him this same exclusive right to realize on his judgment, if he applied for such relief ahead of the other credi-

[1] See Ch. I.

tors There we have one way of looking at the matter, to place the whole law of creditors' rights, in the case of an insolvent debtor, upon the basis of priority in execution, and to make the " race of diligence " — to use the phrase which describes the principle we have heretofore studied — the be-all and end-all of the law.

§ 283. **The Principle of Equal Distribution.** Compare that with the result obtained by viewing the situation from the standpoint of all the creditors instead of merely one of them When we take this position we can reach but one conclusion, that when the debtor is insolvent the right of all the creditors is to an equal distribution of the assets, and the rights of each creditor end with his *pro rata* portion. It is not fair that one creditor should be paid more than another They are all of the same class and they should all suffer equally. It is the universal recognition of this right, however imperfectly expressed or taken for granted it may be in decisions and legislation, that has created the body of law which we may describe under the head of creditors' rights. It is the right of all the creditors that all the debtor's assets should be applied to the payment of his debts, and that equal distribution should be made in the application.

§ 284. **Judicial Recognition of This Principle.** That the courts have recognized this as a worthy principle, however incapable they might be to enforce it in all cases without statutory aid, cannot be denied On numerous occasions we find judges putting this thought into language which is of value to our inquiry, however more or less it might have been connected with the particular cases in which it was used. Thus in Wilson *v* Webb,[1] EYRE, C. B., puts the thought in its negative aspect; equity, says he, will never lend its aid to defeat fair creditors. To the same effect is Constantein *v.* Blache[2] In overruling the plea to the bill of discovery filed in Chambers *v* Thompson,[3]

[1] 2 Cox Ch 3   [2] 1 Cox Ch 286.
[3] 4 Bro C C 434 — See discussion of this case in Ch I

Lord LOUGHBOROUGH remarked that the distribution of assets effected by bankruptcy is merely giving the creditors their own In Pickstock v Lyster,[1] Lord ELLENBOROUGH describes a general assignment as "a discharge of the moral duty attached to the character of debtor to make the fund available for the whole body of creditors." On the same foundation rest the cases which uphold the right of creditors to effect combined action, by means of a reorganization committee, when their debtor's affairs have gone wrong.[2] And the alacrity with which the courts uphold composition agreements of the debtor with his creditors whereby time or other favor is extended the debtor by an agreement signed by all his creditors, and declare that any secret favor shown one creditor over the others is a fraud upon their rights under the agreement, is further demonstration of the favor with which the courts view any arrangement which tends to the equal benefit of all. That rule was laid down at an early date and has been consistently applied to the present day.[3] There the equity court is hampered by none of the limitations which we shall presently consider, it has an agreement to start with, and into that agreement it reads the strongest terms of good faith and fiduciary obligation on the part of each creditor toward the others. In short, this principle lies ready for general use, so far as may not be forbidden by limitations of jurisdiction.

§ 285 **Common Ground of the Two Principles.** Thus we have two lines of thought upon this subject, one resting entirely on the idea of priority, the basis of the other being equality. These ideas harmonize, however, to a certain extent. The rights which they embody are equally capable of invasion by fraudulent conduct on the debtor's part of the various sorts that we have considered in the previous chapters It is obvious

---

[1] 3 M & S 371
[2] Cont Trust &c. Co. v Allis-Chalmers Co, 200 Fed 600, Clarke v Centl of Ga Ry. Co, 66 Fed 16, Fowler v Jarvis-Conklin Co, 63 Fed. 888
[3] Spurrel v Spurrel, 1 Atk 108; Constantein v Blache, 1 Cox Ch 287, Security &c. Co. v. Fust National Bk, 203 Fed. 632

that any case of fraudulent conveyance or of reputed ownership wrongs the creditors as a class to an equal degree with each individual among them.

§ 286 **Relation of the Preferential Transfer to the Two Systems** But in addition to these common wrongs, there is another, which the debtor is capable of inflicting upon the creditors as a class, but which is not a wrong upon the interest of any individual creditor. That is the preferential transfer. If the debtor pays or secures one of his creditors in full or in part when he is unable to pay or secure all of the others to an equal degree, he has violated the rights of these others, if each of them is entitled to equality of treatment. But if the right of each neglected creditor is simply to get paid if he can, and to use the processes of law and equity to that end upon the principle of first come first served, then it is obvious that the preferential transfer effects no invasion of his right. His fellow has simply been more diligent. Any creditor who sought to recover the property preferentially transferred, after putting himself in a position to make the attack by obtaining a judgment, would secure the right of priority which necessarily follows the assertion of his judgment, and the result would be that he would receive a preference instead of the creditor selected by the debtor. "A preference given by an insolvent debtor to a *bona fide* creditor cannot be avoided by an attaching creditor . otherwise it would simply amount to giving a preference to the attaching creditor, instead of to the creditor or creditors selected by the debtor." [1] Hence the well-settled rule that "at common law a debtor in failing circumstances has the right to prefer certain creditors to whom he is under special obligations, though by such preference the fund for the payment of the other creditors be lessened or even absorbed." [2] But the pref-

---

[1] Sawyer v Levy, 162 Mass 190, 38 N E 365.
[2] Huntley v Kingman, 152 U S 527, 14 S Ct 688, Meaux v Howell, 4 East 1, Pickstock v Lyster, 3 M. & S. 371, Dodge v McKechnie, 156 N Y 514, 51 N. E 268

erential transfer is a recognized wrong upon the right of the creditor when viewed in the light of the principle of equal distribution. The place of this principle in our law shall be our approaching study, and in connection with that, we shall address ourselves to the doctrine concerning preferences, as constituting part of the system of liquidation by which equality of distribution is secured.

CHAPTER XV

EQUALITY OF DISTRIBUTION AS ACHIEVED BY THE DEBTOR'S VOLUNTARY ACT

§ 287 Debtor cannot Secure Equal Distribution by Suit
288 The General Assignment
289. It must Prescribe Immediate Distribution.
§ 290 Weakness of the General Assignment
291 Validity of Preferences in General Assignment
292 Status of Assignee

§ 287. **Debtor cannot Secure Equal Distribution by Suit.** We have seen that it is impossible by means of either execution or judgment creditor's bill to obtain equality of distribution, because both these methods of procedure rest entirely on the idea of priority No creditor first on the ground can be compelled to relinquish his gain, and naturally he cannot be expected to do so of his own free will Nor is there any method of procedure known to courts of equity by which the debtor can secure this result. True, there is the equity jurisdiction which is invoked by means of a "bill of peace" to prevent a multiplicity of suits; but obviously a debtor who confesses the justice of the claims against him cannot maintain such a suit.[1] That failing, no other equitable remedy can possibly suggest itself.

§ 288. **The General Assignment.** There was only one thing which a debtor could do of his own motion, and that lay entirely outside of legal procedure. We refer to the general assignment The courts of common law and the Court of Chancery recognized the right of a debtor to make a general assignment of his property to a third person in trust for the payment of

[1] Weber v. Weber, 90 Wisc 467, 63 N W 757, see generally Pomeroy, "Equity" (3d ed), Sec 250.

his creditors Such an arrangement was perfectly valid so far as the courts of common law and of equity were concerned, to use the language of LE BLANC, J , [1] " a party, independently of the bankrupt statutes, may convey away his property for the benefit of all his creditors." " It is not the debtor who breaks in upon the rights of the parties by this assignment," said Lord ELLENBOROUGH in the same case, " but the creditor who breaks in upon them by proceeding in his suit." The only limitation that certain of the courts placed was that at least some of the creditors should assent to the arrangement, otherwise, it being without adequate consideration, it is in the view of these courts a fraudulent conveyance [2] But subject to perhaps such requisites as that, there was no doubt that a general assignment for the benefit of creditors, as such, was valid under the Statute of Fraudulent Conveyances, and imposed duties upon the assignee which an equity court would fully enforce.[3]

§ 289 **It must Prescribe Immediate Distribution.** Beyond this limit the courts would not go If the instrument was anything else than a trust for immediate distribution, then the Statute of Fraudulent Conveyances engulfed it as tending by its operation to hinder, delay and defraud the creditors, however in name it may have purported to be for their benefit This view is expressed in the language of the Illinois court,[4] that " the placing of the property in the hands of assignees for any other purpose than to enable them to distribute it or its proceeds among creditors, must necessarily have the effect to, in some degree, hinder and delay creditors in the collection of their debts " If then a debtor who represents himself to be

---

[1] Pickstock v Lyster, 3 M & S 371.
[2] Griffith v. Ricketts, 7 Hare 299, Garrard v. Lauderdale, 3 Sim 1; Tittle v Van Leer, 89 Tex 174, 29 S W 1065, 34 S W 715, Russell v Woodward, 10 Pick 408 (*semble*)
[3] Goodson v. Ellison, 3 Russ 583, Brandenburgh v Thorndike, 139 Mass 102, 28 N E. 575, Barcroft v Le Sieur, 48 Mo 418
[4] Gardner v Conn Nat Bank, 95 Ill. 298

solvent makes an assignment, the case is bound to be within the
statute, to our way of thinking, and to such effect is the weight
of authority. As said by the New York court "No assignment was ever made by a debtor who supposed himself to be
solvent, with a view or for the purpose of selling and converting
his property into money more speedily than it could be done by
process of law If such were his design, he would effect it
himself without the intervention of an assignee The real
object is to gain time — to prevent the speedy sale and conversion which an execution would inevitably accomplish The
debtor who, believing himself more than solvent, places his
property beyond the reach of the process of the law, whatever
may be the pretence under which he cloaks the act, in the language of the Statute of Frauds 'hinders' and 'delays,' and
ultimately defrauds, his creditors. It is no answer to this
argument to say that the debtor provides an ample fund for
the payment of the debt, and that the creditor is ultimately to
be paid in full. The law gives the creditor the right to determine whether his debtor shall have further indulgence, or
whether he will pursue his remedy for the collection of the debt.
The deferring of payment is, generally, an injury to the creditor,
and he may be overwhelmed with bankruptcy for the want of
the fund which is locked up by the voluntary assignment of his
debtor. It is mockery to such a creditor to say that the assignment is made for the benefit of creditors "[1] Therefore an
assignment which directs that a business, forming the debtor's
chief asset, be continued indefinitely, the creditors to be paid off
as profits accrue, is obviously to be condemned under the
statute,[2] whereas it is equally true that such an arrangement is
guiltless if it merely authorizes the continuance of the business

[1] Van Nest v Yoe, 1 Sandf Ch 4, aff'd 11 N Y 302, Gardner v
Conn Bank, 13 R I. 155, First Nat Bank v Hughes, 10 Mo App
7 Contra is Munson v Ellis, 58 Mich 331, 25 N W 305

[2] Gardner v Conn Nat Bank, supra, Owen v Body, 5 A & E
28, Dunham v. Waterman, 17 N Y 9, Webb v Armistead, 26 Fed.
70.

as an interim measure to its winding up and liquidation.[1] In short, the distinction is the same as exists in the case of an equity receivership to which we shall later come, liquidation should be the object of the assignee's custody and not the continuance of the assignor's affairs with the hope of satisfying his debts as a matter of the wayside. And from the broader standpoint, it may be repeated that however the courts may differ on the particulars of its application, they all agree on the doctrine that the general assignment must be for the creditors' benefit solely, and not that of the debtor. The test should be whether the instrument departs from the simplicity of a direct and unequivocal devotion of the property of the assignor to the payment of his debts, and contains reservations and conditions intended for his ease and advantage.[2] If, then, the assignor provides that no creditor shall participate in the benefits of the trust unless he releases the whole of his claim, it would seem that the assignment is a fraudulent transfer. That was the decision in Grover v. Wakeman;[3] and while this point is of little importance nowadays, in view of the widespread existence of statutes governing the general assignment, it is of importance as indicating the extremes to which the courts went in considering this method of liquidation as a common law proposition.

§ 290 **Weakness of the General Assignment** The value of the general assignment as a method of liquidation is indicated by the considerations already advanced. So far from being able to build up a wholesome branch of liquidation law on this foundation, the chief effort of the courts lay in detecting the frauds that debtors attempted by the use of the general assignment. Purely as a result of this, the courts administering the statutory system of liquidation known as bankruptcy came to look with great disfavor upon the general assignment. They suspected any attempt by the bankrupt to distribute his prop-

---
[1] Robbins v Butcher, 104 N Y. 575, 11 N E 272; Talley v Curtain, 54 Fed 43, Woodward v Marshall, 22 Pick 468.
[2] Grover v Wakeman, 11 Wend. 187   [3] *Supra*.

erty among his creditors; hence the rule soon became fixed that a general assignment for the benefit of creditors was in itself a fraud on the bankrupt act[1] As a result, when the statutes made the general assignment an act of bankruptcy, it was held to justify an adjudication, and does to this day, entirely irrespective of whether or not the bankrupt was actually insolvent at the time he was so ill-advised as to try to save the expense of a bankruptcy.[2]

§ 291. **Validity of Preferences in General Assignment.** Another reason why the bankruptcy courts condemned the general assignment is of even more interest to us, and that has to do with the matter of preferences The kind of wrong which the debtor can inflict by way of the preferential transfer went absolutely unchecked by the doctrine governing even the valid general assignment In the very instrument itself the debtor had the right to prefer any creditors he might please, that, as we have seen, was his common law right, and why should he not exercise it, when turning over the balance of his property to his unpreferred creditors, if he could exercise it against their taking his property under their writs? No courts ever answered that question but in one way The instrument of assignment itself may direct that certain creditors shall be paid ahead of the others, and "neither law nor equity will inquire whether the objects of the debtor's preferences are more or less meritorious than those for whom he has made no provision,"[3] or he may himself effect a preferential payment of part of his debts and make a general assignment of the remainder of his property.[4] As we shall see, one of the chief features of the development of the bankruptcy system has been a growth of doctrine under

---

[1] Small v Oudley, 2 P Wms 427, Kettle v Hammond, 1 Cooke, "Bankrupt Laws," 86, Stewart v Moody, 1 C. M. & R. 777; Barnes v Rettew 8 Phil 133, Fed Cas 1019

[2] West Co v Lea, 174 U S 590, 19 S Ct 836.

[3] Grover v Wakeman, supra; Pickstock v. Lyster, supra, Huntley v Kingman, 152 U S 527, 14 S Ct 688

[4] Cross v Carstens, 49 Ohio St 548, 31 N E. 506.

which the preferential transfer suffers condemnation. The two systems thus differed on a vital point, and, as was natural, the system resting on the debtor's voluntary act had to give way before the system which was framed primarily in the interests of the creditors, in each case where a conflict should occur

§ 292. **Status of Assignee.** Equally important is another difference between the two systems As we shall see, the procedure in bankruptcy results in the appointment of a judicial representative of the creditors, nowadays called the trustee in bankruptcy, who has the right, in behalf of the creditors, to get all property which the debtor had fraudulently or preferentially transferred prior to the bankruptcy. No such power belonged to the assignee under a general assignment He had no status with regard to the debtor's affairs other than as derived from the deed of assignment He could administer such property as passed to him by the deed, but nothing else Consequently, if the debtor had previously transferred property in fraud of the very creditors for whose benefit the assignment of the remaining property was made, the assignee had no standing to sue for the recovery of the property which had been fraudulently conveyed. The short answer to his suit was that he had never acquired any rights in this property because it had not been transferred to him, he was the trustee for the creditors' benefit, but only to the extent of the property he received [1] The assignee was " but the hand of the assignor in the distribution of his estate " [2] And obviously such a person was in no sense the representative of the creditors or clothed in their behalf with rights which could be exercised *in invitum*.

[1] Pryor v Hill, 4 Bro C C 138, Wright v Wigton, 84 Pa St 163, Fouche v Brower, 74 Ga 257

[2] Ludington's Petition, 5 Abb N. C 307; Marbury v. Brooks, 7 Wheat 556

CHAPTER XVI

EQUALITY OF DISTRIBUTION (*CONTINUED*). THE JURISDICTION OF EQUITY

§ 293. Inadequacy of Common Law Process
294. Insolvency Alone Gives no Jurisdiction to Equity
295. Basis of Equitable Jurisdiction — a Limited Fund Dedicated to the Payment of Debts.
296. First Exercise of Jurisdiction — Administration Bill.
297. The Grounds of Jurisdiction.
298. Conditions Imposed upon Plaintiff
299. Jurisdiction Applied to Land as well as Personal Property
300. Equal Distribution Effected by Such Proceedings
301. Remains of This Jurisdiction in America
302. Survival of Jurisdiction in Federal Courts
303. Value of This Equitable Power under Modern Conditions
304. Administrative Jurisdiction of Corporate Assets
305. The "Trust Fund Doctrine" as a Description of Jurisdiction
306. Illustrations in the Case of Partnership
307. Illustrations in the Case of Statutory Liability.
308. The Jurisdiction Arises in View of Insolvency
309. This Jurisdiction Limited in Exercise to America

§ 310 Administration is not Dissolution
311 The Plaintiff cannot have Priority.
312. "Collusion" not of Itself Improper.
313. Jurisdiction Limited to Liquidation
314. Creditors' Committees Lawful.
315 Jurisdiction not a Model of Perfection
316 Distribution of Property in Possession
317 Rights of Prior Lienor
318 Disposition of Pending Suits
319 Effect of Judgment Recovered after Receiver is Appointed
320 Disposition of Property not on Hand.
321. Can Fraudulent Transactions be Set Aside?
322 Receiver the Person to Sue in such a Case, if Any
323. The Question Considered from Standpoint of Principle.
324 The Supreme Court's View
325 Precedents in Such Matters
326 Cases Distinguished
327 Extent of Court's Powers
328 Reasoning in Support of Contrary View.
329 Answer to These Contentions

§ 293. **Inadequacy of Common Law Process.** So obvious is it that the common law process is incapable of affording any compulsory method of liquidation that the topic may be passed with a sentence None of the writs authorized before the Statute of Westminster II, and no writ capable of issuance in any "action on the case," can provide the machinery necessary for a compulsory liquidation of the affairs of a debtor.

§ 294 **Insolvency Alone Gives no Jurisdiction to Equity** Nor was the jurisdiction of equity ever extended so as to allow the creditors of an insolvent debtor to bring him and his property into court for a general liquidation. As we have seen, no solvent debtor holds his property in any trust for his creditors — all they have is a right of realization "While in a certain sense it may be said that every man's property is a trust fund for the payment of his debts," says the New York court,[1] "no action in equity has ever been maintained by a creditor at large to seize and administer the estate of a debtor for the benefit of creditors generally Bankruptcy proceedings are the only means to attain such an object." Nor does the mere insolvency of the debtor add anything on this score; nothing still remains but the ordinary right of realization as we have already considered it On this we need add nothing to the authority of Case v. Beauregard[2] There it was held that there is nothing in the nature of a partnership to give the creditors an equity in the firm property so as to enable them to follow it into the hands of third persons by means of a bill in chancery; the court saying:

"It is indispensable, however, to such relief, when the creditors are, as in the present case, simple contract creditors, that the partnership property should be within the control of the court, and in the course of administration, brought there by the bankruptcy of the firm, or by an assignment, or by the creation of a trust in some mode This is because neither the partners

[1] Marsh v Kaye, 168 N. Y 196, 61 N E. 177.
[2] 99 U. S 119.

nor the joint creditors have any specific lien, nor is there any trust that can be enforced until the property has passed *in custodiam legis.* Otherwise the property can be followed only after a judgment at law has been obtained and an execution has proved fruitless "[1]

§ 295 **Basis of Equitable Jurisdiction — a Limited Fund Dedicated to the Payment of Debts.** There is only one limitation on this general rule of exclusion; or, to put it affirmatively, there is only one principle on which a Court of Chancery can act by way of liquidation That principle may be invoked whenever, by operation of law or agreement, there exists a limited fund dedicated to the payment of debts, whether of one sort or another. In any such case, the actual or probable insufficiency of the fund completely to meet the purposes for which it was intended will induce the court to take jurisdiction over it, and actuate its disposition under the direction, or by the hands of, an officer of the court. That is a well-established branch of the court's jurisdiction, however lacking may have been the chancellors in the exposition of its basis But that there is such a jurisdiction cannot be doubted, it will sufficiently appear as we proceed with our examination of the instances in which it has been unquestioningly exercised.

§ 296. **First Exercise of Jurisdiction — Administration Bill** This jurisdiction was first made known in the case of decedents' estates, and the bill which instituted any such liquidation was known as a creditors' administration bill. The scope of this bill, and the practice in such cases, are really not for us to discuss, that has all been done in a notable book from which the following summary has largely been drawn [2]

§ 297 **The Grounds of Jurisdiction** Three causes contributed to the jurisdiction of equity in this class of cases. (1) the inadequacy of the courts having jurisdiction over probate mat-

[1] To the same effect was Lord Eldon's decision in Exp Ruffin, 6 Ves. 119
[2] Langdell, "Brief Survey of Equity Jurisdiction," 2d ed., pp. 125, *et seq.* See also Jenks, "Short History of English Law," pp 230-5.

ters; (2) the inadequacy of common law procedure for the protection of the executor, and (3) the harsh rules of the common law affecting the succession of the creditors to the property of their deceased debtor. The ordinary tribunals for handling the affairs of a deceased person were the ecclesiastical courts, but, as has been well said, " if the Church courts had ever afforded adequate process in such cases, the contempt into which they had fallen since the Reformation, and the increasing efficiency of the Common Law Remedies, had virtually robbed them of their jurisdiction."[1] The ecclesiastical court preserved its jurisdiction to grant probate or letters of administration, but beyond that it could not go. It had no power to compel an accounting from the executor,[2] and on the other hand, the executor was not afforded the protection he needed in the administration of the decedent's affairs. For instance, there was no way for him to bar claims by any short notice, and if he depended on the ecclesiastical court he would never know when he had the claims of all the creditors in his hands. In England this situation long continued, and it was not until the present day that he was allowed to bar claims by advertising.[3] Nor

---

[1] Jenks, "Short History," 226. As an instance of the contempt with which the Court of Chancery treated the ecclesiastical courts see Backhouse v Hunter, 1 Cox Ch 342 To such a point had these courts sunk that in the eighteenth century the proof of a will was not made by a certified copy furnished by the ecclesiastical court Instead of that, the practice was to obtain from the Chancery Court an order compelling the prothonotary to give the will itself to the solicitor who desired it, upon his giving a bond to return it undefaced, Forder v Wade, 4 Bro Ch 476, Lake v Causfield, 3 Bro Ch 263

[2] "The Court of King's Bench held (strangely enough) that the ecclesiastical courts had jurisdiction only to compel an executor to file an inventory, — not to compel him to file a sufficient and proper inventory, and hence, if one of those courts attempted to do the latter, the King's Bench would grant a prohibition, on the application of the executor The creditor, therefore, could only obtain such an inventory as the executor chose to swear to and exhibit "— Langdell, 139 This narrow range of the ecclesiastical court continued in England through all the statutory reformations, and even at the present day, as a result, the administration of decedents' estates is entirely in the hands of the Chancery Division, Maitland, "Equity," 192

[3] Stat 22-23 Vict c 35, Maitland, "Equity," 197.

were the common law courts equipped with the administrative powers sufficient for the convenience or protection of any parties in interest. If at any time the executor was sued on a debt owing by his testator, the court presumed that he had assets in his hands sufficient to pay the debt and put the burden upon him to show that he had none. On the other hand, the creditors were equally embarrassed in endeavoring to work out their rights by the medium of such a court. The issue tried in a common law court as to whether assets were in the executor's hands did not admit of an accounting, by which the executor would first exhibit a statement of his actions and then be subject to examination thereon. No creditor could act for all, it was each for himself as always in a court of common law, and with no process of discovery to aid an inquiry which of necessity must be instituted in the dark. The executor, of course, handled only the decedent's personal property, but similar difficulties existed in the case of his real estate. In the hands of the heir, land was subject only to debts evidenced by instruments under seal or to such debts as the debtor's will specifically charged upon the land. In the case of a decedent who happened to own real estate, when most of his debts were not under seal, great injustice would thus result. It was to the interest of the simple-contract creditors, at least, that some method be devised by which all the testator's assets could be applied to the payment of his debts.

§ 298. Conditions Imposed upon Plaintiff. All of these difficulties resulted in the Court of Chancery taking jurisdiction over such cases. Of course a creditor always had the option to come in on his own behalf alone on the same basis as though his debtor were living and he had filed a judgment creditor's bill,[1] but if he did that, the executor would have the right to show that debts outranking his had been paid or were credited against the assets.[2] Hence, as a condition to securing the general administration of the estate, the plaintiff was considered as

[1] Langdell, 169.   [2] *Ibid*, 168.

agreeing that all other creditors should be paid off on an equality with himself,[1] and therefore he came in, not for a decree against the executor for payment out of which the latter could recoup himself from the assets, but simply for a direction that the assets in the executor's hands be turned into court for equal distribution among the creditors.[2]

§ 299 **Jurisdiction Applied to Land as well as Personal Property.** The court thus having established its jurisdiction, it became the universal practice to invoke it. And while the executor, as such, only administered the personal property of the testator, yet as the heir who succeeded to the real estate stood in practically the position of the executor, as succeeding to property which should be charged with the payment of debts, the practice was to join the heirs of the testator with the executor and thus bring into the court both the land and the personal property for general distribution.[3]

§ 300 **Equal Distribution Effected by Such Proceedings** Once the property was in court, the latter had full control over it and its distribution. The other creditors were not brought in as parties, but advertisement was made for them to prove their claims before the master and share in the distribution. The basis of the suit being equality, the court worked it out by means of the well-known doctrine of marshaling and subrogation, so that both the land and the personal property were used to pay the testator's debts.[4] Of course, the court could not effect a system of equality entirely to its liking. Debts under seal outranked simple debts in England until Hinde Palmer's Act,[5] although a specialty debt without consideration was postponed,[6] and always personal property was considered as the primary fund for the payment of debts.[7] But compen-

---

[1] Langdell, 169 [2] *Ibid*, 170 [3] *Ibid.*, 184 [4] *Ibid*, 189
[5] Stat 32-33 Vict c 46; Maitland, "Equity," 196
[6] National Trust Co *v* Miller, 33 N J Eq 155, Maitland, "Equity," 197
[7] An idea that extends even to the laws of those States which allow the taxpayer, in order to ascertain the taxable basis of his personal

sation for these defects can be found in the fact that the court, having gathered a fund into its possession for administration, always felt itself empowered to secure the equal distribution it desired by means of enjoining the prosecution of any action against the executor which otherwise would result in a judgment giving priority to the particular plaintiff.[1]

§ 301 **Remains of This Jurisdiction in America.** Thus in the eighteenth century the situation was that whenever a man died leaving assets, whether real or personal, the Court of Chancery had jurisdiction to administer his affairs for the benefit of his creditors.[2] This jurisdiction passed to us as part of our inheritance, and we find frequent instances of its exercise,[3] but it has been gradually limited by the tendency of our States to increase the jurisdiction of their probate courts. In almost every American commonwealth, the probate court of to-day not only has jurisdiction to grant probate of wills and letters of administration, but to receive and pass upon the accounts of executors, distribute the assets in their hands, and discharge them from their trusts. There still remain, of course, various limitations, even to-day the Legislature of New York seems unwilling to grant the surrogate's court the full powers of the Court of Chancery,[4] but in so far as the particular probate court of a State may have jurisdiction, the State's chancery courts

property, to deduct from its market value the amount of his current indebtedness. People v Board of Assessors of Albany, 40 N Y 154, 162 "The personal estate is the primary (and only) fund for payment of debts, and cannot be exonerated from the claims of creditors, unless some other fund be substituted, which is sufficient for that purpose The clear intention, to be collected from the context, is to govern" — Kenyon, M. R., in Webb v. Jones, 1 Cox Ch 245

[1] Langdell, 173-7

[2] "The Court of Chancery had not merely acquired a share of administrative jurisdiction before the end of the seventeenth century, but had, by the end of the eighteenth century, practically secured the lion's share of that jurisdiction" — Jenks, "Short History," 229.

[3] E g Brown v M'Donald, 1 Hill Eq 297 ; Cleveland v Chambliss, 64 Ga 352

[4] See Re Brown, 79 N Y Misc 675, 141 N Y S 318; Rutherford v Alyea, 54 N. J Eq. 411, 34 Atl. 1078.

are apt to refuse to exercise the jurisdiction which they once possessed.[1]

§ 302. **Survival of Jurisdiction in Federal Courts** A curious survival of the ancient jurisdiction, however, may be found in the practice of the federal courts As is well known, these courts took over the powers exercised by the English Court of Chancery, and such powers too, as the English court was wont to exercise at the date of our independence, and these prerogatives, as they have always considered, can in no case be defeated by subsequent State statutes giving equivalent remedies to common law or probate courts of the State in which the suit may arise.[2] It follows that once the probate court has issued letters of administration, then the federal courts have coördinate jurisdiction with the probate court over all matters affecting the distribution of the assets in the executor's hands[3] — a juris-

---

[1] An interesting example of the encroachments which legislation has made upon the old chancery jurisdiction is to be seen in the jurisprudence of New York The necessity for the plea of *plene administravit*, by which the executor when sued at law pleads lack of assets to pay the plaintiff's debt, has been removed by statute In one place the statute (now Sec 1824 of Code of Civ Pro) abolishes this plea, and allows the creditor to recover a judgment for the full amount of his debt, but the other part of the statute (now Code Civ Pro Secs. 1825-6) forbids a judgment creditor from issuing execution without permission of the surrogate's court which has jurisdiction over the estate. The order of the surrogate is a final determination that "the assets are abundant to justify the order" (*Re* Clarke, 2 Abb. N. C 208) and cannot be collaterally attacked (Mount v Mitchell, 31 N Y 356) On the other hand, whatever the surrogate's court lacks, the Supreme Court, in the exercise of its general equitable jurisdiction, still has power to supply (Blood v Kane, 130 N Y 514, 29 N E 994; Bankers' Surety Co v Meyer, 205 N Y 219, 98 N E 399) "Ordinarily, where the surrogate's court has ample power to protect the rights of the parties by enforcing a just and proper administration of a decedent's assets, the Supreme Court will not undertake the administration of his estate But it is well established that when a surrogate's court with its limited jurisdiction is unequal to the task of grappling with special circumstances the Supreme Court will entertain jurisdiction and avoid a failure of remedy or a miscarriage of justice" (Bankers' Surety Co v Meyer, *supra*)

[2] McMullen Lumber Co. v. Strother, 136 Fed 295

[3] Payne v Hook, 7 Wall 425, Waterman v Bank, 215 U. S 33, 30 S Ct 10, Pulliam v. Pulliam, 10 Fed 23; Lecouturier v Ickelheimer, 205 Fed. 682.

240   THE RIGHTS AND REMEDIES OF CREDITORS.   [CHAP XVI.

diction, too, which "cannot be defeated or impaired by laws of a State undertaking to give exclusive jurisdiction to its own courts."[1] Whether they have jurisdiction to set aside the probate of a will once granted is still a matter of some doubt,[2] but it seems clear that, pending the probate of the will or issuance of letters, the federal courts may properly appoint a receiver of the decedent's affairs[3] Of course, this jurisdiction is not exclusive, but is only concurrent with that of the probate court, and hence it will be defeated by any prior decision of that court to which the present plaintiff was a party.[4]

§ 303. **Value of This Equitable Power under Modern Conditions** With this exception, which comes from our curious system of dual jurisdiction in civil matters, it is apparent that the present range of equitable jurisdiction over decedents' estates is very limited in our country at the present day. But as the most ancient branch of this jurisdiction, it deserved mention first, as the progenitor of another branch of more practical importance to-day, its study is of equal value. Speaking broadly, the reason why the Chancery Court habitually administered the property of a deceased debtor, was that the decedent's property had been left in the air, by his death, without adequate protection So long as a decedent lived, he could handle his own affairs, and the let-alone instinct of the common law, illustrated by its encouragement of the race of diligence to which we have referred, left the property in the care of the man who owned it. If he did not pay his creditors, that was a matter for them to work out by means of the ordinary process for the collection of debts. But when he died the property passed into

---

[1] Lawrence v Nelson, 143 U S. 215, 12 S Ct 440
[2] *In re* Broderick's Will, 21 Wall. 503, McDermott v. Hannon, 203 Fed 1015
[3] Underground Electric Rys v. Owsley, 176 Fed 26.
[4] Johnson v Waters, 111 U S. 640, 4 S. Ct 619, Arrowsmith v. Gleason, 129 U S 86, 9 S Ct 237. The recent case of McCauley v McCauley, 202 Fed 280, where the court refused to take jurisdiction because accounting proceedings were already pending in the State court, would seem wholly wrong

the hands of the executor, or if real estate, of his heir, who received it charged with at least a moral duty of first paying the debts attributable to it, this duty, of necessity, being limited to the assets in his hands This, of course, was not a trust No one ever claimed that an executor or heir was in the position of a trustee nor is that at all the question. The court saw before it a fund dedicated to the one purpose of immediate administration It took jurisdiction simply for the purpose of administration, because no other court could do it, and because without the aid of the court the person charged with the administration could not adequately perform his duty

§ 304 **Administrative Jurisdiction of Corporate Assets.** In this country it is a principle of almost universal sway that the assets of an insolvent corporation are a trust fund for the payment of its debts It is not the present purpose to go into a general discussion of this hackneyed theme Whether the doctrine, taking it by and large, fails of justification in sound reason, certainly to an extent it has a sound basis, and that appears when the theory is considered from the standpoint of administration The estate of an insolvent corporation is like that of a decedent in one fundamental respect. Of course mere insolvency does not end the corporate life, a chancery winding-up does not have that effect,[1] nor does even bankruptcy take away the company's charter existence.[2] But that does not affect the really important feature of resemblance, that in each case there is present a limited fund dedicated to the primary purpose of distribution among creditors The stockholders and directors are not personally liable to the company's creditors, the latter can look only to the corporate funds for payment. Whenever we have such a case, there we have a

---

[1] Bank of Bethel v Bank, 14 Wall 383, 400, Continental Securities Co v Interborough R T Co, 165 Fed 945, Detroit etc Ry. v Campbell, 140 Mich. 384, 103 N W 856

[2] *In re* Jacobson & Son Co , 196 Fed. 949, Coburn v Boston Paper Co., 10 Gray 243, Wood & Selick v Vanderveer, 55 N Y App Div 549, 67 N. Y S 371

jurisdiction which may be invoked by the bill of any creditor who chooses to ask the court, on behalf of himself and all the other creditors equally, to gather in and distribute the corporate assets on the basis of equality and by the use, if need be, of the equitable doctrines of marshaling Such a bill, to use the words of the Supreme Court, is "quite sufficient to enable a court of equity to administer the property and marshal the debts." [1]

§ 305 The "Trust Fund Doctrine" as a Description of Jurisdiction. If we take it simply from this standpoint of administration rather than entangle ourselves in the reasoning attendant upon viewing it as a rule of substantive law, the trust fund doctrine, while narrowed in scope, acquires much more of a logical outline The Supreme Court evidently meant to give the doctrine but little if any wider range when it decided that the "trust" in the case of an insolvent corporation was "rather a trust in the administration of the assets after possession by a court of equity than a trust attaching to the property, as such, for the direct benefit of either creditor or stockholder." [2] At any rate, this point of view is sufficient to justify this equity jurisdiction, as resting entirely upon the existence of a limited fund for purposes of distribution among creditors [3]

§ 306. Illustrations in the Case of Partnership This is illustrated by two notable cases. In Case v. Beauregard [4] it was held, as we have seen, that there is nothing in the nature of a

---

[1] Union Trust Co v Illinois Midland Ry, 117 U. S. 434, 459, 6 S. Ct 809
[2] Hollins v Brierfield Coal Co, 150 U. S 371, 383, 14 S Ct. 127
[3] Recently Noyes, J., has described "the evolution of the creditor's bill into the proceeding by which courts of equity undertake the general administration of the estates of corporations" as springing from the judgment creditor's bill, Penn Steel Co v N. Y C Ry, 198 Fed. 721, 737. It is submitted that if the jurisdiction had started with that, it would never have got a real start, because, as we have seen, the idea of priority is inseparable from the conception of the judgment creditor's bill The courts required a judgment as proof of the debt in the present class of cases, but they did not take jurisdiction to enforce the judgment   [4] supra

partnership to give the creditors an equity in the firm property so as to enable them to follow it into the hands of third persons by means of a bill in chancery. On the other hand, when the New York legislature provided for special partnerships, that is, partnerships where the liability of a partner is limited to the amount which he contributes to the capital of the firm, Chancellor Walworth held that upon such a concern becoming insolvent, its assets became impressed with a trust for the benefit of its creditors, and that the court, on the application of any creditor, should wind up the affairs of the firm for the benefit of all[1]. The Chancellor said that "whenever the legislature creates new rights in parties, for the protection and enforcement of which rights the common law affords no remedy, and the statute itself does not prescribe the mode in which such rights are to be protected, this court, in the exercise of its acknowledged jurisdiction, is bound to give to a party the relief to which he is equitably entitled under the statute."[2]

§ 307 Illustrations in the Case of Statutory Liability. Equal demonstration is afforded by the cases involving the liability which the laws of some States impose, it may be upon the directors, it may be upon the stockholders, of corporations for the payment of corporate debts. Where the statute limits this liability by ratio, so that the extraordinary indebtedness thus laid upon individuals will not suffice fully to pay the creditors of the corporation, then the apportionment of the liability is for an equity court to determine on a general administration bill of the same character as that which we have discussed,[3] and the court, incidentally, may restrain any creditor from suing at law.[4] But where the statute puts no limit to the liability, so that each director or stockholder shall be liable for all the

[1] Innes v. Lansing, 7 Paige, 583
[2] Innes v. Lansing, supra, See also Whitcomb v Fowle 7 Abb. N C 295
[3] N. Y &c Ry Co v Beard 80 Fed. 66, Bauer v Platt, 72 Hun 326.
[4] Pfohl v Simpson, 74 N Y 137

corporate debts, then no general administration suit will lie, and equity has no jurisdiction.[1]

§ 308 **The Jurisdiction Arises in View of Insolvency.** There we have the entire idea So long as no artificial limits are placed upon the responsiveness of the debtor to the demands of his creditors, there is no room for equity jurisdiction. The fact that he is insolvent, while in effect limiting his ability to pay all his debts in full, never was considered as a sufficient reason for equity taking up the general administration of the debtor's affairs So with an insolvent partnership, since a partnership has never been more than a mere association of persons whose liability for debts is unlimited. But it is quite a different thing when the State sanctions any association, whether corporation or limited partnership, which at best does business with but a limited fund beyond which no creditor can reach. So long as this fund is adequate for the payment of debts, there is no need to consider any special administrative powers of equity, because, by means of execution or judgment creditor's bill, each creditor can come into his own [2] But when those assets become insufficient to meet the liabilities, then the administrative jurisdiction of an equity court may be invoked by any creditor for the benefit of all.

§ 309 **This Jurisdiction Limited in Exercise to America.** Under the vast jurisdiction which has thus arisen, the affairs of thousands of corporations have been administered, and there has been created in this country a body of "receivership" law whose size would astonish an English practitioner For this branch of equity jurisdiction is peculiarly American. In England the increase in use of the corporate form of conducting business brought with it the admirable winding up provisions of the Companies Acts, so that it was never necessary for the

---

[1] Marsh v Kaye, *supra*
[2] Carson v Alleghany Glass Co, 189 Fed. 791 The Supreme Court has frequently declared that the "trust" does not attach to the assets of a solvent corporation See McDonald v Williams, 174 U S. 397, 19 S. Ct. 743.

English Chancery Court to work out its own jurisdiction in such cases.¹ A bill for such a purpose was once filed, it is true, but the court denied its power to wind up the affairs of a public service company.² With us, on the other hand, this jurisdiction is certainly as frequently exercised in the case of public service companies as of other corporations.³ "The practice has become particularly well established in the case of quasi-public corporations where the interests of the public require continuous and continued operations, and where, generally, the bankrupt act is not available." ⁴

§ 310 **Administration is not Dissolution** In this connection several distinctions should be observed. For instance, the bill cannot pray a dissolution of the corporation in the sense that its charter life shall be ended In many States at the present day,⁵ jurisdiction has been conferred upon courts of equity to entertain proceedings by the creditors of an insolvent corporation for the double purpose of distributing its assets and ending its corporate existence.⁶ But in the absence of such

---

¹ Evans v Coventry, 5 De G M & G 911, though often cited in support of the trust fund theory seems to have no application The plaintiff held a policy in a life insurance company and relief was granted on the theory that his policy gave him an equitable charge on the company's funds A similar case was Towle v American Bldg & Loan Soc, 60 Fed 131; but neither case has any real bearing on the point of interest to us. In two instances English judges have used this theory very ingeniously in order to avoid the strict English doctrine of *ultra vires*, *In re* Guardian Bldg Soc, L R 23 Ch Div 440, *In re* Birkbeck Bldg Soc, 28 Times L R 451; see also 57 Sol. Journ. 167 But as we have said, it was never necessary for the English courts to go further than this

² Gardner v. London, etc Rv, L R 2 Ch App 201, 212

³ Union Trust Co. v Illinois Midland Rv, 117 U S 434, 458; American Brake Co v Pere Marquette Rv., 205 Fed 14

⁴ Noyes, J, Penn Steel Co v N. Y City Rv Co, 198 Fed 721, 737, n 9

⁵ E g New Jersey Corporation Law, Sec 65, and New York General Corporation Law, Secs 101-2

⁶ The federal courts have held that the presence of such a State statute confers upon them the same jurisdiction, Land Title & Trust Co v. Asphalt Co, 127 Fed 1; Jacobs v Mexican Sugar Co, 130 Fed 589.

statute, no court of equity has such power; and such instances must be carefully distinguished from the jurisdiction of the court in the cases of which we speak No statute authorizes a bill of the present kind, and no statute governs the procedure. True, the courts in matters of administration on such a bill follow as nearly as possible the practice in bankruptcy as a safe and convenient guide,[1] but it has never been suggested that they are compelled to do so.

§ 311. **The Plaintiff cannot have Priority.** Another distinction occurs in this connection. As is already apparent, a bill of the character now under consideration is essentially different from the ordinary kind of judgment creditor's bill.[2] The fact that a corporation is insolvent does not deprive the creditor of the right to file a judgment creditor's bill and make the same claim of priority that he could in the case of any other insolvent debtor. He has, indeed, the option to file either the one bill or the other. As the Supreme Court has said:[3] "It was his privilege, under the law, to sue for his own benefit, and it was within the power of the court, for his protection as a judgment creditor, to place the property of the debtor company in the hands of a receiver, for administration under its orders." But the creditor must make his choice at the outset, for if he files a bill for general administration, he has no claim of priority. Once he has made his decision, he must abide by it, and the nature of his choice must be gathered from the allegations of his bill. The question then is whether the plaintiff chose to come into court for a general administration of the corporation's affairs for the benefit of all the creditors equally with himself, or whether he chose as a judgment creditor to ask nothing but the application of such assets as could be found to the payment of his own claim.[4]

[1] Conklin v U. S. Shipbuilding Co, 136 Fed 1006
[2] Professor Langdell draws this distinction at the outset of his discussion Langdell, 125 n
[3] Sage v Memphis etc Ry, 125 U. S 361, 376, 8 S Ct 887
[4] Haehnlen v Drayton, 192 Fed 300

§ 312 "**Collusion**" **not of Itself Improper** It is perfectly proper for this jurisdiction to be invoked by "collusion." If the corporation is insolvent, for its own protection it can lawfully procure a friendly creditor to file a bill against it [1] and there is nothing objectionable in this sort of collusion If the debt is really owing to the plaintiff as he alleges, it is right for the defendant to admit it, this admission cannot deprive the court of jurisdiction, otherwise no court could ever enter a decree *pro confesso*, and finally, the motive which induces the plaintiff to file his bill in one court rather than another, or to file his bill at all, is entirely immaterial.[2] This reasoning, in which all courts seem to concur, has not been without its consequences The fact that one hand guides both bill and answer led at an early date to the practice, where no creditor had yet secured a judgment, of letting a simple-contract creditor file the bill, since any possible objection, it is held, is waived by the general answer of the corporation which always accompanies the bill to the files of the court [3] As a result, such a bill is almost invariably filed by a friendly creditor, the corporation puts in an answer admitting its allegations, and thereupon a receiver is appointed to take charge of the defendant's assets Thenceforward the suit proceeds toward the goal of final distribution, and this is its only terminus, unless meanwhile, by means of some reorganization arrangement to which the creditors consent, the bill is dismissed and the receivership terminated.

§ 313 **Jurisdiction Limited to Liquidation** This practice, as might have been expected, has led to some strange misconceptions regarding the nature of a "receivership case" It is all very well for a leading textbook to speak of "friendly re-

---

[1] Sage v Memphis etc Ry, 125 U S 361, 8 S Ct 887, Hollins v Brierfield Coal Co, 150 U S 371, 14 S Ct 127; Re Metropolitan Ry. Receivership, 208 U. S 90, 28 S Ct. 219 So could an executor procure the filing of a bill by a friendly creditor. Langdell, 171.

[2] The Supreme Court thus sums up the reasoning of the earlier cases, Re Metropolitan Rv. Receivership, 208 U S 90, 28 S Ct 219

[3] Sage v Memphis etc Ry, 125 U S 361, 8 S Ct 887, Horn v. Pere Marquette Ry, 151 Fed 626.

248   THE RIGHTS AND REMEDIES OF CREDITORS.   [CHAP. XVI.

ceiverships" as an institution with us,[1] but the vulgar error[2] that the courts will allow a receivership for any other purpose than a winding up, should never be tolerated There is no such thing as a nursing receivership Long ago Lord Eldon pointed out, in the case of a partnership dispute, that a court of chancery had no right to appoint a receiver simply to enable the parties to adjust their affairs[3] No more has a court of chancery to-day the power to appoint a receiver merely to enable a corporation to tide over its difficulties,[4] or to enable its creditors and bondholders to effect a plan of reorganization.[5] If the record or the conduct of the parties shows that the object was any other than liquidation, the court will refuse jurisdiction, if the liquidation is unduly delayed, the court will divest itself of jurisdiction so as to let in the other creditors according to their common law priorities.[6] Emphatic language has been used on this point many times. "We are not aware," says the New York court, "of any statute or law which justifies the continuance of the receivership for the purpose of giving the corporation time to raise money to pay its debts"[7] As our

---

[1] Alderson, "Receivers," 5
[2] An error which sometimes creeps even into judicial opinions See Schumert & Warfield v Brewing Co., 199 Fed 358.
[3] Waters v Taylor, 15 Vesey 10
[4] Duncan v Treadwell Co, 82 Hun 376.
[5] Gutterson & Gould v Lebanon Steel Co, 151 Fed. 72, Burton v Peters Salt Co, 190 Fed 262
[6] East Tenn etc R R v Atlantic R R, 49 Fed 608, Merchants' & Planters' Nat Bank v Trustees, 63 Ga 549, Wilmer v Railroad Co, 2 Woods 409, Schloss v Schloss, 14 N Y App Div 333, 43 N Y S 788, Mercantile Trust Co v Baltimore etc R R., 89 Fed 606 Even the jurisdiction of a bankruptcy court can be defeated in this way, Acme Harvester Co. v. Beekman, 222 U. S 300, 32 S Ct. 96 In one case the receiver, because of his cooperation in such a purpose, was deprived of his compensation, Campau v Driving Club, 144 Mich 80, 107 N W 1063
[7] Duncan v Treadwell Co, 82 Hun 376, 377, 31 N Y S 340. In Gardner v London etc Ry, L R 2 Ch App 201, 212, Cairns, L J, said
"Now I apprehend that nothing is better settled than that this court does not assume the management of a business or undertaking except with a view to the winding up and sale of the business or under-

highest tribunal has said, " a court is a very unsatisfactory body to administer the affairs of a railroad as a going concern, and . the possession of such property by the court through its receivers should not be unnecessarily prolonged " [1]

§ 314. **Creditors' Committees Lawful** This is perfectly consistent with the encouragement the courts give the creditors to combine their interests by means of a reorganization committee,[2] and their view that it is proper for the receiver, so far as consistently may be, to coordinate his efforts with those of the committee [3] That is merely by the way, of course the creditors should be allowed to save expense by withdrawing the assets from court if they can all agree on a good way of doing it. But that is quite a different thing from saying that the court takes jurisdiction for any such purpose. The court does no such thing, it takes jurisdiction only to liquidate, and liquidate it will unless meanwhile the assets are withdrawn by the consent of all in interest

§ 315. **Jurisdiction not a Model of Perfection** The system of judicial administration thus created is perfect as far as it goes, and it goes as far as it possibly may But it has its limitations.

taking The management is an interim management, its necessity and its justification spring out of the jurisdiction to liquidate and to sell, the business or undertaking is managed and continued in order that it may be sold as a going concern, and with the sale the management ends "

In *In re* Receivers Philadelphia etc. R R , 14 Phila 501, 502, Butler, J , said

"The modern practice prevailing to some extent, elsewhere, of transferring corporate property to the custody of the courts to be thus held and managed for an indefinite period of years, to suit the convenience of the parties, whereby general creditors and stockholders are kept at bay, I regard as a mischievous innovation "

"In this class of cases, if it later develops that the receivership is being managed with a view to primary liquidation and incidental operation, the remedy is not to conclude that there was no jurisdiction to appoint the receiver, but to direct the receiver to perform his duty " — Burton v Peters Salt Co , 190 Fed 262, 265

[1] *Re* Metropolitan Ry Receivership, 208 U S 90, 111, 28 S Ct 219
[2] Continental etc Trust Co v Allis-Chalmers Co 200 Fed 600
[3] Clarke v Central R R., 66 Fed 16, Fowler v Jarvis-Conklin Co , 63 Fed 888

§ 316. **Distribution of Property in Possession.** So far as concerns property in the debtor's possession, the creditors' rights are clear The court, of course, has the power to limit the time for claims to be filed with the receiver or a master appointed for such purpose,[1] and, after a final distribution has been made, will protect its distributing officers against the attacks of belated creditors.[2] The creditors who are thus duly in court are entitled to a distribution of the assets in hand on a basis of absolute equality, land and goods going as one, but of course prior liens must be duly respected. A creditor is only entitled to what his debtor has, and if the debtor's property has been saddled with a valid lien, the creditor can only realize on the debtor's equity of redemption

§ 317. **Rights of Prior Lienor.** The party holding such a prior lien may do one of two things If he desires to realize on his lien while the receivership lasts, he must come into the equity court for leave to proceed, because to do otherwise would result in an intolerable interference with the receiver's possession [3] But if the lienor chooses to stay out, resting upon his lien, he cannot be compelled to come in The court must administer the property subject to the lien, and it can be enforced, after the closing of the receivership, against any one who may have purchased the charged property on the liquidation sale. That has frequently been held in the case of judgment creditors' bills, and the same principle must apply to the present form of procedure [4] A winding up of this kind is therefore of

---

[1] Smith v Jones Lumber Co, 200 Fed. 647.

[2] Farrell v Smith, 2 B & B 337, Halsted v Forest Hill Co., 109 Fed 820; Woodruff v Jewett, 115 N Y 267, 22 N E 157; Walsh v Raymond, 58 Conn 251, 20 Atl 464, Keene v Gaehle, 56 Md 343

[3] *In re* Tyler, 149 U. S 164, 13 S. Ct. 785; Wiswall v Sampson, 14 How. 52, Wabash R. R. Co v Adelbert College, 208 U. S. 38, 28 S. Ct. 182

[4] Chautauqua County Bank v Risley, 19 N. Y 369; Hillyer v. Le Roy, 179 N. Y. 369, 72 N. E. 237, Jackson v Holbrook, 36 Minn 494, 32 N W. 852 As has been said. "A debtor's conveyance of his real estate to a receiver, although it may be compulsory, is in its nature simply and purely the creation of a trust for the payment of the debts

little avail if the filing of the bill is too long delayed, because, once the race of diligence starts, the successful judgment creditors may secure liens which the Chancery Court perforce must recognize. Indeed, it is a familiar allegation in bills of this sort that certain of the creditors have already entered suit against the corporation and others are about to do so, all of which, if left alone, will result in preferences to one or the other which the court must then recognize to the injury of the other creditors. It follows that the only thing that can cut short this race is for the court to take jurisdiction over the debtor's affairs and appoint a receiver as an interim measure.

§ 318 **Disposition of Pending Suits.** Of course the appointment of the receiver does not of itself stay the suits pending against the debtor, nor is it good practice for the court to enjoin their further prosecution. In one form or another the creditor must finally liquidate his claim, as the court must receive it whenever it is liquidated so long as that process is completed prior to the decree settling the list of distributees.[1] If the creditor chooses to liquidate his claim by plenary suit rather than before the master appointed to make up the list of distributees, that is a right with which the equity court is not inclined to interfere.[2] Apart from all questions of jurisdiction[3] the Chancery Court should not enjoin the prosecution of such an action to judgment.[4]

---

on which the proceedings in equity are founded. But no creditor having a statutory lien by judgment can be compelled to take the equitable remedy. He may, if he prefer, stand upon his lien and the means which the law has given him of enforcing it." — Chautauqua County Bank *v* Risley, 19 N. Y. 369, 374–375.

[1] N Y Security & Trust Co *v* Lombard, 73 Fed 537, Penn Steel Co *v* N Y City Ry, 198 Fed 721.

[2] Honegger *v* Wettstein, 94 N Y 252; Wilder *v.* New Orleans, 87 Fed 843.

[3] For example, the federal courts are broadly forbidden by statute from enjoining the maintenance of a suit in a State court. See Nelson *v.* Camp, 191 Fed. 712.

[4] Mercantile Trust Co *v* Pittsburg R R, 29 Fed 732, Earle *v* Conway, 178 U. S 456, 20 S Ct 918.

§ 319 **Effect of Judgment Recovered after Receiver is Appointed.** But when the creditor, thus left alone, enters up his judgment, his freedom of action ends. He will not be allowed to avail himself of any remedies under that judgment which would make for inequality, or, to put it from the more familiar point of view, interfere with the receiver's possession of the debtor's assets. One thing the creditor is allowed to do with his judgment, and that is to prove it as a claim before the master and thereby share *pari passu* with the other creditors [1]

§ 320 **Disposition of Property not on Hand** Thus, so far as property on hand is concerned, equality of distribution is generally assured. The same result is achieved with respect to property which is not on hand but which is owned by the debtor The Chancery Court through its receiver can summarily gather in all concealed, lost, or "forgotten" property. No one can withhold property from the receiver's possession unless under a colorable claim of right If a colorable claim is made, then the receiver must proceed against the claimant by plenary suit, but in all other cases the court has the power summarily to take the property away from the claimant and give it into the receiver's possession [2]

§ 321 **Can Fraudulent Transactions be Set Aside?** We have now made the circuit of this winding up jurisdiction which the

[1] Tracy *v* The Bank, 37 N Y 523, Mercantile Trust Co *v* Pittsburg R R 29 Fed 732, Wilder *v* New Orleans, 87 Fed 843 It must be remembered that the appointment of a receiver on a bill of this sort takes all the property of the company into the exclusive cognizance of the court which appoints the receiver The appointment of the receiver relates back from the filing of his bond to the date of his appointment "and actual seizure by him is not necessary to cut off rights which attach only after the order of appointment '— Horn *v* Pere Marquette Ry , 151 Fed 626

[2] Horn *v* Pere Marquette Ry., 151 Fed 626; Underground Electric Rys *v* Owsley, 176 Fed. 26, Wheaton *v* Daily Telegraph, 128 Fed 61, Dexter Horton Nat Bank *v.* Hawkins, 190 Fed 924 This point is of most value in averting conflicts between the federal and the State courts Where the two actions pend in the same court, and that court has jurisdiction of both law and equity, this rule of comity is unnecessary, as it presents them only "a question of administration of assets," Cass *v* Sutherland, 98 Wis 551, 74 N W. 337.

equity courts have created. But in doing this we have not discovered a complete system for effecting equality of distribution. Firstly, not all cases are embraced within it. The estates of decedents and the estates of corporations and limited partnerships are thus covered, but there are living debtors to be reckoned with, and common law partnerships. And even when we have a case within these bounds, we find the court lacking power in a most serious aspect. The receiver must fairly distribute the property in his possession; he can defend his right of possession and he can gather all the available assets into his possession. But the court's powers fail when it comes to the case of any of the wrongs which the debtor may have inflicted upon the creditors prior to the filing of the bill. If the debtor has fraudulently conveyed or encumbered any part of the property, or used it to prefer one creditor over the other, can the wrong thus inflicted be redressed by this method of procedure?

§ 322. **Receiver the Person to Sue in such a Case, if Any.** This question can only be answered with another. In order that the property thus fraudulently treated may be made available for equal distribution among the creditors, it must be brought into the estate already in the hands of the equity court. Somebody must bring a suit for that purpose, as the representative of the court, or, if one pleases to have it so, as the representative of all the creditors. The court therefore must appoint such a representative, and the receiver would naturally be chosen. So the question is, can the chancery court clothe its receiver with such powers?

§ 323. **The Question Considered from Standpoint of Principle.** On principle, this question must be answered in the negative. The Statute of Fraudulent Conveyances never was intended as anything but an aid to the enforcement of a judgment already obtained. The doctrine of reputed ownership, which started with a bankruptcy statute in England and with us rests upon a principle of estoppel, must in logic take the same course, because, as we have seen, it is not until the creditor has secured judgment that he is entitled to complain of the debtor's conduct respecting his property. Of preferences we shall speak presently, for the moment let us confine ourselves to cases of fraudulent conveyance and reputed ownership, for which redress, be it repeated, the creditor must first have obtained a judgment The right of priority is inseparable from the judgment, to assert one is to maintain the other, and one cannot be abandoned without the other The receiver, of course, takes no title to the assets in his charge, and even if he should, his title would come from the debtor corporation, which cannot itself repudiate its own acts. Nor are we helped by assuming that the receiver represents the creditors rather than the debtor, because the essence of this winding up jurisdiction is that these creditors do not occupy the position of judgment creditors but have waived all rights of priority based thereon, and, as simple-contract creditors without liens, are the beneficiaries of a fund in court. For the court to empower its officer to set aside a fraudulent transaction is to impeach its jurisdiction, because the officer, in order to bring such an action, must represent persons who have not abandoned the right to attack the fraudulent transaction — in other words, persons who still insist upon their priorities.

§ 324. **The Supreme Court's View** This point is strongly made by the Supreme Court in Myer v. Car Co[1] There a receiver appointed in a foreclosure action, instituted upon a mortgage which covered all of the property of a railroad company, attempted to set aside a contract of conditional sale under which certain equipment had been delivered, upon the ground that the contract had not been recorded as provided by the laws of the State where the delivery occurred. The recording act of that State provided that such agreements, when unrecorded, should be void as against the creditors of

[1] 102 U. S 1.

the vendee The court, assuming for the purpose of argument that the receiver represented the creditors, held that he could not attack the transaction because the recording act should be construed in the same way as the Statute of Fraudulent Conveyances, and that the rule with respect to that statute was clear "Until suit was commenced, the parties were at liberty to deal as they pleased with the property conveyed, and the rights of creditors were determined by the condition in which the property was when they interfered . The rights of the parties were fixed at the moment the property was taken by the court through its receiver into its own possession At that time these appellants were not either execution or attaching creditors " [1]

§ 325 **Precedents in Such Matters** Precedents lead us to the same result. The uniform practice in the case of a decedent's estate negatives the idea that a receiver can be clothed with any such power. In spite of the fact that the decedent's affairs had been taken into administration on a winding up bill, no creditor who discovered that the decedent had fraudulently transferred or encumbered property thought of asking the equity court to use its receiver for the purpose of setting the transaction aside Nor, on the contrary, was it ever considered that the death of the debtor or the pendency of the winding up bill barred any diligent creditor from filing a judgment creditor's bill to set aside the fraudulent transaction, and secure the same priority therein that he would have secured had the debtor still been living.[2] The only point that ever arose in this connection was whether it was necessary for the creditor to go through the form of obtaining a judgment against the executor as a prerequisite to filing his judgment creditor's bill This point, however, occasioned little difficulty In Cleveland v Chambliss [3] it was held that it was not necessary for the creditor to show a judgment, where he had been en-

[1] Myer v Car Co , *supra* , Fosdick v. Schall, 99 U S 235
[2] Hogan v. Walker, 14 How 29.   [3] 64 Ga 352

joined from bringing an action by the same court during the pendency of the administration bill. In like manner it was held that the filing of a proof of claim is sufficient to excuse the absence of a judgment, whether it is filed with the executor,[1] or with the master who had been appointed in the administration suit to receive the creditors' claims.[2] If the creditors, said the New Jersey court, "had exhausted their remedy at law against the estate of which he died seized and possessed, this court should be open to them to enable them to reach, if necessary for the satisfaction of their debts, any property which in fraud of their rights he may have placed in the hands of others."[3]

§ 326 **Cases Distinguished** Doubtless many books and opinions affirm the right of a chancery receiver, as the representative of the creditors, to maintain suits to set aside fraudulent transactions. But the cases commonly cited for such a view have been classified as cases[4] "where the receiver by force of some statute can act for creditors; where the act complained of was *ultra vires* and not binding upon the corporation; where the receiver was appointed in a proceeding prosecuted by the creditors which was supplemental to execution, and the receiver had the rights of the creditors at whose instance and to secure whose claims he was appointed, and where the receiver was suing for property or assets that belonged to the debtor." Of course, a receiver may sue to recover property belonging to the corporation but withheld from him, but he must sue in the debtor's name,[5] and is bound by all the defenses available against the debtor.[6] Of course, he can sue in his own name to protect his own right of possession, or to

[1] Haston *v* Castner, 29 N J. Eq 536, Hills *v.* Sherwood. 48 Cal. 386
[2] Brown *v* M'Donald, 1 Hill Eq 297.
[3] Haston *v* Castner, *supra*
[4] Republic Life Ins. Co *v* Swigert, 135 Ill 150, 25 N. E 680.
[5] Hayward *v* Leeson, 176 Mass 310, 57 N E 656, Yeager *v* Wallace, 44 Pa St. 294
[6] Auten *v* City Electric Co , 104 Fed. 395.

redress injuries to the property in his charge,¹ and that is all that the broad language in Davis v Gray ² really means And of course if a statute authorizes him to sue to set aside a fraudulent transaction he may do so, but the very existence of such a statute shows what the law would be in its absence ³

§ 327 **Extent of Court's Powers** The most, it is conceived, that the Chancery Court, unaided by statute, can do in this sort of case is to exclude the participant in this wrongful transaction from sharing in the distribution of the estate until he has thus been restored to the level of the other creditors Thus, in Wilson v Paul ⁴ a creditor who had received a part payment by way of a preference was excluded from the distribution until the dividends received by the other creditors reduced their claims proportionately This measure of relief, however, is so apt to be useless in most cases that it cannot be seriously reckoned with.

§ 328. **Reasoning in Support of Contrary View** Undoubtedly, however, there is considerable authority in this country in favor of the contention that a chancery receiver of the class we have described may properly maintain an action to set aside a fraudulent transaction of the debtor.⁵ This is somewhat on the idea that the Chancery Court has the power to consider its officer as clothed with all the powers of a levying creditor, but so vested in the equal behalf of all, and it is needless to say that any such action by the receiver would be by way of bill in the court of his appointment Historically there is

---

¹ *Re* Sacker, L R 22 Q B D 179 For example, in behalf of the creditors who are participating in the creditors' suit, the receiver may properly be heard in opposition to bankruptcy proceedings instituted by other creditors against the corporation, *Re* Hudson River Power Co , 173 Fed 934, aff'd 183 Fed. 701

² 16 Wall 203

³ See Yeager *v.* Wallace, 44 Pa. St 294 , Porter *v* Williams, 9 N Y 142

⁴ 8 Sim. 63

⁵ Duplex Press Co *v* Clipper Pub Co , 213 Pa St 207, 62 Atl 841, H K Porter Co *v* Boyd, 171 Fed 305, Am Can Co *v* Erie Preserving Co , 171 Fed 540, Phila Warehouse Co *v* Winchester, 156 Fed 600, Franklin Bank *v* Whitehead, 149 Ind 560, 49 N E. 592

some figment of support for this view. In Rider *v* Kidder[1] Lord ELDON held that the narrow view of Lord Thurlow, that choses in action were not within the "equity" of the Statute of Fraudulent Conveyances,[2] would not apply to a case where the debtor died after making the transfer, because as soon as a man died a trust arose in his property for the benefit of his creditors, the executor being in the position of a trustee whose duty it was to gather in all the assets for the benefit of his creditors. And, on the reasoning that a bankrupt was virtually dead and a trust arose in his property for the benefit of his creditors, the same result was reached under the Bankrupt Act in Norcutt *v.* Dodd.[3] In other words, the basis of both those cases was that as against a trust estate for the benefit of creditors the fraudulent transferee was in the position of wrongfully withholding property from a fund, and that therefore the court on its usual principle of administering trust estates would require him to restore it to the estate. There was confusion as well among the common law courts on this point. As we shall hereafter see, there yet exists some difference of opinion whether the executor of a deceased debtor may recover property which the decedent had fraudulently transferred[4] And the same confusion existed with regard to the position of the heir. At one time Lord Macclesfield considered that while the Statute of Fraudulent Devizes[5] forbade a testator from devising his land so as to keep it from descending to the heir and thus being subject to the specialty and judgment debts, yet if the debtor in his lifetime should convey the land to the heir, the latter could not be held because literally he could plead that nothing came to him by descent[6] But this decision was much criticized[7] and the better view

[1] 10 Vesey 360
[2] *Supra*, Ch IV.
[3] 1 Cr & Ph 100
[4] *Infra*, Ch XIX.
[5] 3 & 4 Wm & Mary c 14.
[6] Paislow *v* Weedon, 1 Eq. Cas Abr 148, pl 7
[7] See Brunsden *v* Stratton, Prec. Ch. 521; Jones *v* Marsh, Cases temp Talbot 64.

seems to have been that "the assets were considered to have descended notwithstanding the feoffment"[1] This view seems strengthened as well by the case of Leonard v Bacon[2] which in full is this

"*Formedon* — The tenant pleads *non tenure*, and upon this they were at issue, and it was found that, before the writ purchased, the tenant enfeoffed divers persons, to the intent to defraud them which had cause of action for the same lands, and notwithstanding he took the profits. And this verdict was adjudged for the demandant, for the feoffment was void against him by the Statute of 13 Eliz c 5"

§ 329. **Answer to These Contentions.** These considerations, however, seem of little weight As for Lord Eldon's view that a decedent's estate is a trust for his creditors, and hence all property the decedent had fraudulently removed should be brought back, that may be true enough, but it must be remembered that the action in which those words were used was brought by a creditor, not by a receiver As for the view that a bankrupt estate is a trust for the creditors, and that hence property which the bankrupt had fraudulently transferred should be restored, that is quite true, but the proceeding there was brought by the statutory assignee. That an executor can recover such assets does not answer the same question when asked concerning a receiver who, unlike an executor, has no title that a court of law can recognize Whether creditors without judgment can charge their debts on land devised to their debtor's heir is really an academic question, because, as has been said, "as such debts do not bind the heir, but merely the personal assets, such creditors would gain nothing by avoiding the voluntary conveyance of the ancestor, since if the land were construed to descend upon the heir as assets, they would not be assets to satisfy demands

---

[1] Dyer 295 b pl 16, Robertson "Fraud Conveyances," 596; Manhattan Co. v. Osgood, 15 Johns 162.
[2] Cro. Eliz 233.

upon simple contract."[1] However reason or precedent be raked, no justification can be found for the practice of tolerating suits by chancery receivers to set aside fraudulent transfers The most the court should do, it is believed, is to allow the receiver, if he has come into possession of property upon which claim is made by an outside person, to set up the fraudulent transfer by way of defense or estoppel[2] That, however, is quite a different thing from tolerating an affirmative action by the receiver

[1] Robertson, "Fraud Conveyances," 592
[2] As in Phila Warehouse Co. v Winchester, *supra*.

CHAPTER XVII

BANKRUPTCY AS A METHOD OF EFFECTING EQUALITY OF DISTRIBUTION

§ 330	The System which is Needed	§ 342	View in Some Jurisdictions
331	Bankruptcy Legislation Produces This System.	343	Origin of Doctrine Concerning Preferences
332	Early English Legislation	344	Trustee can Enforce All of the Creditors' Rights
333	Interpretation of These Statutes	345.	Position of Trustee under the Recording Acts.
334	The Creditors' Representative	346	Contrary Doctrine of Yeatman v Savings Institution
335.	Forcing the Creditors to Come In	347	Early Decisions under Present Statute.
336	Double Object of the System.	348	The Amendment of 1910
337.	Annulment of Outstanding Judicial Liens	349	Trustee the Sole Representative
338	Annulment of Judicial Liens as Bearing on Status of Trustee	350.	Trustee's Status with Respect to Claims
339.	Right of Trustee to Attack Fraudulent Conveyance	351.	Trustee's Status with Respect to Stockholders' Liability
340.	Cognate Character of Statute of Fraudulent Conveyance and First Bankrupt Act	352	Different Aspects of the Situation
		353	Procedure of Trustee
341.	Concurrent Jurisdiction of Law and Equity	354	Trustee's Status with Respect to New York Statutory Trust

§ 330. **The System which is Needed** The conclusion to which our discussion has led us is that the only way to secure equality of distribution is to devise some method of procedure that will do two things · (1) bring the debtor's property into the court as a fund for equal distribution, and (2) by means of suit for the equal benefit of all the creditors, increase this fund with property which the debtor had previously transferred in breach of his obligation to hold his assets for equal distribution. That was our quest, and we followed it among the powers of chancery as revealed to us in its practice, for obviously the common law was a barren field of research. We found that there was a certain winding up jurisdiction in chancery, but its limits were very narrow. The Chancery Court could distribute the estate of a deceased debtor; but what of a living debtor? In our country equity courts habitually wind up the affairs of corporations, but what of individual traders and unlimited partnerships? And finally, in sound logic, no reason can be found for the extension of this winding up jurisdiction beyond property which the debtor has actually on hand; there is no way, in strict reason, by which property fraudulently transferred can be restored to the estate for final distribution.

§ 331. **Bankruptcy Legislation Produces This System.** Thus at last we reach the bounds of the court's powers, and must look elsewhere for the remedy. But we need not look far. The remedy lies near at hand in the shape of legislation, of so ancient an origin as to be a part of the body of the law in every sense, and a commonplace of everyday thought. We refer to the various statutes on the subject of bankruptcy and insolvency. In so far as mere information is concerned we might halt there; but if the rights of creditors are a subject worth studying at all, it will not do to stop an inquiry into their nature with a mere reference to existing legislation. For this legislation in its modern form is complex, and its history contains much that is fascinating. Here we are at the point where not only the common law, but the jurisdiction of equity itself, breaks down, yet complete relief is afforded by legislation of a far more ancient origin than some of the basic doctrines of equity. Sir George Jessel reminds us that we know the names of the chancellors who invented many of these doctrines, but no one knows the names of the men who first gave us, through Parliamentary enactment, a new body of law in the form of bankruptcy legislation "It is obvious," says Fry, J,[1] referring to the Statute of Fraudulent Conveyances, "that the intent of the statute is not to provide equal distribution of the estates of debtors among their creditors, there are other statutes which have that object" It is with these statutes that we propose now to deal, but necessarily in a most limited way, and only with reference to their primary feature of securing equality of distribution by means of creating a representative of the creditors and clothing him with rights exceeding their own.

§ 332 **Early English Legislation** Twenty-eight years before the Statute of Fraudulent Conveyances, the first bankrupt act was introduced into the jurisprudence of England[2] From a practical standpoint, however, bankruptcy legislation really commenced in the same year as the Statute of Fraudulent Conveyances, because in that year, 1570, was also enacted an act nominally amending, but really superseding, the Statute of Henry.[3] In the following reign the Elizabethan Act was much extended by two statutes;[4] and these three acts for two centuries formed the basis of all subsequent bankruptcy law During succeeding years many changes were made, and notable indeed were those introduced by Sir Samuel Romilly's Acts,[5] but, until a general revision was made in 1824,[6] the statutes of Elizabeth and James formed the foundation of the English system of bankruptcy,[7] and for the purposes of our discussion we need not go much further than the state of the bankrupt laws at the time Lord Eldon took the Great

---

[1] *In re* Johnson, 20 Ch Div 389, 392
[2] (1542) Stat 34-35 Hen VIII, c. 4
[3] Stat 13 Eliz. c. 7.
[4] Stat 1 Jac I, c 15, Stat 21 Jac. I, c 19
[5] Stat 46 Geo. III, c 135, Stat 49 Geo III, c 121
[6] Stat 6 Geo IV, c 16
[7] Compare the treatment of the law in Cooke, "Bankrupt Laws" (4th ed), London, 1799, and 1 Comyn's Dig (1780), s v Bankrupt, with the preface to Eden, "Bankruptcy," published after the enactment of the Revising Act of 1824.

Seal, because on that model was framed our own system, however more complex in the nature of things it may be.

§ 333 **Interpretation of These Statutes.** Nothing is more characteristic of the method by which our law grows than this legislation; in working out a system of real justice under it, says Eden,[1] "the courts were driven into innumerable anomalies" Its original object was not so much to relieve the creditors from an intolerable situation, as to punish the bankrupt for putting them there, insolvency of the debtor was not so much the actuating cause of the commission as the debtor's having done something to hinder his creditors in realizing their claims The acts of bankruptcy prescribed by the statutes of Elizabeth and James, and the vindictive punishments provided for the bankrupt, show this only too well[2] Therefore the statutes contemplated that the Chancellor, to whom this jurisdiction was committed — a most fortunate omen of progress — could act of his own motion in declaring a man bankrupt, but the reader can imagine the result so long as an English-bred lawyer should preside in that forum "*Ex cautela*," says Baron Comyn,[3] "the Chancellor, before the commission is granted, usually requires a petition of the creditors, and an affidavit that they believe him to be a bankrupt" Through all such inconsistencies, and by means of being inconsistent, progress has steadily been made toward rendering the bankrupt law "a system for the regulation of mercantile insolvency"[4] such as it is to-day, and of necessity must be. It seems to be true, as an eminent judge has said,[5] that the bankruptcy system is "an example of what most of us have probably had occasion to note, that both the Parlia-

---

[1] Eden, "Bankruptcy" 12
[2] "We find that in the earlier statutes bankrupt traders are dealt with very much as if criminals," Lord Fitzgerald, in Colonial Bank *v* Whinney, 11 App. Cas 439
[3] 1 Comyn's Dig, *s. v* Bankrupt, D I
[4] Eden, "Bankruptcy" 12
[5] Christian, L J, in *In re* Hickey, 10 I. R Eq. 117, 129.

ments and the judges of those older times were bolder in initiative than their modern successors," — certainly this quality was essential if a new body of law was to be built

§ 334. **The Creditors' Representative** We now reach the point of immediate interest to us, the creation of the creditor's representative and his powers It was natural enough to create such a representative, because there had to be some one to care for the bankrupt's property until such time as a distribution could be effected The bankrupt could not be left in the custody of this property for an instant, because originally bankruptcy was a proceeding *in invitum*. The bankrupt, according to the original conception, was a person to be punished for having reached the point of being unable to meet his debts, and for having committed acts which would frustrate the creditors' endeavor to reach payment of their debts by ordinary process of law. The statutes therefore took from the bankrupt his property by force of law, and acted directly upon the legal title thereto, transferring it from the bankrupt to a person selected by the court. In the words of an ancient writer,[1] it was considered "that the bankrupt has been guilty of a fraud, and that he is therefore an improper person to be intrusted any more with the management of his own estate," and hence other persons are appointed "in place of the bankrupt, to whom, for the safety of the creditors, the commissioners are to convey the bankrupt's property." From the first these statutes had the widest of range as to the bankrupt's estate Not only his chattels, but also his land and his choses in action, passed to the assignees. The second section of the Act of Elizabeth includes as the bankrupt's estate "all that the bankrupt might depart withal," and this was always "largely and beneficially expounded for the relief of creditors"[2] Thus by bankruptcy, as well as the remedies we have already considered, is it fulfilled that the creditors are entitled to

[1] 1 Cooke "Bankrupt Laws" 283
[2] Higden *v.* Williamson, 3 P Wms. 132.

realize upon all property to which the debtor enjoys the like right.

§ 335. **Forcing the Creditors to Come In.** The next thing was to force the creditors to come in and share the proceeds of the property on a basis of equality. Originally it was provided that creditors could come into the bankruptcy within four months after the adjudication, but on condition that they contributed to the expense of the commission [1] This, together with the fact that no system then existed for the discharge of the bankrupt from even the debts thus proven against his estate, led to a most unfortunate doctrine of election The creditor, it was considered, could stay out of the bankruptcy, and could sue the debtor and take him in body execution, or seize any goods he might have which were not in the hands of the assignee This idea persisted even after the amending acts which allowed the debtor his discharge,[2] and was very long in dying. In 1732, an attempt was made to cover the difficulty by a statute,[3] which provided that all costs of the bankruptcy should be paid out of the estate, and that the debtor should be eloigned from any imprisonment under execution by showing his discharge It was not, however, until Sir Samuel Romilly's Act,[4] that this doctrine of election actually became " an object of curious research instead of a fund from whence any practical knowledge was to be derived." [5]

§ 336. **Double Object of the System.** The aim of the courts then, in their task of working these statutes into a practical system of law, was to divide all the debtor's assets among his

[1] Stat 1 Jac I, c. 15, Sec. 4.
[2] The first of which was Stat. 4 Ann, c. 17.
[3] Stat 5 Geo II, c 30
[4] Stat 49 Geo. III, c 121, Sec. 14, continued by Stat 6 Geo. IV, c. 16, Sec 59
[5] Eden " Bankruptcy " 111 See *Re* Gallison, 2 Low 72, Fed Cas 5203 At present the bankrupt courts have power to stay suits that are pending against the debtor, English Act of 1883, c 10, American Act of 1898, Sec 11a , and in America even after such a suit has gone to judgment the bankrupt may have it vacated, Boynton *v* Ball, 121 U. S 457, 7 S. Ct. 981; Hill *v* Harding, 107 U. S. 631, 2 S Ct 404.

creditors and make all the creditors come into the distribution.
In the words of Lord Hardwicke,[1] the right of the honest bankrupt to a discharge should be fully commensurate with the right of the creditors to divide up his estate. To attain this end it is obvious that creditors should share fairly, and that no man should prove for more than his due, nor should he be paid more thereon than his neighbor. Hence, an early statute[2] provided that bond creditors could prove only for what was justly due them, without respect to the penalty named therein, even if judgment for that penalty had been recovered. In like wise the race of diligence, the scramble for priority must be stopped, and here we reach a scene of progress not yet ended.

§ 337. **Annulment of Outstanding Judicial Liens.** To start with, it is obvious that the race of diligence must perforce be checked by the passage of the debtor's affairs into the custody of the court. No liens may be gained after that has happened. So far as the assets on hand are concerned that was clear from the beginning, for the assignee took the property in the condition it was in on the date of the act of bankruptcy, however secret that may have been. "The property shall be vested in the assignee by relation from the first act of bankruptcy, as to the avoidance of all *mesne* acts."[3] This harsh doctrine was softened in many respects, and in our times has been legislated into limbo, but it had this good result, that it cut off all liens which the diligent judgment creditor had acquired during the period between the act of bankruptcy and the adjudication, because an action at the suit of the assignee lay against the sheriff who levied under any such judgment.[4] Finally, Sir Samuel Romilly's Acts provided that executions should be valid, if levied over two months before the adjudication of bankruptcy, and all levied within this period should likewise avail,

---

[1] *Ex parte* Groome, 1 Atk 115
[2] Stat. 21 Jac 1, c 19, Sec 9
[3] 1 Comyn's Dig s v Bankrupt, D 26
[4] Smith v Milles, 1 T. R 475, Cooper v Chitty, 1 Burr 20.

if taken without notice of the act of bankruptcy.[1] These enactments, substantially followed in our earlier Acts of 1800 and 1841, had important results It was considered that the statutes meant, so far as was justly possible, to provide a clear *glacis* around the bankruptcy so as to reduce priorities and accomplish the system's aim. Each creditor must, so far as could be required, lay down his claim of priority and come in as a simple claimant. In the average case the pressure of creditors is followed by the debtor's bankruptcy within thirty to ninety days, or just as soon as the impatient creditors have time to bring suit and enter up their judgments thereon   Hence, by avoiding all judgments entered within such a period, a substantial leveling would be accomplished and there would be few priorities left   That was the idea, but the courts could not completely enforce it; instead, they leveled only those priorities that had been obtained "in contemplation of bankruptcy," or practically under such circumstances as to constitute a fraudulent execution under the Statute of Fraudulent Conveyances; perhaps there was a difference in this respect, but it is hard to find [2] To us of the present day the distinction is of little importance, because our present Act contains provisions [3] which, as construed by the Supreme Court in Wilson v Nelson,[4] automatically destroy all liens obtained through judicial proceedings, within four months prior to the adjudication, without regard to fraud, intent or anything else   This is indeed the "high-water mark" of bankruptcy legislation; the Act of 1867 [5] operated only on attachments, and the present English Acts are still read in the old light.[6]

[1] Stat 46 Geo. III, c 135, Sec 1, Stat 49 Geo III, c 121, Sec 2 See Eden, "Bankruptcy," 203, *et seq*
[2] Morgan v Brundrett, 5 B. & Ad 289; Buckingham v McLean, 13 How. 151, Wilson v City Bank, 17 Wall 473
[3] Secs 67f and 3a.
[4] 183 U S 191, 22 S. Ct 74
[5] Sec 14.
[6] See opinion of Hotchkiss, Referee, in *Re* Rung Furniture Co 10 Am. B R 44, Collier Bankr (8th ed) 74

§ 338. **Annulment of Judicial Liens as Bearing on Status of Trustee.** But whatever the modern differences may be, this tendency toward a leveling of judicial liens bears directly on our immediate subject of inquiry. We have seen that the bankruptcy system creates a representative to receive the debtor's property, and he receives it of necessity in the same plight and condition that the bankrupt left it in. The assignee can get no higher rights in an honest contract than the bankrupt, where the latter is bound, there also is the assignee bound [1] Of this general proposition no doubt has ever been expressed, but it has its limitations. If it were carried to the extreme, the assignee would be in the same position as an assignee for the benefit of the creditors who, as we have seen, could take only what the debtor gave, and hence could not claim whatever the debtor had given to others, however fraudulently. But the courts never went to that extreme On the contrary, it was in bankruptcy only that all frauds upon the creditors' rights could be corrected, and that through the medium of the assignee

§ 339. **Right of Trustee to Attack Fraudulent Conveyance.** It is in connection with the law of fraudulent conveyance that we can best appreciate the status of the assignee as the representative of the creditors It is settled law that he can recover for the benefit of the estate property which the bankrupt had fraudulently conveyed, and effect this recovery by means of a plenary suit. No court has ever doubted that, yet few have ever tried to explain it Nowadays, explanation is unnecessary, because the modern acts [2] expressly vest the trustee with the title to all property fraudulently conveyed. But even when the statutes were silent the assignee had this right to recovery, yet no judge thought it necessary to say much about it. Undoubtedly, as said by Jessel, M. R., [3] "the trustee in seeking

---

[1] See *supra*, § 59.
[2] E g Secs 67 and 70 of our Act of 1898
[3] *Ex parte* Butters, L R. 14 Ch Div 265

270   THE RIGHTS AND REMEDIES OF CREDITORS.   [CHAP. XVII

to set aside a transaction as fraudulent under the Statute of Elizabeth, is claiming by a higher and better title than the bankrupt himself, for the bankrupt is a party to the fraud " Such descriptive matter, however, does not answer the question, whence comes this higher right? It is likewise illuminating that the trustee always gets out of the bankrupt's shoes when it comes to any transaction which he, the trustee, is empowered to avoid,[1] and that the assignee " represents both the corporation and its creditors." [2] But that is no answer to our inquiry Perhaps Lord Loughborough comes nearest to the point when he says that " assignees have all the equity the creditors have, and may impeach transactions which the bankrupt himself would be estopped from impeaching ",[3] but, so far as reason goes, we find our answer only in an ultimatum, — " assignees have frequently been allowed as creditors under the Statute of Fraudulent Conveyances without question." [4]

§ 340 **Cognate Character of Statute of Fraudulent Conveyances and First Bankrupt Act**   There is, however, a rational basis for all this. In working out what finally came to be the real purpose of the bankrupt acts, equality of distribution, Parliament and the courts cooperated in discouraging the creditors from obtaining priorities by means of judgment. The more creditors without judgment, the better it was for an easy administration of each case   Yet it would not do to deprive creditors of their only means of righting the wrong inflicted upon them by a fraudulent conveyance, without providing, as part of the new dispensation, an effective substitute. The basic bankruptcy statute, as we have seen, was enacted in the same year as the Statute of Fraudulent Conveyances, the two laws were only two chapters apart on the Parliamentary

[1] Claridge v Evans, 137 Wis 218, 118 N W. 198, 803; Carey v. Donohue, 209 Fed. 328
[2] Chubb v. Upton, 95 U S 665
[3] Anderson v Maltby, 2 Vesey Jun 244
[4] May, " Fraudulent Conveyances," 171

roll, and obviously must be read together What was more natural than to say that, as a fraudulent conveyance is, by the terms of chapter 5, " void, frustrate and of no effect " against creditors, and as chapter 7 vests the assignee with title to the bankrupt's property, this assignee is therefore vested with the title to the property fraudulently conveyed? Our present Bankrupt Act incorporates both chapters in one, but logically no real difference is made, certainly statutes of the same session have just as close a kinship. By a later statute,[1] a fraudulent transfer by means of a deed was made an act of bankruptcy, but this really added nothing to the law, because a fraudulent conveyance by any other method was equally open to the assignee's attack [2] The doctrine must therefore be left on this broad basis, that the two statutes work together It follows that those cases in our country which hold that, although the present Bankrupt Act in its definition of a fraudulent conveyance [3] limits it to an act happening within four months prior to the bankruptcy, nevertheless the trustee may recover property fraudulently conveyed at an earlier period,[4] are correct, and those to the contrary [5] lack sound basis The trustee should be allowed to sue under the reënactment of the Statute of Fraudulent Conveyances as found in the laws of the State where the transaction occurred; in short the State law and the federal Bankrupt Act should be made to coordinate so as to avoid the conclusion that Congress, by enacting the Bankrupt Act, intended to suspend in the various States a

[1] Stat 21 Jac I, c 15, Sec 2
[2] Martin v Pewtress, 4 Burr. 2477, Dutton v Morrison, 17 Vesey Jun 194.
[3] Sec. 67
[4] Manning v Patterson, 156 Fed. 111, Re Toothaker Bros, 128 Fed 187, In re Schenck, 116 Fed 554; Sharp v Fitzhugh, 75 Ark. 562, 88 S. W. 929; Hunt v Doyal, 128 Ga. 416, 57 S E 489.
[5] Murphy v Murphy & Co, 126 Ia 57, 101 N. W 486, semble. Thomas v. Roddy, 122 N Y. App. Div. 851, 107 N. Y. S 473; Woods v Klein, 223 Pa St. 256, 72 Atl. 523; In re Ceballos & Co., 161 Fed 445.

fundamental law which, taken in connection with a bankrupt act, materially aids in securing equality of distribution

§ 341 **Concurrent Jurisdiction of Law and Equity.** There seems never to have been any difference of opinion between the common law and the chancery courts on this point. Technically, the Chancellor, in the exercise of his bankruptcy functions, did not sit as an officer of the Court of Chancery, but he was the same man for all that, and it was not long before the distinction was of little importance Moreover, the Court of Chancery, either by means of proceedings by petition in the bankruptcy or by bill filed by or against the assignee, was soon defining for the use of future generations the position of the assignee, laying it down that this officer took all that the bankrupt had in the way of assets, both legal and equitable, and, on the other hand, that he took this estate subject to all outstanding equities with respect to it.[1] From this it turned to the assignee's position with respect to property which had been fraudulently transferred, taking jurisdiction of bills filed by assignees to get in property out of their natural reach, or by claimants against property which the assignees, by self-help alone, had gathered in. It was really the volume of this kind of business rather than of judgment creditors' suits, which justified the remark of Kenyon, M. R., that the Court of Chancery had coördinate jurisdiction with courts of law over matters affected by the Statute of Fraudulent Conveyances [2] In course of time, the assignees began to institute such actions in the courts of common law, particularly in the case of personal property, and no technical argument appears to have been made against their recovery, probably because bankruptcy was the only branch of law where the common law courts were on common ground with the Court of Chancery

[1] As an early example, see Parker v. Dykes, 1 Eq. Cas Abr 54; See also 6 Col Law Rev. 562, et seq
[2] Hobbs v. Hull, 1 Cox Ch 445, see also Pratt v Curtis, Fed. Cas. 11375

and, hence, both disposed to yield to its opinion, and able to follow it in the use of their own processes The only limit, therefore, that the common law courts put upon such suits was that "a demand and refusal were necessary to maintain the action." This was only right, because the assignees "might either affirm or disaffirm the contract, and if they thought proper to disaffirm it, they ought to have demanded the goods, a refusal to deliver which would have been evidence of a conversion "[1]

§ 342. **View in Some Jurisdictions** So complete has been the acquiescence of the common law courts in the view that the bankruptcy assignee may recover property fraudulently conveyed, that in our country there is a distinct tendency to restrict him to his common law remedy Thus, in Massachusetts[2] and New York,[3] the courts refuse to tolerate suits in equity by an assignee whose object is merely the recapture of property fraudulently conveyed; there must be more than that in the case before equity will give aid The federal courts have never taken this step and equity still has concurrent jurisdiction within their halls,[4] but it would seem that, if they had it to do over again, the national courts would have drawn the same sort of dividing line [5]

§ 343 **Origin of Doctrine Concerning Preferences.** We might stop at this point, and regard as superfluous another line of reasoning which leads to the same result, were it not true that upon it rests also the modern bankruptcy doctrine which forbids preferences Preferences are expressly avoided by our present Bankrupt Act,[6] as they are by the English statute of our times;[7] but long ago the law of preferences had become established, as a result of Lord Mansfield's view of the policy

---

[1] Nixon v Jenkins, 2 H Bl 135; Young v Billiter, 8 H L C. 682
[2] Pratt v Wheeler, 6 Gray 520, see Bigelow, "Fraudulent Conveyances," 467 n
[3] Allen v Gray, 201 N Y 504, 94 N. E. 652
[4] Wall v. Cox, 101 Fed 403
[5] Parker v Black, 151 Fed 18
[6] Sec. 60
[7] Act of 1883, Sec. 48.

of bankruptcy legislation. The Chief Justice considered that the primary end of such statutes would be defeated if the debtor, prior to his affairs being brought into court for administration, could with impunity place his property beyond its reach, or himself pay such creditors as he pleased. The courts had already mooted this topic in holding general assignments to be against the policy of the Bankrupt Act,[1] but it remained for Lord Mansfield to carry the doctrine to its logical result, that either a preference or a fraudulent conveyance was impliedly forbidden by the statute, and hence the assignee was entitled to the property constituting the subject matter. As to fraudulent conveyances, he first laid down this rule in Martin v Pewtress,[2] saying that "a trader can't alter the property of goods, by a criminal fraudulent transaction, to the prejudice of his creditors" Respecting preferences, he is reputed to have first expressed himself at *nisi prius* in Kettle v. Hammond,[3] and the King's Bench, with himself presiding, followed this with a series of striking decisions[4] The same doctrine was applied by the Supreme Court of Massachusetts in a case arising under our National Bankrupt Act of 1800[5] " If indeed it be true," said Sedgwick, J , "as it undoubtedly is, that every attempt to defeat the public law is fraudulent and void, it then follows that the delivery of property to a creditor, in contemplation of bankruptcy, is fraudulent, notwithstanding the delivery is made in satisfaction of a *bona fide* debt " That is the basis of the law of preferences, and even when the statutes, as nowadays, expressly forbid them, the idea remains the same. Thus the Supreme Court, construing those provisions of the National Act of 1867 which undertook to forbid preferential transfers, considered the act which it

---

[1] 1 Cooke, "Bankrupt Laws," 86.
[2] 4 Burr 2478
[3] Reported in 1 Cooke Bankr 86
[4] Alderson v Temple, 4 Burr 2235; Worseley v Demattos, 1 Burr 467, Rust v Cooper, 2 Cowp 629, Hassels v. Simpson, 3 Doug 361
[5] Locke v Winning, 3 Mass. 325.

was intended to forbid as one committed "to prevent the property from coming into the hands of the assignee in bankruptcy and from being distributed under the bankrupt law"[1]

§ 344 **Trustee can Enforce All of the Creditors' Rights.** So by one line of reasoning or another, we reach the conclusion that the trustee in bankruptcy is the representative of the creditors' rights in every sense of the word, and by plenary suit, instead of ancillary proceedings, he may redress those wrongs for the benefit of all the creditors. It follows that, if any statute confers additional rights on the creditors, the trustee will succeed to those rights In view of this the incoming of the recording acts should have caused no difficulty, but nevertheless they did, and it is necessary that we examine this trouble

§ 345. **Position of Trustee under the Recording Acts.** Briefly, towards the middle of the nineteenth century, both in England and our States, statutes were adopted making void as against creditors various transactions affecting the title to personal property when unaccompanied by change of possession, unless public record of the details were made. Obviously, such statutes stand on the same ground with the Statute of Fraudulent Conveyances: all are for the benefit of creditors, and none can be availed of by a creditor unless he has a judgment.[2] In plain common sense, should not an assignee in bankruptcy succeed to the same right? At first, there was but one answer In Bingham v Jordan [3] it was held that an assignee was entitled to attack an unrecorded transfer, on the ground that the policy of these statutes was the same as that of the Statute of Fraudu-

---

[1] Gibson v Warden, 14 Wall 244. In utter forgetfulness of all this, however, the Supreme Court of late years has swung around to the view that a preference is nothing but *malum prohibitum* in the strictest sense of the term Coder v Arts, 213 U S 223, 29 S. Ct 436; Van Iderstine v Nat Discount Co, 227 U S 575, 33 S. Ct. 343 But that cannot unmake history

[2] Myer v. Car Co, 102 U S 1, Skilton v Coddington, 185 N Y. 80, 77 N E 790

[3] 1 Allen 373

lent Conveyances and that the assignee represented the creditors under the one as under the other. The same view was taken by the New York Court of Appeals in Southard *v.* Benner.[1] Indeed, the trustee should be considered, not of course as a purchaser in any sense of the word, as Lord Hardwicke pointed out years ago in Walker *v* Burrows,[2] but as "a creditor armed with an attachment or execution."[3] If we view the trustee in this light, we will have no more difficulty with the recording acts than we had with the Statute of Fraudulent Conveyances

§ 346 **Contrary Doctrine of Yeatman v. Savings Institution.** In spite of all these considerations the Supreme Court in Yeatman *v.* Savings Institution[4] held that an unfiled chattel mortgage was valid as against the trustee in bankruptcy, because he did not occupy the status of a judgment creditor. Thus the Supreme Court and the New York Court of Appeals came to differ radically. One held that the trustee in bankruptcy had all the rights of a judgment creditor, and consequently could attack anything which was by statute made void as against creditors. The other held that, while he had that status with regard to fraudulent conveyances and preferences, he did not have that status with regard to any State law beyond such a point. This difference of opinion still existed when the Act of 1867 was repealed, and it revived with the passage of the Act of 1898

§ 347 **Early Decisions under Present Statute** It was undoubtedly to remedy this defect that the present Bankrupt Act provides in Sec. 67a that "claims which for want of record or other reasons would not have been valid liens as against the claims of the creditors of the bankrupt, shall not be valid liens as against his estate," and also provides in Sec. 70 that

---

[1] 72 N Y. 424· Skilton *v.* Coddington, 185 N. Y. 80, 77 N E. 790
[2] 1 Atk. 93
[3] Zartman *v.* Bank of Waterloo, 189 N Y 267, 82 N. E 127.
[4] 95 U S 764

the trustee shall be vested with the title to all property which, prior to the filing of the petition, could by any means have been transferred or which might have been levied upon and sold under judicial process against him [1] Yet, notwithstanding these provisions, a federal court, sitting in New York, held that an unfiled chattel mortgage was valid as against the trustee, except in behalf of such creditors as might meanwhile have obtained judgment, because it was the intention of the statute that only judgment creditors should attack such transactions [2] Then the New York Court of Appeals in Skilton v Coddington [3] repeated the view which it had expressed in Southard v Benner,[4] that under the New York law the trustee in bankruptcy did occupy the position of a judgment creditor with regard to the recording acts; whereupon the federal court took the same view.[5]

The law thus stood that a trustee in bankruptcy cannot avail himself of a State recording act unless the State courts have decided that a trustee in bankruptcy occupies the position of a judgment creditor [6]

§ 348. **The Amendment of 1910.** This *impasse*, however, has been relieved by Congress. In 1910, Sec 47a of the statute was amended so as to declare that the trustee, as to all property not in the custody of the court, is " vested with all the rights, remedies and powers of a judgment creditor holding an execution returned unsatisfied." As the Massachusetts court pointed out in Denny v Lincoln [7] the Massachusetts insolvency law contained such an express provision It has now been determined that the present amendment, while not affecting a valid lien which need not be recorded,[8] does " vest in the trustee

[1] See 6 Col Law Rev 562
[2] *In re* N. Y Economical Printing Co , 110 Fed. 514
[3] 185 N Y 80; 77 N E. 790
[4] 72 N Y 424.
[5] *In re* Gerstman, 157 Fed 549
[6] See 6 Col Law Rev 562
[7] 13 Metc 200.
[8] *In re* East End Mantel Co , 202 Fed 275.

for the interest of the creditors the potential rights of the creditors of that class "[1] Thus the judicial errata are cured, and we are brought back to where we started, with all the creditors' rights, however conferred, fully vested in the bankruptcy trustee.

§ 349 **Trustee the Sole Representative.** The trustee is considered the representative of the rights of the creditors, and their sole representative. The estate of the debtor having passed into the custody of the law, and equality of distribution being the object, it would not do to allow any creditor thenceforth to proceed with his remedy with respect to the assets Consequently, no single creditor can bring an action to set aside a fraudulent transfer in his own name or right. This is true even though the trustee most unreasonably refuses to bring the action, as the only remedy of the creditor in such a case is to have the court remove the trustee and appoint some other trustee who will institute such an action [2]

§ 350 **Trustee's Status with Respect to Claims.** In connection with the distribution of the assets, the trustee is interested as well in the size of the claims upon which distribution is to be made. The entire matter of distribution being in his hands as an officer of the court, he is the proper person to object to any claim that has been improperly made.[3] We may repeat,

---

[1] *In re* Bazemore, 189 Fed 236.
[2] Davis *v* Snell, 3 L T 394; Glenny *v.* Langdon, 98 U. S. 20; Moyer *v* Dewey, 103 U S 301, McMaster *v* Campbell, 41 Mich. 513, 2 N W 836, *In re* Pitts, 9 Fed 544 The same rule applies of course to a statutory receiver, Idding *v* Bruen, 4 Sandf Ch 417
[3] *In re* Lewensohn, 121 Fed 538, *In re* Sully, 152 Fed 619 In like manner, a chancery receiver has standing to object to claims, Thom *v* Pittard, 62 Fed 232; McGregor *v* The Bank, 124 Ga 557, 53 S E 93, Bosworth *v* Association, 174 U S 182, 19 S Ct 625· Of course, if the trustee refuses to make such an application a creditor can apply for the proper relief (*In re* Mexico Hardware Co, 197 Fed 650), if he does so promptly, *In re* Pittsburgh Lead Co, 198 Fed 316 If, however, without objection a creditor has been allowed to proceed with objections at his own expense, an order of disallowance will not be disturbed, merely because it has been procured by such means, *In re* Canton &c. Co, 197 Fed. 767. If a late decision is well founded,

therefore, as a broad proposition that all the distributive rights of the creditors in the debtor's property are fully vested in the trustee, and he may assert those rights, by any action appropriate therefor, in anything affecting the *quantum* of the debtor's property for distribution.

§ 351. **Trustee's Status with Respect to Stockholders' Liability.** And here again, of course, we meet the same proposition which has confronted us throughout this discussion, that the creditors can have no more than the debtor has unless a statute gives them more. Statutes give them more, as we have seen, and shall see, in cases of (*a*) fraudulent transactions, (*b*) reputed ownership and (*c*) preferential transfers. There is another broad instance where the statute enlarges the creditors' rights, and that is the case of corporate stock. When a corporation becomes insolvent and a trustee in bankruptcy or statutory receiver is appointed the question arises of the stockholders' liability to contribute to the corporate estate. This proposition may take one of several angles.

§ 352 **Different Aspects of the Situation.** It may be that a shareholder has subscribed but has failed to pay at the time of the bankruptcy the full amount of his agreed subscription of stock. This constitutes a contract liability, and there is no difficulty in sustaining the right of the trustee to enforce it because, undoubtedly, the corporation itself could enforce

there may occasionally arise equitable considerations sufficient to preclude all of the creditors from being represented by the trustee In Cornell *v* Nichols Co, 201 Fed 320, an estate had no money with which to prosecute a suit for property which had been fraudulently conveyed The receiver applied to the creditors for a contribution in order to put him in funds with which to prosecute the action, but did not meet with an unanimous response It was held that the fruits of this litigation should be distributed only among the creditors who thus contributed It was perhaps consistent with this doctrine for the courts to hold that the trustee had no standing to object to an application for the debtor's discharge, because his concern was solely with the distribution of the debtor's assets and not with the debtor's liberty from his debts, but this restriction has been removed by the amendment of June 25, 1910, to Section 14, subdivision B See *In re* Reiff, 205 Fed 399.

such a liability.¹ And also if in this regard, under the provisions of a statute regulating the consideration for which stock may be issued, the directors issue stock to themselves without paying therefor, the trustee may treat the matter as though these directors had purloined property of the corporation. In such a case he has, of course, a common law election of remedies, suing either in tort or upon the quasi contract obligation to pay the value of the property, viz. the par value of the stock.² But if the stockholder has paid less for his stock than par value under express agreement with the corporation to that effect, the situation is somewhat different. Under the rule in certain jurisdictions, as England and Massachusetts,³ this amount may be recovered on the theory that the agreement was a fraud on the other subscribers and the creditors. Under the New York rule⁴ a precisely opposite result has been reached. The Supreme Court has committed itself no further than to hold that the corporation itself cannot sue for the unpaid difference,⁵ but it expressly left open all other questions. At an earlier day, however, it had held that the trustee in bankruptcy could recover such amounts for the benefit of the creditors, the agreement in question being a fraud on them,⁶ and that seems to represent the prevailing view.⁷ In New York, on the contrary, it has been flatly held that a trustee in bankruptcy cannot recover this amount for the benefit of the company's creditors in the absence of a statute of the State where the corporation was organized, which expressly authorizes the

¹ Babbitt v. Read, 173 Fed 712
² Lanphere v Lang, 157 N Y App Div 306, 141 N. Y. S. 967.
³ Erlanger v New Sombrero Phosphate Co, L R 3 A. C. 1218, Old Dominion Copper Co v Bigelow, 188 Mass 315, 74 N. E 653
⁴ Christensen v Eno, 106 N Y 97, 12 N. E. 648, Southworth v. Morgan, 205 N Y. 293, 98 N E. 490
⁵ Old Dominion Copper Company v Lewisohn, 210 U. S 206, 28 S Ct 634.
⁶ Scoville v Thayer 105 U S 143
⁷ In re Munger etc Co, 168 Fed 910, Cumberland Lumber Co v. Clinton Hill Lumber Co, 57 N. J Eq 627, 42 Atl 585; Lewisohn v. Stoddard, 78 Conn 575, 63 Atl 621.

trustee to recover such amount. In the latest case the court clearly states this view that the trust fund doctrine cannot apply to this differential, because the corporation has agreed that it was never to be paid. "The capital or capital stock which it thus segregates is not the capital stock authorized or named in the charter of the corporation . . . and as there is not a fund or security in the nominal or potential shares there is none in the case of the nominal value over the subscribed value of the shares . The doctrine does not create or fulfill subscriptions. It lays hold of the assets of an insolvent corporation and in doing that, it compels subscribers to fulfill their legal obligations and perform their legal duties; but it does not alter these duties or obligations, it does not make invalid or unlawful a subscription which, apart from it, was valid and lawful "[1] In New York the liability of stockholders for anything other than what they have agreed to pay, whether for the differential between their subscription and the par value of the stock, or for a double liability imposed upon them by statute in event of the corporation's failure, exists purely by virtue of a statute, and it is according to the terms of the statute alone that the court must decide whether the statute intends the liability to be enforced by the trustee or by the creditors individually This has been held in New York with respect to such double liability as is imposed on stockholders of banks under Section 303 of the Banking Law, and on stockholders of business corporations and creditors under Section 56 of the Stock Corporation Law, and the courts have concluded that a trustee in bankruptcy has no cause of action to recover this statutory amount, but that it can be recovered only by the creditors individually, just as though the company's assets had never passed into the hands of the trustee [2]

§ 353 **Procedure of Trustee.** In any case where the trustee is entitled to sue there are two steps to be taken The first

[1] Southworth v Morgan, 205 N Y 293, 98 N. E 490
[2] Breck v Brewster, 153 N Y App Div 800, 138 N Y. S 821

is to define the amount of the deficiency which should be recovered That means that a preliminary assessment must be made by the court, and it is only upon the basis of such an assessment that the second step in the matter can be taken [1] The judgment of the court in making this assessment determines once and for all the necessity therefor; and upon such assessment the proofs of claim allowed by the court are conclusive as to the amount of the corporation's indebtedness.[2] Hence the assessment thus made is binding upon the stockholder as to the footing of the assets and liabilities, the amount of the differential upon which he is to be charged for liability, and the aggregate assessment required [3] But all other questions are left open for decision, including whether as a matter of law upon the footing of the facts found by the assessing court and upon the law as applicable thereto, the subscriber is liable for the differential at all [4]

§ 354. **Trustee's Status with Respect to New York Statutory Trust** Another instance of a statute limiting the representation of the creditor by the trustee is to be found in the case of the income of a *cestui que* trust under the New York statute. As we have already seen, the creditors of one who is the beneficiary of a trust created pursuant to the New York statutes, can reach only such surplus of income from the trust estate as may be above the reasonable living expenses of the debtor, the amount thereof to be determined by the court In Butler *v* Baudoyne [5] it was held that a trustee in bankruptcy did not acquire any rights in the income, and that the only persons

---

[1] *In re* Remington Automobile Co , 153 Fed. 345; Scoville *v* Thayer, 105 U S 143, *In re* Munger etc Co., 168 Fed 910, Rosoff *v* Gilbert Transportation Co., 204 Fed 349, and cases there cited.

[2] *In re* Remington Automobile Co , 153 Fed 345.

[3] *Ibid* , Howarth *v* Angle, 162 N Y. 179, 56 N. E 489, Great Western Telegraph Co. *v.* Purdy, 162 U. S 329, 16 S. Ct. 810.

[4] Southworth *v* Morgan, 205 N. Y. 293, 98 N. E. 490, Mettinger *v* Hendricks, 208 Fed 824.

[5] 84 N Y. App Div. 215, 82 N. Y. S. 773, aff'd 177 N. Y. 530, 69 N. E 1121.

having any rights are the judgment creditors A peculiar situation then occurred in *In re* Tiffany.[1] The debtor, who was the beneficiary of such a trust, applied for his discharge in bankruptcy. The creditors opposed the discharge on the ground that they had not yet had time to institute actions to reach his surplus income and that the bankrupt's intervening discharge would bar their actions Consequently the court in the exercise of its discretion adjourned the application for a discharge pending the actions to reach the surplus income Thus the same difficulty was presented, with respect to the New York statutory trust, that we saw arise with regard to the New York recording acts. Only judgment creditors could act, but it was considered that the trustee did not represent the judgment creditors This difficulty has been cured by the 1910 amendments to Sec 47a of the Bankrupt Act in the same manner as the other difficulty has been cured The statute having now expressly defined the trustee's status as that of a judgment creditor with an execution returned unsatisfied, the federal courts consider that it is unnecessary to take the same course that they followed in the Tiffany case inasmuch as the trustee now may proceed in the State courts for the benefit of the creditors.[2]

[1] 147 Fed 314

[2] *In re* Morris, 204 Fed 770

CHAPTER XVIII

THE BANKRUPTCY TRUSTEE UNDER THE PRESENT NATIONAL ACT

§ 355 Present National Bankrupt Act
356 Voluntary Bankruptcy
357. Acts of Bankruptcy
358 The Fraudulent Conveyance
359 Concealment of Property
360 The Preferential Transfer
361 To Suffer or Permit, while Insolvent, a Creditor to Obtain a Preference through Legal Process, and not to Vacate it Five Days before Sale or Final Disposition of Property Taken under Process
362 Debtor's Inaction with Respect to the Levy may Constitute Act of Bankruptcy.
363. Date of Lien
364 Lien of "Equitable Levy."
365 Other Acts of Bankruptcy
366. The Time Limit for the Occurrence of the Acts
367. Relationship of Bankruptcy to Solvency
368. Acts of Bankruptcy Unaccompanied by Insolvency
369 Appointment of Receiver as Act of Bankruptcy.
§ 370 What is Insolvency?
371. Real Nature of Statutory Definitions
372 Illustrative Cases
373 Further Illustration — Appointment of Receiver
374 Territorial Limitations of Federal Courts
375 The Federal District as the Unit of Jurisdiction
376 Jurisdiction of the District Court
377 Character of Proceedings Prior to Adjudication.
378 Appointment of Receiver in Bankruptcy
379 Ancillary Receivership.
380. Title of the Trustee
381 Extraterritorial Powers of Trustee.
382. Similar Powers of National Bank Receiver
383 Recognition of Title of Foreign Trustee to Personal Property — English Rule
384 Title of Foreign Trustee to Real Estate.
385 Title of Foreign Trustee to Personal Property — American Rule.

§ 355. **Present National Bankrupt Act** The American bankruptcy system exists by virtue of an act of Congress. Its authority is Section 8 of Article I of the Constitution, which confers upon Congress the power to pass laws looking to a uniform system of bankruptcy. The Act under which we live was enacted in 1898 and with various amendments, most notable of which were those of the years 1903 and 1910, still remains in force. The constitutionality of this Act has been fully upheld and its uniformity from a constitutional standpoint has been vindicated, the Supreme Court justifying one of its most conspicuous features, viz the allowance in full of all exemptions which the debtor is allowed by the laws of the State where he resides.[1]

§ 356. **Voluntary Bankruptcy** This statute allows both voluntary and involuntary bankruptcies. Of the voluntary procedure there is little to say, except to note that until the amendment of 1910 to Section 4, a corporation could not become a voluntary bankrupt. In practice, however, this made little difference, as a corporation desiring liquidation under the Act could easily commit an act of bankruptcy by confessing in writing its inability to pay its debts and its desire of being adjuged a bankrupt, whereupon three friendly creditors could file a bankruptcy petition against it It is more important, for the purpose of this work, that we confine ourselves to the practice in involuntary proceedings as more directly affecting the creditors' rights to a distribution by use of the means which the Act provides

§ 357 **Acts of Bankruptcy** In order for the creditors to proceed, it is necessary that within four months prior to the filing of the petition the debtor should have committed an act of bankruptcy These are prescribed by Section 3a of the act. In addition, there must be present at the time the act of bankruptcy is committed a condition of insolvency. This is a general proposition, but it has its exceptions which will presently be noted Why the concurrence of an act of bankruptcy with insolvency is generally required involves a recurrence to the history of bankruptcy legislation which has already been set forth Originally, as we have seen, the object of bankruptcy proceedings was not so much the winding up of an

[1] Hanover Bank v Moyses, 186 U S. 181, 22 S Ct 857

insolvent's estate as the relief of creditors from fraudulent acts of the debtor tending to the impairment of their remedies The Bankrupt Act, in other words, was in the nature of a criminal statute, and the common law conception of the overt act as a necessary feature of a crime led, perhaps unconsciously, to the requirement that there should be no bankruptcy unless the bankrupt had committed some overt act showing his fraudulent intent Several such acts as originally specified survive to this day in the English Act of 1883 [1] The four other acts of bankruptcy prescribed by the present English statute are (*a*) a general assignment, (*b*) a fraudulent conveyance, (*c*) a preferential transfer, and (*d*) notice by the debtor to any of his creditors that he has suspended or is about to suspend payment of his debts These savor of the modern spirit, and so nearly approach the acts of bankruptcy prescribed by our modern

---

[1] This Act prescribes (Sec 4) as acts of bankruptcy, among others, the following

"(*d*) If with intent to defeat or delay his creditors he does any of the following things, namely, departs out of England, or being out of England remains out of England, or departs from his dwelling house, or otherwise absents himself, or begins to keep house.

"(*e*) A debtor commits an act of bankruptcy if execution has been levied by seizure of his goods under process in an action in any court, or in any civil proceeding in the High Court, and the goods have been either sold or held by the sheriff for twenty-one days Provided that where an interpleader summons has been taken out in regard to the goods seized, the time lapsing between the date at which said summons is taken out and the date at which the sheriff is ordered to withdraw, or any interpleader issued order thereon is finally disposed of, shall not be taken into account in calculating such period of twenty-one days

"(*f*) If he files in the court a declaration of his inability to pay his debts or presents a bankruptcy petition against himself

"(*g*) If a creditor has obtained a final judgment against him for any amount and execution thereon not having been stayed has served on him in England, or by leave of the court elsewhere, a bankruptcy notice under this act, requiring him to pay the judgment debt in accordance with the terms of the judgment, or to secure . and he does not within seven days after service of the notice . . . either comply with the requirements of the notice or satisfy the court that he has a counterclaim which equals or exceeds the amount of the judgment debt and which he could not set up in the action in which the judgment was obtained "

statute that further parallels in this regard would seem to be unnecessary. Turning, therefore, to our statute, let us take up successively the acts of bankruptcy which it prescribes in Section 3a.

§ 358. **The Fraudulent Conveyance.** The fraudulent conveyance, as defined in this section, was intended to embrace all of the elements of a fraudulent conveyance as defined in Section 67e and also in the Statute of Fraudulent Conveyances, with, of course, the exception that the latter allows a past consideration to support a transfer, whereas the present Act of necessity does not, otherwise it would justify preferential transfers, as we have already pointed out. Although in Section 3a a saving clause in behalf of the purchaser does not appear, yet, nevertheless, a fraudulent conveyance is not an act of bankruptcy unless all of the elements as prescribed by the tests we have already examined are present [1]

§ 359 **Concealment of Property.** In addition to the fraudulent conveyance, this section also includes as an act of bankruptcy the concealment or removal of the bankrupt's property. This, of course, is not technically a fraudulent conveyance, because it applies to property which the debtor is hiding from his creditors instead of transferring or encumbering by means of transactions affecting the title thereto. In a case of this sort, where no title has passed, it is obvious that nothing need be shown except the title of the debtor to the property and an act on his part with respect to its physical disposition indicating his intention to conceal or remove it

§ 360 **The Preferential Transfer.** Here the transferee's knowledge or notice is dispensed with. All that it is necessary to show is that the debtor, while insolvent, paid or secured one claim to the exclusion of others. In other words, all the elements of a preference which we shall hereafter examine need not appear when the preference is asserted as an act of bankruptcy But of course it is otherwise when the trustee tries to take

[1] Githens v Schiffler, 112 Fed. 505, Lansing Works v Ryerson, 128 Fed. 701.

the preference away, or prevent the transferee from proving his claim for any balance that may remain. That is because Congress has not amended Section 3 as it did Sec. 57g so as to take it out from the rule of Pirie v. Trust Co.,[1] of which we shall have more to say in Chapter XX

§ 361 To Suffer, or Permit, while Insolvent, a Creditor to Obtain a Preference through Legal Process, and not to Vacate it Five Days before Sale or Final Disposition of Property Taken under Process. This requires no action on the part of the debtor in permitting the judgment Whenever there is a judgment and levy the debtor is absolutely required to pay it off five days before the resulting judicial sale In default of that, he should file a petition of voluntary bankruptcy and get the lien wiped off under Section 67f, which vacates all judicial liens obtained within the four months' period [2] The preference may consist of a judgment constituting a lien on real estate,[3] or an attachment under which goods are seized.[4]

§ 362. Debtor's Inaction with Respect to the Levy may Constitute Act of Bankruptcy. By the precise terms of Section 3a, the preference does not operate until there is a sale But by reading this section together with Section 25 (defining " transfer ") Section 60a (defining a preference), and Section 67f, nullifying all liens obtained within the four months' period, the courts have extended this section so as to make it a preferential act on the debtor's part merely to let the judgment remain until just before the expiration of the four months' period, although the judgment creditor may be taking no steps to enforce it.[5]

[1] 182 U S 438, 21 S Ct 906   Re Riggs Rest Co , 130 Fed. 691; Alter v Clark, 193 Fed 153, 160
[2] Wilson v Nelson, 183 U S 191, 22 S Ct 74, Bradley Co. v White, 121 Fed 779 As to the four months' period, see *supra* § 337.
[3] Re Tupper, 163 Fed 766.
[4] Folger v. Putnam, 194 Fed 793 , Re Truitt, 203 Fed. 550.
[5] Folger v Putnam, 194 Fed 793; Re Tupper, 163 Fed 766. But if the lien subsisted before the four months' period, the debtor s inaction within that period cannot make it a preference, Colston v Austin &c. Co., 194 Fed. 929

§ 363. **Date of Lien.** In connection with this point, the reader must be careful to ascertain when, according to the general principles affecting the lien in question, it actually is obtained Thus, the Circuit Court of Appeals of the Second Circuit has held that a mechanic's lien filed under the Lien Laws of New York does not take effect within this section as a judicial lien at the date of filing As the court construed the State laws in question, the person entitled to the benefit of the statute for material supplied toward the improvement of real estate acquires his lien as an inchoate thing from the moment that the materials were delivered, having after that time a statutory period within which to perfect his lien by filing notice thereof in public office, and hence the lien is obtained from the moment the materials are supplied rather than from the time when the notice of lien is filed That was the decision in *In re Emshie*.[1] Whether or not it accurately represents the law of the State may be called into some question in view of some recent decisions,[2] but of course this is a matter entirely governed by the law of the particular State

§ 364 **Lien of " Equitable Levy."** From a broader standpoint, however, the decision in *Metcalf v. Barker*[3] is valuable. There it was held that the equitable levy under a judgment creditor's bill, whose nature we have already discussed, is acquired from the moment the bill is filed, and that hence, although a decree confirming the priority of the plaintiff in an action is entered within four months prior to the time when the judgment debtor was adjudged a bankrupt, nevertheless the judgment creditor has a lien which was not obtained by judicial proceedings within this statutory period if the bill was filed at an earlier date.

[1] 102 Fed 291
[2] See Tisdale Lumber Company *v* Read Realty Company, 154 N Y App Div 270, 138 N Y S 839, where it is held that the lien is not inchoate prior to the filing of the notice, from certain points of view
[3] 187 U. S 165, 23 S. Ct 67

§ 365   **Other Acts of Bankruptcy** These require no extended discussion, at this point. They are. — (1) the execution of a general assignment for the benefit of creditors. As we have already seen,[1] this, as the Supreme Court has considered, is an act of bankruptcy irrespective of the debtor's solvency. (2) Written admission of inability to pay debts, and willingness to be adjudged a bankrupt on that ground. This is an oblique method of voluntary bankruptcy. (3) The appointment of a receiver of the debtor's property on the ground of the debtor's insolvency This act of bankruptcy was added by the amendment of 1903 In connection with it have arisen certain questions concerning the definition of insolvency, of which we shall speak later

§ 366   **The Time Limit for the Occurrence of the Acts** The statute does not allow one to be adjudged a bankrupt unless within a certain period prior to the filing of the petition the act of bankruptcy has occurred, and this period is fixed at four months This accords with the current of English legislation, three months being prescribed by the present act, and under former acts a shorter period averaging two months. The idea, of course, is that a party whose affairs are in a fair way to require the administration which the statute provides, reaches the downward point within a period when his overdue bills and accounts would become due, and, as business is conducted on the basis of an average period of from thirty to ninety days' credit, the arbitrary period of four months will strike a fair average [2] Under Section 3b, this time does not begin to run until, in case of fraudulent conveyance, preference, or assignment, (*a*) the recording of the transfer if such is either required or permitted by law, or (*b*) the date when the transferee takes "notorious, exclusive or continuous possession," (*c*) unless

---

[1] *Supra*, § 290
[2] In computing this time the practice is to exclude the first day and include the last, *Re* Stevenson, 94 Fed. 110; *Re* Dupree, 97 Fed. 28.

the creditors meanwhile have had actual notice of the transfer
This we have considered elsewhere [1]

§ 367. **Relationship of Bankruptcy to Solvency** Section 3c applies to the first act of bankruptcy, a fraudulent conveyance. It allows the debtor to show that however he was insolvent at that time, or left insolvent by the transaction, it is academic because now, at the time of the filing of the petition, he is solvent. By the plain words of the statute here, the burden of proof is on the bankrupt to show the fact of supervenient solvency.[2] If the debtor sustains this burden of showing that he is solvent at the time of the proceeding, there is no need of the bankruptcy proceedings and the court must dismiss them [3]

§ 368. **Acts of Bankruptcy Unaccompanied by Insolvency.** Two acts of bankruptcy are not accompanied by the requirement of insolvency. The first of course is the written admission of inability to pay debts and willingness to be adjudged a bankrupt. Necessarily there would be no use in requiring the creditors to prove insolvency in such a case, because the debtor has admitted that he is insolvent and has stated that he is willing to be adjudged a bankrupt on that ground The other is the general assignment. In common with the English courts and notwithstanding the express language of Section 3c, the Supreme Court, as we have seen, has established the rule that the general assignment is an act of bankruptcy as such without proof of insolvency.[4]

---

[1] *Infra*, Ch. XX.

[2] *Re* Larkin, 168 Fed. 100; *Re* Steinmeyer, 108 Fed 591; *Re* Pease, 129 Fed 446.

[3] Elliott *v.* Teoppner, 187 U S 327, 23 S Ct. 133. While the burden of showing insolvency is on the petitioners, yet they are aided by Section 3d, which requires the bankrupt, if he tenders the issue of his insolvency by traversing the petition, to appear with his books and submit to examination. Under this he must produce all books and papers bearing on his financial condition, Bogen *v* Potter, 129 Fed 553, and they are all competent, though not conclusive evidence against him, *Re* Docker Foster Co, 123 Fed. 190; Smith *v.* Moore, 199 Fed 680.

[4] *Supra*, § 290.

§ 369. **Appointment of Receiver as Act of Bankruptcy.** In like manner, although it has not as yet been conclusively determined, it would seem that the Act of Bankruptcy which is added by the amendment of 1903, viz., the appointment of a receiver of the debtor's property on the ground of insolvency, would exclude the requirement of proof on this head in the bankruptcy proceeding. But that is not so. In two cases the bankrupt has been allowed to be heard on the question of insolvency at the time the receiver was appointed.[1] In a later case it was intimated that while the appointment of a receiver would at least be presumptive evidence of insolvency at the time he was appointed, still the bankrupt should be heard on whether since that time he has become solvent.[2]

§ 370. **What is Insolvency?** As defined by our Bankrupt Act, insolvency is whenever the aggregate of the debtor's property, exclusive of property fraudulently transferred or concealed, shall not at a fair valuation be sufficient in amount to pay his debts.[3] The Act of 1867 did not define insolvency, but the Supreme Court construed it to mean a case where the bankrupt could not pay his debts as they matured in the course of business.[4] In the same manner, under the New Jersey Corporation Law[5] which allows the appointment of a receiver on the ground of insolvency, or where the corporation suspends its ordinary business for want of funds to carry it on, it has been held that insolvency means inability to pay debts as they accrue in the course of business.[6] In providing for voluntary bankruptcy the English statute in section 8 says "A debtor's petition shall allege that the debtor is unable to pay

[1] Blue Mt etc Co v Portner, 131 Fed. 57, *In re* Belfast etc. Co., 153 Fed 224
[2] *In re* Pickens etc Co., 158 Fed 894.
[3] Sec 1, subd. 15
[4] Toof v Martin, 13 Wall 40; Buchanan v. Smith, 16 Wall 277, 308
[5] Sec 65
[6] Skirm v Eastern Rubber Co, 57 N J Eq 179, 40 Atl 769; Ft. Wayne Electric Co. v. Franklin etc Co, 57 N. J Eq 7, 41 Atl. 217.

his debts." That is the common law definition of insolvency. It is really harder on the debtor than our new bankruptcy test, because, as is pointed out by SHAW, C. J.,[1] it is much easier to show that one cannot pay his debts in ordinary course than to show that the total of his assets would at some future time be insufficient in amount to pay his debts by means of liquidation.

§ 371. **Real Nature of Statutory Definitions.** In truth, however, both views of insolvency are not so much definitions as mere tests.[2] In its ultimate analysis, insolvency is such a condition of the debtor's property that he is unable to meet all his obligations according to their terms. Under our present bankruptcy definition it has held that the debtor's business assets must be valued as though they were owned by a going concern[3] But if the courts had followed the statute literally, they would have considered the valuation of assets as those of a stopped concern, because, to appraise assets on the basis of a going concern predicates appraisal of the future and the concern's ability to meet future debts as they accrue.

§ 372 **Illustrative Cases.** Statutory tests therefore cannot be rigidly applied, if a common sense solution of the particular case is to be had. This is illustrated by the difficulty the New York courts have had with the statutory test prescribed by Section 66 of the New York Stock Corporation Law, wherein preferences are defined. According to a strict reading of the statute, the only test of the company's insolvency, and hence of the transfer in question being preferential, is whether the corporation refused to pay its obligations as they fell due. It would follow that if the corporation is insolvent, and yet for the present is able to meet its obligations as they accrue, no preferential transfer made during this period can later be

[1] Thompson v. Thompson, 4 Cush. 127.
[2] Eden, 'Bankruptcy," p. 4
[3] Chicago Title etc. Co v Roeblings Co., 107 Fed. 71, Butler Paper Co v Goembel, 143 Fed 295

attacked by the receiver appointed in the dissolution proceedings which may finally result. The Court of Appeals refused to follow the strict test,[1] but nevertheless a lower court recently reached the absurd result above outlined.[2] It is fortunate, indeed, that this decision has recently been reversed and the statutory test practically nullified.[3]

§ 373 **Further Illustration — Appointment of Receiver** Another illustration of the difficulty of adhering to a strict statutory test is afforded by the cases under the Act of Bankruptcy which was created by the amendment of 1903, viz. where a receiver has been appointed of the property of the debtor because of his insolvency. As all of the State courts follow the common law definition of insolvency or inability to pay debts as they accrue, this question arises — should we, in considering whether an act of bankruptcy has been committed, define the insolvency in the light of the statutory test, or of the common law test on which the court acted when it appointed the receiver? No authoritative answer can yet be given. All that can be said is that there are several cases which foot up as follows: (1) if the order appointing the receiver states that he is appointed because of the debtor's insolvency, it is conclusive, and no evidence can be admitted to impeach it,[4] otherwise it is dubious,[5] (2) if the order does not so specify, but the record in the State court shows that application was made on such ground, it is likewise conclusive,[6] (3) if the application does not show it then the entire record may be viewed to ascertain the ground upon which the receiver was appointed;[7] (4) if neither the order nor the record shows

[1] O'Brien v. East River Bridge Company, 161 N. Y. 539, 56 N. E. 74
[2] Cæsar v Bernard, 79 N Y Misc. 224, 139 N. Y. S 974.
[3] Cæsar v Bernard, 156 N Y App. Div 724, 736, 141 N. Y. S. 659, 668
[4] Blue Mt etc Co v Portner, 131 Fed. 57.
[5] Schumert v Brewery Co , 199 Fed. 358.
[6] Hooks v Aldridge, 145 Fed. 865.
[7] *In re* Belfast etc. Co , 153 Fed 224.

it, and it appears that the court had no jurisdiction to appoint a receiver because of insolvency, then it is not an act of bankruptcy [1]

§ 374. **Territorial Limitations of Federal Courts.** The United States courts, which have exclusive jurisdiction in bankruptcy, are territorially limited in their respective jurisdictions Congress, under its power to establish inferior courts of the national government, could have given them jurisdiction as wide as the Union itself, but instead of that, from the time of the judicature act of 1789 to the present day, the limits of the federal courts of first instance have marched with the limits of the States.

§ 375. **The Federal District as the Unit of Jurisdiction** The judiciary act of 1789 divided the whole United States into thirteen districts. Each district consisted of a State, because there were then only thirteen States in the United States. Later, as time went on, additional districts were created as States were added; and then, as the population of certain States increased, they in turn were divided into several districts. This process of subdivision is still going on; but whether Congress creates two districts in a State or one, each is a jurisdiction foreign to the other in the same sense that one State is to another

" By the general provision of the laws of the United States the circuit courts cannot issue any process beyond the limits of their districts " [2] Of course, as PARKER, J , said many years later, there is " no doubt that Congress may provide for service of process out of the district, as this is a regulation of practice

---

[1] *In re* Spalding, 139 Fed 244 There a receiver had been appointed under the New York Code in a judgment creditors' action to set aside a conveyance in fraud of creditors The Federal court held that this was not an act of bankruptcy because the Code conferred no power upon the courts to appoint a receiver of an individual's property on the single ground of insolvency, although such power was conferred in the case of a corporation, and that it did not appear from the record that such appointment had been made on grounds of insolvency

[2] See Toland *v* Sprague, 12 Peters 300; Beekman *v* Hudson River Ry. Co., 35 Fed 3

296   THE RIGHTS AND REMEDIES OF CREDITORS   [CHAP XVIII

subject to legislative control." [1] But it does not appear that Congress has done so in all cases. On the contrary all the legislation on the subject since the days of the Judiciary Act shows that there never was any intention on the part of Congress to give any circuit or district court any jurisdiction outside of its district, with certain minor exceptions that have appeared of recent years.[2]

§ 376   **Jurisdiction of the District Court**   Upon the district court, Congress by the act of 1898 conferred all bankruptcy jurisdiction. Undoubtedly this statute "is very comprehensive of the whole scheme of bankruptcy ",[3] nevertheless its limita-

---

[1] U S v Crawford, 47 Fed. 561, 563
[2] By the act of March 3, 1875, it was provided that "when a State contains more than one district every suit not of a local nature in the circuit or district courts thereof against a single defendant inhabitant of said State, must be brought in the district where he resides, but if there are two or more defendants residing in different districts of the State, the suit may be brought in either district and a duplicate writ may be issued against the defendants directed to the marshal of any districts in which any defendant resides," etc   And again, that when a part of the real or personal property against which a suit may be brought to determine liens "shall be within another district but within the same State," the suit may be brought in either district in the State But that is a different thing from giving concurrent jurisdiction to the two districts   By Section 615 of the Revised Statutes, a cause may under certain circumstances be transferred from one circuit "into the circuit court of the next adjoining State or the next adjoining circuit court " See May v Le Clair, 18 Fed 49. This statute would seem to recognize, rather than deny, that the circuit court sitting in another district within the State is an adjoining court and not any part of its neighbor   The Judicial Code of 1911 (Section 56) modified this rule only to the extent of providing that where a Circuit consists of one or more districts situated in different States, a receiver appointed by the district court in one of such districts shall have power to act in other districts of said Circuit   Judge Lurton had already construed the existing statutes to authorize such a procedure, Horn v Pere Marquette Railway Company, 151 Fed 626, but his decision had never been unreservedly accepted by the bar, so that the amendment removed a source of considerable doubt   But even under the present state of the statutes, it may be laid down as a general proposition that the district court (which is now the federal court of first instance in all cases) has no civil jurisdiction outside of its district other than as provided by the recent statutes above mentioned   See Judicial Code of 1911, Secs 51–59
[3] Wood v. Wilbert etc. Co , 226 U S 384, 33 S. Ct 125.

§ 376]   THE BANKRUPTCY TRUSTEE   297

tions are many. For a long time it was considered that by the very creation of a bankruptcy system Congress intended to vest the district court with jurisdiction to entertain all suits by the trustee in bankruptcy affecting the estate. But in Bardes v. Hawarden Bank,[1] it was held that no plenary suit by the trustee for the recovery of property belonging to the bankrupt estate, or fraudulently or preferentially assigned by the bankrupt, could be instituted in the district court without the consent of the defendant By the act of February 5, 1903, Sections 60b and 67e were amended so as to give the district court jurisdiction of suits by the trustee in bankruptcy to recover property which had been the subject of either a fraudulent conveyance or a preference.[2] But even now this jurisdiction is limited, so that if the trustee desires to attack a fraudulent transfer made outside of the four months' period (which according to the best authority he can do as we have already seen), he cannot file his bill in the district court without the consent of the defendant. Acting under the State law, as he must do in such a case, he is like any other litigant, and can come into the federal courts only if they have jurisdiction under the Judicial Code of 1911 by reason of diversity of citizenship or otherwise.[3] With these jurisdictional limitations

[1] 178 U. S. 524, 20 S. Ct. 1000.
[2] Harris v Trust National Bank, 216 U S 382, 30 S. Ct 296
[3] Wood v Wilbert etc Company, 226 U S 384, 33 S Ct 125 In like manner the matters of appeal are still limited If, whether by means of a plenary suit by the trustee, Knapp v Milwaukee Trust Company, 216 U S. 545, 30 S Ct 412, or the intervention of a person claiming the title to the property held by the trustee of which the trustee has possession, Grooy v Dockendorff, 231 U S 513, 34 S Ct 106, a controversy arises with respect to the title of the trustee to property, thus involving the question whether the property has been fraudulently or preferentially transferred, the case is appealable as of right to the Supreme Court from the Circuit Court of Appeals If, on the other hand, the controversy does not involve the trustee's title so that his status under the Bankrupt Act is directly involved, then the case is not appealable to the Supreme Court unless it should see fit to grant a writ of *certiorari* under the Circuit Court of Appeals Act of 1891 In other words, the controversy must really respect the validity or construction or effect of a federal statute in order to be appealable as of right to the Supreme Court, Shulthis v. McDougal, 225 U S 561, 32 S.

298   THE RIGHTS AND REMEDIES OF CREDITORS.   [CHAP XVIII.

in mind, we are able to appreciate the distinctions which confront us when we attempt the consideration of the practice leading up to the appointment of the final representative of the creditors in the shape of the trustee.

§ 377. **Character of Proceedings Prior to Adjudication**
While an adjudication of bankruptcy is a proceeding *in rem* directly affecting the title to the bankrupt's estate, and is binding upon all persons whether or not they were parties thereto,[1] the proceedings prior to the adjudication are of quite a different character.[2] The petition is filed in the district court which, as we have seen, is a court with local jurisdiction. This institutes a proceeding *in personam*,[3] which does not divest the bankrupt of the title to his property.[4] Indeed, the framers of the Act recognized this by forbidding preferential transfers after the filing of the petition as well as before.[5] By

Ct. 704. It follows that in a suit for conversion of goods alleged to belong to the bankrupt estate, where the title of the trustee is in no wise disputed except as an incidental result of the issues thus raised, the final judgment is not appealable as of right to the Supreme Court, Spencer *v* Duplan Silk Co., 191 U S. 526, 24 S Ct 174, nor is a suit on a forthcoming bond given to the trustee for the return of property to which the latter asserted title, Lovell *v*. Newman, 227 U. S. 412, 33 S Ct 375

[1] Strawhan *v*. Wheritt, 7 How 627; Michaels *v*. Post, 21 Wall. 398; Chapman *v*. Brewer, 114 U S 158, 5 S. Ct. 799

[2] Most unfortunately for the sake of clear thinking, the Supreme Court let fall the dictum that "the filing of a petition is a caveat to all the world, in fact an attachment and injunction," Mueller *v* Nugent, 184 U. S 1, 22 S. Ct. 269, but the court has later declared that this remark "was made in regard to the particular facts in that case," York Mfg Co *v* Cassell, 201 U S 344, 26 S. Ct 481, Jones *v* Springer, 226 U S. 148, 33 S Ct 64

[3] Hence if the bankrupt wins his case and the petition is dismissed, no parties acting for him can have any judicial allowance out of his property, because the dismissal of the petition ends the court's connection with the case, *Re* Ward, 203 Fed. 769

[4] The protection from civil arrest in creditors' suits, afforded by Section 9 of the statute, is intended as protection to a confessed bankrupt, and while a party is contesting the proceedings which would lead to his being declared a bankrupt he is not entitled to this protection, Chase *v* Farmers etc Bank, 202 Fed. 904.

[5] See Sec 60b.

way of rhetoric, it may be said that the bankrupt "holds his property in a sort of trust capacity for his creditors" during this period,[1] but, in that sense, so may any insolvent debtor be said to hold his property. As a practical matter the bankrupt can manage and handle his property as he pleases until an actual adjudication of his bankruptcy is made. Of course if he transfers it for no consideration, or under circumstances which would constitute it a fraudulent conveyance, the property may be reached after his adjudication, but any fair trade made by him during this period will be upheld. In short, the mere pendency of the bankruptcy petition against the debtor does not put a check on his conduct of his affairs.[2]

§ 378. **Appointment of Receiver in Bankruptcy.** On the other hand, if the creditors fear that during this intervening period the bankrupt's covert dealings with his property may change the *status quo* to their detriment, they have their relief in the provisions of the Act which allow the court, at any time after the petition has been filed, to appoint a receiver for the custody of the bankrupt's property.[3] After adjudication, and before there has been time for the appointment of a trustee, a receiver will be appointed without any special inquiry into the bankrupt's circumstances,[4] but prior to the adjudication an application for the appointment of the receiver should be determined upon the same considerations that appeal to a chancery court in any other case where such relief is requested.[5] Of course, if there is a receiver, that means that the assets are in the court's custody, and any interference therewith is a contempt. Therefore after knowledge of the receiver's appointment, people deal with the bankrupt and his property at their peril.[6]

[1] *In re* Banks, 207 Fed. 662
[2] Tiffany *v.* Lucas, 15 Wall. 418; Tiffany *v.* Boatman's Institution, 18 Wall. 375
[3] Sec. 2
[4] *In re* Huddleston, 167 Fed. 428
[5] *In re* Oakland Lumber Company, 174 Fed. 634; *In re* Heim Milk Company, 183 Fed. 787; Faulk *v.* Steiner, 165 Fed. 861
[6] *Re* Lufty, 156 Fed. 873; *Re* Ehrich's Brewery, 158 Fed. 644; *Re* Alton Mfg Co, 158 Fed. 567. The amendment of 1910 to Section

§ 379. **Ancillary Receivership.** This receiver has no powers outside of the district of the court which appointed him, except as, under the present dispensation afforded by the Judicial Code of 1911 he may have powers in an adjoining district located within the same Circuit.[1] If, then, the debtor owns property which is located in districts of other States, it is necessary to resort to some form of ancillary proceedings to obtain judicial custody of such property. While the National Bankrupt Acts always contemplated that only one petition in bankruptcy is proper, and that in the district which has jurisdiction over the bankrupt by reason of his residence or, in the case of a corporation, the location of its principal place of business,[2] it was also recognized that in cases of scattered assets the federal courts of the districts where the property is located should give aid to the creditors' representative in his efforts to gather in the estate. In the case of a bankruptcy receiver, however, there has been considerable difference of opinion among the federal courts. Some prescribed as the proper practice that the petitioning creditors should file a secondary bankruptcy petition in the federal court sitting within each district where the bankrupt's property was located, and under such petitions obtain the appointment of receivers in those districts.[3] Other courts held that a receiver in bankruptcy "not only derives his powers from the bankruptcy statute, but the jurisdiction of the court appointing him is, as to such receiverships, coextensive with the United States", and hence he has the same rights outside of his district that he has within them, and is entitled by virtue of such rights to such

---

59g takes away from the proceedings prior to adjudication much of their former private character. Until then the petitioners could withdraw the proceedings without notice to the other creditors. Re Levi, 142 Fed 642. Now it cannot be done without notice to all the other creditors.

[1] Boonville Bank v Blakey, 107 Fed 891: *In re* National Mercantile Agency, 128 Fed 839; *In re* Dunseath, 168 Fed 973

[2] Lothrop v Drake, 91 U S 516, Babbitt v Dutcher, 216 U. S 102, 30 S Ct 372

[3] *Re* Benedict, 140 Fed 155, *Re* Dunseath, *supra*

orders and injunctions as he may need, in the districts where he is seeking to obtain possession of the property, from the federal courts sitting in those districts.¹ These difficulties were removed by the amendment of 1910 to Section 2 of the Bankrupt Act, which now empowers district courts sitting in bankruptcy, among other things, to "exercise ancillary jurisdiction over persons or property within their respective territorial limits in aid of a receiver or trustee appointed in any bankruptcy proceedings pending in any other court of bankruptcy." Despite this section, we still find cases where ancillary receivers were appointed, such a case being *In re* Lipman ² The correct practice under this amendment, however, would seem to have been followed in the Musica bankruptcy There the bankruptcy petition was filed in the New York district Certain property being located in New Orleans, the receiver appointed by the New York District Court appeared by counsel in the district court for Louisiana and obtained an order confirming his appointment as receiver, upon which he filed a petition against the persons having the property in their custody The Circuit Court of Appeals, Fifth Circuit, held that this was the proper procedure, saying that "the court below had ancillary jurisdiction of the proceedings, if not under the bankruptcy law as originally enacted, certainly by virtue of the amendment of June 25, 1910" ³ On the other hand, it seems to have been considered as settled that a bankruptcy receiver cannot bring suits to gather in property belonging to the estate where genuine adverse claims are set up by the persons in possession of the property ⁴ This doctrine does not seem to be affected by the amendment of 1910, because that amendment did not upset the principle that the receiver should act only in matters relating to the preservation of the estate rather than its collection The distinction seems

---

¹ *Re* Dempster, 172 Fed 353, *Re* Muncie Pulp Co, 151 Fed 732
² 201 Fed 169.
³ Musica *v* Prentice, 211 Fed 326
⁴ Booneville Bank *v* Blakey *supra*, Guaranty Title etc Co *v* Pearlman, 144 Fed 550

to be " that the collection of the estate belongs to the trustee; but its preservation pending the election of a trustee is the duty of the receiver, and in many cases the property of the bankrupt can only be safe from disposition by the receiver's taking it into his immediate actual possession "[1]

§ 380 **Title of the Trustee** Without a receivership, there is no way to disturb the debtor's enjoyment of his assets until the appointment of a trustee He continues to own them even after he is adjudged bankrupt The statute effects no transfer of title until the trustee is appointed by the creditors' vote at their first meeting, an event that occurs after the adjudication Then a curious *ex post facto* process is effected by the statute. Upon the trustee's qualification his title relates back to the date of adjudication [2] Therefore, one who purchases from the bankrupt is liable to have his title upset by the relation back of the trustee s title.[3] The qualification of the trustee vests him, as though it had been actually transferred, with the legal title to all the bankrupt's property [4] He needs no muniment of title, even to the debtor's real estate, other than a certified copy of the order approving his bond [5] If this, together with a certified copy of the adjudication, is filed in the proper record office it operates as a transfer of the bankrupt's real property.[6] Thus the trustee stands clothed with legal title to all the bankrupt's assets. He needs no ancillary appointment in other States, because his title prevails in all,[7] derived as it is from a statute which Congress has passed in the exercise of its constitutional

---

[1] *Re* Dempster, *supra*

[2] Sec 70 Meanwhile the bankrupt is owner of his real estate even within the transfer clause of a fire insurance policy, Fuller *v*. Jameson, 98 N Y. App Div 53, 90 N Y S 456, aff'd 184 N. Y. 605, 77 N. E 1187, Fuller *v* Ins Co., 184 Mass 12, 67 N. E 879. Likewise, the bankrupt can sue on debts due him, Rand *v.* Iowa etc. Ry., 186 N Y 58, 78 N. E 574, Griffin *v.* Mutual Life, 11 Am. B R. 622.

[3] Bank *v* Sherman, 101 U. S. 403; Greenhall *v* C T. Co , 180 Fed. 812

[4] Sec 70.   [5] Sec 21e.   [6] Secs 21e, 47c.

[7] Bankrupt Act Secs 70e, 67e.

power to enact laws providing for a uniform system of bankruptcy throughout the United States.

§ 381 **Extraterritorial Powers of Trustee** The trustee of course remains an officer of the court of his appointment, and over him and the assets in his hands it has the full powers of a liquidating court. With respect to all other courts in the United States, whether State or federal, the trustee is in the position which was accorded to the English assignee in bankruptcy by the common law and chancery courts of that realm They recognize him as vested, by law, with the title to all the bankrupt's estate, and with the right to bring possessory or other actions looking to the restoration to the estate of property fraudulently or preferentially transferred In addition, the federal courts in other districts are empowered to grant him ancillary aid, by way of summary proceedings of the same nature that the court of his appointment might be able to give him were the property located within the territorial bounds of its jurisdiction.[1]

§ 382. **Similar Powers of National Bank Receiver.** There is only one other representative of creditors who has this wide roving power, and he derives it from a source of the same nature, an act of Congress We refer to the receiver of a national bank Of the liquidation of national banks we shall speak in Chapter XIX, the status of the receiver appointed in such a proceeding is exactly like that of the trustee in one respect. He, like the trustee, can sue in any court of the Union without the necessity of obtaining an ancillary appointment,[2] and, while the statute makes the receiver act under the direction of the Comptroller of the Currency, that does not mean that he must obtain that official's leave for every act on his part It simply means that he is subject to the direction of the Comptroller who can revoke or reverse his action, but it does not mean that as a

---

[1] Babbitt v. Dutcher, 216 U S 102, 30 S Ct 372, Re Rathfon, 200 Fed 108, Stanton v. Wooden, 179 Fed 61; See Re Wood, 210 U S 246, 28 S Ct 621

[2] Hayden v Brown, 94 Fed 15.

condition precedent to his action he must have the Comptroller's direction.¹ The statute indeed requires the direction of the Comptroller and an assessment by the latter when it comes to enforcing the statutory liability of the stockholders.² But it is very different when the receiver finds a preferential transfer or a transfer in fraud of the bank's creditors. In that case he fully represents all the creditors and may attack any such transaction, however the corporation itself would have been estopped to do so by reason of its technical corporate consent.³ In any such case as that the receiver needs no previous fiat from the Comptroller in order to institute such an action.⁴

§ 383 **Recognition of Title of Foreign Trustee to Personal Property — English Rule.** Whether the title of the trustee can be asserted to such of the debtor's property as may be in a foreign country, is a point upon which our courts differ from those of

---

¹ Kennedy v Gibson, 8 Wall 506, Turner v. Richardson, 180 U. S. 87, 21 S Ct. 295.

² Kennedy v Gibson, *supra*

³ Cockrill v Abeles, 86 Fed 505, Bank v. Kennedy, 17 Wall 19; Allen v Luke, 141 Fed 694, Kennedy v Gibson, *supra*

⁴ Hayden v. Thompson, 71 Fed 60. It must be remembered, however, that although these powers of winding up are vested in the Comptroller the powers of the federal courts sitting in chancery to wind up by means of a creditors' bill have not thereby been ousted, Snohomish County v Puget Sound Bank, 81 Fed 518, King v Pomeroy, 121 Fed 287 And likewise when it comes to the statutory liability of the stockholders of a corporation, unless a statute expressly confers such a right upon a statutory representative of the creditor the latter acquires no right in their behalf to sue to enforce this liability, as we have already seen The National Bank Act, however, does confer on the receiver the power to bring this action, and in Kennedy v. Gibson, 8 Wall 498, it was held that these provisions were exclusive so that the receiver appointed by the Comptroller is the only party who can bring such an action, no right in that respect remaining in the creditor This rule, however, was abolished by the Act of June 30, 1876, which authorized the creditors to enforce this liability at their option by means of a representative bill in chancery Harvey v Lord, 10 Fed 236 This much being allowed by the statute, it was later held that as a measure of convenience for the creditors, the Chancery Court, on a bill filed by one, could appoint a chancery receiver, and vest him with the right to maintain such an action for the benefit of all the creditors who may come into the suit Richmond v Irons, 121 U S 27, 7 S Ct 788, King v. Pomeroy, 121 Fed 287

England. In Hunter v Potts¹ an English bankrupt owned personal property which was located in Rhode Island, and an English creditor, disregarding the bankruptcy, sued the bankrupt in the Rhode Island courts, and levied on this property under a writ of attachment. It was held that the English bankruptcy assignees could recover the proceeds of the attachment by means of an action against the creditor in question, the court basing its decision on the fiction that the location of personal property is the domicile of the owner. Previously Lord Hardwicke had taken the same view,² and later Lord Eldon followed it,³ so that it became and still is the established rule in England that a bankrupt's personal property, wheresoever located, passes, by the adjudication of bankruptcy, to his trustee.

§ 384. **Title of Foreign Trustee to Real Estate.** As the fiction upon which this doctrine rests does not apply to land, both the English and the American courts were never of the view that a bankruptcy had any extraterritorial effect upon the title to foreign real estate.⁴ The only course was for the bankrupt to specifically convey his foreign lands to the trustee, but in the absence of an express statutory direction to the bankrupt to perform such an act the bankruptcy courts had no power to compel him to execute such a transfer.⁵ In later days this difficulty was cured by legislation. Our present Act⁶ requires the bankrupt to "execute to his trustee transfers of all his property in foreign countries", and the English statute of to-day legislates into the trustee the title to land located outside the realm.⁷

[1] 4 T R 182, aff'd 2 H Bl 402.
[2] McIntosh v Ogilvie, 4 T R 193 n.
[3] Bank of Scotland v Cuthbert, 1 Rose 462; Cockerell v Dickens, 2 Rose 291
[4] Oakey v Bennett, 11 How 33
[5] *Ex parte* Blakes, 1 Cox Ch. 398; Phelps v McDonald, 16 Nat. B R 217
[6] See 7
[7] See Sec 168 of Bankrupt Act of 1883, which effectually applies at least to land located in all the British Colonial possessions Collender v Colonial Secretary, (1891) A C 460

§ 385. **Title of Foreign Trustee to Personal Property — American Rule.** On the question of personal property the American courts repudiate the English doctrine. In Harrison v. Sterry [1] the counterfoil to Hunter v. Potts [2] was presented. It was held that where an English owner of personal property located in America had been adjudged bankrupt by the English courts, this constituted no bar to a creditor levying upon the local personal property under a judgment rendered by an American court. This decision has been followed by the various State courts who have had occasion to pass upon the question, [3] and the difference of opinion is one which will always remain between the courts of the two nations.

[1] 5 Cranch 289
[2] *Supra.*
[3] Blake v Williams, 6 Pick 286, Abraham v Plestoro, 3 Wend. 538, see *Re* Waite, 99 N Y 433

CHAPTER XIX

METHODS OF JUDICIAL LIQUIDATION OTHER THAN BANKRUPTCY

§ 386. Necessity of Statutory System
387. Bankrupt Acts as Confined to Traders
388. Insolvency Acts
389. Dual System thus Created, and its Omissions
390. Conflict in American Ideas
391. Resulting Complexity of American System
392. Common Law Position of Executor
393. Confusion in Early English Decisions
394. Conflict in American Decisions
395. Doctrine under Modern Statutes
396. Original Status of Committee
397. American Legislation
398. Jurisdiction of Chancery Court under Modern Statutes
399. Enforcement of Claims
400. Assignee's Status under American Legislation
§ 401. Duty of Assignee under Such Statutes.
402. Modern American Legislation
403. Illustration — Practice under New York Statute.
404. Status of Receiver.
405. Resemblance of National Statute to English Statutes
406. Federal Banks as Local Institutions
407. Creative Legislation
408. Statutes Afford Complete System for Winding up
409. Summary of Winding up Provisions
410. Statute Secures Equal Distribution
411. Appointment of Receiver — State Control
412. Judicial Control of Receiver
413. Tendency to State Control in Laws Governing State Banks

§ 386. **Necessity of Statutory System** The bankruptcy system, one would think, should have become universal in its scope, however narrowly its application might originally have been restricted In an exact sense that was not its destiny, for bankruptcy as such was always jealously restricted to certain classes of the economic state In a broader sense, however, and tested by the principle of representation which has already been discussed, the system has spread beyond the domain of bankruptcy by the name of bankruptcy. There was always a certain dislike for the word bankruptcy, in part because of the quasi-criminal nature of the early statutes, but all men finally realized the necessity of a statutory system of distribution and representation. That was the case in England, that became the case in this country.

§ 387. **Bankrupt Acts as Confined to Traders.** With exceptions so modern as to be negligible for their effect upon American legislation, the English bankrupt acts were confined in application to persons engaged in commerce, or, as they were called, traders. The Statute of Henry VIII was not thus limited and did not thus confine itself, but, as has been said,[1] "it appears to have been so regarded in practice, for one of the first cares of the Statute of Elizabeth is to define the class of merchants capable of being made bankrupt." The basic definition made in the first section of that Act continued through all the changes of later amendments, that a trader was one "using or exercising the trade of merchandise by way of bargaining, exchange, re-exchange, bartery, chevisance or otherwise, in gross or by retail, or seeking his or her trade of living". In later days it became necessary to widen this definition. For instance, by the Statute 21 James I, c. 19, Sec. 2, scriveners were brought within the acts, as persons "using the trade or profession of a scrivener, receiving other men's moneys or estates into their trust or custody"; and this led to bankers, through having taken up the trade of scriveners, being brought within the definition, together with brokers,[2] so that finally, as a result of these inclusions, the Revising Act of 1824 defines as a trader,[3] "all persons using the trade of merchandise by way of bargaining, exchange, bartering, commission, consignment or otherwise, in gross or by retail, and all persons who, either for themselves or as agents or factors for others, seek their living by buying or selling, or by

[1] Jenks, "Short History of English Law," p. 383
[2] Stat. 5 Geo II, c. 30, Sec. 39, Eden, "Bankruptcy," 6.
[3] Stat. 6 Geo. IV, c. 16, Sec. 1

buying or letting for hire, or by the workmanship of goods or commodities." But wide or narrow, the distinction was always present in those years of evolution, and traces of this distinction, and of a certain favoritism displayed by the legislators in its application, survive with us to this day. While the Statute of George II brings in, as subject to the Bankrupt Act, bankers, brokers and factors, it carefully exempts "farmers, graziers and drovers." To this day, with us, farmers and persons engaged chiefly in tillage of the soil are exempt from involuntary bankruptcy; and it was not until 1910 that our act was amended so as to allow corporations, though not chiefly engaged in mercantile pursuits, to be adjudged bankrupt [1]

§ 388 **Insolvency Acts.** But while the name of bankruptcy was odious, its principle became attractive after the debtor's discharge was made a part of the system. The pressure of the common law led the debtor who was not subject to the bankruptcy régime provided for traders to press Parliament for relief of the same nature, though of another name. It may very well be that imprisonment for debt was unknown to ancient common law, but it was of little avail to a debtor to urge such a point, in view of the successive statutes which extended the writ of capias to actions upon debts as well as trespass, so that any creditor could levy his execution upon the debtor's body and keep the debtor in prison until the writ was satisfied by the payment of the adjudged amount. The imprisonment of the debtor for a short space constituted an act of bankruptcy, so that if the debtor came within the trading class, his other creditors could bring his affairs into the bankruptcy court for distribution, but if the prisoner was merely a "poor debtor," and not a trader, no such relief could be had. Finally, however, the well-known legislation for the relief of insolvent debtors began. Its origin was ancient, certainly as old as the bankrupt laws, but the first permanent statutes which established a court for the administration of the debtor's property, and appointed an

[1] Act of 1898, Sec. 4, *infra* § 457.

310   THE RIGHTS AND REMEDIES OF CREDITORS.   [CHAP. XIX.

assignee for its reception, were the famous Acts of 1813 and 1814 [1] In common with the bankrupt acts, these insolvency laws were revised in the following reign, [2] but even before that, to use the words of an American counsel speaking in 1817, the situation in England was that "a legal system of insolvency was established, and courts possessing a peculiar jurisdiction, clearly and practically contradistinguished from bankruptcy, decided cases of insolvency in one room of Guildhall, while commissioners of bankruptcy were deciding cases of bankruptcy in another" [3]

§ 389 **Dual System thus Created, and its Omissions.** This dual system provided in effect a method of getting the debtor into a court empowered to redress the creditors' wrongs, as well as to distribute the property on hand. There were only two omissions One was the corporation. It could neither be a bankrupt nor a poor debtor, because the original conception of the corporation allowed no room for its winding up in a commercial sense, and all that Parliament ever concerned itself with was to keep the stockholders in the great incorporated monopolies from being considered as traders and thus subject to individual bankruptcy [4] The potential danger of this omission,

---

[1] Stat 53 Geo III, c. 102 and Stat 54 Geo. III, c 23
[2] Stat 7 Geo IV c 57
[3] Mr Hunter, *arguendo* in Sturges v Crowninshield, 4 Wheat, 122, 142 The succeeding Statute of 1838, 1-2 Vict c. 110. Sec 59, forbade preferences, and vested in the assignee the title to the property thus transferred; and it was also held that the assignee could recover property which the debtor had fraudulently conveyed, Doe v Ball, 11 M & W. 531; Young v Billiter 8 H L C. 682.
[4] Thus in the time of the Protectorate, a statute which recited that "divers noblemen, gentlemen and persons of quality, no ways brought up to trade or merchandise, do oftentimes put in great stocks of money into the East-India Company, or Guiney Company and the fishing trade," goes on to provide that such a person shall not be "reputed a merchant or trader within any statute or statutes for bankrupts," Stat 13-14 Car II, c 24 Sec 3, and after the establishment of the Bank of England, a series of acts were passed exempting its stockholders from adjudication in bankruptcy as traders, Stat 7-8 Wm. III, c 31, 8-9 Wm III, c 20, 5 Anne, c 13 "There are several other acts containing the same clause upon incorporating trading companies," 1 Cooke, " Bankrupt Laws," 12.

however, was not of real importance, because, with the increased use of the corporation as an instrumentality of ordinary commerce, came the Companies Acts with their admirable winding up provisions, so that in England at the present day the bankruptcy of corporations is entirely covered by a separate statutory system. The other omission was the deceased or lunatic debtor of which we have treated elsewhere.[1] To some extent, as will appear from the more or less parenthetical references that have already been made, that is also our system, allowing for the many complexities which always appear when the common law's American progress is examined.

§ 390. **Conflict in American Ideas.** Confronted by the same pressing needs and with the demands of the mercantile community just as insistent, our courts and legislatures were forced to work with tools not already fashioned to their hands. There was, as we have seen, a prejudice in England against the application of the term bankrupt to a debtor, but there was also a prejudice against the fraudulent methods by which many debtors who were bankrupts achieved their freedom.[2] The American colonies, although always tempted to protect the local debtor against his foreign creditor, really tried in some instances to enact fair bankruptcy laws, but the Privy Council seemed to frown upon these attempts.[3] There were then, and always have been, in this country, men who believed in the necessity for a general system of bankruptcy.[4] On the other hand, there were

---

[1] *Infra*, § 457.

[2] The recitals of a statute, 5 Geo II, c. 30, indicate the prevalence of such practices. In Lewis v. Chase, 1 P. Wms. 620, the bankrupt, in order to get the consent of a creditor to his discharge, gave him a bond for the amount of the debt, and Parker, L. C., held the bond was valid. Doubtless to overcome this case, which Lord Mansfield, in Trueman v. Fenton, 2 Cowp. 544, declared "smelt of the certificate," this statute was adopted, which among other things forbade all such acts. See 11.

[3] See 14 Columbia Law Review, p. 509.

[4] Thus Madison says in "Federalist," No. 41: "The power of establishing uniform laws of bankruptcy is so intimately connected with the regulation of commerce, and will prevent so many frauds where

and are many who prefer to deal with the problem from quite a different standpoint, such as in the past has found expression in "stay laws" which were not merely a feature of colonial legislation, but have appeared in economic crises until a comparatively late day.[1] Even to-day at every session of Congress bills are introduced to repeal the present Act.[2]

§ 391. **Resulting Complexity of American System** As a result of this conflict of thought we have had no less than four successive national bankrupt acts, and also, we have had no less than four periods where this country was without a bankrupt act. Bearing in mind the peculiar nature of our Union, as a result of which a State bankruptcy act stops in its operations at the borders of the local court's jurisdiction and can operate only on property included therein,[3] we can imagine the difficulty of fairly distributing the assets of a debtor who has been compelled to disregard the fact that when, in the course of his business, he crosses an imaginary line, he is going into a foreign country so far as jurisdiction over his tangible property is concerned. That is bad enough, but aggravation is added when we attempt to unify the laws of the different States with regard to the administration of the affairs of an insolvent If every State had an insolvency law like that of Massachusetts (upon whose model two of our bankrupt acts have been framed) there would be some comfort in the repeal of the national Act, however little may be the excuse for such a course since the statute has been

the parties or their property may lie, or be removed into, different States, that the expediency of it seems not likely to be drawn into question " And writing in 1889 at a time when there was no Federal Bankrupt Act in force, Mr Woodrow Wilson, in "The State," p 494, speaks of the need of a uniform national system

[1] See for instance the stay law, adopted by the State of Georgia on Dec 13 1866, which was held to be unconstitutional in Aycock v Martin, 37 Ga 124

[2] See the report of the Committee on Commercial Law at a recent session of the American Bar Association (Rep. Am Bar Ass'n, vol 38, p 478) where mention is made of three different bills introduced in the last Congress to repeal the Bankrupt Act.

[3] See *infra*, ch XXII

shorn of the features which led to the repeal of the Act of 1867.[1] But there never was such uniformity in State legislation, as is apparent from a glance at a compilation which appeared for the convenience of practitioners after the repeal of the previous national Act.[2] With us, therefore, the Bankrupt Act is by no means of universal application, and there are many cases where we must look to State laws for a representative having the same status as a bankruptcy trustee, though under a different name and appointed by a different court

A Personal Representatives of a Deceased Debtor

§ 392 **Common Law Position of Executor.** At common law an executor or administrator in no sense represented the creditors of the decedent. If he did not choose to pay any creditor, the latter had no common law right to do anything other than bring assumpsit or debt against the executor. In such an action against the executor, the latter must set up as an affirmative defense lack of sufficient assets to pay the debt If he fails to thus plead, the judgment may be satisfied out of the executor's own property, whether or not the estate is ample for his reimbursement[3] On the other hand, the creditor has no protection against the executor if the latter should choose to prefer one creditor over another.[4]

§ 393. **Confusion in Early English Decisions** With such a common law conception of the executor's status, it would follow that he could not set aside any fraudulent conveyance made by his testator, because by the same token he would be attacking his own conveyance, since he was the successor of the testator

---

[1] It is generally known that the ostensible ground for the repeal of the former act was the excessive allowances granted by many of the federal courts to receivers and counsel.

[2] R J Moses, "Compilation of State Insolvency Laws" (N Y 1879)

[3] Rock v Leighton, 1 Salk 310; Ramsden v Jackson, 1 Atk 292, Leonard v Simpson, 2 Bing N C 176

[4] Maitland, "Equity," 198

And so it was determined in Hawes v Leader.[1] In that case the intestate made a gift of his goods to cheat his creditors, continued to remain in possession of the goods and finally died When the administrator qualified, the fraudulent grantee brought replevin for goods, to which the administrator pleaded the Statute of Fraudulent Conveyances. A demurrer to the plea was held good In the case as reported by Yelverton, the chief ground of the judgment was that the deed was void only as against creditors, but that it remained good as against the party himself, and his administrators.[2] In Bethel v Stanhope[3] it was said that if the donee in such a case as Hawes v Leader should take the goods from the administrator, "it is a trespass against the administrator for which he hath his remedy, and they are always assets in his hands" This dictum seems to be overruled by Hawes v. Leader, which is a later case, but it is stated as sound doctrine by an ancient writer.[4]

§ 394. Conflict in American Decisions. Hawes v. Leader was followed at an early date in New York.[5] In a later case, however,[6] the court doubted its former judgment, saying that the rule of Bethel v Stanhope would seem sound In Massachusetts the doctrine of Bethel v Stanhope was followed[7] and it has also received the approval of the courts in several other jurisdictions,[8] while in Michigan a statute conferring upon executors this right of action has been stated to be declaratory of the

---

[1] Cro. Jac 270; Yelv 196
[2] "This ground of the decision is mentioned by Yelverton in his report of the case with *Quod Nota*, and he was counsel for defendant, and his reports are among the best of the old authorities " — Osborne v Morse, 7 Johnson 161, 164
[3] Cro. Eliz 810.
[4] Robertson, "Fraudulent Conveyances," 592, 593.
[5] Osborne v. Morse, 7 Johnson 161.
[6] Babcock v Booth, 2 Hill 181
[7] Holland v Cruft, 20 Pick 321, Harmon v Osgood, 151 Mass. 501, 24 N. E 401
[8] Buehler v. Gloniger, 2 Watts Pa 226, Doney v. Clark, 55 Ohio State 294, 45 N. E 316, Estes v Howland 15 R I. 127, 23 Atl 624, Webb v Atkinson, 122 N. C 683, 29 S. E. 949

common law.[1] In other jurisdictions the doctrine of Hawes v Leader has been followed[2] Thus two conflicting views originated at an early date, and have continued even to the present day. In England, the later cases certainly follow the doctrine of Bethel v. Stanhope, a decision precisely on all fours with it being Shears v Rogers[3] But, extraordinary to relate, in Edwards v Harben[4] it was held that the executor could hold the fraudulent grantee who had taken possession of the goods as an executor *de son tort*, the court citing as authority for this position, not the case of Bethel v Stanhope, but the case of Hawes v. Leader.

§ 395. **Doctrine under Modern Statutes** This confusion, however, has been minimized with us by statutes in many of the States expressly conferring this power upon the executor At an early date in New York a statute was adopted, abolishing the common law doctrine of holding an intermeddler with the testator's goods as an executor *de son tort*[5] In Babcock v. Booth,[6] it was held that "this statute takes away the remedy which the creditor formerly had against the fraudulent vendee, and transfers the action to the personal representative of the vendor. He may now sue or controvert the validity of the sale in any other legal form, where that course is necessary for the payment of debts of the testator or intestate " The statute marked the movement in America toward making "executors

---

[1] Beith v Porter, 119 Mich 365, 78 N W 336
[2] Kinnemon v. Miller, 2 Md Ch 407; Backhouse v Jett, 1 Brock Va 500; Anderson v Brown, 72 Ga 713
[3] 2 B. & Ad 362
[4] 2 T. R 585
[5] This statute is as follows

"No person shall be liable to any action as executor of his own wrong, for having received, taken or interfered with the property or effects of a deceased person; but shall be responsible as a wrong-doer in the proper action to the executors or general or special administrators of such deceased person for the value of any property or effects so taken or received, and for all damages caused by his acts to the estate of the deceased "— 2 R S. 449, Sec 17, now Sec 112 of The Decedents' Estate Law

[6] 2 Hill 181

and administrators have a new character, and stand in a different relation from what they formerly did to the creditors of the deceased persons with whose assets they were intrusted They are not now the mere representatives of their testator or intestate, they are constituted trustees and the property in their hands is a fund to be disposed of in the best manner for the benefit of the creditors." [1] Consequently, as stated in the case last cited, " whatever difficulty there might be in allowing an executor or administrator to set up a fraud, when considered as the mere representative of the testator or intestate, there can be none when he is regarded in the further capacity of a trustee for creditors and is necessarily acting for their benefit " [2] The same result was reached in Virginia under a similar statute.[3] Later in New York a further statute was made, expressly conferring upon the executor or administrator the right to disaffirm, treat as void and resist any act done, or transfer or agreement made, in fraud of the rights of any creditor interested in the estate. The same statute conferred a similar right upon assignees for the benefit of creditors and receivers.[4] Under

[1] Dox v Backentose, 12 Wendell 543
[2] Babcock v Booth, 2 Hill 181
[3] Shields v Anderson, 3 Leigh 729
[4] Laws of 1858, Chapter 314, Sec 1. In its present form this Statute appears as Section 19 of the Personal Property Law as follows.

"Disaffirmance of fraudulent acts by executors and others An executor, administrator, receiver, assignee or trustee, may, for the benefit of creditors or others interested in personal property, so held in trust, disaffirm, treat as void and resist any act done, or transfer or agreement made in fraud of the rights of any creditor, including himself, interested in such estate or property, and a person who fraudulently receives, takes or in any manner interferes with the personal property of a deceased person, or an insolvent corporation, association, partnership or individual is liable to such executor, administrator, receiver or trustee for the same or the value thereof and for all damage caused by such an act to the trust estate A creditor of a deceased insolvent debtor, with a claim exceeding in amount the sum of one hundred dollars, may, without obtaining a judgment on such claim, in like manner, for the benefit of himself and other creditors interested in said estate, disaffirm, treat as void and resist any act done or conveyance, transfer or agreement made in fraud of creditors or maintain

this statute it was held that if the executor refused to sue upon the demand of a creditor, the latter had the right to sue himself, joining the executor as a party defendant, to set aside the fraudulent transfer, and have the property held under it administered as assets to pay debts [1] Such a suit must be for the benefit of all the creditors, thus essentially differing, as we can see, from the judgment creditor's action which may be brought in the case of a living debtor [2] Under other statutes [3] it is the duty of an executor or administrator to subject land to payment of debts if the personal property is insufficient Consequently, land which has been fraudulently conveyed may be reached by the administrator or executor for the benefit of creditors by the joint force of the two statutes [4] Similar statutes have been enacted in many other States, and the same result has been reached under them.[5] In like manner statutes have been adopted in some States making in general terms the executor or administrator the trustee for the decedent's creditors, and such statutes serve the same purpose [6]

an action to set aside such act, conveyance, transfer or agreement Such claim, if disputed, may be established in such action. The judgment in such action may provide for the sale of the property involved, when a conveyance or transfer thereof is set aside, and that the proceeds thereof be brought into court or paid into the proper surrogate's court to be administered according to law "

[1] Bate v. Graham, 11 N Y 237, Harvey v. McDonnell, 113 N. Y 526, 21 N. E 695 But such an action cannot be brought against the debtor alone, the executor must also be joined as a party Lichtenberg v. Herdtfelder, 103 N Y 302, 8 N E 526

[2] Crouse v. Frothingham, 97 N Y 105, Spelman v Freedman, 130 N. Y 421, 29 N. E 765

[3] Code Civ. Pro § 2950

[4] Lichtenberg v. Herdtfelder, 103 N Y 302. 8 N E. 526 Barton v Hasner, 24 Hun 467; National Bank v. Levy, 127 N. Y 549, 28 N. E. 592

[5] Doe v Clark, 42 Iowa 123 Martin v Crosby, 11 Lea 198; McLean v Johnson, 43 Vt 48, Beith v. Porter, 119 Mich 365, 78 N W 336

[6] Frost v Libby, 79 Me 56, 8 Atl 149; Doney v Clark, 55 Ohio St 294, 45 N E 316.

B. *Committee of a Lunatic*

§ 396. Original Status of Committee Originally the committee of a lunatic's property partook even more of the character of the Roman heir than did an executor, because there was no distributive duty cast upon him with respect to the lunatic's property. The procedure in the case of an appointment of a committee was governed by an ancient statute [1] which conferred upon the person to be designated by the Crown, usually, but not necessarily the Chancellor,[2] the property of the lunatic, he to be maintained with the income, and the residue to be delivered to him when he should return to his right mind. It follows that the committee simply carried on the property and affairs of the lunatic in the same way in which the latter left them. As Chancellor Kent says: "There was no special authority given to the court or to the committee of the lunatic to sell or mortgage his real estate for the payment of his debts."[3] The court did not conceive that to be any part of its duty, nor had it the power to authorize such a thing.[4] The pressure of the creditors, however, in the case of insolvent lunatics, led to legislation which has tended toward the application, by one method of procedure or another, of the lunatic's estate to the payment of his debts. In England this legislation commenced with the statute 43 Geo. III, c. 75 which authorized the Chancery Court to make such application. Under the practice which thus arose, the court applied the funds of the lunatic, over and above what was necessary to his support, to the payment of his debts, the creditors seeking distribution of the fund by means of a petition to the court.[5]

§ 397 American Legislation. In America, legislation in this matter has taken two courses. In some States, as New Hamp-

---

[1] 17 Edw II, c 9 and 10
[2] Oxenden *v* Lord Compton, 2 Ves Jr 73-74, Brasher *v.* Van Cortlandt, 2 Johns Ch 242.
[3] Brasher *v* Van Cortlandt, 2 Johns. Ch 242
[4] Oxenden *v.* Lord Compton, 2 Ves Jr 73-74
[5] *Ex parte* MacDougall, 12 Vesey 384, *Ex parte* Hastings, 4 Vesey 182.

shire,[1] the committee of an insolvent lunatic may bring the estate in for distribution under the State insolvency act. In other States, legislation, more nearly approaching that of England, has resulted in charging upon the committee himself the duty of distribution. Conspicuous among these States is New York. At an early date in New York[2] the charge of the person and estate of the lunatic and his maintenance was committed to the Court of Chancery, and the duty of providing for the payment of the debts was especially enjoined. This put upon the committee appointed by the Chancery Court the duty of administering the estate for the benefit of the lunatic's creditors as well as the lunatic. The statute required the committee to exhibit under oath, within six months from his appointment, an inventory of the estate, debts and credits of the lunatic. It also provided that if the personal property of the estate should be insufficient for the discharge of the lunatic's debts, the committee should show that fact by way of a petition to the chancellor. Thereupon, if the personal property should appear to be insufficient, it was made the duty of the chancellor to cause so much of the real estate to be sold as was necessary for the discharge of the debts. "These provisions," said Chancellor Kent, "render the payment of the debts out of the lunatic's property no longer a matter of discretion, but a duty, and they contemplate the committee as being charged (though undoubtedly under the control and direction of this court) with a trust to be performed for the benefit of creditors, and an agency in the payment of the debts and the administration of the estate."[3]

§ 398. **Jurisdiction of Chancery Court under Modern Statutes.** Under subsequent statutes in New York,[4] the same doctrine applies. So when the court appoints the committee of a lunatic in New York, it does so in pursuance of a power once vested

---

[1] Hawkins v. Learned, 54 N. H. 333
[2] 1 N. R. Laws 147.
[3] Brasher v. Van Cortlandt, 2 Johns. Ch. 242
[4] Now appearing as Code of Civil Procedure, Section 2364.

in the Crown by the Statute 17 Edward II, c. 9, afterwards in the High Court of Chancery by the Statute 43 Geo. III, in the Court of Chancery of New York by the old statute above cited, and now vested in the Supreme Court by the people of the State.[1] As stated in a modern case. "The jurisdiction confided to the court over the persons and estates of lunatics carries with it as a necessary incident, after inquisition found and the appointment of the committee, a power to direct the application of the estate of the lunatic to the payment of demands existing against it"[2]

§ 399 **Enforcement of Claims.** The way a creditor establishes his claim is by suit against the committee, if the latter does not recognize his claim That practice was authorized in Brasher v. Van Cortlandt[3] and has been consistently followed in New York. The court does not permit a lunatic to be sued; and if the creditor, after notice of inquisition found and the appointment of a committee, proceeds in such a suit, the judgment he may recover therein is void[4] On the other hand, after the appointment of the committee, the court, on his application, will perpetually stay any action against the lunatic. In other words, the creditor's only remedy after the appointment of a committee is by a suit against the committee as such. If, in such an action, the creditor is successful, his judgment can be satisfied only out of the assets in the hands of the committee, and will rank equally with the other unsecured claims against the estate, but not higher[5] If the estate is insolvent, then we have the word of the highest court that "it cannot be doubted that when the assets are insufficient to pay all the debts in full the same rule of equality should be applied",[7] and

---

[1] Sporza v. German Bank, 192 N Y S 84 N. E. 406.
[2] Matter of Otis, 101 N Y 580, 5 N. E 571
[3] 2 Johns. Ch 242
[4] Matter of Delahunty, 28 Abb N C. 45.
[5] Grant v. Humbert, 114 N Y App Div 462, 100 N Y. S 44.
[6] Re Waterbury, 8 Paige 380
[7] Matter of Otis, 101 N Y 580, 5 N E 571

therefore ratable distribution must be made as in every other case of insolvency administration.¹ But the question whether such an official can sue to set aside a fraudulent transfer in behalf of the creditors has never come up for decision in New York

C Assignee for Creditors

§ 400. **Assignee's Status under American Legislation** As we have already seen, an assignee for the benefit of creditors has no standing to attack fraudulent transfers This is, of course, still the rule in the absence of a statute giving him the higher right, but in many of the States the general assignment has been made use of as a method of effecting a statutory distribution of the debtor's assets among the creditors. This result is accomplished by the enactment of a statute authorizing a general assignment, providing for its recording in public office, and to a more or less degree prescribing the rights and duties of the assignee and of the creditors thereunder   " It is now too late," says the court in Grover v Wakeman,² " to agitate the question, whether these assignments, either partial or general, are sustained by considerations of true wisdom and policy. Reflecting men have differed upon that subject; but the better opinion seems to be, that in the absence of a general bankrupt system, the interests of a commercial community require that they should be sustained   They have accordingly grown into use, and have been sanctioned by judicial decisions in most of the States of the Union. They have become thoroughly incorporated into our system " This method, however, had its difficulties   At common law, as we have seen, the assignee was but " the hand of the assignor in the distribution of the estate " By dint of presuming the assent of the creditors to the assignment, the New York courts worked out the assignee's position as more that of a trustee for the creditors than of an agent for the debtor   Still,

¹ Matter of Wing, 83 Hun 284, 31 N Y. S 941.
² 11 Wend 187

legislation was necessary, among other things, "for the prevention of fraud.¹ Such a statute exists in New York,² which may be taken as a fair sample of the statutes on this subject in the different states. The assignee under such a statute represents the creditors for whose benefit the assignment is made, and hence he is not bound by the assignor's acts, as he would be were the statute not of force.³

§ 401 **Duty of Assignee under Such Statutes.** In New York the statute which we have discussed in connection with executors confers the same rights upon an assignee for the benefit of creditors, respecting the debtor's fraudulent transaction. Indeed the statute is broader even than that because, as stated by the Court of Appeals Any executor, administrator, assignee, or other trustee of an estate, or the property and effects of an individual, may for the benefit of creditors or others interested in the estate or property so held in trust, disaffirm and treat as void all transfers in fraud of the rights of any creditor or others interested and maintain all necessary actions for that purpose . . . This act gave a new remedy in favor of creditors at large by giving to an assignee or trustee for their benefit a statutory right to property conveyed in fraud of creditors, and this statutory right took the place of a specific lien of individual creditors required by law as a condition of their right to contest the validity of the transfer '⁴ Accordingly it is so clear that an assignee has this right, that it is also his duty to institute such proceedings in the proper case, and his omission to do so is chargeable against him as negligence ⁵ It is not only

---

¹ Ludington's Petition 5 Abb N C 307
² Debtor and Creditor Law Sections 2-29. The history of this legislation is given in Ludington's Petition, *supra*.
³ Tams *v* Bullitt 35 Pa 308; McMahon *v* Allen, 35 N. Y 403, Hubbard *v*. Tod, 171 U S. 474, 19 S Ct 14, Taylor *v*. Lauer, 127 N C 157, 37 S E 197
⁴ Southard ι Benner 72 N Y. 424
⁵ Lichtenberg *v* Herdtfelder 103 N. Y 302 8 N. E. 526, Reynolds *v* Ellis, 103 N. Y. 115, 8 N. E. 392; Loos *v* Wilkinson, 110 N. Y. 195, 18 N E. 99.

the assignee's right to bring such an action but it is his duty, and consequently " his negligent omission of his duty would constitute a breach of trust."[1]

D Statutory Receivers of Insolvent Corporations

§ 402 Modern American Legislation In a number of States there are statutes governing the distribution of the assets of an insolvent corporation Were it not for such statutes, a corporation might pass through bankruptcy or a chancery receivership and still continue to exist because, as we have seen, neither of these processes affects its corporate life When the use of the corporation, as an instrument of commerce, came to be general, it was recognized that its insolvency should be a reason for determining not only the continuance of its use of its current assets, but of terminating its corporate life, so that in all respects this business association should no longer exist after it had failed in its purposes of existence A fair example of such a modern statute is to be found in New Jersey It empowers the Court of Chancery to appoint a receiver of the property of any corporation which has been dissolved [2] and also it is provided that whenever any corporation " shall become insolvent or unable to continue ordinary business for want of funds to carry on the same," the court shall appoint a receiver on application of a creditor or a stockholder. In New York the matter is covered by two statutes One, formerly Section 1784 of the Code, provides for sequestration proceedings, and the other provides for the dissolution proceedings. At present they are all grouped within the general corporation laws of the State [3] Sequestration proceedings are now governed by the General Corporation Law [4] which provides thus " Where final judgment for a sum of money has been rendered against a

[1] *In re* Cornell, 110 N Y 351 18 N. E 142
[2] Corporation Law, Sec 56.
[3] General Corporation Law, Secs 65 and 66
[4] See 100

corporation created by or under the laws of the State, and an execution issued thereupon to the sheriff of the county, where the corporation transacts its general business, or where its principal office is located, has been returned wholly or partly unsatisfied, the judgment creditor may maintain an action to procure a judgment sequestrating the property of the corporation, and providing for a distribution thereof."

§ 403 **Illustration — Practice under New York Statute.** The statute governing dissolution proceedings is, in the fullest sense of the word, a winding up statute. It provides [1] that " in either of the following cases, an action to procure a judgment, dissolving a corporation, created by or under the laws of the State, and forfeiting its corporate rights, privileges and franchises, may be maintained." These cases are. " (1) Where the corporation has remained insolvent for at least one year (2) Where it has neglected or refused, for at least one year, to pay and discharge its notes or other evidences of debt (3) Where it has suspended its ordinary and lawful business for at least one year (4) If it has banking powers, or power to make loans on pledges or deposits, or to make insurances, where it becomes insolvent or unable to pay its debts, or has violated any provision of the act, by or under which it was incorporated, or of any other act binding upon it " This proceeding must be brought by the Attorney-General in the name of the people, but if the Attorney-General omits to bring the action for sixty days after application has been made to him by a creditor or stockholder, such creditor or stockholder may, on obtaining leave from court, maintain the action himself [2]

§ 404 **Status of Receiver** In all such cases no doubt has ever been expressed of the power of such a receiver to attack

---

[1] General Corporation Law, Sec 101

[2] *Ibid*, Sec 102 It may also be noted here that under recent amendments in New York the creditor need not resort to sequestration proceedings as formerly, but can at his option resort to supplementary proceedings, Laws of 1908, c. 278, Rabbe *v* Astor Trust Company, 61 Misc. 650 114 N Y S 131

fraudulent transactions. Whether he may be able to attack preferential transfers depends, as we shall see, upon the statute in the particular case, but as to fraudulent conveyances and such other transactions as the creditors themselves can attack, there is no question but that the receiver represents them for that purpose [1]

E. *Receivers of Banks*

§ 405. **Resemblance of National Statute to English Statutes** Banking institutions in this country are of two kinds, those created under the national law and those created under State laws. The law regarding the distribution of the assets of national banks closely approaches both the English Companies Acts and the English Bankrupt Act of 1883. It resembles the English Companies Acts because it is part of a general corporation law completely covering both organization and distribution, and it resembles the English Bankrupt Act of 1883 in that, with respect to distribution, it carries to the same degree the idea of State control, which a distinguished writer has recently pointed out with respect to the English statute [2] Within the current year the basic act, as modified by several later amendments, has in turn been greatly modified by the National Currency Law, but in its winding up provisions the old statute remains unimpaired

§ 406 **Federal Banks as Local Institutions** Prior to the Civil War there was no such thing as a local bank chartered by the United States government. The last charter of the old Bank of the United States, whose history was so intimately connected with the early days of the Republic, expired in the administration of President Jackson and was not renewed That institution, however, never approached in its model the

---

[1] Hayes v Pierson, 65 N J Eq. 353, 15 Atl 1091, 58 Atl 728, Briggs v Spalding, 141 U S. 132, 11 S Ct. 924, Movius v Lee, 30 Fed 298, Alexander v. Relfe, 74 Mo 495; Vail v Hamilton, 85 N Y. 453

[2] Jenks, "Short History of English Law," p 387.

326   THE RIGHTS AND REMEDIES OF CREDITORS.   [CHAP. XIX.

idea afterwards embodied in the present National Bank Acts
It was more a central institution on the models of the national
banks of the great European nations. The banking business
under the present statute, on the other hand, from a legal aspect,
is conducted by local institutions organized for the purpose of
doing business in a particular city or town.

§ 407 **Creative Legislation.** By the Act of March 3, 1863,[1]
this system was first launched; but a substitute for this statute
was found the following year in the Act of June 3, 1864,[2] which
in most of its administrative provisions continues to-day. As
the Supreme Court has said, " the object of the Act, as its title
imports, was to create a national currency, secured by a pledge
of the bonds of the United States,"[3] and to make these notes
the sole circulating medium in this country, Congress, by the
Act of July 13, 1866,[4] imposed a tax on all circulating notes
issued by State banks amounting to 10 per cent of their par
value The constitutionality of this prohibitive statute was
upheld in Veazie Bank v. Fenno [5]

§ 408 **Statutes Afford Complete System for Winding up** In
order to secure uniformity in the law concerning every operation
of these banks from beginning to end, Congress endeavored to
create a complete code similar to the present English Companies
Acts, governing not only the chartering, organization and operation of each bank created under the Act, but also all matters
relating to the winding up of its affairs should such become necessary by reason of its insolvency or otherwise. To quote
from the Supreme Court.

"We consider that act as constituting by itself a complete
system for the establishment and government of national
banks prescribing the manner in which they may be formed,
the amount of circulating notes they may issue, the security

[1] 12 Stat. L 670
[2] 13 Stat L 111
[3] National Bank v. Colby, 21 Wall 609
[4] 14 Stat. L 146, now U. S. R S. Sec 3412.
[5] 8 Wall 533.

to be furnished for the redemption of those in circulation, their obligations as depositaries of public moneys, and as such to furnish security for the deposits and designating the consequences of their failure to redeem their notes, their liability to be placed in the hands of a receiver and the manner, in such event, in which their affairs shall be wound up, their circulating notes redeemed, and other debts paid or their property applied towards such payment Everything essential to the formation of the banks, the issue, security, and redemption of their notes, the winding up of the institutions, and the distribution of their effects, are fully provided for, as in a separate code by itself, neither limited nor enlarged by other statutory provisions with respect to the settlement of demands against insolvents or their estates." [1]

§ 409 **Summary of Winding up Provisions** Turning then to the provision of the statutes of interest here concerning the winding up of the bank, we cannot do better than to repeat this summary contained in Chemical National Bank v Armstrong [2]

"By section 5234, Rev. St, and Section 1 of the Act of June 30, 1876 (19 Stat. 63), it is made the duty of the Comptroller of the Currency to appoint a receiver to wind up a national banking association whenever the Comptroller shall, after examination, have become satisfied of its insolvency. It is the duty of the receiver thus appointed to take possession of the books and effects of the bank, liquidate its assets, and pay the money thus realized into the treasury of the United States Section 5235 makes it the duty of the Comptroller thereupon to give notice by public advertisement for three months, calling on all persons having claims against the association to present the same, and to make legal proof thereof Section 5242 declares void all transfers of its property by the national bank after the commission of the act of insolvency, or in contemplation thereof, to prevent distribution of its assets in the manner provided in said national banking act, or with the view to prefer any creditor, except in payment of its circulating notes. And it further provides that no judgment or injunction shall be issued against the bank or its property before final judgment in

[1] Cook County Nat Bank v. U S., 107 U S 445, 44S, 2 S Ct 561
[2] 59 Fed 372

328   THE RIGHTS AND REMEDIES OF CREDITORS   [CHAP XIX.

any suit, action, or proceeding in any State, county or municipal court Section 5236 provides that, after making full provision or the redemption of the circulating notes of the association, the Comptroller shall make a ratable dividend of the money so paid over to him by such receiver on all such claims as may have been proved to his satisfaction or adjudicated in a court of competent jurisdiction, and as the proceeds of the assets of such association are paid over to him, shall make further dividends on all claims previously proved or adjudicated, and the remainder of the proceeds, if any, shall be paid over to the shareholders of such association or their legal representatives in proportion to the stock by them respectively held The suspension of the bank, and its seizure by the Comptroller and his appointee, the receiver, work, by operation of law, a transfer of the title to the assets of the bank from the bank to the Comptroller and receiver, in trust to reduce the assets to money and apply them, as directed by the national banking act, first, to the redemption of the circulating notes of the bank, and second, in ratable distribution to the creditors of the bank."

§ 410 **Statute Secures Equal Distribution** In its operation the statute, therefore, is precisely like the statutes of bankruptcy In the Supreme Court's language, "all rights, legal or equitable, existing at the time of the commission of the act of insolvency which led to the appointment of the receiver, other than those created by preference forbidden by Section 5242, are preserved; and no additional right can thereafter be created, either by voluntary or involuntary proceedings. The distribution is to be 'ratable' on the claims as proved or adjudicated, that is, on one rule of proportion applicable to all alike. In order to be 'ratable' the claims must manifestly be estimated as of the same point of time, and that date has been adjudged to be the date of the declaration of insolvency" [1]

§ 411 **Appointment of Receiver — State Control.** The idea of State control appeared in the amending Act of June 30, 1876. Under its provisions not only the initiative act is by an officer of State, but the actual appointment of a receiver is depart-

[1] Merrill v. Nat'l Bank of Jacksonville, 173 U. S 131, 19 S Ct 360.

mental instead of judicial. The court has nothing to do with the appointment of the receiver, and the Comptroller, in making the appointment, does not perform a judicial act. On the contrary his decision is that of the head of a department of government over which the courts have no control, and, consequently, his decision is final.[1] Prior to this statute the original act[2] gave the stockholders the right by a two thirds vote to put the concern into voluntary liquidation and appoint an agent for that purpose. But the later Act of 1876, giving the Comptroller power to appoint a receiver as above stated, controls the first act to the extent of giving him the prior right, and the stockholders' action must be deferred until the Comptroller decides not to act.[3] Putting the statutes together, then, it may be said that the Comptroller always has the prior right to appoint a receiver, who liquidates the estate for the benefit of the creditors After that the stockholders can proceed to a voluntary liquidation of the remaining assets by means of an agent appointed by a two thirds vote. But this agent can be appointed only when the receiver certifies that the allowed claims of all creditors have been paid.[4] The agent represents the bank itself so that he can be sued by a creditor, just as the bank could have been sued before the insolvency happened, without the permission of the Comptroller or of any court[5] The rights of the shareholders' agent therefore, are of little interest here because, as we have seen his appointment is predicated on the practical elimination of the creditors by their payment in full The party of interest to us is the receiver whom the Comptroller appoints

---

[1] Bushnell v Leland, 164 U S 684, 17 S Ct 209, Price v Abbott 17 Fed. 606, Washington Bank v Eckels, 57 Fed 870
[2] U S R S Sec 5220, 19 Stat L 63, c. 156
[3] Washington Bank v Eckels, 57 Fed 870
[4] Before the agent starts upon the performance of his duties the creditors must furnish a bond satisfactory to the Comptroller condition for the payment in full of all claims not then on file with the Comptroller The rights of such creditors are not limited however to suit upon this bond. Guaranty Co. v Hanway, 104 Fed. 369.
[5] Barton v McKinnon, 179 Fed. 759.

330   THE RIGHTS AND REMEDIES OF CREDITORS.   [CHAP XIX.

§ 412. **Judicial Control of Receiver.** From the fact, as above seen, that this receiver is not an officer of the court, but is an administrative officer appointed by the head of a department without a judicial determination, he is not subject to the same measure of protection from the equity courts as is enjoyed by a receiver appointed by the court. Thus, in a certain case the Comptroller appointed a receiver, who liquidated the property for the benefit of all the creditors that he believed to be such, and was then discharged by the Comptroller. Thereupon the shareholders appointed an agent to finish the liquidation; but a creditor who had been left out sued the person who had been the original receiver, to establish his claim. This party applied to the federal court for an injunction staying the action on the ground that he was no longer the receiver and that the court should protect him. But the Supreme Court held that the petitioner was not entitled to protection, because he never had been a court official, and had never derived any of his powers from any act of the court.[1]

§ 413. **Tendency to State Control in Laws Governing State Banks.** Of recent years some of the States have followed this model in their banking laws, especially in the idea of departmental control over matters of liquidation. The Act of Massachusetts is so well-known a pioneer in this respect as to need little comment. Perhaps more interest will therefore attach to the recent act of the Legislature of New York.[2] Since its origin was the scandal attaching to previous receiverships of banks in the shape of expenses of administration,[3] the statute removes from the courts their former power to entertain dissolution proceedings in the case of banking or "monied" corporations. The present statute[4] authorizes the Superintendent of Banks, a State official having charge of all matters concerning the gov-

[1] *In re* Chetwood, 165 U. S 441, 17 S Ct 385
[2] Now to be found in the Banking Law, Consolidated Laws of 1909, c. 2. New Jersey has a similar Statute, Laws of 1913 c 171
[3] *In re* Union Bank, 204 N. Y. 313, 97 N E 737.
[4] Secs 19, 190.

ernment of banks incorporated under the statute, to take charge of the affairs of any such institution which may have become insolvent, and wind them up for the benefit of its creditors, by a " new and simple method " [1] Thus, as in the case of the national bank, a departmental officer takes charge of the affairs of an insolvent institution and liquidates them Undoubtedly in such liquidations he acts subject to the governance of the courts, and is entitled to seek their aid and advice, but the initiative is always with him [2] The Superintendent himself, being the liquidator under this system, has the power as a representative of the creditors to enforce all of their rights, including cases of fraudulent transfers [3]

[1] Van Tuyl v Robin, 80 N. Y Misc 360, 142 N Y S 535
[2] In the recent case of *In re* Bologh, 185 Fed 825, Holt, J says "By this and other general provisions in the banking law it appears that although the superintendent of banks in taking possession of the assets of a banking institution acts by virtue of the authority conferred upon him by law, and in taking such possession is not acting strictly as an officer of a court, nevertheless his general administration of the trust is subject to the supervision and control of the State Supreme Court in most respects"
[3] Van Tuyl v Scharman, 208 Fed 53, Van Tuyl v Robin, 80 N. Y. Misc. 360, 142 N Y. S 535.

CHAPTER XX

THE PREFERENTIAL TRANSFER AS INFRINGING THE RIGHT TO EQUAL DISTRIBUTION

§ 414. General Considerations.
415 Preferences in Connection with the Trust Fund Doctrine.
416 State Laws Forbidding Preferences
417. Preferences Forbidden by National Bank Acts.
418 Preferences under the National Bankrupt Act
419 Superfluous Definitions in Statute
420 Spirit of the Statute
421. National Bankrupt Act as Model
422. Passive Preferences
§ 423. Definition of "Transfer."
424 Illustrative Cases.
425. Illustrative Cases Continued
426 Exchange of Values No Preference.
427 Test is the Diminution of the Debtor's Estate
428 Set-off as an Exception
429 Time Limit.
430 Time Limit with Respect to the Recording Acts
431 Interpretation of Statute as to Time Limit for Recording Transfer

§ 414. **General Considerations.** Having considered the different kinds of creditors' representatives as they exist under the several State or federal systems, it is in order to consider the preferential transfer as a wrong which may be inflicted upon the right to equality of distribution As we saw, the preference was lawful at common law, and the English Court of Chancery felt that it was unable to afford more than negative relief even in the exercise of its administrative jurisdiction On the other hand, the doctrine became settled that a preferential transfer could be set aside by an assignee or trustee in bankruptcy, because it is impliedly forbidden by such bankrupt act as may be in force. That doctrine, however, was never extended beyond a case involving the presence of a bankrupt act as such.

§ 415 **Preferences in Connection with the Trust Fund Doctrine.** In our country, indeed, the attempt was made to carry it further in the case of a corporation. If we couple the trust fund theory of corporate assets with the fact that a corporation exists only by virtue of a statute, does it not follow that a preferential transfer by the corporation involves an act transgressing the spirit of the statute, which contemplates, not only that the corporate assets shall be a trust fund for the creditors, but that the fund shall be equally distributed among the creditors? That question, which involves a great many inferences, was nevertheless answered affirmatively in Ohio [1] But, in Connecticut at an earlier day an emphatic negative was put upon the proposition,[2] and this case has been followed by most of the State courts [3] So, outside of the domain of bankruptcy as such, there is no such wrong as a preferential transfer, unless it is forbidden by statute.

§ 416. **State Laws Forbidding Preferences.** In many States, indeed, preferences are distinctly allowed, to more or less degree, even in winding up acts The general assignment laws of some States permit preferences to be created by the debtor to the extent of one third of his estate; in other States they are forbidden [4] It is needless to say that a State like Massachusetts, which possesses a complete bankruptcy statute of its own, will take care to forbid preferences, by the terms of the statute itself;[5] but other States have no such models, and therefore it may be said that, so far as State systems of liquidation are concerned, the inquiry should be for the State statute forbidding

---

[1] Rouse v Merchants Bank, 46 Ohio St 493 See also Joseph v Raff, 82 N Y App Div 47, 81 N Y S 546, aff'd 176 N Y 611, 68 N. E 1118, a case involving a foreign corporation not governed by the present New York statutes forbidding corporate preferences

[2] Catlin v Eagle Bank, 6 Conn 233

[3] Covert v Rogers, 38 Mich 363, Dana v Bank, 5 W & S 223 Whitwell v Warner, 20 Vt 425, Dabney v The Bank, 3 S C 124, Reichwald v Hotel Co, 106 Ill 439, Planters Bank v Whittle, 78 Va 737, Buell v Buckingham, 16 Iowa 284 The Arkansas Supreme Court says that "such preferences, when they are meritorious, so far from furnishing an argument against the deed, conduce rather to uphold it," Ringol v Biscoe, 13 Ark 563

[4] See list of these States in Bigelow, "Fraudulent Conveyances," p. 678, et seq

[5] See Crafts v Belden, 99 Mass 535

preferential transfers. At the present day preferences in the case of corporations are covered in a great many States by statute. Thus in New York [1] and in New Jersey [2] are statutes which are to the same effect and have received substantially the same interpretation.[3] The New Jersey statute as well has been the model for adoption in some of the newer States, such as New Mexico.[4] These statutes, as interpreted by State and federal courts, are substantially to the same effect as the federal statute to which we will presently come, and therefore may be left with this mention.[5] They are all of comparatively modern origin,[6] but it is to be hoped that all of the States will follow the example thus afforded.

§ 417. **Preferences Forbidden by National Bank Acts** In like manner the National Bank Acts forbid preferences [7] and their provisions have received substantially the same construction as those of the successive Bankrupt Acts.[8] The object of their winding up provisions is to secure equality of distribution among the general creditors of the bank, and to that end the Act contains very comprehensive provisions forbidding preferences.[9] As stated by the Supreme Court [10] "the act evidently

---

[1] Stock Corporation Law, Sec 66. With limited partnerships, State laws forbid preferences (*supra*, § 306, Burdick, 'Partnership," 2d ed, 411)

[2] Corporation Law, Sec 64

[3] Quenn *v* Weaver, 38 N Y App Div 628, 56 N Y S 998

[4] See Centr Electr. Co *v* Socorro Co, 209 Fed 534

[5] Regina Music Box Co *v* Otto, 65 N J Eq 582, 56 Atl. 715, Varnum *v* Hart, 119 N Y 101, 23 N E 183; Gordon *v* Southgate, 109 N Y App Div 838, 96 N Y S 717.

[6] Thus in New York, the first statute forbidding corporate preferences was limited to banks (Laws of 1882, c 409) It received the strong support of the courts National Shoe & Leather Bank *v.* Mechanics National Bank, 89 N Y 467, Kingsley *v* First Natl. Bank, 31 Hun 329 But as it did not apply to foreign corporations, the Court of Appeals was left free in such cases to follow its own views; and in such cases it sustained preferences as being sanctioned by the common law, Coats *v* Donnell, 94 N Y 168.

[7] U S R. S. Sec. 5242.

[8] National Bank *v.* Colby, 21 Wall 609, Case *v* Bank, 2 Woods 23 Fed Case 2489; Casey *v* Societe, 2 Woods 77 Fed Case 2496; Robinson *v* Bank of Newberne, 81 N Y. 585

[9] U S R S Sec. 5242 [10] National Bank *v* Colby, 21 Wall. 609

intends to secure equality among them in the division of the proceeds of the property of the bank. This design would be defeated if a preference in the application of the assets could be obtained by adversary proceedings."

§ 418. **Preferences under the National Bankrupt Act.** As we have seen, for many years after the bankruptcy doctrine concerning preferences was enunciated by Lord Mansfield, the English statutes continued to be silent on the subject. It was not necessary for the statute to speak, unless by way of codification of a doctrine already shaped out by the courts, and this codification was long in coming. At the present day the Bankrupt Acts of both England [1] and this country [2] do address themselves to the subject; but they have added nothing to the idea which the courts had already put forth concerning the essential nature of the preference, and but little to its details of application, with one exception which will presently be noticed. Our present Act [3] defines a preference as occurring where the debtor within four months prior to the filing of the petition or between petition and adjudication, (a) procures or suffers an adverse judgment, or (b) transfers property, if the effect of such judgment or transfer is to enable one creditor to obtain a greater percentage of his debt than any others of the same class. The four months' period dates from the recording or registering of the transfer or judgment, if such is required by law. After thus defining a preference, the Act [4] confers upon the trustee the power to recover the property thus transferred if the creditor had reasonable cause to believe that a preference was intended. In another place [5] creditors holding preferences as above defined are not allowed to prove their claims until after the surrender of the property which they had thus wrongfully received.

§ 419. **Superfluous Definitions in Statute.** The above is the present state of the Act, after certain amendments made in

[1] Bankrupt Act of 1883, Secs 48-9
[2] Bankrupt Act of 1898, Secs 57, 60
[3] Sec 60a
[4] Sec. 60b
[5] Sec 57g.

1903 and 1910 Prior to that there was much confusion as to whether creditors holding a preference, but innocently, which could not be taken away from them, under Section 60, could yet prove their claims, under Section 57g, without surrender of their preferences,[1] and whether the four months' period ran from actual transfer or public registration of the same The fault of our recent legislation, in other words, has been excess of particularity The idea of the preferential transfer had been evolved before the statutes spoke, it would have been better had they never spoken, for with us, at least, in excess of zeal to define the legislator has raised obscurity. The extreme analysis of our present statute was clearly unnecessary; for it has added nothing to the law. As with a fraudulent conveyance, so with a preference — its essence is the unjust diminution of the debtor's estate, rather than a matter of "conveyances," "transfers," and the like Thus there need not be a transferor and another person as transferee One person, holding property in one capacity, can unlawfully prefer himself as acting in another capacity; thus A, as trustee for X, may prefer himself. A, as trustee for Y [2]

§ 420. **Spirit of the Statute.** The aim of the courts, in allowing trustees in bankruptcy to set aside preferential transfers, was to secure that equality of distribution which is of the essence of the bankruptcy laws; the same object those laws still seek to attain, and all their provisions must be read in that light Hence Section 60c of the present act allows a preferred creditor to offset, against the trustee's attack, fresh credits which he may have extended to the bankrupt That works for equality, as the diminution of the estate caused by the preferential transfer has to that extent been made good [3]

§ 421. **National Bankrupt Act as Model.** We will, therefore,

---

[1] See Pirie v. Trust Co, 182 U S 438, Jaquith v Alden, 189 U. S. 78, 23 S Ct 649, McKey v Lee, 105 Fed 923

[2] Clarke v Rogers, 228 U S 534, 33 S Ct 587; Bush v. Moore, 133 Mass 198.

[3] Kaufman v Tredway, 195 U. S 271, 25 S Ct. 33.

have less trouble with this subject, if we approach it from such a point of view. And as all statutory definitions of preferences in effect endeavor to attain the same end, it is unnecessary for us to examine each in detail, we may deal with the whole subject by the study of one of these statutes alone. We shall, therefore, for convenience, address ourselves to the present National Bankrupt Act, in so far as it deals with the preferential transfer.

§ 422 **Passive Preferences** As we have said, a preference, under the National Act, divides itself into two classes.' First, where property is transferred, and, second, where the debtor procures or suffers a judgment to be entered against himself The latter branch of the subject is not important, because under Section 67f of the Act every judgment obtained against the bankrupt, within the same four months' period as is prescribed for a preference, is avoided by the adjudication of bankruptcy. This Section controls the contradictory subdivision C of Section 67, and has the effect of avoiding every judgment obtained within the period whether the bankrupt procures or suffers it to be entered or whether it is entered against his will [1] We are remitted, therefore, in our consideration of preferences, to that feature which consists essentially of the "transfer" of property.

§ 423 **Definition of "Transfer."** As defined by the first section of the Bankrupt Act, "transfer" has a very wide meaning This, however, was not necessary so far as the courts' conception of a preference is concerned, because, just as in the case of a fraudulent conveyance, the courts have always given "transfer" a wide meaning "It is not," says the Supreme Court, "the mere form or method of the transaction that the Act condemns, but the appropriation by the insolvent debtor of a

---

[1] *In re* Richards, 95 Fed 258 If, however, the trustee elects to consider a piece of land as not part of the estate, then the statutory lien of a judgment thereon is not vacated, McCarty *v* Light, 155 N Y. App Div 36, 139 N. Y S 853.

portion of his property to the payment of a creditor's claim, so that thereby the estate is depleted and the creditor obtains an advantage over other creditors." [1]

§ 424. **Illustrative Cases.** A few instances will suffice. Thus an accepted draft drawn by the bankrupt on one indebted to him may be a preference, since it operates as a transfer of funds [2] It is the result of the transaction that the court looks at, not the transaction itself If the result is to lessen what the other creditors will get compared to what the preferred creditor gets, then we have a preference It does not matter how that is done. The court simply considers the fact that such is the result of the transaction The Act expresses it in terms of percentages, as the Supreme Court has noted in the case above cited, but whether we express it in percentages or otherwise, we must look to the result of the transaction to see whether a preference has occurred Thus, as in the English case already considered,[3] the transfer of firm assets to one partner, to enable his individual creditors to come in ahead of firm creditors, is a preference.[4] And however with a wicked intent an entirely fictitious transaction appears by book entries, but nothing in fact leaves the estate, no preference has been effected [5] On the other hand, if a transfer of property has really taken place, then the result cannot be affected by means of book entries showing that no transfer has occurred.[6]

§ 425. **Illustrative Cases Continued.** Two cases more to illustrate this contention, and we are done In Aiello v. Crampton,[7] A owned most of the stock of B corporation, and the

---

[1] Nat'l Bank of Newport v Nat'l Herkimer County Bank, 225 U S. 178, 32 S Ct 633.   [2] Re Hines, 144 Fed 543
[3] Ex parte Mayou, 4 De G. J. & S. 664
[4] Re Waite, 1 Low 207, Fed. Cas. 17011, see Re Perlhefter, 177 Fed 299 If an insolvent firm dissolves and distributes its assets among its members, that may well constitute a preferential transfer as against the partnership creditors, Re Head, 114 Fed 489
[5] In re Steam Vehicle Co , 121 Fed 939.
[6] Rock Island Co v Freeman, 83 N Y Misc 7, 144 N. Y S. 317.
[7] 201 Fed 891

bankrupt was indebted to both. But a payment to B corporation was held not to operate as a preferential payment on the debt owing to A. In Keystone Warehouse Co. v Bissell [1] the situation was more complicated. The bankrupt was a milling company engaged in blending flour The vendors of the flour shipped it consigned to themselves in care of the defendant warehouse company They made drafts on the bankrupt for the price, which they sent, with bills of lading attached, to a bank for collection The defendant warehouse company's custom was to receive the flour and store it in numbered compartments for the various vendors until the drafts were paid and then, upon receiving notice of that, to hold the flour for the account of the bankrupt, which would withdraw it as needed in its business. The bankrupt, without the knowledge of the defendant warehouse company, took flour without drafts having been paid The defendant stopped the bankrupt from taking any more flour from the warehouse and called upon it to make good the shortage, which the bankrupt was unable to do Thereupon an arrangement was made as follows The warehouse company paid to the banks, which held drafts and bills of lading, $8000 The bankrupt gave its note to the warehouse company for $8000 and turned over to it, as collateral, all the flour remaining in the warehouse and also some other property' It was held that this was preferential because the defendant was not a creditor of the bankrupt, since it held the flour which had been stolen merely as bailee It was bailee for the shippers or the banks. True, it could have sued in its own name for the stolen flour, but such a suit would have been really as trustee for the owner, to whom it would be bound to turn over the proceeds. The warehouse company was not a creditor of the bankrupt until it took the latter's note, and this transfer was made as collateral for the note as a part of the transaction in which the note was given.

§ 426 **Exchange of Values No Preference** It follows that although the creditor may have been given something from the

[1] 203 Fed 652

debtor's estate, yet if he, as part of the same transaction, relinquishes to the estate something of equal value, there is no preference in that transaction If there was substantial equality of value in the substitution no preference has been effected [1] It is from this point of view that we can uphold the numerous cases deciding that a bankrupt who pays the running expenses of his business, such as rent, power, heat, etc , is not thereby preferring the creditors who furnish these products. If he did not pay them, he would have no business for his other creditors to get anything from, and in the long run, therefore, the business, as a going concern, being preserved to them by means of these payments, in effect the estate has not been diminished [2]

§ 427 **Test is the Diminution of the Debtor's Estate.** These last cases again show us that the definition given by the present act is not scientific, and if the courts had confined themselves strictly to its terms, such cases as the above could not be sustained, because there is no doubt that the creditors in the shape of the landlord, the power company and the heating company, do receive a greater percentage of their debt than the other creditors of the same class. The courts, however, upheld such transactions because the net result was that the estate was not diminished The test is the diminution of the estate available for the other creditors, rather than the percentage received by the preferred creditor. Such is the rule which is of general application, with one exception.

§ 428 **Set-off as an Exception.** That exception is in the case of set-off In its general aspect, we have already discussed set-off. Its origin, as we have seen, was ancient, at common law, in bankruptcy and in the jurisdiction of the courts of equity.

---

[1] Sawyer v. Turpin, 91 U S 114, In re Reese Brick Co, 181 Fed 641, Lindley v Ross, 200 Fed 733; De Land v Bank, 119 Iowa 368, 93 N W 304 If this quid pro quo turns out to be of less value because of later but unanticipated events, there is still no preference, Engel v. Union Square Bank, 182 N Y 544, 75 N E 1129

[2] In re Locke, 1 Low 293; In re Columbia Real Estate Co, 205 Fed 980, In re Douglas Co, 131 Fed 769, In re Perlhefter, 177 Fed 299, Goodlander etc. Co. v, Atwood, 152 Fed. 978

As we have seen, it was always allowed in bankruptcy, and it is allowed to-day by the express language of the Bankrupt Act.[1] The Act forbids a set-off of mutual debts and credits only where the person indebted to the bankrupt estate buys a claim against it for the purpose of set-off.[2] Outside of the limitations imposed by the act itself, set-off is freely allowed although technically and strictly it operates to effect a preference.[3] But the set-off must be of mutual debts. Thus a debt owing to A as trustee for B cannot be offset against a debt owing by A individually.[4]

§ 429. **Time Limit.** The statute provides a limit of time within which a preference if given shall be wrongful. Obviously there must be such a limit and a short one at that, because otherwise the ordinary processes of business would be greatly hindered. The present statute prescribes four months prior to the filing of the petition in bankruptcy. The English statute gives a period of three months. The State laws on the subject, and the National Bank Act, fix no time limit, but rather tend to reach back to the time when the insolvent condition of the debtor becomes manifest to its management. The test, in other words, is whether the concern, so far as its officers could gather from their reasonable knowledge of the situation, was continuing, and expected to continue, in the due and ordinary course of its business.[5]

§ 430. **Time Limit with Respect to the Recording Acts.** With the Bankrupt Act, the time limit ordinarily would commence with the actual transfer of the property, however secret might have been the transaction.[6] But the increasing importance of

---

[1] See 68.
[2] Re Shults, 132 Fed 573.
[3] N Y County Bank v. Massey, 192 U. S 138, 24 S Ct 199; Studley v Boylston Bank, 229 U S 523, 33 S Ct 826; Continental Trust Co. v. Chicago etc Co, 229 U. S 435, 33 S Ct 829, explaining Western Tie Co. v Brown, 196 U S. 502, 25 S Ct 339.
[4] Western Tie Co. v Brown, 196 U S. 502, 25 S. Ct 339.
[5] McDonald v Chem Nat Bk, 174 U S 610, 19 S Ct 787; Ball v. German Bank, 187 Fed. 750.
[6] Re Perrin, 7 Nat. Bankr. Reg. 283, Fed. Cas. 10995; Burdick v. Jackson, 7 Hun 488.

the registration acts of modern times has led Congress to make this modification in the present law, — that if a transfer is required by law, that is by the State law, to be recorded, " such period of four months shall not expire until four months after the date of the recording or registering of the transfer "[1] In a case within this proviso, therefore, although the transfer might have been made six months prior to the bankruptcy, yet if it is not recorded until within four months prior thereto, it is a preferential transfer, although as between the parties the complete title vested at a date outside of the statutory period

§ 431 **Interpretation of Statute as to Time Limit for Recording Transfer.** This proviso has received a very sensible construction. The whole question in any such case is whether the law of the State where the transaction occurred required the registration in order for the transaction to be valid as against the creditors of the transferor Unless the law of the State requires the transfer to be recorded in order to be valid as against the creditors of the grantor or mortgagor, the case is not within the proviso; and, although the deed or mortgage is recorded within the four months, no preference occurs unless the actual transfer occurs within the four months.[2] On the contrary, a case where the State laws require a registration of the instrument in order that it may be valid as against the creditors of the transferor, as in the case of a chattel mortgage, is clearly within the terms of the statute [3] In some States, as New York and Kansas, the registration laws make a distinction between a chattel mortgage and a conditional sale The latter to be valid as against the creditors of the mortgagor must be recorded, whereas the former does not need recording for such a purpose. Consequently, in the case of any transfer of personal property the question is simply whether the transaction, from its legal

---

[1] Sec 60a
[2] *In re* Hunt, 139 Fed 283, Claridge *v* Evans, 137 Wis 218, 118 N. W 198, 803, Dean *v* Plane, 195 Ill 495, 63 N E 274
[3] *In re* Reynolds, 153 Fed 195, Loeser *v* Savings Bank, 148 Fed. 975; see Bradley *v* Benson, 93 Minn 91, 100 N W 670

aspect, constituted a chattel mortgage, — that is, a transfer of title to goods possessed by the debtor, — or a conditional sale arrangement — that is, a transaction where the debtor never had the title to the personal property, but acquired merely its possession under a contract to vest the title to him upon his making certain payments or performing certain acts. The particular case with regard to the proviso of Section 68 must be determined according to this criterion.[1] Indeed, from a broader point of view, the matter may be shortly disposed of in this way: no preference at all occurs in such a case because the bankrupt transfers no property. The essence of a conditional sale transaction is that the bankrupt gets no title to the property, and if he gets no title he can transfer none. "In this respect," says BREWER, J., "a conditional sale differs from an unconditional sale with a mortgage back. In such a case the vendee has everything, except as limited by the terms of the mortgage; here he has nothing except as expressed in his contract."[2] This distinction is pointed out in the second of the cases above cited as follows: "There could be no preference without a transfer by the bankrupt of his property. If there were any transfer in this case it is evidenced by these instruments . . . but they transferred no property of Bell. They expressly refrained from transferring any to him."[3]

[1] Big Four Company v. Wright, 207 Fed 535; Baker Company v. Bailey, 209 Fed. 603
[2] Hall v. Draper, 20 Kan 137
[3] Big Four Company v. Wright, *supra*

CHAPTER XXI

PREFERENCES (*CONTINUED*) POSITION OF THE TRANSFEREE

§ 432 "Intent to Prefer."
433 Test is the Result of the Transfer.
434 "Reasonable Cause to Believe"
435 Ordinary Standard of Prudence
436 Transfer Pursuant to Previous Obligation
437. Transfer must be in Payment of, or as Security for, a Previous Debt
438 Transfer is by Way of Performance or Recognition of Obligation.
439 Restoration of Embezzled Trust Funds

§ 440 The Transfer must be of Debtor's Own Property
441. Explanation of Doctrine of Equitable Lien
442 Illustrative Cases
443. Agreement in the Alternative
444. Putting Mortgagee in Possession
445 Property must be Identified
446 Promise to Give Security
447 Relation of Broker and Customer.
448 Illustrative Cases
449 Contract must have Mutuality.
450. Good Faith Essential

§ 432. "**Intent to Prefer.**" The zeal for the particular which inspired the framers of our present Bankrupt Act led them, in defining the preferential transfer, to speak of the debtor's "intent to prefer." The Act,[1] as amended in 1910, provides that a preferential transfer shall be voidable by the trustee, and he may recover the property or its value from the transferee, if the latter, at the time when he received the transfer, had had reasonable cause to believe that a preference was thereby intended. Under the Act of 1867 the transferee was required to have reasonable cause to believe that the debtor was insolvent, but the effect is the same under each statute.

§ 433 **Test is the Result of the Transfer.** The only real difference between the English and the American doctrine of pref-

[1] Sec 67d

erences appears at this point. In England the courts always allowed payments which were made under pressure or constraint, and this led to a certain extent to an examination of the debtor's intent. With us there is no such distinction, and it is not necessary to show any intention on the part of the debtor[1] As is said by the Circuit Court of Appeals, Second Circuit, "the result of the transfer and not the mental attitude of the transferor is made the test."[2] As is said by the New York court, "when a trustee in bankruptcy has proven that a debtor who is insolvent has made a payment, the effect of which will be to give one creditor a preference over others of the same class, and has supplemented this by evidence from which a jury would have the right to find that the creditor receiving the payment had reasonable ground to believe that it was intended thereby to give a preference, he has established all that the statute requires in support of his cause of action He need not go further, as the plaintiff herein was required to do, and seek to prove the intent of the debtor in making the payment"[3]

§ 434 "**Reasonable Cause to Believe.**" On the other hand, in ascertaining whether the transferee had reasonable cause to believe that the effect of his transfer would create a preference, we have practically the same situation as obtains under the doctrine of fraudulent conveyance In brief, it must be shown that such facts as would have put a reasonable man on inquiry were brought to the transferee's attention Mere grounds for suspicion of insolvency are not enough There must be reasonable cause to believe, and not mere surmise, or conjecture[1] "A man may have many grounds for suspicion that his debtor is in failing circumstances," says the Supreme Court, "and yet

---

[1] Benedict v Deshel, 177 N Y 1, 68 N E 999, Pirie v Chicago Title etc Co, 182 U S 838, 21 S Ct. 906. See 19 Harvard Law Review, p 572, et seq
[2] Alexander v Redmond, 180 Fed. 92
[3] Benedict v Deshel, 177 N. Y. 1, 68 N E 999
[4] In re Pettingill, 135 Fed 218, Grant v Monmouth Bank, 97 U S 80, Merchants Bank v. Cook, 95 U S 343; Carey v Donohue, 209 Fed 328.

have no cause for a well-grounded belief of the facts He may be unwilling to trust him further; he may feel anxious about his claim and have a strong desire to secure it, and yet such belief as the Act requires may be wanting "[1] On the other hand, it is equally true, as is said by Judge Hough, that " knowledge is not necessary, nor even belief, but only reasonable cause to believe, which is a very different thing "[2] Thus, if the debtor has a reasonable hope of being able to go on, then, even though the facts upon which that hope are based are known to the transferee, he does not receive a preferential transfer when he gets security. People are entitled to take the ordinary things of life as they find them, and if the debtor himself had reason to hope that he would be able to continue in business, his transferee should not be held to a higher standard.[3] On the other hand, if the debtor's hope of being able to go on is not reasonably based on facts, then the transferee, if charged with notice of the facts upon which this hope is unwisely founded, is receiving a preference.[4] Thus, in a case where a transferee's belief in his ability to go on rested on the hope that certain other creditors from motives of self-interest would aid him by loans sufficient to pay off his existing debts, a creditor who took security for his debt in the hope that the other creditors would extend this aid, received a preferential transfer.[5] The best of intentions will not help the transferee in such cases; he is held to a different test from that of benevolence.[6]

§ 435. **Ordinary Standard of Prudence.** — The creditor, we repeat, is held to the ordinary standard of prudence If facts come to his attention sufficient to put him upon inquiry, that inquiry, of course, he cannot avoid by willful abstinence. To

---

[1] Grant v Monmouth Bank, 97 U. S. 80.
[2] Pratt v Columbia Bank, 157 Fed. 137.
[3] Grant v Monmouth Bank, 97 U S. 80.
[4] Re Deutschle & Co., 182 Fed 435.
[5] Alexander v Redmond, 180 Fed 92, *In re* Mayo Contracting Co, 157 Fed. 469
[6] Montague v. Hotel Gotham Co, 208 N Y 442, 102 N E. 513

use the language of the Supreme Court, he cannot continue "recklessly with guilty knowledge"[1] Nor can he, to use the expressive language of another case, "travel as near to the edge of actual knowledge as it would be possible to go without obtaining it"[2] If the means for ascertaining the debtor's affairs are at hand, if the transferee has the opportunity to examine his books and does not do so, then he is held to the knowledge which such an examination would have disclosed[3] As has been said, "notice of facts which would incite a man of ordinary prudence to an inquiry under similar circumstances, is notice of all the facts which a reasonably diligent inquiry would disclose"[4]

§ 436. **Transfer Pursuant to Previous Obligation** — We now pass to a more difficult question It is whether a transfer pursuant to a previous obligation may constitute a preferential transfer. In one sense this question should answer itself, because every preferential transfer is a transfer in pursuance of a previous obligation. But the question is broader than that, as we shall see.

§ 437 **Transfer must be in Payment of, or as Security for, a Previous Debt.** — Unless the debtor gives property in exchange for, or as collateral security for, a debt contracted at the same time and as part of the same transaction, the transaction cannot be preferential, because the essence of a preference is a transfer either in payment of or as security for a pre-existing debt.[5] Thus, a mortgage to secure future advances cannot constitute a preferential transfer The mortgage has no validity as a lien until the advances are made; and hence in legal effect the lien is created *pro tanto* as each advance is made. This transfer is essentially distinct from a preferential transaction.[6] On the

---

[1] Clements v Moore, 6 Wall 786
[2] *In re* McDonald, 178 Fed 487
[3] *In re* Pease, 129 Fed 446, Singer v Jacobs, 11 Fed. 559
[4] Coder v. McPherson, 152 Fed 951
[5] Tiffany v Lucas, 15 Wall. 418, Tiffany v Boatmen's Institution, 18 Wall 413
[6] *Ex parte* Ames, 1 Low, 561.

other hand, of course, a mortgage which is given in part for past and in part for future advances will be good only as collateral for the future advances, if the other elements of a preference are present.[1]

§ 438. **Transfer is by Way of Performance or Recognition of Obligation.** — Essentially, therefore, a preferential transfer is nothing but the performance of a contract obligation either as it originally stood or as modified by later agreement If a man pays his debt in full, he is doing nothing but what his contract bound him to do   If he pays it in part, he is doing part of what he is required to do by his contract of debt   If he gives security for his obligation, he is, while not performing it, at least acting in modification of it. It follows that to have a preference at all we must have a pre-existing obligation which is either discharged in whole or in part, or secured, by the transfer complained of.

§ 439. **Restoration of Embezzled Trust Funds** — This is emphasized rather than confused by the conflict of authority upon the question whether a trustee, who has embezzled his beneficiaries' trust property and afterwards restores it, can be considered by that act as giving a preferential transfer. The English courts hold that such restitution of stolen funds does not constitute a preferential transfer.[2] In the Second Federal Circuit this rule was followed,[3] but that decision has been overruled, and the contrary view has been taken, by the Supreme Court in Clarke v Rogers [4] The court, there, it would seem, adopted the proper course of reasoning, by starting with the inquiry whether the trustee's act in embezzling his client's property gave the latter a provable claim against the trustee's estate in bankruptcy   In short, the court's first inquiry was, did a debt arise from the trustee to the beneficiary as a

---

[1] *In re* Wolf, 98 Fed 84
[2] *Ex parte* Stubbins, 17 Ch Div 58   *In re* Lake, (1901) 1 K. B. 710, *In re* Black Pool Motor Car Co , (1901) 1 Ch 77.
[3] McNaboe *v* Columbia Co , 153 Fed. 967.
[4] 228 U S 534, 33 S Ct 587

result of the former's tortious act? The court's reasoning in other words was that for a preference we must have a person who had a provable claim, as otherwise no wrong has been done the other creditors. If a man has not a provable claim he is not entitled to share in the distribution with them, and therefore he has not been preferred. This emphasizes again the real scope of a preference as compared with a fraudulent transfer In a fraudulent transfer, as we have seen, from the broad point of view it makes no difference who the transferee is In the case of a preference the transferee must be of the same class as the persons injured, and, therefore, a creditor.

§ 440 **The Transfer must be of Debtor s Own Property** — The cases just discussed are of equal importance in showing that a preference consists of paying the debtor's own property to the transferee If the debtor gives to the transferee something that belonged to the transferee anyhow, then he is not preferring the transferee, because while the creditors are entitled to all that the debtor has, it must follow, on the other hand, that they are not entitled to anything that the debtor has not If the debtor has in his possession property which belongs specifically to some one else, and which he is under the duty to turn over to that person, then the creditors are not injured by the transfer because they would not be entitled to the property in any event. In Clarke v Rogers[1] the trustee did not turn over to his beneficiary the identical property which he held in trust. That property had been wasted, so he turned over its equivalent out of his own pocket If the trustee had taken the former course it would not have resulted in a preference, but as he took the latter, it did The beneficiary was not in position to say that he was merely receiving his own, because at the moment of the embezzlement the beneficiary had the election between two courses, (a) following specifically his property, and (b) taking its equivalent in value from the trustee's own assets It is true that this election need not be manifested at that moment,

[1] *Supra*

indeed this point of manifestation may be preserved to the very end of the whole matter.[1] But still there is a point when this election is no longer available. In the case of interest here it occurs when the payment is made and received. Then the beneficiary, knowing that he is paid out of the trustee's own pocket, instead of merely receiving his specific property back, has taken the position of a creditor and has received payment of his debt. This distinction is emphasized by Atherton v. Green.[2] To the bankrupt, a private banker, the defendants sent a note for collection. The bankrupt, being insolvent, collected the note and pocketed the proceeds. A few days later he transferred real estate to the defendants with directions to hold it until they had definite notice of the closing of his bank. It was held that this constituted a preferential transfer, as the defendants' acceptance of the real estate was based upon their recognition of the misappropriation as creating an indebtedness.

§ 441 **Explanation of Doctrine of Equitable Lien.** This distinction gives the key to the problem presented by the cases where a transfer is sought to be supported on the theory of an equitable lien. In any case where by virtue of a transfer or a contract specific property is set apart in the legal ownership of A for the sole use of B to be transferred to him on conditions, or the income paid to him, a court of equity treats A as being the trustee for B and under the duty to transfer that property to B upon the conditions being fulfilled. Upon this basis, therefore, if A has contracted to sell real estate or personal property of a peculiar nature to B, a court of equity treats A merely as holding the property in trust for B; and, upon B's application and the conditions of the contract being fulfilled, the court will compel the specific performance of the trust by the transferee. In like manner, if an agreement has been made by A to give a lien upon his property in the shape of a mortgage, and, by reason of

---

[1] Richardson v Shaw, 209 U S 365, 28 S Ct 512; Thomas v. Sugarman, 218 U S 129, 30 S Ct 650
[2] 179 Fed 806

failure to comply with some technical rule of law, an instrument has been executed or a transfer made which does not comply with the requirements of law governing such instruments and yet money has been advanced on the faith of the agreement to give this security, a court of equity will compel specific performance of the obligation thus created.[1] It follows that where the debtor is so situated as a trustee for another that a court of equity would have enforced the trust as against him had he not been insolvent, the fact of his insolvency can give his creditors no equity in the trust property which can prevail over the prior equity of the *cestui que* trust. They should not be able to take what he himself could not hold, and hence the court, as against the creditors of a bankrupt trustee, will enforce the same equity which they would have enforced as against the bankrupt.

---

[1] "There can be no doubt," said the New York Court of Appeals, "upon the authorities that where one party advances money to another upon the faith of a verbal agreement by the latter to secure its payment by a mortgage upon certain lands, but which is never executed, or which, if executed, is so defective or informal as to fail in effectuating the purpose of its execution equity will impress upon the land intended to be mortgaged a lien in favor of the creditor who advanced the money for the security and satisfaction of his debt. Some of these cases hold that the lien of the party who has advanced money under such circumstances is analogous to that of the vendor of real estate for the unpaid purchase money . . . The right of the vendor and that of the person who has advanced the money are not essentially different, and each would seem to commend itself with equal force to the conscience of a court of equity. The doctrine of equitable mortgages is not limited to written instruments intended as mortgages, but which by reason of formal defects cannot have such operation without the aid of the court, but also to a very great variety of transactions to which equity attaches that character. It is not necessary that such transactions or agreements as to lands should be in writing in order to take them out of the operation of the Statute of Frauds for two reasons, first, because they are completely executed by at least one of the parties and are no longer executory, and, secondly, because the statute by its own terms does not affect the power which courts of equity have always exercised to compel specific performance of such agreements." — Sprague v Cochran, 144 N Y 104, 38 N E 1000; Biggs v French, 1 Sumner 504, Lord Portarlington v Soulby, 3 Atk 104.

§ 442. **Illustrative Cases** This is illustrated by a number of cases. In Taylor v. Taylor[1] the bankrupt mortgaged copyhold land, but the surrender was not presented to the lord of the manor, as the custom of the manor required in cases of that kind. The mortgagor then became bankrupt and died. After his death, the surrender was tendered, but the lord refused to accept it, because by the custom of the manor all surrenders were to be void if not presented within twelve months after they were made. The court held that the surrender should be performed. Even more striking is *Ex parte* Pollard.[2] There it appeared that the bankrupts owned certain land in Scotland, and were indebted to Pollard. They gave Pollard a memorandum to the effect that the land should stand as security for the debt, and deposited the title deeds with Pollard. This memorandum operated as a mortgage neither under Scottish nor English law, and it appeared that the Scottish law did not recognize our equity doctrine of an equitable mortgage, above referred to. Pollard filed a petition praying that the proceeds of the sale of this land be applied to the payment of his debt. The Court of Review denied the petition.[3] On appeal, the Lord Chancellor reversed this judgment, and said:

"The only parties resisting the creditor's claim are the assignees, who are bound by all the equities which affect the bankrupts. To deny to the creditor the benefit of this security would be an injustice which, if unavoidable, would be much to be regretted. In giving effect to it, I act upon the well-known rules of equity in this country, and do not violate nor interfere with any law or rule of property in Scotland, as I only order that to be done which the parties may by that law lawfully perform."[4]

[1] 2 Vern. 564.
[2] Mont. & Chitty 239.
[3] 3 Mont. & Ayrton 340.
[4] A similar state of facts arose in *Ex parte* Holthausen, L. R. 9 Ch. App. 722, the land being located in Shanghai. The court held that the security should be enforced. This principle has been enforced in America in numerous instances, Burdick v. Jackson, 7 Hun 488; Cross-

§ 443. **Agreement in the Alternative.** — In another case it has been held that an agreement in the alternative, to give a mortgage or personal endorsement satisfactory to the mortgagee in lieu thereof, may be specifically enforced if the debtor has not exercised the option The nonexercise of the option, the court said, " remitted the plaintiff to such remedy for the total noncompliance of the contract as the doctrine above stated will afford him " [1]

§ 444 **Putting Mortgagee in Possession.** The same principle applies in cases where, when a chattel mortgage has been given or goods sold under conditional sale, the debtor puts the creditor in possession of the property covered by the instrument. In such a case as that, no preferential transfer has occurred, because the agreement gave the creditor the right to take possession upon default, and the voluntary act of the debtor in transferring it was nothing but a compliance with the terms of the agreement.[2]

§ 445 **Property must be Identified**   With this principle in view, we can proceed now to the qualifications   The principal one is that the property in question must be clearly identified. The reason for this is obvious. The basis of this doctrine, as we have seen, is the jurisdiction of equity to enforce a trust, as equity acts only *in personam* by compelling the delivery or transfer of property. It is obvious that the property which is to be the subject of the transfer must have been clearly identified by the original arrangement. Nothing less than that will suffice, and the courts have shown of late times a tendency toward applying this test even more strictly than of former times   Thus, in MacDonald *v.* Daskam[3] a person holding a mortgage upon property made a fresh loan with an agreement

---

well *v* Allis, 25 Conn 301; Williams *v* Clark, 47 Minn 53; *In re* Wood, 5 N. B. R 421, Fed Case 5271, Nicholson *v* Schmucker, 81 Md. 459, 32 Atl. 182

[1] Bridgeport Ice Co *v* Meader, 72 Fed 115.

[2] Duplan Silk Co *v* Spencer, 115 Fed 689, Sabin *v.* Camp, 98 Fed 974   [3] 116 Fed. 276

that all existing policies of insurance which had been taken out upon the mortgaged property should stand as collateral for the new loan. The court held that this was an enforceable trust, saying "It is true that the statement in the notes does not indicate the particular insurance, but this is made clear by the evidence which shows that all the policies were in the keeping of the insurance agent for the parties interested and that in all of them the loss was made payable to Edward Daskam, mortgagee."

§ 446. **Promise to Give Security.** From this premise certain conclusions are clear. A mere general promise to give security is of no avail,[1] nor even a promise to repay a debt out of a particular fund.[2] Those cases are quite different from the case where money is advanced for the purchase of property with the agreement that the loan shall be secured by the purchased property or its proceeds when sold [3] All of this is well stated in Sexton v Kessler [4] which we have already examined in another connection [5] In that case a New York house wishing to draw from time to time upon an English firm set aside certain bonds and stocks for the latter's account. The New York house placed these securities in a package marked "escrow" for account of the English house These securities were withdrawn by the New York house from time to time, but in each instance fresh securities were substituted of a market standard sufficient to support the drawings of the New York house. Each time a purchase was made and the purchased security thus set aside, the New York house advised the English house. It was held that the English house had a lien upon this security, and hence its removal to Manchester on the eve of the failure of the New York house could not constitute a preference The Supreme Court gives these as its reasons·

[1] Pollock v. Jones, 124 Fed 163.
[2] Torrance v. Bank, 66 Kansas 177, 71 Pac 235.
[3] Sabin v. Camp, 98 Fed. 974, See Greey v. Dockendorff, 231 U. S. 513, 34 S Ct 166
[4] 225 U. S. 90, 32 S. Ct. 657.
[5] *Supra*, Ch. XI.

"A general promise to give security in the future is not enough. But the present was a more limited and cautious dealing. It was confined to specific identified stocks and bonds on hand, and purported to give an absolute present right, qualified only by possible substitution and perhaps by right of partial withdrawal if the remaining securities had risen sufficiently in value. It purported not to promise but to transfer,
. . There can be no doubt, as was said by the court below, that before the bankruptcy the English house has an equitable right, at least, to possession if it wanted it "

§ 447. **Relation of Broker and Customer** Even further than that has the Supreme Court gone. In Richardson v. Shaw[1] the court adopted the New York view, that a stockbroker who purchases stocks on margin for his customer does not occupy the position of vendor, but, on the contrary, purchases the stock as agent for his customer, advancing for that purpose his own funds sufficient to make up the difference between the whole amount of the purchase price and the amount given him by the customer as margin. It follows that while the broker has a lien upon this stock for the amount which he had advanced towards its purchase, he holds the stock, subject to this lien, in trust for the customer. The custom of the Exchange does not require the broker to keep this stock specifically apart for the account of the customer, but on the contrary allows him to purchase the stock in question together with a quantity of other stock for other customers, and, in order to acquire the funds for such purchases, to borrow from other sources and hypothecate all his mass of stocks then on hand for such purpose. Nevertheless he holds this mass in trust for his different customers in the same manner as the keeper of a grain elevator holds the grain, although it may all be mixed in one bin From this it follows that " the customer is held to have such an interest that a delivery to him by an insolvent broker is not a preference."[2]

§ 448. **Illustrative Cases** Within a later time, however, the court has shown a tendency to draw the line tighter Let

[1] 209 U. S. 365, 28 S. Ct 512.   [2] Richardson v. Shaw, *supra*.

us first examine Union Trust Co v Bulkeley [1] There A agreed to loan B $15,000, lending $10,000 at once and $5,000 shortly afterward To secure this, the borrower assigned all of his book accounts on hand, and agreed to assign all other book accounts which might accrue to him until the account was paid. It was held that this created an equitable lien on all the accounts later acquired, because in the first place, the borrower was bound to loan up to $15,000, and secondly, the amount of book accounts to be assigned could be definitely ascertained by the fact that the borrower had agreed to assign all This case, however, should be measured with the recent decisions of the Supreme Court in National City Bank v Hotchkiss and Mechanics & M Bank v Ernst [2] In each of these cases it appeared that, pursuant to a long-established custom, the bankrupt, a stockbroker, borrowed money from his bank at the opening of business hours, with the agreement that before the close of business on that day he would transfer to the bank, as collateral for that loan, all of the securities which he should acquire during the course of the day's business It was held that this created no equitable lien The court's reasoning lights up so many of the dark places that we quote from it at length.

"In the present case it is agreed that it was expected and understood that no portion of the clearance loan was to be used for any purpose other than to clear securities But, on the other hand, by consent of the bank, as it seems, the loan was put into the general deposit account, which was drawn upon for general purposes, at least, to the extent of the balance above the loan; the securities released were not kept separate, but were used like any other; and no separate account was kept of money received from deliveries of stock so received What happened as between these parties was simply that all moneys received in the course of the day, from whatever source, went into the firm's deposit account with the bank. .
A trust cannot be established in an aliquot share of a man's

[1] 150 Fed 510.
[2] 231 U S 50, 34 Sup Ct. Rep 20; Mechanics & M. Bank v Ernst, 231 U. S. 60, 34 Sup Ct Rep. 22

whole property, as distinguished from a particular fund, by showing that trust moneys have gone into it On similar principles a lien cannot be asserted upon a fund in a borrower's hands, which, at an earlier stage, might have been subject to it, if, by consent of the claimant, it has become a part of the borrower's general estate. But that was the result of the dealings between these parties, and it cannot be done away with by a wish or intention, if such there was, that alongside of this permitted freedom of dealing on the part of the bankrupts, the security of the bank should persist."

§ 449 Contract must have Mutuality For such a contract likewise there must be mutuality The parts of the agreement must balance each other so that there will be equality in its enforcement, otherwise, while there may be a legal contract, there is nothing which could be considered enforceable by a court of equity This is illustrated by Vickers v Vickers [1] In that case the defendant bought the plaintiff's business, giving the latter an option of repurchase, during the defendant's life, upon a valuation to be fixed by appraisement The plaintiff was to name one appraiser and the defendant the other, and if the two appraisers could not agree they were to select an umpire. The plaintiff, within the defendant's lifetime, elected to purchase, and gave the defendant notice; but the defendant refused to appoint an appraiser on his part, and the plaintiff filed a bill for specific performance. The court dismissed the bill, holding that it was impossible to decree specific performance, since "there is no existing contract until this valuation has taken place." This point is illustrated by several comparatively recent cases In *In re* Mandel [2] the bankrupt from time to time hypothecated its accounts receivable with the Jefferson Bank, the latter itself collecting these accounts as they became due. The bankrupt also had the usual business account with the same bank. As the bank collected on the "receivables," it would credit the borrower's business account with the surplus of

[1] L. R 4 Eq 5 9.   [2] 127 Fed 863

the deposit account. "It was agreed that the bank's lien for each advance should extend to all property of the bankrupt left with the bank as security or otherwise, and upon all collateral to any loan or otherwise, which collateral should also be held for any other liability to the bank, whether then existing or thereafter contracted." Shortly prior to the bankruptcy, the bankrupt borrowed $1000 on some fresh " receivables," the bank then having reasonable cause to believe that the bankrupt was insolvent. It was held that these accounts could stand as collateral only for the $1000 presently advanced upon them, and could not be applied toward any deficiency claim on the previous assignments. To the same effect are many other decisions of equal weight.[1]

§ 450 **Good Faith Essential** And finally, let us observe that this doctrine of equitable lien will not be enforced where there is any doubt of the good faith of the parties. A mere oral agreement cannot be brought forward as a cover or excuse for the failure to make a real agreement. There must be something more positive than this, or the court is very apt to entertain doubt as to the good faith of the parties. Thus in *In re* Stiger[2] the court refused to believe that there had been an oral agreement to assign accounts. In several cases the pertinent inquiry has been made, why was not the oral agreement to give a mortgage or deed carried out? If it appears to the court's mind that the oral agreement was designedly not carried out because its consummation by an open transfer would have excited inquiry and suspicion on the part of the creditors, then the situation is the same as if an actual agreement had been made and carefully withheld from public notice, in order to allow the borrower to gain credit by his ostensible ownership[3]

[1] Matthews v Hardt, 79 N. Y. App Div 570, 80 N. Y. S ,462, Hilton v. Ernst, 38 N Y. App. Div. 94, 57 N Y S. 908, aff'd 161 N. Y. 226, 55 N. E 1056; *Re* Cotton Mfrs Co , 209 Fed. 629
[2] 209 Fed. 148.
[3] Lathrop Bank v. Holland, 205 Fed 143; Citizens Trust Co v. Tilt, 200 Fed 410, *In re* Great Western Manufacturing Co , 152 Fed 123.

CHAPTER XXII

RELATION OF NATIONAL AND STATE SYSTEMS OF JUDICIAL LIQUIDATION

§ 451 Supremacy of National Bankrupt Act
452. Jurisdiction of Admiralty an Exception
453. Question of Supremacy is One of Jurisdiction
454. Test for Determining Conflict of Jurisdictions
455. Conflict Relates to Administration
456. National Statute Suspends only the Decisions of the Particular Case
457. Limitations of Bankruptcy Jurisdiction
458. Other Courts' Powers are Territorially Limited
459. Average Case Raises Question of Conflict of Laws
460. Question in Connection with Jurisdiction where Debtor Resides.
§ 461 Difficulty of Suing Absent Debtor
462 Powers of Receiver outside Jurisdiction — Federal Rule.
463. Powers of Receiver outside Jurisdiction — Conflict among State Courts
464. Powers of Statutory Receiver outside Jurisdiction.
465. Priority of Local Judgments.
466 Ancillary Receivers
467. Nature of Ancillary Suit
468 Duties of Ancillary Receiver.
469 Powers of Ancillary Court
470 Jurisdiction of Federal Courts
471 Dependent Jurisdiction of Federal Courts.

§ 451. **Supremacy of National Bankrupt Act.** Ever since Sturges *v* Crowninshield[1] it has been an axiom that while a national bankruptcy act is in force it is the supreme law for the distribution of an insolvent's effects Further than this have the federal courts gone, in a late decision the Supreme Court has even refused to allow a federal court, sitting in chancery, to administer the affairs of an insolvent corporation to the exclusion of proceedings instituted to the same end under the Bankrupt Act[2]

[1] 4 Wheat. 122. See also *Re* Klein, 1 How 277 n.
[2] U S Fidelity etc Company *v* Bray, 225 U S. 205, 32 S Ct 620

§ 452. **Jurisdiction of Admiralty an Exception** The only limit to this exclusiveness of the bankruptcy proceedings is the admiralty jurisdiction of the federal courts. Property in the custody of a federal court sitting in admiralty cannot be removed into the bankruptcy jurisdiction, for the reason that the one jurisdiction is derived from just as high a source as the other, as both are derived from the federal Constitution.[1] With this exception, however, the supremacy of the bankruptcy jurisdiction is unquestioned.

§ 453. **Question of Supremacy is One of Jurisdiction.** We must, however, be careful in the application of this idea of supremacy; because here, as elsewhere, the issue must arise in a practical manner. The point of conflict is connected with the custody of the debtor's property. At that point, all other jurisdictions must yield; and the bankruptcy court must be given complete control over the administration of the debtor's estate.[2] Beyond that the bankruptcy court should not go. It should not prohibit proceedings in another court unless to allow their continuance would mean an interference with the administrative powers of the bankruptcy court. It follows that no such proceedings will be stayed unless it appears that such a course is necessary for the benefit of the estate as distinct from the interest of any persons therein concerned, whether the bankrupt's creditors or others.[3] But when any such danger appears to the estate, then the bankruptcy court has full power by means of injunction to stop any further procedure in the rival court. This is illustrated by the case where a corporation,

---

[1] The Philmena, 200 Fed 859, *In re* Hughes, 170 Fed 908, Paxon v. Fleming 63 Fed 132; Matter of Froment, 110 N Y App Div. 72, 96 N. Y S 1061, 184 N Y 568, 77 N. E 9 The same principle was laid down by the Supreme Court in Moran v Sturges, 154 U S 256, 14 S Ct 1019, with respect to the jurisdiction of a State court in dissolution proceedings as against the jurisdiction of a federal court sitting in admiralty.

[2] *In re* Knight, 125 Fed 35, Hookes v Aldridge, 145 Fed 865; Exploration Mercantile Co v Pacific etc. Company, 177 Fed 825

[3] *In re* Mercedes Import Company, 166 Fed. 427, *In re* Federal Biscuit Company, 203 Fed. 37.

whose affairs have been brought into the bankruptcy court by means of a petition seasonably filed, applies for dissolution proceedings in the State court, or application is made by a creditor for that purpose. In spite of the fact that bankruptcy, as we have seen, does not dissolve the corporation's charter, the federal courts will stay such proceedings Laying all distinctions aside, the dissolution proceedings will result in the State court taking custody of the corporate assets for the purpose of distribution, and thus will interfere with the bankruptcy proceedings, because for a winding up under bankruptcy it is necessary that the federal court have complete control of all the corporate assets and affairs.[1] As the Supreme Court has said, "the bankruptcy law is paramount, and the jurisdiction of the federal courts in bankruptcy, when properly invoked in the administration of the affairs of insolvent persons and corporations, is essentially exclusive [2]

§ 454. **Test for Determining Conflict of Jurisdictions** Enough has already been said, it is believed, to give a test for determining whether a given State statute is affected by the presence of a national bankrupt act under the rule of Sturges v Crowninshield [3] All modern bankrupt acts allow a discharge to the debtor who has honestly turned his affairs in for distribution, yet it is well settled that a State law looking to the distribution of an insolvent's assets may be affected by the national act, although it contains no provision for the debtor's discharge.[4] On the one hand, it is the prevailing rule that insolvent debtors' acts are not affected by a national bankrupt act if all they do is to allow an insolvent debtor, imprisoned under a writ of capias, to be discharged from further imprisonment under the detaining writ, and under judgments on all other debts which

---

[1] Morehouse v. Giant Powder Co , 206 Fed. 24 , *In re* Watts, 190 U S 1, 23 S Ct 718
[2] *In re* Watts, supra
[3] *Supra*
[4] *Re* Salmon, 143 Fed 395; *Re* Hall Company, 131 Fed 992 , *In re* Reynolds, Fed. Cas 11723

he may then owe, on condition that he surrender his property for statutory distribution among his creditors [1] On the other hand, a statute providing for the general distribution of the assets of an insolvent debtor among his creditors is suspended by the Bankrupt Act [2] And so with respect to the general assignment. As we have seen, it was considered as a fraud upon any bankrupt act, and is an act of bankruptcy entirely irrespective of the debtor's insolvency Yet the Supreme Court's view seems to be that a statute which merely authorizes a general assignment for the benefit of creditors, but does not discharge the insolvent from arrest or imprisonment, or oblige the creditors to come in and prove under it, is not suspended by the Bankrupt Act [3] If, on the other hand, the assignment is made in pursuance of a statute which authorizes a distribution of the property in defiance of the creditors who do not choose to come in under the assignment, so that in effect the assignment is merely a method of getting the property into court for distribution, then the law is suspended by the Bankruptcy Statute [4]

§ 455 **Conflict Relates to Administration** There are apparent inconsistencies in all of this, is reconciliation possible? It is submitted that reconciliation is possible, and that the touchstone may be found in the discussion which has gone before. The national courts are really not concerned with the abstract question whether a State law is suspended. They are concerned only with obtaining freedom for themselves — elbow reach, so to speak — in doing their duty in a particular case arising under the national act. If the bankruptcy jurisdiction of the federal court is invoked in a particular case that court's duty is to take complete control of the insolvent's affairs. So

---

[1] Stockwell v Silloway, 100 Mass 287; 105 Mass. 517; Steelman v Mattix, 36 N. J. Law 344; Jordan v. Hall, 9 R I 218, 222, Berthelon v Betts, 4 Hill 577
[2] *In re* Pickens, 158 Fed. 894; Griswell v Pratt, 9 Metcalf 16.
[3] Mayer v Hellman, 91 U. S 496
[4] Shryock v. Bashore, 13 Nat Bankruptcy Reg 481; Ketcham v. McNamara, 72 Conn 709, 46 Atl 146; Rowe v. Page, 51 N H 190.

far as a State court is handling those affairs under a statute authorizing such a thing, then the federal court has the superior right to the administration and can deprive the State court of it. To that extent the law authorizing the State court to proceed is not pleadable as a bar to the progress of the bankruptcy. A general assignment, as we have seen, was always considered both in this country and in England as a fraud on the bankrupt acts and as void. Hence what difference does it make whether a State law authorizes it or not? The general assignment, under the terms of the Bankruptcy Act, is made an act of bankruptcy provided it occurs within a certain period of time prior to the filing of the bankruptcy petition. Suppose that the petition is not filed until after that period; obviously it is immaterial whether or not the State law authorizing the practice under the general assignment is suspended by the Bankrupt Act, because the transaction did not constitute a fraud upon the statute, nor was it an act of bankruptcy, and the bankruptcy court therefore must leave it alone. That seems to be the effect of Mayer v Hellman [1]. On the other hand, if timely application to the bankruptcy court is made, there can be no doubt that the general assignment may be set aside. If the State law is urged in its support it may be said that the State law is suspended. If there is no State law, but the principles of the common law are invoked, then it may be said that the transaction constituted a fraud upon the Bankrupt Act. The statutes authorizing the discharge of insolvent debtors held in prison under a writ of capias may or may not be suspended by the Bankrupt Act. If, in the particular case, the bankruptcy court has not taken jurisdiction, there is no reason why these laws should be considered as suspended, and this is certainly a better reason than the historical reasons advanced in some of the decisions. It is true that a system of insolvency administration existed side by side with the bankruptcy administration in question — that we have already seen — but a history of insolvency legisla-

[1] *Supra*

tion would not furnish a workable basis of distinction. The answer, it is submitted, in all such cases must depend upon whether or not the bankruptcy court is acting in the particular case.

§ 456 **National Statute Suspends only the Decision of the Particular Case.** In other words, properly considered, a bankrupt act never suspends the State statute, but only the decision of the particular case therein. If the debtor's affairs are brought in for administration under the State law and no creditor invokes the Bankrupt Act, there is no reason why the State court should hesitate. It should proceed with the administration of the assets until the bankruptcy court calls upon it to halt. This view, carefully stated by Vice Chancellor STEVENSON in Singer v National Bedstead Company,[1] seems to meet the difficulties of the situation and the apparent conflict of the authorities. Upon this ground can be based the line of cases which hold that a creditor who has participated in the State court administration is estopped to file a bankruptcy petition,[2] on any other hypothesis these decisions would be untenable. Also it follows that the liquidator appointed by the State court is entitled to his disbursements and all reasonable charges for preserving the debtor's property to the date when the bankruptcy court has gathered the estate into its exclusive custody.[3] The assignee may be considered as the agent of the debtor during this period,[4] that matters little, — but it is only fair that his expenses should be paid. And finally, this reasoning enables us to understand the undoubted rule that upon the repeal of the National Bankrupt Act the State

[1] Singer v National Bedstead Company, 65 N J Eq 290, 55 Atl 868
[2] Simonson v Sinsheimer et al., 95 Fed 948, In re Faithing, 202 Fed. 557, Boese v King, 108 U. S. 379, 2 S. Ct 765, see also In re Salmon, 143 Fed. 395
[3] Randolph v Scruggs, 190 U. S 533, 23 S Ct 710
[4] Whittlesey v Becker etc. Co , 142 N. Y App Div. 313, 126 N Y. S 1046, Cohen v. American Surety Company, 192 N. Y 227, 84 N E 947.

§§ 456-457] SYSTEMS OF JUDICIAL LIQUIDATION.   365

laws-need no re-enactment, but that their full benefits may be obtained on the application of any party having interest in the distribution of the debtor's effects.[1]

§ 457. **Limitations of Bankruptcy Jurisdiction.** The Bankrupt Act does not apply to all classes of debtors. Neither a wage earner, farmer nor tiller of the soil can be adjudged an involuntary bankrupt. Nor can a man be adjudged an involuntary bankrupt if he was insane when he committed the act of bankruptcy.[2] So if the debtor dies prior to adjudication, the proceedings abate.[3] Bankruptcy courts originally had nothing to do with the administration of a decedent's estate, and our present Act likewise abstains.[4] The present English Bankrupt Act allows it[5] and so do the bankrupt acts of some of our States,[6] but that is a modern innovation. With respect to corporations as well the Bankrupt Act has certain limitations. Prior to 1910 it applied only to corporations chiefly engaged in mercantile pursuits; and this led to some remarkable distinctions, the courts holding that neither a waterworks company,[7] a real estate company[8] nor a restaurant

---

[1] Lathrop Foundry *v.* Highland, 128 Mass 128; Torrens *v.* Hammond 10 Fed 900.

[2] *Re* Ward, 161 Fed 755. And even if he was sane when he committed the act, but insane at the time of adjudication, the court's jurisdiction is very doubtful, *Re* Funk 101 Fed 244, *Re* Murphy, Fed Cas 9946, *contra*, *Re* Weitzel, Fed Cas 17365, *Re* Pratt, Fed Cas 11371. Certainly a lunatic may not file a voluntary petition, *Re* Marvin, Fed Cas 9178; *Re* Weitzel, Fed Cas. 17365. *Re* Eisenberg, 117 Fed 786; *Re* Stein, 127 Fed 547.

[3] Sec 8

[4] *Re* Temple, Fed Cas 13825, Briswalter *v* Long 14 Fed 153, *Re* Pierce, 102 Fed 977. The only exceptions were where an executor continues a business pursuant to the will, *Exp* Garland, 10 Vesey 110, *Exp* Richardson, 3 Madd 99, and the estate of a partnership, *Re* Pierce, 102 Fed 977. If one partner dies his survivor can be adjudged bankrupt both individually and as surviving partner, but no assets in the administrator's hands can be touched, *Re* Pierce, 102 Fed. 977.

[5] Sec 125

[6] See Hawkins *v.* Learned, 54 N H 333

[7] *Re* N Y etc Water Co , 98 Fed. 711

[8] *Re* Kingston Realty Co , 160 Fed 445.

company¹ were subject to adjudication. The Act, in other words, was limited to corporations "dealing in merchandise, goods, or chattels that are the subject of commerce." In 1903 the Act was amended so as to include corporations engaged in mining, printing and publishing; but still these subtleties continued until 1910, when Section 4a was drastically amended so as to apply to all corporations except banks, insurance companies and railroads. Yet even this leaves a broad domain untouched by the Bankrupt Act.

Wherever we have such an excepted case we must look to the State law for relief.² When we reach this point we cross the border of a national act of uniform operation

§ 458. **Other Courts' Powers are Territorially Limited** If all of the debtor's property is located within the State where he resides the State law is adequate for the relief of the creditors so far as it goes, subject, of course, to such criticism as it may deserve by reason of its omission to forbid preferential transfers and its deficiency in providing ample powers to the creditors for the examination of their debtor with respect to property which he has concealed or fraudulently transferred³ The federal courts, in respect to their chancery jurisdiction, are subject to the same limitations as State courts. As we have seen,

---

¹ *Re* Wentworth Lunch Co , 191 Fed. 84.

² Sheperdson's Appeal, 36 Conn 23 As stated in an early case, "the legislatures of the several States have competent authority to pass laws for the relief of all persons who are not comprehended within the Act of Congress," Clark *v* Ray, 1 H & J 318, 320, Wilson *v.* State Savings Bank, 56 N H 466

³ The strongest criticism that can be made of the average State insolvency law is its deficiency in providing the same free examination of the debtor and his confederates as is afforded by Section 21a of the Bankrupt Act The average State court is generally loath to give, to such provisions of the State Act as may allow discovery proceedings, the same broad effect that the federal courts have given to the above cited section of the Bankrupt Act. See *In re* Union Bank of Brooklyn, 204 N. Y 313, 97 N E. 737, a case dealing with the discovery section of the new banking law — the decision in which was promptly followed by legislative amendment expressly conferring upon the creditors the rights which the Appellate Court had denied them, New York Laws of 1912, c. 104.

each federal court is bound by the limits of its district, and no district can be more than coterminous with the State to which it is affiliated. Thus, neither the powers of a State court nor the powers of a federal court can extend beyond persons and property located within its jurisdiction, that may be taken as a truism of our American jurisprudence [1]

§ 459 **Average Case Raises Question of Conflict of Laws.** Thus, in the average insolvency case, we are forced into the consideration of a question of conflict of laws, because there are few debtors of the present day whose assets are confined to the State of their residence In the case of the average failure, whether of a corporation or the individual trader, it will be found that much property of the debtor's belonging is located outside of the jurisdiction where his person may be found, and thus immediately the relief which can be afforded in such cases becomes a vital matter of inquiry

§ 460. **Question in Connection with Jurisdiction where Debtor Resides.** Let us start with the jurisdiction of the debtor's residence. If the debtor is a corporation, the courts of its State have jurisdiction to liquidate its affairs by way of dissolution proceedings or a chancery receivership If the debtor is an individual, the courts of his State have jurisdiction to wind up his affairs by means of the local insolvency law of whatever nature it may be. Having put this debtor's affairs in course of administration into the courts of the particular jurisdiction, the creditors must try to reach abroad into other States to gather in the assets located there The choice must then be made between a fresh suit in the foreign State, against the debtor by the creditors, and a suit against the debtor by a representative of creditors who has been appointed in the primary proceedings in the home State

§ 461 **Difficulty of Suing Absent Debtor.** The first alternative involves the search for a statute of the foreign State author-

[1] Pennoyer *v* Neff, 95 U S 714, St. Clair *v* Coxe, 106 U. S. 350, 1 S. Ct 354; see § 21, *supra*

368   THE RIGHTS AND REMEDIES OF CREDITORS.   [CHAP. XXII.

izing suit against an absent defendant. As we have seen,[1] there was no power, according to the weight of authority, in a court of equity to gather in the property of an absent debtor for the benefit of his creditors, or in fact to take any jurisdiction respecting the property. Statutes exist in most States nowadays, authorizing such a procedure, but there are also limiting statutes which sometimes seriously hamper the procedure of the creditors. Thus, in New York the Code [2] forbids an action by a nonresident against a foreign corporation in the courts of the State unless the cause of action arose within the State, and this may very well hamper the right of nonresident creditors to come into New York to reach the property of a nonresident debtor.[3]

§ 462   **Powers of Receiver outside Jurisdiction — Federal Rule.** The easiest course for the creditors, therefore, is to adopt the other alternative, and cause their representative, who has been chosen in the State of the primary proceedings, to go abroad after the assets. When this representative passes the bounds of the jurisdiction of his appointment he can act freely with respect to property which he may find in the other jurisdiction, so far as he is not compelled to invoke the aid of the courts. Thus, if he has already obtained the custody of the property and is about to take it into his own jurisdiction for administration, the courts of the other State are not apt to interfere with his possession thus obtained [4]. But when it is necessary for him to sue in the courts of the foreign State to reach property of the debtor located within that jurisdiction he must face serious obstacles to his suit.

If the representative is a receiver appointed by a court of chancery in the primary jurisdiction he cannot, in sound reason, exercise these powers outside of the jurisdiction of the court

[1] §§ 21-2
[2] Sec. 1780
[3] Trotter v. Lisman, 199 N Y 497, 92 N E 1052
[4] In re Fitch, 160 N. Y 87, 54 N E 701, see High on Receivers, pp 189, 194, 202-3

which appointed him. A court of chancery can confer no title upon a receiver, it can do nothing but protect him in the custody of the property which it has authorized him to seize. Obviously, therefore, when this person goes into another jurisdiction and institutes an action for the recovery of property which belongs to the debtor, he is stopped at the outset of his action by the charge that no court in that jurisdiction has authorized him to take the property, nor is the plaintiff helped by any decree of his home court which appointed him as receiver and authorized the suit in question, because that decree cannot run beyond the limits of the jurisdiction of the court which rendered it. Carrying this doctrine to its logical extreme, the Supreme Court has held that a chancery receiver, whether appointed by the State court or a federal court, cannot sue for the recovery of property of the debtor outside of the jurisdiction of the court which appointed him.[1]

§ 463. **Powers of Receiver outside Jurisdiction — Conflict among State Courts.** On this subject the State courts are in conflict. As the Supreme Court says,[2] we find with these courts "numerous and conflicting decisions as to the rights of a receiver to sue in a foreign jurisdiction upon the practice of comity." Thus, in New York and New Jersey this right is accorded the foreign receiver,[3] while in other States this right is denied him. In New York it has been held that a foreign receiver is amenable to service of process and suit in this State

---

[1] Booth v. Clark, 17 How. 338; Great Western Mining Co. v. Harris, 198 U. S. 561, 25 S. Ct. 770. Of course if the debtor transfers the title of all of his assets to the receiver the latter can then sue in another jurisdiction, but he then has the right to sue not because of his being receiver, but because of the transfer, Hawkins v. Glenn, 131 U. S. 319, 9 S. Ct. 739. It has recently been held that a receiver who obtains a judgment against the debtor may sue upon that judgment in a foreign jurisdiction because then his claim is as a judgment creditor and not as receiver, McBride v. Oriental Bank, 200 Fed. 895, Trotter v. Lisman, 209 N. Y. 174, 102 N. E. 575.

[2] Great Western Mining Company v. Harris, *supra*.

[3] Howarth v. Angle, 39 N. Y. App. Div. 151, 57 N. Y. S. 187, 162 N. Y. 179, 56 N. E. 489; Hurd v. Elizabeth, 41 N. J. Law 1.

For instance, a creditor residing in New York can sue a foreign receiver for a judgment establishing the creditor's right against the assets in his custody, although in the event of his success he necessarily must enforce his judgment in accordance with the laws of the State of the receiver's appointment [1] It also seems to be established that such jurisdiction can be obtained by serving the managing agent of the debtor corporation if the foreign receiver has, under the orders of the court of his appointment, continued the business of the corporation within the State where the service is effected [2]

§ 464 **Powers of Statutory Receiver outside Jurisdiction.** Quite a different status is that of a receiver who owes his powers to some statute as distinct from the mere equity powers of the court. If the receiver is appointed by virtue of a statute which vests in him the property of the debtor, in other words is a statutory representative of the creditors in the same way as is a trustee in bankruptcy, then there is no question of comity in the matter. The courts of the different jurisdictions must recognize the officer, and he is entitled to sue in any jurisdiction for the recaption of assets belonging to the estate, because in effect the State of his appointment has legislated the title to the assets into this representative, and the Constitution requires that full faith and credit be given to this statute by the courts of every other State.[3]

§ 465 **Priority of Local Judgments** But in connection with either class of liquidator, whether chancery receiver or statutory liquidator, a rule of priority applies which no constitutional doctrine can overcome. In some States, as we have seen, a chancery receiver is allowed to institute recaption proceedings. In all States a statutory receiver may do so,

---

[1] LeFevre v Matthews, 39 N. Y. App Div 232, 57 N. Y S 128; Pruyn v McCreary, 105 N Y App Div 302, 93 N Y S 995.

[2] Jacobs v Blair, 157 N Y App Div 601, 142 N Y S 897, Ernest v. Pere Marquette Railroad Co , 176 Mich 398, 142 N. W 567

[3] Relfe v Rundle, 103 U S 222, Bernheimer v Converse, 206 U S. 516, 27 S Ct. 755

§§ 464-465] SYSTEMS OF JUDICIAL LIQUIDATION. 371

but until he actually gets within his custody the property in question by using the processes of the foreign jurisdiction, it is well settled that intervening attachments and judicial liens upon the property, obtained by diligent local creditors, take priority.[1] The only difference of opinion which has arisen in this connection occurs in the case where such a priority is obtained, not by a resident of a particular State, but by one who himself is a foreigner. In some States it is held that a foreign creditor will not be allowed priority if he is a resident of the same State in which the primary proceedings are instituted, because he should be bound by the law of the domicile which was common to him as well as to the creditors who obtained the original receivership.[2] In other States no such distinction is recognized.[3] "We have refused," says the New York court,[4] "to adopt the distinction made in some of the States, and have placed the right of a creditor coming here from the State of the common domicile upon the same footing as that of a citizen or resident creditor, and have sustained the lien of an attachment issued here at the instance of a foreign creditor after proceedings in insolvency had been instituted in the State of the common domicile of the insolvent and creditor."[5] This discrimination is subject to no check by the federal Constitution. Undoubtedly a State cannot in its insolvency statutes provide for preferring domestic over foreign creditors,[6] but when it comes to a question of self-help such as is afforded

---

[1] People v. Granite Association, 161 N. Y. 492, 55 N. E. 1053; Barth v. Backus, 140 N. Y. 230, 35 N. E. 425; Faulkner v. Hyman, 142 Mass. 53, 6 N. E. 846.
[2] May v. Wannamaker, 111 Mass 202; Moore v. Bonnell, 31 N. J. Law 90; Sanderson v. Bradford, 10 N. H. 260.
[3] Hibernia National Bank v. Lacombe, 84 N. Y. 367; Barth v. Backus, 140 N. Y. 230, 35 N. E. 425.
[4] Barth v. Backus, supra.
[5] To the same effect are McClure v. Campbell, 71 Wisc. 350, 37 N. W. 343; Rhawn v. Pierce, 110 Ill. 350; Boston Iron Works v. Boston Locomotive Works, 51 Me. 585; Upton v. Hubbard, 28 Conn. 274.
[6] Blake v. McClung, 172 U. S. 239, 19 S. Ct. 165, 176 U. S. 59, 20 S. Ct. 307.

by the situation above discussed, there is no basis on which the federal courts could say that any unconstitutional discrimination was practised If they were to undertake that, they would also have to attack the whole common law system under which the "race of diligence" among creditors is sanctioned wherever a statute is not at hand to stop it.

§ 466. **Ancillary Receivers.** The only way to prevent such difficulties is to stop the race of diligence by the use of the same methods that we have already examined, namely, by putting the property into the custody of the local chancery court by means of proceedings ancillary to the proceedings of the primary jurisdiction. Ancillary letters of administration are a commonplace thing for the aid of executors or administrators of a decedent who has died with assets in another jurisdiction than that in which the primary letters have been issued upon his estate [1] The difficulties which have been already outlined in the case of other representatives of creditors have led to a similar practice being adopted by both the State and federal courts in aid of any representative of creditors, whether he be a chancery receiver or a statutory receiver An ancillary suit may be instituted in the courts of any jurisdiction where property of the debtor may be found, and the local court of equity on such application will take the debtor's local property into its own custody by the appointment of its own receiver. This jurisdiction is freely exercised by State courts in aid of proceedings pending in the courts of other States or in the federal courts of other States [2] In like manner

[1] The situation is the same with a foreign executor as with the committee of a lunatic If the decedent or incompetent has property within the jurisdiction, the courts should issue ancillary letters of administration, Hoes v N Y etc R. R , 173 N. Y 435, 66 N. E 119, Evans v Schoonmaker, 2 Dem Sur. Rep N Y 219, or appoint an ancillary committee, as the case may be, *In re* Fowler, 2 Barb Ch. 305. In any such case the court will act promptly at the behest of creditors, *Re* Fowler, *supra*; *Re* Gennert, 96 N Y App Div 8, 89 N Y S 37.

[2] Trust Co v. Miller, 33 N J Eq 155, Buswell v Supreme Sitting, 161 Mass 224, 36 N E. 1065; Baldwin v. Hosmer, 101 Mich. 119, 59 N W 432.

the local federal courts of any State where the debtor's property is located will exercise this equitable jurisdiction in aid of proceedings pending in State courts of other States, or in federal courts of other States.[1] Of course this ancillary jurisdiction will not divest the priority of local judgments which we have discussed in Section 465. Ancillary receivers will be instructed to respect the priority of such judgments in the disposition of property in their custody,[2] but on the other hand the ancillary court should be prompt to exercise jurisdiction in order to prevent such judgments from being obtained, and priority thus secured by local creditors.[3]

§ 467. **Nature of Ancillary Suit** Such a suit must be pleaded upon the same cause of action as is stated in the original jurisdiction. It is not a suit for the appointment of a receiver, but a suit for a winding up in the same way as the original suit was, and the appointment of the local receiver is asked for merely as an interim measure. In other words, the presence of the assets within the foreign State justifies the plaintiff in the original suit going into the foreign State and there instituting a plenary and coterminous suit. Thus an ancillary receiver should be appointed only in a plenary suit instituted by bill of complaint, as distinct from an informal proceeding instituted by way of petition,[4] for an ancillary order made in the latter way is void and open to collateral attack.[5] In the ancillary bill the court must be just as fully informed of the cause of action as was the original court,[6] and the only person who can bring the action is the original plaintiff. The foreign receiver naturally cannot bring an action for the appointment of an ancillary receiver because he is not the real party in interest

---

[1] Sands v. Greeley, 88 Fed 130
[2] Patterson v. Lind, 112 Ill 207; Taylor v. Insurance Co., 96 Mass 353; Willitts v Waite, 25 N Y 577.
[3] Sands v. Greeley, *supra*
[4] Mercantile Trust Co v Kanawha Ry Co, 39 Fed 337.
[5] Fairview etc Co v Ulrich, 192 Fed 894
[6] Bluefields S S Co v Steele, 184 Fed 584.

374   THE RIGHTS AND REMEDIES OF CREDITORS.   [CHAP XXII.

for such a purpose, nor, as we have seen, has he the proper standing for a suit outside of his own jurisdiction.[1]

§ 468. **Duties of Ancillary Receiver**   When the ancillary receiver is appointed he works under the direction of his court, with respect to property located within its jurisdiction, just as if it were an original court; and uses his court for the collection of assets within the jurisdiction just as the original receiver uses his.[2]   He must also account to his court just as an original receiver accounts to his own, and not to any other court [3]

§ 469. **Powers of Ancillary Court.**   It has been held that the ancillary court has jurisdiction to establish the status of a person as a creditor,[4] although of course the ancillary court finally turns over the assets to the court of primary jurisdiction, which determines the status of the creditors and the method of distribution   And the ancillary court will not hear a motion to vacate the receivership on grounds which more properly should be urged to the court which appointed the original receiver [5]

§ 470   **Jurisdiction of Federal Courts.**   The federal courts have carried this doctrine of ancillary receivership to the point that, although in ordinary chancery matters they cannot take jurisdiction unless the plaintiff is a citizen and resident of a State different from that of the defendant, nevertheless a federal court may entertain an ancillary bill although the diversity of citizenship does not exist on the record thus constituted   If the proper requisites exist for the jurisdiction of the primary

---

[1] Mahon v. Ongley Elec Co , 156 N Y 196, 50 N. E 805   This distinction is well brought out by PUTNAM, J , in Conkling v U. S Ship Bldg Co , 123 Fed 913 , McGraw v Mott, 179 Fed. 646
[2] Brown v. Allebach, 156 Fed 697 ; Gunby v. Armstrong, 133 Fed 417
[3] Loeser v Dallas, 192 Fed 909
[4] Pfahler v. McCrum, 197 Fed. 684
[5] Re Hayes, 192 Fed. 1018   As a matter of fact the practice is generally to appoint the same person as receiver, 3 Street, "Federal Equity Practice," Sec. 2697 , McGraw v Mott, 179 Fed. 64. In the Second Circuit the practice is to add a local co-receiver, and to require the foreign receiver to give a bond conditioned, among other things, upon his coming within the jurisdiction at any time the court may order, Lotte v American Silk Co., 159 Fed 499.

federal court, then the jurisdiction of the ancillary court is founded on the jurisdiction of the first, and hence diversity of citizenship is not necessary for the second court.[1]

§ 471 **Dependent Jurisdiction of Federal Courts** This ancillary jurisdiction must not be confounded with the dependent jurisdiction which is also exercised by the federal courts in cases of chancery liquidation It is a well-settled rule of comity, as between the federal and the State courts, that the court which has acquired jurisdiction of a fund by means of a receivership has the exclusive right to administer it [2] If, then, a federal court has thus acquired jurisdiction over a fund, a dependent jurisdiction is of necessity entailed upon it concerning all questions of the disposition of the estate [3] The only limit on this doctrine is the statute [4] which allows any one to sue a federal receiver without previous leave of the court. The Supreme Court construed this statute as authorizing such a suit to be brought in the State court,[5] but the statute applies only to acts done by the receiver while in possession of the debtor's property. For acts of his predecessor in title, whether it be the debtor or a prior receiver, the old rule applies that the receiver cannot be sued without leave of the federal court, and the latter, in giving permission, can prescribe that such a suit can be brought in its own court [6] And any judgments obtained against the receiver are still within the control of the federal court to the extent that that court has the right to determine the manner and time of their payment.[7]

[1] Gableman v. Peoria etc Ry , 179 U. S 335, 21 S Ct. 171 ; Bluefields Co v Steele, *supra*.
[2] Stirling v Seattle &c Ry Co., 198 Fed 913 , Virginia Iron etc Co v Alcott, 197 Fed 733
[3] White v Ewing, 159 U. S 36, 15 S Ct 1018 , Porter v Sabin, 149 U S. 473, 13 S Ct 1008 ; Compton v Golden Cycle Co., 141 Fed. 610 , Compton v Jesup, 68 Fed 263
[4] Acts of 1887 and 1888, 24 St at L c 373, p 552 ; 25 St. at L c. 866, p 433 (Now comprised in Judicial Code of 1911, § 66)
[5] Gableman v Peoria etc Ry , 179 U S 335, 21 S. Ct. 171.
[6] Bottom v National Ry Building etc. Assn , 123 Fed 744 , Love v. Railway Co , 178 Fed. 507 , Holmes v Dowie, 177 Fed 182 , Rice v Durham Water Co , 91 Fed 432   [7] Wilcox v Jones, 177 Fed. 870

CHAPTER XXIII

EXPENSES OF ADMINISTRATION

§ 472 Government does not Meet All the Expenses
473 Expenses not Taxable as Costs
474. Expenses are Chargeable against the Estate.
475 Services of Counsel
476 Expenses of Administration as a Primary Charge.
477 Method of Estimating these Charges
478 Allowances to Counsel other than Those Employed by the Liquidator
479 Requisites for Allowance to Counsel.
480 Continuance of Business by Liquidator
481 Necessity of Receiver Borrowing Money to Continue Business
§ 482. Cannot Displace Vested Lien without Holder's Consent
483. Liquidator's Pledge as against Rights of General Creditors Rule in Bankruptcy
484. In the Absence of Statute
485. Rule in the Case of Railroad Companies
486. This Rule should Apply to All Public Service Companies
487. Receiver's Certificates
488 Deficiency in Operation of Public Service Company.

§ 472 **Government does not Meet All the Expenses.** The liquidation of a debtor's estate is not free of expense As we have seen, there necessarily must be a liquidating officer of some sort, and, in addition, generally the case requires the services of officials in the shape of masters or the like. These persons are specially appointed for the particular cases in which they are to act The system prevailing in the State and federal courts allows no governmental salaries to any such special official, and he, whether he is the master or referee who passes upon the validity of claims in the distribution, the distributing officer, or the auctioneer who is usually employed by the master to conduct the sale of such real property as the debtor may have, must be paid for his services from some source other than government funds

§ 473 **Expenses not Taxable as Costs.** Necessarily the common law, even as it knew no way of effecting equality of distribution, was ignorant of any method by which such expenses could be met. It is obvious that these expenses are not taxable as costs against any party to the litigation, whether he be the creditor who instituted the proceedings, or the creditors who proved their claims therein. Indeed, costs even in litigation *inter partes* were unknown at common law, and it required several ancient statutes, the first of which was the Statute of Gloucester, to authorize the imposition of costs as a penalty which the unsuccessful party to litigation must pay.[1] This system of costs was adopted by the Court of Chancery to cover ordinary litigation therein, the court, however, reserving a discretionary power with regard to taxing costs in each case, instead of following the strict rule of the common law that the unsuccessful party must pay his adversary's costs. But expenses of administration are not taxable as costs, because they do not fall within the terms of any statute authorizing costs; and therefore, if they are to be allowed, it must be by virtue of some other principle than is expressed in the statute.[2]

§ 474 **Expenses are Chargeable against the Estate.** The principle on which the court acts in allowing the expenses of administration rests on an entirely different idea from that which instigated the statutory system of taxable costs. The rule of costs is founded altogether on the idea of punishment. The party who pays them gets no *quid pro quo*, and is a loser by the transaction, however just it is that he should pay them. The allowance of expenses rests on the opposite idea that he who receives a benefit, through the court but at the hands of another, should meet his share of the attendant expense. A

---

[1] See 3 Blackstone, "Commentaries," 399; Lehigh Valley R. R. v McFarland, 44 N J Law 674.
[2] Equitable Life Assur Co v Hughes, 125 N Y. 106, 26 N E. 1; Stevens v. Centr. Bank, 168 N Y 560, 566, 61 N. E 904; Louisville Co v Smith, 154 N Y App Div. 386, 139 N. Y S 357; Lee Co v Penberthy Co, 109 Fed 964.

378 THE RIGHTS AND REMEDIES OF CREDITORS. [CHAP. XXIII.

striking instance of this is to be seen in Cornell v. Nicholls Co.[1] There it was held that where an estate had no money, but certain creditors contributed the necessary funds for the receiver to prosecute a suit in behalf of the estate, only those who had thus contributed could share in the property recovered by means of the suit It follows that the expense of administering the estate should be met from the funds which constituted the estate That is the only fair way of meeting the difficulty, and it is the way which the chancery courts have followed from an early date. In the language of the Supreme Court [2] " a trust estate must bear the expenses of its administration."

§ 475. **Services of Counsel.** Among these expenses are included what are commonly known as allowances to counsel. In many cases it is necessary for the liquidator to avail himself of the services of learned counsel, either to advise upon the legal aspects of the different problems that present themselves in the course of administration, or to prosecute or defend litigation affecting the estate. These disbursements the liquidator is entitled to charge upon the estate. Of course, wherever he can lawfully compel other persons to pay them, as where in litigation against a third party he is successful and can tax his costs at common law, the estate in his hands should be relieved *pro tanto*, but, in so far as he is unable to collect costs from the third party, the liquidator is entitled to indemnity from the estate in his hands [3] Likewise, if any attempt is made to remove the liquidator, he is entitled, upon successfully showing that the application is ill founded, to indemnity from the estate for the legal expenses which he thus incurred [4]

§ 476 **Expenses of Administration as a Primary Charge.** For the reasons already given, these expenses of administration are primary charges upon the estate, and must be paid in full before the creditors are entitled to receive anything by way

---

[1] 201 Fed 320. [2] Trustees v Greenough, 105 U. S 527.
[3] Conrad v. Hamner, 9 Beav 3
[4] Cowdrey v Galveston etc. R R. Co., 1 Woods 331, Fed Case 3293.

of distribution.¹ If the estate is insufficient to meet these charges, who should pay the difference? The answer seems clear. The party who brought about the situation should pay for what he caused. The original plaintiff is bound to pay these charges in the same way that he is bound to pay the statutory court charges in the shape of filing fees, and hence is personally liable to the receiver and other court officials for their services and disbursements in connection with their work upon the estate.²

§ 477. **Method of Estimating these Charges.** With regard to disbursements made or incurred by the liquidator, the only question for the court's determination is whether the liquidator's expenses were reasonable, having in view his primary duty of speedily bringing the estate to a close. Having ascertained the out-of-pocket expenses in the matter, the court's next duty is to fix the compensation of the various nonsalaried officials who have served in the administration of the estate. Some jurisdictions have statutes which are applicable in this regard. The National Bankrupt Act fixes the compensation of receivers, trustees and referees on a scale of percentages regulated by the size of the estates in their charge,³ and in New York the compensation of a receiver appointed in dissolution proceedings, and the compensation of a general assignee, are likewise fixed on a commission basis.⁴ In other States a similar percentage system is followed by the courts, although no statute authorizes it.⁵ In New York, also, the compensation of counsel representing the receiver appointed in corporate dissolution proceedings is regulated by statute,⁶ but this law is by no

¹ Buell v. Kanawha etc Co., 201 Fed. 762; Gallagher v. Gingrich, 105 Iowa 237, 74 N. W. 763.
² McIntosh v. Ward, 159 Fed 66, see High, "Receivers," 4th ed., p. 963, and following.
³ National Bankrupt Act of 1898, Secs 41 48.
⁴ New York General Corporation Law, Secs 277, 278; Debtor and Creditor Law, Sec 26.
⁵ See High, "Receivers," 4th ed., Sec 785.
⁶ General Corporation Law, Sec 242.

means a uniform model among the States. In all cases where a statute does not prescribe the compensation of any such official, it is the court's duty to award him such compensation as the court deems adequate, having in mind the nature of the services rendered and the size of the estate [1] But whether a statute governs the court in regard to the award of compensation or not, it is clear that the official who is to be rewarded has no right or assignable interest in the estate. His rights are fixed when an order is made directing the payment of the compensation to him, and not until then.[2]

§ 478 **Allowances to Counsel other than Those employed by the Liquidator** The court also may properly impress upon the estate the reasonable fees of any counsel who, although nominally acting for another client has through his services succeeded in either (1) bringing the estate into the court, (2) augmenting it, or (3) preserving or defending it. The doctrine which governs this practice is of ancient origin. As stated by the Supreme Court [3] it amounts to this, that "where one of many parties having a common interest in a trust fund, at his own expense takes proper proceedings to save it from destruction and to restore it to the purposes of the trust, he is entitled to reimbursement, either out of the fund itself, or by proportionate contribution from those who accept the benefit of his efforts" The origin of this rule, as the Supreme Court points out, lay in the ancient practice of the Court of Chancery in cases involving a charitable use, where the court was wont to allow to the relator, upon whose information the Attorney-General filed the bill to have the charity administered, a bill of costs "as between solicitor and client," that is, a bill of costs allowing the fees of counsel and all expenses in addition

---

[1] For an illustrative case see opinion of Holt, J , in *In re* Sully, 133 Fed. 997
[2] Haigh *v* Grattan, 1 Beav 201, *Re* Worthington, 141 N. Y. 9, 35 N E 929; Colonial Bank *v.* Sutton, 79 N. Y Misc 244, 139 N Y. S 1002
[3] Trustees *v* Greenough, *supra*

to ordinary taxable disbursements [1] The English Chancery
applied the same rule to administration suits on creditors' bill,
allowing to the plaintiff, who filed the original bill which resulted in the estate being brought into court for administration,
reimbursement from the estate for all of his counsel fees and
expenses In the words of Knight Bruce, V. C , the other
creditors should contribute to this expense by allowing it to
be taken from the estate, because " they having come in and
proved, and obtained the benefit of the suit which was instituted
on their behalf, as well as that of the plaintiff, it cannot be just
that in such a suit — a suit instituted for the benefit of all
creditors — one alone should bear the burden, when others
have the benefit." [2] The same doctrine was applied in bankruptcy, an allowance being made to the creditors who filed the
bankruptcy petition which resulted in the adjudication [3] This
rather difficult subject of so-called allowances often shows
itself in different phases, but the basic principle is always the
same

§ 479. **Requisites for Allowance to Counsel** In the first
place the estate must be properly in court. Not only must
the court have jurisdiction to administer the estate, but the
reason for its being in court must appear Hence, if it develops
in administration under a creditors' bill that the corporation
defendant was solvent, and that there was really no necessity
for the proceeding having been brought, then there is no reason
for giving the plaintiff an allowance for his counsel fees in bringing the fund into court. The debtor, being solvent, should be
turned out of court with his estate, and the distributing court

---

[1] Attorney-General v Brewers Co , 1 P Wms 376, Attorney-General
v. Old South Society, 13 Allen 474 "Of course, it is well understood
that costs as between solicitor and client include all reasonable expenses
and counsel fees, and are not like costs as between party and party,
confined to the taxed costs allowed by the fee bill " — Trustees v Greenough, *supra*
[2] Thompson v Cooper, 2 Collver 87
[3] Worrall v Harford, 8 Ves Jr 4; *In re* Williams, 2 Natl Bank
Reg 28; see Trustees v. Greenough, *supra*

should leave the matter alone, in short, it should not allow administration expenses out of a fund which does not need administration.¹ Secondly, the question must be asked whether the counsel was working for the benefit of his primary client in opposition to the interests of the estate, or was working in the interests of the estate, his primary client's interest being identical therewith. The test would be, therefore, whether the estate was preserved or augmented through the efforts of counsel, or whether the estate really benefited nothing by the services of the counsel.² As stated by the Michigan court, if the services " were adverse rather than beneficial to the trust fund . . they are not justly chargeable to that fund." ³

§ 480 Continuance of Business by Liquidator So far we have spoken of the expenses attendant strictly upon liquidation. The complexities of modern business conditions, however, often require that expenses be incurred, which from one standpoint are expenses of liquidation but in another sense may bear a more doubtful character. In the ordinary case of liquidation the receiver finds simply a lot of property which requires no daily expenditures, except the expenses necessary for maintenance, until it can be turned into money by means of judicial sale. But the debtor's principal asset may very well consist of a going business, whose value as a whole is more intimately connected with the continued operation of the business than the valuations of the physical properties used in its operation. From a business point of view, in a case of that sort it is essential that, pending the day when the assets can be turned into money by means of a judicial sale, there be preserved, not merely certain physical properties, but that intangible thing which

---

[1] Huff v. Bidwell, 195 Fed 430: Stanton v Hatfield, 1 Keene 358, Germania etc Co v Virginia etc Co., 108 Va. 393, 61 S E 870

[2] Wead v. Central of Georgia Ry Co., 100 Fed. 62, Matter of the Attorney-General, 91 N Y 57, Savage v Sherman, 87 N. Y. 277, Sprague v Moore, 136 Mich 426, 99 N W. 377, Campau v. Detroit Driving Club, 144 Mich 80, 107 N. W 1063.

[3] Sprague v. Moore, supra

connects them in a system, namely, the business in which these physical properties find their use

§ 481. **Necessity of Receiver Borrowing Money to Continue Business.** To continue the business would require daily expenditures on the part of the liquidator, which perhaps the income from the business might suffice to meet. But it often happens that the reason why the debtor's affairs have passed into the hands of the court is that while his business is good he has insufficient working capital, and therefore, if his business is to be continued, it is necessary to borrow additional capital. In such a case, if the receiver is to continue the business it will be necessary for him to borrow, and he cannot borrow without security. Hence the problem in such cases is whether the court can authorize the receiver to borrow money, giving as security either such of the estate as may not be covered by existing liens, or such portion of the estate as may be covered by existing liens, under an agreement that the lender shall have a lien prior to all secured creditors.

§ 482. **Cannot Displace Vested Lien without Holder's Consent.** Taking the latter proposition first, it is apparent that no court can hypothecate property which is covered by an existing lien, in such manner that the lien of the new lender shall be superior to that of an outstanding mortgage, unless the holder of that mortgage should consent. Nor has any bankrupt statute ever undertaken to authorize such a confiscation of property. The bankruptcy court cannot authorize the trustee to hypothecate property to secure a loan for the continuance of business, unless such hypothecation be made subject to existing liens, or the holders of those liens consent to the hypothecation and agree to subordinate their security to that of the new lender.[1] Of course this prior lender may consent to a subordination of this kind; it may be to his interest to do so,[2] and his consent

---

[1] *Re* Clark etc Company, 173 Fed 652.
[2] Where the mortgage secures an issue of bonds, the mortgage proper being held by the trustee for the benefit of the holders of the bonds,

may be implied as if he institutes a foreclosure proceeding and expressly requests such subordination in his bill, or submits an order authorizing the continuance of the insolvent's business.[1]

§ 483. **Liquidator's Pledge as against Rights of General Creditors Rule in Bankruptcy.** The next question deals with the power of the court to authorize its liquidator to borrow money upon the pledge of general assets Such a lien of course would rank ahead of the claims of the general creditors, and the extent to which the court can go in authorizing it is an important consideration The present Bankrupt Act affords no difficulty in cases of administration under its provisions, because it expressly empowers the federal courts sitting in bankruptcy to "authorize the business of bankrupts to be continued for limited periods by receivers, marshals or trustees, if necessary for the best interests of the estates"[2] Of necessity this empowers the court, in a proper case, to authorize the trustee or receiver to borrow money for necessary working capital[3] Nevertheless, the court's action should not savor of paternalism, and therefore it should not authorize such a course without a hearing at which the creditors should have an opportunity to express their views, and then only if a majority of the creditors are in favor of the proposition[4]

§ 484 **In the Absence of Statute** In the absence of statutory sanction such as is afforded by the Bankrupt Act, the question is more difficult. If all of the creditors consent, the court should have no trouble in directing the receiver to continue the business and to incur the necessary debts for that purpose But if the creditors should differ as to the advisability of such a course, then the court must look to its own powers in the mat-

the trustee has power to consent to a subordination of the lien in behalf of all the holders of bonds issued under the mortgage, Kent v Lake Superior etc Co, 144 U S 75, 12 S Ct 650.

[1] St Louis etc Ry Co v Holbrook, 73 Fed. 112, Davenport v. Alabama etc Ry., 2 Woods 519, Fed Case No 3588.

[2] Bankruptcy Act of 1898, Sec 2

[3] Re Restein. 162 Fed 986

[4] In re Burlein Cornice etc Co., 133 Fed. 958.

ter. Undoubtedly it should obtain the views of the creditors,[1] but in the end, unless practical unanimity against such a course appears on the part of the creditors, the court is compelled to inquire into its own powers in considering whether such a course be adopted. What are its powers in this regard?

§ 485. **Rule in the Case of Railroad Companies** In the case of railroads, the Supreme Court at an early date pronounced in favor of the court's inherent power to impose such a charge upon the estate. The court may authorize the receiver to continue the transportation business which the debtor corporation had conducted, and if necessary to borrow money for that purpose, making the debt thus constituted a prior lien upon the physical properties of the company, ranking even ahead of such mortgages as may be outstanding The reasons for that doctrine were stated as twofold. In the first place a railroad is a peculiar species of property, for " not only will structures deteriorate and decay and perish if not cared for and kept up, but its business and good will will pass away if it is not run and kept in good order " This reasoning, however, would apply to the case of the average manufacturing or trading concern, and is not peculiar to the transportation business The court, however, also assigns as a reason what is really the fundamental point of distinction, that a railroad is a matter of public concern, since " the franchises and rights of the corporation which constructed it were given not merely for private gain to the corporators, but to furnish a public highway, and all persons who deal with the corporation as creditors or holders of its obligations, must necessarily be held to do so in the view that, if it falls into insolvency and its affairs come into a court of equity for adjustment, involving the transfer of its franchises and property by a sale into other hands, to have the purposes of its creation still carried out, the court, while in charge of the property, has the power, and under some circumstances it

[1] See Union Trust Company v. Illinois Midland Company, 117 U S 434, 6 S Ct 809

386   THE RIGHTS AND REMEDIES OF CREDITORS.   [CHAP. XXIII.

may be its duty, to make such repairs as are necessary to keep the road and its structures in a safe and proper condition to serve the public"[1] The doctrine announced in this case has been so frequently applied in subsequent cases as to become a matter of axiom. It is always recognized that in the liquidation of a railway corporation, the power to continue the business of the corporation, and borrow the money which is necessary therefor, is vested in the court as a matter of course. To quote the language of Mr. Justice BREWER in a later case, "If at the instance of any party rightfully entitled thereto, a court should appoint a receiver of property, the same being railroad property, and therefore under an obligation to the public of continued operation, in the administration of such receivership, the receiver might rightfully contract debts necessary for the operation of the road, either for labor, supplies or rental, and make such expense a prior lien on the property itself."[2]

§ 486. This Rule should Apply to All Public Service Companies. To confine this doctrine to the case of a railroad corporation would not savor of sound logic, for the distinction of necessity must be upon broader lines than that. The Texas court would seem to be rightly advised when it applied the same rule to a waterworks company;[3] and the Supreme Court, in a comparatively late declaration, inclines to a broader classification than its earlier decisions outline[4] The rule should include every public service company whose franchise has a value in excess of the value of its physical properties, but is

[1] Union Trust Company v Illinois Midland Company, *supra*.
[2] Kneeland v American Loan etc Co, 136 U. S. 89, 10 S. Ct. 950; see also Pennsylvania Steel Co v New York City Ry. Co., 198 Fed. 721
[3] Ellis v Vernon etc Light & Water Co, 86 Tex 109
[4] Atlantic Trust Company v Chapman, 208 U. S 360, 28 S. Ct. 406, where the court after quoting the language used in Farmers' Loan Company v Oregon etc Ry. Company, 31 Ore 237, 48 Pac. 706, says "That it is true, was the case of the railroad receivership, but what is said is equally applicable to other quasi-public corporations having public duties to perform, as in the case of water and irrigation companies."

subject to forfeiture if the business of the company is discontinued. In any such case the continued business of the company is the major asset in the hands of the court, rather than the properties which are used in its operation. With a corporation whose business is not founded upon such a franchise the situation is entirely different There is no doubt that the court cannot authorize continuance of the business of a corporation which cannot be classed as a public service company, unless all of the creditors consent, the opposition of any creditor is fatal to the proposition [1] That sort of company is under no public obligation to continue its business, and whether its business should be continued is a matter for the unanimous decision of its creditors. After all is said and done, in the case of either a public service company or a private corporation, the primary end of the court's activities is to liquidate. A public service corporation cannot be liquidated without the continuance of its business, because of the ties upon the franchises which constitute the principal asset But with a private corporation there are no such ties, and there is no public service franchise as the bed rock of its business structure While in the case of a public service corporation the continuance of the business is necessarily an integral feature of the liquidation, that is not the case with a private company. Under the present Bankrupt Act, in view of its provisions which we have noted above, no such distinction is possible between public service and other corporations; [2] but in the absence of statute, there can be no doubt that such is the distinction that all courts must perforce observe.

§ 487. **Receiver's Certificates.** It remains to say a word about a method of borrowing the necessary funds which has

---

[1] Farmers' Loan & Trust Company *v.* Grape Creek Coal Company, 50 Fed 481. Raht *v* Attrill, 106 N. Y 423, 13 N E 282; Hooper *v* Central Trust Company, 81 Md. 559, 32 Atl 505, International Trust Company *v* United Coal Company, 27 Colo 246, 60 Pac 621, High, " Receivers," 4th ed , p 378 n.

[2] *In re* Erie Lumber Co 150 Fed 817.

become sanctioned by long use We refer to the system of "receiver's certificates." In a case where it is lawful for the liquidator to borrow money, and the loan is to be of any considerable amount, it is easier to finance such a loan by dividing it into integral parts than to have it represented by one instrument of obligation Consequently, it is customary for the court to order that the receiver issue his certificates in the shape of promissory notes, which shall constitute a first lien upon the estate Such instruments must be discharged, together with the other expenses of operation, at or before the time of distribution. These certificates, although negotiable in form, on their face put the purchaser on inquiry as to the receiver's authority to issue and charge them as a lien upon the estate. The purchaser, therefore, should advise himself as to the terms of the order authorizing the issuance of the certificates, and, whether or not he does so advise himself, he is nevertheless bound by the terms of the order It is in that connection that the Supreme Court describes these certificates as not being negotiable instruments, because, as the court says, "its records are accessible to lenders and subsequent holders."[1] In short, the receiver's certificate is negotiable in the sense that it may well be made payable to bearer, or transferable to order, like a promissory note; but it is not negotiable in the sense that any purchaser may assert innocence of the limitations imposed by the order authorizing their issuance[2]

§ 488. **Deficiency in Operation of Public Service Company.** If the expenses thus incurred by the receiver in the operation of a public service company pass the point where the estate is able to defray them, should the parties who brought the suit into court bear the deficiency? That was the proposition in Atlantic Trust Company *v.* Chapman.[3] There a bill was filed

---

[1] Union Trust Company *v* Illinois Midland Co , *supra*, *In re* Burkhalter, 182 Fed 353
[2] Stanton *v* Ala etc Ry Co , 2 Woods 506, Fed. Case No. 132966, Bernard *v* Union Trust Co , 159 Fed 620
[3] *Supra.*

to foreclose a mortgage upon the properties and franchises of a public service company. The lower court from time to time authorized expenses of operation, which finally exceeded the amount realized by the sale of the property under the foreclosure decree. The Circuit Court of Appeals held that the plaintiff who had instituted the foreclosure action was personally liable to the receiver for reimbursement of the deficit thus resulting [1] But the Supreme Court reversed this decree, giving as its reason that because a public service company's franchises require continued operation of the corporate business, even though its assets are in course of liquidation, it follows that the party whose bill brings the fund into court for administration is not responsible for the expenses incurred in operation after his bill is filed.[2] Thus far the Supreme Court is in accord with the views of the courts of Oregon which it expressly adopted,[3] but the Supreme Court added the suggestion that in a case where the expenses of operation were likely to exceed the value realizable from the property on liquidation sale, the court might consistently require the plaintiff, as a condition to the appointment of a receiver, to give security for the possible deficit.

[1] 145 Fed 820
[2] Atlantic Trust Company *v.* Chapman, 208 U S 360, 28 S Ct 406.
[3] Farmers' Loan Co *v.* Oregon etc Company, *supra*.

CHAPTER XXIV

DISTRIBUTION OF DEBTOR'S ESTATE. GENERAL CLAIMS

§ 489. Creditors Primary Parties in Interest.
490. Claims Capable of Assertion
491. Tort Claims
492. Judgments Founded on Torts
493. Interest on Claims
494. Mode of Establishing Claims
495. No Time Limits for Establishing Claims in Absence of Statute
496. Peculiarities of New York Rule
497. Protection of Distributing Officer
498. Liquidating Point for Claims
499. Corporate Dissolution — Conflict of Rules
500. Bankruptcy — Development of English Doctrine
501. Bankruptcy — American Doctrine.
502. Restrictions of Early American Statutes.
§ 503. Restrictions on Contingent Claims should be Enforced only in Aid of Creditors
504. Contingent Claims in Cases of Corporate Dissolution.
505. Ranking of Contingent Claims in Cases of Decedents Estates and of Corporate Dissolution
506. Confusion in New York and Minnesota Cases
507. Whether Debtor's Liquidation is a Breach of His Contract.
508. Right of Adoption, in General.
509. What Obligations may be Adopted
510. Time Allowed Liquidator for Choice
511. Effect of Rejection
512. Effect of Adoption.
513. Exception in Case of Public Service Companies

§ 489 Creditors Primary Parties in Interest The only persons interested in the debtor's estate are those to whom the debtor is under some sort of obligation, as distinct from those who are under obligations to the debtor; the latter are not parties in interest with respect to his estate.[1] When the claims of those to whom the debtor is under obligation have

---

[1] *In re* Sully, 152 Fed 619; Piquet *v* Swan, 3 Pick 443, *In re* Brown, 47 Hun 360, Chicago etc Railway Co *v* Gould, 64 Iowa 343, 20 N W 464, Ford *v* Gilbert, 44 Ore 259, 75 Pac 138

been discharged, the creditors' representative holds what overplus may remain as trustee for the debtor,[1] but as long as these claims remain open the representative's obligation is to their holders. These claims divide themselves into three classes, (1) general claims, (2) claims entitled to priority of payment, and (3) claims which are secured by collateral of one type or another. This chapter shall deal with the first class.

§ 490 **Claims Capable of Assertion** The first distinction is between the claim which is due at the time the debtor's affairs pass into the control of the distributing court, and the claim which at that time is incapable of assertion because no breach of the debtor's obligation has yet occurred The courts are nearly unanimous in their agreement as to the kind of claim which may be considered as matured It must be a claim which arises from a contract or a quasi-contractual obligation, and is capable of ascertainment as to amount on its face, or by a simple process of liquidation

§ 491. **Tort Claims.** If the obligation of the debtor arises from a tort as distinct from a contract, no one can say at any given time how much money the debtor owes until this amount has been fixed by the verdict of a jury and a judgment entered upon it, though the tort consists of an injury to a property right The present English Bankrupt Act of 1883 [2] states this distinction by excluding from the list of provable claims " all demands in the nature of unliquidated damages arising otherwise than by reason of a contract, promise or breach of trust " In other words, " unliquidated damages occasioned by tort " never have constituted a provable claim [3]

§ 492 **Judgments Founded on Torts.** On the contrary, it never was doubted that a judgment is a provable claim though based upon a cause of action in tort, because the judgment is a debt of record for an amount clearly specified, and

---

[1] Charman *v.* Charman, 14 Vesey 580 , Wealing *v* Ellis, 1 De G. M & G 596; Johnson *v* Norris, 190 Fed 459.   [2] Sec. 37.
[3] Hun *v.* Carey, 82 N Y. 66; *In re* Wiggers 2 Biss 71

capable of immediate computation at any given time by the simple addition of interest to the principal amount unpaid Hence a tort creditor who has recovered judgment prior to the transfer of the debtor's affairs into the hands of the distribution court is a creditor in every sense of the word [1]

§ 493. **Interest on Claims** As a general rule, after property of an insolvent is *in custodia legis* interest thereafter accruing is not allowed on debts payable out of the fund realized by a sale of the property. That is not because the claims had lost their interest-bearing quality during that period, but is due to the fact that in case of receiverships the assets are generally insufficient to pay debts in full If all claims were of equal dignity and all bore the same rate of interest from the date of the receivership to the date of the final distribution, it would be immaterial whether the dividend was calculated on the basis of the principal alone or of principal and interest combined. But some of the debts might carry a high rate and some a low rate, and hence inequality would result in the payment of interest which accrued during the delay incident to collecting and distributing the funds As this delay was the act of the law, no one should thereby gain an advantage or suffer a loss. For that and like reasons, in case funds are not sufficient to pay claims of equal dignity the distribution is made only on the basis of the principal of each debt But that rule does not prevent the running of interest during the receivership; and if, as a result of good fortune or good management, the estate

---

[1] *In re* Charles, 4 East 197; Bass *v* Gilbert 2 M & S 70. The form of the proceedings which may have resulted in the entry of the judgment is immaterial All that is required in this connection is a final mandate of a court awarding to the plaintiff the right to acquire from the defendant's property a definite sum of money Hence, a judgment for a fine, based upon the defendant's contempt in disobeying an order of court made for the benefit of the other party, is provable in bankruptcy if the record shows that the fine was imposed, not so much for the punishment of the debtor, as for the indemnification of the creditor for the wrong which his property suffered through the contemnor's acts, Van Wezel *v* Van Wezel, 3 Paige 38, People *v.* Spaulding, 10 Paige 284, People *v* Sheriff, 206 Fed. 566.

proves sufficient to discharge the claims in full, interest as well as principal should be paid.[1] Even in bankruptcy, despite the argument that the debtor's liability on the debt and its incidents terminates at the date of adjudication, it has been held that in the rare instances where the assets ultimately proved sufficient for the purpose, the creditors are entitled to interest accruing after adjudication.[2]

§ 494. **Mode of Establishing Claims** In order that the court may properly distribute the estate, the beneficiaries must properly identify themselves Under the Bankrupt Act this method of identification is simple. The proof of claim is filed with the referee appointed in the particular bankruptcy proceeding Any objection to it is resolved in a summary manner on issues made up by the proof of claim and the objection, the burden being upon the objecting party.[3] Unfortunately such a simple method of procedure does not obtain in many other forms of liquidating practice From the very fact that the liquidating officer is considered as a trustee for the administration of the debtor's affairs, there is a tendency to require the creditor, if his claim is objected to by the distributing officer, to sustain his claim by means of a plenary suit against the officer Such a suit, while in form merely an action upon the claim, in reality is " an action to establish and ascertain the status of a plaintiff as a creditor, . . and as such entitled to share in the distribution of the assets in the hands of the receiver . . . and to procure an adjudication for the guidance of the receiver in administering the estate."[4]

[1] Thomas v Western Car Co, 149 U S 95, 13 S Ct 824, Tredegar Co v S A L Ry Co, 183 Fed 290, Am. Iron etc Co v S A L Ry. Co, 34 Sup Ct Rep. 502 The same rule applies to claims which are entitled to priority under the principles discussed in the next chapter, ordinarily they are not entitled to interest, People v Am. Loan & Tr Co., 172 N Y 371, 65 N E 200

[2] Re John Osborn's Sons Co, 177 Fed 184, Johnson v. Norris, 190 Fed. 460

[3] Whitney v Dresser, 200 U S 532, 26 S Ct 316

[4] Ludington v Thompson, 153 N Y 499, 47 N. E 903, White v Knox, 111 U S 784, 4 S Ct 686, Empire State Co v. Carroll County,

§ 495. **No Time Limits for Establishing Claims in Absence of Statute** But that is quite another thing from saying that the beneficiaries must prove their claims within any given period of time In the absence of express statute or order, there can be no time limit which can bar a beneficiary from his proof, because no time runs in favor of the trustee of an express trust against the claim of a beneficiary Therefore, under the early English bankrupt acts, as no time limitation was prescribed for the filing of claims with the assignee, it was held that the courts could not create any arbitrary period In the words of Sir John Leach, V. C , " the statute of limitations did not run against a creditor, the commission was a trust for the benefit of all the creditors, and it was a known principle that the statute did not run against a trust " [1] And this principle has been applied to other distributing officers.[2]

§ 496 **Peculiarities of New York Rule.** The New York courts, however, have not been thorough in their application

---

194 Fed 593 So strongly has this method of procedure intrenched itself with the State courts, as distinct from the simple method provided by the Bankrupt Act, that the present New York Banking Law expressly sanctions this method of procedure by providing (Section 190) that upon any claim rejected by the superintendent in the liquidation of a bank "an action . . must be brought within six months after" such rejection. In New York, the costs awarded to the plaintiff in such an action are entitled to priority of payment as an expense of the receivership, Camp *v.* Niagara Bank, 2 Paige 283 , *Re* Carnegie Trust Co , 161 N Y App Div 280, 146 N Y S 809

[1] *Ex parte* Ross 2 Glyn & J 46.
[2] It has been applied to an assignee for the benefit of creditors, Minot *v* Thatcher, 9 Met. 348 , to a receiver in dissolution proceedings, Ludington *v* Thompson, 153 N Y 499, 47 N. E 903 , to a chancery receiver appointed on a creditors' bill for general administration, Kirkpatrick *v* McElroy, 41 N J Eq. 539, 7 Atl 647; Sterndale *v.* Hankinson, 1 Sim 393; Wrixon *v* Vize, 3 Dru & War 104, and to a receiver under the National Bank Act, Riddle *v* First National Bank, 27 Fed. 503 This, however. must not be confused with the equally well-settled doctrine, that the appointment of a receiver for the estate of A will not stop the running of the statute of limitations upon a claim which B may have against A, since the mere fact that a receiver is in charge of A's estate is no obstacle to B bringing suit against him, Anon, 2 Atk 15 , Harrison *v* Dingman, 2 Dru. & War 295; White *v.* Megraw, 92 Ill App 293

of this well-founded principle While they apply it to the case of a receiver, they refuse to consider an executor in the same light, although, as we have seen, there is a New York statute which confers upon the executor the same trust obligations as rest upon a bankruptcy assignee or receiver. Nevertheless, in New York the statute of limitations resumes its course upon the claim of any creditor from the moment that letters of administration have been issued upon the estate of the deceased debtor, the courts saying that at the moment a representative of the debtor comes into existence against whom suit can be brought, the reason for considering the statute as suspended ceases [1] Likewise has this been held of claims against the committee of a lunatic,[2] although, as we have seen, the New York statutes place the committee of an insolvent lunatic's estate in the position of a true distributing officer.

§ 497. **Protection of Distributing Officer** But with such exceptions as are thus afforded, the rule above stated seems to be so firmly fixed in principle and precedent that it may be said to apply to the case of every distributing officer, and hence claims can be filed with him at any time after his appointment, unless time limits are prescribed by statute or order in the particular case. If, prior to the appearance of a particular beneficiary on the scene in the shape of a creditor filing a proof of claim, the officer has distributed the assets in his possession under due order of court, the court will not permit the belated creditor to participate in aught save such assets as may remain on hand, and will protect its representative from what would otherwise be the consequences of his premature distribution [3] From this has grown the practice of the distributing courts to make, at an early date in the course of the proceedings, an

---

[1] Christophers v Garr, 6 N Y. 63
[2] Sanford v. Sanford, 62 N Y 553; Grant v Humbert, 114 N Y. App Div 462, 100 N Y S 44
[3] Farrell v Smith, 2 B & B 337, Halsted v Forest Hill Co 109 Fed 820, Woodruff v Jewett, 115 N Y 267, 22 N E 157, Walsh v Raymond, 58 Conn 251, 20 Atl. 464, Keene v Gaehle, 56 Md. 343.

396   THE RIGHTS AND REMEDIES OF CREDITORS.   [CHAP XXIV.

order requiring all creditors to prove their claims before the appointed officer within a certain time limit, and authorizing distribution upon the basis of claims filed in obedience to such an order A time limit is likewise prescribed by the present bankrupt acts   Our statute [1] requires proof of each claim to be made within one year after the adjudication of bankruptcy ; nor need the trustee wait until the expiration of the year before paying any dividends   On the contrary, it is proper for him to pay dividends from time to time upon the claims as filed, leaving later claimants to participate as they may in the assets remaining after the payment of the dividends already declared [2]

§ 498 Liquidating Point for Claims   Let us now consider the allowance of unmatured claims   Obviously there should be a point as of which the liquidation of such a claim must be settled   The old bankrupt acts fixed it as of the date when the docket of claims was made up,[3] and our present Bankruptcy Act fixes it as of the date of the filing of the bankruptcy petition.[4] With national banks, the point is the date when the receiver of the bank is appointed, because that is the time when the assets are taken into the custody of the Comptroller for distribution [5]

§ 499. Corporate Dissolution — Conflict of Rules. In proceedings for corporate dissolution, there are two points of view. The New York courts hold to the date when the action is instituted   Their view is that " the judgment relates back to the commencement of the action and becomes effective as of that time   It is the day on which the court practically takes possession of the assets of the company for the purpose of distribution among its creditors, and consequently is the day on which the rights of creditors should be ascertained and the value of their claims should be determined." Such hard-

[1] Sec 57n
[2] *In re* Coulton, 206 Fed 906.
[3] Kittier *v.* Raynes, 1 Cox Ch. 105.
[4] Sec. 63a.
[5] White *v.* Knox, 111 U. S. 784, 4 S. Ct. 686.

ship as may result from the strict application of this rule is justified by the assertion that any other rule "would so far retard and delay the distribution of the assets as to make their administration practically impossible "[1] The New Jersey courts have decided that the proper point is the time when the assets are distributed Against the reasoning of the New York courts, the New Jersey Chancellor places the view that by the statute " a complete collection of assets is contemplated, and a full and final distribution of them is made possible " That being the situation, " natural justice demands that those who suffer from breaches of contract should be included in the distribution; even if the breaches and consequent damages follow the insolvency."[2] This was followed by one of the federal courts in the distribution of corporate assets under State law [3] A little beyond this lies a recent decision of the Circuit Court of Appeals for the Second Circuit "We think," says NOYES, J, "this rule very nearly correct, although it probably goes too far in permitting the proof of claims up to the time of distribution. All claims ought to be in before the accounts are made up for distribution, and there should be no opportunity for uncertainty, delay or expense in reopening and recasting them A narrower rule can be adopted which would obviate any difficulty in this regard and which would be simple, equitable, and workable It is this: Claims which when presented within the time limited by the court for their presentation are certain or are capable of being made certain by recognized methods of computation, should be allowed. Claims which are not then certain should be disallowed because they afford no basis for making dividends. . Claims should be divided into two great classes. So, without laying stress upon the question whether claims are (1) past due, (2) immature, or

---

[1] People v. Commercial Alliance Life Insurance Co., 154 N. Y 95, 47 N. E. 968.
[2] Spader v Mural Decoration Co , 47 N J Eq. 18, 20 Atl. 378
[3] N. Y Security etc. Co. v. Lombard Co., 73 Fed. 557.

(3) contingent, the real way we should divide them with respect to the question of provability is into these two classes. (1) claims of which the worth or amount can be determined by recognized methods of computation at a time consistent with the expeditious settlement of the estates, (2) claims which are so uncertain that their worth cannot be ascertained The second class of claims cannot be proved. They may be highly meritorious, but they cannot share in the estate because their amounts cannot be ascertained The first class of claims ought to be proved and share in the estate, and this whether they are overdue accounts, immature notes, or claims for damages for breach of contract coinciding with or following the receiver "[1] This well-reasoned case develops a doctrine of liquidation consistent with the different aspects of the law of creditors' rights already considered It is regrettable that our Bankrupt Act is incapable of the same interpretation.

§ 500 **Bankruptcy — Development of English Doctrine.** In bankruptcy proceedings there is a divergence between the statutes of England and America. The early English acts permitted no claim to be proven which was not susceptible of immediate computation at the time of the bankruptcy. In other words, the original requirement for a claim to participate in dividends, was that it should represent an overdue obligation. The first judicial protest against this narrow doctrine was voiced by Lord Hardwicke[2] and it was echoed by Lord Eldon[3] It was not, however, until the act of 1824[4] that English bankrupt statutes were altered so as to permit the proof of an immatured claim Since that time, to use the words of LORD HALSBURY,[5] Parliament was " engaged in the effort to exhaust every conceivable possibility of liability under which a bankrupt might be, to make it provable in bankruptcy

[1] Pa Steel Co v. N. Y City Railway Co, 198 Fed. 741.
[2] *Ex Parte* Groome, 1 Atk 115.
[3] *Ex Parte* Barker, 9 Ves Jr 109
[4] 6 Geo. IV, c 16
[5] Hardy v. Fothergill, L. R 13 A C 351.

against his estate and relieve the bankrupt for the future from any liability in respect thereof." The English Act of 1869, of which Lord Halsbury spoke in the passage above quoted, contained, in respect to the allowance of unmatured claims, a provision which was substantially reenacted in Section 37 of the present act of 1883.[1] This admits all claims except (1) in cases where the court considers that it is impossible to estimate in any way whatsoever the amount of the claimant's damages, and (2) claims upon contracts capable of specific performance or restraint by equitable procedure.[2] The first of these exceptions is provided for in the statute. "Such a case," says Lord Manhaghten, "is conceivable, but it is one, I think, very unlikely to occur."[3] The second was furnished in a dictum by Lord Selborne[4] which was later followed by the Court of Appeals.[5] But with these exceptions, says VAUGHN WILLIAMS, L J , "no amount of difficulty in the estimate of its value would justify the exclusion of a proof of debt."[6]

§ 501. **Bankruptcy — American Doctrine.** Our bankruptcy legislation furnishes an even more interesting history in this respect. The National Acts of 1841 and 1867 were both broader, as regards the proof of unmatured claims, than our

[1] "'Liability' shall, for the purposes of this act, include any compensation for work or labor done, any obligation or possibility of an obligation to pay money or money's worth on the breach of any express or implied covenant, contract, agreement, or undertaking, whether the breach does or does not occur, or is or is not likely to occur or capable of occurring before the discharge of the debtor, and generally it shall include any express or implied engagement, agreement, or undertaking, to pay, or capable of resulting in the payment, of money or money's worth, whether the payment is, as respects amount, fixed or unliquidated, as respects time, present or future, certain or dependent on any one contingency or on two or more contingencies; as to mode of valuation, capable of being ascertained by fixed rules, or as matter of opinion" To a similar effect is Section 206 of the present Companies' Acts

[2] Hardy v Fothergill, supra   [3] Ibid

[4] Ibid

[5] *In re* Reis, (1904) 2 K B 769, aff'd under name of Clough v. Samuel, (1905) A. C 441

[6] *In re* Reis, *supra;* see 10 Columbia Law Review, 709

existing statute.[1] Under the English law of to-day, any claim liable to occur under a contract existing at the time of the bankruptcy, is provable against the bankrupt's estate, and barred by his discharge. The American statute,[2] on the other hand, allows no claim to be proved against the bankrupt's estate unless either (1) it existed, as a fixed liability, against the bankrupt prior to the filing of the petition, or (2) the bankruptcy itself, as a matter of substantive law, unaided by any provision of the statute, may be said to operate as a breach of the contract, and thus give rise to a fixed liability. Section 63a allows proof of a fixed liability, arising on a judgment or a written instrument, although not payable at the time of the bankruptcy, provided an appropriate rebate of interest is credited thereon. This one class of unmatured claims is sanctioned under our bankruptcy practice. But with respect to all other kinds of unmatured claims, our statute gives no relief. Section 63b provides that "unliquidated claims against the bankrupt may, pursuant to application to the court, be liquidated in such manner as it shall direct, and may thereafter be proved and allowed against his estate." But an unliquidated claim is quite a different thing from an unmatured claim. The term "unliquidated," as used in the statute, applies merely to the assessment of damages on a matured claim. In other words, an unliquidated claim exists only in the case where the bankrupt has broken a special contract, thereby causing damage

---

[1] Dunbar v Dunbar, 190 U S 340, 23 S Ct. 757, *In re* Roth, 181 Fed. 667

[2] Our present act defines provable debts substantially as follows (Section 63a):

"1. A fixed liability as evidenced by a judgment or instrument in writing absolutely owing at the time of the filing of the petition, whether then payable or not, with any interest thereon which would be recoverable at that time or with a rebate of interest upon such as were not then payable and did not bear interest (4) founded upon an open account, or upon a contract express or implied, and (5) founded upon provable debts reduced to judgment after the filing of the petition and before the consideration of the bankrupt's application for a discharge"

to the claimant, but the amount of these damages had not been judicially ascertained at the time the bankruptcy petition was filed. An unmatured claim is of quite a different character, and is not covered by Section 63b. That section, as the Supreme Court has said, "adds nothing to the class of debts which might be proved under paragraph A of the same section (Section 63a). Its purpose is to permit an unliquidated claim, coming within the provisions of Section 63a, to be liquidated as the court should direct."[1]

§ 502. **Restrictions of Early American Statutes.** The previous acts were not free from restrictions. Thus, under the Act of 1841, the Supreme Court held that damages for breach of a covenant for title, which had not occurred until after the bankruptcy, were not provable.[2] On the other hand, under the Act of 1867, it was held that damages on a bond were provable in bankruptcy, although the breach did not occur until after the filing of the petition.[3] From these decisions and the decision in French v. Morse[4] came the doctrine that a contingent claim was provable if the contingency respected the cause of action alone, but it was not provable if the existence of the demand upon which the action could be based was likewise contingent. Even with these limits, however, these acts were broader than our present statute, which sweeps the law back to where it had been in the earlier days of English legislation.

§ 503. **Restrictions on Contingent Claims should be Enforced only in Aid of Creditors.** But however stringent or liberal they may be, no restrictions on the proof of a contingent claim should apply except in behalf of the creditors who have provable claims. Neither the debtor, nor any person interested in the debtor's estate in any capacity other than that of a present creditor, should be allowed to object to proper provision being

[1] Dunbar v. Dunbar, 190 U. S. 340, 23 S. Ct. 757
[2] Riggin v. Magwire, 15 Wall. 549
[3] Wolf v. Stix, 99 U. S. 1
[4] 2 Gray 111.

made for the satisfaction of a contingent claim against the time of its maturity This principle was recognized by LORD HARDWICKE when, in the liquidation of a decedent's estate, he directed the executors to set aside from the estate funds sufficient to meet unmatured claims, saying that "wherever a demand is made out of assets, certainly due but payable at a future time, the person entitled thereto might come against the executor, to have it secured for his benefit and set apart in the mean time, that he might not be obliged to pursue these assets through several hands."[1] While this decision was afterwards limited in England[2] it has met with a very favorable response in America.[3]

§ 504. Contingent Claims in Cases of Corporate Dissolution. The same principle governs the case of corporate dissolution where, in the end, the assets are more than sufficient to pay the company's debts In any such case it is clear that the stockholders should receive no dividends until all outstanding claims, however incapable of proof at that time of liquidation, have been provided for Sufficient assets should be reserved in the hands of the liquidator to meet these claims whenever they should mature, so that the persons whose interests make up the interests of the debtor corporation should not profit by the abstraction of funds from their primary purpose of meeting the debts of the corporation. This rule was laid down in an English case[4] where JAMES, V. C., held that while assets would not be impounded for future rent as against the claims of creditors it was proper to impound the assets before allowing a distribution to be made to the stockholders Some States cover this by statute. In New York dissolution proceedings the

---

[1] Johnson *v* Mills 1 Ves. Sr. 282.
[2] King *v*. Malcott, 9 Hare 692
[3] Petrie *v*. Voorhis, 18 N. J Eq 285, Bankers Surety Co. *v* Meyer, 205 N. Y. 219, 98 N E 399, Cobb *v* Kempton, 154 Mass 266, 28 N E. 264.
[4] *In re* Telegraph Construction Company, L. R 10 Eq. 384, *Re* New Oriental Bank, (1895) 1 Ch 753

receiver is directed to retain funds "for the purpose of canceling and adjusting any open or subsidiary engagements" of the company [1] On the other hand, a contingent claim should not be allowed as against the claims of other creditors with matured claims, they should not be required to wait for a contingency that may never occur Such is the distinction that exists in the courts of most of our States [2]

§ 505 **Ranking of Contingent Claims in Cases of Decedents' Estates and of Corporate Dissolution** This distinction is most apt to arise in the case of a decedent's estate or the dissolution of a corporation, where not only is there a limited fund for distribution, but there is no longer the personal responsibility of the debtor In a case of that sort, there is still no reason why a contingent claim should rank with claims susceptible of liquidation. The most the court should do is indicated in the case above cited; it should not require the creditors with matured claims to wait, but, after they have been satisfied, it should not allow the distribution of the estate's overplus until provision has been made for the ultimate satisfaction of all contingent claims Where the debtor is still in existence, the question of this secondary ranking of contingent claims seldom arises because (a) the debtor's estate would not be in this course of distribution were the debtor solvent, and therefore the secondary ranking, as a practical matter, would be vain, and (b) the

---

[1] General Corporation Law, Sec 257
[2] People v. Metropolitan Surety Co , 205 N Y 135, 98 N E 412, and cases there cited; Goding v Rosenthal, 180 Mass 43, 61 N E. 222; Funerald v Johnson, 71 Me 437 , Meyer v. Attorney-General, 32 N J Eq 815 The New York Court of Appeals says, in its most recent declaration on this subject "The claimant will also be entitled to his proper dividend from any surplus that may remain after all claims in existence, when the action for dissolution was commenced, are paid and discharged. . The contest is between creditors of the corporation, not between the claimant and the corporation His contract is not impaired, for it is still of full force," People v Metropolitan Surety Co , supra   To the same effect is Wells v Hartford Manilla Co , 76 Conn 27, 55 Atl. 599, where an unmatured claim was not allowed in competition with the claims of creditors, but the claims of stockholders were postponed beyond it

contingent claim, if not provable, by the same token is not barred from future assertion against the debtor and such fresh estate as he may afterwards acquire.[1] But while for these practical reasons the question has arisen more often in cases where the debtor ceases to exist coincidently with the liquidation of the estate than where the debtor's existence continues, the rule should be the same in any case where the necessity arises for its application. Purely contingent claims should be given a secondary rank when they apply for admission, the debtor's continuance or cessation of existence being a matter of accident rather than a point of distinction.

§ 506 **Confusion in New York and Minnesota Cases** Failure to steer this course has placed the New York and Minnesota courts on rather bad shoals General assignments stand on no different footing than bankruptcy proceedings with regard to the provability of future claims. Future claims, in fact, cannot be proven in a general assignment any more than in bankruptcy without such special authority as the present English statute affords [2] So far the Minnesota and New York courts are clear. Thus the Minnesota courts held that rent not yet accrued could not be proven against the lessee's estate under a general assignment.[3] But in a later case the court held that where the lessee was a corporation and was subjected to dissolution proceedings, the lessor could prove for rent for the unexpired term [4] The court distinguished its earlier decision by saying that the assignor in a general assignment " continued liable for the rent notwithstanding the insolvency proceedings; but in the case at bar, a corporation has by its voluntary dissolution practically committed suicide, when its estate is ad-

---

[1] Phenix Nat Bank v. Waterbury, 197 N Y 161, 90 N. E 435, Ames v. Moir, 138 U. S. 306, 11 S. Ct 311; Boot v Wilson, 8 East. 311
[2] Matter of Hevenor, 144 N Y. 271, 39 N E. 393, Wilder v. Peabody, 37 Minn 248, 33 N W 852
[3] Wilder v Peabody, *supra*
[4] Kalkhoff v Nelson, 60 Minn 284, 62 N. W. 332.

ministered it ceases to exist." The New York court went to the same extent,[1] saying that " the situation of a receiver placed in the possession of the assets of an insolvent corporation by force of the decree of the court and with the broad and equitable powers conferred by statute, bears little comparison with the situation of an assignee under a general assignment for the benefit of creditors whose scope of powers and duty is prescribed by that instrument." The hopeless confusion into which these decisions fall cannot be relieved; the most that can be hoped is that other courts will not attempt a similar course.

§ 507 **Whether Debtor's Liquidation is a Breach of His Contract** This question of the provability of a contingent claim solves itself where the debtor's passage into the distributing court may be considered as a breach of his contract One ground of the Minnesota court's decision above cited was that the insolvent corporation, by procuring dissolution proceedings to be instituted, had committed a breach of a rent covenant upon which the claim in question was predicated [2] This view is directly opposed to the pioneer case of Deane v Caldwell,[3] where it was held that the death of the tenant cannot in any event accelerate rent under a leasehold. " Before the day at which rent is covenanted to be paid," said the court, " it is in no sense a debt; it is neither *debitum* nor *solvendum;* for if the lessee is evicted before that day, it never becomes payable." [4] Some leases provide that on the tenant's bankruptcy the landlord may reënter and relet the estate at the tenant's charge. In the case of such a lease, there is a tendency to allow the landlord to prove a claim for " the full amount of the damages which should be ascertained by the reletting,"[5] but this view

---

[1] People v St Nicholas Bank, 151 N Y 592, 45 N E 1129
[2] Kalkhoff v. Nelson, *supra*.   [3] 127 Mass 242
[4] This case has been generally followed, Watson v Merrill, 136 Fed 359; Wilson v Trust Co, 114 Fed 742, *Ex parte* Houghton, 1 Low 554, Fed Cas 6725
[5] *Ex parte* Houghton, *supra*, (*semble*), *In re* Roth, 181 Fed 667

has been unsparingly, and we think soundly, criticized in other quarters.[1] The real question should be, not what the parties have stipulated, but whether the bankruptcy of a party will constitute a breach of the contract from the nature of the contract itself. In the latter case, of course, the parties may agree as to the liquidation of the damages; but if the bankruptcy would not be a breach in the absence of express stipulation, then a stipulation as to the damages in such a case is a penalty rather than a provision for damages capable of proof.[2] It may, therefore, be laid down as a safe proposition that no open contract of the debtor should be considered as giving rise to a provable claim against his estate, to rank equally with the claims of other creditors, unless (a) such a course is justified by the express provisions of a statute like the present English Bankrupt Act or (b) the contract is of such a nature that, upon the ordinary principles of the law of contracts, the judicial liquidation of the debtor's affairs may be considered a breach of its terms, resulting in damages susceptible of precise computation. On this last point the cases are in a state of confusion with regard to classifying contracts of varying natures, which we may properly leave to the writers upon contract law for solution.[3]

§ 508. **Right of Adoption, in General.** In the present connection we are interested in another right which is of equal importance, and often in actual conflict, with the right to prove a claim upon an open contract. We refer to the so-called right of adoption which every liquidating officer possesses. There can be no doubt that even in a case where the bankruptcy of one party to a contract operates as a breach of his obligations

---

[1] Watson v Merrill, *supra*, Re Merwin 206 Fed 116
[2] Re Merwin, *supra*
[3] See portion of article of "Unmatured Claims in Bankruptcy," 10 Columbia Law Review, at p 715, *et seq*, Re Swift, 112 Fed 315: Re Buffalo Mirror Co, 15 Am B R 122, Re Neff, 157 Fed 57, Harding v Mill River Corp, 34 Conn 458, Re Inman, 171 Fed 185, 175 Fed. 312, People v Globe Insurance Co., 91 N Y. 174, Re Silverman, 101 Fed 219, Carr v Hamilton, 129 U S 252, 9 S. Ct 295

thereunder, the opposite party is not bound to treat it as a breach. He may "at his election treat it as a breach of contract," [1] but he is not bound to; and if he takes the contrary course the contract remains an open obligation which the debtor must perform at its appointed time, or be liable in damages for its breach [2] The debtor's open contract, therefore, remains open unless it is of such a nature that the bankruptcy operates as a breach of its terms, and even then it remains open unless the opposite party elects to consider it as terminated by the breach thus effected. But this election cannot be made if the contract is capable of adoption by the liquidating officer, and he does adopt it. At that point the right of adoption prevails, and it is necessary that we ascertain just what that right is.

§ 509. **What Obligations may be Adopted.** When the court assumes control of the debtor's affairs, its liquidating officer is entitled to take charge of all things upon which the creditors are entitled to realize. In a broad sense, as we have seen, this would include all the debtor's rights which are capable of assignment. In the case of any unfulfilled or open contract to which the debtor is a party, the liquidator may consider that it is to the benefit of the estate to have this contract performed. Of course the contract must require something to be done on the part of the debtor, or be free from any default of his, because if at the time the liquidator takes charge the contract is in default on the debtor's part, it presents no question of adoption, but rather gives the opposite party a claim provable against the estate.[3] And if the contract is of such a personal nature as not to be assignable, or the burdens thereby laid upon the debtor cannot be discharged by the acts of any one save himself, then the assignee cannot adopt it or perform it, because the debtor could not have assigned its rights or have had any one

---

[1] Jessel, M. R., in Re Northern Counties Ins Co, 17 Ch D 337
[2] See cases cited in § 505, *supra*
[3] Hurley v Atch oto Ry Co, 213 U S 126, 29 S Ct 466

else perform its obligations If, on the other hand, the contract is of such a nature that the liquidator may perform the debtor's obligations and collect such payments as may become due, he may, if he pleases, assume the entire undertaking and be entitled to all its benefits upon the performance of all its obligations. The courts however do not allow this to the opposite party's hurt. In adopting the contract the liquidator is not entitled to the benefit of credits allowed to the debtor, the original party, on the supposition of his continued solvency Thus an outstanding contract for the sale of goods by installments to the debtor may be adopted upon condition that payments be made in cash on delivery instead of being made upon credit dates contemplated by the agreement, since the insolvency of the vendee, while not being equivalent to a rescission or breach of the agreement, yet " relieves the vendor from his agreement to give credit, and payment may be substituted "[1] Subject to these limitations, this right of adoption is enjoyed by all classes of liquidators A trustee in bankruptcy was always considered as having the right to continue outstanding engagements, because he is the statutory successor to the insolvent in all the latter's property rights.[2] A general assignee likewise has the same power, because the assignment passes to him all of the assignee's outstanding obligations[3] The same right, by a series of decisions of the Supreme Court, has been extended to a receiver appointed in a chancery winding up,[4] and the court has stated that in this respect there is no difference between a statutory assignee and a chancery receiver.[5]

§ 510. **Time Allowed Liquidator for Choice** Whether to adopt or reject any such open contract, therefore, lies within

[1] Re Niagara Radiator Co, 164 Fed 102; Vandegrift v. Cowles Engineering Co, 161 N. Y 435, 55 N E. 941
[2] Bourdillon v Dalton, 1 Esp 236; Turner v. Richardson, 7 East 33, Dushane v Beall, 161 U S 513, 16 S Ct 637
[3] New England Iron Co v Gilbert Elevated Co, 91 N Y. 153.
[4] Sunflower Oil Co v Wilson, 142 U S 313, 12 S Ct 235; Quincy Railroad Co. v Humphrey, 145 U S 82, 12 S Ct 787
[5] Dushane v Beall, 161 U S 513, 16 S. Ct 637

the choice of every liquidating officer. Naturally he is entitled to a reasonable time within which to make his election. His appointment alone does not vest in him the obligations of these open contracts On the contrary, "upon taking possession of the property, he is entitled to a reasonable time to elect whether he will adopt the contract, and make it his own, or whether he will insist upon the inability of the insolvent to pay, and return the property in good order and condition "[1] Meanwhile the contract remains in suspense The liquidator is entitled to his period of consideration, and the delay thus entailed adds nothing to the rights of the opposite party, it creates no breach of the agreement that the liquidating court will allow to be asserted.[2] In the words of the Circuit Court of Appeals, First Circuit,[3] "the holder of the contract is entitled to treat it as abandoned as of the date when the receiver was appointed, subject, however, to an obligation to wait a reasonable time for the purpose of ascertaining what would ultimately be decided by the receiver" This was strikingly brought out in Wells v Hartford Manilla Co[4] There an insolvent company had agreed to purchase a quantity of pulp from the plaintiff in installments The receiver took some time to consider whether he would go on with the contract, but finally decided not to do so, and thus notified the opposite party. That party then filed a claim on the contract, claiming that the estate in the receiver's hands was responsible for any damages the delay had occasioned. The court, however, held that the claim was not allowable, saying that "this conclusion, if sound,

---

[1] If during this period the liquidator should occupy or use any of the property forming part of the subject matter of the contract, the court would require him, as a matter of equity, to pay the reasonable value of such use or occupation, but beyond that he is under no liability, Sunflower Oil Co v Wilson, *supra*

[2] Wells v Hartford Manilla Co, 76 Conn 27, 55 Atl 599, Malcomson v Wappoo Mills, 88 Fed. 680; U. S Trust Co v Wabash Railway Co, 150 U S 287, 14 S Ct 86

[3] Commonwealth Roof Co. v North American Co, 135 Fed 984

[4] *Supra.*

would seem to reduce the privilege of election, which a receiver admittedly enjoys, to microscopic proportions."

§ 511. **Effect of Rejection** If the liquidator elects to reject the contract under his consideration, the estate has nothing more to do with it. The contract itself remains the debtor's contract, and whether a proof of claim thereon can be properly filed with the liquidator depends, as we have elsewhere said, upon whether the bankruptcy of the debtor can be considered as a breach of the contract. In like manner, any property of the debtor which may have been so connected with his outstanding engagement that to accept the one would amount to adopting the other, is rejected from the estate along with the rejected contract of which it was part, and thenceforth the liquidator has nothing to do with it, in point of law. Hence an intervening conveyance of property by the debtor, made in the chance that the liquidator would reject the property, is perfectly good, in the event of the liquidator's rejection even under the terms of the Bankrupt Act [1] This is illustrated by the recent case of McCarty v. Light [2] There the bankrupt owned certain real estate which was subject to the statutory lien of a judgment which had been recovered against the bankrupt immediately prior to the filing of the bankruptcy petition. The trustee decided that the operation of the property would be too burdensome, and decided not to adopt it as part of the estate. It was accordingly held that the lien upon the property was not vacated by virtue of Section 67f of the Bankrupt Act, which vacates all liens recovered within four months prior to the filing of the petition, and that the judgment creditor accordingly might enforce the rights conferred upon him by this lien as against persons to whom, after the trustee's rejection, the bankrupt had conveyed the property

§ 512. **Effect of Adoption** On the other hand, if the liquidator adopts the contract he becomes the substitute of the debtor

[1] Sessions v Romadka, 145 U. S. 29, 12 S. Ct 799
[2] 155 N. Y App Div 36, 139 N Y. S 853

thereon, and all property connected with it becomes part of the estate for administration. No proof of claim for breach of the contract can be filed but on the other hand the liquidator must perform it according to its terms If he fails to perform it, then the opposite party has a claim for damages which the liquidator must pay, recouping from the estate as the court may choose to allow him according to the circumstances.[1] The estate, in short, is substituted for the debtor upon the contract, with the individual liability of the liquidator as a last resort.

§ 513. **Exception in Case of Public Service Companies** An exception, however, has been made in the case of public service companies, due in part to the fact that the public interest requires that a company engaged in public service operations under a special franchise should continue its operations even though it is insolvent, or have them continued during liquidation by the receivers in charge. If then a public service operation, such as a railroad, is under lease, and the affairs of the lessee company are in course of winding up, the receiver of the lessee company performs his full duty by turning over to the lessor the net earnings of the leased line, even though those earnings do not equal the stipulated rent, and, if the receiver cannot operate the leased line except at a loss, the lessor must make good the difference. So long as the lessor " assents to the performance of its public duties " by the receiver of the lessee, it is unfair for the lessor to require more than the net earnings; and it should make good any losses, for if it is not satisfied with that, " it can demand to have its property back again " [2]

[1] Bourdillon v Dalton, *supra*, Turner v Richardson, *supra;* Dayton Hyd Co v Felsenthal, 116 Fed 961 *In re* Wiseman, 159 Fed 236.
[2] Penn Steel Co v N Y City Ry Co., *supra*, and cases there cited.

CHAPTER XXV

DISTRIBUTION (*CONTINUED*) PRIOR CLAIMS

§ 514. Nature of Prior Claims.
515. Debts Due Government.
516. Government Debts in National Bank Liquidation
517. Marshaling of Government Debts.
518. Statutory Priorities in General
519. Landlord's Lien on Tenant's Goods
520. Priority of Landlord's Lien
521. Priority of Labor Claims.
522. Priority of Supply Claims in General
§ 523. Equitable Doctrine in Case of Public Service Companies
524. The Decision in Fosdick v Schall
525. Time within which Supplies must be Furnished
526. Necessity for Liquidator to Obtain Further Credit
527. Whether Doctrine Applies to Case Instituted by Creditor's Bill
528. State Laws Embodying the Doctrine

§ 514 **Nature of Prior Claims** In the distribution of the estate among the creditors whose claims have been presented, the liquidator is apt to find certain of them asserting the right to be paid in full before anything is paid upon account of other claims of different nature. Any such claim of priority must rest upon some applicable statute or principle of law which is entirely extraneous to the doctrines we have heretofore considered In the last chapter we saw that the practice is, or should be, to postpone the payment of unmatured claims to the overplus remaining from the estate after the payment of the matured claims. But that sort of ranking does not rest on the same basis of priority as the claims we are about to consider. The claim of priority proper asserts no comparison between the favored debt and the others, nor any principle of justice or equity that, as a result of the comparison, would prescribe that the one be paid ahead of the other On the contrary, the claim of priority rests on something quite apart from all that, it invokes a statute or rule of public policy that requires that certain debts be paid though all others go unpaid There are certain claims which, by virtue of one or the other of these forces, the court must direct to be paid in full before the assets in its charge can be applied to the payment of other claims on a basis of equality

§ 515. **Debts Due Government.** First among these come debts due to the State; and these may be divided into two classes. (a) debts due by way of taxes, and (b) debts due by way of contract At common law there was no distinction between these classes. All debts due to the Crown were entitled to payment in any case ahead of all other debts.[1] And that is the general rule to-day, debts due to the United States whether upon contract or by taxation coming first, and debts due a State of the Union coming second[2]

§ 516. **Government Debts in National Bank Liquidation** An interesting distinction, however, has resulted from federal legislation. By the Act of Congress of 1797[3] all debts due the United States government were given priority in payment over all other debts, whereas at a later day the national bank legislation gave preference, in the winding up of a national bank, to labor claims and nothing else The result of this legislation is that in the case of a national bank the government is entitled to no priority for indebtedness due it, save only in the case of advances made by the Treasury in redeeming the notes of the bank.[4] But with this exception, the rule of priority is the only rule that the liquidator can properly

---

[1] American Bonding Co. v Reynolds, 203 Fed 356
[2] *In re* Carnegie Trust Company, 206 N Y. 390, 99 N E 1096, Matter of Niederstein, 154 N Y App Div. 238, 138 N Y S. 952, People v Metropolitan Surety Company, 158 N Y App Div 647, 144 N Y S 201, Pittsburgh v S S Trust Co., 208 Fed 984
[3] U. S R. S Sec 3466; Compiled Statutes of 1901, p 2314
[4] Cook County Co v United States, 107 U S 445, 2 S Ct 561; Guarantee etc. Co v Guaranty etc Co, 224 U S 152, 32 S Ct 457 Thus, public funds on deposit in such a bank have no priority in the event of its failure, Lucas County v Jamieson, 170 Fed 338.

follow in the satisfaction of debts due the national and State governments

§ 517. **Marshaling of Government Debts.** But on the other hand, the courts have never hesitated to shift the burden of this debt to the proper source by means of the equitable doctrine of marshaling. From an early date it was the practice of the Court of Chancery, in the administration of decedents' estates, to throw upon the debtor's real estate, which was not reachable by his simple contract creditors, the burden of meeting Crown debts, so as to leave the personal property free to meet the claims of the creditors whose debts were not under seal [1] The same rule to-day applies whenever necessary. Thus in a recent case it was held that a debt due for taxes upon the bankrupt's estate could be shifted entirely to the real estate, although it was mortgaged, and thus relieve the unsecured creditors from the obligation of meeting the debt out of the property available for their claims, so that the mortgagee would be compelled to meet the taxes out of the property constituting the security for his claim [2] In like manner a court should be constrained, by the same equitable principles, to hold that a surety on a debt due the State is entitled, upon his paying the debt, to be subrogated to the right of priority which the State had enjoyed. Consequently the estate should reimburse this surety before it pays a dividend upon the general claims [3]

§ 518 **Statutory Priorities in General** In addition to the priority which it can claim of inherent right upon debts due to it, the average American State of late years has undertaken to confer by statute the right of priority upon claims of a certain general nature. These priorities may be divided into two classes, (1) for labor furnished to the insolvent, and (2) for supplies and material furnished to the insolvent.

[1] Saggitary v Hyde, 1 Vern 455 [2] *In re* Oxley, 204 Fed 826
[3] U S. Fidelity etc Co v Carnegie Trust Co., 161 N. Y. App Div. 429; Same v Borough Bank, 161 N. Y. App. Div. 479.

§ 519. **Landlord's Lien on Tenant's Goods.** But before we come to these priorities, which are wholly of American growth, let us deal with a peculiar right of priority which, though originating in statute, had so ancient an origin as to be part of our common law inheritance, with the result that it exists to-day in such States as have not abolished it by statute. We refer to the "lien" of a lessor, for rent in arrears under his lease, upon such chattels of the lessee as may be located upon the demised premises. This lien is unlike all other common law liens in that it is not possessory, but is simply a right of seizure and sale. In short, it is a right of realization for the rent in arrears, enforceable without the aid of a judgment, and by the landlord's action alone.[1] From the moment that the rent day arrives, the landlord has the right to enter the leased premises and seize the chattels located thereon, and, as statutes of an early date[2] prohibit the tenant's removal of the goods so as to defeat the distress, the landlord was rightly considered as having a lien or specific right of realization upon them from the day when the default in rent payment occurred.

§ 520. **Priority of Landlord's Lien.** This right, wherever it still exists, must be respected by any liquidating court, whether it be a national court of bankruptcy or a State court. In the words of Bradley, J.,[3] the landlord's right of distress "being commonly called a lien, and being a peculiar right in the nature of a lien which is greatly relied on as an essential condition of all leases . . . the courts have regarded it as fairly to be classed as a lien within the true intent and meaning of the Bankrupt Act, and have allowed the landlord a priority over the general creditors to the extent of the goods subject to his right of distress." This lien is a common law right of the land-

---

[1] In some States, as Georgia, statutes compel the landlord to procure his distress warrant from a justice of the peace instead of acting under his own warrant, as the English statute allowed him to do See Flury v Grimes, 52 Ga 341

[2] E.g Stat 8 Anne, c 14

[3] Austin v O'Reilley, 2 Woods 670, Fed Cas No 665.

lord, and the creditors, of course, can acquire in the chattels in question no higher right than the tenant had, so that the act of the landlord in seizing the chattels in no way can be considered as a preferential or fraudulent transfer of them. He is, therefore, entitled to make his seizure even after the chattels have passed into the hands of the liquidator, because, as we have seen, the liquidator can acquire no better right than the creditors would have had.[1]

§ 521 **Priority of Labor Claims** Let us now turn to the priorities given claims by latter-day statutes The first class, as we have said, comprises labor claims These have priority by virtue of the average statute, whatever may be the nature of the business in which the debtor was engaged, and irrespective of the nature of the debtor, whether corporate or individual. In nearly every State may be found such a statute, the claim of the class prescribed ranking next, in order of priority, to debts due the national or State government.[2] Such priorities are respected in a chancery winding up as well as in a statutory proceeding [3] and may be considered, therefore, as having full application to any liquidation in a court of the State where the statutes have force. The National Bankrupt Act also allows priorities of this kind for wages due to laborers, clerks and salesmen,[4] and, as if this were not enough, it goes to the length of allowing priorities to claims according to their rights in this regard under the law of the State where the administration of the particular case occurs [5] One would infer that as a

---

[1] Longstreth v. Pennock, 20 Wall 575, Henderson v. Mayer, 225 U. S 631, 32 S Ct 699; Austin v O'Reilley, *supra*, *Re* West Side Paper Co , 162 Fed 110

[2] See for example of such State laws *In re* Blackstaff Engineering Co , 200 Fed 1019; *In re* Erie Lumber Co , 150 Fed. 817 , *In re* Rheinstrom etc Co , 207 Fed 118; Am etc Co v Angelasto, 136 Fed 399; *Re* Barnett, 153 Fed. 673. These statutes are intended to protect the claims of laborers and persons furnishing clerical help as distinct from persons acting in an executive capacity, *In re* Greenberger, 203 Fed 583, Matter of Stryker, 158 N Y 526, 53 N E 525

[3] Oliphant v St Louis etc Co , 22 Fed 179

[4] See 64, subd 4.

[5] See 64, subd. 5.

result the bankruptcy court would give full effect to all the
State's priority laws in so far as they might have wider range
than the provisions of the Bankrupt Act, and that, indeed,
seems to be the prevailing view.¹ The Circuit Court of Appeals
for the Second Circuit furnished an apparent discord in the
shape of *In re* Slomka,² but the exception is more apparent
than real. The bankrupt had made a general assignment,
which, as we have seen, is considered as an offense against the
Bankrupt Act It was held that the bankruptcy court could
not give priority to a certain claim which did not fall within
Section 64 of the Bankrupt Act, although it did come within
the language of the priorities accorded by the New York
statute,³ because the latter statute governed, by its terms,
cases of administration under a general assignment only
The reasoning of this case, however, has the false premise that
a general assignment is void *ab initio* in the eye of a bankruptcy
court This view, as we have seen, is not well founded, so that
the cases which hold to the contrary of the decision of *In re*
Slomka seem to have the better foundation. A similar difference of opinion exists regarding another statute of New York
This statute applies to the liquidation of an insolvent banking
corporation, and directs that the deposit accounts of receivers
and trustees shall be entitled to priority of payment out of the
assets The federal courts consider that this statute was not
intended to apply to the case of a federal receiver who deposited
funds in a New York State bank,⁴ but a contrary decision has
been reached by the New York State courts⁵

§ 522. **Priority of Supply Claims in General.** We come now
to the other class of priorities, for supplies furnished the debtor

---

[1] *In re* Erie Lumber Co , 150 Fed 817, and cases there cited
[2] 122 Fed 630
[3] Labor Law, Sec 9, applying to corporate receiverships , Debtor
and Creditor Law, Sec 27, applying to general assignments
[4] *In re* Bolough, 185 Fed 825.
[5] Morris *v.* Carnegie Trust Co , 154 N Y App. Div 596, 139 N Y.
S 969

418   THE RIGHTS AND REMEDIES OF CREDITORS.   [CHAP XXV.

prior to the bankruptcy. Here the lines are tighter. Everywhere this claim or "lien" as it is often called, is limited to cases where the debtor is a corporation Where the courts enforce the claim independently of statute a further limitation appears, because the doctrine which exists without the aid of statute applies only to the case of a public service company which enjoys special franchises granted to it by the State.[1] The statutes in many States have gone further,[2] but as these statutes at least are of origin contemporaneous with the doctrine established by the courts, it would seem best to deal with the judicial doctrine first

§ 523. **Equitable Doctrine in Case of Public Service Companies** Stated in general terms, the doctrine is this: where the affairs of a public service company are being wound up by any distributing court, debts owing for supplies and materials necessary for running expenses, contracted within a period of six months prior to the receivership, are entitled to priority of payment. As the doctrine is still in process of formulation, it would be impossible, within the space allotted for the present purpose, to adequately cover all of its features, and it will do only to mention it for purposes of a most general description

§ 524 **The Decision in Fosdick v Schall** The doctrine started with Fosdick v. Schall.[3] There the Supreme Court held that a claim for rent of cars used by a railroad company, should be paid out of the assets in the hands of the receiver appointed on the foreclosure of an underlying mortgage. This was the court's reasoning: Certain public interests inherent in the operation of railways demand that unsecured debts for labor, equipment and supplies should be protected The

---

[1] Wood v Guarantee Trust Co , 128 U. S. 416, 9 S Ct. 131; Spencer v. Taylor Creek Co , 184 Fed. 635

[2] E g. Virginia has a statute dating back to 1877, which gives a lien for the purchase price of supplies furnished to a mining or manufacturing corporation See Fidelity etc. Co. v. Roanoke Iron Co., 81 Fed 439.

[3] 99 U. S 235

blanket mortgage which lies at the bottom of all railway financing, under which not only the money necessary for construction purposes, but the working capital of the railroad are supplied, would, if given full effect, prevent the payment of any unsecured creditors should the railroad prove to be a losing proposition, and yet the railroad could not continue without a certain amount of credit being given it for current supplies necessary for its daily operation. Hence, whether the parties to the mortgage intended it or not, equitable considerations required that the current earnings of the railroad should be detached from the lien of the mortgage and applied to keeping down these debts. From that it would follow that if the debts in fact had not been kept down, then as a condition to giving the mortgagee, upon the railroad's default in the payment of interest under the mortgage, the relief which a court of equity could extend him by means of a foreclosure proceeding, he should be required to allow the court to meet these debts out of the railroad's earnings This, as we have intimated in another place,[1] is a logical result of the extreme length to which the Supreme Court had previously gone in supporting the "after-acquired property clause" of a railway mortgage. It had gone too far, it had recognized a use of the mortgage which, though logical in itself, was a perversion of the original ideas of financing, and the court called a halt at this point. Such was the doctrine of Fosdick v Schall It has been the parent of multitudinous decisions ranging from another Supreme Court decision rendered at the same term [2] to its decisions of the present day,[3] during which period the court's real task has been to give the doctrine some sort of a practical outline

§ 525. **Time within which Supplies must be Furnished** The first limitation laid upon this general rule related to the time within which these protected debts must arise, with the result

---

[1] *Supra*, § 276   [2] Hale v Frost, 99 U S 39S.
[3] *E g* Gregg v. Metropolitan Trust Company, 197 U S 183, 25 S Ct. 415.

that at the present day the outside limit is definitely fixed at six months prior to the receivership.[1] The second limitation is as to the purposes for which the materials have been supplied. If these purposes are concerned with the construction of the line, as distinct from its operation, there is no lien.[2] Thirdly, the lien is limited to the earnings, as distinct from the corpus of the property; hence if the road has never earned anything and has never been operated, then there is no lien.[3] But this limitation has been followed by nothing savoring of the artificial. If there were earnings, then, whether they are in hand or not at the date of liquidation, the lien must be paid, if necessary, out of the corpus of the estate.[4]

§ 526. **Necessity for Liquidator to Obtain Further Credit.** Of late the Supreme Court has announced still another limitation which logically proceeds from its idea, as expressed in the early cases, that it is necessary for the public that a public service company should continue its operations even though in difficulties. Since to do this it is necessary that the company should continue to purchase supplies, it follows that when the concern passes into the hands of the court, the latter will instruct its officer to continue the operation of the plant for the benefit of the public. Putting these ideas together, the Supreme Court has announced that there is no lien unless, in order to continue the operation of the road, it will be necessary as a matter of business for the receiver to pay off the previous indebtedness which the company owed to the persons extending credit to it for the necessary supplies, in order that the receiver may continue to make such purchases so as to continue the operation of the system.[5]

[1] Central Trust Co v East Tenn. Railroad, 80 Fed 624; Union Trust Co v Illinois Midland Railroad, 117 U S 434, 6 S Ct 809.
[2] Porter v Steel Co., 122 U S 267, 7 S Ct 1206
[3] St Louis Railroad v Cleveland Railway, 125 U S 658, 8 S Ct. 1011; Niles Tool Co v. Railway Co., 112 Fed 561
[4] Burnham v Bowen, 111 U S. 776, 4 S Ct 675
[5] Gregg v Metropolitan Trust Co., 197 U S 183, 25 S Ct 415; Carbon Fuel Co v Chicago etc. Railway, 202 Fed 172

§ 527. **Whether Doctrine Applies to Case Instituted by Creditor's Bill** On the other hand, the original basis of the doctrine has been entirely obscured by decisions to the effect that in liquidation under a creditor's bill the same lien for supplies should be recognized. In Whelan v. Enterprise Transportation Company [1] it was held in the First Federal Circuit that this lien should be recognized only as against the vested lien of a mortgage creditor, and hence the doctrine of Fosdick v Schall does not apply to the case of a winding up under a general creditor's bill That seems eminently right, for why should one creditor be preferred over another, when the basis of the rule was the power of the chancery court to compel a mortgagee to do equity as a condition to giving him relief by means of a foreclosure? In strictness of reason, the rule of Fosdick v. Schall should not be applied to the winding up bill of a general creditor who claims no specific lien But while this view finds support in a comparatively recent dictum of the Supreme Court [2] it must be said that the decisions of the lower federal courts present strong authority to the effect that this lien will be recognized as against the rights of general creditors, even in the absence of any mortgage covering the corporate assets [3]

§ 528 **State Laws Embodying the Doctrine.** Thus the so-called doctrine of Fosdick v Schall, from a rule announced by the federal courts for their own guidance, has spread to the State courts, which have adopted it with no show of reluctance; and finally the rules thus announced have passed into the statutes of many of the States.[4] So, in Kentucky, priority is given by statute to persons extending supplies not only to public service companies but to any business or manufacturing corporations, and the federal courts, sitting in that State in

---

[1] 175 Fed 212.
[2] Kneeland v. American Loan Co , 136 U. S 89 10 S. Ct 950
[3] Pennsylvania Steel Co. v N Y City Railway Co , 208 Fed. 168, Berwind-White Coal Mining Co v. Metropolitan S. S. Co , 183 Fed 250; American Trust Co v. Metropolitan S S Co , 190 Fed 113.
[4] See supra, § 522

bankruptcy, are thus compelled to recognize this priority in the case of an ordinary mercantile corporation,[1] although they have managed to construe the statute as limiting the lien to the case of a manufacturing business as distinguished from a mercantile business [2]

[1] *In re* Floyd etc. Co., 200 Fed. 1016.
[2] *In re* Starks etc Co., 171 Fed. 834

CHAPTER XXVI

DISTRIBUTION (CONTINUED) SECURED CLAIMS

§ 529. Secured Creditors have Interest in the Liquidation
530. Position of Secured Creditor in Absence of Liquidation
531. Liquidation does not Deprive Mortgagee of Right to Realize on Security.
532. Rights of Mortgagee when Property is in Liquidator's Possession
533. Chancery Practice in Such Cases.
534. Expenses of Preserving Property, and Liquidator's Charges
535. Relative Positions of Mortgagee and Liquidator

§ 536. Bankruptcy Rule — English Legislation.
537. American Bankruptcy Rule, and Practice Thereunder
538. Security Given by Surety — Federal Rule
539. Defect of Bankruptcy Rule
540. Limitations of Doctrine of Marshaling
541. Early Chancery Doctrine
542. Later Chancery Doctrine — Rule of Mason v Bogg
543. Prevalence in America of Rule of Mason v Bogg.
544. Degree to which Rule of Mason v Bogg now Obtains
545. Problem of Notes Secured by Promissor's Bonds

§ 529. **Secured Creditors have Interest in the Liquidation** Judicial liquidation is not necessarily for the benefit of the unsecured creditors alone, for it may very well be that certain of the creditors hold security which they received in a legitimate manner. It matters not, for our present purpose, whether the security agreement partakes of the nature of a pledge or of a mortgage. In any such case the estate is none the less indebted to the secured creditor, or mortgagee, as we shall for convenience call him, because of the fact that the latter has security for his claim. A debt is a debt, and the security is a mere incident thereto; and this fact cannot be overlooked in the administration of the debtor's estate.[1]

[1] Myer v Car Co, 102 U S. 1. Even in a jurisdiction where a real estate mortgage is considered as passing the legal title, the mort-

§ 530. **Position of Secured Creditor in Absence of Liquidation**
If the debtor's affairs had not passed into the hands of the court, the secured creditor, at any time, could have brought suit upon his claim without waiving or abandoning his right to the security. He could push such a suit into a judgment and hold his security as collateral for the judgment; also he could issue execution on the judgment and realize upon it as far as he might go and then look to his original collateral to make good the difference.[1] That is the way a court of equity would regard the matter, and the courts of law take no contrary view. In short, if the security proves inadequate to satisfy the claim, the mortgagee may recover against the debtor as a general creditor for the deficiency. If, on the other hand, the security is more than ample in money value to pay off the debt in question, the debtor has a substantial interest in the mortgaged property which is commonly described as his "equity," or equity of redemption.

§ 531. **Liquidation does not Deprive Mortgagee of Right to Realize on Security.** So far as realizing upon his security goes, the fact that the debtor's affairs are in liquidation does not alter the mortgagee's rights. Even though his debtor were a corporation and in the hands of a court empowered to terminate its charter life as well as distribute its assets, still the mortgagee can proceed to realize on his security by foreclosure.[2] By failing to participate in the distributive proceedings as a creditor, he does not jeopardize his right to look to his security for payment; the most he might forfeit is his right to share in the general assets for the amount of any deficiency that may result from the realization of his security.[3]

gagee, in the view of a court of equity, holds the title simply by way of security for his debt. See Campbell *v* Holyland, 7 Ch Div 166; Barnard *v* Onderdonk, 98 N. Y. 158; Roberts *v.* Lawrence, 16 Ill App 433

[1] Evertson *v* Booth, 19 Johns. 486, Lockhart *v.* Hardy, 9 Beav. 349.

[2] *In re* Binghamton Company, 143 N. Y 261, 38 N E. 297.

[3] Bennett *v.* Calhoun etc Assn , 9 Rich Eq (S C.) 163.

But of this right thus to realize on his security the mortgagee cannot be deprived, however it may inconvenience the liquidator or disappoint the expectations of the creditors.[1] If the property is in the mortgagee's possession, the full meed of his rights with respect thereto may be secured without the permission of the distributing court. While indeed the latter may enjoin him from proceeding for a time long enough to enable the liquidator to ascertain whether the mortgagee holds his security by virtue of a valid lien, it is undoubtedly true that the court cannot thus suspend the mortgagee's rights longer than the reasonable circumstances of such a case may require.[2]

§ 532. **Rights of Mortgagee when Property is in Liquidator's Possession.** On the other hand, if the mortgagee had left the debtor in possession of the charged property, there is no reason why, upon the debtor's affairs passing into the hands of the court, the liquidator may not take possession of the property, since, as we have seen, he is entitled to take possession of any asset that he may find, having the option later to reject or abandon it. If the property is thus in the possession of the liquidator, the court undoubtedly has power, to facilitate administration between the liquidator and the mortgagee, to order the property sold. In any such case, however, this sale can in no wise affect the rights of the mortgagee; his lien attaches to the money received from the sale, and the court will not allow the liquidator to use or divert it.[3] The mortgagee has no recourse but to foreclose his lien by means of direct proceeding in the liquidating court. He comes into the court, not as a general creditor, not as a claimant, but for the simple purpose of foreclosing his lien, and the court will order the proceeds to be turned over to him to the extent of his debt.[4]

[1] Gay v. Hudson River Co., 184 Fed 689.
[2] *In re* Mertens, 144 Fed 818
[3] *In re* Hershberger, 208 Fed 94
[4] Greey v Dockendorff, 231 U S. 513, 34 S. Ct. 166, Ward v First Natl Bank, 202 Fed 609

§ 533. **Chancery Practice in Such Cases.** That, undoubtedly, is within the power of any liquidating court, but as a matter of practice it is only exercised by courts of bankruptcy. As distinct from that is the practice of the chancery courts, which is to hold the property and give the mortgagee permission to foreclose his lien by plenary suit in the same court, joining the creditors' receiver as a party defendant to such suit. If, in the foreclosure suit, the mortgagee asks for the appointment of a receiver of the mortgaged property it is customary to appoint one, and direct the general receiver to turn over to him the property in question.

§ 534. **Expenses of Preserving Property, and Liquidator's Charges.** This practice tends to avoid the disputes which were frequent, under the bankruptcy method, about the expenses and charges of the creditors' representative. It was claimed that the bankruptcy trustee, who had taken possession of mortgaged property and sold it under order of the bankruptcy court, was entitled not only to reimbursement out of the fund for expenses incurred in connection with the preservation of the mortgaged property, but also to take the same compensation out of the fund as though it constituted part of the general estate. Though this proposition was vigorously denied by several courts[1] the Bankrupt Act[2] was amended in 1910 so as to give the trustee this right. This really does no harm other than in forcing the bankruptcy trustee upon the mortgagee as a receiver and caretaker of the mortgaged premises and their proceeds. But it would seem fairer to give the mortgagee his own choice in that regard.

§ 535. **Relative Positions of Mortgagee and Liquidator.** Meanwhile, what is the position of the parties? The mere fact that the debtor's equity of redemption has passed into the liquidator's hands neither accelerates the maturity date of the debt so as to entitle the mortgagee to immediate foreclosure

---

[1] See Re Anders Push Button Co., 136 Fed. 995, and cases there cited. [2] Sec. 48.

or suit, nor does it excuse a default which may subsequently occur in the payment of the debt when it does fall due [1] The liquidator, therefore, is presented with the choice of adoption or rejection of the equity of redemption If he elects to accept the equity as part of the estate for liquidation, then he takes it *cum onere*, and must pay the interest on the mortgage debt as it falls due. This works no undue preference or priority in favor of the mortgagee, since the general creditors are entitled to nothing more than their debtor has, and he held his equity in the mortgaged property subject to the obligation to pay interest on the mortgage debt or suffer foreclosure [2] If, therefore, the liquidator does not keep down the interest on the mortgage debt, or allows the principal sum to get in default, the mortgagee is in the position of having an overdue debt secured by a mortgage. He holds security, it is true, to which he can look for payment of his debt if it is sufficient for that purpose, but none the less he is a creditor also Then arises this question, Should the court allow the mortgagee to prove against the estate for the full amount of his debt and also to realize his debt out of the security by foreclosure, or should it compel him to avail himself of the security so far as it would go by means of foreclosure, and prove against the estate only for the difference in monetary amount that may be thus caused?

§ 536 **Bankruptcy Rule — English Legislation.** Bankruptcy legislation answered this question at an early date The basic act of Elizabeth [3] directed that the bankrupt estate be applied to "the true satisfaction and payment of such creditors, that is to say to every of the said creditors a portion rate and rate alike according to the quantity of his or their debts." While this language provided for equality of distribution, it could not be described as exactly meeting the question above pro-

---

[1] Mulcahey *v.* Strouse, 151 Ill App 70
[2] Am. Iron etc Co. *v* Seaboard A L Co , 233 U S 261, 34 Sup Ct. Rep. 502, Centr. Trust Co *v.* Condon, 67 Fed 84.
[3] 13 Eliz c 7, Sec 2

pounded But the later statute of James[1] specifically forbade creditors, whether "having security" or not, to prove "for any more than a ratable part of their just and true debts with the other creditors of the said bankrupt" To quote the language of Mr. Justice Gray,[2] "the object of this provision would appear to have been to put all debts, whether by specialty or by simple contract, upon an equal footing in the ratable distribution of a bankrupt's estate, and to permit the real amount only of any debt, and not any larger sum named in a bond or other specialty, to be proved in bankruptcy." There never seems to have been any doubt with the English courts that the bankruptcy rule was as Mr Justice Gray described it Indeed, an early writer traces this rule practically to the statutes which the learned justice quotes, saying that Parliament's intention, in all the statutes concerning bankrupts, was that the creditors should have an equal proportion of the bankrupt's effects, and hence creditors of every degree must come in equally[3] The only way of attaining that end was to force the secured creditor to adopt the course above outlined, and that has been the policy of all English legislation This idea has persisted throughout subsequent English legislation, and to-day is expressed in the current Bankrupt Act[4]

§ 537 **American Bankruptcy Rule, and Practice Thereunder.** In our country the bankruptcy rule is the same as that of England, being provided for nowadays by Sections 57a and 57h of the present Bankrupt Act These provisions have been taken in connection with Section 57n, which requires each proof of claim to be presented within one year from the adjudication of bankruptcy, unless it is liquidated by litigation and final judgment is rendered within thirty days after the year's expiration, in which event the claim must be presented within

[1] 21 James I, c 19, Sec 8
[2] Merrill v National Bank of Jacksonville, 173 U. S 131, 19 S. Ct. 360
[3] Cooke, "Bankrupt Laws," 4th Lond ed , vol. 1, p 119.
[4] Bankrupt Act of 1883, Sec. 639, 2d sch.

sixty days thereafter. This, in the view of the Circuit Court of Appeals, Second Circuit, requires the secured creditor to present, within one year from the adjudication, his claim for the difference between the face of his debt and the appraised value of his security, even though it would be necessary after that time to liquidate the lien by the sale of the hypothecated property [1] In other words, "if a secured creditor delays filing his claim until after the year, because the security is being liquidated, he loses all right to file it at all." [2] If, however, the right of the lienor to hold his security is meanwhile attacked by the trustee, then the creditor is not required to file his proof of claim until after final judgment in that litigation, because he is precluded from doing so at an earlier date by the provisions of Section 57g to the effect that creditors holding preferences shall not be allowed to prove their claims until they have surrendered such preferences. This has been construed as justifying the lienor in surrendering the mortgaged property only after a decision has been rendered against him, holding that he received his security by way of preferential transfer or fraudulent conveyance.[3] Accordingly in *In re Baker Notion Co.*[4] JUDGE HAND allowed a proof of claim to be filed at the conclusion of litigation between the mortgagee and the trustee on the question whether the mortgagee was a preferred creditor So, under these authorities, the test is whether within the year the trustee has attacked the creditor's right to hold the security If he has, then the creditor need not file his claim until the successful termination of the suit; but, if the trustee has not attacked the security, then the creditor must file his claim within a year after the adjudication of bankruptcy

§ 538 **Security Given by Surety — Federal Rule** The bankruptcy rule does not apply, however, to the case of a

[1] *In re* Sampter, 170 Fed 938
[2] *In re* Baker Notion Co , 180 Fed 922
[3] Keppel *v* Tiffin Bank, 197 U. S 356, 25 S Ct 443; Page *v.* Rogers, 211 U. S 575, 29 S Ct 159
[4] *Supra*

creditor who holds security given by another person than the debtor In that case it has always been the rule in bankruptcy that the creditor may file a proof of claim in full. For instance, if the debt of the bankrupt has been guaranteed by a third party, who in turn has afterwards become bankrupt, the creditor may prove his claim against both estates in full, the only limitation being that the total of the dividends must not exceed the amount of his debt with interest, and the same rule applies to any other security given by a third person.[1] This principle was recently applied to a case where a creditor sold goods to the bankrupt and a third person guaranteed the payment of the purchase price and gave security for his guaranty[2] The question, said the learned judge, "comes down to this May the creditor in the first instance prove, or must the surety take up the balance and sue afterwards?" The court held that the creditor might prove in the first instance, for this reason — "The surety has no rights which the creditor originally had not. Subrogation is only a fiction, by which he is said to be an assignee of the creditor's claim. Hence, if the creditor has no right, neither has the surety, and the bankrupt would enjoy a wrongful immunity. The original error arises from regarding the security as a fund which should exonerate the estate The statute does not so regard it (Sec. 1, subd 23) and the law is well settled that a surety's security does not exonerate the estate." The reasoning contained in the above quotation sufficiently sets apart the case of guaranteed suretyship from the case where the principal debtor has furnished the security, and allows our return to the original proposition, that in bankruptcy the secured creditor is required to realize first upon his collateral, and may prove against the estate for the deficiency only, if a deficiency should fairly result from the procedure thus enjoined.

[1] *In re* Noyes, 127 Fed 286; Swarts *v* Fourth National Bank, 117 Fed 1; *In re* Mertens, 144 Fed 818.
[2] *In re* Keep Shirt Co., 200 Fed 80

§ 539 **Defect of Bankruptcy Rule** Other liquidating courts, however, have had difficulty with the question of adopting this bankruptcy rule It is undoubtedly true that if one creditor has two securities to which he can resort, and another creditor has but one of these funds for his security, a court of equity will compel the former to resort to that fund which the latter cannot reach. This is true marshaling; the court's jurisdiction resting, not on any contractual or trust relation between the parties, but on its general power to prevent injustice in cases where the common law is inadequate for relief.[1] And by the exercise of this power the courts have frequently given relief to creditors, indeed, the flexibility of the winding up jurisdiction of equity is due in large part to its possession of this power We have already had occasion to note instances of its exercise [2]

§ 540 **Limitations of Doctrine of Marshaling.** But there is a strict qualification to the use of this great power, a qualification indeed which almost suggests itself "A court of equity," says SPENCER, C. J, "will take care not to give the junior creditor this relief if it will endanger thereby the prior creditor, or in the least impair his prior right to raise his debt out of both funds." [3] This is well illustrated by the litigation which arose in England after the American Revolution. A number of our States had adopted acts which confiscated the property of Tories, and, with the proceeds of the sale of this confiscated property, provided funds for the payment of the Tories' debts owing to American creditors, and only American creditors. In a case where a bankrupt Tory owned American property Lord Thurlow compelled his American creditors to resort to this property first, leaving the Tory creditors to satisfy their claims out of the rest of the estate.[4] The difficulty with

[1] Lanoy v Duke of Athol, 2 Atk 446, Hayes v. Ward, 4 Johns Ch. 132
[2] See the instances mentioned in Chapter XVI, and the example, with respect to taxes upon mortgaged property in Chapter XXV
[3] Evertson v Booth, 19 Johns. 486, Coker v Shropshire, 59 Ala 542
[4] Peters v Irving, 3 Bro C C. 55, Wright v. Nutt, 3 Bro C. C. 326.

this decision, however, was that it carried the doctrine of marshaling too far, in that it compelled the creditor to go outside of the English courts into a foreign country for the satisfaction of his claim. Lord Eldon, as Mr. Scott, argued the case in behalf of the American creditors before Lord Thurlow, and strenuously protested in favor of the freedom of a creditor to collect his claim under the process afforded by the English courts; and afterwards, when he became chancellor, he overruled Lord Thurlow's decision.[1] With this limitation in mind, that marshaling is never compelled at the unjust cost of the prior lienor, can we say that the bankruptcy rule, by which a secured creditor must resort first to his security or else surrender it, should be adopted by a court which is not constrained by statute as is a court of bankruptcy? That is a very hard question to answer, as the equity courts of England and this country found when they came to answer it.

§ 541. **Early Chancery Doctrine** At first the English courts of equity were disposed to adopt the bankruptcy rule. SIR JOHN LEACH, V. C., decided that it was the equity of the unsecured creditors to require the secured creditor to realize fully on his security before he could prove his claim on a parity with the other creditors.[2] This decision has been followed in several of our States.[3] As matter of principle, this doctrine must find its sole justification in the view expressed by PARKER, C. J., of Massachusetts, that the secured creditor under any other rule "would in fact have a greater security than the pledge was intended to give him, for originally it would have been security only for a proportion of the debt equal to its value; when by proving the whole debt, and holding the pledge for the balance, it becomes security for as much more than its value as is the dividend which may be received on the whole debt."[4]

[1] Wright v Simpson, 6 Vesey 726
[2] Greenwood v Taylor, 1 Russ & Mylne 185
[3] Amory v. Francis, 16 Mass. 309, Wurtz v. Hart, 13 Ia. 515; Wheat v Dingle, 32 S C 473, 11 S E 394.
[4] Amory v Francis, supra

§ 542 **Later Chancery Doctrine — Rule of Mason v. Bogg** This, however, did not continue to be the equity rule in England. Sir John Leach's decision was overruled by LORD COTTENHAM in the notable case of Mason v. Bogg [1] There it was held that the secured creditor has the right to prove his claim fully with the other creditors and to realize on his security as well, subject only to the proviso that the total amount he might realize should not exceed the amount of his debt with interest Thus the two opposite ideas originated, that of equity which allowed the secured creditor to pursue both his remedies at the same time, and that of bankruptcy which required the secured creditor to come in only for the balance of his claim Undoubtedly Lord Cottenham inclined to the bankruptcy rule, but he professed himself unable to follow it because he felt that he could not interfere with the plain legal right of the mortgagee [2]

§ 543 **Prevalence in America of Rule of Mason v. Bogg** The views of Lord Cottenham have prevailed with the majority of the courts of our country, so that outside of the rule in bankruptcy and the rule in the few States which followed the decision of Sir John Leach, and thus adopted the bankruptcy rule as applicable to all cases of liquidation, the rule of Mason v. Bogg prevails. In such jurisdictions the mortgagee can prove against the estate for the full amount of his claim provided that he gives credit thereon for such amounts as he may meanwhile realize by the application of his security [3] These authorities rest on the proposition which is well put by TAFT, J, "that the collateral shall be security for the whole debt and every part of it, and therefore is as applicable to any balance which remains after payment from other sources as to the original amount due" [1] The federal courts, in short,

---

[1] 2 Mylne & C1 443   [2] Mason v Bogg supra
[3] Merrill v National Bank of Jacksonville, 173 U S 131 19 S Ct 300, People v Remington & Sons, 121 N Y 328, 24 N. E 793 Chemical Natl Bank v. Armstrong, 59 Fed 372 and cases there cited, Commercial Trust Co v Robert H Jenks Co, 194 Fed 732
[4] Chemical Natl Bank v Armstrong, 59 Fed 372, 377.

have given full approval to the rule of Mason *v.* Bogg, and apply it to all cases which are not governed by the National Bankrupt Act, hence, among other things, it applies in winding up proceedings under the National Bank Act.[1] Thus in our country two radically opposite rules exist, and in all probability one will never yield to the other

§ 544. **Degree to which Rule of Mason** *v* **Bogg now Obtains.** Similar conflict existed for many years in England. As the view of LORD COTTENHAM was adopted in winding up proceedings under the Companies Acts [2] the result was that, outside of the bankruptcy courts, a mortgagee stood in one position toward the debtor's estate, whereas if the debtor's estate was in bankruptcy his position was entirely different As JESSEL, M R, said, the English courts were in the absurd situation " of having different rules in the case of living and of dead bankrupts " [3] Finally, by the Judicature Acts of 1873 and 1874, the bankruptcy rule was applied to all distributive proceedings, whether in chancery or bankruptcy, so that to-day in England the position of the secured creditors toward the estate of the insolvent debtor is governed by the bankruptcy rule in all courts and in all proceedings [4] Thus the bankruptcy rule has finally vindicated itself in England With us, despite the strong reasoning of MR JUSTICE GRAY in Merrill *v.* National Bank of Jacksonville [5] and the reasoning of the Massachusetts court in Amory *v.* Francis,[6] the bankruptcy rule prevails only in winding up proceedings under the National Bankrupt Act and in liquidation proceedings in a few of our States, whereas the chancery rule, which has been abolished in England, prevails in the majority of our States, and with the federal courts in all proceedings outside of bankruptcy It is to be regretted that the bankruptcy rule, which undoubtedly makes more for justice, has

[1] Merrill *v* National Bank of Jacksonville, *supra;* Chemical National Bank *v.* Armstrong, *supra.*
[2] *In re* Withernsea Brick Works, L R. 16 Ch 337.
[3] *In re* Hopkins, 18 Ch Div 370
[4] See Maitland, "Equity," p. 195.
[5] *Supra*
[6] *Supra.*

not secured as sweeping a victory with us as it has finally attained in England.

§ 545. **Problem of Notes Secured by Promissor's Bonds** A question has arisen of late, however, having its origin in the modern free-handed uses of bonded indebtedness in corporate financing, which would occasion difficulty under either theory. The practice has become common, at a preliminary stage in corporate financing, for the parties interested to raise a temporary loan on the note of the corporation, secured by a larger amount, in face value, of its mortgage bonds. In effect the creditor in such a case has the unsecured note of the corporation for a certain figure, and, though the amount of his loan equals only the face of the note, he also has the secured obligation of the corporation for a much larger sum. The rights of the creditor in the event of default upon such a loan have given rise to considerable difference of opinion. Some courts impatiently override the technicalities of the situation, and view the creditor as after all a creditor only for the smaller amount, with the additional right to realize as a secured creditor only up to that amount. In other words, although he holds the corporate bonds as collateral, the secured creditor is held not to be entitled to avail himself of the security of the bonds to the same extent that he would be if they were bonds of a third person. Thus in Dickinson v Kempner,[1] a pledgee having sold such bonds where there had been no default, it was held that the pledgor had an adequate remedy at law because there was nothing to give a court of equity jurisdiction, the bonds being mere choses in action and capable of being compensated for in money, so that to all intents and purposes the proceeding had for its ultimate object the recovery of a money judgment against a solvent pledgee. The court, however, admitted that if the object of the bill had been to set aside the sale and recapture the bonds, the situation might have been different. In *In re* Matthews,[2] HOLT, J., sitting in bankruptcy, held that

[1] 193 Fed 204 [2] 188 Fed. 445

the court should restrain the pledgee from selling the bonds upon the pledgor's default caused by his bankruptcy, saying that " after bankruptcy it would be unjust to the other creditors to permit the trust company, by selling these bonds, to apparently establish a large additional indebtedness for which there was no consideration." This decision, however, was in effect overruled by the Circuit Court of Appeals,[1] the court without further opinion resting its decision on Jerome *v* McCarter.[2] In its broad effect, Jerome *v* McCarter seems to give the pledgee the fullest of rights in such cases. Judge Holt's argument, as we have noted, was that the pledgee, by selling the bonds on the pledgor's default, would create, in the hands of whosoever might buy them, an additional indebtedness which, in the end, the estate must meet. In Jerome *v* McCarter it was squarely held, however, that the pledgee has this right, the Supreme Court saying that " the position that the pledgee could not sell the pledge after the adjudication of bankruptcy, is quite untenable; . . . the Bankrupt Act has taken away no right from a pledgee secured to him by his contract." That is all true in strict logic, and of course the high authority of the court that spoke carries the issue, but it is to be regretted that practices of this kind cannot be stopped by anything short of special statutes which as yet do not exist.

[1] *In re* Iron Clad Mfg Co, 192 Fed 318.
[2] 94 U S 734.

CHAPTER XXVII

THE DEBTOR'S DISCHARGE

§ 546 No Discharge at Common Law
547. Equity can Give no Discharge
548 Discharge under English System of Bankruptcy
549 Discharge in Present National Bankrupt Act
550. Discharge of Judgments — Tort Claims
551 Test is whether Party could have Sued *Ex Contractu*
§ 552 Certain Judgments not Barred by Discharge
553 Creditor must have Notice of Bankruptcy
554 Effect of Discharge
555. Promise to Pay Discharged Debt
556 Extraterritorial Effect of Discharge
557. Intervening Removal of Creditor

§ 546 **No Discharge at Common Law** The common law idea of the discharge of a debt involves only its payment or its merger into a judgment resulting from a suit thereon And as the judgment in turn could be discharged only by the debtor's voluntary payment of the amount it called for, or by the sheriff "making" that amount out of the debtor's property by sale under a writ of execution, the end of the matter, from the common law standpoint, is that every debt is either made good out of the debtor's property, or remains a debt Statutes of limitation in time appeared, and gave the debtor a personal defence to stale claims, judgments became dormant after a certain number of years and were presumed to have been paid unless revived by process of *scire facias*, but, barring such things as that, the general proposition remains as we have stated it

§ 547. **Equity can Give no Discharge** Nor did a court of chancery take any different view, it recognized no other way of discharging a man from his debts than by satisfying them.

When it exercised its administrative jurisdiction upon the affairs of a corporate debtor, it never coerced creditors into giving a discharge of their claims; the most it could do would be to see that the debtor was entitled to credit for the amount of dividends received by its creditors. Of course in the case of a decedent's estate or the dissolution of a corporation, this question cannot arise, since there is no longer a debtor in existence to be sued or to acquire property in addition to that which is in the court's hands for distribution. As a practical matter, the question is academic in the case of a chancery winding up of a corporation's affairs on creditor's bill, because a corporation which has passed through such an ordeal is, from a business point of view, but a fly-blown name, and not fit for further use, but no court, in its final decree in such a case, would think of granting the company a discharge from further suit upon any creditor's balance of claim remaining after the receipt of dividends. It may therefore be affirmed, as an indubitable proposition, that no debtor may be discharged from any balance that may remain due upon his debts, after his existing affairs have been judicially liquidated, unless a statute grants him that right, as an incident to the liquidation.

§ 548 **Discharge under English System of Bankruptcy.** As we have seen,[1] the English bankrupt acts, at an early date, accorded to the bankrupt his discharge This right of the debtor to a discharge, as we have also seen,[2] made the principle of bankruptcy attractive, it led, in fact, to the parallel system of liquidation afforded by the insolvent debtor's acts. It led, too, as we have seen, at least in England, to the movement for the allowance of unmatured claims[3] In short, the situation of the English bankrupt was this The bankruptcy put into the trustee's hands all of his property which then existed in every conceivable shape, and also all of the property which he might acquire up to the closing of the estate and final distribu-

[1] *Supra,* c. XVII.
[2] *Supra,* c XIX.
[3] *Supra,* c XXIII.

tion.¹ On the other hand, the movement was growing to secure the bankrupt a discharge, not only from his debts presently owing, but from all claims that might thereafter become due by reason of any of his past transactions. At the present day the English bankruptcy passes all of the debtor's property which he might acquire up to the date of his discharge,² and, as we have seen, with very minor exceptions, all unmatured claims are barred by his discharge.

§ 549. **Discharge in Present National Bankrupt Act.** Our present Bankrupt Act is not of this symmetry. In the matter of unmatured claims, as we have seen, it is very deficient. It is more favorable to the bankrupt with regard to the property that passes under the bankruptcy, since it leaves to the bankrupt all property that he may acquire after the adjudication of bankruptcy, a date which necessarily precedes the bankrupt's discharge by a considerable interval of time.³

§ 550. **Discharge of Judgments — Tort Claims.** The courts acting under the Bankrupt Act make a distinction with respect to judgments. While all judgments are provable against the estate of the bankrupt, there are certain judgments which the creditor is allowed to prove, but from which, on the other hand, the debtor cannot obtain his discharge. The present Bankrupt Act⁴ provides that a discharge in bankruptcy shall release a bankrupt from all of his provable debts, with certain exceptions. As a general proposition whatever is provable is dischargeable. As the Supreme Court has said, "whether the discharge of the defendants in bankruptcy shall operate as a discharge of the plaintiff's debt, it not having been reduced to judgment, depends upon whether the debt was provable under the bank-

---

¹ Consequently a second bankruptcy could not occur until the estate had been fully administered under the first, *Ex parte* Brown, 4 Bro. C. C. 211.
² Bankrupt Act of 1883, Sec. 44.
³ Bankrupt Act of 1898, Sec. 70.
⁴ Sec. 17. A judgment for alimony is expressly excluded from proof by Sec. 63a. See Audubon *v.* Shufeldt, 181 U. S. 575, 21 S. Ct. 735; Wetmore *v.* Markoe, 196 U. S. 68, 25 S. Ct. 172.

ruptcy."[1] The Act allows any liability evidenced by a judgment to be proven,[2] but forbids a discharge of any judgment based upon a cause of action for obtaining property by false pretenses or willful and malicious injuries to person or property.[3] This was not intended, however, to enlarge the class of provable debts, but rather was intended to preclude the possibility of claims for certain torts being discharged, whether they were reduced to judgment or not[4] The rule has always been that a tort claim as such cannot share in a bankruptcy unless it has been reduced to judgment Yet certain tort claims are admitted to proof and are dischargeable in bankruptcy, on the other hand, there are certain tort claims which, though reduced to judgment are not provable The point of distinction is whether the claim is "accompanied with contractual liability "[5]

§ 551 **Test is whether Party could have Sued Ex Contractu** The original distinction was along the line of malice If malice was the gist of the action, then even a judgment for a tort was not a provable debt in bankruptcy.[6] The modern distinction, however, may be expressed in more scientific language. The test is not so much what the gist of the action for tort is, but whether the injured party could have sued *ex contractu*. If the case is such that " there is a claim arising out of contract but of such a nature that there is at the same time an independent remedy in tort " then the claim is provable[7] This reasoning

[1] Tindle v. Birkett, 205 U S 183, 27 S. Ct 493
[2] See 63a.
[3] See 17a
[4] *In re* New York Tunnel Co , 159 Fed 688 , Brown v United States Button Company, 149 Fed 48
[5] *Re* New York Tunnel Company, 159 Fed. 688
[6] Thus, under the Illinois Insolvency Law a judgment for seduction was held not be dischargeable, People v Greer, 43 Ill 213 - And under the Act of 1867 a similar ruling was made, Howland v Carson, 28 Ohio St 625
[7] Grant Shoe Company v. Land, 212 U S 445, 29 S Ct. 332 In Clarke v. Rogers, 228 U. S 531, 33 S Ct. 587, the question, whether a preference had been committed because a trustee who had embezzled trust funds chose to make restitution prior to the bankruptcy, resolved itself into the question whether the person receiving the preference was

has been applied to Section 17 of the Bankrupt Act, which excepts from the discharge a provable debt accompanied by fraud, embezzlement, misappropriation or defalcation on the part of the bankrupt " while acting as an officer or in any fiduciary capacity " Such claims are provable, but the Act excepts them from discharge The present Act has gone further, and excepts liability for obtaining property by false pretenses The Act of 1841 [1] discharged the bankrupt from debts " which shall not have been contracted in consequence of a defalcation as a public officer or as executor or administrator, guardian or trustee or while acting in any other fiduciary capacity " [2] The Act of 1867 [3] provides that no debt " created by the fraud or embezzlement of the bankrupt or by his defalcation as a public officer or while acting in a fiduciary character " shall be discharged, but provides that the creditor can prove his debt and receive dividends thereon on account of the claim The present Act, as we have seen, uses different language. " The intent of Congress in changing the Act of 1867 seems to have been to restore the Act of 1841, which extended the benefits of the law to every debtor who had not been guilty of defalcation as a public officer or in a fiduciary capacity, the Act of 1898 adding to the excepted clause those against whom a judgment for fraud had been obtained " [4] But under all these statutes it has been held that the fiduciary capacity which the statute intends to describe must be that of an express trust, as distinct from the obligation arising from an implied or resulting trust Hence a factor who embezzles the proceeds of sales is not considered as indebted

---

a creditor with a provable claim, so that the result of the Act would be to prefer him over other creditors of the same class In holding that he was a creditor, the court points out that his claim against the embezzling trustee was one which, enforceable only in equity though it may be, was in the nature of a claim in contract rather than tort, and therefore was a provable claim

[1] Sec 1
[2] See Crawford v Burke, 195 U S 176, 25 S Ct 9
[3] Sec 33
[4] Crawford v Burke, *supra*

in a trust capacity, and his liability is discharged by his bankruptcy.[1]

§ 552. **Certain Judgments not Barred by Discharge.** In any case where the claim is barrable by the discharge, the fact that the creditor elects to sue in tort makes no difference. "All debts originating on an open account or upon a contract express or implied are provable, though the plaintiff elects to bring his action for fraud."[2] On the other hand, a judgment for damages resulting from malicious and willful injury to property, while provable as a claim in bankruptcy, would not be barred by discharge. Thus a judgment for criminal conversation with the plaintiff's wife on the part of the bankrupt invades a property right and is provable, but is not discharged under the present Act.[3]

§ 553. **Creditor must have Notice of Bankruptcy.** In order for the discharge to bar the particular creditor, it is only fair that he should have shared in the distribution of the bankrupt's estate, or at least have had a reasonable opportunity of doing so. In short, he should have had notice of the bankruptcy. To that end our statute requires the referee, to whom the proceedings are referred after the adjudication, to advertise for claims for a stated period and to mail notice to all creditors named in the schedules filed by the bankrupt. Creditors have one year from the date of adjudication in which to file claims. If a creditor is not named in the schedule and has no reasonable notice of the bankruptcy, then, while he is barred from participating in the distribution of the assets in the trustee's hands, he is not barred from subsequently suing the bankrupt.[4] This provision has been liberally construed in favor of the creditor,

---

[1] Chapman v. Forsyth, 2 How. 202; Neel v. Clark, 95 U. S. 704; Hennequin v. Clews, 111 U. S. 676, 4 S. Ct. 576; Forsythe v. Vehmeyer, 177 U. S. 177, 20 S. Ct. 623; Crawford v. Burke, 195 U. S. 176, 25 S. Ct. 9.
[2] Crawford v. Burke, 195 U. S. 176, 25 S. Ct. 9.
[3] Tinker v. Colwell, 193 U. S. 473, 24 S. Ct. 505; See also Kavanaugh v. McIntyre, 210 N. Y. 175.
[4] Sec. 17.

so that if his address or name are stated, but improperly, the creditor is not barred, and on the other hand he has no interest in the debtor's discharge or standing to apply for its vacation.[1]

§ 554. **Effect of Discharge.** The discharge, when effected, has a limited value in terms of principle. It does not destroy or limit the debt, that remains in full force and vigor despite the discharge, and the latter's only effect is as a personal defence to the debtor which he, and only he and his personal representatives, may plead.[2] Nor, as we have seen, is it a bar against any particular debt, unless two things concur, (a) the debt was provable in the particular bankruptcy in which the discharge was granted, and (b) the creditor participated in that bankruptcy, or had proper notice of its pendency. In view of this the Supreme Court was on firm ground when it recently held that the mere existence of the debtor's discharge in bankruptcy raised no presumptive bar of *res adjudicata* against the assertion of a particular creditor that the discharge was not pleadable against his claim.[3]

§ 555. **Promise to Pay Discharged Debt.** Such being the nature of the discharge, it is easy to understand how the rule originated that a subsequent promise to pay a debt, barred by a discharge in bankruptcy, requires no fresh consideration in order for an action to be brought upon default in payment. This doctrine, which formerly enjoyed a well-recognized vogue both in England[4] and America,[5] really violates no principle of the law of contracts. The new contract was not the basis of the suit, as the sounder practice was to declare on the original debt, reserving the new promise to use by way of replication to

---

[1] Birkett v. Columbia Bank, 195 U S 345, 25 S Ct 38; Guasti v. Miller, 203 N Y 259, 96 N E 416.
[2] Moyer v. Dewey, 103 U S 301.
[3] Friend v. Talcott, 228 U S 27, 33 S Ct 505.
[4] Williams v. Dyle, Peake N P 68; Wennell v. Adney, 3 B & P 249; Leaper v. Falton, 16 East 420.
[5] Christie v. Bridgman, 51 N J Eq 331, 25 Atl 929, 30 Atl 429; Maxim v. Moss, 8 Mass 127; Dusenberry v. Hoyt, 53 N Y. 531.

the anticipated plea of the discharge.¹ In short the discharge, being merely a personal defense to an action on the debt, may be waived, and a fresh promise operates as a waiver. This is illustrated by the fact that a debt barred by a composition agreement may not be thus revived, because it is in effect canceled by the agreement,² whereas neither the bankruptcy nor the discharge cancels any of the bankrupt's obligations Beyond illustrating the nature of the discharge, however, this doctrine, though still existent with us, is of little present-day importance. It was abolished by statute in England many years ago,³ and although the present English statute says nothing on the subject, the doctrine is regarded as obsolete⁴ And the Supreme Court, with us, has reduced it to the strictest of limits by requirements as to the nature of proof requisite to support such a promise.⁵

§ 556. **Extraterritorial Effect of Discharge.** This appreciation of the nature of the discharge will help us in our next inquiry, which concerns its extraterritorial effect. This involves not only the discharge under a National Bankrupt Act such as we have at the present day, but the discharge of a debtor under the various methods of liquidation which are prescribed by the laws of our different States. On this subject the English judges differ radically from our Supreme Court They recognize a foreign discharge, at least on a debt of foreign origin, and allow it to be pleaded in their own courts to a suit by an English creditor. Their view is stated in their leading case of Potter v. Brown,⁶ to be that " what is a discharge of a debt in the country where it was contracted, is a discharge of it everywhere " Our Supreme Court denies any extraterritorial effect to such a discharge, except when it is pleaded, in the courts of another juris-

---

¹ See Moyer v Dewey, *supra*
² Stafford v Bacon, 1 Hill 233, see also Straus v. Cunningham, 159 N Y App Div 718, 144 N Y S 104
³ 7 Geo IV, c 57, Sec 61
⁴ Exp Barrow, 18 Ch. D. 464
⁵ Allen v Ferguson, 18 Wall 1
⁶ 5 East 124, 3 East 77.

diction, to a suit by a citizen of the jurisdiction where the discharge was granted In short, the discharge binds only creditors who at the time were fellow citizens of the debtor in the jurisdiction of the court which granted the discharge That was the decision in Ogden v Saunders.¹ As later stated by the Supreme Court, that case decided that " a certificate of discharge under such a law cannot be pleaded in bar of an action brought by a citizen of another State in the courts of the United States, or of any other State than that where the discharge was obtained '²

§ 557 **Intervening Removal of Creditor.** The case is more doubtful where the plaintiff had been a fellow citizen of the debtor at the time the debt was contracted, but had removed from their erstwhile common State before the debtor went into bankruptcy. In Pullen v Hillman³ it was held that such a person was not bound by the subsequent discharge of his debtor The court reasoned that a chose in action follows the person of the creditor, and therefore the State of the debtor's residence cannot deal with the discharge of the debt, and to allow a discharge because the creditor once lived in the same State with the debtor is to forbid him from ever removing from the State On the other hand, in Coler v Cunningham⁴ there is a dictum to the contrary effect. But there seems to be no room for doubt that if the debtor, who once resided in the same State with his creditor, moves into another State and is discharged in bankruptcy, the creditor is not bound by his discharge.⁵

[1] 12 Wheat. 213
[2] Baldwin v Hale, 1 Wall 223, Coler v. Cunningham, 133 U. S. 107, 10 S Ct 269, and cases there cited
[3] 84 Me 129, 24 Atl. 795
[4] *Supra*
[5] Lowenberg v Levine, 93 Cal 215, 28 Pac 941

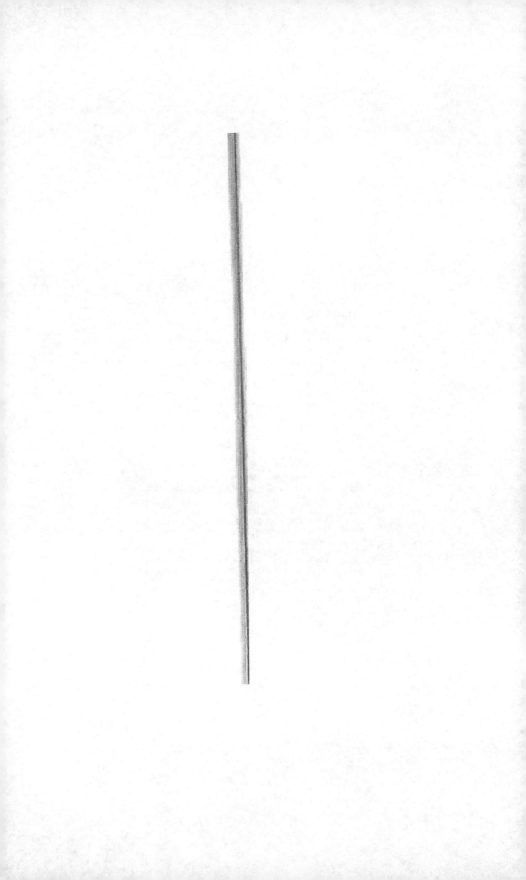

INDEX

[The References are to Sections.]

A

ADMINISTRATOR. (*See* EXECUTOR.)

ADMIRALTY,
  jurisdiction of, as exception to supremacy of Bankrupt Act, 452.

ADOPTION,
  of claims by Liquidator, in general, 508, 509.
  priority of choice of, 510.
  effect of rejection of, 511-513.
  effect of, 509.

AFTER-ACQUIRED PROPERTY CLAUSE,
  nature of, 259.
  legal and equitable views concerning, 260-263, 265.
  limitations of locality of, 264.
  intervening act with respect to, 266.
  New York rule as to, 267-269, 271.
  opposing view regarding, 270.
  view of Federal courts, regarding, 272, 273.
  exception in favor of, in railroad mortgages, 274-276.
  See MORTGAGES.

AGENCY,
  class of, affected by doctrine of reputed ownership, 240.
  method of inquiry in cases of, 244-247.
  disposition of goods in, 248.
  disposition of proceeds of sale in, 249.
  whether sale is absolute or conditional in, 250.
  rule in cases of conditional sale and chattel mortgage in, 251-253.
  recording of agreement of, immaterial, 254.
  false character of such arrangements in, 255.
  different views on, 256.
  See TRUST RECEIPTS.

AGREEMENTS,
  restricting creditors' right of realization, 60.
  See REALIZATION.

ALIMONY,
  divorced wife as judgment creditor for, 71, *n*. 2.

[The References are to Sections]

ANCILLARY RECEIVERS (*See* RECEIVERS)

ASSETS,
    equality of legal and equitable, 13.
    unlawful, 26.
    lawful, available to creditors, 25–27.
    labor not an asset, 28.
    must have existence, 29.
    must be alienable, 36
    Stock Exchange seats as, 49
    contingent remainders as, 50
    tenancy by the entirety as, 50.
    equitable, omitted from Statute of Fraudulent Conveyances, 89, 90
    worthless, 27, 98
    equitable, application of Reputed Ownership Statute to, 187–189.
    See FRANCHISES.

ASSIGNMENT,
    of right to set aside fraudulent transfer, 84
    See GENERAL ASSIGNMENT

ATTACHMENT,
    status of attaching creditor in, 74, *n* 4.

B

BADGES OF FRAUD,
    character of, 146.
    twofold use of, 147.
    retention of possession by vendor as, 148
    sales in bulk as, 149.
    statutes relating to sales in bulk as, 150
    agreements to withhold from record as, 151
    other examples of, 152

BANKRUPT ACT,
    constitutionality of, 355.
    supremacy of National, 451, 452.
    as applied to corporations, 457.
    as applied to decedents' estates, 457
    as limiting administrative powers of State Courts, 458, 459.
    See BANKRUPTCY.

BANKRUPTCY,
    application of English Reputed Ownership Statute to, 184.
    purposes accomplished by, 330, 331
    early English legislation regarding, 332, 333
    as transmuting title to bankrupt's property, 334
    forcing creditors in, 335
    double object of system, 336.
    cognate character of, with Statute of Fraudulent Conveyances, 340
    voluntary, 356.

[The References are to Sections]

BANKRUPTCY, — *continued*
    acts of, 357-365
    connection of with solvency, 367-373
    character of proceedings prior to adjudication in, 377.
    receivers in, 378
    necessity of statutory system in, 386
    acts of, as confined to traders, 387, 457.
    connection of, with Insolvency Acts, 388, 389
    complexity of American legislation regarding, 390, 391
    question of supremacy as relating to jurisdiction in, 453-456
    limitations of jurisdiction in, 457
    as connected with debtor's residence, 460, 461
    See BANKRUPT ACTS; JUDGMENTS, LIQUIDATION.

BANKS,
    status of receivers of national, 382, 411
    chancery receivers of, 382, *n* 4
    resemblance of National Act concerning, to English Statute, 405
    Federal, as local institutions, 406
    winding-up legislation for national, 407-410
    judicial control of receivers of, 412
    legislation affecting State, 413
    preferences forbidden to, by Statute, 417

C

CAR TRUST AGREEMENTS,
    nature of, 219

CHATTEL MORTGAGE,
    analyzed, 241-243
    in cases of complication, 244-247
    See LIENOR; MORTGAGES, RECORDING ACTS

CHOSES IN ACTION,
    application of reputed ownership doctrine to, 189, 204, 205
    See ASSETS

CLAIMS,
    bankruptcy trustee's status with respect to, 350
    chancery receiver's status with respect to, 350, *n*. 3.

COMMERCIAL CUSTOM,
    reasonable use of, in reputed ownership, 195
    in connection with debtor's status in business, 196
    proof of, 197

COMMITTEES OF CREDITORS,
    legality of 314

COMMITTEE OF LUNATIC (*See* LUNATIC)

[The References are to Sections]

CONCEALMENT OF PROPERTY,
 as distinct from fraudulent transfer, 62
 as an act of bankruptcy, 359.

CONDEMNATION PROCEEDINGS,
 creditors must allow for payment in full in, 30, n 1.

CONDITIONAL SALE,
 Reputed Ownership Statute does not apply to, 193.
 erroneous view of certain courts as to reputed ownership doctrine, 199, 203
 analyzed, 241-243
 in cases of complication, 244-247
 statutory rights of vendee, 241, n 2
 See RECORDING ACTS

CONFUSION OF GOODS.
 See PLEDGE.

CONSIDERATION, UNDER STATUTE OF FRAUDULENT CONVEYANCES,
 where on hand, 135
 where debtor has disposed of, 136.
 where debtor uses, to prefer creditor, 137-139.
 where debtor secretes, etc , 140.
 nature of, 141.
 past, 142.
 extent of, 143.

CONSIGNMENTS,
 Reputed Ownership Statute does not apply to, 193.
 position of factor regarding, in case of reputed ownership, 193-204.
 analyzed, 242, 243
 in cases of complication, 244-247.

CORPORATIONS,
 jurisdiction of equity over, source of, 303-307.
 jurisdiction over, in case of statutory liability, 307
 equitable jurisdiction over, in connection with insolvency, 308
 equitable jurisdiction over, limited in exercise to America, 309.
 administration is not dissolution of, 310
 plaintiff cannot have priority in bill for general administration against, 311
 collusion does not affect jurisdiction over, 312.
 jurisdiction over, limited to liquidation, 313
 lawfulness of committees of creditors of, 314.
 limitations of jurisdiction over, 315-329
 state laws forbidding preferences by, 416.
 fraudulent use of, 105
 rights of creditors on foreclosure sale of property of, 106-108.
 rights of creditors against successive, 109, 126.

[The References are to Sections]

CORPORATIONS, — *continued*
    merger of, as constituting fraudulent transfer, 105, n. 3
    See REALIZATION, RECEIVERS, STOCKHOLDERS' LIABILITY, TRUST FUND DOCTRINE.

COURTS
    See JURISDICTION

CREDITOR,
    has no title to debtor's property, 1
    distinction between secured, and general, 2
    judgment, as conferring claim on creditor, 3, 4
    résumé of procedure by, at law and equity, 17
    entitled to whatever debtor can sell, 25
    present and subsequent, 70, 157.
    tort claimant as present, 71
    contract creditor as present, 72
    distinction between, and purchaser with respect to Recording Acts, 209–213
    See CLAIMS; ESTOPPEL, EXECUTION, JUDGMENT, SUBSEQUENT CREDITORS, TORT CLAIMS

CUSTOM
    See COMMERCIAL CUSTOM.

D

DEBTOR,
    has no relationship with creditor in broad sense, 1.
    See CREDITOR.

DECEDENTS' ESTATES,
    administration bill, first exercise of equitable jurisdiction over, 296
    grounds of jurisdiction over, 297.
    conditions imposed upon the plaintiff in suit against, 298
    as subject matter of jurisdiction, 299.
    equal jurisdiction over, effected by bill, 300
    remains of equal jurisdiction over, in America, 301
    federal jurisdiction over, 302
    application of this jurisdiction to corporate affairs of, 303
    See CORPORATIONS

DISCHARGE OF DEBTOR,
    not obtainable at common law or in equity, 546, 547.
    in bankruptcy, 548, 549.
    notice to creditor, 553
    effect of, 554
    promise to pay discharged debt as waiver of, 555
    extra-territorial effect of, 556, 557
    See TORT CLAIMS, JUDGMENTS.

DISTRIBUTION
    See EQUALITY OF DISTRIBUTION

452   INDEX

[The References are to Sections]

DONATION,
    inquiry in case of, under Statute of Fraudulent Conveyances, 116
    in cases of partnership and corporate reorganization, 126
    as against subsequent creditors, 158–166
    subrogation in case of, 127
    distinction between purchase and, 128.
    See INTENT.

E

ENCUMBRANCES,
    property must be taken subject to, 30.
    See MORTGAGE, SET-OFF

EQUALITY OF DISTRIBUTION,
    definition of system of, 280, 281.
    principle of, 283, 284.
    common ground of, with selfish system, 285.
    relation of preferences to system of, 286
    cannot be secured by debtor's suit, 287
    not attainable by common law procedure, 15, 293
    not secured by judgment creditor's bill, 16.
    as secured by general assignment, 288
    See DISTRIBUTION; GENERAL ASSIGNMENT, REALIZATION.

EQUITABLE LIEN,
    on chattels not pledged, 239.
    in connection with preferences, 436–450.
    See AFTER ACQUIRED PROPERTY CLAUSE; MORTGAGES;
       PLEDGE, PREFERENCES.

EQUITY,
    no jurisdiction in, conferred by insolvency alone, 294
    basis of jurisdiction in, 295
    See CORPORATIONS; DECEDENTS' ESTATES, PARTNERSHIP

ESTOPPEL,
    of creditors, 115
    as substitute for Reputed Ownership Statute, 200–202

EXAMINATION OF DEBTOR,
    deficiency of State laws in providing for, as compared with bankrupt act, 458, *n.* 3

EXECUTION,
    right of realization conferred by, 6.
    common law limitations concerning, 8
    judgment as original source of, 7
    sale, rights of purchaser under recording acts, 212.
    date of levy of, 15, *n* 3.

EXECUTOR,
    common law status of, with respect to fraudulent transactions, 302–394.

[The References are to Sections]

EXECUTOR, — *continued*
    status of, under modern legislation, 395
    jurisdiction of bankruptcy over, 457, n 4

EXEMPTION LAWS,
    prevalence of, in United States, 52.
    life insurance as a subject of, 53.
    as provisions of the Bankrupt Act, 54.
    former conflict of interpretation of, 55
    present rule as to, 56, 57
    Statute of Fraudulent Conveyances does not apply to property covered by, 97

F

FACTOR.
    See CONSIGNMENT.

FRANCHISES,
    corporate, as available to creditors, 37.

FRAUD, BADGES OF
    See BADGES OF FRAUD.

FRAUDULENT CONVEYANCE,
    necessity of judgment in case of, 73
    necessity of regular process in case of, 75.
    other procedure to attack, 76
    of real estate, procedure in case of, 77
    inadequacy of common law procedure in case of, 78
    jurisdiction of equity over, 64–67
    of real estate, concurrent jurisdiction of equity in case of, 79
    of personal property, concurrent jurisdiction of equity in case of, 80.
    right of action in case of, 82
    necessity of acting in case of, 83
    assignability of rights, in case of, 84
    cognate character of Statute of, and first bankrupt act, 310
    when set aside, restoration of status quo, 58
    definition of, 61
    as distinct from concealment, 62
    inadequacy of common law to deal with, 63
    validity of, as between immediate parties, 86, 87
    validity of, as against third parties, 88
    of equitable assets, jurisdiction over, 91–96.
    transfer of, as test, 99–100, 102, 103
    passivity of debtor in case of, 101
    partnership rights as subject of, 104
    issues which affect transferee in, 112
    merger of corporations as constituting, 105, n 3
    status of transferee's privies in case of, 114
    rights of equity receiver with respect to, 321-329
    concurrent jurisdiction of law and equity over, in bankruptcy proceedings, 341, 342
    as an act of bankruptcy, 358

[The References are to Sections.]

FRAUDULENT CONVEYANCES, STATUTE OF,
    as basis of law, 68, 69
    omission of equitable assets from, 89, 90.
    adequacy of, in cases of reputed ownership, 174-180
    Reputed Ownership Statute as supplement to, 183
    in connection with status of trustee in bankruptcy, 339-344

G

GENERAL ASSIGNEE,
    actual status of, as against fraudulent transactions, 292
    status of, under American legislation, 100, 101

GENERAL ASSIGNMENT,
    Reputed Ownership Statute does not apply to, 192
    as securing equal distribution, 288
    must prescribe immediate distribution, 289.
    weakness of, 290
    validity of preferences in case of, 291
    as an act of bankruptcy, 365

GIFT
    See DONATION.

GOOD FAITH
    See NOTICE.

GOVERNMENT,
    claims against, as available to creditors, 38.
    does not pay expenses of liquidation, 172

H

HOMESTEADS
    See EXEMPTION LAWS.

I

INSOLVENCY,
    relation of, to acts of bankruptcy, 367-369
    definitions of, 370
    nature of statutory definitions of, 371-373
    as connected with jurisdiction of equity, 291.

INSOLVENCY ACTS,
    connection of, with bankruptcy legislation, 388, 389

INSURANCE
    See EXEMPTION LAWS; REALIZATION

INTENT,
    as to subsequent creditors in cases of gift, 158-166
    rule as to, 167-170.
    express, 168
    imputed, 169
    application of rule as to, to contract claims, 171
    application of rule as to, to broad claims, 172

[The References are to Sections]

INTENT, — continued.
    general rule as to debtor's, 117.
    indebtedness of donor as bearing on, 118-125
    as determined by the debtor's financial condition, 133
    as determined by effect of transaction, 134
    See Consideration

INTEREST ON CLAIMS.
    See Liquidation

J

JUDGMENT,
    as constituting claim on debtor, 3-4.
    original source of right of realization, 7
    double effect of, 5.
    procedure in absence of, 18
    exceptions, 19, 21-23
    enforcement of foreign, 20
    transferee cannot attack validity of creditor's, 113
    effect of, as against receiver, 318, 319
    annulment of, by bankruptcy, 337-338
    lien of, as constituting a preference, 361-363, 122
    priority of local, 465.
    founded on tort, enforceability in liquidation, 492
    See Tort Claims

JUDGMENT CREDITOR,
    procedure of, 74
    not protected by recording acts, 211.
    necessity for judgment, 221
    divorced wife as, for alimony, 71, n. 2

JUDGMENT CREDITORS' BILL,
    jurisdiction of chancery over, 10, 11
    representative character of, 14
    pre-requisites to equitable aid by means of, 12.
    lien of equitable levy under, as affected by bankruptcy, 364.
    supplementary proceedings as a substitute for, 17, n. 1.

JURISDICTION,
    territorial limitations of Federal, 374-376.
    See Judgment; Receivers; Trustee, etc

L

LABOR CLAIMS.
    See Prior Claims.

LANDLORD'S LIEN
    See Prior Claims

LIENOR,
    rights of, in case of creditors' bill, 317-319
    has interest in liquidation of debtor's estate, 529.
    position of, in absence of litigation, 530

[The References are to Sections]

LIENOR, — *continued*
    liquidation as affecting right of, to realize on security, 531-544.
    position of, in case of note secured by promisor's bonds, 545

LIMITED PARTNERSHIP (*See* PARTNERSHIP)

LIQUIDATION,
    mortgage foreclosure as, 24 n 1
    Government does not meet all expenses of 472
    expenses, theory on which they are met, 473, 474, 476.
    method of estimating expenses of, 477
    counsel fees in, 475, 478, 479.
    continuance of business in, 480-484
    of railroads and public service companies, 485, 486
    receiver's certificates in, 487.
    deficiency in operation of business in, 476 488.
    status of debtor in, 489
    status of creditor in, 489
    interest on claims in, 493
    method of estimating claims in, 494-497
    maturity of claims in, 498-507
    expenses of preserving hypothecated property in, 534
    in connection with hypothecated property in possession of liquidator, 532-534
    See ADOPTION; LIENOR, PRIOR CLAIMS, JUDGMENT; TORT CLAIMS

LUNATIC,
    original status of committee of, 396.
    status of committee of, under modern legislation, 397-399.
    jurisdiction in bankruptcy over, 457.

M

MARSHALING,
    of partnership assets, 32 34
    of Government debts, 517
    as applied to relation of secured creditor to estate in liquidation, 539, 540

MECHANIC'S LIEN
    effect of, as an act of bankruptcy, 363.
    See JUDGMENT, LIENOR.

MORTGAGE,
    creditor's right to accounting of premises covered by, 35.
    rights of creditors against purchaser at foreclosure sale, 106
    See AFTER ACQUIRED PROPERTY CLAUSE; CHATTEL MORTGAGE, LIENOR; LIQUIDATION

N

NOTICE,
    as connected with good faith, 144
    sufficiency of, 145

[The References are to Sections]

NOTICE, — *continued*
    receipt of, before complete payment, 153-156.
    See BADGES OF FRAUD

O

OWNERSHIP
    See POSSESSION, SECRECY

P

PARTITION SUIT,
    rights of creditors in, 1, *n* 1

PARTNERSHIP,
    rights as subject of fraudulent transfer, 104
    assets transferred to new partnership, 126
    jurisdiction of equity over liquidation of, 306
    winding-up jurisdiction of chancery over limited, 306.
    preferences forbidden to limited, 416, *n* 1
    jurisdiction of bankruptcy over surviving partner in cases of, 437, *n* 4.

PERSONAL PROPERTY
    See RECORDING ACTS

PLEDGE,
    analysis of, 221
    strictly confined to tangible chattels, 228
    of choses in action, 225
    equitable, as pertaining to specific performance, 227
    symbolical delivery and notice of possession of property under, 230, 231.
    requisites as to custodian of property under, 232, 233
    confusion of goods in case of, 243.
    possession by third party of property under, 235, 236
    in connection with warehousing, 237, 238
    as differing from equitable lien on chattels not pledged, 239
    See EQUITABLE LIEN

POSSESSION,
    rule of Twyne's Case as to, 176.
    separation of, from ownership inconclusive, 177
    constructive, in connection with reputed ownership, 229-231
    notice of, in connection with symbolical delivery, 230, 231.

POWER OF APPOINTMENT,
    as available to creditors, 47

PREFERENCE
    where debtor uses proceeds of sale to prefer creditor, 137-139
    validity of, in general assignment, 291
    relation of, to opposing systems of realization, 286
    origin of doctrine concerning, 343
    as an act of bankruptcy, 360-366.

INDEX

[The References are to Sections]

PREFERENCE, — *continued*
    in connection with trust fund doctrine, 415.
    State laws forbidding, 416.
    in the case of limited partnerships, 416, n. 1.
    forbidden by National Bank Acts, 417, 418.
    definition of, under present Bankrupt Act, 418–421, 423–425.
    not created by exchange of values, 426.
    diminution of debtor's estate as test of, 427
    time limit imposed by statute as to, 429–431.
    intent to create a, 432, 433
    reasonable cause to believe transfer would effect a, 434, 435
    whether constituted by transfer pursuant to previous obligation, 436–450
    restoration of embezzled trust funds as, 439
    explanation of doctrine of equitable lien in connection with, 441–450
    See SET-OFF.

PRESUMPTION,
    of reliance in case of reputed ownership, 202
    in case of withholding conveyance from record, 216

PRIOR CLAIMS,
    equitable doctrine of, 523–527
    equitable doctrine of, as supplementary to rule concerning railroad mortgages, 276
    statutes embodying equitable doctrine of, 528
    nature of, 514
    ranking of, 515–517
    marshaling of, 517
    landlords' liens as, 519–521
    nature of statutory, 518.
    supply claims as, 522
    in supplementary proceedings, 16, n. 2.

PRIORITY,
    complainant cannot have, in administration bill, 298.
    complainant cannot have, in corporate administration, 311.

PROOF,
    burden of, under Statute of Fraudulent Conveyances, 131.
    relevancy of, 132.

PURCHASER,
    innocent, proviso in favor of in Statute of Fraudulent Conveyances, 110-111, 129.
    difference between situation of donee and, 128
    protection of *bona fide*, 130
    distinction between, and creditor with respect to Recording Acts, 209, 213.
    on execution sale, rights under Recording Acts, 212.
    See PROOF.

[The References are to Sections]

R

RAILROADS.
See MORTGAGES, PRIOR CLAIMS.

REAL ESTATE,
procedure respecting, in case of Statute of Fraudulent Conveyances, 77.
application of Reputed Ownership Statute to, 185
application of Statute of Uses to, 186
as a subject matter of administration, 299
right of levy on, at common law, 6, n 1, 17, n 2
See FRAUDULENT CONVEYANCES, RECORDING ACTS

REALIZATION, RIGHT OF,
as limited by Statute, 51
illustration of, insurance and banking firms, 51
agreement restricting creditors' rights of, 60
selfish system of, 279.
selfish point of view of, 282.
common ground of, with system of equal distribution, 285.
relation of preferences to, and system of equal distribution, 286.
See INSURANCE, CORPORATION, EQUALITY OF DISTRIBUTION.

RECEIVER,
in equity, rights with respect to prior lien, 317
with respect to pending suits and judgments, 318, 319
rights of, with respect to fraudulent conveyances, 321–329.
status of, with respect to claims, 350, n 3.
status of, in bankruptcy, 378
ancillary, in bankruptcy, 379, 466–469
of corporations, status of, 402–404
status of, in foreign jurisdiction, 462, 463
statutory, powers outside of jurisdiction, 464
ancillary, powers of ancillary courts, 466–469.
ancillary and dependent jurisdiction respecting, 470, 471.
appointment of, as an act of bankruptcy, 365
See BANKS, LIQUIDATION

RECORDING ACTS,
agreement to withhold from record, 151
general value of, 206
relating to real estate, 207–213
as augmenting doctrine of reputed ownership, 214
as to effect of withholding conveyance from record, 215, 216
affecting personal property, 217.
tendency to growth of legislation concerning, 218–223
classification of, 219
different views as to manner of compliance with, 220
relating to personal property, rule of Twyne's Case is basis for, 222

[The References are to Sections.]

RECORDING ACTS, — *continued*
    present English view concerning mortgages as affected by, 278.
    position of trustee in bankruptcy under, 345–348
    See AGENCY, PREFERENCES

REPRESENTATIVES OF CREDITORS,
    have no higher rights than creditors, 59.

REPUTED OWNERSHIP,
    definition of, 173
    application of Statute of Fraudulent Conveyances to, 174–180.
    original clause as to, 181
    in present clause of English Act, 182
    as a supplement to the Statute of Fraudulent Conveyances, 183
    Statute, limitations of, 184–187
    criticisms of English Statute of, 190
    cases not reached by Statute of, 191–194
    commercial custom and use thereof as test of, 195–197.
    absence in America of statutes concerning, 198
    erroneous view of some courts concerning, 199
    estoppel the American substitute for, 201, 202
    exceptions to American rule, 203–205
    constructive possession in connection with, 229–231
    See AGENCY, PLEDGE; PRESUMPTION; RECORDING ACTS, SECRECY

S

SECRECY,
    effect of, 178
    when accompanied by separation of ownership from possession, 179

SET-OFF,
    constitutes no preference, 428
    doctrine of, as against creditors' right of realization, 31.

SPECIFIC PERFORMANCE.
    See PLEDGE, PREFERENCE

STOCKHOLDERS,
    liability of, status of liquidator with respect to, 351–353.

STOPPAGE IN TRANSIT,
    Reputed Ownership Statute does not apply to, 191
    as between principal and factor, 244, n 1

SUBSEQUENT CREDITORS,
    distinction between present and subsequent, 70, 157
    rule in cases of gifts as against, 158–166
    as against purchaser, 167
    express intent as against, 168
    imputed intent as against, 169
    test of imputed intent as against, 167–170.

[The References are to Sections]

SUPPLEMENTARY PROCEEDINGS,
right of priority in, 16, n. 2
as a substitute for judgment creditors' bill, 17, n. 1.

SURETY,
subrogation of, in case of fraudulent transfer, 81
rights in liquidation, when security is given by, 538.

T

TORT CLAIMS,
enforceability of, in liquidation, 491.
judgments founded on, 492
discharge and provability of judgments founded on, in bankruptcy, 550–552.
See CREDITORS

TRUST FUND DOCTRINE,
as a description of jurisdiction, 204, 205
preferences in connection with, 415.

TRUST RECEIPTS,
doctrine of, 257, 258

TRUST,
spendthrift, in connection with creditors' right of realization, 39–46
estate, interest in as attainable by judgment creditor, 11, n. 4
estate, interest in as attainable by trustee in bankruptcy, 354

TRUSTEE IN BANKRUPTCY,
as the creditors' representative, 334, 349
status of, as affected by annulment of lien of judgments, 338
status of, in connection with fraudulent conveyance, 339–344
status of, in connection with preferences, 343
position of, under Recording Acts, 345–348
status of, with respect to stockholders' liability, 351–353
status of, with respect to New York statutory trust, 354
title of, 380
extra-territorial powers of, 381.
title of foreign, 383–385

TWYNE'S CASE,
as illuminating the Statute of Fraudulent Conveyances, 69
rule of, 176.
as basis for Recording Acts relating to personal property, 222.
relation of, to vendor's retention of possession, 148

U

USES, STATUTE OF.
See REAL ESTATE

USURY, -
when creditor can set aside liens as tainted with, 12, n. 1

CPSIA information can be obtained
at www.ICGtesting.com
Printed in the USA
LVHW022230010423
743235LV00002B/69